S0-BOJ-479

A
HISTORICAL COMMENTARY
ON
THUCYDIDES

A
HISTORICAL COMMENTARY
ON
THUCYDIDES

BY

A. W. GOMME
PROFESSOR OF GREEK
UNIVERSITY OF GLASGOW

THE TEN YEARS' WAR

VOLUME II
Books II–III

OXFORD
AT THE CLARENDON PRESS

Oxford University Press, Ely House, London W.1

GLASGOW NEW YORK TORONTO MELBOURNE WELLINGTON
CAPE TOWN SALISBURY IBADAN NAIROBI LUSAKA ADDIS ABABA
BOMBAY CALCUTTA MADRAS KARACHI LAHORE DACCA
KUALA LUMPUR SINGAPORE HONG KONG TOKYO

FIRST PUBLISHED 1956
REPRINTED LITHOGRAPHICALLY IN GREAT BRITAIN
AT THE UNIVERSITY PRESS, OXFORD
BY VIVIAN RIDLER, PRINTER TO THE UNIVERSITY
FROM CORRECTED SHEETS OF THE FIRST EDITION
1962, 1966, 1969

PREFACE

I HAVE many obligations to record: first to three scholars who have, at different dates, read this volume in type or proof, and have not only saved me from many errors, but added much by criticism and discussion—to Mr. D. Mervyn Jones, of Exeter College, Oxford, to Dr. O. Luschnat of Berlin, editor of the new Teubner *Thucydides* (whose first volume, however, reached me too late to use for book ii), and to Dr. A. Wasserstein of Glasgow University; to all of whom I express most sincere thanks. I am most grateful, too, to a number of others, especially to the ever helpful authors of *Athenian Tribute Lists*, Professors Meritt, Wade-Gery, and McGregor, who, among other kindnesses, sent me advance proofs of their financial chapters which were of the greatest value; also to Mr. N. G. L. Hammond, Professor W. P. Wallace, and Sir William Macarthur and the editors of *Classical Quarterly*, similarly, for advance proofs of articles. Sir William Macarthur also helped me with letters and other articles to aid my notes on the pestilence; Professor Meritt generously put at my disposal the results of a recent visit to Sphakteria, Professor Wade-Gery discussed with me the proofs of my commentary on ii. 13 and 15, and Mr. T. J. Cadoux sent me valuable notes on his travels in the Chalkidic peninsula and to the north of it. To Mme de Romilly I owe a great deal, both for her books and for correspondence and discussion with her.

I have to thank as well the Council of the Hellenic Society and the editors of *Hesperia* for permission to reproduce maps from *J.H.S.* and *Hesperia* respectively, to Mr. M. N. Tod and the Delegates of the Clarendon Press for similar permission to reproduce the tables from *G.H.I.* given on pp. 435–6, and to Mr. Tod for a number of corrections of misprints in vol. i which had escaped the diligent eye of the printer's reader. To the Delegates of the Press I owe very great thanks, not only for their continual kindness and help, but their patience during the overlong preparation of this volume.

For it has been too long delayed, from causes which were not all of them within my control. Signs of this may appear in some inconsistencies and repetitions, certainly in the large crop of *Addenda* (which could well have been larger). I can only hope that the last volume will be finished within a much shorter time.

I have written so much, that it has been found necessary to divide this part into two volumes, so that the whole will take four instead of three, as originally planned. But these two volumes are intended to form a unity, a commentary on the History of the Ten Years' War; the numbering of the pages is continuous, and there is one index for both, at the end of vol. iii.

PREFACE

I have been careful in this volume (as I should have been in the first) to have all the *lemmata* printed according to the O.C.T. text. I have recorded all occasions where I disagree with or have doubts about its readings, even in quite small matters, and, owing to the importance of their editions, many of the similar occasions for Stahl, Classen–Steup, and Hude.

I should explain that in the page-headings the words *year*, *summer*, and *winter*, correspond to Thucydides' ἔτος, from the beginning of spring to the end of winter, θέρος, from the beginning of spring to the beginning of winter (i.e. here including ἔαρ and φθινόπωρον), and χειμών. The Julian dates therefore are given as 431 B.C., 430 B.C., etc., for the *summers*, and 431/0 B.C., 430/29 B.C., etc., for the winters. When, in the text, a whole year is meant, whether Thucydidean war-year or an official year, the ordinary form for the Attic year, 431–430 B.C., is used.

A. W. G.

vi

CONTENTS

LIST OF MAPS

Drawn by Phyllis Gomme

BIBLIOGRAPHY OF SHORT TITLES

Arnold = T. Arnold, *Thucydides*, with notes, etc. 3rd ed. Oxford, 1847.

Ath. Ass. = B. D. Meritt and A. B. West, *The Athenian Assessment of 425 B.C.* University of Michigan Press, 1934.

Ath. Studies = *Athenian Studies presented to W. S. Ferguson.* Harvard Studies in Classical Philology, Supplementary Volume i, 1940.

A.T.L. = *The Athenian Tribute Lists*, by B. D. Meritt, H. T. Wade-Gery, and M. F. McGregor, 4 vols. Cambridge, Mass., 1939–53.

Beloch = K. J. Beloch, *Griechische Geschichte.* 2nd ed. Strassburg, and Berlin and Leipzig, 1912–27.

Bender = G. F. Bender, *Der Begriff des Staatsmannes bei Thukydides*, Würzburg, 1938.

Bockh–Frankel = A. Böckh, *Die Staatshaushaltung d. Athener*, 3rd ed. by M. Frankel. Berlin, 1886.

Bohme = Widmann, below.

Bursian = (a) C. Bursian, *Geographie v. Griechenland.* Leipzig, 1862–72. (b) Bursians *Jahresbericht.*

Busolt = G. Busolt, *Griechische Geschichte.* 3 vols. Gotha, 1893–1904. (Vols. i and ii, 2nd ed.)

Busolt–Swoboda = G. Busolt, 'Griechische Staatskunde', in Müller's *Handbuch* (vol. ii, edited by H. Swoboda). 2 vols. Munich, 1920–6.

C.A.F. = Th. Kock, *Comicorum Atticorum Fragmenta.* Leipzig, 1880–8.

C.A.H. = *Cambridge Ancient History*, vols. i–vi. Cambridge, 1923–7.

Classen = J. Classen, *Thukydides.* See Steup, below.

Croiset = A. Croiset, *Thucydide*, Livres i–ii. Paris, 1886.

Delachaux = A. Delachaux, *Notes critiques sur Thucydide.* Neuchâtel, 1925.

Demiańczuk = J. Demiańczuk, *Supplementum Comicum.* Cracow, 1912.

Denniston = J. D. Denniston, *The Greek Particles.* Oxford, 1934.

de Romilly = Jacqueline de Romilly, *Thucydide et l'impérialisme athénien*, Paris, 1947.

Dittenberger = see *S.I.G.*[3], below.

F.Gr.Hist. = Jacoby, below.

F.H.G. = Müller, below.

Finley = John R. Finley, Jr., *Thucydides.* Cambridge, Mass., 1942.

Gomme, *Essays* = A. W. Gomme, *Essays in Greek History and Literature.* Oxford, Blackwell, 1937.

Gomme, *Sather Lectures* = *The Greek Attitude to Poetry and History.* Univ. of California Press, 1954.

Grote = G. Grote, *History of Greece.* 10 vols. London, 1888.

Grundy = G. B. Grundy, *Thucydides and the History of his Age*, vols. i[2] and ii. Oxford, 1948.

Head = B. V. Head, *Historia Numorum.* 2nd ed. Oxford, 1911.

Hill, I. T. = Ida Thallon Hill, *The Ancient City of Athens.* London, 1953.

Hude = C. Hude, *Thucydidis Historiae.* Leipzig, 1898–1901; id., ed. Teubner. Leipzig, 1908–13.

ix

BIBLIOGRAPHY OF SHORT TITLES

Jacoby = F. Jacoby, *Die Fragmente der griechischen Historiker.* i–ii. Berlin, 1923–30; iii A., B. Leyden, 1940–54.

Judeich = W. Judeich, 'Topographie v. Athen', in Müller's *Handbuch.* Munich, 1931.

Kakridés = *I. Θ. Κακριδής, Περικλέους Ἐπιτάφιος.* Thessalonike, 1937.

Kirchner = see *P.A.*, below.

Kock = see *C.A.F.*, above.

Kolbe = W. Kolbe, *Thukydides im Lichte d. Urkunden.* Stuttgart, 1930.

Kromayer–Veith = J. Kromayer and G. Veith, *Antike Schlachtfelder.* Berlin, 1903–31; *Schlachten-Atlas.* Leipzig, 1922.

L. and S. = Liddell and Scott, *Greek–English Lexicon.* New edition, revised by H. Stuart Jones. Oxford, 1925–40.

Leake = W. M. Leake: (1) *The Topography of Athens.* London, 1841. (2) *Travels in the Morea.* London, 1830. (3) *Travels in Northern Greece.* London, 1835.

Luschnat = O. Luschnat, *Die Feldherrenreden im Geschichtswerk des Thukydides. Philologus,* Supplbd. xxxiv. 2. 1942.

Meritt, *A.F.D.* = B. D. Meritt, *Athenian Financial Documents of the Fifth Century.* Univ. of Michigan Press, 1932.

Meritt, *Ath. Cal.* = B. D. Meritt, *The Athenian Calendar in the Fifth Century.* Harvard University Press, 1928.

Meritt, *D.A.T.* = B. D. Meritt, *Documents on Athenian Tribute.* Harvard University Press, 1937. See also *A.T.L., Ath. Ass.*

Meyer (1) = E. Meyer, *Geschichte des Altertums.* Vols. iii (2nd ed.) and iv (3rd ed.: known as iv.² 1). Stuttgart, 1937–9.

Meyer (2) = E. Meyer, *Forschungen zur alten Geschichte.* 2 vols. Halle, 1892–9.

Müller = C. and Th. Müller, *Fragmenta Historicorum Graecorum.* 5 vols. Paris, 1841–85.

Nesselhauf = H. Nesselhauf, 'Untersuchungen zur Geschichte der delisch-attischen Symmachie'. *Klio,* Beiheft 30, 1933.

P.A. = J. Kirchner, *Prosopographia Attica.* Berlin, 1901–3.

Page = D. L. Page, *Greek Literary Papyri,* i (Loeb). London and Cambridge, Mass., 1942.

Pickard-Cambridge = A. W. Pickard-Cambridge, *The Theatre of Dionysus.* Oxford, 1946.

Poppo = E. F. Poppo, *Thucydidis libri octo.* 11 vols. Leipzig, 1821–40.

Powell = *Thucydidis Historiae,* recognovit H. Stuart Jones, 2nd ed. J. E. Powell, Oxford, 1942.

Pritchett–Neugebauer = W. K. Pritchett and O. Neugebauer, *The Calendars of Athens,* Harvard University Press, 1947.

Prott–Ziehen = J. de Prott and L. Ziehen, *Leges Graecorum sacrae.* Leipzig, 1896.

Ps.-Xen. = [Xenophon], *Ἀθηναίων Πολιτεία.*

R.E. = Pauly–Wissowa–Kroll, *Realencyclopädie.* Stuttgart, 1893–.

Robinson Studies = Studies presented to D. M. Robinson: ed. G. E. Mylonás and D. Raymond. St. Louis, 1951 and 1953.

BIBLIOGRAPHY OF SHORT TITLES

Ros = Jan Ros, S.J., *Die ΜΕΤΑΒΟΛΗ (Variatio) als Stilprinzip des Thukydides*. Paderborn, 1938.

Schmid, or Schmid–Stählin = W. Schmid and O. Stählin, *Geschichte der griechischen Literatur*. Munich, 1920–48. (W. Schmid, Band V. ii. 2, Thukydides, Leukippos u. Demokritos, 1948.)

Schwartz = E. Schwartz, *Das Geschichtswerk des Thukydides*. Bonn, 1919.

Shilleto = R. Shilleto, *Thucydidis I et II*. Cambridge, 1872–80.

S.E.G. = *Supplementum Epigraphicum Graecum*, i–xii, 1923–55.

*S.I.G.*³ = W. Dittenberger, *Sylloge Inscriptionum graecarum*, ed. 3.

Steup = J. Steup, *Thukydides* erklärt von J. Classen, bearbeitet von J. S. 3rd to 5th ed. Berlin, 1900–22.

Stuart Jones = *Thucydidis Historiae*. Oxford, 1898.

Tod = M. N. Tod, *Greek Historical Inscriptions*, vol. i, 1933, 2nd ed., 1946; vol. ii, 1948.

Widmann = S. Widmann, *Thukydides*, erklärt von G. Böhme; besorgt von S. W. 5th to 6th ed. Leipzig, 1894.

Wilamowitz = U. v. Wilamowitz-Moellendorf, *Aristoteles und Athen*. Berlin, 1893.

xi

COMMENTARY
BOOK II

1. *The Beginning of the War*

1. ἄρχεται δὲ ὁ πόλεμος ἐνθένδε: all the emphasis is on ἄρχεται—'the war properly so called *begins* at this point; that is, the period in which they no longer communicated with each other without a herald now begins'. ἐν ᾧ can hardly be taken as defining either ὁ πόλεμος or ἐνθένδε, for such a statement would be true of all wars. The scholiast interprets ἐνθένδε as ἀπὸ ταύτης τῆς αἰτίας, which is also wrong. ἐνθένδε points forward to c. 2.

The sentence follows closely on the last of book i; at the same time the beginning of the war is formally announced—Ἀθηναίων καὶ Πελοποννησίων καὶ τῶν ἑκατέροις ξυμμάχων. On the apparent contradiction between this statement, 12. 3 and 19. 1, combined with v. 20. 1, see nn. ad locc.

The name of the war, Ἀθ. καὶ Πελ. here, τῶν Πελ. καὶ Ἀθ. in i. 1. 1, is quite neutral. The later ὁ Πελοποννησιακὸς πόλεμος (first in Strabo) shows the Athenian standpoint, inevitable after Thucydides, just as 'the French Wars' shows the English.

When ancient critics said that Thucydides emulated the 'economy' of Homer (Markell. *Vita*, 35), they may have been thinking, amongst other things, of this beginning, and comparing *Od.* i. 10–11 (and viii. 500).

ξυνεχῶς: by contrast with the previous two years (σπονδῶν ξύγχυσις, i. 146), not the ten years' war by contrast with the later seventeen years as in v. 24. 2 (so Stahl). This is shown by καταστάντες. For this last word see below, n. on iii. 3. 1.

κατὰ θέρος καὶ χειμῶνα: Thucydides gives no definition of 'summer' and 'winter' (cf. nn. on 2. 1, ἅμα ἦρι ἀρχομένῳ, and on 31. 1, περὶ τὸ φθινόπωρον), and no explanation why he adopts this method. The latter he gives briefly in v. 20. See vol. i, pp. 1–8. Dionysios attacked this chronological method, *Epist. ad Pomp.* 773; Π⁸ (the commentary on ii. 1–45, *Ox. Pap.* 853, given also in Hude's edition of the *scholia*) has an interesting reply. See Appendix.

YEAR 1: 431–430 B.C. (CC. 2–46)

2–6. *Theban Attack on Plataia*

Cf. Hdt. vii. 233. 2; Dem. lix. 98–106; Diod. xii. 41.

2. 1. τέσσαρα μὲν γάρ, κ.τ.λ.; a date, and also a statement—'the Thirty Years' Peace lasted less than fifteen years'; cf. i. 87. 6 (vol. i, p. 392). For the treaty, see i. 115. 1.

I

Χρυσίδος ἐν Ἄργει: Hellanikos in his *Priestesses of Hera* made a chronological table (*F. Gr. Hist.* 4, F 74 ff.), and presumably had done so when Thucydides wrote this. (See Jacoby, *Atthis*, 356. 24, 358.) The temple of Hera was just within the territory of Argos on the boundary of Mykenai (Mykenai indeed had more than thirty years before been conquered by Argos—vol. i, pp. 408–9), about 8 kilometres north-east of the city.

Chrysis remained priestess for $8\frac{1}{2}$ years more: iv. 133. 2–3.

ἐφόρου ἐν Σπάρτῃ: one of the five ephors was eponymos, as was one of the nine archons at Athens. But the method of dating events by the eponymos at Sparta did not become usual, at least outside Sparta; there was another method, that of the regnal years of the kings, which was more commonly employed later. It is a pity that Thucydides did not give here the year of Archidamos' reign; it would have saved us much trouble (vol. i, pp. 405–7), or caused us more.

ἔτι δύο μῆνας: this is one of the figures in Thucydides that must be wrong, for (1) the attack on Plataia was at the beginning of spring (see below), in all probability on the night of March 6–7 or 7–8 by the Julian calendar (23. 2 n.), and the end of the archon-year was *c.* July 4 (Meritt, *A.F.D.*, 176); and (2) equally clearly Thucydides must have known that at the beginning of spring an archon had more than two months still to serve. We must therefore adopt Krüger's emendation τέσσαρας (δ being presumably mistaken for δύο); the interval is just four lunar months.

For the significance and purpose of this dating by archon and ephor, see vol. i, p. 8; also H. Bloch in *Ath. Studies*, p. 327, n. 1. The only other parallel in Thucydides is his dating of the end of the war, v. 25. 1, for which he has also the 'natural' dating in v. 20. 1. For the archon-list which was officially published on stone *c.* 425 (vol. i, p. 6. n. 2), see Jacoby, *Atthis*, 171–4. It was not necessarily the first time such a list was published: the one of which we have a fragment may have been copied from an old and worn stone, with archaic lettering, like the Halikarnassian list, *Syll.*³ 1020 (*Atthis*, p. 358). That Herodotos did not use such a list does not prove that one did not exist.

μηνὶ ἕκτῳ: for this figure, which I have argued cannot stand, see i, 125. 2 n. δεκάτῳ is the most probable emendation; ἐνάτῳ possible. In *J.H.S.* lxix, 1949, 85, however, Wade-Gery maintains his defence of μηνὶ ἕκτῳ. He thinks that some emendation of the text in i. 125. 2, ἐνιαυτὸς μὲν οὐ διετρίβη, ἔλασσον δέ, is unavoidable (the parallel with Hdt. vii. 39. 2 being delusive), and we may emend to ἔλασσον δὲ ⟨ἡμίσεος⟩ as easily as to ἔλασσον δὲ ⟨οὐ πολλῷ⟩, and thus make Thucydides contradict stories of Peloponnesian delay and emphasize the comparative speed (ὅμως δέ = 'for all the need of great preparations, they invaded within six months'). But, looking again at the whole passage in i. 125. 2, I find this unconvincing: first, if the decision to go to war was taken in November 432, there is no reason why there should have been stories of delay; secondly, εὐθὺς μὲν ἀδύνατα ἦν ἐπιχειρεῖν ἀπαρασκεύοις οὖσιν has little meaning, unless there was opportunity for invasion within a month or two; and thirdly, ἐνιαυτὸς μὲν οὐ διετρίβη, ἔλασσον δὲ ἡμίσεος is not, in the context, a natural way of saying 'so far were the Peloponnesians from delaying for a year that they invaded Attica within six months, virtually as soon as invasion was possible'.

ἅμα ἦρι ἀρχομένῳ: Thucydides has just said, c. 1, that he will record the events of the war by summers and winters, and the very first of them he records by the spring, without saying to which half of the year it belongs. See Appendix.

ὀλίγῳ πλείους τριακοσίων: Herodotos says 400.

βοιωταρχοῦντες: see n. on iv. 91.

Πυθάγγελός τε - - - Ὀνητορίδου: We know nothing more of these men.

We are left to suppose that the other Boeotarchs had no part in this attack; but not necessarily that they disapproved of it, even after its failure. The Thebans profess to be acting for all Boeotia (κατὰ τὰ πάτρια τῶν πάντων Βοιωτῶν, § 4).

περὶ πρῶτον ὕπνον: a natural indication of the hour—the significant point being that it was night time and early in the night (οὐ γὰρ ἑώρων ἐν τῇ νυκτί, 3. 1)—as ἅμα ἦρι ἀρχομένῳ is a natural indication of the season, for a military event. So αὐτὸ τὸ περίορθρον, 3. 4.

Ἀθηναίων ξυμμαχίδα: see iii. 55. 1, 68. 5 nn. Thucydides says nothing of the military importance of Plataia to either side, nor, except for the hint in the words τῆς Βοιωτίας and κατὰ τὰ πάτρια τῶν πάντων Βοιωτῶν, § 4, of the natural desire of Thebes to include the recalcitrant city within the Boeotian federation. Of the latter we hear something in the Theban and Plataian speeches after the fall of the city (iii. 53–67).

2. ἰδίας ἕνεκα δυνάμεως: the same fault which, in Thucydides' view, brought or helped to bring Athens (ii. 65. 10–12) and many another state (iii. 82. 8) to disaster.

3. Εὐρυμάχου τοῦ Λεοντιάδου: Leontiadas was that Theban noble who brought Thebes over to the Persian side (Hdt. vii. 233);[1] Eurymachos' son, another Leontiadas, surrendered the Kadmeia to

---

[1] Aristophanes the Boeotian (F. Gr. Hist. 379, F 6) said that not Leontiadas but Alexandros was in command of Theban forces at Thermopylai; and Plutarch takes Herodotos (vii. 233) to task for his error (de Hdt. mal. 33, 866 F). But Leontiadas may have been morally responsible for Theban action, as, to compare great things with small, Miltiades was at Marathon.

Phoibidas the Spartan in 383–382 B.C. (Xen. *Hell.* v. 2. 25 ff.). A long-lived and mischievous family.

Eurymachos was as powerful as any man in Thebes, but not at the time in office, or not in the principal office.

4. τίθεσθαι παρ' αὐτοὺς τὰ ὅπλα: cf. iv. 68. 3 and 93. 3 n., as well as θέμενοι - - - τά ὅπλα above; and Graves's n. on iv. 44. 1. Here it is, literally, 'take his place with them'; but the figurative meaning, 'take sides with them', is predominant.

3. 2. κρατήσειν: I do not feel confident that κρατῆσαι, the reading of all the MSS., is impossible—an objective infinitive where there would be no ambiguity of meaning; but the confusion of the future and first aorist infinitives is not uncommon in Thucydides' MSS., and Aineias, *Takt*, 2. 3, quotes κρατήσειν. ⟨ἂν⟩ κρατῆσαι would be as easy an emendation.

τῷ γὰρ πλήθει: 'the majority' here, rather than 'the masses'.

4. αὐτὸ τὸ περίορθρον: 'the darkest hour before the dawn'; cf. n. on 2. 1, περὶ πρῶτον ὕπνον. They waited as long as they could in order to be as well prepared as possible (ὡς ἐκ τῶν δυνατῶν ἑτοῖμα), but must strike while it was still dark.

4. 2. προσβαλλόντων: so we should surely read, with Bekker, Stahl, and Classen, not the MSS. προσβαλόντων (Hude, Stuart Jones), for it is in all respects parallel to χρωμένων and βαλλόντων below.

τελευτῶντος τοῦ μηνός: an indication of time which enables us to date the attack on Plataia with some exactness; but inserted here (almost as an afterthought—'I should have said that it was the end of the month') as a natural, not a calendar, date, to explain the continued darkness. Thucydides does not say, in 2. 1, 'on the last day (or last day but one) of Anthesterion'. Cf. iv. 84. 1 n. See also n. on ἱερομηνία, iii. 56. 2.

τοῦ μὴ ἐκφεύγειν: as Classen says, the genitive must be dependent on ἐμπείρους, as τῶν διόδων on ἄπειροι above; and his defence of this may stand: "dass Th. τοῦ μὴ ἐκφεύγειν sagt, nicht ἐὰν ἐκφεύγειν, hat seinen Grund in der von ihm gewählten Wendung ἐμπείρους ἔχοντες τοὺς διώκοντας statt τῶν διωκόντων ἐμπείρων ὄντων. An jene schliesst sich bei der Gleichheit der Subjekte ohne zu grosse Schwierigkeit das τοῦ μὴ ἐκφεύγειν an."

ὥστε διεφθείροντο οἱ πολλοί: bracketed by some editors (others bracket οἱ only, with A alone of our MSS.; Π⁸ has οἱ π.) on the ground that it is contradicted by 4. 5 and 5. 7 (compared with the number given in 2. 1); but the words may stand. They give the general result of the Thebans' ignorance of the locality and their difficulties in the dark: some attempted to escape by getting over the city wall; a few got away by an unguarded gate; others were killed in the street-

4

fighting; the majority had to surrender unconditionally. διεφθείροντο does not mean 'they were immediately killed'.

3. τῶν δὲ Πλαταιῶν τις: τε, the reading of ABEF, seems preferable here to δέ. Below, § 4 init., the same MSS. again have τε, where δέ is to be preferred. (Classen reads τε, most edd. δέ, in both places.)

4. λαθόντες καὶ διακόψαντες: I think the best way out of the difficulty of the reading is to transpose λαθόντες after τὸν μοχλόν, so that καὶ διακόψαντες may follow γυναικὸς δούσης (Classen compares βαλλόμενός τε καὶ χαλεπῶς, i. 63. 1) and λαθόντες go with ἐξῆλθον, where it rightly belongs. Richards, *C.Q.* vi, 1912, 141, would transpose it after ἐρήμους and add καί before γυναικός.

5. ὃ ἦν τοῦ τείχους, κ.τ.λ.: I do not find the difficulty in these words which others do. The building was so constructed that one of its long sides was formed by the city wall; as it was a large building it had more than one door, and the door nearest to the retreating but still orderly body of Thebans was open. CG among the MSS. omit πλησίον, but Π⁸ had it, and there is no apparent reason for its presence in ABEF if it is not genuine. (Classen objected that if the building was attached to the city wall, the Thebans would have been able to climb from it on to the wall, and hold it till their main forces arrived, or at least attempt to escape that way; he forgot that the building must have had a roof, to be reached only from the outside.) For the construction ὃ ἦν τοῦ τείχους, cf. ὃ ἦν τοῦ ἱεροῦ, i. 134. 1.

In an interesting article on the medieval fortified village of Mesta in Chios (*B.S.A.* xlv, 1950, 16–20), W. A. Eden compares its plan, with a small central square and narrow, crooked streets (normal width, 6 feet 6 inches) and houses built against the fortification wall, with Plataia and probably many other ancient cities that had not been built, or rebuilt, according to the ideas of Hippodamos. This seems exaggerated: wheeled vehicles used the streets of Plataia (3. 3), and the house built against the wall was clearly exceptional. (The objection to this is clear: not to prevent treachery, as Wace, *Mycenae* (Princeton, 1949), p. 57, says, but a besieger who had got to the top of the wall would have an easy descent on to roofs; with a lane along the wall he not only had a difficult jump, but could be more easily caught by defenders.)

5. 1. περὶ τῶν γεγενημένων: since the main body of the Thebans were told only part of the story (§ 4), not the situation in Plataia at the point which the narrative had already reached (4. 8), Classen suggested γιγνομένων here, perhaps rightly. But in 6. 2 τὰ γεγενημένα refers expressly to the beginning of the conflict.

2. σταδίους ἑβδομήκοντα: Thebes is about 12½ km. from the walls of Plataia in a direct line, just about 70 Attic stades of 177 m.; about 10 km., or 58 stades, from the river Asopos, the boundary of

Plataian territory. As likely as not the Theban army marched first by the more important road to Athens, and branched off it southwest to Plataia. On the heavy soil of this part of Boeotia, on unmetalled tracks, it is difficult going after much rain; and there is a good deal of land on both sides of the river which is marshy in wet weather.

οὐ ῥᾳδίως διαβατὸς ἦν: in dry summer weather the Asopos in this part of its course is only a few feet wide, and quite shallow. But its banks are steep and it can readily flow in a flood in wet weather, in winter and spring.

5. ἀποδώσειν αὐτοῖς τοὺς ἄνδρας: many edd. bracket τοὺς ἄνδρας, and we certainly have a superfluity of the words in §§ 5–7. If we should bracket at all, I would extend it to include αὐτοῖς.

7. ἀπέκτειναν τοὺς ἄνδρας: presumably the Plataians, Naukleides and his friends (2. 2), suffered the same fate; they were now traitors, for they had been defeated. Cf. iii. 68. 3, ὅσοι τὰ σφέτερα φρονοῦντες Πλαταιῶν περιῆσαν.

6. 1. ἔς τε τὰς Ἀθήνας ἄγγελον ἔπεμπον: the account of the messengers sent to Athens is certainly confused: 'Plataia now sent a message (after the killing of the prisoners). Messages had been sent immediately to relate what had happened, and Athens sent word not to do anything to the prisoners till she had considered the matter; she had not yet heard that they had been killed. For the first messenger was sent as soon as the Thebans entered the city, and the second just after they had been defeated and captured.' Why did not Thucydides add, 'and later the third message arrived with the news of the executions'?

However, there is no need to suspect the text (Steup's proposal to add περὶ βοηθείας or τιμωρίας to § 1, in order to differentiate this message from the first and second, does not help; for the third must have contained the news as well as a request for help); still less to suppose, with Wilamowitz, that §§ 2–3 are a later insertion by Thucydides. See Steup's note on this point.

7–12. *Final Preparations for War by the Athenians and the Peloponnesians*

7. 1. πρεσβείας τε μέλλοντες, κ.τ.λ.: because of ἑκάτεροι below, this and ποιούμενοι belong to οἱ Ἀθηναῖοι as well as to Λακεδαιμόνιοι (so Wade-Gery, *J.H.S.* lxix. 83–84). Since in 67. 1 we hear of a Peloponnesian embassy to Persia, and in 29 of Athenian alliances with Sitalkes of Thrace and Perdikkas of Macedon, but of no Athenian embassy to Persia before that of 424 B.C. (iv. 50. 3), Herbst and Classen adopt the view of the scholiast here that in fact πέμπειν παρὰ βασιλέα belongs to the Lacedaemonians only and ἄλλοσε πρὸς τοὺς βαρβάρους to the Athenians. This seems unlikely. Actually the first embassy to Persia during the war that we know of is that described in *The Acharnians*. The Peloponnesians also won barbarian allies, for a single campaign, in the north-west (ii. 80. 5–7). Cf. i. 82. 1.

2. ἐπετάχθη: this is the reading of the *recentiores*; ἐπετάχθησαν codd.; ἐπετάχθη σ̄ (i.e. διακοσίας) Herbst. I am convinced that of the many attempts to remedy the reading of the best MSS. here, ἐπετάχθη is the best; the question remains whether Herbst's suggestion is an improvement on this. Diodoros, xii. 41. 1, in a passage narrating the preparations of the Peloponnesians for the war (including an embassy to Persia, πρεσβεύσαντες, not πρεσβείας μέλλοντες πέμπειν, as Thucydides has it), says that they asked for 200 triremes; it may be that Ephoros had read this figure in Thucydides, as his figures for the financial and military resources of Athens were based on 13. 3–7 (where see nn.); and the clause below, ὡς ἐς τὸν πάντα ἀριθμὸν πεντακοσίων νεῶν ἐσομένων, perhaps suggests that a figure was given here. Herbst's reading is therefore decidedly attractive. (The difficulty in the way of the apparently simple remedy adopted by Classen—νῆες ἐπετάχθησαν, with the mistake explained by the later use of ναῦς as a nom. plur.—is that, we are told, in no other of the 130 or so instances of νῆες in Thucydides is the word corrupted to ναῦς. But this is not decisive.) Π⁸ has the following interpretation: ἐ[πέταξάν] φησιν ὁ Θ[ο]υκυδίδης κα[ὶ τοῖς ᾽Ιτα]λιώταις κα[ὶ] τοῖς ἀπὸ Σικ[ελίας οἱ] Λακεδαιμόνιοι ναῦς π[οιεῖσθαι] εἰς τὴν συμμαχίαν. This suggests that there was no figure in his text of Thucydides. No scholiast mentions any grammatical difficulty.

πεντακοσίων νεῶν: an impossible number, whether or not we read διακοσίας above. We cannot imagine that the western states would think of sending even 200 ships and scarcely that the Peloponnesians would ask for as many (they sent 22 in 413!); and there were nothing like 300 in commission among the latter. In 432 the Corinthians and their allies, who include nearly every state that could provide ships for the Peloponnesian League (see below, 9. 3 n.), mustered 150, in a great effort (i. 46. 1, with my note on i. 54. 2). In ii. 66. 1 we hear of a fleet of 100 ships; in iii. 16. 3 of 40; and in viii. 3. 2, from all the cities of the alliance, 100 were ordered. Some have thought that Thucydides wrote 500 in irony, to point to the fruitless optimism of the Peloponnesians; but it does not read to me like that. If the MSS. figure is not wrong, we should have expected him to show the exaggeration, not only of the hopes from the west, but of their own resources. Characteristically, the scholia do not help.

δεχομένους μιᾷ νηί: a regular formula for neutrality in war-time, to admit not more than one warship of a belligerent. Cf. iii. 71. 1, vi. 52. 1.

3. τήν τε ὑπάρχουσαν ξυμμαχίαν: the Delian Confederacy only, as the next clause shows.

Κέρκυραν, κ.τ.λ.: in 9. 4, Kerkyra, the majority of Akarnanians, and Zakynthos are listed among the allies of Athens at the beginning of the war; Kephallenia only joined later in the summer when a large Athenian fleet was in those waters (30. 2). There was only an ἐπιμαχία, not full ξυμμαχία, with Kerkyra (i. 44. 1; cf. iii. 75. 1). The scholiast says here that the ἐπιμαχία was now made a full alliance, as we should indeed suppose from 9. 4, where they are called ξύμμαχοι without qualification, and 24. 1; but from iii. 70. 2, 6 we learn that the original defensive alliance remained in force till 427.

βεβαίως: joined with φίλια by all edd. since Koraës; and this not only suits the rhythm of the sentence but makes good sense—the already existing friendship was to be strengthened or confirmed. But I am not entirely convinced. Classen says that adverbs are often placed at the end of a sentence for emphasis (edd. compare iv. 20. 3); but in Greek emphasis is given by placing a word early in its clause, after, not before, a pause;[1] and we could do well with an emphatic βεβαίως - - - καταπολεμήσοντες, 'we shall then be waging war against the Peloponnese, from every direction, with a secure base'. We may, however, keep βεβαίως (unemphatic) with φίλια, and translate 'seeing that we should then be fighting all around the Peloponnese'. καταπολεμήσοντες must here be simply bello infestare (cf. iv. 1. 2, 86. 5), as Stahl and Classen, not 'exhaust by war, reduce', as L. and S.; or else 'wage war', as sometimes in later Greek. The Athenians were not so confident as to suppose that they would win the war simply by confirming their friendships in the west. These allies were, however, essential if Athens was to attack, as well as to defend by the system of the Long Walls, if she was to make good use of her base at Naupaktos, if she was to extend her empire, or even her influence, in Italy and Sicily. See vol. i, p. 305.

8. 1. νεότης πολλή: Greek warfare being what it was, the many wars in the fifties and forties had not greatly affected the birth-rate, as such modern wars as those of 1870–1 and 1914–18 did; so that the mainly peaceful years since 454 or 453 B.C. had had their natural effect.

---

[1] οὐκ ἀπεικότως below, 8. 1, is emphatic; but there is a pause before it—the two words form almost a separate sentence, 'and not unnaturally', and the next sentence explains only them. So often with εἰκότως: an instance in Thucydides is i. 77. 5; ii. 93. 1 and vii. 57. 5 are similar. Cf. τρόπῳ τοιῷδε, iii. 20. 2, and, for a simpler form, χαλεπῶς δὲ καὶ βιαίως, iii. 23. 4. In i. 125. 2, however, φανερῶς clearly has some emphasis; we must not be too pedantic; and ὡς ἐπὶ πλεῖστον at the close of ii. 35 is a notable instance of an adverbial phrase at the end of a sentence. See G. Thomson, Oresteia, ii, pp. 367–72.

8

ὑπὸ ἀπειρίας: cf. i. 80. 1. The scholiasts, including Π^8, repeat the tag from Pindar.

2. λόγια: λόγιά ἐστι τὰ παρὰ τοῦ θεοῦ λεγόμενα καταλογάδην· χρησμοὶ δὲ οἵτινες ἐμμέτρως λέγονται, θεοφορουμένων τῶν λεγόντων—schol.; and this is doubtless roughly correct, though λόγια were not necessarily in prose (and perhaps not always παρὰ τοῦ θεοῦ λεγόμενα). As Classen says, the true distinction is between ἐλέγετο, 'were on many people's lips', and what the oracle-mongers more solemnly proclaimed. See Ar. Equit. 61, 120, with Neil's notes.

3. Δῆλος ἐκινήθη: Herodotos, vi. 98. 1–3, records another earthquake in Delos, ὡς ἔλεγον οἱ Δήλιοι, also unique, which occurred shortly before Marathon and presaged the evils suffered by the Greeks during the reigns of Dareios, Xerxes, and Artaxerxes, including the internecine wars of the principal Greek states. By this last Herodotos may be referring to the war which began in 431, but perhaps to the fighting between 459 and 445 (see i. 18. 3 n.). In either case Thucydides cannot be referring to the same earthquake; nor, I think, is he correcting Herodotos. See my Essays, p. 122 n. See also Pindar, fr. 87, from a prosodion to Delos (not before 472 B.C., according to Wilamowitz, Sappho u. Simonides, 129, n. 3), where the island is called ἀκίνητον τέρας.

ἐλέγετο δὲ καὶ ἐδόκει: 'it was said and believed', which does not mean that Thucydides believed it, nor that he did not. See i. 23. 3 n.

4–5. ἡ δὲ εὔνοια, κ.τ.λ.: Thucydides does not attempt to conceal the general unpopularity of Athens throughout Greece, both as an imperial (οἱ μὲν τῆς ἀρχῆς ἀπολυθῆναι βουλόμενοι) and as a still aggressive power (οἱ δὲ μὴ ἀρχθῶσι φοβούμενοι); nor does he ever defend the empire either on the ground that it introduced some sort of unity in the Greek world and peace within part of it or because it was materially useful in the suppression of piracy and the encouragement of trade, as, he says, the earlier empires had been (i. 4–8, etc.). But as to where his affections lay, we are not left in doubt. Therein is one tragic note of his History: that the city to which he was devoted, which he, and therefore we, would wish to win the war, was the aggressor.

There is, however, no section of Thucydides' narrative which entirely justifies this statement about the enthusiastic support given to Sparta. We have already heard that at Plataia the majority were for Athens (3. 2); and except in Olynthos, Spartolos, and Poteidaia, and the ill-fated Skione, nowhere were the majority enthusiastic for Sparta; they generally, as in Mytilene, Amphipolis, Akanthos, Mende, Samos, and elsewhere, stood by Athens, shakily in some places, firmly in others—see iii. 47. 2 and n. there; only Brasidas inspired, to some degree, this enthusiasm: iv. 81. 2, 108. 3–6. There is a contradiction between Thucydides' summary and his narrative which is in some respects like that to be observed in ii. 65. 8, 11, iv. 81. 3, and vi. 15. 3-4; on which passages see my article in *J.H.S.* lxxi, 1951, 70-74. But here there is no evidence that the summary is late; it might in fact be an early belief which was later contradicted by events.

προειπόντων ὅτι τὴν Ἑλλάδα ἐλευθεροῦσιν: cf. 11. 2, iii. 32. 2, iv. 85. 1.

ἐν τούτῳ τε κεκωλῦσθαι, κ.τ.λ.: 'everything is at a standstill if I cannot be there'. Cf. Milton, *P.L.* vi. 238 (quoted by Shilleto):

> Each on himself rely'd
> As only in his arm the moment lay
> Of victory.

In i. 141. 7 Perikles had asserted that on the contrary there would be no common energy on the Peloponnesian side. To be orthodox we should compare Herodotos' picture of the sailors of the Persian fleet at Salamis (viii. 86): καίτοι ἦσάν γε καὶ ἐγένοντο ταύτην τὴν ἡμέρην μακρῷ ἀμείνονες αὐτοὶ ἑωυτῶν ἢ πρὸς Εὐβοίῃ, πᾶς τις προθυμεόμενος καὶ δειμαίνων Ξέρξην, ἐδόκεέ τε ἕκαστος ἑωυτὸν θεήσεσθαι βασιλέα.

9. 2. Πελοποννήσιοι μὲν οἱ ἐντὸς Ἰσθμοῦ: Steup objects that whereas 'Peloponnesians within the isthmus' can only be opposed to 'Peloponnesians beyond the isthmus' and Πελοποννήσιοι therefore must mean the whole Peloponnesian alliance (as commonly throughout the *History*), the words πλὴν Ἀργείων καὶ Ἀχαιῶν show that Πελοποννήσιοι is in fact to be taken in its geographical sense. He would therefore bracket οἱ ἐντὸς Ἰσθμοῦ. Herwerden, with perhaps greater probability, bracketed Πελοποννήσιοι (transposing μέν after οἱ). If the received text is to stand, we can only interpret 'the Peloponnesians (I mean on this occasion the Peloponnesians in the geographical sense, those living within the Isthmus)'. Somewhat similar is ἄλλαι πόλεις αἱ ὑποτελεῖς οὖσαι below, 'other states, namely those that were tributary', and νῆες ὅσαι - - -, πᾶσαι αἱ Κυκλάδες.

Ἀχαιῶν: they had more or less decisively sided with Athens before, i. 111. 3, 115. 1.

Πελληνῆς: this was the easternmost of the twelve Achaian cities, neighbour to Sikyon. It acted separately from the rest, and with Sikyon and Corinth, on other occasions (after 421 B.C.): v. 58. 4-60. 3, viii. 3. 2.

ὕστερον καὶ ἅπαντες: their friendship with the Peloponnesians is implied in the account of the naval engagements off their coast in the third year of the war, ii. 83-92 (note πρὸς τῇ γῇ οἰκείᾳ οὔσῃ, 87. 6). For the period after 421, see v. 82. 1, vii. 34. 1.

Λοκροί: only the northern Lokrians, Opountioi and Epiknemidioi: the Ozolai were friendly to Athens, and allies later: iii. 95. 3, 101. 1. Thucydides normally uses Λοκροί only, when meaning the northern group (cf. 26. 1).

Φωκῆς: they had once been supported by Athens against Sparta, and allied with her, i. 107. 2, 108. 3, 112. 5 n., and vol. i, p. 366; they were expected to rejoin their old friends later, iii. 95. 1.

Λευκάδιοι: the only one of the western islands that stood by the Peloponnesians; cf. especially iii. 94. 2.

Ἀνακτόριοι: secured by Corinth in 433 B.C., i. 55. 1 n.

3. ναυτικὸν παρείχοντο Κορίνθιοι, κ.τ.λ.: compare with this list those who assisted Corinth against Kerkyra in 435 and 433, i. 27. 2, 46. 1. Of those who sent ships in 435 Hermione, Epidauros, and Troizen were not only absent in 433, but do not help at sea in 431; all those who joined Corinth in 433, with the exception of Anaktorion with her single vessel, supplied ships in 431, and Sikyon and Pellene as well.

4. Ἀκαρνάνων οἱ πλείους: but not Oiniadai, always at variance with the rest, i. 111. 3, ii. 82, 102. 2–6, iii. 94. 1; nor as yet Astakos, 30. 1.

Κερκυραῖοι: see 7. 3 n.

Ζακύνθιοι: cf. i. 47. 2 n.

ἐν ἔθνεσι τοσοῖσδε: in vii. 57, too, the catalogue of the forces at Syracuse, Thucydides emphasizes the different racial (perhaps one should not translate, but say 'ethnic') elements which faced and fought each other; but here he confuses apparently two things, the geographical division of the empire into its five divisions, Karia (which included its Dorian neighbours), Ionia, Hellespont, Thrace, and the Islands (of which by this time the Karian had been merged with the Ionian),[1] and its ethnic divisions; for Ionia includes the Aioleis of Mytilene and the opposite mainland, the Kyklades were as Ionian as Ionia, and Hellespont and Thrace a mixture of Ionian and Dorian. There is another small difficulty: Euboea was in the Island district, which would suit νῆσοι ὅσαι - - - ἀνίσχοντα, but it was not reckoned among the Kyklades; some editors therefore bracket πᾶσαι αἱ ἄλλαι Κυκλάδες, or Κυκλάδες only.

ὅσαι ἐντός, κ.τ.λ.: the islands within (an area bounded by) Peloponnese and Crete, to the east; but east of the former only, north of Crete. (The scholiast here limits πρὸς ἥλιον ἀνίσχοντα to Κρήτης, and understands by the whole sentence (a) the islands off Peloponnese, which are the Kyklades, and (b) those east of Crete, Karpathos, Kasos, etc.; but this is a wrong translation, and the islands between Crete and Rhodes are included in Δωριῆς Καρσὶ πρόσοικοι.)

πλὴν Μήλου καὶ Θήρας: Melos, as is well known, was assessed, at 15 tal., in the assessment of 425 B.C. (iii. 116, n. ad fin.), though it was

_____
[1] Stahl well compares viii. 96. 4.

not conquered till 416. Cf. iii. 91. 1–2. Thera was similarly assessed in 425 at 5 tal.; but it had paid tribute (3 tal.) in 430–429 and 429–428, and it paid an unknown sum in 422–421; it also paid something in a special category, with Samos, in 426–425 (*I.G.* i.² 65. 20 = *A.T.L.* ii, D 8: below, p. 18), and presumably in other years. This last may have been reparations for war-costs (*A.T.L.* iii. 336–7; and Meritt, *D.A.T.* 36–38). Thucydides does not tell us how Thera came to join the League, a surprising omission after the exception made in this chapter, all the more if there was an expedition against her, opposition, and fighting, ending with submission and an agreement to pay both tribute and reparations.

Melos made a contribution towards Spartan war-costs, perhaps in 427: *I.G.* v. 1. 1 (below, n. on iii. 32. 2).

5. οἱ δὲ ἄλλοι πεζὸν καὶ χρήματα: since Kerkyra, which was an ally, but not in the League, is put among the cities which contributed ships, we must conclude that other allies not in the League (Plataia, the Messenians of Naupaktos, Akarnanians, Zakynthos, and very soon Kephallenia, 30. 2) contributed money and land-troops—the latter of course only when called on, and money probably only when Athens sent military forces to their country; but the two islands may have paid something every year: see below, 13. 3, n. on ἐξακοσίων ταλάντων.

6. ξυμμαχία μὲν αὕτη ἑκατέρων καὶ παρασκευὴ ἐς τὸν πόλεμον ἦν: but it is a meagre and beggarly description, especially of the παρασκευή, with no details of forces, and above all no comparison of the strength of the two sides. Thucydides tells us more of Athens alone in c. 13, but even there not enough.

It is also to be observed that Thucydides in this chapter says nothing of the allies in the west, either on the Peloponnesian side (above, 7. 2 and iii. 86. 2) or on the Athenian (iii. 86. 3; vol. i, pp. 198, 365–6); nor, more surprisingly, of the Thessalians, who sent cavalry in accordance with an old alliance to the help of Athens this very year (22. 2–3). It is easy to say that Thucydides is here thinking only of allies ready to take part in the ensuing campaign, though even this does not avoid the disharmony. This chapter in fact looks like a short note (made at the time?), which was never properly worked into the main narrative. So 7. 1 and 10. 1 are not in full harmony with each other; and cf. n. on 19. 1.

Ullrich, p. vii n., observed that the list of allies fits (so far as it fits at all) only the ten years' war: Elis after 421 was not an ally of Sparta; Argos in 418 was an ally of Athens; and the Italian and Sicilian Greeks are absent (some of whom indeed became allies of Athens before the ten years' war was over).

10. 1. τά τε ἐπιτήδεια: supplies for at most 40 days (57. 2), though

they would expect to get a good deal on the spot, from the enemy land and from the Boeotians (22. 2, iii. 1. 2; cf. iii. 26. 4); on this occasion for perhaps thirty days (see n. on 23. 2). Cf. the agreement between Athens and Argos, Mantineia and Elis, v. 47. 6.

2. τὰ δύο μέρη: two-thirds of the front-line force of each state, the usual contingent in expeditions abroad (47. 2, iii. 15. 1). The Boeotians join later (12. 5).

It is remarkable that Thucydides gives no estimate of the total strength of the Peloponnesian land force. Ephoros (Diod. xii. 42. 3–6) only followed suit. Androtion gave a figure (F 39), but the MS. reading (Schol. Soph. O.C. 698) is, according to Jacoby in *F. Gr. Hist.*, unfortunately corrupt: καὶ μυριάσι, which at once suggests κ̄ for καί, though this gives an absurdly large figure (200,000).[1] Plutarch, *Per.* 33. 5 (and *An Seni, 2 = Mor.* 784 E), says 60,000, which may be based on the figure given by an Atthis, perhaps by Androtion. Apart from this, there is no reason to suppose that the combined force under Archidamos' command exceeded 30,000, and perhaps it did not reach that number.

11. *Speech of Archidamos*

11. 1. τῆσδε οὔπω μείζονα, κ.τ.λ.: repeating what Thucydides has himself said of the magnitude of this war, especially i. 18. 3–19.

2. ἐπῆρται - - - εὔνοιαν ἔχουσα διὰ τὸ Ἀθηναίων ἔχθος: see 8. 1, 4–5.

4. ἄδηλα γὰρ τὰ τῶν πολέμων: a view expressed more than once in speeches in Thucydides—e.g. Archidamos himself, i. 84. 3; the Spartans to the Athenians, iv. 20. 2 (indeed the whole speech); Perikles, i. 140. 1; other Athenians, i. 78. 1, vii. 61. 3. There is no reason to suppose that this was not the historian's own view as well, to suppose, on the contrary, that he thought events happened according to a predetermined and foreseeable cycle,, foreseeable, that is, by those who took the precaution to read his *History*.

δεδιὸς ἄμεινον ἠμύνατο: the MSS. reading is rightly kept by Stuart Jones and others; δεδιός is essential, both in preparing the way for the paradox in § 5, τῷ δ' ἔργῳ δεδιότας, and because it explains why so often a smaller force has beaten a larger one: 'it kept its powder dry'; it 'feared' the stronger forces of the enemy and so took proper precautions, kept itself always ready (παρεσκευάσθαι). The only objection to δεδιός is that in the previous sentence mention has been made not of carefully prepared attacks, but of impulsive ones (δι' ὀργῆς, though that may be combined with keeping your powder dry); and still more that in § 7 this is not only emphasized, but

---

[1] It is sometimes stated that Androtion's figure was 100,000 (e.g. by Bloch in *Ath. Stud.*, p. 347); but this is only one of many possible conjectures. Jacoby's 60,000 (as the basis for Plutarch's figure) is more probable.

explained by what οἱ λογισμῷ ἐλάχιστα χρώμενοι do, which is said to be particularly applicable to the Athenians. But there are other instances in the speeches of γνῶμαι somewhat isolated from their immediate context; cf. i. 77. 5 n.; and in § 6 Athens is declared to be οὐκ ἀδύνατος ἀμύνεσθαι οὕτω and ἄριστα παρεσκευασμένη.

5. τῇ μὲν γνώμῃ - - - τῷ δ' ἔργῳ: a paradoxical example of this well-used antithesis—'keep your hearts high, but do not forget the proper precautions'. (On another occasion it would be easy to reverse the positions of δεδιότας and θαρσαλέους: vi. 34. 9; cf. i. 120. 5; Hdt. vii. 49. 5.) παρεσκευάσθαι, the reading of C (though corrected by a later hand), is surely right, not παρασκευάζεσθαι. Cf. ἀμελέστερόν τι παρεσκευασμένους, § 3 above. 'You must maintain your precautions, be always on the alert.' We must not, however, whittle down the use of δεδιός here and just above; it is conscious exaggeration by Archidamos, like his defence of τὸ βραδύ and ἀμαθία, i. 84. 1–3.

7. ἐν τοῖς ὄμμασι, κ.τ.λ.: if the text is sound, we must take ἐν τῷ ὁρᾶν as parallel with ἐν τοῖς ὄμμασι, and παραυτίκα (like παραχρῆμα, i. 22. 4, ἐς τὸ παραχρῆμα ἀκούειν, not ἐν τῷ παραυτίκα, as L. and S. and some edd.) with ὁρᾶν as infinitive after ὀργὴ προσπίπτει. 'It is at the sight of an experience (or a wrong) to which we are not accustomed, and at the moment of seeing ourselves the victims of it, that excitement and anger take us all.' πάσχοντας is of course rightly in the accusative, agreeing with the understood subject of the infinitive (cf. 7. 2). But ἐν τοῖς ὄμμασι - - - ὀργὴ προσπίπτει is a strange expression; and we should perhaps emend to ἐν ⟨τῷ⟩ τοῖς ὄμμασι taking this first ἐν τῷ with ὁρᾶν, and τοῖς ὄμμασι καὶ ἐν τῷ παραυτίκα together; or to ἐν ⟨τῷ⟩ τ. ὄ. καὶ [ἐν τῷ] παρ. ὁρᾶν. (Thucydides uses παραυτίκα more often with the article, τὸ παραυτίκα, adverbially, than without; but the latter is not uncommon: ii. 49. 8, 64. 5, iii. 76. 5, viii. 48. 3. Only once elsewhere has he ἐν τῷ παραυτίκα, vii. 71. 7.) For the general meaning we might compare Soph. O.T. 1237–8.

οἱ λογισμῷ ἐλάχιστα χρώμενοι: in a different context, the contrary of this was said to be true of Athens—40. 3. But Archidamos had earlier claimed τὸ εὔβουλον for Sparta, and that she was not liable to act on the excitement of the moment, i. 84. 2–3; and to some degree he prophesied truly, both the immediate future, for 21. 2 repeats in narrative the idea expressed here (ἐν τῷ ἐμφανεῖ, ὃ οὔπω ἑοράκεσαν, and δεινὸν ἐφαίνετο; see n. there), and, of course, in the long run. Cf. also iv. 10. 1 n.

8. μᾶλλον ἢ τὴν αὐτῶν ὁρᾶν: cf. 21. 2 and iv. 92. 5.

9. τοῖς τε προγόνοις καὶ ἡμῖν αὐτοῖς: Athens thought more of posterity, 41. 2, 64. 3.

πολλοὺς ὄντας ἐνὶ κόσμῳ χρωμένους φαίνεσθαι: a fine expression of the value of discipline in an army; but also of the totalitarian state, such as Sparta was. Athens had a different ideal, 40. 2, 41. 1; but she equally valued discipline: compare, not only 37. 3, but 89. 9 with κόσμον καὶ φυλακὴν - - - τὰ παραγγελλόμενα ὀξέως δεχόμενοι here. Compare also the Greeks and the Trojans in the *Iliad*: iii. 1–10, iv. 428–38. See below, 21. 2 and 22. 1, for a further note on this speech.

12. *The Last Ambassador sent to Athens*

12. 1. Μελήσιππον: he was one of the three sent on the last embassy to Athens the year before, i. 139. 3, but not there introduced with the formality used here.

εἴ τι ἄρα μᾶλλον ἐνδοῖεν: it took a lot to convince Archidamos; see i. 82. 3, ii. 11. 6–7, 18.

2. τὸ κοινόν: the boule, perhaps, or rather the prytaneis, and the strategoi; but the ekklesia is not ruled out. ἐς τὴν πόλιν is here 'within the city'.

κήρυκα καὶ πρεσβείαν: κῆρυξ has not here its formal meaning, the herald employed only in war-time, as in i. 53. 1, 146, ii. 1; he apparently forms part of a πρεσβεία. (Thucydides has not written μήτε κ. μήτε πρ. which would mean either declaration of ἀκήρυκτος πόλεμος, or 'neither a πρ.', implying that war had not been declared, 'nor a κ.', implying that it had.) Cf. also i. 145, οὐκέτι ὕστερον ἐπρεσβεύοντο.

ἐξεστρατευμένων: Π8 reads ἐκστρατευομένων, which would do as well, since the present may mean 'to be on the march'.

3. ἥδε ἡ ἡμέρα, κ.τ.λ.: another formal note of the beginning of the war; see 19. 1 n. Edd. quote Ar. *Peace*, 435–6, as reminiscent of Melesippos' words—

σπένδοντες εὐχόμεσθα τὴν νῦν ἡμέραν
Ἕλλησιν ἄρξαι πᾶσι πολλῶν κἀγαθῶν,

and Xen. *Hell.* ii. 2. 23, of the enemies of Athens when her walls were pulled down, νομίζοντες ἐκείνην τὴν ἡμέραν τῇ Ἑλλάδι ἄρχειν τῆς ἐλευθερίας. Kassandra only was a true prophet. Compare also Hdt. v. 97. 3 (of the squadron sent from Athens to help the Ionians), itself presumably a reminiscence of *Iliad*, v. 52–53.

4. οὐδέν πω ἐνδώσουσιν: on οὔπω with the future—'they will not yet give way (but they may when they see us actually ravaging their land)'—see Shilleto's note. Steup and others adopt ἐνδωσείουσι (a conjecture which appears in E, according to Hude), partly because of the rarity of οὔπω with the future, partly, they say, because Archidamos is concerned with the present not the future intentions of the Athenians; it is sufficient to answer that he was concerned with their actions, not with their desires (so Böhme, who compares 18. 5).

προύχώρει ἐς τὴν γῆν αὐτῶν: but he did not yet cross the frontier; see 18. 1 n.

5. Βοιωτοὶ δὲ μέρος μὲν τὸ σφέτερον: two-thirds of their hoplite force, like the Peloponnesian states (10. 2), according to most edd. Not necessarily; their agreed share may have been smaller, as they had other commitments; but see n. on iv. 93. 3.

13. *Perikles on the Financial and Military Resources of Athens*

13. 1. πρὶν ἐσβαλεῖν ἐς τὴν Ἀττικήν: cf. 19. 1, 21. 1 nn.
Περικλῆς ὁ Ξανθίππου, κ.τ.λ.: formally introduced, like Archidamos, in 10. 3 and 19. 1 (where see n.), though he has been already prominent in the last part of book i.
δέκατος αὐτός: see vol. i, pp. 178–9.
ὥσπερ καὶ τὰ ἄγη: i. 126. 2–127. 1.
ἀφίησιν αὐτὰ - - - γίγνεσθαι: a characteristically vivid sentence—it is part of his speech (προηγόρευε): 'I surrender them, release them to the state, and let no suspicion lie against me on their account.'
2. ἅπερ καὶ πρότερον: see i. 144. 2, note on ἐκεῖνα, and i. 143 for the general advice here given. For what is here omitted, which we might well have expected, see vol. i, p. 21.
διὰ χειρὸς ἔχειν: 'to keep a tight hold on', as literally in 76. 4; 'not to let the League get loose, or any member of it slip away'.
τὴν ἰσχὺν - - - τῆς προσόδου: Steup, comparing iii. 13. 5–6, δι' ἣν ἡ Ἀττικὴ ὠφελεῖται· ἔστι δὲ τῶν χρημάτων ἀπὸ τῶν ξυμμάχων ἡ πρόσοδος, takes τῶν χρ. τῆς πρ. with τὴν ἰσχύν and ἀπό with τούτων only. In spite of the comparison, the rhythm of the present sentence compels, I feel, the older view that ἀπό governs τῆς προσόδου: literally 'our strength lies in the incoming of their money', the order of words giving the necessary emphasis on τὴν ἰσχύν and τούτων.
γνώμη: sound judgement, which will decide the proper strategy. I do not believe that will-power is included in γνώμη here, as Steup suggests; cf. vol. i, pp. 443–4. As in i. 144. 4, Perikles has in mind the necessity of using judgement; they must not rely on τύχη, on possible good luck if, for example, they were to attack the Peloponnesian army and take it off its guard (see 11. 3–4).
χρημάτων περιουσίᾳ: see i. 80. 4, 83. 2, 121. 5, 141. 2–5. Thucydides ever emphasizes the importance of financial strength in war, as also in the progress of states (i. 2. 2, 7. 1, etc.). Is περιουσία here 'superiority' to the enemy, or 'abundance', or 'accumulated money, capital reserves', as in i. 2. 2, 7. 1, and especially 141. 5? Probably the last, its more usual meaning in Thucydides.
3–5. θαρσεῖν τε ἐκέλευε, κ.τ.λ.: Thucydides' account of Athens' financial resources, income, and capital reserve, has been the subject of much recent study, carried out with great ingenuity and thorough-

ness. Since in the most important, *Athenian Tribute Lists*, ii and iii. (esp. pp. 118-32 and 275-345 of vol. iii), Meritt, Wade-Gery, and McGregor propose a radical correction of the text of Thucydides in § 3, it will be as well first to give an interpretation of the text as it stands in the MSS. and in our editions, with comment on certain details, and afterwards to discuss the new proposal, with which I do not agree.

3. προσιόντων μὲν - - -, ὑπαρχόντων δέ: Thucydides is carefully distinguishing between income and capital; but the latter was readily available, mostly in the form of coined money.

ἑξακοσίων ταλάντων - - - ἀπὸ τῶν ξυμμάχων: the figure, 600 talents, is a matter of considerable difficulty. The MSS. reading is confirmed by Plutarch, *Arist.* 23. 4, who cites Thucydides and thinks (naturally enough) that it shows an increase in the tribute over Aristeides' original 460 tal. (i. 96. 2), imposed by Perikles. (Diodoros gives— from Ephoros—460 tal. for this time, 431 B.C.; for his evidence see below, pp. 19, 28.) The meaning of ὡς ἐπὶ τὸ πολύ must be 'as a rule', 'generally', 'by and large' (opposed here to changes in detail from one year to another), and the phrase goes with the whole sentence, προσιόντων ἑξακοσίων ταλ. κατ' ἐνιαυτόν: cf. Isokr. iv. 154, viii. 35; Plat. *Polit.* 294 A; and in Thucydides, i. 12. 2, v. 107, vi. 46. 4 (especially the last—'not exactly the same vessels on every occasion, but by and large the same'); it does not mean, as Kolbe and Nesselhauf wished (see Nesselhauf, p. 117), 'as to the greater part', to be taken only with φόρου—'the greater part of it tribute'. Yet at no time do our records allow that anything like 600 tal. was paid in tribute at this time (see vol. i, pp. 273-8, and now *A.T.L.* iii, pp. 267-75, 338-9); and in the year 433-432, the nearest year for which we have a complete, or almost complete, list, the latest estimate is just under 390 tal. (*A.T.L.* iii, p. 334); nor is there any reason to suppose that there had been as yet any general increase in the assessment of tribute since Aristeides; indeed since the Thirty Years' Peace there had been some small decrease. Since we should not suppose Thucydides guilty of an error of this magnitude, we must conclude that he means by φόρος here all the revenue contributed by the allies— τούτων τῶν χρημάτων ἡ πρόσοδος above; and there is support for this view. (1) In vii. 57. 4 he includes Samos among the φόρου ὑποτελεῖς; yet Samos never paid φόρος in the strict sense and her name is not on any of our quota-lists; whether money contributed by her at this time (431 B.C.) was part of her reparation payments (i. 117. 3) will be discussed below (p. 33); for the moment it matters little, for even if she had paid the whole of that debt by 431, she was certainly not left to make no contribution to the League (Byzantion, which had revolted with her, returned to her status of tribute-paying member of the League); and we know in fact, from inscriptions

17

as well as from Thuc. vii. 57. 4 ($I.G.$ i.^{2} 65$_{21}$ = D 8 (426–425 B.C.) and perhaps 3244$_{2}$ = $A.F.D.$, p. 139 = Tod 64 (423–422 B.C.),[1] 302$_{18-19}$ = $A.F.D.$, p. 160 (418–417 B.C.), and 297$_{16}$ (of 414–413 B.C.) = $A.F.D.$, p. 89: see ibid., p. 130), that she continued to pay sums in a special category. (2) From $I.G.$ i.^{2} 65 we know that Thera and other cities were paying money in the same category as Samos in 426–425; and though Thera was not doing so in 431 (see above, 9. 4 n.), some of the others may have been; and in 9. 5 we are told that other allies, besides those in the League, paid money contributions (see n. there). (3) In iv. 108. 1 Thucydides says that Amphipolis was valuable to Athens ξύλων τε ναυπηγησίμων πομπῇ καὶ χρημάτων προσόδῳ; Amphipolis did not pay φόρος—at least not in the sense that a quota went to Athena—nor did Eion, at the mouth of the Strymon; so the important revenue they contributed was in addition to the 390 tal. that we know from the tribute-lists. (4) Though Meritt and his colleagues are not with me in this, chiefly because there are a few entries in the quota-lists of moneys paid to commanders in the field ($A.T.L.$ iii, p. 88), I still incline to my view that the very small sum paid regularly by Sestos and one or two other cities, and the occasional absence altogether of Thasos and others from the quota-lists, are probably to be explained by the use of such cities as naval stations and the consequent payments of sums direct to Athenian forces, from which no quota was paid to Athena (see vol. i, pp. 276–8). This is no more surprising than the absence of the payments of Amphipolis and Samos from the quota-lists. (5) There is also the possibility of some increase in payment in 431–430, already voted by Athens in 432–431 as soon as war was seen to be inevitable; for there was some increase, especially in the Hellespont region in 430–429 ($A.T.L.$ iii, pp. 70, 352), and no fragments exist of the 431–430 quota-list to disprove the suggestion that the increase was made earlier. If it had already been voted in 432–431, Perikles could have included it in his reckoning.

All these contributions together, which are certainly ἀπὸ τῶν ξυμμάχων τῇ πόλει πρόσοδος, would amount to a considerable annual sum. And besides these there is the revenue coming direct to Athena and the other gods on the Akropolis of Athens from their property abroad, within the allies' territory, property which had generally come to her when land was confiscated after an unsuccessful secession, as later in Lesbos in 427, when she got land bringing in 10 tal. a year (iii. 50. 2); we know that there were τεμένη Ἀθηνᾶς μεδεούσης in Euboea (Hestiaia, and probably in Chalkis and Eretria), Samos, and Aigina. (See my note in $C.R.$ l, 1936, 6–8.)

How much came to the gods in this way we cannot say, and it is

---

[1] I am not in fact sure of Meritt's [παρὰ] Σαμ[ίον] here in place of the older [πρὸς] Σαμ[ίος]. Pritchett–Neugebauer, p. 102, print the latter.

18

idle to guess; but it is not wrong to suppose that all these profane and sacred moneys accruing to Athens from one source or another within the empire amounted to 200 tal. yearly, and with the 390 tal. tribute attested by the quota-lists made up the 600 tal. given here as the annual revenue from the allies.

ἄνευ τῆς ἄλλης προσόδου: Xenophon, *Anab.* vii. 1. 27, reports a speech in which he said that when Athens entered on the Peloponnesian war she had 300 triremes, at sea and in the arsenals, a large reserve fund of money, and a revenue from home and abroad of 1,000 tal. This seems to be in general based on Thucydides, and, if accurate, gives us the additional figure that we need, viz. 400 tal. for the internal revenue—unless, of course, as is possible enough, like Ephoros he took 460 tal. to be the revenue from abroad, and therefore 540 or thereabouts to be the figure for the internal revenue. *A.T.L.* iii, p. 333, says that Perikles "implies that the 'other revenue' was not available for war purposes. This other revenue was doubtless sacred money used for games, festivals, and the like, and profane money too used for internal purposes". I can see no such implication; on the contrary, since these words are part of the "encouragement" for the war, the internal revenue was part of Athens' general financial resources, on the basis of which the war was to be waged; and this is also the meaning of Xenophon. Obviously a good deal of the 400 tal., or 540 tal., would be used for internal purposes—for secular public buildings, for the dicasteries, for the supervision of the markets, and the like—but perhaps not for sacred festivals, the expenses of which more probably came from the private incomes of the temples (unless this income is included in ἡ ἄλλη πρόσοδος)—but how much it is impossible to say. Athens had spent, and continued to spend, *some* money on her navy—her own contribution to the imperial forces. See below, pp. 31–32, 42–43.

We should bear this sum, 400 or 540 tal. for Athens' internal revenue, in mind in connexion with the tribute paid by the allies; and as well the 200 tal. raised by εἰσφορά in 428 (iii. 19. 1). No one of the allied states in the League paid more than 30 tal. φόρος, and all of them together paid no more than half as much again as Athens' own revenue (600 :: 400 tal.); or, more significantly, omitting the many very small contributors, taking only those who paid ½ tal. or more tribute (φόρος in the strict sense), we can see that about 80 states paid, in 433–432 B.C. (list 22 in *A.T.L.*), about 340 tal., less than Athens' own internal revenue, and this for the privilege of being relieved of further payment for defence. It is clear that the tribute cannot have been a heavy financial burden on the subject allies as a whole, nor a large addition to their ordinary budgets, even if one or two (Aigina, with 30 tal. ?) were severely taxed; it was the infringement of autonomy, being φόρου ὑποτελεῖς at all, not αὐτοτελεῖς (v. 18. 2), and having the amount of their tribute decided by another state, that was resented, where resentment was felt.

ἐν τῇ ἀκροπόλει: this will, or should, include the "treasury of the Goddess" and "the treasury of the Other Gods", according to the now accepted date, 434-433, of the decrees of Kallias (I.G.i.[2] 91-92 =Tod, 51 = A.T.L. ii, D 1-2), as well as the treasury of the Hellenotamiai. See A.T.L. iii, pp. 332-3; and below, n. on τὰ ἐκ τῶν ἄλλων ἱερῶν, § 5, and pp. 31-32.

ἀργυρίου ἐπισήμου: all rentals from temple-lands or money from the sale of produce, all fines, and all tribute from the allies, came in the form of coin; and the last in Attic coin at this time, if the terms of the coinage decree of c. 450 were enforced (A.T.L. ii, D 14; cf. my vol. i, pp. 205-6, 383-4; E. S. G. Robinson, Hesp. Suppl. viii, 1949, 324-40. For doubts about the date of this decree, see Tod, J.H.S. lxix, 1949, 105, who shows some good reasons for a date later than 438).

ἑξακισχιλίων ταλάντων: the equivalent of ten years' revenue from imperial sources, of six years' revenue perhaps from all sources; the largest sum, 9,700 tal. mentioned below, equal to about sixteen and ten years' revenue respectively.

τὰ γὰρ πλεῖστα: 'the largest sum that had been on the Akropolis at any one time.' See below, p. 27.

ἔς τε τὰ προπύλαια - - - καὶ τἆλλα οἰκοδομήματα - - - ἀπανηλώθη: the Propylaia is the only building mentioned by name for two reasons: (1) that it was the most recent, work on its construction continuing until the outbreak of war; and (2) it was in this sense the most splendid of Athenian buildings, or the most significant instance of their splendour, that whereas magnificent temples were known, even if the Parthenon surpassed them all—that of Zeus himself at Olympia was but a generation old—such a gateway to a sacred precinct was unique in its fine extravagance. It was thus more than once singled out for praise in the fourth-century writers: Dem. xiii. 28; Aischines, ii. 105; Dem. Phal., F. Gr. Hist. 228 F 8 (Cic. de Off. ii. 60); Dem. xxii. 13 mentions both Propylaia and Parthenon. For estimates of the cost of the buildings, and some discussion on what are included in 'the other buildings', see below, pp. 22-25.

καὶ ἐς Ποτείδαιαν ἀπανηλώθη: two preliminary points should be noticed: first, that expenditure on a war is from the capital reserve. This is in accord with our inscriptional evidence, both direct records of war expenditure, e.g. Ἀθεναῖοι ἀ[νέλοσαν - - - ἐς τὸν] πρὸς Σαμίο[ς πόλεμον] in 440-439 B.C. (I.G. i.[2] 293 = Tod, 50 = A.F.D., p. 47), or [Ἀθεναῖοι ἀνέλ]οσαν ἐς Κόρκ[υραν τάδε] in 433-432 (i.[2] 295 = Tod, 55 = A.F.D., pp. 69-71), or [Ἀθεναῖοι ἀνέλ]οσαν ἐς Μα[κεδονίαν καὶ Ποτείδαιαν καὶ ἐς Πελοπόννησον] in 432-431 (i.[2] 296 = A.F.D., pp. 80-83), where the money is actually found by the treasurers of Athena

20

(who looked after the reserve fund in the Akropolis), and records of the *logistai*, i.e. of loans, and interest due on loans, made by the treasurers of Athena to the state during the war, almost all for war purposes (*I.G.* i.² 324: below, pp. 432 ff.); all these payments, like those for the buildings, come from the reserve. Secondly, no mention is made of the Samian and Kerkyra wars, the expenses of which had been met in the same way as those of the Poteidaian campaign.¹ The absence of Samos can be at least theoretically explained if she had paid in reparations the whole cost of the war (1,276 tal.) by 431 B.C.; for the reserve fund would in that event have got back what it had spent (Kolbe, 74–75); but most scholars would deny that more than a small part of the debt had yet been repaid (see below, p. 33). The absence of Kerkyra can, it seems, only be explained by the small cost of the expedition (the total is doubtful: 76 tal. according to the received view); and some of it may have been repaid by Kerkyra— perhaps its cost from the time of its leaving Zakynthos, the last Athenian ally before Kerkyra, till its return there. (Cf. v. 47. 6 = *I.G.* i.² 86. 20.)

Theoretically again, we might suppose that the Samian war-costs are omitted because the highest total, 9,700 tal., was reached after 439; in that event most of the cost of the Parthenon (and the Parthenos statue) would also be excluded. It is, however, virtually impossible to believe that the fund was at its maximum after so much had been spent. By a similar argument in reverse, we may note as well the absence of the cost of the Koroneia and Euboea campaigns of 447 and 446; but this may not have been heavy, for they were short and were on land;² the maximum in the reserve may well have been reached in 446 or 445, though more probably in 447 before large expenditure on the buildings had begun.

The total cost of the siege of Poteidaia was 2,000 tal. and more (ii. 70. 2). The initial expenses in 432 will have been high, for they include those of three fleets, triremes and transports (i. 59. 1, 61. 1, 64. 2), as well as the early cost of the exceptionally paid hoplites (iii. 17. 4). Compare the high initial costs of the Sicilian expedition (3,000 tal. were voted in 416–415: *I.G.* i.² 99. 25–28; 300 tal. was sent out in 415–414, and 120 tal. in the winter of 414–413: Thuc. vi. 94. 4, vii. 16. 2. See *A.T.L.*, iii. 356–7). In *A.T.L.* iii. 340 and 342, n. 73, it is calculated that 400 tal. had been spent by the early spring of 431, the time of Perikles' speech; we need not bind Thucydides so closely

¹ *A.T.L.* iii, p. 329, draws a distinction between loans and gifts from Athena's treasury for the Samos and Kerkyra campaigns; but that does not affect us here—either would reduce the amount in the reserve fund in the spring of 431.

² *A.T.L.* iii, p. 340, suggests that land-campaigns may have cost more. Not initially, at any rate, for the hoplites supplied their own armour and mustered with three days' rations; and an army, save in exceptional cases such as the Sicilian expedition, would expect to live off the land.

to a date for ἔτι τότε ἑξακισχιλίων ταλάντων, but in any case I should put the figure a good deal higher, 800, perhaps as much as 1,000 tal. If we are right to ignore all other military expenditure, this would leave rather less than 3,000 tal. for the sum spent on the Propylaia and other buildings.

Heliodoros the antiquary (of the second century B.C.? see Jacoby in *R.E.*, s.v.) is reported by Harpokration and Souidas as saying that the Propylaia was completed (ἐξεποιήθη) in five years, cost 2,012 (or 2,011) tal., and had five gates (*F. Gr. Hist.* 373 F 1). The first statement is nearly true: that is, Philochoros (F 121) says that building began in 437–436, and it would fit the inscriptional evidence if it stopped in 433–432, though this is not certain (*I.G.* i.² 363–7; for some new readings, see *A.T.L.* iii. 329–31)—and the Propylaia was not *completed*. The statement of cost therefore should also be reliable, and it looks, so exact is it, to be based on epigraphic or other official evidence. Yet it must be very far from the truth. If the Propylaia cost 2,000 tal., the Parthenon cost very much more: its style of building is similar, it is a good deal larger, and it was adorned with a great variety of sculpture (only its substructure may have cost less, as Kolbe argues, if this had most of it been built in Kimon's time). The gold and ivory statue cost perhaps 750 tal. (see below, on αὐτῆς τῆς θεοῦ, § 5); and there are other buildings, certainly the Odeion for example (Plut. *Per.* 13. 9), to be included in τἆλλα οἰκοδομήματα; perhaps also all or some of the other temples which belong to this period (see below on τὰ ἐκ τῶν ἄλλων ἱερῶν, § 5); and though none were of the same splendour as the Akropolis buildings, yet together they must have cost a considerable sum.

There is, moreover, another way to approach the problem. We have some figures for the cost of the fourth-century temple and tholos at Epidauros (*I.G.* iv.² 102–3): that was smaller than the Parthenon and was built of stone, not marble, and required a far lower degree of accuracy in the masonry; but much of its material had to be transported for as long distances as that for the Akropolis, and the cost of this at least may therefore have been as great. Some figures are directly comparable: e.g. the similar payments to the overseer (ἀρχιτέκτων). R. W. Stanier has recently published an article making the comparison between the Akropolis and the Epidauros temples: *J.H.S.* lxxiii, 1953, 68–76. The figures suggest a sum of something like 50 tal. for the Asklepieion, and therefore that the cost of the Propylaia and the Parthenon must be reckoned in hundreds, not thousands of talents (in spite of the fine rhetoric of λίθους πολυτελεῖς καὶ ἀγάλματα καὶ ναοὺς χιλιοταλάντους, Plut. *Per.* 12. 2, which is doubtless contemporary), 200 to 250 tal. perhaps, and 300 to 500 tal., respectively.¹ This would give a maximum of 750 tal., and,

¹ I am a layman in these matters; but it is not unreasonable to expect that

22

with the gold and ivory statue (§ 5 n.), of perhaps 1,550 tal. for these two buildings.

A.T.L. iii, p. 124, n. 15, accept 2,012 tal. as a true figure obtained from the official record, but of a total spent on all the Akropolis building (including the Parthenos statue) of which the Propylaia was the last, and would be the last mentioned item, either Heliodoros or the lexica which quote him being responsible for the mistake of applying it to the Propylaia alone. This may be true, though Heliodoros' error would be a remarkable one, and Harpokration's quotation does not read like a mistaken summary; if so, and if *c.* 3,000 tal. were spent on building altogether (above, p. 22), about 1,000 tal. were spent elsewhere than on the Akropolis.

4. χρυσίου ἀσήμου καὶ ἀργυρίου, κ.τ.λ.: uncoined gold and silver from dedications, public and private, in the temples, equipment for festivals, and the Persian spoils (these last really a special form of public dedication). We possess annual records, made by the boards of ταμίαι, from 434–433 to 407–406 B.C., of the sacred objects belonging to Athena and stored in the three parts of the Parthenon (Pronaos, Hekatompedon, and Parthenon proper—the inner cella), and of those belonging to the other Gods, also now stored on the Akropolis (*I.G.* i.² 232–92, 310; Tod, 69, 70, 78). The greater part of Athena's treasure consisted of objects—statuettes, cups, crowns, and the like—in gold and silver, with their weights recorded; of that of the other Gods, coined money; uncoined bullion, gold or silver, is rare. The objects might be melted down, and the metal sold or made into coin; and Thucydides presumably has this in mind. The total value, however, of the objects recorded in these inscriptions is not more than 20 tal. silver; and much the greater part of the 500 tal. worth mentioned here must have been stored elsewhere, and not recorded (or the record is lost)—it will have been, most of it, bullion.

It may be noted that these gold and silver dedications were not in fact melted down till the last desperate days of the war, in 406–405, and not all then (Tod, pp. 171, 172).

5. τὰ ἐκ τῶν ἄλλων ἱερῶν: the 'Treasury of the Other Gods', similar

architects should be able to tell us that if the Propylaia cost *x*, the Parthenon (the building only, not the sculpture) cost $x + \frac{1}{4}x$ or whatever it should be; that the Parthenon should not have cost more than so many times what the Epidauros temple cost; and that, since we have detailed figures for some of the costs of the Erechtheion, including its sculpture, we could make some calculations for the other buildings. It is to be borne in mind what the problem is: not, did the Propylaia cost 150 or 200 or 300 talents? but, did it cost 200 or 2,000? Beloch, ii.² 335–6, asserted the lower figures, while so good a scholar as Kolbe (pp. 78–85) accepted Heliodoros' figure, 2,012 tal., for the Propylaia and thought the Parthenon might have cost *less*, about 1,200 tal. I cannot believe either of Kolbe's figures in themselves, nor their relation to each other; but it is for the experts to say.

to the Treasury of Athena and administered by a similar board of $\tau\alpha\mu\iota\alpha\iota$, had been instituted in 434–433 by the first decree of Kallias ($I.G.$ i.[2] 91 = Tod, 51 = $A.T.L.$ ii, D 1), and was placed on the Akropolis, sharing the Opisthodomos with Athena's treasury. If Thucydides is being strictly accurate, it should therefore have been already included in the moneys on the Akropolis, in § 3; and $A.T.L.$ iii, p. 333, assumes this to be the case, and that the money in 'the other temples' here mentioned is that at Eleusis, at Rhamnous in the Amphiareion, at Sounion and elsewhere in Attica. This is probably correct; but it should be added that, unless these places were strongly garrisoned, or Peloponnesian and Boeotian piety could be firmly trusted, not only not to loot the temples but not to 'borrow' from them as they had proposed to borrow from Delphi and Olympia (i. 121. 3), it is not very likely that these treasures were left in out-lying parts of Attica. All, at least all the money and bullion, will have been brought within the walls; and the most convenient place for storing it was the Akropolis; and we know from $I.G.$ i.[2] 324, lines 55–97, that many at least of the treasuries from the temples outside Athens were included in that of 'the Other Gods'. (See, however, $I.G.$ i.[2] 313, 314, records of the Eleusinian treasures of 408–407 and 407–406—after the triumphant return of Alkibiades to Athens and the celebration of the Mysteries once more in the tradi-tional manner—in which the objects are divided between the Akro-polis, the Eleusinion in Athens, and Eleusis.) If this is so, $\grave{\epsilon}\nu$ $\tau\hat{\eta}$ $\mathring{\alpha}\kappa\rho o\pi\acute{o}\lambda\epsilon\iota$ above, § 3, will refer only to treasuries officially, so to speak, at home on the Akropolis.

I referred above to a number of new temples, outside the Akro-polis, which were built, to judge from their style, during this period, 447 to 432, or are so recorded by ancient writers: the Hephaisteion, that of Ares in the agora, those at Rhamnous and Sounion, and the $telesterion$ at Eleusis (Plut. $Per.$ 13. 7; Dinsmoor, $Hesp.$ ix, 1940, 47). If all of these were built from funds in the possession of the sanctuaries, their expense will not fall within the 3,700 tal. referred to in § 3. It is generally, but silently, assumed that this is so; but if it is the case, these sanctuaries must have had con-siderable sums at their disposal, and this will be of some significance in the discussion of the size of Athena's own treasury (below, p. 28); and the joint treasury of the Other Gods established in 434–433 will have had in it only what was left after large expenditure.

$\mathring{\eta}\nu$ $\pi\acute{\alpha}\nu\upsilon$ $\grave{\epsilon}\xi\epsilon\acute{\iota}\rho\gamma\omega\nu\tau\alpha\iota\,\pi\acute{\alpha}\nu\tau\omega\nu$: 'if we are excluded from all.' From what? from the sea? or the Laureion mines? Perhaps it is not so definite; but Perikles is thinking of an almost desperate situation.

$\alpha\mathring{\upsilon}\tau\hat{\eta}\varsigma$ $\tau\hat{\eta}\varsigma$ $\theta\epsilon o\hat{\upsilon}$ $\tauo\hat{\iota}\varsigma$ $\pi\epsilon\rho\iota\kappa\epsilon\iota\mu\acute{\epsilon}\nuo\iota\varsigma$ $\chi\rho\upsilon\sigma\acute{\iota}o\iota\varsigma$, $\kappa.\tau.\lambda.$: see $I.G.$ i.[2] 354–62 (cf. Tod, 47) for the expense accounts of the statue, from 447–446 to 438–437, when it was dedicated. Dinsmoor, $'E\phi.$ $'A\rho\chi.$ 1937, 501–11, gives the most detailed account of them, and concludes that the total cost, gold, ivory, and other materials, and the work, was 847 tal. 700 dr. + ; and this figure has been quoted by others as authoritative. It is, I think, too high. Philochoros, F 121, gives 44 tal. as the weight of the gold; this looks like an accurate statement (but see below, p. 186, for this fragment of Philochoros) and Thucydides may be giving a round number (Diodoros, xii. 40. 3, says 50 tal., and this is probably from Ephoros), or his MSS. may be at fault, $\langle \tau \acute{\epsilon} \sigma \sigma \alpha \rho \alpha \ \kappa \alpha \grave{\iota} \rangle$ τεσσαράκοντα being an easy emendation. Gold then stood at 14 to 1 of silver ($I.G.$ i.^{2} 355, which records the purchase of gold for the statue); so 40 tal. cost 560 tal. of silver, 44 cost 616 tal. This leaves 230 tal. (847—616) as the cost of the other material (ivory and wood mainly), freight, and salaries of artists and workmen—an incredible sum; and in fact Dinsmoor's total figure is, as he says, only the mean between two epigraphically possible extremes, namely

ΓΗ Η Η [Η Η Ρ 4 4 4 4 Ρ] | Γ Δ Δ - - - = 995 tal. 520+

and

ΓΗ Η Η [4 4 4 4 Τ Τ Τ Τ] | Γ Δ Δ - - - = 744 tal. 520+

Obviously a figure very near the lowest possible, 744 or 748 tal.+, is much more probable than 850 tal. Even this leaves 130 tal. for the ivory, freight, and salaries; and 130 tal. is a very large sum— 780,000 dr. See below, pp. 45–47; and Addenda.[1]

περιαιρετὸν εἶναι ἅπαν: almost inevitably the foolish story grew that Perikles and Pheidias had cunningly so devised the statue that the gold could be removed and weighed, anticipating the expected attack on the artist for putting some of it into his pocket (Plut. $Per.$ 31. 3). Of course gold on a wooden statue is, in the nature of things, removable and replaceable.

So far as we know, and in this case our ignorance is practically decisive, the Athenians did not make use of this considerable gold reserve, even in the closing stage of the war, nor, when one might think it would be an even greater temptation, in the difficult first years of the peace: neither the Thirty nor the restored democracy proposed it.[2]

---

[1] Dinsmoor thinks that $I.G.$ i.^{2} 354, which contains these figures, is the last of the series and therefore to be dated in 438–437, in spite of certain archaic features in the lettering. But it may be a little earlier (as in $I.G.$): much the largest disbursement, for the gold, would have been made early in the making; and though the fine style of the lettering suggests a monument, the absence of title for the whole (unless there had once been another stone fitted above?) is against its being final.

[2] There is no good $evidence$ that they ever borrowed or looted Athena's golden dress. True the wicked Lachares was said by someone in a comedy to have stripped her bare, γυμνὴν ἐποίησε τὴν Ἀθηνᾶν Λαχάρης, and true that a later historian ($Ox. Pap.$ xvii. 2082; see Ferguson, $C.P.$ 1929, 1–20; $F. Gr. Hist.$ 257 A) and Pausanias, i. 25. 7, both supposed this to mean that the statue had been

μὴ ἐλάσσω ἀντικαταστῆσαι πάλιν: this refers, I feel sure, only to the gold and silver ἀναθήματα, public and private, of §§ 4–5, which belong to the temples, not to the reserve fund of § 3, which was only deposited with Athena. Yet from about this time, perhaps for the expenses of the squadron to Kerkyra and certainly for all war operations after 431, money taken from this fund was called a loan, and not only that, but a loan at interest; so that the erection of a new reserve fund after 421 was treated as a repayment of the principal and interest of the various loans made during ten or twelve years. See nn. on *I.G.* i.² 324, below on iii. 116 and v. 19. 2. It may be (if it is desirable to pin Thucydides to a detailed accuracy) that the decision to treat the money taken from the fund in 433–432 and 432–431 as a loan to be repaid was only taken after the war had broken out.

The Text of 13. 3

In *Historia*, ii, 1953, 44–63, I have argued against the reading and interpretation of § 3 given in *A.T.L.* Some of the problems have already been discussed in the above notes on §§ 3–5; a summary of the essential argument of my paper in *Historia* follows. It will be clear to all students of Athenian finance how much in this is owed to Kolbe, *Thuk. im Lichte d. Urk.*, c. ii, even though he was writing before Wade-Gery's discovery of the relationship between the two Kallias-decrees, *I.G.* i.² 91 and 92 (*J.H.S.* li, 1931, 57–85).

The scholion on Aristophanes' *Ploutos*, 1193, in the Venetus and Ravenna MSS., quotes Thucydides, ii. 13. 3 in this form: ὑπαρχόντων δὲ ἐν τῇ ἀκροπόλει αἰεί ποτε ἀργυρίου ἐπισήμου ἑξακισχιλίων ταλάντων· τὰ γὰρ πλεῖστα τριακοσίων ἀποδέοντα περιεγένετο· ἀφ' ὧν ἔς τε τὰ προπύλαια καὶ τἆλλα οἰκοδομήματα καὶ ἐς Ποτείδαιαν ἐπανηλώθη. (R. has ἄγει ποτέ for αἰεί ποτε; V. has τά for τριακοσίων, presumably by mistake for ζ̄.) This is translated in *A.T.L.* (iii, p. 131): "And there was, he said, a regular standing amount of 6,000 talents on the Akropolis. (The greater part of this, actually 5,700 talents, was in

stripped; but, apart from the bias of the charge at a time of acute party strife, the verse could have been as justly written had Lachares emptied her treasury (as the Athenians had nearly done in 421, and did by 406), still more if he had melted down gold and silver dedications. If he did take it, when were the Athenians prosperous enough, or what shy, retiring prince was generous enough, to replace it?

(The same rhetorical question is the answer to Dinsmoor's most unconvincing theory that the Parthenon was so badly burnt in a fire c. 165 B.C. that the gold of the statue must have melted, and the ivory been destroyed (*A.J.A.* xxxviii, 1934, 93–106). He assumed that Attalos II, or some other of the philathenian princes of the time, may have restored it: that is, that though the Attalid dedications on the Akropolis were known and much talked about, and Attalos', like Antiochos', splendid generosity to Athens trumpeted abroad, this little act was forgotten. This is to sacrifice *history* to archaeological theory.)

26

fact still there. There had been extra disbursements from it for the Propylaia and other buildings and for Poteidaia.)" There are three variations from the reading of our MSS. of Thucydides: αἰεί ποτε for ἔτι τότε, περιεγένετο for μύρια ἐγένετο, and ἐπανηλώθη for ἀπανηλώθη. The authors of A.T.L. maintain that the scholiast's reading is both linguistically superior and alone consonant with the facts. For the language, they point out that αἰεί ποτε is a phrase found several times in Thucydides, ἔτι τότε but rarely; and they assert that οἱ πλεῖστοι, τὰ πλεῖστα, etc., always means 'the majority' in him (though not in Herodotos, Isokrates, or Plutarch), never 'the maximum', 'the largest number', and that if he wanted a word for the latter he used πλεῖστοι, etc., without the article. The former of these is pure accident;[1] the latter argument, I think, shows misunderstanding: the difference between οἱ πλεῖστοι and πλεῖστοι in Greek is grammatical, not semantic, whether 'the maximum' or 'the majority' is the meaning; an easy example is iv. 31. 2, μέσον δὲ - - - οἱ πλεῖστοι αὐτῶν καὶ Ἐπιτάδας ὁ ἄρχων εἶχε, and 33. 1, οἱ περὶ τὸν Ἐπιτάδαν καὶ ὅπερ ἦν πλεῖστον: οἱ πλεῖστοι and ὅπερ ἦν πλεῖστον mean the same troops, and this could be either the majority of the Spartan troops or the largest of the three detachments into which they were divided. Further, the meaning of the last sentence, ἀφ᾽ ὧν - - - ἐπανηλώθη, seems to me forced: 'from this (the 6,000 tal., not the sum just mentioned) extra payments had been made' which had the effect of bringing a reserve which had been constant at 6,000 tal. to 300 tal. less, when the greater part of the payments, those on the buildings, had not only been made over the whole period of fifteen years from 447 to 432, but had been so managed, according to A.T.L., that, offset by the yearly surplus of the tribute, the reserve had been kept constant. The only extra disbursement would have been that for Poteidaia. We must keep ἀπανηλώθη; and the authors of A.T.L. do not, of course, set much store by this variation.

But much the greatest linguistic difficulty is that τὰ πλεῖστα τριακοσίων ἀποδέοντα is a meaningless phrase: it should be translated 'the greater part less 300 tal.', not 'the greater part, that is, the sum just mentioned less 300 tal.' We should need τοσαῦτα or τὰ πάντα (cf. vii. 57. 4, τὸ πλεῖστον Ἴωνες ὄντες οὗτοι πάντες - - - πλὴν Καρυστίων, the passage cited in A.T.L. to justify their translation), or the figure, from which a figure can be deducted; in fact, I am sure that Thucydides would have written τοσαῦτα γὰρ καὶ ὀλίγῳ ἐλάσσω περιεγένετο to express this meaning. A number then has been dropped by mistake in the scholion; which will not surprise us (as in the Venetus τριακοσίων has itself disappeared); the figure was mistaken for the short

___

[1] I doubt too whether αἰεί ποτε ('traditional', 'of long standing', κατὰ τὴν Ἀθηναίων αἰεί ποτε φιλίαν, iii. 95. 1, etc.) would be used here in the sense required by A.T.L.

form of $\pi\epsilon\rho\iota$ and $\pi\epsilon\rho\iota\epsilon\gamma\acute{\epsilon}\nu\epsilon\tau o$ was the result; and the question becomes, is there good reason to doubt that the figure was $\mu\acute{\nu}\rho\iota\alpha$ as given by our MSS. of Thucydides? The later literary evidence supports it: for Ephoros mentioned 10,000 tal. as the sum on the Akropolis from which 4,000 tal. had been taken for the Propylaia and the Poteidaia campaign (Diod. xii. 40. 2—this is expressly from Ephoros: 41. 1), and Isokrates (viii. 69, xv. 234) and Demosthenes (iii. 24), more simply, as the amount once on the Akropolis. Diodoros (xii. 38. 2) and Isokrates (viii. 126) also speak of a sum of 8,000 tal., 'collected from the allies and placed on the Akropolis'; we need not attribute the confusion to Ephoros—he may easily have thought that 8,000 tal. was the accumulated sum in 454 when the treasury of the League was transferred to Athens, and that the reserve had grown to 10,000 by 431.

The authors of *A.T.L.*, however, say that there is evidence that, in fact, there never had been at any time a sum of 9,700 tal. in the reserve fund, nor anything like it, and that the fund had been kept fairly constant at 6,000 tal. since the Peace of Kallias in 450–449; and that Thucydides could not have been ignorant of this. (In this last point I am altogether with them.)[1] They rely for this on the papyrus fragment of a commentary on Demosthenes xxii known as *Anonymus Argentinensis* (first published by B. Keil, Strasbourg, 1902; see a better text in Wilcken, *Hermes*, xlii, 1907, 374–418; *A.T.L.* ii, D 13), and on *I.G.* i.[2] 91, the financial decree of Kallias (*A.T.L.* ii, D 1; Tod, 51). But the restoration, the interpretation, and the value of this torn piece of papyrus are all alike doubtful; and the interpretation of the relevant clause in Kallias' decree is by no means certain. The *A.T.L.* restoration of the papyrus (most conveniently now to be read in Andrewes and Meiggs's edition of Hill's *Sources*, Oxford, 1951, p. 51) is to be translated as follows: '(on Dem. xxii. 13, the building of the Propylaia and the Parthenon) thirty-three years after

---

[1] S. Accame, in *Riv. d. Filol.* xxx, 1952, 245 (in an article which appeared too late for me to use in my paper in *Historia*) has a variation of Beloch's view that Thucydides was so ignorant of Athenian finances that he thought the reserve fund at its maximum to have been 9,700 tal. (whereas *we* know so much better), and to have reached this maximum in 433: namely that Thucydides by an oversight (*una svista*: comparable to 'the oversight' in § 6 below, when he 'gives 29,000 as the total hoplite population when he should have given it as the total of adult males of all classes') gave the figure 9,700 tal., as a maximum, though it was really the total of all moneys paid in by the Hellenotamiai between 448–447 and 432–431: this sum was, in fact, 9,656 tal. (*A.T.L.* iii. 338–40). Thucydides so accurate, yet so slipshod; for what did the year 448–447 mean to him? This sum of 9,656 tal. was not, as far as we know, even the result of additions or calculations made in Athens; it belongs only to the present decade of scholarship; some of the items are very doubtful, and it is largely the result of the same calculations as those by which the impossibility of Thucydides' maximum has been argued.

the Persian wars they began to build the temples (i.e. 447–446 B.C.):[1] they accomplished this and what else was necessary when in the archonship of Euthydemos (i.e. 450–449 B.C.)[2] Perikles moved a decree to touch ($\kappa\iota\nu\epsilon\hat{\iota}\nu$, as restored: cf. Thuc. ii. 24. 1) the 5,000 tal. accumulated from the phoros according to Aristeides' assessment which was stored in the public treasury ($\dot{\epsilon}\nu\ \delta\eta\mu\sigma\sigma\dot{\iota}\omega\ \dot{a}\pi\sigma\kappa\epsilon\dot{\iota}\mu\epsilon\nu a$).' It is argued that there was no separate fund, available for war, in $\tau\dot{o}\ \delta\eta\mu\dot{o}\sigma\iota\sigma\nu$ (below, p. 31), and this 5,000 tal., therefore, represents the whole reserve of the League and of Athens in 450, all saved from the surplus of the tribute; Athena may have had an additional 1,000 tal. in her private treasury (see esp. *A.T.L.* iii. 281, 327–8). But Ephoros gave 8,000 as the figure of the accumulated surplus of League funds in 454. The explanation of this apparent discrepancy is to be found in the clause of Kallias' decree (ll. 3–4), 'now that the 3,000 tal. which had been voted have been taken ($\dot{a}\nu\epsilon\nu\dot{\epsilon}\nu\epsilon\gamma\kappa\tau a\iota$) to the Akropolis for Athena'. What, ask the authors of *A.T.L.*, were these 3,000 tal.? It was not a sum to be collected in a day. They find that probably in the decree of 449 referred to in the papyrus, Perikles moved (1) that the accumulated surplus of the tribute be used for the buildings (as we know he did), and (2) that, since these buildings would cost about 3,000 tal. and take fifteen years to complete, i.e. the cost would average 200 tal. a year, the sum of 200 tal. annual surplus of the tribute be placed every year in Athena's treasury, not only making again a total of 3,000 tal., which was 'placed with Athena' (the Kallias decree), but *with the effect of keeping the reserve practically level* at 6,000 tal. (5,000 from the Aristeidean tribute, and 1,000 in Athena's 'privy purse'), $\dot{\upsilon}\pi a\rho\chi\dot{o}\nu\tau\omega\nu\ \dot{\epsilon}\nu\ \tau\hat{\eta}\ \dot{a}\kappa\rho\sigma\pi\dot{o}\lambda\epsilon\iota\ a\dot{\iota}\epsilon\dot{\iota}\ \pi\sigma\tau\epsilon - - - \dot{\epsilon}\xi a\kappa\iota\sigma\chi\iota\lambda\dot{\iota}\omega\nu\ \tau a\lambda\dot{a}\nu\tau\omega\nu$. (A Fifteen-Year Plan which in its optimistic accuracy has not been equalled by any modern statesman.) Ephoros' 8,000 tal. is a mistake arising out of these two figures of 5,000 and 3,000; there had never been such a sum in the treasury.

I find it impossible to accept these conclusions. First, there are two difficulties inherent in the scheme itself: one is that the theory that no collection of tribute was made in 449–448 is still maintained in *A.T.L.*, yet Perikles moved his decree (to put into the reserve 200 tal. a year from the tribute) in the previous year, 450–449, towards its close. This is just possible if Athens had proclaimed, towards the end of 450, 'we are summoning a Panhellenic Congress

---

[1] It is to be noted that 'after the Persian wars' ([$\dot{\upsilon}\sigma\tau\epsilon\rho\sigma\nu\ \tau\hat{\omega}\nu\ \Pi\epsilon\rho\sigma\iota]\kappa\hat{\omega}\nu$) should be after 479–478, and 33 years after would be 446–445. The figures $\overline{\Lambda\Gamma}$ on the papyrus are in fact extremely doubtful.

[2] Euthynos was the true name of the archon of 450–449, but the two names were often confused, as by Diodoros, who calls both this Euthynos and the archon of 426–425 Euthydemos. The latter was the name of the archon of 431–430. (Andrewes and Meiggs, though printing *A.T.L.*'s restoration of the papyrus, give 431–430 as the date of Euthydemos; *A.T.L.* gives 450–449.)

[see vol. i, pp. 366–7], and there will be no tribute to pay next year'; and then in the early summer of 449, 'the Congress has failed; we must maintain our large fleet and rebuild our temples ourselves, so tribute will be resumed in 448–447'; but it is difficult. I do not myself believe that the collection of tribute was suspended for a year;[1] but if A.T.L. is right in this, the difficulty remains. Secondly, there must, on any theory, have been a drop in the reserve fund of 1,000 tal. at least between 440 and 439, when the heavy expenses of the Samian war had to be met and no reparations had yet been paid; and if A.T.L.'s view is correct that Samos paid reparations only at the rate of 50 tal. a year (see below, p. 33), there would have been still some 700 tal. less in 432 than in 439. This is inconsistent with the view that there were always about 6,000 tal. in the fund from 448 to 432, and that only the extra expenditure at Poteidaia had brought the sum down to 5,700 in 431.

But there are more important arguments. Both the date and the content of the papyrus decree are obviously quite uncertain; Perikles could have moved a decree about the accumulated reserve of the Aristeidean tribute in 431 (archonship of Euthydemos) as well as in 449; and since we do not know the length of line, many other restorations are possible: e.g. a statement that the buildings were completed after fifteen years ($\mu\epsilon\tau$’ $\check{\epsilon}\tau\eta$ $\overline{\Lambda\Gamma}$ | [$\dot{\epsilon}\pi\grave{\iota}$ $T\iota\mu\alpha\rho\chi\acute{\iota}\delta\sigma\upsilon$ $\mathring{\upsilon}\sigma\tau\epsilon\rho\sigma\nu$ $\tau\hat{\omega}\nu$ $\Pi\epsilon\rho\sigma\iota$]$\kappa\hat{\omega}\nu$ $\mathring{\eta}\rho\xi\alpha\nu\tau\sigma$ $\sigma\mathring{\iota}\kappa\sigma\delta\sigma[\mu\epsilon]\hat{\iota}\nu$, $\dot{\epsilon}\pi\sigma\acute{\iota}$[$\eta\sigma\alpha\nu$ $\delta\grave{\epsilon}$ $\mu\epsilon\tau\grave{\alpha}$ $\delta\epsilon\kappa\alpha\pi\acute{\epsilon}\nu\tau\epsilon$ $\check{\epsilon}\tau\eta$]), and a mention of a decree in 431 ([$\dot{\epsilon}\pi\grave{\iota}$ δ’ $E\mathring{\upsilon}$]$\theta\upsilon\delta\acute{\eta}\mu\sigma[\upsilon]$), not to use the reserve without a special vote of the ekklesia ([$\check{\alpha}\nu\epsilon\upsilon$ $\dot{\alpha}\delta\epsilon\acute{\iota}\alpha\varsigma$ $\mu\grave{\eta}$ $\kappa\iota\nu\epsilon\hat{\iota}\nu$]: cf. I.G. i.[2] 92, the second Kallias decree = Tod, 51 B, line 16, and 302, the payments from Athena's treasury for state purposes in 418–417 B.C. = Tod, 75, lines 15, 28, 30, 33, 57).[2] This would not be very accurate, nor relevant to Demosthenes; but neither is the next note in the papyrus, which is about old and new triremes. We do not, in fact, know the value of the papyrus any better than we know its missing letters, as Wilcken pointed out; and, even if the A.T.L. restoration is correct, it is wrong in principle to correct Ephoros' 8,000 tal. for the surplus of 454 B.C., however unreliable a writer he was, by the doubtful evidence of the papyrus. This figure in Ephoros may come from a good source (as his 10,000 tal. less 4,000 in 431 comes, I am sure, from Thucydides); and, if it does, it is clear that the maximum may at one time have reached 9,700 tal., perhaps in 448–447, before big expenditure on the buildings had begun and before the campaigns of 447 and 446.

[1] C.R. liv, 1940, 65–67 (see vol. i, p. 275. n. 4 and Addenda). S. Accame in his article cited above (p. 28 n.), 223–45, has argued that the missing year is not 449–448 but 447–446. This may be right, but I still do not agree that no tribute was collected.

[2] This, with a reference to Thuc. ii. 24, was Cavaignac's original view, adopted at first by Meritt in A.F.D., p. 175.

We may go further; for it is not difficult (in my view) to keep both the 5,000 tal. of the papyrus and Ephoros' 8,000, by supposing that the former alone was the figure of the accumulated surplus from the tribute, the latter includes 3,000 tal. the surplus of the public treasury of Athens (perhaps the private treasuries of Athena and of the Other Gods as well); this implies only a small error in Ephoros, or, perhaps, in Diodoros, in implying that the whole sum of 8,000 tal. came from the allies. If this is right, then by 434 (the probable date of the Kallias decree) the sum of 3,000 tal. had been taken from the public treasury, $\tau\grave{o}$ $\delta\eta\mu\acute{o}\sigma\iota\sigma\nu$, and placed on the Akropolis under the guardianship of Athena, partly for the sake of simplicity of administration of a large reserve fund, partly to protect the fund from sudden, ill-considered votes of the ekklesia; for Athena's money could not be touched without a special vote (cf. 24. 1 below for another and even more careful precaution for the special reserve).[1] This, however, according to A.T.L. iii. 337, and other writers (see e.g. G. H. Stevenson, J.H.S. xliv, 1924, 1–9), cannot be, for there was no money in $\tau\grave{o}$ $\delta\eta\mu\acute{o}\sigma\iota\sigma\nu$, or at least no sum worth considering; for, if there had been, the expenses for the Samian war of 440 would have been met from it, and there would have been no need to borrow from Athena (I.G. i.[2] 293: Tod, 50; S.E.G. x. 221: see vol. i of this Commentary, p. 356). This argument I believe to be due to a misunderstanding of Athenian principles of war-finance. The war with Samos was a matter for the League, just as much as the wars with Naxos c. 468 and Thasos in 465, as Eurymedon and the Egyptian and Cyprus expeditions had been; it was, therefore, financed from the funds of the League, which since 454 had been under the care of the treasurers of Athena. Similarly the restoration of the sacred buildings destroyed by the Persians: that was a Hellenic affair, and, since the failure of the Panhellenic Congress, Hellenic obligations had been undertaken by the Delian League, which was a Hellenic League (its treasurers were Ἑλληνοταμίαι, though they were Athenian officials). Where Athens drew the line between Athenian and League affairs, especially wars, between 476 and 434, we do not know; the public treasury of Athens, from its reserve fund, may have financed Kimon's campaign in aid of Sparta during the Helot revolt, the wars against Corinth and Boeotia, Tolmides' periplous to Naupaktos, the expedition to Delphi—any or all of these; but whatever they did in these cases, there is no reason to suppose that there was not, before 434, a considerable sum in Athens' own treasury, $\tau\grave{o}$ $\delta\eta\mu\acute{o}\sigma\iota\sigma\nu$,[2] and it was this

---

[1] If my suggested restoration of the papyrus, ἄνευ ἀδείας μὴ κινεῖν, is on the right lines (and I lay no stress on it; I only give it to show how doubtful any restoration inevitably is), the author may have confused this decree of Thuc. ii. 24. 1, which does belong to 431, with the earlier one which is referred to in the second Kallias decree.   [2] Not after 434: see l. 25 of the decree.

sum, or much the greater part of it, 3,000 tal., which was put into the care of Athena's treasurers in 434. It is one of my major differences with the authors of *A.T.L.* and others, that they believe Athens herself incapable both of putting money in reserve and of spending any of their own on wars (including League wars) after 476. On the contrary: If they could be persuaded to spend the silver from Laureion on ships in 483, they were capable of doing the same after the League was founded and of building a reserve fund (it must have been mainly by Athenian initiative that the reserve fund of the League was formed); into this would be placed the considerable sums won in booty after one-tenth had been set aside for Athena; and they could tax themselves by special εἰσφοραί before 434 (the second Kallias decree, Tod, 51 B, line 16) as well as during the Peloponnesian war. (There is no reason to suppose that this last stopped with the increase in the tribute in 425: see below, n. on iii. 19. 1.) The Athenians were as ready to spend their money as their energies and their lives in the service of the empire.

The table below gives a rough picture of what the changes in the total reserve funds in Athens may have been between 454 and 431, in accordance with the arguments given above; the figures are, some of them, conventional, and assume accuracy in Ephoros and the *Anonymus Argentinensis* and *A.T.L.*'s date for Perikles' decree mentioned in the latter; and Athena's private treasury is ignored:

Date	In State Treasury	In Athena's Treasury	Totals
	tal.	tal.	tal.
454–453	3,000	5,000	8,000
447–446	3,700[1]	6,000[2]	9,700 (acme)
441–440	3,300[3]	5,000[4]	8,300
439–438	3,300	3,200[5]	6,500
434–433	3,300	3,400[6]	6,700
434–433	300[7]	6,400	6,700 (Kallias decree)
432–431	300	5,400[8]	5,700

[1] i.e., in the course of seven years, with additions (perhaps from εἰσφοραί) and expenses for the Delphi and Koroneia campaigns.

[2] Annual additions from tribute, but large expenses in Cyprus.

[3] After the Thirty Years' Peace there was perhaps no εἰσφορά or other special tax; some expenses in war against Peloponnesians and perhaps Euboea.

[4] Expenses for Parthenon, the Parthenos statue, and Odeion; perhaps for other buildings.

[5] Expenses for Samos and Byzantion, and for buildings.

[6] Expenses for Propylaia and other buildings, and perhaps for campaigns (e.g. Pontos? See vol. i, pp. 367–8); but reparations from Samos (below).

[7] A token figure only; the transference of 3,000 tal. to Athena's treasury may have emptied τὸ δημόσιον of all its reserve.

[8] More reparations from Samos, but heavy expenses on Propylaia and the Poteidaia campaign.

There is one other matter to be discussed. As stated above (p. 21), most scholars reject out of hand the notion that Samos could have paid the whole of her indemnity, 1,000 or 1,200 tal. or more (see i. 117. 3 n.), by 432–431; *A.T.L.* argues for an annual rate of 50 tal. for twenty-six years; but I am not so sure. Samos was, for Greece, a wealthy state; she had had rich friends in Asia and Egypt and had suffered no violent destruction, as Athens had; she will have shared in the booty won by the League at the Eurymedon and elsewhere. The internal revenue of Athens was, according to such evidence as we have (which is not very good; above, p. 19), about 400 or 540 tal. a year; she could raise 200 tal. from εἰσφορά in a year without difficulty; she had, in my view, a large reserve from these sources, accumulated since the Persian war, amounting perhaps to 3,000 tal. (above, p. 31); the treasuries of her gods, especially Athena's, but not hers only, had had funds with which some of the temples were rebuilt (above, p. 24). Further, Lesbos and Chios between them had manned 55 triremes in the crisis of 439 and Samos herself 50 (i. 116. 1, 2; 117. 2); each trireme represented perhaps 3 tal. of tribute,[1] and though we should not believe that these three states kept this number of ships regularly in commission, yet we must allow to them a contribution to the League equivalent to at least 70 tal. each for Lesbos and Chios, and 90 for Samos. By analogy, and this is all that we have for argument, it seems probable enough that Samos now with no 'defence budget' of her own, could have found perhaps half the sum for reparations from reserve funds ('borrowed' from Hera, as Athens borrowed from Athena for her war expenses), and 100 tal. a year from revenue; which would mean full repayment by 431.[2] This is much the easiest explanation of the silence about Samian expenses in § 3; and the later Samian payments (above, p. 17) are more easily explained as her contribution to League expenses, though we do not know why Samos, Thera, and some other states were placed in a special category (*I.G.* i.² 65). We must keep a balance in these things. Athens was doubtless the wealthiest state in the Aegean area; but she was not unique in being wealthy. See Addenda.

6. ὁπλίτας δὲ τρισχιλίους καὶ μυρίους: figures confirmed in 31. 2.
τῶν ἐν τοῖς φρουρίοις: not only in the frontier forts of Attica, such

---

[1] Mr. M. Holroyd of Oxford, in a most interesting paper read at the Joint Meeting of Classical Societies at Cambridge in 1951, argued for this equivalence of 3 tal. and one ship; he noted what a large proportion of tributes from the larger cities of the League was of 3 tal. or multiples or simple fractions of 3 (18, 15, 10½, 9, 6; 1½) and how rare are 5 and 10.

[2] It is not necessary to suppose that (on the assumption that half the sum was taken from reserve) this was paid at once, as I stated in my *Historia* paper, p. 62, which is perhaps inconsistent with Thucydides i. 117. 3. The reserve fund could have been 'touched' for 100 tal. a year for five or six years.

as Oinoe (18. 1–2) and Panakton (v. 3. 5), but those overseas (24. 1, iv. 7, 104. 4, 110. 2; *I.G.* i.² 93. 11–17: vol. i, pp. 380–2; *A.T.L.* iii. 143–4).[1] For the forts in Attica, see the articles mentioned in vol. i, p. 14, n. 1; and in addition, Scranton in *A.J.A.* xlii, 1938, 525–36; J. H. Kent, *Hesp.* x, 1941, 346–7. The latter points out that these forts were only garrisoned in war-time (see 18. 2 below) and were only of local importance; they could interfere with raiders, but were of no use to prevent invasion. How indeed could they be when invaders were not dependent on one or two roads only both for their own marching and for subsequent supplies? See below, 18. 1 n.[2]

How many oversea garrisons, ἐν τῇ ὑπερορίᾳ, there were we do not know; a good many, but the number must not be exaggerated, as it has often been, for example (to take a recent case) by A. S. Nease in his paper in *Phoenix*, iii, 1949, 102–11; who says that every Athenian official, even a ὁρκωτής, implies a garrison. Thucydides' narrative shows that there were no garrisons in Olynthos, Spartolos, or Poteidaia in 432, nor in Akanthos, Galepsos, Argilos, Stagiros in 424, in Mytilene in 412 or in Samos in 411. They should not be assumed except in places of strategical importance (e.g. Sestos and Byzantion) and where they are expressly mentioned.

τῶν παρ' ἔπαλξιν: i.e. those who manned the walls of Athens and Peiraeus and the Long Walls, when necessary, as explained below.

ἑξακισχιλίων καὶ μυρίων: this figure has been either radically emended (as by bracketing καὶ μυρίων) or treated as a childish error of Thucydides, by most scholars, because it implies, they say, that the number of citizens in the thirty age-classes, 20 to 49, was very little more than those in the twelve classes, 18–19 and 50–59 (the oldest and youngest of § 7). I have defended it at length in *C.Q.* xxi, 1927, 142–51; and for

---

[1] The authors of *A.T.L.* have given up the view that by the Treaty of Kallias, 450–449 B.C., the cities of Asia Minor who were members of the League also paid tribute to Persia (my vol. i, pp. 334–5), but maintain their opinion that Athens agreed to withdraw all her garrisons there. They think, however, that she was "able to circumvent this embarrassment by the expedient of colonization", for we know of an ἀποικία to Kolophon and probably of another to Erythrai (my statements, vol. i, pp. 344, n. 1, and 376, are to be corrected): see *A.T.L.* iii. 143–4, 283–4. They have an important page on the distinction between ἄποικοι and κληροῦχοι, a distinction observed, they argue, always officially, and generally by careful writers, as by Thucydides; if they are right, this must correct much loose writing, including my own. But, for the present at least, I find it difficult to believe that Athens could, so soon after the treaty (for the colony to Kolophon is dated to 447–446), get round so important a clause in this manner. Colonists could not have been in effect very different from a garrison. See further nn. on iii. 34, and V. Ehrenberg's article, *C.P.* xlvii, 1952, 143–9, in which he disputes the rigid distinction made in *A.T.L.*

[2] Eupolis, fr. 341, has a line, καὶ τοὺς περιπόλους ἀπιέν' ἐς τὰ φρούρια. The schol. on Aischines (ii. 167) who quotes this, identifies the peripoloi with the epheboi, who did garrison duty for a year in the fourth century. This may not be true of the fifth: see iv. 67. 2 n.

its relation to the hoplite strength of Athens at other times and to that of other classes of the population, see my *Population of Athens in the Fifth and Fourth Centuries B.C.* (Oxford, 1933). The general outline of the objections and of my defence are as follows. I assume for the moment, as I assumed in 1933, that the hoplites ἐν τοῖς καταλόγοις comprise the thirty age-groups, 20–49, not a smaller number, e.g. 20–44; but see below, p. 37.

We have to obtain the numbers of *citizen* troops in the different age-classes. Since the 'oldest and youngest' of the cavalry and of the men in the garrisons will have been available for defence of the walls, we may, in order to get at the relative numbers of active and reserve citizen troops, add the cavalry and τοὺς ἐν τοῖς φρουρίοις to the 13,000 hoplites to get the front-line strength. The cavalry were 1,000 strong, § 8 n.; no number is given for οἱ ἐν τοῖς φρουρίοις, but they cannot well have been fewer than 1,000. The total active force is thus at least 15,000. From the reserve figure of 16,000 we must subtract the metics; in 31. 2 we are told that 3,000 metic hoplites marched with the citizen army into the Megarid in the autumn of this year; which leaves 13,000 for the citizen reserve. But the active army consisted of men of the years 20 to 49 inclusive, thirty age-groups, the reserve of the youngest, the recruits of 18 and 19, and the oldest, 50–59 inclusive, twelve age-groups only, of which the ten oldest would be weaker in numbers than any of the rest. The ratio 15,000 to 13,000 is impossible (something like 3 to 1 is what is required); hence, it is argued, the figure ἑξακισχιλίων καὶ μυρίων cannot stand.

This argument, however, assumes that the 15,000 active troops comprise all the citizens, of hoplite census or over, of the age-groups 20–49—a paper-figure only, and one a good deal larger than any possible total of troops in the field. For there were, at any one time, a considerable number who did not in fact serve in the ranks: (*a*) the exempt—bouleutai and other officials who were hoplites and under 50, and trierarchs and tamiai in the navy (cf. 24. 2)—certainly some hundreds;[1] and (*b*) the unfit. These last must have been numerous, especially in the older classes, the men over 40; for all hoplites 'on active service', στρατευόμενοι, were front-line troops, who must be able to march and fight in heavy armour; none were in the baggage-train or 'L. of C.' troops or the like—all these services, such as they were, were performed by the light-armed (cf. iv. 90), or by civilians ('camp-followers'). Athens was quite exceptional in calling on men up to the age of 49 for foreign service in the front line; Sparta stopped at 40, so did Rome, and so, in normal circumstances, do modern countries which have adopted conscription. For the exempt and the unfit together we must allow not fewer

---

[1] For the ταμίαι of the navy (πεντηκόνταρχοι), see Ps.-Xen. 1. 2, Eupolis, fr. 195, and Dem. l. 18–19, 24–25.

35

than 3,000, who would not in fact march with the rest on active service, though all, or nearly all, would be available for manning the walls in their turn. But Thucydides says quite expressly that 10,000 citizen hoplites did march into the Megarid at a time when 3,000 others were engaged in Chalkidike (31. 2); and there is no independent reason for doubting this. The 3,000 exempt and unfit men, if we are right to assume such a figure, must then be added to the 15,000 to get the total of citizens of 20–49 of hoplite census or over: this will then be c. 18,000.

It is similarly assumed that the 3,000 metics of 31. 2 also comprise the total number of metics of hoplite census between 20 and 49. This is an even less probable assumption than the other. For, though none would be exempt for official duties, many would be unfit and untrained (especially the recent arrivals), and there is no reason to suppose that the metics were well organized as a military force; they did not normally serve abroad (this invasion of the Megarid was the first occasion and there were not many afterwards; see iv. 90. 1 n.), and they were all technically in the reserve, as is here stated. It would not be rash to assume 5,000 metics in all, of 20–49 years of age and of hoplite census, of whom 3,000 were sufficiently well organized to join the Athenian army.[1] Besides these there were also the metics of 18–19 and 50–59 who could be called on to help man the walls: at least 1,500, if there were 5,000 of 20–49.

In order to get the number of *citizens of 18–19 and 50–59* among the 16,000 who 'mounted the ramparts', we must subtract from this figure the 3,000 unfit and exempt citizens of 20–49, the 5,000 metics of 20–49, and the 1,500 'oldest and youngest' metics; the result is 6,500, which in relation to the 18,000 citizens of 20–49 is about the right figure. I take the 15,000 (the hoplites ἐν ταῖς τάξεσι—cf. iii. 87. 3—the cavalry, and οἱ ἐν τοῖς φρουρίοις) to be effective strength, and the 16,000 to be paper strength. That is to say, though Thucydides' figures for the troops which invaded the Megarid, for those who were in Chalkidike under Phormion, and for the cavalry, are *round* figures (the exact numbers may have been 9,895, 2,982, and 993), they are real; they do not represent the paper strength of Athenians of hoplite and cavalry rank between the ages of 20 and 50; whereas for the manning of the walls I assume a general summons (when invaders were in Attica) to all available men.

For this satisfactory result, which is obtained not in order to save Thucydides' figures, or those of his MSS., but by making certain

---

[1] Professor A. H. M. Jones suggests to me that the 3,000 who joined in the invasion of the Megarid took the place of the 3,000 citizen hoplites who were in Chalkidike. This is an attractive suggestion, and, if right, shows clearly that the number does not necessarily show the strength even of the organized metic hoplites. See further p. 37 below for Jones's views on this passage in Thucydides.

assumptions that are necessary or probable in themselves, all that we have to assume in addition is that since the oldest and youngest and the metics technically formed the reserve, though others of military age were liable to service in it, they are so called here; just as in i. 105. 4 we are told that it was a force consisting of the oldest and youngest who marched against Corinth, when the active troops were elsewhere, yet certainly not only men of 50–59 and 18–19 were included.[1]

A. H. M. Jones has objected (by letter) to my treatment of this problem in the following particulars; he thinks that my figures for citizen hoplites are too large by comparison with those for Delion in 424 and with the 9,000 in 411 (Lysias, xx. 13; *Population*, p. 7), and my suggested 5,000 metics of hoplite census and military age too small; and that there was no class or group of men within the front-line age-groups who were known as 'fit for garrison duty only', 'unfit for active service beyond the frontiers', as I assume, the only men of military age not on the $\kappa\alpha\tau\acute{\alpha}\lambda o\gamma os$ being the cripples, $\acute{\alpha}\delta\acute{\upsilon}\nu\alpha\tau o\iota$; that, therefore, my figures to explain the 13,000 hoplites and the 16,000 for manning the walls will not do. To solve the problem of these figures he suggests (1) that the age-groups of the front-line hoplites were not 20–49, but 20–44 or even 20–39; and (2) that the cleruchies regularly (in war-time) sent their hoplite forces to Athens and that they are included in the 13,000 (and their 'youngest', in Athens for training, are among the 16,000, but not of course their 'oldest'); for this see too his article in *Past and Present*, 1952 (No. 1), n. 23 on p. 27. He also maintains that metic hoplites regularly served abroad with the citizen-troops, as part of the same army.

It may be that we have all along been wrong to assume that active service at Athens lasted till a man reached the age of 50; in 431 his 45th birthday may have been the upper limit (Sokrates was 44 or 45 when he fought at Delion). This would at once do away with any difficulty in the proportions of 13,000 and 16,000 discussed above. (Limits of 20–39 in 431, with 20–44 in 424, seem to me very improbable; of course age-groups *called up* might, and did, vary in different campaigns; but it would imply a different basis of reckoning for our present passage, $\acute{o}\pi\lambda\acute{\iota}\tau\alpha s$ $\tau\rho\iota\sigma\chi\iota\lambda\acute{\iota}ovs$ $\kappa\alpha\grave{\iota}$ $\mu\upsilon\rho\acute{\iota}ovs$ $\epsilon\grave{\iota}\nu\alpha\iota$, and for $\pi\alpha\nu\delta\eta\mu\epsilon\acute{\iota}$ in iv. 90. 1; and we are not justified in assuming such a change.) For the 'permanently unfit', the number of these would of course be considerably reduced if the active service age-limit was 45, not 50; but there would, in the nature of things, be some hundreds who would be a source of weakness rather than of strength to an army, and (together with the temporarily sick) did not in fact join up and were not afterwards prosecuted for $\acute{\alpha}\sigma\tau\rho\alpha\tau\epsilon\acute{\iota}\alpha$. And we should believe

---

1 Myronides himself may have been under 50: see the note on Eupolis' *Demoi* in vol. iii. Cf. also iii. 106. 1 n. on $ov\acute{\sigma}\eta s$ $\acute{\epsilon}\rho\acute{\eta}\mu ov$.

Thucydides when he tells us that 10,000 citizen hoplites took part in the Megarid campaign. A similar question is involved in the 4,000 who sailed with Perikles in 430 when the pestilence was at its height (56. 2). Theoretically there are three ways in which this figure can be interpreted: let us assume 4,000 to be the figure for those in the 20–29 classes (not counting those then in Chalkidike); then (1) the ekklesia may have voted for the call-up of these classes, and in that event not more than 2,000 to 2,500 actually sailed; or (2) the vote was for a call-up of the 20–35's, of whom there were, say, 6,000 on the κατάλογος, and 4,000 responded and sailed; or (3) the vote was for 4,000 to sail, and powers were given to Perikles, with perhaps one or two other strategoi, to muster them as best he could. I am convinced that either the second or the third of these is right; we are not entitled to assume that 4,000 is a misleading paper figure.

As to the cleruch-hoplites (except for the recruits of 18–19, who may have come to Athens for training, though we hear nothing of them), the fact that some, from Imbros and Lemnos, are specially mentioned on four occasions, iii. 5. 1, iv. 28. 4, v. 8. 2, and vii. 57. 2, and from Aigina and Hestiaia on one of them (vii. 57. 2),[1] as well as men from Andros, Tenos, and Karystos, and the Aiginetan ἔποικοι at viii. 69. 3, is an indication that when they are not mentioned, they were not present, and that no other cleruchs were present even on these occasions (certainly not any from Chalkis, Eretria, or Andros on the expedition to Sicily—see vii. 57. 2–4); and of the four occasions, on two of them the Lemnians and Imbrians were called up not because they were in Athens, but because they were near the scenes of action, Mytilene and Amphipolis. This is natural: cleruchs were certainly liable to military service, but generally near their own homes. The third occasion, Sicily, was altogether exceptional; only iv. 28. 4, and perhaps viii. 69. 3, might suggest (if other evidence supported the suggestion) a regular contingent of cleruch-hoplites in Athens; and then only a contingent, not their full force. For casualty-lists in which Imbrians and Lemnians are recorded, separately from Athenians, see I.G. i.[2] 947 and 948. (For 949, see iv. 38. 5 n.) See Busolt–Swoboda, 765, n. 1.

That the MSS. are not at fault here is highly probable, for Ephoros gave figures similar to, but not identical with, those of Thucydides: 12,000 active troops and 17,000 in the reserve—that is, he did not idly copy an already mistaken figure in his text of Thucydides (Diod. xii. 40. 4).[2] That Thucydides would not have supposed the

---

[1] The Hestiaies are called specifically ἄποικοι, apparently distinguished from the others. See above, p. 34, n. 1.

[2] It is possibly of some significance that Diodoros' 17,000 reserve troops are described as τοὺς ἐν τοῖς φρουρίοις ὄντας (just before this he has adopted from Thucydides his description of the first-line troops as χωρὶς συμμάχων καὶ

total number of citizens of 18–19 and 50–59 to be nearly equal to those of 20–49 is, we may say, certain. An ignorant or thoughtless man might suppose that the numbers in every age-group were exactly equal to each other; but this would mean a ratio between active and reserve of 30 to 12, not of 15 to 13. And Thucydides was neither ignorant nor thoughtless. Before he published anything, or wrote anything but his current notes, he had been strategos, and responsible for mustering troops; he would know all about the exempt and the unfit, not to mention the *embusqués*, that is, about paper figures and effectives ἐν ταῖς τάξεσιν. And in v. 64. 3 he tells us that in the Mantinean campaign of 418 B.C. the Spartan command sent home *one-sixth* of their force, and that this included the oldest and the youngest.

7. τοῦ τε γὰρ Φαληρικοῦ τείχους στάδιοι ἦσαν, κ.τ.λ.: the purpose of this digression is to explain why so many were needed to man the walls (when the enemy was encamped sufficiently near that a sudden attack might be made). The total length to be garrisoned, according to Thucydides, was 148 stades, or about 26,000 metres, that is practically 2 metres per man, or 4 metres if duty was taken turn and turn about. No wonder he thought it desirable to tell his readers the length of the walls.

But these figures too have been disputed, by so careful a scholar as Judeich (pp. 155–60); there are certainly difficulties, but in this case I believe the present answer to the objectors to be that we do not know enough to assert that Thucydides' figures (or the MSS. figures) are wrong. (1) The Long Walls to Peiraeus. The line of these is known, and the length given is about right: see i. 107 n. ὧν τὸ ἔξωθεν ἐτηρεῖτο: because, as long as the Phaleric wall was there, only the outer, northern wall had to be guarded against a land attack. (2) The line of the Phaleric wall is quite uncertain, for no remains have been found; but I believe that the old view that it left the city wall east of Mouseion Hill and went direct to the east end of the Bay of Phaleron (as given, e.g., in the map in *C.A.H*. v, opp. p. 165) to be correct, and Judeich's objections to be unsound (see vol. i, p. 312); 35 stades is about right for this. (3) The line of the city wall is in general uncertain, especially on the north; on the south the fifth-century wall between the western slopes of the Pnyx and the top of Mouseion Hill seems to have been found (Thompson and Scranton, *Hesp*. xii, 1943, 301–83); but this section, together with that down from Mouseion Hill eastwards to the beginning of the Phaleric wall, is the part that did not have to be garrisoned. As the rest of the line is drawn on most maps, 43 stades, the figure given here, is too much.

τῶν ἐν τοῖς φρουρίοις ὄντων); that is, Ephoros may have added 1,000 men to Thucydides' 16,000 in the reserve, by including the garrisons in the latter category.

Judeich proposed that we should read 33 stades for the city wall, or rather for that part of it which was not between the Peiraeus and Phaleric Long Walls, and 45, instead of 35, for his line for the Phaleric wall. (4) The wall of Peiraeus itself (see i. 93. 3–7 nn.). The existing remains, which are of the restoration by Konon in 394, are some 78 stades long; but the Themistoklean wall may have been shorter, 60 stades, if it was drawn across the peninsula of Akte (the south-western portion of which was probably not inhabited) and not round its coastline. But the statement that half this length was garrisoned is difficult. The purpose of this garrisoning of the walls was primarily to guard against attacks by land, not by sea (defence at sea was the business of the navy, including the special reserve fleet that was soon to be created, 24. 2; or, if the enemy did force a landing, it would not be the reserve, but the front-line troops who would be called on to resist him; that is one reason why Judeich's difficulties over the Phaleric wall are not well founded); and the only sections of the Peiraeus walls which needed to be manned for this purpose are those from the starting-point of the northern long wall westwards to Eetioneia, and from that of the southern long wall southwards and eastwards to the west coast of Phaleron Bay. These sections, however, are not 30 stades long; by the Kononian line they are less than 20, and no trace of any other line has been found. This is not a case where we may suppose a MS. error in a numeral, because, as stated, 60 stades for the whole length of the wall is credible, and a smaller figure (40 stades) would not be long enough. We must suppose that parts of the Peiraeus circuit wall, where it protected the νεώσοικοι particularly in Zea and Mounichia harbours and the entrance to the principal bay (the commercial harbour), were guarded against sudden raids by sea, which in a short time might do much damage (we may compare *Acharnians*, 915–24, though the sabotage there imagined is plotted from the land, as well cc. 93–94 below); a similar raid on the open roadstead of Phaleron Bay would not be nearly so dangerous.

8. ξὺν ἱπποτοξόταις: since there were 1,000 cavalry (see e.g. Ar. *Equit.* 225), there were 200 of these mounted archers; they were of course citizens. But we do not know what tactical use was made of them—they were a newly formed force; but to what purpose? Xenophon says that they went ahead of the cavalry (*Mem.* iii. 3. 1); and this may have been true in the fifth century as well, for it would correspond to the use made of light-armed, slingers and stone-throwers, in company with hoplites (cf. vi. 69. 2). The only mention of them elsewhere in Thucydides is at v. 84. 1, when 20 *hippotoxotai* go to Melos in a force of 1,200 hoplites (with 1,500 more from the allies) and 300 *toxotai*, but no cavalry, and at vi. 94. 4, when, in response to a request from Nikias and Lamáchos for cavalry (vi.

40

74. 2), 250 men are sent to Sicily, whose mounts are to be provided on the spot, and 30 *hippotoxotai*. What they did when they got to their posts, especially the 20 sent to Melos, we do not know. Sitalkes king of Thrace had large numbers in his army, ii. 96. 1; and we can guess *their* tactical value. See Busolt–Swoboda, ii. 979, n. 4; and above, vol. i, pp. 327–8.

Lysias, xv. 6, implies that aristocrats would not naturally serve in this force of mounted archers instead of the cavalry; it was rather less dignified. Aristophanes, *Aves* 1179, speaks of innumerable mounted archers in the City of the Birds, all citizens, at least all birds (hawks).

In *Hipparch.* 9. 3 Xenophon advocates the establishment of a force of 200 foreign *hippeis* in the service of Athens, as a useful addition to the 1,000 citizen cavalry; for they might give an example to the latter of discipline and courage; he had observed the good effect of foreign cavalry at Sparta and elsewhere. It may be that, as no mention is made of the 200 *hippotoxotai*, this force had ceased to exist.

Xenophon's words are καὶ εὐπειστότερον ἂν πᾶν τὸ ἱππικὸν ποιῆσαι καὶ φιλοτιμότερον πρὸς ἀλλήλους περὶ ἀνδραγαθίας. We do not usually suspect the cavalry of lack of courage; for their indiscipline, see the passage in Lysias cited above and, more definitely, *Mem.* iii. 5. 16–19. Yet both the *Hipparchikos* and the *Hippike* show a high degree of skill in riding, and good order on the march, at least at festivals, such as could only be attained by hard training and some discipline. It is, however, possible, as other military and especially aristocratic corps have shown, to combine skill and discipline in one respect with indiscipline in another.

ἑξακοσίους δὲ καὶ χιλίους τοξότας: these citizen bowmen in action are mentioned more often than the mounted men, sometimes in conjunction with a force from other Greek states or from Thrace: for example, ii. 23. 2, 400 *toxotai* on the *periplous* of the Peloponnese; iii. 98. 1, in the Aitolian war (probably Athenian, but perhaps Akarnanians); 107. 1, sixty of them in Amprakia; iv. 9. 2, 32. 2, and 36. 1, at Pylos (perhaps half of the 800 were Athenians: cf. 28. 4); 129. 2, 600 in Chalkidike; v. 84. 1, 300 in Melos; and some probably on the Sicilian expedition, but in the narrative allied and citizen bowmen are not distinguished (vi. 22, 25. 2, 69. 2; in vi. 43 the force consists of 480, of whom 80 were Cretans; but the other 400 were not certainly all Athenian); viii. 71. 2, perhaps Athenian. See also *I.G.* i.² 929, ad fin. (Tod, 26: 4 *toxotai* of Erechtheis), 949. We hear occasionally of non-citizen τοξόται apparently regularly employed at Athens (Andok. iii. 5, 7); and they were often to be found there in war-time on particular occasions (e.g. iv. 28. 4, viii. 98. 1), and on campaigns (iv. 28. 4, vi. 43, 69. 2).

Although light-armed forces belonging to other states are often mentioned, special mention of *toxotai* is comparatively rare: i. 49. 1 (Corinth and Kerkyra), iii. 2. 3 (Mytilene, from Pontos), iv. 55. 2 (Sparta), vi. 20. 4 (Syracuse), vi. 67. 2, vii. 33. 1 (Kamarina). τριήρεις τὰς πλωίμους τριακοσίας: these, if all manned at once (cf. iii. 17, with nn.), would require over 50,000 rowers and 3,000 ἐπιβάται, all the latter and such of the rowers as were Athenian drawn from the *thetes* of Athens; the navigating officers (i.e. excluding the *tamias* and the trierarch), four to each vessel, were Athenian (i. 143. 1). We do not know at all in what proportion the citizen and foreign rowers stood to each other; it doubtless varied from time to time; and money rather than political pressure seems to have secured the foreigners—at least Athens was able to recruit men for the fleet in the fourth century, when she was less able to exert pressure, as freely as in the fifth.

Thucydides does not give us a total either of trained Athenian rowers or of the population from which they were drawn, as he does, roughly, for the hoplites in §§ 6 and 7 (the total of hoplites in the ranks and in the reserve). The circumstances of the two services were different: the total number of sailors could be easily computed from the number of ships in commission, but neither were all sailors Athenian or metic, nor all Athenian *thetes* sailors, whereas all hoplites were Athenian or metic and all Athenians and metics of hoplite or richer class were (theoretically) liable for service as hoplites, in the ranks or in the reserve (or in the cavalry). Similarly we do not have the number of *thetes* who died in the pestilence (iii. 87. 3), or of those who were levied *en masse* for field work in the Boeotian campaign of 424 (iv. 90, 94), because they were not organized into a military force.

We do not know either how many ships were normally in commission in peace-time. Plutarch (*Per.* 11. 4) tells us that sixty were regularly in commission for eight months in the year (manned, perhaps, by citizens only, for training). This, at the rate of expense prevailing in 415 B.C., would have cost 480 tal. a year (vi. 8. 1). The sailors on the Sicilian expedition were, exceptionally, paid 1 dr. a day (vi. 31. 3); if we assume that the rowers were paid in peacetime, before 431, one half-drachme a day, the total cost of these triremes would be about 300 tal. or more; for 120 ships, 600 tal.; and 600 tal. would exhaust all the yearly income from the allies, and leave nothing to be put to reserve. Since, however, in this period large sums were put into reserve, if 120 ships were kept in commission, a large part of the expense was borne by Athens herself; and, though many have disputed this, I do not doubt that this was in fact done, and that on many particular occasions, as the expedition to the Pontos and the Samian war, Athens contributed largely. I do not mean that we have any direct evidence for 120 ships kept in commission, nor that we must place implicit trust in Plutarch's statement; but the fleet was kept in being, and it was ready, ships and men, when war broke out. For this, good maintenance and training were necessary.

9. ἔλεγε δὲ καὶ ἄλλα, κ.τ.λ.: there are, as noted above, difficulties in the figures of Athenian resources which Thucydides gives in this chapter; there are also certain specific omissions, such as the amount of ἡ ἄλλη πρόσοδος in § 3 and the numbers of the θητικὸς ὄχλος which supplied rowers to the fleet, and of allied contingents (§ 8); but, besides this, he omits most of what alone could give us an understandable picture of those resources. For figures by themselves mean nothing; we must have something else with which to compare them, to which to relate them; and though doubtless his contemporary readers could have supplied for themselves much which we cannot, they too will have been left in the dark on some of the major problems involved.

For example, we are not given any comparable figures for the revenue of enemy states, even of Corinth whose social structure was in many ways similar to that of Athens; we have only had, in the speeches of Archidamos and Perikles in book i, a general picture of the difference between the two sides; and, valuable as that is, and though it shows that Thucydides thoroughly understood the essential financial and economic conditions which determined the general strategy of the war, it does not help us to appreciate the particular figures of Athenian resources given in this chapter, and therewith the degree of Athenian financial superiority.

Secondly, what is the relation of the stated revenue to the annual expenditure, at least on military services, both in peace-time and during the war, or to what in 431 B.C. was estimated to be the probable expenditure? That is, we require the other side of the budget— how much did 600 tal. a year, or 600 plus ἡ ἄλλη πρόσοδος, provide of the annual state expenditure? That it provided a surplus in peacetime is a certain conclusion from the fact that a large reserve had been built up; but Thucydides does not tell us the average amount of the surplus over a period of years. Still less—and this perhaps we should not expect of him—does he relate this state revenue to the total income of Athens, state and private, or rather of the whole empire, which would give some idea of what further resources there were on which to draw: an important element in the financial problem in relation to the imposition of εἰσφορά in Athens and the increased assessment of tribute on the allies in 425 B.C. In the course of his narrative he gives some figures of expenditure on particular campaigns, e.g. the 2,000 tal. on the siege of Poteidaia (70. 2); he mentions the 1,000 tal. put into special reserve (24. 1), and the 200 tal.

43

raised by the first εἰσφορά (iii. 19. 1). But no more than that, especially, nothing of the rate of expenditure of the large reserve fund. The true significance of the figures which he does give in this chapter is therefore not stated; the reserve of 6,000 tal. is equivalent to ten years' annual income obtained from the allies—that is all that we know from him. His contemporary readers will have known a little more: very roughly, how much greater was Athenian financial strength than that of any other city.

Similarly with his figures for military strength, apart from his omissions on the Athenian side: he does not give the total of enemy forces, either in hoplites and cavalry, or in ships, with which to compare them; we can only infer from him, from separate figures which he gives elsewhere, that in hoplite strength for the first invasion the enemy must have outnumbered the 10,000 available Athenian hoplites by about three to one (see 10. 2 n.); and we have only optimistic hopes about the fleet (7. 2). We have details of enemy strength in many campaigns, from 435 onwards, but no sum total here. And on the other side, the casualties: Thucydides gives most carefully the Athenian losses in many battles and campaigns, and most important of all, those of the hoplite and cavalry forces from the pestilence, but he does not give the total losses of the army and navy for the whole or for some part of the war, nor of the total population from the pestilence, though these last affected future recruitment so severely.

Thirdly, he gives no comparison *in time*: he has insisted that Athens (and perhaps the Peloponnesians as well) was stronger both financially and in military resources in 431 than ever before (i. 19, etc.); but he nowhere says by how much their revenues and their numbers had increased since 479 or 463 or 445, nor at what rate.

From a few official documents and statements in other writers (which will be more fully discussed in their proper places) we know something from which to supplement the information given here by Thucydides. We know for example that in the course of the Archidamian war over 4,700 tal. was taken from the reserve fund of 5,000 tal.—'borrowed from Athena' (the special reserve of 1,000 tal. not being touched till 412 B.C.—viii. 15. 1), besides 900 tal. from 'the Other Gods' (*I.G.* i.² 324, Tod, 64: below, p. 432), but not whether other sums were being paid in; that considerable sums were 'repaid' to Athena between 421 and 415 B.C. (vi. 26. 2, and, perhaps, Andok. iii. 8–9); that there was a large increase in the tribute in 425 (i.² 63, Tod, 66: below, p. 500); and we know a little of the expenses of the Sicilian expeditions (i.² 99 = Tod, 77 B; 302 = Tod, 75). We must not of course forget that Thucydides was absent from Athens after 425 B.C. and could have no access to official documents kept there before his return in 404; and that in the confused times immediately after that he was probably unable to get true figures for expenditure or for income (e.g. from the harbour dues instituted in 413: vii. 28. 4), or for military forces and casualties; and he will not invent, and hence, for example, will only state in the most general way the expensiveness of the Sicilian expedition (vi. 31. 5). Had he lived to complete his work, he would doubtless have given more figures than he does, certainly for particular campaigns, perhaps for the ten years' war and for the twenty-seven years' war as a whole. But that does not excuse him for not giving the necessary *comparisons* in this chapter which alone would put life and substance into the figures which he does give.

Finally, we desire one thing more, though here no criticism lies against Thucydides. Can we say what the figures mean in terms of *value*? It means nothing at all to convert a talent into sterling or dollars according to its silver content (quite apart from the modern changes in the gold value of silver); to get at the value of a talent we must have some idea of its purchasing power, or, better, of its relation to current personal incomes. I believe that we know enough to enable us to give some meaning to the figures. We know, for example, some special rates of pay of hoplites and sailors during the war (iii. 17. 4, vi. 31. 3). We know that in 409–407 B.C. skilled men in the building trade, stonemasons and others employed by the state (whether free, citizen or metic, or slave), were paid 1 dr. a day for each day of work, like the hoplite and the sailor on special occasions; the ἀρχιτέκτων, or overseer in charge of the work, 1 dr. a day for every day (36 or 37 dr. per prytany); unskilled labour $\frac{1}{2}$ dr. a day, the normal pay of the sailor (*I.G.* i.² 373–4). We do not know indeed whether wages were about the same twenty years earlier: they may have been increased in the interval owing to a rise in the prices of food during the war, especially of imported wheat, or have been depressed owing to Athens' financial difficulties after 413; but we can probably say with sufficient confidence for our purposes that, if the number of holidays in the year were not more then than now, i.e. about 100, this 1 dr. a day in Athens corresponds roughly to the £1 5s. to £1 10s. a day (£7 10s. to £8 a week) earned on an average (excluding overtime) by skilled workers in Great Britain at the present time (1952)[1] (except that the Athenian was not paid for the holidays). That is a very rough approximation indeed, and we have not taken into account the comparative values of subsidized food

[1] By "corresponds to" I do not mean "has a similar purchasing power", because the ancient Athenian and the modern Englishman purchase very different things. It is rather a social correspondence; and it gives an idea of the comparative value, in terms of money, of man-hours. But a good deal of research is still needed, and would probably yield profitable results, into the actual purchasing power of the drachme at different times and in different places—how much food, clothing, and so forth it could buy.

45

or houses, social and health services in this country and of subsidized festivals, gymnasia, etc., in Athens (38. 1, below; Ps.-Xen. 1. 13), and on the other side the taxation which pays for these subsidies. But the approximation is, I think, close enough to put some meaning into the statements that the revenue from the allies was 600 tal. (= 3,600,000 dr.) yearly, that other Athenian revenue was 400 or 540 tal. (2,400,000 or 3,240,000 dr.), that the reserve in coin at its highest point reached 9,700 tal. (58 million dr.), of which perhaps 3,000 tal., or 18 million dr., was spent in the course of fifteen years on the Parthenon, the Propylaia, and other buildings. An impressively large sum, this last, whether reckoned in terms of the annual revenue of the state, or in man-hours (if 1 dr. a day for skilled work and $\frac{1}{2}$ dr. for unskilled is correct for this period)—hours spent in quarrying and transporting as well as in building (Plut. *Per.* 12. 6— see below)—and including the money spent in the purchase of gold and certain other materials from abroad.

We should, however, go a little more into detail for these 'man-hours', in relation to the total adult male population of Attica in 431, from 18 to 60 years old, citizen, foreign, and slave. This I have calculated to be 135,000 (of whom perhaps 30,000 were domestic servants—and so not available for this work?). It is a very rough calculation, but, I think, gives a *maximum* (*Population of Athens*, 26). We take 1 dr. and $\frac{1}{2}$ dr. a day as the rates of pay (or some near figure—5 to 7 and $2\frac{1}{2}$ to $3\frac{1}{2}$ obols), and, to get an average, we must include the higher-paid sculptors and other artists, though since on the Erechtheion these were paid, not daily, but for the finished work we cannot give for them a daily rate; still, if we take 1 dr. as the average day's pay for every man employed, we may not be far wrong, and we may even be exaggerating: the average may have been 5 or even $4\frac{1}{2}$ obols. We want to get the total paid for work on these buildings *in Attica*. For that we must subtract from the total spent (3,000 tal. at the maximum) the sums paid for gold and ivory and some other materials which came from abroad, and perhaps for the freight (allowing, that is, that some of the freight-charges were paid to foreign shipowners): not more than 700 tal. (above, p. 25); since 3,000 tal. is a maximum, say 2,200 tal. at least spent in Attica—all of it, as far as we know, for work done, none, for example, to landowners for the privilege of quarrying the marble of Pentelikos. This was spent in a period of sixteen years, 447-446 to 432-431; that is, $137\frac{1}{2}$ tal. or 825,000 dr. a year on the average. If men worked on 250 days in the year (the solar year: again probably a maximum), this would mean that an average of 3,300 dr. was paid each day, i.e., if a drachme a day is correct for their pay, an average of about 3,300 men were employed, day in day out, for these sixteen years, for all the work of quarrying and woodcutting, transporting the

46

material to the Akropolis, and building and decorating—ὅπου γὰρ ὕλη μὲν ἦν λίθος, χαλκός, ἐλέφας, χρυσός, ἔβενος, κυπάρισσος, αἱ δὲ ταύτην ἐκπονοῦσαι καὶ κατεργαζόμεναι τέχναι, τέκτονες, πλάσται, χαλκοτύποι, λιθουργοί, βαφεῖς χρυσοῦ, μαλακτῆρες ἐλέφαντος, ζωγράφοι, ποικιλταί, τορευταί, πομποὶ δὲ τούτων καὶ κομιστῆρες, ἔμποροι καὶ ναῦται καὶ κυβερνῆται κατὰ θάλατταν, οἱ δὲ κατὰ γῆν ἁμαξοπηγοὶ καὶ ζευγοτρόφοι καὶ ἡνίοχοι καὶ καλωστρόφοι καὶ λινουργοὶ καὶ σκυτοτόμοι καὶ ὁδοποιοὶ καὶ μεταλλεῖς, ἑκάστη δὲ τέχνη, καθάπερ στρατηγὸς ἴδιον στράτευμα, τὸν θητικὸν ὄχλον καὶ ἰδιώτην συντεταγμένον εἶχεν, ὄργανον καὶ σῶμα τῆς ὑπηρεσίας γινόμενον, εἰς πᾶσαν ὡς ἔπος εἰπεῖν ἡλικίαν καὶ φύσιν αἱ χρεῖαι διένεμον καὶ διέσπειρον τὴν εὐπορίαν. An equally impressive figure, 3,300 from a total of fewer than 150,000 men; and it shows even more clearly that we cannot allow more than c. 3000 tal. for the total expenditure, and therefore 2,012 tal. for the Propylaia alone is out of the question. In fact I think it must be too high: the number of men who were at any one time at work on the Erechtheion in 408 and 407, skilled and unskilled, is to be calculated in tens rather than in hundreds, and though conditions at that time were very different from those of 447 to 431, there is a natural limit to the numbers who can work together on a building such as the Parthenon or the Propylaia. True, very large numbers would be employed on transport, of marble and stone within Attica, of other marble from Paros and timber probably from Macedonia or Thrace; it is on record that a rich man in 329 B.C. lent one thousand ζεύγη to the state when the stadion and theatre at Athens were rebuilt (I.G. ii.² 351), and each of these must have had a driver, and we know from the building records at Delphi and Epidauros what a heavy proportion transport, both by land and by sea, took of the total cost; but, even so, for the whole period of sixteen years it is difficult to believe in the figure 3,000 for a *daily* average. We must (I should suppose—we can hardly do more than surmise in these matters) assume a higher average pay than 1 dr. a day, either by assuming a higher rate of pay for skilled and unskilled workers than was the rule on the Erechtheion in 408 or by allowing a good deal more for the sculptors and other artists—sculpture on the Parthenon particularly must have taken a large part of the total cost—and probably more for sea-transport; or by making both these assumptions. If we raise the average paid to each man, skilled and unskilled workers and the artists, to $1\frac{1}{2}$ dr. a day—and we can hardly go higher—the average daily number employed would be 2,200: a sufficiently impressive figure.

14–17. *The Athenians withdraw behind their Walls*

14. 1. τὴν ξύλωσιν: not movable furniture (which would be included in ἡ κατασκευή), but such wooden fixtures (doors, shutters for

47

unglazed windows, and dressers, perhaps barns as well) as could be taken down. (Cf. J. H. Kent, *Hesp.* xvii, 1948, 293.) Edd. generally take this with ἐσεκομίζοντο as well as with καθαιροῦντες, which I doubt. We do not in fact know the details of this migration, what was left for the enemy to use or destroy. ἡ κατασκευή includes all farm implements. Cf. Hdt. i. 17. 2, οἰκήματα μὲν τὰ ἐπὶ τῶν ἀγρῶν οὔτε κατέβαλλε οὔτε ἐνεπίμπρη οὔτε θύρας ἀπέσπα: this, however, is said of the invader (Alyattes, invading Miletos). The Milesians obligingly sowed every year, for Alyattes to reap; the Athenians probably did not. διεπέμψαντο: it is difficult to distinguish between the aorist here and the imperfects above, unless it implies, for the cattle, a single, organized operation, aided perhaps by the state for the transport by sea, while individual families were left to find their way to Athens, with their belongings, as best they could. The ὑποζύγια will have been used first to help the transport.

For those who believe that Athens publicly, or Athenian citizens, owned the greater part of the land of Euboea, ἐς τὴν Εὔβοιαν here might be thought to be some confirmation. See vol. i, pp. 344–7; and to the articles there referred to add Hampl, *Klio*, xxxii, 1939, 13–18, and Raubitschek, *Hesp.* xii, 1943, 31, n. 65: the latter shows from new frr. of *I.G.* i.² 326 that some land in Euboea was owned by one of the Hermokopidai in 415. He would be a rich man; and this hardly affects the question of Athenian ownership. See also iii. 104. 2 n.

15. 1. ἑτέρων μᾶλλον: not more than agricultural and socially and economically backward states, but than those of similar development to Athens, Corinth, Argos, Chalkis, Miletos, and many others.

ἐπὶ γὰρ Κέκροπος: another example to show that Thucydides did not doubt the truth, in outline, of the Greek 'myths', though he might interpret the story in his own way. See i. 9. 1, 4 nn.

κατὰ πόλεις ᾠκεῖτο: here πόλις has its own 'political' meaning, 'they lived in independent, or almost independent communities' (αὐτοὶ ἕκαστοι ἐπολίτευον καὶ ἐβουλεύοντο); in τῶν ἄλλων πόλεων and ἐς τὴν νῦν πόλιν οὖσαν and μιᾷ πόλει ταύτῃ (§ 2) it probably combines both the political and the topical meaning; in § 3 it is topical only; cf. 16. 2 (political only) and 17. 1 and 3 (topical), where we have τὸ ἄστυ as well. Cf. i. 5. 1 n., and contrast i. 10. 2—Sparta, politically centralized, but οὔτε ξυνοικισθείσης πόλεως - - -, κατὰ κώμας δὲ οἰκισθείσης.

πρυτανεῖα - - - ἄρχοντας: the place of meeting of those holding office; and 'officers' in the most generalized meaning of the word, including councillors, magistrates, and king, according as these were imagined for primitive times. The πρυτανεῖον also contained the central hearth of the state (cf. Hdt. i. 146. 1).

48

ὥσπερ καὶ Ἐλευσίνιοι μετ' Εὐμόλπου: cf. Pausanias, i. 5. 1.

It is clear that, whatever may be the truth of the matter, Thucydides did not think that Eleusis, any more than the rest of the Attic communities, retained any independence after the reign of Theseus, the generation before the Trojan war. He would appear to have the authority of the Catalogue of *Iliad* ii behind him; and presumably there were no traditions of any subsequent warfare within Attica.

2. μετὰ τοῦ ξυνετοῦ: it is interesting to note the others who are expressly called ξυνετοί by Thucydides—Archidamos (i. 79. 2), Themistokles (i. 74. 1, 138. 2–3), Brasidas (iv. 81. 2), the Peisistratids (vi. 54. 5), Hermokrates (vi. 72. 2), the oligarchs of 411 B.C. (viii. 58. 4), Perikles by implication (ii. 34. 6, 8); cf. vi. 39. 1 (some thought that democracy could not be ξυνετόν), and n. on iii. 82. 5.

The tradition in Athens about Theseus, whether reliable or not, was singularly precise and vivid (see, for later times, Paus. i. 3. 3). That it was he, that is, a king, and one reigning before the Trojan war, who made of Attica one πόλις, has been doubted in modern times, and is doubtful; but no sure alternative has been established.

ἓν βουλευτήριον - - - καὶ πρυτανεῖον: presumably separate buildings, the former the Council-chamber proper, the latter the place of meeting of King and office-holders (his 'ministers' in modern usage) and the centre of the state. See below, p. 59.

ἁπάντων ἤδη ξυντελούντων: ξυντελεῖν does not necessarily imply subordination, as Croiset says; it only denies independence (cf. n. on αὐτοτελεῖς, v. 18. 2). States which ξυντελοῦσι, might be subordinate to another who does not ξυντελεῖ, as the members of the Delian League to Athens; but, as here, all ξυντελεῖς might be equal members of one state, federal or single.

μεγάλη γενομένη: 'a powerful state', not 'a large city', for the people continued most of them to live in the country, even though πόλις just above has partly a topical meaning (cf. n. on κατὰ πόλεις, above).

ξυνοίκια: a festival that was probably held on the 16th Hekatombaion, not long before the Panathenaia and perhaps thought to have had some connexion with the latter, for Theseus was believed to have founded it too after the union of Attica (Plut. *Thes.* 24. 2–4; Schol. Ar. *Peace*, 1019; A. Mommsen, *Feste d. Stadt Athen*, 35–40).

ποιοῦσιν: as edd. have explained, the active means 'appoint the festival', not celebrate it, which would be ποιοῦνται. But we should have expected the middle. ποιεῖται below (§ 4) may be passive of the middle rather than of the active sense.

3. τὸ δὲ πρὸ τοῦ: this reading (CG) is preferable to τὸ δὲ πρὸ τούτου of ABEFM; and it means, I believe, 'in earlier times', not 'before Theseus', as most have taken it. Thucydides mentions in proof the oldest shrines and festivals, and he is surely not distinguishing between those existing before and after Theseus, but only contrasting with later ones, especially for example those built or instituted by the Peisistratidai. Such a distinction, one would suppose, would have greater significance for us, with our new archaeological knowledge, than for Thucydides; if he was making it, it would be interesting as showing his and his contemporaries' opinions about the past; but what, in that case, was his picture of Athens between the age of Theseus and that of Kylon?

ἡ ἀκρόπολις ἡ νῦν οὖσα πόλις ἦν, κ.τ.λ.: 'what is now the akropolis was the city, together with the area below it, especially to the south.' Herwerden bracketed the second ἡ, and Hude transposed it before πόλις; not only unnecessarily (as Steup says), but wrongly. Compare the slightly different construction of τῆς νῦν ἀγορᾶς οὔσης, v. 11. 1. For τὸ πρὸς νότον, see the discussion on §§ 4 and 5.

4. τὰ γὰρ ἱερά, κ.τ.λ.: some mention of Athena's temple, and of her oldest temple (as Stahl and others), must have been made; e.g. τὰ γὰρ ἱερὰ ⟨τὰ ἀρχαιότατα⟩ ἐν αὐτῇ τῇ ἀκροπόλει ⟨τά τε τῆς Ἀθηνᾶς⟩ καὶ ἄλλων θεῶν ἐστι. The oldest shrine of Athena was that in which her wooden ξόανον had long been preserved (Paus. i. 26. 6), identified with the house of Erechtheus which she visited in Homer (Od. vii. 78–81), or where, in her shrine, Erechtheus was honoured with sacrifices by Athenian youths (Il. ii. 549–51). The other shrines on the Akropolis which were, or were thought to be, of great antiquity included probably those of Brauronian Artemis (Paus. i. 23. 7), Zeus Polieus (id. i. 24. 4), Poseidon and Boutes (id. i. 26. 5).

Verrall, Studies in Greek and Latin Scholarship, 62–64, argued that the insertion of τὰ τῆς Ἀθηνᾶς was unnecessary, for the goddess has been mentioned shortly before (τῇ θεῷ ἑορτὴν ποιοῦσιν), and wrong: for Thucydides is at the moment concerned only with the other gods, his argument being that at a time when the Akropolis was practically the whole city, their shrines also had to be there, if they were not to be outside the city altogether. This is logical; but the passage still needs emendation: as it stands (with only τὰ ἀρχαιότατα added) it means 'for the oldest shrines are on the Akropolis itself and are of other gods'; that is, if we do not supply τά τε τῆς Ἀθηνᾶς, we need καὶ ⟨τὰ τῶν⟩ ἄλλων θεῶν—'the oldest shrines, including those of other gods besides Athena, are on the Akropolis itself'.

τὰ ἔξω: those outside the Akropolis precinct, not, however, excluding the possibility that some of them were outside the later city-walls as well, though not distant from them. Kallirroe, for example, from the nature of things, may have been outside. But I cannot agree with Wilamowitz (Herm. xii, 1877, 617), who is followed by Steup, that τὰ ἔξω must mean sanctuaries outside the later city-walls; see Judeich, p. 57 n. (This has its effect on the argument about the identification of τὸ τοῦ ἐν Λίμναις Διονύσου, for which see below, p. 51.)

τοῦτο τὸ μέρος: this means, surely, τὸ ὑ. α. πρὸς νότον μ. τ. See below.

τὸ τοῦ Διὸς τοῦ Ὀλυμπίου: the only known *hieron* of Olympian Zeus at Athens was that south-east of the Akropolis, founded it was said by Deukalion when the waters of the great flood disappeared under the earth near by (Paus. i. 18. 6–8); where the Peisistratids began, but did not finish, the building of a great temple. This was outside the later city-walls.

τὸ Πύθιον: a shrine, with a statue, of Pythian Apollo was near the sanctuary of Zeus Olympios (Paus. i. 19. 1); and this also is the only certainly known Python in Athens. It was probably to the south-west of the Olympieion, on the right bank of the Ilissos, near where the altar set up by the younger Peisistratos "in the precinct of Pythian Apollo" (Thuc. vi. 54. 6) was found; and there is other evidence for the precinct in this neighbourhood. See Judeich, p. 386; Mitsos, *Hesp.* xvi, 1947, 262.

τὸ τῆς Γῆς: two sanctuaries of Ge to the south of the Akropolis are known, one of Ge Olympia within the *peribolos* of the Olympieion (Paus. i. 18. 7), perhaps to the south-west of the temple near the Itonian Gate (Plut. *Thes.* 27. 6: see Frazer's note on Pausanias), the other of Ge Kourotrophos, somewhere on the way along the south side of the Akropolis between the Asklepieion and the entrance to the Akropolis (Paus. i. 22. 3; Judeich, p. 285, n. 4); there is no way of deciding which of these two, if either, Thucydides means by the oldest sanctuary of Ge (reading ⟨τὰ ἀρχαιότατα⟩ above). There was also an ἄγαλμα of Ge within or near the sanctuary of the Semnai on the Areiopagos, i.e. west of the Akropolis (Paus. i. 28. 6).

τὸ ⟨τοῦ⟩ ἐν Λίμναις Διονύσου: Pausanias, i. 20. 3, says that the oldest sanctuary of Dionysos at Athens was that adjoining the theatre, also to the south of the Akropolis, and that within it were two temples, and two statues, one of Dionysos Eleuthereus, the other the gold and ivory statue made by Alkamenes. Doubtless the temple to Eleuthereus, connected with the arrival of Dionysos in Athens from Eleutherai, whence had come the ancient ξόανον (Paus. i. 38. 8), was "the oldest". The foundations of two temples have been excavated, one of the sixth century B.C., the other dating about 420; but the sanctuary was doubtless much older than the earliest stone temple. There was another sanctuary of Dionysos containing a statue of Pegasos of Eleutherai, who introduced him to Athens, on the road from the Dipylon gate to the agora (Paus. i. 2. 5).

There is, however, no explicit evidence to identify the sanctuary of Dionysos in the Marshes with that near the theatre, and nothing to support this view except the statements of Thucydides that the one and of Pausanias that the other was the oldest sanctuary of the god, and the fact that both were to the south of the Akropolis.

Demosthenes, lix. 76, also says that the sanctuary in the Marshes was the oldest and most venerable in Athens; and Isaios, viii. 35, confirms that it was within the walls. Against the identification is the fact that the area to the south of the theatre is not at all marshy; and that the name of the sanctuary was in accord with the natural surroundings seems to be shown by the chorus of frogs in Aristophanes (209 ff.). It is possible enough that Pausanias is wrong in saying that the sanctuary by the theatre was the oldest. On the other hand, it would be difficult to find a site within the walls of the city which could be called marshy or would attract frogs; and the nearest place to the city which might attract them is the bed of the Ilissos, which even in dry weather has many pools, especially below the spring Kallirroe, and the sanctuary of Dionysos by the theatre is the nearest of his known sanctuaries to the Ilissos—about 500 metres distant. If Pausanias is wrong in saying that the oldest of the sanctuaries was πρὸς τῷ θεάτρῳ, there may have been another not far off and nearer the river.[1]

It has also been argued that since the *hieron* in the Marshes, or at least the temple or other sacred building within it, was only open to the public on one day, the 12th Anthesterion, every year (Dem. l.c.), it cannot be identical with that near the theatre, which must have been open at least during the Lenaia and the city Dionysia (see e.g. Frazer, ii. 215). This is a weak argument. The whole theatre area was sacred to Dionysos; but the "oldest sanctuary" was clearly distinct from the rest and could have been separately closed, and, if of special sanctity, may have been more particularly closed at the time of the great dramatic festivals (whether for the reason given by Demosthenes or for another), to keep out the crowds.

Whether the sanctuary of Dionysos ἐπὶ Ληναίῳ was identical with that ἐν Λίμναις (Frazer, ibid., Judeich) is a different question, which does not concern us here, unless Dörpfeld is right in identifying them and placing the shrine, with Enneakrounos, west of the Akropolis. For this, see n. on τῇ κρήνῃ, § 5, below.

τὰ ἀρχαιότερα Διονύσια: Π⁸ has τὰ ἀρχαιότατα Δ., and this is perhaps to be preferred. The festival is the Anthesteria (celebrated by Dikaiopolis in *The Acharnians*), distinguished here by implication from the Lenaia and the city Dionysia and doubtless from others as well. See Pickard-Cambridge, *Dramatic Festivals*, 16 ff. [τῇ δωδεκάτῃ]: the second of the three days of the Anthesteria called the Feast of *Choes*, especially sacred to Dionysos. It was the day on which the sanctuary of Dionysos in the Marshes was open to the public (Dem. lix. 76; see above).

The words have been bracketed as an (understandable) scholar's

---

[1] Π⁸ quotes Philochoros(?) or Apollodoros(?) (see *F.Gr.Hist.* iii. B, 328, F 229 and p. 744) as saying that the sanctuary was so called διὰ τὸ ἐκλελιμνάσθαι [τὸν τόπον].

note, because with them $\mu\eta\nu\dot{o}s$ $\mathcal{A}\nu\theta\epsilon\sigma\tau\eta\rho\iota\hat{\omega}\nu os$ would be required. But Π^8 had them; and Steup defends them on the strength of three instances of $\dot{\epsilon}\nu$ $\mu\eta\nu\iota$ with the day of the month in inscriptions (Dittenberger, *Or. Gr. Inscr.* i, p. 90).

$\overset{\text{v}}{\alpha}\lambda\lambda\alpha$ $\iota\epsilon\rho\dot{\alpha}$ $\tau\alpha\upsilon\tau\eta$ $\dot{\alpha}\rho\chi\alpha\hat{\iota}\alpha$: we have no evidence which these were.

5. $\tau\hat{\eta}$ $\kappa\rho\dot{\eta}\nu\eta$, $\kappa.\tau.\lambda.$: in the case of the four sanctuaries mentioned in § 4, other evidence, archaeological and literary, strengthens, or is at least reconcilable with, Thucydides' statement that the oldest shrines were situated below and to the south of the Akropolis; and I have given above the hitherto generally accepted explanations. But the Enneakrounos fountain presents an unsolved and perhaps insoluble problem. See Judeich, 55–60 and 193–201, who gives full references to discussion (up to 1934) both of this passage in Thucydides and of the site of the fountain in particular; recent excavations in the agora have been fruitful indeed, but do not, in my view, bring us any nearer a solution.

There are three main elements in the problem. (1) On the left bank of the Ilissos, south-west of the Olympieion and not far from the probable site of the Python (see above), is a spring; and a spring called Kallirroe in this area is mentioned in the pseudo-Platonic dialogue *Axiochos* 364 A (of the fourth century B.C.?)[1] and by various later writers from the eleventh century down to our own day. One of the lexicographers, *Etym. Magn.*, s.v. '$E\nu\nu\epsilon\dot{\alpha}\kappa\rho o\upsilon\nu os$, definitely identifies Kallirroe on the Ilissos with Enneakrounos. This would of course suit Thucydides' geographical description excellently. Herodotos' reference to Enneakrounos, vi. 137. 3, also fits well: he tells the Athenian story that the Pelasgoi, anciently living at the foot of Hymettos, attacked the women of Athens at the fountain— it would suit if this were to the south-east of the city, in the Hymettos direction, and outside the walls.[2] On the other hand, excavations at this spring by Skias ($\Pi\rho\alpha\kappa\tau\iota\kappa\dot{\alpha}$, 1893, 111; '$E\phi$. $\mathcal{A}\rho\chi$., 1893, 103–4, 1894, 133), though perhaps not very thorough excavations (see Judeich, p. 196. 1), discovered no evidence at all for a Peisistratid fountain-house. Kratinos, fr. 186, from *Pytine* (423 B.C.),

$$\overset{\text{v}}{\alpha}\nu\alpha\xi \text{ } \mathcal{A}\pi o\lambda\lambda o\nu, \text{ } \tau\hat{\omega}\nu \text{ } \dot{\epsilon}\pi\hat{\omega}\nu \text{ } \tau\hat{\omega}\nu \text{ } \dot{\rho}\epsilon\upsilon\mu\dot{\alpha}\tau\omega\nu\cdot$$
$$\kappa\alpha\nu\alpha\chi o\hat{\upsilon}\sigma\iota \text{ } \pi\eta\gamma\alpha\dot{\iota}, \text{ } \delta\omega\delta\epsilon\kappa\dot{\alpha}\kappa\rho o\upsilon\nu o\nu \text{ } \tau\dot{o} \text{ } \sigma\tau\dot{o}\mu\alpha,$$
$$'I\lambda\iota\sigma\dot{o}s \text{ } \dot{\epsilon}\nu \text{ } \tau\hat{\eta} \text{ } \phi\dot{\alpha}\rho\upsilon\gamma\iota,$$

seems also to point to Enneakrounos by Ilissos—Kratinos' flow of language going one better than Peisistratos' fountain. And in Polyzelos' $\overset{\text{v}}{\iota}\xi\epsilon\iota$ $\pi\rho\dot{o}s$ '$E\nu\nu\epsilon\dot{\alpha}\kappa\rho o\upsilon\nu o\nu$, $\epsilon\overset{\text{v}}{\upsilon}\delta\rho o\nu$ $\tau\dot{o}\pi o\nu$ (fr. 2, Kock, i, p. 790),

[1] H. Leisegang, in *R.E.* xx. 2 (1950), 2366.
[2] Herodotos is guilty of an anachronism in calling the fountain Enneakrounos in a story of primitive Athens, and would be guilty of another and consistent anachronism if he was thinking of the later circuit-wall of the city.

εὔυδρος suits the Ilissos region much better than the agora or Dörpfeld's Dionysion ἐν Λίμναις.

(2) Pausanias definitely places the κρήνη 'called Enneakrounos', οὕτω κοσμηθεῖσαν ὑπὸ Πεισιστράτου, in the agora (or Kerameikos, as he calls the agora): see i. 8. 5–6, 14. 1, 5—'the statues of Harmodios and Aristogeiton; the Odeion (now discovered by the American excavators almost in the centre of the agora); near by is Enneakrounos; above it—or beyond it (ὑπέρ)—are the temples of Demeter and Kore and of Triptolemos'; etc.[1] There is no sign of any displacement in his MSS., nor that, although his direction is not as clear as we should like, he has here deserted his usual geographical arrangement of his material; and though his first book is not so systematically arranged as his later ones, he makes his movements reasonably clear—for example, the two approaches to Athens, from Phaleron and from Peiraeus (1. 4–2. 1 and 2. 2), the two roads by which he went from the prytaneion to the south-east of the city (18. 3–4, 20. 1). Moreover, he gives a description of the district by the Ilissos (18. 4 and 19. 6) and makes no mention there of Enneakrounos or of any other fountain-house or spring. American scholars have claimed that the remains of Enneakrounos are those of a fountain-house on the north slopes of the Areiopagos, which would fit Pausanias' evidence fairly well. Mitsos in excavating south of the Olympieion has found remains of aqueducts of the sixth century, but no fountain-house (B.C.H. lxiii, 1939, 294).[2]

[1] Pausanias goes from the NW. entrance of the agora along the west side southwards as far as the Tholos (i. 3. 1–5. 1). Thence ἀνωτέρω are the statues of the eponymoi (5. 2), various other statues, the temple of Ares, the tyrannicides (8. 2–5). The position of the last is approximately known from other evidence; and the temple of Ares must therefore be the building whose foundations have now been discovered NW. of the Odeion. That is, Pausanias must turn on his tracks, and go northward when he reaches the Tholos; and he must mean this by ἀνωτέρω (upwards on the map by the convention which has always put the east to the right: as early perhaps as Il. xxiv. 54), though the slope is actually a gentle downhill. I much prefer this interpretation to the emendation ἀπωτέρω suggested by the Americans (see p. 129 of the article by Vanderpool mentioned below, n. 2). I owe many thanks both to Mr. Vanderpool and to Prof. Homer Thompson for help given me on the spot in the agora, and in discussion.

[2] See E. Vanderpool, 'The Route of Pausanias in the Agora', Hesp. xviii, 1949, 128–37; which gives a very clear account of the present theories. Not that Pausanias is at all faultless: he says here that Enneakrounos was (in his day) the only πηγή in Athens, otherwise the inhabitants used φρέατα, wells and cisterns; but he himself mentions a κρήνη within the sanctuary of Asklepios on the south slopes of the Akropolis (i. 21. 4: I.G. i.² 874 is its boundary mark) and a πηγή below the Propylaia (i. 28. 4: Klepsydra, on the NW. slopes). (In Thucydides' day there were certainly several κρῆναι: 52. 2, and cf. 48. 2.) His omissions are remarkable: the stoa of Attalos (in whom he was interested: i. 8. 1, etc.), the middle and south stoai of the agora, the Roman agora with its propylon, the stoa of Eumenes, the arch of Hadrian, the "monument of Agrippa", the temple of Rome and Augustus east of the Parthenon. And his description of the Erech-

54

(3) Finally, as is well known, Dörpfeld claimed to have found Enneakrounos in the course of his excavations in the hollow between the Areiopagos and the Pnyx, due west of the Akropolis. He certainly found a large water-basin supplied both by the rather weak springs which flow here from the foot of the Pnyx (which he identified with Kallirroe) and by a long underground conduit, of sixth-century date, which brought water probably from the Ilissos springs well above Athens, through the Olympieion and south of the Akropolis; this he argued was the work of the Peisistratids, and to it they added the fountain-house Enneakrounos. In the complex of foundations of buildings and walls excavated in this same area, Dörpfeld claimed to have found as well the Dionysion τὸ ἐν Λίμναις (which he identified with that ἐπὶ Ληναίῳ) and the Eleusinion, the oldest agora and oldest Prytaneion. There was no inscriptional evidence to confirm these identifications. He argued as well that a site due west of the Akropolis was reconcilable both with Thucydides' statement that the oldest shrines outside the Akropolis and the Kallirroe were in a mainly southern direction, and with Pausanias' itinerary: Pausanias, he thought, left the agora by the road west of the Areiopagos (i. 8. 6) and returned to it later (i. 14. 6). The former is doubtful, the latter quite arbitrary (not only would Pausanias have indicated his direction, but he must have mentioned not only the Areiopagos but the sanctuaries discovered by Dörpfeld, if these included the Dionysion and the Eleusinion: the difficulties are well put in E. A. Gardner, *Ancient Athens* (1907), 141–51; see also Frazer, *Pausanias*, ii. 212–15, v. 495–9; Judeich, p. 199, n. 3; it is now finally disproved by the discovery of the Odeion (above, p. 54) in the agora and of the probable whereabouts of the Eleusinion to the south-east of the agora (see below, 17. 1 n.; and *Hesp.* ix, 1940, opp. p. 308, for a plan of the agora as a whole). This considerably weakens Dörpfeld's whole case for his siting of Enneakrounos; but, since Pausanias is not reconcilable with Thucydides, if we decide that the latter's account is to be preferred, our conclusion is that Pausanias was misinformed, the fountain which he saw not being the Enneakrounos; and if so, the question of the true site of the fountain is still open and Dörpfeld, shorn of his anyhow weakest arguments, may be right. See Pickard-Cambridge, *Dram. Fest.*, 20–22.

Some of the American excavators maintain not only that

theion is extremely confused (though here there may be some lacuna in the MSS.). But his general topographical order is clear enough. In his account of Corinth too, a meagre one for this fine new Roman town, he does not mention the large stoai which he must have passed (ii. 2. 6–3. 5).

On some plans of the agora excavations the fountain-house (at the western end of the South Stoa) has been labelled Enneakrounos; but on the most recent (1954) it is called SW. Fountain-house, for another has been found near the east end of the same stoa. See p. 63, n. 1; and Addenda.

Pausanias was right about Enneakrounos, that it was in the agora and so north-west of the Akropolis, but that the other shrines mentioned by Thucydides, that of Zeus Olympios, the Pythion, the shrine of Ge and (presumably) that of Dionysos in the Marshes, were in this quarter too, and Thucydides, or the text of Thucydides, is wrong. Thus A. W. Parsons, *Hesp.* xii, 1943, 192, wrote: "Every visitor to Athens is familiar with the north face of the Acropolis as it looks from the streets of the town below; he has seen the sheer rock wall above the tree-covered slope with the dark shadows of the sanctuary-caves near its western end. But not everyone, approaching the Beulé gate of the Acropolis has turned aside to take the path to the left around the slope at the base of the north-west cliffs. He who has, will have paused at the broad ledge directly below the caves and the Propylaia—it is an obvious resting-place—to reflect for a moment about the region where he stood. Here in antiquity was the place where peripatos [the road or path along the north slope] and Panathenaic Street met; above were the Olympion and the Pythion, somewhere near by, the sanctuary of Ge; further along the slope—green to-day as it was in antiquity—were the Aglaurion and the shrine of Aphrodite 'in the Gardens'; below stretched that mysterious area, the Pelargikon. Here surely, was the very heart of primitive Athens, Athens before Theseus—after the Acropolis itself, the oldest and most sacred part of the city. (Thucydides, ii. 15, where πρὸς νότον must be a mistake or a corruption. Thucydides wrote, or intended to write, πρὸς βορρᾶν (or πρὸς ἄρκτον, cf. Belger, *B.Ph.W.* xiv, 1894, 93). It is the duplication of certain sanctuaries, which appear both on the north slope of the Acropolis, and south of it, toward the Ilissos, that may have caused the error, and is certainly responsible for its perpetuation; the question has often been discussed . . ., most recently by O. Broneer, whose paper is summarized in *A.J.A.* xiv, 1941, 92.)" The Olympion and Pythion are, on this view, the two cave-sanctuaries high up in the cliff above the spring Klepsydra, the third cave, to the east, being that of Pan; the sanctuary of Ge is presumably thought to be connected with the image of Ge in or near the shrine of the Semnai (see above, n. on τὸ τῆς Γῆς, § 4); it is not clear where the upholders of this view locate Dionysos in the Marshes.[1]

[1] For the Pelargikon, see 17. 1 n.; for the Aglaurion, Paus. i. 18. 2, Judeich, p. 303; and for Aphrodite in the Gardens, Paus. i. 19. 2 and 27. 3—the two passages are not related to each other—see Judeich, p. 424: Pausanias clearly indicates its position to the SE. or east of the Akropolis, somewhere between the Olympieion and Kynosarges, outside the walls therefore, as seems to be indicated by *I.G.* i.[2] 324, l. 85 (l. 80 in Meritt, *A.F.D.*, p. 141). For the argument that it lay below the north slope of the Akropolis, which is more in consonance with Pausanias' second notice of it, see Broneer, *Hesp.* ii, 1933, 329 ff., iv. 126-7.

56

To this opinion there are several objections. (1) It is a pretty argument in a circle to say (in effect) that, since the words πρὸς νότον suit perfectly at least three of Thucydides' τεκμήρια (Olympieion, Pythion, Ge) and perhaps all five, they are corrupt or a mistake, owing to a natural confusion. (2) I very much doubt whether, if Thucydides had meant the cave-sanctuaries in the Akropolis cliff, he would have said that the Olympieion and Pythion were situated 'towards this quarter of the town', i.e. to the north; he would have included them among the oldest shrines of the Akropolis itself, where they belong. Compare the description of Klepsydra, below these caves, as κρήνη ἐν ἀκροπόλει by Istros, F 6. (3) Keramopoullos' identification of one of the caves with the sanctuary of Zeus Olympios (Ἀρχ. Δελτ. xii, 1929, 86 ff.), accepted by Parsons, is based on Strabo, ix. 2. 11, p. 404 (see below), and is not supported by any archaeological evidence. We do not know to what god it was sacred, if to any. (4) The westernmost cave was sacred to Apollo, but to Apollo ὑπ' ἄκραις or Ὑπακραῖος or ὑπὸ Μακραῖς, not as far as we know to Apollo Pythios; many inscriptions have been found giving the god his proper title (I.G. ii.² 2891–931; Oliver, Hesp. x, 1941, 252–3. All these dedications too are late—first to third centuries A.D.).

The passage in Strabo is some evidence: the Pythaïstai at Athens used to look in the direction of Mt. Parnes for lightning as a sign for them to start the Pythaïs to Delphi; they watched from the hearth (ἐσχάρα) of Zeus Astrapaios, ἐστὶ δ᾽ αὕτη ἐν τῷ τείχει μεταξὺ τοῦ Πυθίου καὶ τοῦ Ὀλυμπίου. The natural interpretation of this is a part of the circuit-wall of the city south-east of the Akropolis (so Judeich, pp. 386–7, without misgiving); but this would be a very odd place from which to watch Mt. Parnes, for it is low-lying and faces the wrong direction. Hence Keramopoullos' argument that τὸ τεῖχος is the Akropolis wall, and that the site of the altar was just above the three caves on the north-west cliff, one of which was sacred to Apollo; and that the second must therefore be τὸ Ὀλύμπιον. But the argument is very weak, for we cannot suppose that Strabo is speaking from direct knowledge: no one doing so would say "the wall between the Olympion and the Python" (two very well-known sanctuaries to the south-east of Athens) when he meant "the wall of the Akropolis at a place above the two caves which are sacred to Apollo and to Zeus". Strabo then is anyhow vague; and the archaeological evidence is definitely against this interpretation of him. No remains of a hearth which might be that of Zeus Astrapaios have been found.

The other evidence cited for a Pythion in this neighbourhood is Pausanias' statement (i. 29. 1) that the sacred ship carried in the Panathenaic procession was displayed near the Areiopagos, combined with Philostratos' description (Vit. Soph. ii. 1. 7) of the route taken

57

by the procession[1]—from the Kerameikos round the Eleusinion and past the Pelargikon to the Pythion, where the ship was moored. This perhaps means a difference of opinion between Pausanias and Philostratos about the place where the ship was kept in the intervals between one procession and another (so Frazer, ii, p. 373); but even that is uncertain, and it would not be very important if it were true. And a route "past the Pelargikon to the Pythion" is strangely described if, as Parsons believed, the former was in this quarter too and the Pythion a cave high up in the cliff apparently within its area. That Euripides should relate in *Ion* (283-6) how 'the Pythian god' met Kreousa in the cave is no evidence that the cave was known as τὸ Πύθιον, especially as in that passage and elsewhere in the play (13, 494, 937) he says that the rocks were called Μακραί.[2]

Finally, I believe that Thucydides is contrasting the early with the later growth of the city. From at least Peisistratid days, this development had been to the north of the Akropolis;[3] there especially were the agora and the public buildings, and the Themistoklean circuit wall made the development in this direction clear enough. Thucydides is not saying, 'Primitive Athens was smaller in extent than the present city, but it extended in the same direction'; but 'unlike the present city it extended mainly to the south'.

[1] For the course of the Panathenaic Street from the Dipylon through the agora to the western approach to the Akropolis, see *Hesp.* ix, 1940, pl. i, and Vanderpool, *Hesp.* xviii, 1949, 134-6.

[2] If there ever was a Pythion north of the Akropolis it is most likely to be identified with the shrine of Apollo Patroos (Paus. i. 3. 4; Frazer, ii, p. 65; *Hesp.* vi. 77-115).

The open paved court just below and to the east of Klepsydra, which was excavated by Parsons, is a puzzling affair; no inscription helps us to identify it. Parsons thought that it was closely connected with the cave of Apollo, and that it was some kind of *pompeion* where certain of the gear for the Pythaïs was kept, "and where some parts of the procession would have been prepared while the larger units formed in the street outside" (ibid., pp. 233-7). The shape of the court, its restricted size, the absence of roofed buildings, and the very steep and narrow steps connecting it with the street outside, make a *pompeion* the last explanation I should have thought of; and the absence of direct connexion with the cave makes it doubtful if it had anything to do with Apollo. One would surmise as more probable some connexion with Klepsydra.

[3] But perhaps not much earlier; at least the sixth-century graves found to the SW. of the agora (*Hesp.* ix, 1940, 302-4; x. 6) seem to show that the area immediately NW. of the Akropolis was not then within the city.

Broneer again, *Hesp.* Suppl. viii, 1949, 47-59, suggests that the imaginative picture of primitive Athens drawn by Plato in *Kritias*, 111 E-112 E, has some foundation in fact; and amongst what may be true is the statement that the 'hoplite class' (the guardians) lived in the northern section of the then Akropolis (which extended as far as the Eridanos to the north and the Ilissos to the south), with gardens and gymnasia in the south. But, even if Plato meant that there was history behind his fancy, we are here concerned only with *Thucydides'* view of early Athens, which may have differed from Plato's, and may have been more correct.

For all these reasons, I am convinced that $\pi\rho\dot{o}s$ $\nu\acute{o}\tau o\nu$ must stand as what Thucydides wrote and intended to write. It follows that there is a conflict of evidence between him and Pausanias as to which fountain-house was the Enneakrounos; and there is no doubt which of the two is right. Thucydides must have known, and Pausanias may easily have been misinformed; it is possible that the Peisistratid fountain was no longer in use in his day.[1] Whether the remains discovered by Dörpfeld can be considered to be the foundations of Enneakrounos depends (in the absence of any inscriptional evidence and of definite archaeological proof) on the exact interpretation of $\tau\dot{o}$ $\dot{v}\pi'$ $a\dot{v}\tau\dot{\eta}\nu$ $\pi\rho\dot{o}s$ $\nu\acute{o}\tau o\nu$ $\mu\acute{a}\lambda\iota\sigma\tau a$ $\tau\epsilon\tau\rho a\mu\mu\acute{\epsilon}\nu o\nu$, of $\pi\rho\dot{o}s$ $\tau o\hat{v}\tau o$ $\tau\dot{o}$ $\mu\acute{\epsilon}\rho os$ $\tau\hat{\eta}s$ $\pi\acute{o}\lambda\epsilon\omega s$ $\mu\hat{a}\lambda\lambda o\nu$, and of $\tau a\acute{v}\tau\eta$ (§ 6, ad fin.), and of the relation between this sentence, $\kappa a\dot{\iota}$ $\tau\hat{\eta}$ $\kappa\rho\acute{\eta}\nu\eta$, $\kappa.\tau.\lambda.$, and what has just preceded: i.e. what $\pi\rho\dot{o}s$ $\nu\acute{o}\tau o\nu$ $\mu\acute{a}\lambda\iota\sigma\tau a$ implies here. We must not suppose that $\pi\rho\dot{o}s$ $\nu\acute{o}\tau o\nu$ can *include* a purely western direction, nor that, however often the Greeks were mistaken about the direction of coastlines and mountains, there could be any doubt about what was to the south of the Akropolis; but Thucydides may have meant that though the greater part of the ancient city extended to the south, some of the ancient shrines and other places of importance which he mentions adjoined that part to the west. I do not myself, however, think this probable; and I believe still that Enneakrounos was somewhere to the south. Dörpfeld went further, arguing that $\pi\rho\dot{o}s$ $\tau o\hat{v}\tau o$ $\tau\dot{o}$ $\mu\acute{\epsilon}\rho os$ does not mean $\tau\dot{o}$ $\dot{v}\pi'$ $a\dot{v}\tau\dot{\eta}\nu$ $\pi\rho\dot{o}s$ $\nu\acute{o}\tau o\nu$ $\tau\epsilon\tau\rho a\mu\mu\acute{\epsilon}\nu o\nu$, but only 'towards, near the Akropolis' (so Verrall, pp. 65–66: see above, p. 50). This is wholly improbable. See the judicious remarks of Mrs. Hill in *The Ancient City of Athens*, 1953, pp. 62–63, 195 (written before the discovery of the second fountain-house in the agora (above, p. 55, n.)).

It is noteworthy that, apart from Enneakrounos, Thucydides mentions only sacred buildings as $\tau\epsilon\kappa\mu\acute{\eta}\rho\iota a$, and especially that he does not give the site of the first or of the Thesean *prytaneion* and *bouleuterion*; for he has stressed their political importance. He may have thought that, obviously, the first *prytaneion* was on the Akropolis (Judeich, 63). He does not mention the tomb of Theseus either (Plut. *Thes.* 36. 4),[2] nor the Areiopagos as the oldest seat of justice

[1] Hitzig and Blümner, in their edition of Pausanias (i. 14. 1), point out that it is not likely that there were two *nine-headed* fountains, one the Peisistratid foundation, and the other not. This must be conceded; but I do not suppose that either Pausanias or his informant was very particular about the fountain they saw; Pausanias does not describe it in detail.

[2] Where was this tomb? or where was it said to be in Thucydides' day? Plutarch says it was $\dot{\epsilon}\nu$ $\mu\acute{\epsilon}\sigma\eta$ $\tau\hat{\eta}$ $\pi\acute{o}\lambda\epsilon\iota$ $\pi\epsilon\rho\dot{\iota}$ $\tau\dot{o}$ $\nu\hat{v}\nu$ $\gamma\upsilon\mu\nu\acute{a}\sigma\iota o\nu$, the resort of humble men who would be protected by the good Theseus. For the older *prytaneion*, as for the 'old agora' (perhaps west of the Akropolis, near Dörpfeld's Lenaion), see Judeich, 62–63.

59

(Hellanikos, F 1). It is also noteworthy that three of his τεκμήρια (Olympieion, Pythion, and Enneakrounos), and the Akropolis temples, were closely associated with the Peisistratids, and that his knowledge of this did not make him think that these places had not been important before; and conversely, that though he must have known of the development of the agora and its public buildings in the sixth century, especially in connexion with the Panathenaia, he did not exaggerate its antiquity. Nor does he mention a Θησεῖον; was that shrine comparatively recent? He does not record, we may note especially, either the elaborate drainage channels in the agora which belong to the sixth century (Thompson, *Hesp.* ix, 1940, 267, 300–1; see also suppl. iv, 1940, index) or Klepsydra, which, once called Empedo and a simple well, fed by a perennial spring, had been known since neolithic times and had recently, since the Persian invasion, been elaborately reconstructed (*Hesp.* viii, 1939, 223–5); but then, unlike Enneakrounos, though its history was similar, they were not in the quarter of the town in which Thucydides was for the moment interested.

It does not of course follow from this that Thucydides was right in thinking that the earliest extension of the city outside the Akropolis was to the south. We must believe him that the sanctuaries which he mentions were a good deal older than the sixth century, but we can hardly suppose that he could in every case distinguish between different degrees of antiquity in the traditions. We know also that the excavations in the agora have shown so far that there was but little building, sacred or profane, public or private, in that area (that is, the area which, together with that to the east of it, would naturally be described as τὸ ὑπὸ τὴν ἀκρόπολιν πρὸς βορρᾶν μάλιστα τετραμμένον) earlier than the sixth century. But there have been found extensive cemeteries of the geometric period, from *c.* 1000 B.C. onwards, both north of the Areiopagos (R. S. Young, *Hesp.* suppl. ii, 1939) and near the Dipylon. Of the Mycenean period (L.H. iii from *c.* 1400 to 1200 B.C. and earlier) large finds of pottery, indicating a fairly populous settlement, have been made in Broneer's fruitful excavations on the north slope of the Akropolis (*Hesp.* ii, 1933, 351–72, iv. 109–21, viii. 317–433), including that found in the remarkable well constructed in the thirteenth century and soon closed, as well as in the Klepsydra; and in the chamber-tombs on the northern slopes of the Areiopagos (*Hesp.* ix, 1940, 274–93; xvii, 1948, 150).[1] Similar remains, covering a long period of time, have been found on the south slope by Italian scholars (*Annuario*, iv–v, 1921–2, 490; *Boll. d'Arte*, iv, 1924–5, 88–89). But there is no reason to suppose that any direct tradition of these settlements survived to Thucy-

[1] See R. S. Young, 'Late Geometric Graves', *Hesp.* suppl. ii, 1939, and 'Sepultura intra Urbem', *Hesp.* xx, 1951, 67-134.

dides' day; one tomb in particular (*Hesp.* ix), perhaps that of a royal princess, was closed soon after its first use, and remained unknown till its excavation. There are also remains of the Mycenean period, scanty when compared with those of Mykenai and Tiryns, and other Peloponnesian and Boeotian cities, on the Akropolis itself, including the 'Pelasgic' fortification wall (Judeich, 54–55, 115–18. See now, Hill, *Anc. City of Athens*, 8–31, for a clear summary of the remains of the bronze and early iron ages in this area). Nothing of this except the last was actually known to Thucydides; all he would have heard was that there had been no public buildings in the region north of the Akropolis earlier than the sixth century, and no tradition of any, whereas on the Akropolis itself and to the south-east of it there had also been much Peisistratid activity, but *there* there was the Homeric, and perhaps other tradition as well, of earlier buildings. We may, if we like, doubt his general conclusion.

τὰ πλείστου ἄξια: some scholars, notably Steup, have objected that, if the earliest inhabitants only used the spring for the most important purposes, firstly, they are not distinguished from Thucydides' contemporaries, and secondly, it would not be proof of their living in the quarter near the spring; for, for important purposes, like the later Athenians, they would make longer journeys. Torstrik emended to τὰ πλεῖστα [ἄξια]¹ (*Philol.* xxxi, 1872, 86); Steup suggests transferring τὰ πλείστου ἄξια to the second half of the sentence before τῶν ἱερῶν. Neither is necessary (Torstrik's is the better for the sense; but, as Steup says, we should have rather τὰ πολλά); Thucydides is contrasting a use for *generally* important purposes, secular as well as sacred, with the purely religious use in his own day—though, on the other hand, we are not to believe that this elaborate fountain was used only for religious purposes in the fifth century, but simply that all inhabitants of Athens (who lived mostly away to the north of the Akropolis), wherever they got their water for drinking and washing, used it for these purposes. Π^8 had the MSS. reading.

6. καλεῖται δέ, κ.τ.λ.: familiar instances of this are to be found in official inscriptions, where πόλις is regular for the Akropolis, and in Aristophanes' *Lysistrate*. Thucydides only has πόλις in this sense in quotations of official documents, v. 18. 10, 23. 5, 47. 11; contrast vi. 55. 1, which only refers to a document.

16. 1. τῇ τε οὖν, κ.τ.λ.: the narrative resumed from c. 14, with a summary of the statement in 14. 2–15. 2.

The reading μετεῖχον is supported directly by the scholia, including

¹ All recent editors except Stuart Jones and Powell say that AB here read τὰ πλεῖστα ἄξια (corr. a₂), which would give some support to Torstrik's emendation; but these two are silent, which should mean that the variant has been wrongly reported.

Π^8, which say simply that Thucydides uses the dative instead of the genitive after it; and indeed this is the only explanation if μετεῖχον is right. But it is scarcely possible (it may be significant that Dionysios does not notice it); and since we can do without a verb, most editors content themselves with bracketing it and confessing that no reason can be given for its appearance early in Thucydides' text. The verb we expect is ἐχρῶντο. (Of all conjectures, Weil's is perhaps the most attractive: ⟨πρὶν ἢ τῆς πόλεως⟩ [better, τῶν Ἀθηνῶν] μετεῖχον.)

τε οὖν is the reading of all our MSS., and there is no need, with most edd., to adopt Krüger's δ' οὖν (after a digression, as i. 3. 4, vii. 59. 2). If another verb should take the place of μετεῖχον, there is no difficulty; if not, τε - - - καί combine the causal dative τῇ αὐτονόμῳ οἰκήσει with the causal participles γενόμενοί τε καὶ οἰκήσαντες, giving, that is, the connexion between the period of local *political* independence, before Theseus, with that of political unity but dispersed living; Steup's objection that the original autonomous organization could not be a cause why the later Athenians οὐ ῥᾳδίως τὰς μεταναστάσεις ἐποιοῦντο is no more valid than an objection that οἱ πλείους τῶν ἀρχαίων cannot reasonably be a subject to ἐποιοῦντο. It only adds to the awkwardness of the sentence to read δ' οὖν, and hence to understand καὶ ἐπειδὴ ξυνῳκίσθησαν as 'even after the political union', with, in consequence, τῇ - - - οἰκήσει a causal dative to ἐν τοῖς ἀγροῖς - - - οἰκήσαντες, explaining διὰ τὸ ἔθος.

πανοικεσίᾳ: in our MSS. and in Π^8 before γενόμενοι; transferred by Lipsius and by most editors, including Stuart Jones, before τὰς μεταναστάσεις: cf. iii. 57. 2, and πανοικίη, Hdt. vii. 39. 1, viii. 106. 3, ix. 109. 2, in all of which there is reference to movement (with the whole household) or to destruction. I agree with Classen that the change is not compelling; but it is attractive, for there is not much point in saying that they used to *live* πανοικεσίᾳ in the country ('without a separate house in Athens'? so Croiset).

17. 1. τὸ ἄστυ: the town as opposed to the country, οἱ ἀγροί (as ἀστεῖος to ἄγροικος), not, as so frequently, Athens in relation to Peiraeus.

τά τε ἐρῆμα τῆς πόλεως: the uninhabited, empty, not 'deserted', parts of the city.

τοῦ Ἐλευσινίου: the location of this sanctuary seems to be now fixed, to the south-east of the agora, c. 100 metres south-east of and above the east end of the south stoa. Remains of a building (fifth century?) have been found, though nothing, whether simple walled enclosure with an altar and a few small buildings (with doors and roof: see *I.G.* ii.² 1672; *Hesp.* xiv, 1945, 89–93; Judeich, 288–90), or one containing a temple, that can be positively identified; but a number of inscribed dedications to the Eleusinian goddesses have been found in this quarter, and, what is more important for deciding the site, five votive deposits of *kernoi*, vases peculiar to the worship of Demeter and Kore (*Hesp.* viii, 1939, 207–11; Pritchett, ibid. ix. 112, n. 48; ibid. 267–8; xvii, 1948, 88 ff.; xviii. 134–5). From Xen. *Hipparch.* 3. 2–4 we must assume a wide road, fit for the rapid movement of cavalry in a procession (at the Panathenaia), and where the galloping horsemen can be seen and admired, stretching from the Hermai in the north-west quarter of the agora to the Eleusinion. This does not help us much to identify the site—we have only to remember that the stoai to the east and south of the agora and the Odeion in the centre, which appear in our plans, were not there in the fourth century; and Pausanias' description, i. 14. 1–3, ναοὶ δὲ ὑπὲρ τὴν κρήνην ὁ μὲν Δήμητρος καὶ κόρης, κ.τ.λ., would be very misleading (whether ὑπέρ here means 'above' or 'beyond'), if the κρήνη were, as some of the excavators have thought, the building once identified with Enneakrounos (above, p. 54); but the second fountain-house, the one found near the east end of the South Stoa (see n., below), would suit—the Eleusinion would then be above or beyond it. But the Eleusinion was below the Akropolis (*I.G.* ii.² 1078); we are told that the Panathenaic ship passed the Eleusinion on its way from the agora to the Akropolis (Philostratos, *Vit. Soph.* ii. 1. 5), and we know that the Panathenaic Road passed near the site in question from the inscription cut in the north face of the bastion of Mnesikles west of the Propylaia (see Vanderpool, *Hesp.* xviii, 1949, 134–5); so, whatever may be the truth about Enneakrounos or Pausanias' κρήνη, the site of the Eleusinion seems to be assured.[1]

For some details about the rites of the city Eleusinion, see L. Jeffery, *Hesp.* xvii, 1948, 86–111.

τὸ Πελαργικόν: this spelling is confirmed for the fifth century by *I.G.* i.² 76. 55 (Tod, 74), and is found in the better MSS. of Herodotos, v. 64. 2 (the siege of the Peisistratidai on the Akropolis), and of Ar. *Av.* 832, and in Arist. *Ἀθπ.* 19. 5; C alone of Thucydides MSS. has it here, the rest Πελασγικόν. See also Philochoros, F 99, on which Jacoby has a long comment. But what is the meaning of the name Πελαργικόν, and what the relation between the two names and between this place below the Akropolis and the old circuit-wall of

_____

[1] Recent excavations have uncovered the foundations of this second fountain-house of the sixth to fifth centuries just south of the eastern end of the Hellenistic south stoa: H. Thompson in *A.J.A.* lvii, 1953, 21–25. This suits the relation of Enneakrounos to the Eleusinion as described by Pausanias, though of course it does nothing towards settling the problem whether Pausanias was right about the former. The newly discovered fountain was apparently fed by the same aqueduct as the other. Thompson himself only says that one or other of the two must be Pausanias' Enneakrounos. See Addenda.

the Akropolis itself said to have been built by the Pelasgoi (Paus. i. 28. 3; Kleidemos, $F.$ $Gr.$ $H.$ 323, F 16),[1] and where exactly this Pelargikon was, it is impossible to say. Herodotos, vi. 137. 1, mentions, from Hekataios (F127), the building of the Akropolis wall by the Pelasgoi; and this, one would suppose, was the same wall as τὸ Πελαργικὸν τεῖχος within which (ἐν τῷ Πελαργικῷ τείχεϊ) the Peisistratidai were besieged by Kleomenes in 511 b.c. (Hdt., and Ἀθπ., loc. cit.), or at least part of it. Thucydides, on the other hand, is clearly distinguishing the Pelargikon from the Akropolis wall. It is possible that the Peisistratidai had built a wall, or used an older wall, to form a bastion below the Akropolis in order to enclose either the Klepsydra or the spring on the south slope (Paus. i. 21. 4: above, p. 54, n. 2) or both; for the Akropolis itself is notoriously lacking in a good water-supply, and Herodotos says (but with what authority?) that the Peisistratidai were well supplied with both food and water and would have held out against Kleomenes if it had not been for the accident of the capture of their children (v. 65). This bastion will have been destroyed after the expulsion of the tyrants, or by the Persians, and not rebuilt; yet its boundaries had been preserved, and the area within them left uninhabited in obedience to the oracle mentioned below.[2] See Judeich, 113–20.

Exactly where this Pelargikon was cannot be determined, for no trace of any wall or boundary has been discovered. It is assumed that it was below the Akropolis to the west—to the west and southwest by Dörpfeld in accordance with his view on the site of Enneakrounos and the oldest centre of Athens, to the north-west by Parsons in accordance with his view (above, pp. 56–58). All I think that we can say with some probability is that it can hardly have been due west where the main entrance to the Akropolis lay; for though this area may not have been built upon, it was necessarily much frequented and could hardly have been described as ἀργόν; also that the area did not include the Areiopagos.[3] We know from the second part of the decree, $I.G.$ i.² 76 (Tod, 74), that in $c.$ 418

---

[1] Some ancient writers, at least, identified the two: Strabo, ix. 2. 3, p. 401.

[2] When the new walls were built round the Akropolis after the expulsion of the Persians, it was not necessary to include the springs within the circuit because the Akropolis was henceforward to be not a fortress but a sacred precinct. In fact after this time the walls never included a good spring except for the short period during which the Greeks were besieged there by the Turks in 1825-6 (Parsons, $Hesp.$ xii, 1943, 223-6); nor as far as we know had they done so before the tyrants, except for a brief time in the late Mycenean age (above, p. 60). We may note, however, that Lachares managed to hold out for a long time within the Akropolis walls.

[3] Mrs. Hill, $Anc.$ $City$ of $Athens,$ pp. 16, 74, 124, 131-3, defines it as a narrow strip running north, west, and south of the Akropolis, above the $peripatos,$ starting from the Anakeion on the north slope westwards, and ending at the western boundary of the Asklepieion on the south slope.

64

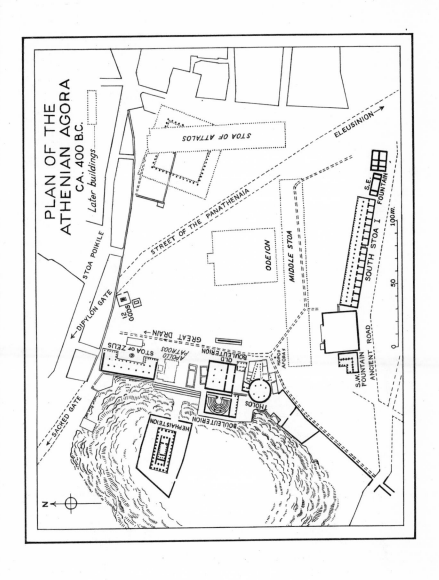

PLAN OF THE
ATHENIAN AGORA
CA. 400 B.C.
Later buildings

STOA POIKILE
DIPYLON GATE
SACRED GATE
STREET OF THE PANATHENAIA
STOA OF ATTALOS
ELEUSINION
ODEION
MIDDLE STOA
12 GODS
GREAT DRAIN
STOA OF ZEUS
APOLLO PATROOS
OLD BOULEUTERION
HOROS AGORA
THOLOS
BOULEUTERION
HEPHAISTEION
S.W. FOUNTAIN
ANCIENT ROAD
SOUTH STOA I
S.E. FOUNTAIN

B.C.[1] it contained $\iota\epsilon\rho\acute{a}$ whose boundaries were to be defined, and that altars were not to be set up in it without authorization by boule and demos, and the removal of stones or earth from it was to be stopped. We can imagine the need for such regulations after the occupation of the area during the Archidamian war.

We know also that the section of the 'Pelasgic' wall round the Akropolis just within and to the south of the Propylaia which stands today to a height of 4 m. (the thickness of the wall varies between 4 and 6 m.), was expressly preserved in the fifth century, when it may have been 10 m. high; for the south-east corner of the southern wing of Mnesikles' Propylaia was worked in order to fit with it (Judeich, p. 115; G. Stevens, *Hesp.* v, 1936, 447–58). But this can hardly have anything to do with the Pelargikon as Thucydides understood it; for to him it is clearly only an area below the Akropolis which was declared $\dot{a}\rho\gamma\grave{o}\nu$ $\ddot{a}\mu\epsilon\iota\nu o\nu$, not one which included the Akropolis.

If it be true that the Pelargikon was an area below the northwest cliffs of the Akropolis, including the cave of Pan, the supposed Pythion (above, pp. 56–58, 64), and the spring of Klepsydra, as Parsons thought, and Frazer on Pausanias i. 28. 3 (ii, pp. 357–8), it is to be noted that Thucydides did not use it as evidence for the site of the primitive city: which is natural enough if he thought that the site was the Akropolis and the region south of it.

τὸ Πελαργικὸν ἀργὸν ἄμεινον: according to the scholiast the curse dated from 'Pelasgian' times, because the Pelasgians who had lived in Attica attacked Athens; they were driven out and the place where they had lived was cursed from thenceforth. We have no means of knowing whether Thucydides was thinking of any such legend, or (assuming, as is almost certain from the official use in *I.G.* i.[2] 76, that he wrote Πελαργικόν, not Πελασγικόν) whether he connected the area with the Pelasgoi at all. Pollux, viii. 101, says that the fine for cutting wood or hay, or burying the dead, in the Pelargikon, was 3 dr.; if this is correct for the original 'curse', it must have been not earlier than the sixth century because it is expressed in terms of money, but perhaps early in that century because of the smallness of the amount (it was 500 dr. in *I.G.* i.[2] 76); see Judeich, p. 119, n. 1.

2. καί μοι δοκεῖ, κ.τ.λ.: "attende scriptoris animum liberalem"— Stahl. I am not so sure: true, Thucydides rejects the common superstition that the oracle was foretelling this war (conveniently without

---

[1] The date of the inscription is uncertain, and some have argued for one before the Peloponnesian war. But Dinsmoor now puts it in 416–415 B.C. (*Archons of Athens*, 335–8, 341. Dinsmoor included a study of the Pelargikon in his major work on the western section of the Akropolis, a work not yet published—Lord, *History of the American School at Athens*, 1947, 165–7).

naming it); but he seems to have accepted the view that the oracle could, to some degree, know the future. Cobet, indeed, conjectured $\pi\rho o\hat{\eta}\delta\epsilon$ for $\pi\rho o\acute{\eta}\delta\epsilon\iota$, and this is adopted by Hude and Steup, on the ground that, as the latter puts it, $\pi\rho o\acute{\eta}\delta\epsilon\iota$ "passt nicht zu dem freien Standpunkt, den Thukydides, c. 54, in Bezug auf das Orakelwesen einnimmt". But this is not only to manufacture the evidence for a theory, but $\pi\rho o\hat{\eta}\delta\epsilon$ itself implies foreknowledge. It does not of course require much foresight to say simply 'it will be a bad day for Athens when the Pelargikon is occupied'.

$a\acute{\iota}\ \xi\nu\mu\phi o\rho a\acute{\iota}$ might refer specifically to the plague, or more generally to the hardships of the war (variatio with $\delta\iota\grave{a}\ \tau\grave{o}\nu\ \pi\acute{o}\lambda\epsilon\mu o\nu$ below); but not to final defeat. The word does not help us to date the composition of this chapter.

3. $\grave{\epsilon}\nu\ \tau o\hat{\iota}s\ \pi\acute{\nu}\rho\gamma o\iota s$: vividly put by Aristophanes, Eq. 792–3:

$$\kappa a\grave{\iota}\ \pi\hat{\omega}s\ \sigma\grave{\nu}\ \phi\iota\lambda\epsilon\hat{\iota}s,\ \hat{o}s\ \tau o\hat{\nu}\tau o\nu\ \acute{o}\rho\hat{\omega}\nu\ o\grave{\iota}\kappa o\hat{\nu}\nu\tau'\ \grave{\epsilon}\nu\ \tau a\hat{\iota}s\ \phi\iota\delta\acute{a}\kappa\nu a\iota\sigma\iota$$
$$\kappa a\grave{\iota}\ \gamma\nu\pi a\rho\acute{\iota}o\iota s\ \kappa a\grave{\iota}\ \pi\nu\rho\gamma\iota\delta\acute{\iota}o\iota s\ \acute{\epsilon}\tau o s\ \acute{o}\gamma\delta o o\nu\ o\grave{\nu}\kappa\ \grave{\epsilon}\lambda\epsilon a\acute{\iota}\rho\epsilon\iota s.$$

4. $\grave{\epsilon}\kappa a\tau\grave{o}\nu\ \nu\epsilon\hat{\omega}\nu\ \grave{\epsilon}\pi\acute{\iota}\pi\lambda o\nu\nu$: see 23. 2 n.

18–23. First Invasion of Attica. Attack on Oinoe

18. 1. $\grave{\epsilon}s\ O\grave{\iota}\nu\acute{o}\eta\nu\ \pi\rho\hat{\omega}\tau o\nu$: cf. Hdt. v. 74. 2, who calls Oinoe and Hysiai (captured by the Boeotians in 507 B.C.) $\delta\acute{\eta}\mu o\nu s\ \tau o\grave{\nu}s\ \grave{\epsilon}\sigma\chi\acute{a}\tau o\nu s\ \tau\hat{\eta}s\ \grave{A}\tau\tau\iota\kappa\hat{\eta}s$. (Hysiai was not an Attic deme in the technical sense established by the new organization of Kleisthenes; Oinoe was, in the coastal trittys of Hippothontis, with Eleusis; there was another Oinoe, in Aiantis, near Marathon.) Its site is uncertain; for we have no specific archaeological evidence, and the literary evidence is vague. All we know from Thucydides is that it was on the Boeotian (not apparently the Megarian) border (§ 2, below), and that Archidamos had not crossed into Attica before he reached it; he must, therefore, have marched direct from Megara northwards by one of the two passes across the Kerata range, and crossed the Megarian–Boeotian frontier somewhere west of the point where the three frontiers met.[1] Unfortunately we do not know where this was. The line of the ancient road from Eleusis to Thebes, even if not the same as that of the modern in its first part (see L. Chandler, J.H.S. xlvi, 1926, 13–14), certainly coincided with it in its passage over Kithairon by the Dryoskephalai pass, at the southern end of which are the well-known remains of the fortress now called Gyphtokastro. One must suppose that, since the accession of Plataia to the Athenian alliance, this pass was in Athenian hands; and direct communication between Megara and Boeotia must have been by one or other of

---

[1] N. G. L. Hammond has found and described one of these routes. He also would locate Oinoe near the village of Víllia. His article is to appear in B.S.A. xlix (1954).

the steep and narrow paths that cross Kithairon between Dryos-kephalai and the coast of the Corinthian Gulf (see my *Essays*, c. ii, pp. 21–22). Oinoe must therefore have been some miles west of Dryoskephalai, and cannot have been Gyphtokastro, as Leake thought (ii. 129–30), nor, *a fortiori*, the ruins called Myoúpolis, with which it has often been identified, which are some four miles farther to the east of Gyphtókastro.[1] Note that it is on the very borders, for Archidamos does not think that he has invaded Attica by attacking it (19. 1).

Thucydides does not tell us why, unless only to delay matters (§ 5), Archidamos chose this route by which to invade Attica, instead of the direct way from Megara to Eleusis by which many enemies had come in the past (i. 114. 2; Hdt. v. 74. 2, when the Boeotians joined in the invasion by seizing Oinoe and Hysiai). It is generally assumed, for example, by Grote, that he did so in order to get into touch with the Boeotians; but Thucydides does not say this, and a simple reading of his narrative (10. 1, 12. 5, 13. 1 above) suggests that the Boeotians were already with Archidamos before he left Megara. It was not that the Athenians were holding the narrow pass along the shore between the Megarian frontier and Eleusis. Nor does Thucydides explain what purpose was served by the frontier fort at Oinoe ($a\mathring{v}\tau\hat{\varphi}\ \phi\rho ov\rho i\varphi$ - - - $\dot{\epsilon}\chi\rho\hat{\omega}\nu\tau o$, § 2), why Archidamos wanted to capture it and why it was so obstinately defended (for its ultimate loss to Athens by treachery, see viii. 98); nor why Athens did not have a similar fort on the direct Eleusis road. It is wrong to speak of such a fort 'commanding' or 'controlling' a pass, as though it could prevent an enemy using the pass; for in normal Greek warfare an army was not dependent on a long train of supplies, whether of food or muni-tions. The contrast in this respect between the purpose of these frontier fortresses and, for example, those of the Low Countries in Louis XIV's wars, is complete. See vol. i, pp. 13–14, 16, and below, 23. 3 n.

1 Gyphtókastro used generally to be identified with Eleutherai (Strabo, ix. 2. 31, pp. 411–12; Paus. i. 38. 8); but there is no evidence that the latter was a strong fortress, and recent scholars have agreed that Gyphtókastro is Panakton. See v. 3. 5 n. ($\tau\hat{\eta}s\ Bοιωτίας$ is used below, § 2, in a geographical not a political sense, and will have included the Plataiis; but this does not greatly affect the issue, especially if Archidamos chose this way into Attica in order first to get into touch with his Boeotian allies, for which purpose he or they must have marched west of the Plataiis.) Miss Chandler, l.c., p. 12, says that according to Philochoros the Megarid stretched from the Isthmus to "the Python at Oinoe". If he had said this, the problem would have been simplified, for it would have provided evidence that the fort in Oinoe was exactly where the three frontiers met; unfortunately, Strabo, ix. 1. 6, p. 392, who is responsible for the quotation of Philochoros, F 107, only says $\mu\epsilon\chi\rho i\ \tau o\hat{v}\ \Pi v\theta iov$, nothing about Oinoe, and it is only modern conjecture which places the shrine in Oinoe, a conjecture presum-ably based on Philochoros, F 75 (from schol. Soph. *O.C.* 1047), which mentions the Python in the other Oinoe, near Marathon.

ἥπερ ἔμελλον ἐσβαλεῖν: a warning that the war was about to begin; see 19. 1 n. In the event they appear to invade by the normal route, by Eleusis (19. 2); but presumably they went from Oinoe to the main Thebes–Athens road which did go through Eleusis.

Professor W. Wallace has argued that the fort of Oinoe was to the north of the Kithairon range, within Boeotia therefore geographically, like Plataia and Hysiai, though controlled by Athens, and that the Peloponnesians went there by sea from Corinth to Siphai (iv. 76. 3) or a nearby harbour in Boeotia and thence by a comparatively easy route to the northern end of the Dryoskephalai pass (in *Studies in Honour of G. Norwood*, Phoenix, Toronto, 1952, 80–84). He tells me that since writing his article he has examined ancient remains of a wall and some pottery on a ridge just east of the old line of the road from Thebes up to the pass (the present road makes a wide westward bend into the village of Kriekoúki), and suggests that this may be Oinoe. He stresses the difficulty of the road direct from Megara to the passes over Kithairon, and argues that the sea-route was the easier and more natural one to take, and Thucydides' omission of express mention no more surprising than his failure (by the ordinary interpretation) to state the land-route taken; and that one reason at least why the Peloponnesians returned through Boeotia (23. 3) was to reach Siphai and the transports. I do not, however, find this convincing. The Peloponnesians took this land-route, presumably, after Tanagra (i. 108. 1–2); and its difficulties are not greater than those on the majority of routes, in some part or other of their courses, to which Greek armies were (and are) well accustomed, for example, to take some of the most familiar, those from Corinth, Argos, and Elis into Arkadia, or Brasidas' from Phokis to Herakleia, or indeed the much frequented road from Corinth via Megara to Eleusis by which so many Peloponnesian armies invaded Attica.[1]

We need not, I think, suppose that the whole of the Peloponnesian army marched to Oinoe; half or more may have stayed in the Megarid and joined the others later at Eleusis. As to the site of Oinoe, as far as the evidence goes, Wallace may be right to look for the fort on the Boeotian side of the range; but the *deme* was in all probability on the southern slopes, for Athens, though she controlled parts of Boeotia, did not incorporate them (neither Hysiai in this region nor Oropia to the east), and one would suppose that the fort was on the borders of the deme. It is also to be noted, as Wade-Gery

---

[1] It is often stated that Hadrian's was the first carriage-road along this route; if so, it was certainly very difficult in the fifth century. But I think a carriage-road of some kind was much older. One is reminded of the often repeated statement that the Allies, in 1916, were the first to build the road from Itéa to Brálo, whereas what they did was to destroy the old road with their heavy lorries and then rebuild. See also Hammond's paper (above p. 66 n.).

68

pointed out, that the Boeotians took Panakton (v. 3. 5) when Oinoe was still in Athenian hands (viii. 98), which would be surprising if Gyphtókastro was Panakton (see above, p. 67 n.).

μηχαναῖς τε καὶ ἄλλῳ τρόπῳ: presumably in the manner, though on a smaller scale, of the attack on Plataia, cc. 75-77.

2. ἐτετείχιστο: 'was a fortified place', before the war began, not 'had been fortified' with the implication 'shortly before the war' (Shilleto).

3. αἰτίαν τε: δέ, the reading of C⟨G⟩, seems here preferable to τε, for a new line of thought is begun.

ἐν τῇ ξυναγωγῇ τοῦ πολέμου: a phrase reminiscent of the Homeric συνάγειν Ἄρηα, etc., as edd. note. Classen thinks that it comprises all that was done to bring about the clash with Athens from the first conference at Sparta (i. 67-88) to the summoning of the allies to the Isthmos (ii. 10. 1), and that only thus can a proper meaning be given to τοῦ πολέμου; this is unnecessary, and καί before ἐν τῇ ξυναγωγῇ is against it; and οὐ παραινῶν προθύμως πολεμεῖν does not refer particularly to the advice he gave at the first conference.

4. ἐδόκουν οἱ Πελοποννήσιοι: the Athenians had in fact been already moving into the city for some time; cf. 13. 1 and 14. 1 (Classen).

τὴν ἐκείνου μέλλησιν: edd. have noted the rich variety of words (most of them verbal nouns of the kind Thucydides affects) used to describe Archidamos' conduct as the Peloponnesians saw it— ἐπιμονή, 'waiting about', σχολαιότης, 'leisurely progress on the march', ἐπίσχεσις, 'the hold-up at Oinoe', μέλλησις, 'his delays or hesitations'. ἐν τῇ καθέδρᾳ (§ 5), however, I think means only 'during this siege'. Finally, Archidamos still 'held his hand' (thinking incidentally that the Athenians 'would hesitate to see the destruction of their land', κατοκνήσειν, another word that might have been used of himself).

5. ἀνεῖχεν: [- - - με]ταφορικῶς [ἀπὸ τοῦ τὰ ὅπλα ἀν]έχειν, ἀφ' οὗ [καὶ ἀνοχαὶ αἱ ἐκε]χειρίαι—Π⁸. Though this may be a wrong explanation, the meaning seems right—'he held his hand', rather than 'he continued' (with the siege), as L. and S. Similarly, vii. 48. 3.

19. 1. οὕτω δὴ ὁρμήσαντες ἀπ' αὐτῆς, κ.τ.λ.: a formal statement, as formal, and nearly as full, as that introducing the Theban attack on Plataia (2. 1)—and accurately dated, like that, both by reference to the last important event noticed and by the 'natural' chronology of the seasons; succinctly expressed, ἐσέβαλον ἐς τὴν Ἀττικήν—the irrevocable step, 'war was unleashed'—and with the leader of the invading army given his most formal title, even though he has not only been formally introduced before as the army commander (10. 3), but has by his personality and his policy been the central figure of the last chapter. With this last compare the more easily understandable formality of i. 139. 5, Περικλῆς ὁ Ξανθίππου, κ.τ.λ. (and ii. 13. 1),

after the previous mention of him, i. 127. 1, 3 (not to speak of i. 111. 2, 114. 1–3, 116. 1–117. 2, for those passages are of a different context and perhaps written at a different time); and ii. 29. 7 after §§ 1 and 4 (Sitalkes and Perdikkas). Compare, too, the effect of such repetition in Herodotos, in a different kind of narrative, e.g. i. 43. 2, 45. 3.

Since in cc. 7–11, 13–17 Thucydides relates the last preparations for war (note esp. 13. 9), in c. 12 and, in effect, c. 18 last-minute efforts to avoid it, and emphasizes in cc. 2–6 that the attack on Plataia took place ἐν σπονδαῖς (2. 3, 5. 4, 5; 7. 1 compared with i. 87. 6, 88; cf. iii. 56. 2), it would appear that at one time at least he considered this moment of invasion to be the true beginning of the war and the Plataian episode, cc. 2–6, only the last and the most provocative of the αἰτίαι καὶ διαφοραί which preceded it; which is the natural conclusion also to draw from i. 125. 2, πρὶν ἐσβαλεῖν ἐς τὴν Ἀττικὴν καὶ τὸν πόλεμον ἄρασθαι φανερῶς. On the other hand, 10. 1 looks like the natural result of τὰ ἐν Πλαταιαῖς, the war having already begun, though it is also the natural result of the resolutions taken in the previous year. Note also 9. 1, ἐς τὸν πόλεμον καθίσταντο, as though the war had not begun 'at this point' (1. 1), namely the Theban attack on Plataia. Moreover, not only, as already said, does 12. 3 also look like the beginning, but in 12. 4 both Archidamos' conception of the situation seems inconsistent with c. 18 and the expression, οὕτω δὴ ἄρας τῷ στρατῷ προυχώρει ἐς τὴν γῆν αὐτῶν, anticipates 19. 1, οὕτω δὴ ὁρμήσαντες, κ.τ.λ. It may be that Thucydides altered his first draft of cc. 1–22 more than once, and that he only decided later to put the attack on Plataia among the events of the war proper as fitting better with his chronological scheme, 'year by year and by summers and winters'; by which scheme the attack was naturally taken as the first event of year 1, rather than as the last of the earlier series. Cf. 22. 1 n. (p. 77); also v. 20 nn., and Appendix.

ἡμέρᾳ ὀγδοηκοστῇ μάλιστα: μάλιστα shows that ὀγδοηκοστῇ is a round number; so what is, literally, '79 days after' may be interpreted as 77–80 days after, i.e. by our calendar, May 23–26 if the attack on Plataia was on March 6 or 7 (2. 1 n. on ἔτι δύο μῆνας). As will be seen later (23. 2 n.), the earliest possible date is to be preferred.

This date is properly described as θέρους καὶ τοῦ σίτου ἀκμάζοντος, 'the summer being well on its way [it being now summer—whether Thucydides here means to include the spring in τὸ θέρος or not] and the corn getting ripe'. The Attic harvest begins in the last days of May, and it is already summer time (τὸ καλοκαῖρι, as it is now called) in May. See n. on iii. 3. 1, τοῦ πολέμου ἄρτι καθισταμένου καὶ ἀκμάζοντος, which shows that θέρους ἀκμάζοντος does not mean 'when the

70

summer was at its height', i.e. in July, nor even midsummer (see Appendix).

2. Ἐλευσῖνα καὶ τὸ Θριάσιον πεδίον: this emphasizes how Archidamos went out of his way to attack Oinoe, whether simply to delay the war or for some military reason; for he now descends to the same district which he would have reached first had he entered Attica by the usual route. We are to suppose that the sacred precinct of Eleusis itself was spared.

τοὺς Ῥείτους καλουμένους: see Paus. i. 38. 1–3, Frazer ad loc. It was thought to be the old boundary between Eleusis and Athens, and here was fought the battle between Eumolpos and Erechtheus (15. 1, above).

ἐν δεξιᾷ ἔχοντες τὸ Αἰγάλεων ὄρος: the Reitoi are in the south-east corner of the Thriasian plain, at the foot of Mt. Aigaleos, and from there the direct road to Athens turns east and crosses the hills by the comparatively low pass of Daphné. It was not, however, the purpose of the Peloponnesians to attack the city, but to ravage the country; and they consequently turn back and march northwards, 'with Aigaleos on their right', and round the northern end of the hills eastwards to Acharnai. See vol. i, p. 13 n. (For the extent of the hills covered by the name Aigaleos, see Dow's article mentioned below.)

διὰ Κρωπιᾶς: the site of Kropia is not known; but it should be placed in the open country to the north of Aigaleos, Thucydides naming it in order to make clear the route followed by Archidamos. So already Leake, i. 25; Bursian, i. 335.[1]

No mention is made by Thucydides (or by any other ancient writer) of the remarkable wall which runs from south to north across this open country to the foothills of Mt. Parnes, below Phyle. This wall has now (at last) been adequately described, by Sterling Dow, *Hesp.* xi, 1942, 193–211. It is 4,200 metres long, its southern part best preserved, the centre mostly destroyed; there were in addition watchtowers on higher hills to north and south. Its date and purpose are alike uncertain, except that, to judge from its construction, it may well be earlier than 480, and was somewhat hastily erected, and that it faced west, that is, it was designed to meet an enemy

[1] It is natural to suppose that Kropia is the district of the small deme Kropidai. But there are difficulties. Kropidai was in Leontis phyle, and if identified with Kropia must have been of the inland trittys; for the coastal trittys included Sounion and Phrearrioi. The location of the inland trittys is indeed quite uncertain (my *Population of Athens*, p. 59), but it is difficult to place it so that Kropia form part of it, unless it can be squeezed in between the northern boundary of the city-trittyes to the south, Acharnai (Oineis, inland trittys) on the north and NE., and Phyle, Thria, and Kothokidai (all Oineis, coastal trittyes) to the north and west. See map at end of *Population of Athens*. Wade-Gery, *Mélanges Glotz*, 884, n. 3, accepts this position, putting the Leontid trittyes SW., NW., and NE. of Acharnai, and identifying Kropia and Kropidai.

coming from the Thriasian plain. R. L. Scranton, *Greek Walls*, 39–42, 154–5, puts it in the eighth century, at a time, he argues, when Eleusis was independent of Athens, and this was the Athenian frontier wall; but, as Dow says, what evidence is there that Eleusis was independent so late as this (see 15. 1 n.)? Dow himself, for historical reasons, arguing that it was built in a hurry, not for a permanent garrison (permanent in war-time, that is, like Oinoe and other frontier fortresses), but as a field-work to meet a particular danger, makes the in itself attractive suggestion that it belongs to 506 B.C., built to meet the Peloponnesian invasion and while the enemy were debating policy at the Isthmos (Hdt. v. 75), much as, by the different strategy of seventy-five years later, the Athenians left their villages and towns for the city while the enemy were collecting their forces for the invasion. The same sort of tactical purpose is shown by the defensive wall built across the pass of Thermopylai in 480 (Marinátos, *A.J.A.* xliii, 1939, 698–700)—another pass wide enough and level enough for hoplite fighting (vol. i, p. 13)—and the design of the two walls is not dissimilar. Dow's negative arguments against other dates, however, are not strong: not before Peisistratos, for Athens was then too weak [but therefore needed a wall to defend herself?]; not Peisistratos, for his policy was peaceful [but 'a strong defence will help to keep the peace'?], not 490–480 [but why not?]; not between 479 and 457 (after which time the construction of the Long Walls changed the strategy completely), because Sparta and Athens were at peace [but Themistokles and the circuit-wall of Athens?]. So its date remains quite uncertain; all we should say is that it was probably remote enough, or else late enough, for the silence of the historians about it to be understandable.

Dow also suggests that the destruction of the centre part of this wall may have been due to the Peloponnesians on this invasion. But if so, it must have been thought still to serve some purpose, and we should expect Thucydides or Herodotos to have mentioned it.

ἐς Ἀχαρνάς, χωρίον μέγιστον, κ.τ.λ.: Acharnai had 22 bouleutai (in the fourth century); Melite may have had 17 or 18; but no other deme had for certain more than 12 in the fifth and fourth centuries. Quite important demes had 5 or 6; and there were numerous small ones with but 1 or 2 (*Population of Athens*, 56–65). The great difference in size of the demes, and the extreme subdivision into many very small demes of much of the city area, are among the surprising elements in Kleisthenes' artificial reorganization and redistribution of the citizen body.

(All our good MSS., except C, but including G¹, have χῶρον here, not χωρίον. χῶρος is rare in Attic prose, but is used four or five times by Thucydides (see 20. 4, 25. 2, vii. 78. 4), and should perhaps be read here, not, as Classen has it, "weil von dem Demos, dem Bezirk, die Rede ist, nicht von der Ortschaft"; but because the use of diminutives generally and this one in particular was becoming so common in Thucydides' day and increased so greatly in later times, that it is difficult to believe that any copyist would have written χῶρος here, had not Thucydides used it, in an archaic sense. He uses χωρίον of course as well, often enough. Cf. Lykourgos, c. Leocr. 96, and Shilleto's n. here.)

ἐμμείναντες: an interesting use of the aorist participle with an imperfect verb, of which we have another example in iv. 109. 5. Not 'when they had settled there', as most edd. (see Classen's note), a meaning which ἐμμένειν does not have in Thucydides (cf. 23. 3, iii. 1. 3, viii. 31. 4), but the timeless aorist, 'by a long stay', similar to περιδεῖν τμηθεῖσαν or τμηθῆναι (18. 5, 20. 2), 'look on at the destruction of their land', and διαφθαρέντα, 20. 4. Cf. Forster Smith's rendering, "where they remained for a long time ravaging the country".

20. 1. ὡς ἐς μάχην ταξάμενον: bracketed by Stahl, on the ground that it is inconsistent with what we have just been told (στρατόπεδόν τε ἐποιήσαντο) and with Archidamos' future actions; and Classen suggested transposing the clause after οὐ καταβῆναι. The latter is clearly wrong, for it would imply that Archidamos did not want a battle; and there is no real inconsistency, for since the Peloponnesian aim was to provoke a battle, they must get ready for it. The phrase is in accord not only with § 2, but with the orders given by Archidamos in 11. 4, 6.

ἐς τὸ πεδίον: the plain of Athens, to the north and west of the city, where the lands of the nobility were particularly to be found (see Hdt. i. 59. 4; Arist. Ἀθπ. 13. 4; my *Population of Athens*, 37–39). Acharnai was to the north of the plain among the foothills of Mt. Parnes, though some of its extensive territory may have included part of the plain. See Wade-Gery (above, p. 71 n.), 885–6; who reads Π[εδ]ιέων as the name of the trittys on *I.G.* i.² 899, and this must be Acharnai (a reading strengthened by *Hesp.* ix, 1940, 55, no. 3).

ἐκείνῃ τῇ ἐσβολῇ: contrast 55. 1 below, and cf. iii. 1. 2.

2. ἀκμάζοντάς τε νεότητι πολλῇ καὶ παρεσκευασμένους - - - ὡς οὔπω πρότερον: cf. i. 1. 1, 18. 3–19; and more particularly, ii. 8. 1 and 11. 6. See 22. 1 n.

περιδεῖν τμηθῆναι: an awkward repetition from 18. 5. In fact I feel that c. 18 sits ill with 19 and 20, though the beginning of 19 fits well enough. See 22. 1 n.

4. τρισχίλιοι γὰρ ὁπλῖται ἐγένοντο: this is another figure which cannot stand. The natural interpretation of ὁπλῖται in this context is hoplites in the active army, ἐν ταῖς τάξεσιν. Of these Athens had 13,000 in all (13. 6). If we take it more loosely to include hoplites in

73

the reserve, and cavalry as well, that is all between 18 and 60, there were, according to my calculations from Thucydides' own figures, some 24,000 in all (c. 18,000 between 20 and 49, and c. 6,000 oldest and youngest: see 13. 6 n.). Since the ten phylai were approximately equal in population, and the hoplite army was based on the phylai, with ten approximately equal regiments, the phyle Oineis will have had a total paper strength of 2,400 (hoplites and cavalry up to the age of 60). The Acharnians had 22 bouleutai of the 50 from Oineis (19. 2 n.) and on this ratio should have had fewer than 1,100 hoplites and cavalry; in the epheboi list of c. 330 B.C. from the agora (Pritchett, *Hesp.* suppl. viii, 1949, 273–8) they had 22 or 24 out of a total of 53 to 55 for the phyle, i.e. about the same proportion of epheboi as of bouleutai; perhaps, if they were a richer deme than most in the phyle and had relatively more hoplites and fewer thetes, they may have had 1,200 (for the 22 bouleutai represent the whole citizen population of the deme). This is the maximum; and it is only reached by assuming that ὁπλῖται does not mean here hoplites in the active army (Acharnai could hardly have more than 850 ἐν ταῖς τάξεσιν). The MS. error is inexplicable; it is perhaps worth noting that, by the old system, 3,000 was written XXX, 1,200 XHH, and the H's may have been corrupted into X's.

Whatever their number, Pindar too, like Aristophanes, could write admiringly of their quality: Ἀχαρναὶ δὲ παλαίφατοι εὐάνορες (*Nem.* ii. 16).

ἐκείνῃ τῇ ἐσβολῇ: see § 1 n.

οὐχ ὁμοίως προθύμους: an expectation singularly falsified; for six years later the Acharnians were as warlike and as hostile to any compromise with the Spartans as ever, and this too after the ravages of the plague.

Indeed, there was to be very little στάσις at Athens before 411; and it was short-lived then and not very helpful to the enemy (viii. 71. 2). See 65. 10–11 n.

21. 1. καί τινα ἐλπίδα εἶχον: 'did in fact have some hope.'

Πλειστοάνακτα, κ.τ.λ.: see i. 114. 2; but this passage is written without reference to that. Note particularly δι᾽ ὃ δὴ καὶ ἡ φυγὴ αὐτῷ ἐγένετο, a well-known event, but not mentioned in book i. See *A.T.L.* iii. 301–3 for a summary of the situation: the real bribe to Pleistoanax was the offer to surrender, or to discuss the surrender of, Megara, Troizen, and Achaia.

τέσσαρσι καὶ δέκα ἔτεσιν: so 2. 1 (for the treaty followed not long after the Peloponnesian retreat); but again, and more noticeably, this is written without reference to the earlier passage. Cf. 22. 1 n.

2. ὃ οὔπω ἑοράκεσαν οἵ γε νεώτεροι: they were more fortunate than the citizens of most Greek states. Athens was almost beginning to think herself powerful enough to be, like Sparta, immune from invasion. Cf. 11. 8, ἐπιόντες τὴν τῶν πέλας δῃοῦν μᾶλλον ἢ τὴν αὐτῶν ὁρᾶν. A little earlier in this same year, a chorus of Euripides had sung of the ἱερᾶς χώρας ἀπορθήτου τε (Medea 825).

11. 7 generalizes that feature in human conduct of which we have here a concrete example (note especially ἐν τῷ ἐμφανεῖ, ἀνηρέθιστο and ἐν ὀργῇ εἶχον). See 22. 1 n. on ὀργῇ τι μᾶλλον.

καὶ μάλιστα τῇ νεότητι: in Aristophanes (Acharnians, Wasps, Lysistrate) it is the older generation rather, whom he so sympathetically mocks, who are the fiery warriors.

3. κατὰ ξυστάσεις: at informal meetings.

οἱ δέ τινες: the minority ('others, some only').

χρησμολόγοι τε, κ.τ.λ.: as in 480 B.C.

οὐκ ἐλαχίστην μοῖραν: an unnecessary repetition (one would have thought) from 20. 4, μέγα μέρος ὄντες.

ἐκάκιζον: here specifically 'attacked him for cowardice', as Shilleto notes; cf. i. 105. 6. Plutarch, Per. 33. 7, quotes lines from Hermippos' contemporary comedy (fr. 46) to illustrate this (the whole chapter is interesting, following Thucydides closely for the facts, and adding details)—βραχέα φροντίζων (ὁ Περικλῆς) τῶν καταβοώντων καὶ δυσχεραινόντων. καίτοι πολλοὶ μὲν αὐτοῦ τῶν φίλων δεόμενοι προσέκειντο, πολλοὶ δὲ τῶν ἐχθρῶν ἀπειλοῦντες καὶ κατηγοροῦντες, πολλοὶ δ' ᾖδον ᾄσματα καὶ σκώμματα πρὸς αἰσχύνην ἐφυβρίζοντες αὐτοῦ τὴν στρατηγίαν ὡς ἄνανδρον καὶ προϊεμένην τὰ πράγματα τοῖς πολεμίοις. ἐπεφύετο δὲ καὶ Κλέων ἤδη διὰ τῆς πρὸς ἐκεῖνον ὀργῆς τῶν πολιτῶν πορευόμενος εἰς δημαγωγίαν, ὡς τὰ ἀνάπαιστα ταῦτα δηλοῖ ποιήσαντος Ἑρμίππου·

> βασιλεῦ σατύρων, τί ποτ' οὐκ ἐθέλεις
> δόρυ βαστάζειν, ἀλλὰ λόγους μὲν
> περὶ τοῦ πολέμου δεινοὺς παρέχει,
> ψυχὴν δὲ Τέλητος ὑπέστης;
> κἀγχειριδίου δ' ἀκόνῃ σκληρᾷ
> παραθηγομένης βρύχεις κοπίδος,
> δηχθεὶς αἴθωνι Κλέωνι.

Fr. 47, not continuous with this, is yet in the same vein—'the war is on'. The comedy will not have been produced before the spring of 430; but perhaps later, for the attacks on Perikles continued. Kleon, true to the demagogue's principle enunciated by Disraeli, began his career by attacking those in power.

It is worth referring to two other fragments of lost comedies though their significance is not certain: (1) Kratinos, fr. 460 (doubtfully his: see Kock), may mean that the poet was taxiarch of his phyle, Oineis (which included Acharnai), and was reproached for cowardice because he obeyed the orders of the strategoi and stayed within the walls; and he may well have attacked Perikles as responsible for this. (2) The newly discovered fragment which may be from Eupolis' Προσπάλτιοι has some reference to the sending of troops by or in aid of the deme (see Page, *Greek Lit. Pap.*, Loeb, i, p. 216); but to me an 'army of Prospaltioi' (a deme not far from Athens) seems to be the sort of absurdity that we find in Polemon's army in Menander's *Perikeiromene.*

Note what Thucydides omits: Kleon's part in these attacks (cf. 65. 4 n.); Perikles' answer, δένδρα μὲν τμηθέντα καὶ κοπέντα φύεται ταχέως, ἀνδρῶν δὲ διαφθαρέντων αὖθις τυχεῖν οὐ ῥᾴδιόν ἐστι (with which, however, cf. 62. 3, below); and, of course, all reference to comedy as illustrating the moods and opinions in Athens at this time.

Another question is suggested by this account of Athenian tempers at the invasion of 431: why was the position of Athens in 446, when Pleistoanax invaded (i. 114), so desperate, that apparently only a bribe, or genuine concessions, could save her (*A.T.L.* iii. 301–3)? Why was not the same strategy, of retirement behind the walls, adopted? The Long Walls had been completed some years before, and this was what they were for. One can only suppose that the Athenians at that time were not prepared, τῇ γνώμῃ, for the sacrifice of their homes as they were, however reluctantly, in 431; that Perikles had had a long and hard task to persuade them (13. 2). (This difference between the two occasions, incidentally, is one of the strongest arguments against the view that the Old Oligarch's pamphlet was written before 431: see 2. 16; *Ath. Stud.* 224–8.)

22. 1. ὁρῶν μὲν αὐτοὺς πρὸς τὸ παρὸν χαλεπαίνοντας: as later, 59. 3; but on that occasion Perikles did summon the assembly.

ἐκκλησίαν - - - οὐδὲ ξύλλογον οὐδένα: ξύλλογος here clearly means 'informal meeting of citizens' (Latin *contio*), as at iii. 27. 3; elsewhere, as 59. 3, it means a formal ekklesia, just as in i. 67. 3 it means a meeting of the apella at Sparta. Arnold quotes Plat. *Gorg.* 456 B, λόγῳ διαγωνίζεσθαι ἐν ἐκκλησίᾳ ἢ ἄλλῳ τινὶ συλλόγῳ; but Plato is more specifically thinking of the law-courts than of informal meetings.

There is no evidence that the strategoi had the power (as Classen supposes, from this passage) to disallow the regular ekklesiai; what Perikles refused to do was to summon a special meeting, which in a crisis the strategoi could do and which they did next year (59. 3), and to address the people in any way. Note that in both passages Perikles speaks for the whole body of strategoi. Kahrstedt, *Untersuch. z. Magistratur in Athen*, 1936, p. 268, however, maintains that Perikles, though with no special legal powers, yet by his influence prevailed with the boule (and his fellow strategoi) not to call the normal ekklesia; he is followed in this by Hignett, *History of the Ath. Const.*, Oxford, 1951, pp. 246–7.

ὀργῇ τι μᾶλλον ἢ γνώμῃ: again recalling Archidamos' speech, II. 4,

76

7-8; cf. 20. 2, 21. 2 nn. I have the impression that these chapters (20-22), containing Archidamos' plan and its near success, were not written at the same time as Archidamos' speech, that Thucydides later decided to put these ideas into speech form. C. 18. 3-5, which also gives Archidamos' plan in some detail, would also belong to the earlier draft.[1] That is to say, the repetitions found here seem to me different in kind from the general concordance of speech and narrative to be found in Thucydides, e.g. i. 33. 2, 42. 2, and 44. 2, or iv. 10. 3, 4 and 11. 3, 12. 2 (de Romilly, pp. 25, 30, 151). I have already suggested that 19. 1 belongs to a different plan from 1. 1, 2. 1, and 12; the opening chapters of book ii seem to show signs of a remodelling which was never completed. It does not necessarily follow that the two drafts, if there were two, or three, were separated from each other by a long period of time; and the remodelling does not affect Thucydides' fundamental conception of his *History*. On the other hand, if I am right about the relation of cc. 21-22 to the speech in c. 11, it may affect the problem of the origin of the speeches.

2. ἐν Φρυγίοις: Π^8 says that this was a τόπος δήμου Ἀθμονέων, which may well be correct (Athmoneis was a few miles to the north-east of Athens). Steph. Byz. s.v. says carelessly it was between Attica and Boeotia (perhaps by mistake for Oinoe).

τέλει ἑνί: cf. iv. 96. 5, of the Boeotian cavalry at Delion. We do not know its size; we only know that the Attic cavalry was organized by phylai, and so had ten squadrons, each led by a φύλαρχος, on the model of the infantry (Ἀθπ. 30. 2, 31. 3, 61. 5). A τέλος may have been one of these squadrons.

καὶ ἀπέθανον, κ.τ.λ.: the monument to the Thessalians who fell was still to be seen in Pausanias' day, i. 29. 6. It is generally supposed that the monument to Athenian cavalry mentioned by Pausanias a few lines later was also to the dead of this battle (ἱππεῦσιν ἀποθανοῦσιν ἡνίκα συνεπελάβοντο οἱ Θεσσαλοὶ τοῦ κινδύνου). This may be right; but we have no evidence that the cavalry of Athens had separate monuments in the Kerameikos—we should expect that their dead would be named with the others on a single monument for all the casualties of the year—and the context of Pausanias suggests that he may mean a battle against Kleomenes (cf. Hdt. v. 63-64); for, though there was no organized cavalry at Athens at that time, some Athenian nobles may have fought, or marched, on horseback with the Thessalians, and may have been so represented on a tomb.

---

[1] I cannot agree with Steup that 18. 3-5 is a passage added later, because 19. 1 would follow more easily from 18. 2 ("wo ebenfalls οἱ Πελοποννήσιοι Subjekt ist") than from the end of 18. 5. The first sentence of 19. 1 takes its precise form just because it is a resumption from a short digression; we must have at least the last sentence of c. 18.

77

For *Anth. Pal.* vii. 254 (an epitaph ascribed to Simonides), which has been thought to have been written for the cavalry who fell here, or for all the casualties of this year, and for the inscription thought to contain the casualty list, see below, 34. 1 n.

ἀσπόνδους: they did not therefore admit their defeat, though the Peloponnesians, by setting up a trophy, asserted their victory.

3. κατὰ τὸ παλαιὸν ξυμμαχικόν: see i. 102. 4, 107. 7. But the last appearance of the Thessalians as allies, at Tanagra, had not proved likely to lead to a renewal of the alliance, except perhaps by a change in the party in power in the Thessalian states (cf. ἀπὸ τῆς στάσεως ἑκάτερος below). They are not listed among the allies of Athens in 9. 4; and perhaps their appearance on this occasion was as unexpected as it proved to be, for this war, unique. Hermippos, fr. 41, may be a reference to it. But how did they reach Athens? not surely by land, through Thermopylai, Phokis, and Boeotia (cf. iii. 92. 6); yet for cavalry to come by sea required careful preparation.

For later indications, and indications only, of the alliance, see iii. 92–93, iv. 78, 132, v. 13, and viii. 3.

Λαρισαῖοι, κ.τ.λ.: a characteristic piece of detail, of little significance in itself, and not made significant in any degree by explanation. It is just a note made by Thucydides at the time. The explanation required is not only, what proportion were these of all Thessalian cities? and how do they fit in with those who betrayed Athens at Tanagra? but, why are separate cities, apparently, acting at all? It was with τὸ κοινόν of all Thessaly that the old alliance had been made; in a time of war, normally, it was the federal government which took action and elected a single ταγός as commander-in-chief; but here we have contingents from different cities, and not from all. There was a separatist tendency in Thessaly as elsewhere in Greece; and differences of policy, particularly in relations with foreign states (Macedon always, Athens at this time and later, in the days of Jason of Pherai), sharpened it. The last we have heard of Thessaly was the expulsion of the βασιλεύς, i.e. the ταγός, Orestes of Pharsalos, by the anti-Athenian party, c. 455 (i. 111); the next that we shall hear is the aid given to Brasidas by the same faction, then dominant, and a weak resistance to it by the constitutionalists who would appeal to τὸ κοινόν (iv. 78). See Busolt-Swoboda, ii. 1480–2.

[Παράσιοι]: I doubt whether the critical note in Stuart Jones is correct in saying that Π^8 did not have this (Π^9 has it).

ἀπὸ τῆς στάσεως ἑκάτερος: again we expect an explanatory note. (Some edd. suppose στάσις to mean some constitutional division of the state. There is no evidence of this, and an explanatory note would be more than ever necessary.)

ἐκ δὲ Φαρσάλου Μένων: Daochos I of Pharsalos was constitutional 'ruler of all Thessaly' for twenty-seven years, about this time, and it has been suggested by Dittenberger, $S.I.G.^3$ 274, that these twenty-seven years were those of the Peloponnesian war. See below, iv. 78. 1, 3 nn. This does not seem to be consistent with the present passage, not so much because it is Menon who leads the forces of Pharsalos, as because the cities are acting separately (see above). Daochos may have been *un roi fainéant*; or he may have been elected after this time. In any case, he was not a very effective commander-in-chief.

23. 1. Βριλησσοῦ: more generally known as Pentelikos. The Peloponnesians followed the upper valley of the Kephissos, and went thence (as road and railway go to-day) by Dekeleia (which, according to the pretty story in Herodotos, ix. 73, they did not ravage) into Oropia (§ 3).

2. ὄντων δὲ αὐτῶν ἐν τῇ γῇ: the date lacks precision, more particularly as we are not told how long the invasion lasted (Thucydides is giving only the military situation—the presence of the invaders did not hinder the Athenian naval expedition); but since the longest invasion lasted 40 days (ii. 57. 2), and the first seems to have been normal (ὅσου εἶχον τὰ ἐπιτήδεια, § 3), we may suppose a length of 30 to 35 days. Thucydides clearly means that the ships sailed after the Peloponnesians had left Acharnai, that is after they had been in Attica for some time, 10 days at least, more probably 20. (Classen suggests that ἔτι has fallen out before ἐν τῇ γῇ; which is possible.) This would bring us to June 2–15 as the date when the expedition sailed, if the invasion began May 23–26 (19. 1 n.).

From $I.G.$ i.² 296. 33 ff. (cf. vol. i, p. 423; Meritt, $A.F.D.$ 71–81; $C.R.$ lv, 1941, 59–67) we know that money was paid to the three strategoi mentioned here by Thucydides, in at least four instalments, during the period covering the last eight days of the ninth prytany and the first days of the tenth, of the year 432–431 B.C., i.e. from May 20 to May 31, 431 ($A.F.D.$ 176); the first of these payments was made to the generals direct, the subsequent ones to them through the Hellenotamiai. It has generally been supposed that this difference of formula meant that payments through the Hellenotamiai were made after an expedition had sailed (this would be a possible explanation, for example, in the case of the payments for the fleets which sailed against Macedonia and Poteidaia recorded on the earlier part of this same inscription); but this will not suit here, if ὀγδοηκοστῇ ἡμέρᾳ in 19. 1 is to be kept.[1] For the attack on Plataia cannot be put earlier than shortly before the new moon of March 8; and we cannot alter ὀγδοηκοστῇ by much, to ἑξηκοστῇ for example, because the consequent date May 3–6 for the invasion, which would suit

---

[1] See Hubbell, $C.P.$ xxiv, 1929, 217–30 (esp. 223). Meritt's argument against this view, however, from the payment to Phormion (if it was to Phormion) in the fourth prytany ($Ath. Cal.$ 110) is weak.

May 20 for the departure of Karkinos' fleet, is too early to be described as θέρους καὶ τοῦ σίτου ἀκμάζοντος. We do better, therefore, to keep the MSS. reading ὀγδοηκοστῇ in 19. 1, and to conclude that Karkinos sailed not earlier than June 2 and perhaps not before June 15, and to look for some other explanation of the payments through the Hellenotamiai. This may anyhow be necessary; for if this fleet set sail immediately after the first recorded payment, it is difficult to understand both why further payments were necessary so soon, and when the three later instalments were sent to the fleet. More probably these frequent instalments were paid before the departure of the fleet. Or else the calendar equations in $A.F.D.$ are wrong.

τὰς ἑκατὸν ναῦς: 17. 4.

χιλίους ὁπλίτας: generally supposed to be the epibatai who were a normal part of the trireme's crew, and generally, at this time, 10 to a trireme; they fought in naval battles, to protect the ship and the rowers. But if they are meant here, there was no need to mention them; and epibatai were normally thetes (13. 8 n., p. 42). Clearly this is a special body, consisting of 1,000 hoplites and 400 bowmen, whose function will be fighting on land. Cf. iii. 91. 3.

Καρκίνος ὁ Ξενοτίμου: $K.$ Θορίκιος on the inscription, in accordance with official custom. He was the tragic poet often mocked by Aristophanes and the other comedy-writers. See $P.A.$ and $R.E.$, s.v.

Πρωτέας: Αἰξωνεύς on the inscription (and on i.² 295). He had been strategos in 433–432 B.C. and was one of the commanders of the first squadron to Kerkyra, i. 45. 2. Nothing more is known of him.

Σωκράτης: Ἁλαιεύς on the inscription. Nothing more is known of him either.

It is clear that these three strategoi must already have been elected to serve for the following year, 431–430, as well; for they set sail only a few days before the end of their present year of office, if that, as is generally believed, coincided with the conciliar·year.

3. ὅσου εἶχον τὰ ἐπιτήδεια: they were not dependent on a regular supply from the Peloponnese, which would have entailed a long line of communications to defend; see vol. i, pp. 13, 16 and n. on Οἰνόη, 18. 1, above. They probably got much from Boeotia.

οὐχ ᾗπερ ἐσέβαλον: i.e. they marched westwards through Boeotia (probably to secure further supplies); but presumably then crossed Kithairon, either by the pass west of Plataia, and thence descended to Megara by the road by which they had left it when they marched against Oinoe, or by the main Thebes–Athens road till they were within a short distance of Eleusis (18. 1 n.). (But see above p. 66, n.)

τὴν γῆν τὴν Γραϊκὴν καλουμένην: like Eleutherai and Salamis, the land of the Oropioi, conquered by Athens probably in 506 ($C.A.H.$ iv. 162–3), had never been incorporated in Attica; the inhabitants indeed remained subject to Athens (here and iv. 99) in a sense in which Eleutherai and Salamis, it seems, were not—a recognition by Athens that the inhabitants were Boeotian, or at least not Athenian. Before its conquest by the Boiotoi, it had belonged to Eretria (actively interested again in 412–411 : viii. 60), before that perhaps to the Graioi (whoever they were); for the name Graia is as old as the *Catalogue of Ships* (*Il.* ii. 498). See Wilamowitz, *Hermes*, xxi, 1886, 91 ff.

It is curious that both here and at iii. 91. 3 the word $\Gamma\rho\alpha\ddot{\iota}\kappa\dot{\eta}$ has been corrupted in our MSS., including here the papyrus fragment of the first century A.D., to $\Pi\epsilon\iota\rho\alpha\ddot{\iota}\kappa\dot{\eta}$ (for $\pi\epsilon\rho\alpha\dot{\iota}\alpha$?) and $\pi\dot{\epsilon}\rho\alpha\nu\ \gamma\hat{\eta}$, which suggest an Eretrian outlook.

Since Oropos, which had in it a garrison, was won by treachery by the Boeotians in the winter of 412–411, it is a natural assumption that this sentence was written before 411 (Wilamowitz, *Herm.* xii, 1877, 343 n.). It is of the same kind as that in i. 56. 2, where see note, and contrasts with $Ai\gamma\iota\nu\hat{\eta}\tau\alpha\iota$, $o\dot{\iota}\ \tau\dot{o}\tau\epsilon\ Ai\gamma\iota\nu\alpha\nu\ \epsilon\dot{\iota}\chi o\nu$, vii. 57. 2.

24–33. *Athenian Counter-measures*

24. 1. $\phi\upsilon\lambda\alpha\kappa\dot{\alpha}\varsigma\ \kappa\alpha\tau\epsilon\sigma\tau\dot{\eta}\sigma\alpha\nu\tau o$: not further defined; but since they were established after (which does not here mean, in consequence of) the departure of the Peloponnesians, they must be garrisons outside mainland Attica, e.g. in Salamis (cf. 93. 4), Naupaktos (69, unless all the garrison duties there were undertaken by the Messenians), and doubtless elsewhere in the empire; for Oinoe was already garrisoned, and we cannot doubt that the same was true of Panakton, Phyle, Oropos, and such other fortresses as the Athenians then had on their land frontier. Later special care was taken to guard Peiraeus (93. 4); but this was in consequence of the alarm caused by the threatened raid by sea, and the previous carelessness had been due to over-confidence; and some new garrisons were sent, as to Atalante (32). On $\delta\iota\dot{\alpha}\ \pi\alpha\nu\tau\dot{o}\varsigma\ \tau o\hat{\upsilon}\ \pi o\lambda\dot{\epsilon}\mu o\upsilon$, Classen says, "nach c. 13. 7 muss hierzu hinzugedacht werden: 'während der Zeiten, wo kein Feind im Lande sein werde' ", as though Thucydides was only thinking of Attica and fortresses were garrisoned only when there was no enemy to guard against; but $\dot{\epsilon}\phi\dot{\upsilon}\lambda\alpha\sigma\sigma o\nu$ in 13. 7 refers to the special precautions needed on the Athens–Peiraeus circuit-walls; the garrisons here referred to are included in $o\dot{\iota}\ \dot{\epsilon}\nu\ \tau o\hat{\iota}\varsigma\ \phi\rho o\upsilon\rho\dot{\iota}o\iota\varsigma$ of 13. 6.

It is also clear that garrisons were not sent to the cities of the empire in peace-time, except to a few most exposed to attack; and that their primary purpose was military, to ward off the external enemy, not to secure obedience (cf. iv. 88. 1 n.). See *A.T.L.* iii. 147, where it is suggested, too, that the Hellespontophylakes were established at this time (cf. *I.G.* i.² 57, 36–37 = *A.T.L.* ii, D 4 = Tod, 61 : 426–425 B.C.).

διὰ παντὸς τοῦ πολέμου: possibly written soon after 421, and referring to the ten years' war only.

χίλια τάλαντα: see 13. 3 n.

νηίτη στρατῷ: a formal expression (recurring in a speech, iv. 85. 7), with a poetical colour, like ναύφαρκτος στρατιά in the Athenian decree of this year, *I.G.* i.² 296. 30 (above, 23. 2 n.). The wording here is certainly very close to that of the decree as passed in the assembly.

θάνατον ζημίαν ἐπέθεντο: the Athenians took strong precautions against their own rashness and thoughtlessness. The middle instead of the more common active, presumably because they were imposing this limitation on themselves; yet it is difficult to see any distinction between the meaning here and in viii. 67. 2, where also there is a limitation placed on a normal privilege of all citizens.

The reserve was kept intact till the revolt of Chios in 413 B.C., when it was necessary for the clause containing the penalty to be first repealed because there had not yet been any attack on Athens by sea.

2. τὰς βελτίστας: to be taken closely with the preceding words— not a hundred new triremes every year, but every year the best hundred. It was a strange provision for so active a people, and marks a strongly defensive policy—unless it is a sign of confidence that their next best vessels would be good enough (as they proved) against the enemy.

When this provision (μετὰ τῶν χρημάτων) was revoked we do not know, certainly long before 413. Presumably the 100 ships, or some of them, set sail in the winter of 429–428 (94. 2) and in the following summer (iii. 16. 1).

τριηράρχους: they would be exempt from other military service during their year of office, to compensate for the financial burdens which this policy laid on them.

25. 1. Κερκυραῖοι: not compelled to help the Athenians in this enterprise by the terms of the defensive alliance (i. 44. 1), but presumably persuaded by the embassy mentioned in 7. 3 (see n. there). This was the only time they were involved in the war before 427: see 85. 5 n.

πεντήκοντα ναυσί: not half the number they were able to man in 435 and 433, when many of their ships, old-fashioned most of them, were lost; but nearly the total they manned in 427, and certainly as many as they were likely to send to help the Athenians in a raid. See vol. i, pp. 191–4.

ἄλλοι τινὲς τῶν ἐκεῖ ξυμμάχων: Akarnanians, Zakynthians, and particularly the Messenians of Naupaktos, who are mentioned below (§ 4); see 9. 4.

ἄλλα τε ἐκάκουν: Diodoros, xii. 43. 1 (see below, § 5 n.), says τὴν καλουμένην Ἀκτὴν ἐδῄου καὶ τὰς ἐπαύλεις ἐνεπύριζε, and there *may* have been some evidence for this. Akte will be those parts of the Argolic peninsula, as Epidauros and Hermione, which were hostile to Athens.

ἐς Μεθώνην τῆς Λακωνικῆς: a fortified town on the south-west coast of the westernmost of the three peninsulas in the southern Peloponnese. Walls of the fourth century or later (built after the recovery of Messenian independence) still stand in places to a great height, partly restored and decorated by the Venetians in the seventeenth century.

On τῆς Λακωνικῆς, see i. 10. 2 n.

ἀνθρώπων οὐκ ἐνόντων: λείπει πολλῶν, schol. Either this is true (cf. the schol. on τὰ ἐρῆμα, 17. 1 : τὰ ὀλιγάνθρωπα) or ἄνθρωποι here means 'garrison'. Herwerden would insert πολλῶν, Classen ἀξιομάχων; but cf. iii. 106. 1, οὔσης ἐρήμου, which means only, 'after the *army* had left'. Perhaps, however, τοῖς ἐν τῷ χωρίῳ below suggests that there is something wrong with the text; καὶ ἀ. οὐκ ἐν. may be an adscript explanatory of ἀσθενεῖ, and should be deleted (as Mervyn Jones suggested to me), though I am not convinced of this.

2. φρουρὰν ἔχων: a special Spartan use of the word for a small *mobile* force. Cf. iv. 55. 1, 56. 1 ; Xen. *Hell.* iii. 2. 23, 5. 6, etc. (Classen, Croiset).

μετὰ ὁπλιτῶν ἑκατόν: a small number of hoplites was sufficient to defend a walled town (vol. i, pp. 16–18).

ἐσκεδασμένον - - - καὶ πρὸς τὸ τεῖχος τετραμμένον: for two reasons I find this unsatisfactory. The two participles are inconsistent with each other ('scattered over the country' and 'with their minds concentrated on the siege' or better, 'on the attack') ; it is not said that part of the force was scattered and the rest attacking. And had the Athenians been engaged in the attack—which was an attempt to capture the place by surprise—Brasidas would not have been able so easily to slip through them. What we expect and do not find is (1) Athenian attack and failure of first assault, and (2) their forces in consequence scattered to ravage and plunder, καὶ ⟨οὐκέτι⟩ πρὸς τὸ τεῖχος τετραμμένον. (We cannot suggest the insertion of the simple negative only; it would be inconsistent with προσέβαλον, unless the attack had been called off in consequence of failure, and we had been told this.)

πρῶτος τῶν κατὰ τὸν πόλεμον: if we may supply ἐπαινουμένων from ἐπηνέθη, there is no need to adopt Herwerden's πρώτου; and a copyist's error of πρῶτος for πρώτου is less likely than the reverse, πρώτου for πρῶτος. ἐπηνέθη means 'received the thanks of the state'.

Brasidas is one of the few individuals in the *History*, and Thucydides takes the trouble to mention his first success; for though not important, it was characteristic, and gave a hint of the future. He had not been so careful about Kleon's first appearance (21. 3 n.).

83

3. τῆς Ἠλείας ἐς Φειάν: like Methone, not further described by Thucydides.

τριακοσίους: a common number for such select troops for special missions; cf., in Thucydides, iii. 22. 7, iv. 70. 2, 125. 3 (Classen). **αὐτόθεν ἐκ τῆς περιοικίδος:** Pheia was in Pisatis, and Pisatis was subject to, and not fully incorporated with, Elis proper, ἡ κοίλη Ἦλις, to the north in the valley of the Peneios.

Since with the text as we have it the 300 λογάδες are said to come from both Elis and the perioikis, and this is both unlikely in itself and, if true, unnecessarily complicated in expression (why not simply προσβοηθήσαντας Ἠλείων τριακοσίους λογάδας?), Wilamowitz, *Herm.* xxxv, 1900, 558 n., suggested reading τοὺς αὐτόθεν and taking Ἠλείων with τῆς περιοικίδος. Classen proposed inserting πλῆθος (πολλούς would be more attractive) after περιοικίδος. It seems more probable that by τῶν αὐτόθεν - - - Ἠλείων, Thucydides means not the Pisatai, but Eleans living, as landowners, in Pisatis (or, perhaps, rich Pisatai who had altogether accepted Elean domination and been received by the Eleans into full citizenship); so that the first objection to the sentence as we have it vanishes. The second, the unnecessary elaboration, amounts to little; there is a lot of such unrelated detail in Thucydides.

4. ἐν ἀλιμένῳ χωρίῳ: It is a little strange that the fleet did not anchor straightway in the harbour, which would have been as convenient a base for the raiding by land-forces, unless it was thought to be defensible and defended on the sea-approaches.

5. ἐκλιπόντες Φειάν: nothing in the narrative of this chapter suggests that this expedition had any purpose beyond that of doing as much harm as possible to the Peloponnese by a series of raids, in retaliation for the destruction in Attica, and to weaken Peloponnesian morale; it does not appear that if the Athenians had captured Methone they would have held on to it and so anticipated their success at Pylos. For clearly they had enough hoplites to have held Pheia against almost any assault provided that they were prepared to send regular supplies there. A policy of raiding was sensible enough, in the circumstances of this war; for it brought home to the Spartans, and more forcibly to the allies of Sparta, that ravaging the territory of your enemy (which was to prove of such little use against Athens) was a game that two could play (i. 143. 4). But a permanent post would have been more effective, as the capture of Pylos and of Kythera proved. On the other hand, no one in Athens in 425 (certainly not Kleon, and probably not Demosthenes) expected that Pylos and Sphakteria would have so profound an effect in Sparta; and we must remember that it was in cutting off and then capturing the Spartiates on Sphakteria, even more than by their hold on Pylos, that Athens won her decisive—or nearly decisive—victory. In 431 Perikles may well have thought that a permanent post at Methone (to be maintained only with considerable effort) would not have done more than make raiding, within a restricted area, easier; Pheia, much farther from Athens, would have been even more costly to hold, though both posts would have been valuable places of call on cruises round the Peloponnese (vol. i, p. 19). As events proved, what might have been a decisive result—the revolt of the helots of Lakonia (or, with much less effect, of the Pisatai from Elis)—did not in fact take place; and it is arguable that, after 421, Athens wasted her efforts in holding on to Pylos for as long as she did. See H. D. Westlake in C.Q. xxxix, 1945, 75–84, with whose arguments I in general agree; but I do not know why he thinks that Thucydides did not understand Athenian strategy, which was hardly a state secret known only to a few strategoi to whose company Thucydides was not admitted.

Diodoros' chapter about this expedition (xii. 42. 7–44) is worth comparing, for it is typical. In the first place it is wrongly dated, in 430–429. Diodoros has already dated the beginning of the war, including the attack on Plataia and the Peloponnesian invasion, in the archonship of Euthydemos, 431–430, and in the same year the Athenian naval expedition; and this is only wrong in the manner in which all his dates tend to be wrong, since he equates the archon-year with the Roman consular year, which began in March (see vol. i, pp. 4–5, 52–53). He states that the expedition was a triumphant success. But he then gives the details of the fleet's activities (from Thucydides), the attacks on Methone and Pheia, and on Kephallenia (below, c. 30), as well as other events of this campaigning season (cc. 26, 27, 31, 33), to the following summer, 430 B.C., and the archonship of Apollodoros, in which, more correctly, he also places the second Peloponnesian invasion and the pestilence. Secondly, he gives one additional detail which may be correct (see § 1 n. on ἄλλα τε ἐκάκουν), and for the rest an uninspired narrative with conventional rhetorical adornment. This he probably took direct from Ephoros and abbreviated; we need not attribute to the latter the misdating as well. The adornment includes a statement that Perikles quietened his angry countrymen by promising to get rid of the Peloponnesians from Attica without loss, and so sent out the fleet under Karkinos and others; which, by its raiding, did have the effect of making them withdraw hastily from Attica; and Perikles won great popularity for his fine generalship. Is this only Ephoros? or did he have evidence, from comedy or later speech, that such things were said at the time?

The briefer and much more intelligent narrative of Plutarch, writing as a biographer, Per. 34. 1–2, may also be compared.

26. 1. περὶ τὴν Λοκρίδα: Opous and Epiknemidian Lokris, as in 9. 2.

Εὐβοίας - - - φυλακήν: see 32 below.

Κλεόπομπος: strategos again next summer, 58. 1, perhaps in the same official year (431–430), but in all probability in the following year as well; see n. ad loc. Nothing more is known of him; he may have been related to Kleinias, father of Alkibiades; but his deme is unknown.

2. Θρόνιον - - - ἐν Ἀλόπῃ: Strabo, ix. 4. 4, p. 426; Leake, ii. 176–7; Bursian, i. 189–90. (Classen's note on Θρόνιον is "weiter von der Küste entfernt: daher τῆς τε παραθαλασσίου - - - καὶ Θρ." But τε connects more probably with ὁμήρους τε ἔλαβεν αὐτῶν, or with καὶ ἐν Ἀλόπῃ, and Thronion is included in the coastal district.)

Wilhelm, S.E.G. iii. 52, suggests reading [ἐν Ἀλ]όπει instead of [ἐν Σιν]όπει in the small fragment, I.G. i.² 944 (see vol. i, p. 367, n. 1), and takes the stone to be part of the casualty list of this, the first year of the war; and he has been supported by Raubitschek, Hesp. xii, 1943, 25–27, who publishes what he believes to be another fragment; cf. S.E.G. x. 415. (So A.T.L. iii. 117, n. 9.) See 34. 1 n. on τῶν - - - πρώτων ἀποθανόντων, for a discussion of this view; here I will only say that, since the reading ἐν Ἀλόπει involves setting the caption in line with the list of names, whereas in the next line but one (for only one man fell at - - - όπῃ) the caption is set off by one space, and since with the older reading, ἐν Σινόπει, the line would be set off in the same way, I feel no confidence at all in the new reading.

27. 1. οὐχ ἥκιστα τοῦ πολέμου σφίσιν αἰτίους εἶναι: a stronger expression than we should expect from i. 67. 2, 139. 1, 140. 3. It is not here a question of Thucydides' own view of the cause of the war (de Romilly, 29–30); it is that we should not suppose from book i that Aigina was so important in common opinion. His treatment of the Megarian decree is similar: see vol. i, pp. 465–7.

τῇ Πελοποννήσῳ ἐπικειμένην: 'because it lay close to the Peloponnese'; cf. iv. 53. 2 (Kythera and Lakonike). It has been objected by many that this reason for the Athenian action suggests, and only suggests, an intention to use Aigina as a base for offensive action against the Peloponnese (cf. again Kythera), whereas a much more powerful motive was probably the danger of a Peloponnesian landing on the island, where they would have found a friendly population, and hence the threat, because of its proximity, to Attica: Περικλῆς τὴν Αἴγιναν ἀφελεῖν ἐκέλευσε τὴν λήμην τοῦ Πειραιέως, Arist. Rhet. iii. 10, 1411 a 15; nimis imminebat propter propinquitatem Aegina Piraeeo, Cic. de Off. iii. 11. 46. Classen, therefore, proposed ⟨τῇ τε Ἀττικῇ καὶ⟩ τῇ Π.—'as near to Attica as to the Peloponnese'; with this we can suppose that the danger to Athens was in mind in both halves of the clause.

ἐποίκους: perhaps here used, instead of ἀποίκους, particularly to mean 'settlers who must keep watch'. Meritt, Wade-Gery, and McGregor, A.T.L. iii. 285, nn. 45, 46, in an important note, argue for a clear distinction between colonists (ἄποικοι) and klerouchoi sent out from Athens; according to them, these settlers were not κληροῦχοι, and did not retain Athenian citizenship, and hence were called Αἰγινῆται (with the necessary explanation) in vii. 57. 2. Above, p. 34, n. 1.

The original inhabitants were restored in 404 B.C. by Lysandros, Xen. Hell. ii. 2. 9.

For the sake of those who still believe that Aigina 'at one time' had 470,000 slaves (Aristotle, ap. Athen. vi. 272 c), we may ask what happened to them on this occasion? Did the new Athenian settlers find themselves each having to look after 1,000, or at least 500, slaves, and feed them?

It is well known that Ar. Ach. 652–4 suggested to ancient scholars, who have been followed by many modern, that Aristophanes, or rather his father, for he was not yet of age, was one of the settlers in Aigina (or, to others but not to me, that Kallistratos was). Others have supposed that his mother was from Aigina, and that he was born after the citizenship law of 451 B.C.; hence Kleon's γραφὴ ξενίας against him (schol. Ach. 378). It is possible that Telekleides, fr. 43, ὅδ' ἀπ' Αἰγίνης νήσου χωρεῖ δοθιῆνος ἔχων τὸ πρόσωπον (where Herwerden's οἴκαδε for νήσου—or ἐνθάδε?—is attractive) refers to him; but see 56. 6 n. I feel that there is some jest in the reference to the island that we cannot now understand, and that this explanation of the passage is too simple. Schol. Ach. 653 shows how little the ancient scholars knew.

2. τὴν γῆν νέμεσθαι: to occupy and cultivate, but not to own, perhaps. In v. 41. 2 the Lacedaemonians νέμονται αὐτήν, without reference to the expelled Aiginetans.

κατά τε τὸ Ἀθηναίων διάφορον: by Classen interpreted to mean Spartan hostility to Athens, like κατ' ἔχθος τὸ Λακεδαιμονίων in a converse case, i. 103. 3; and Ephoros may have so understood it (διὰ τὸ καὶ τοὺς Ἀθηναίους δεδωκέναι τοῖς ἐκ Μεσσήνης ἐκβληθεῖσι κατοικεῖν Ναύπακτον, Diod. xii. 44. 3); but it is more probably Aiginetan hostility to Athens which prompted Spartan help, the more so since the Aiginetans are the subject of the second half of the sentence; and see iv. 56. 2, ad fin. Indeed, if τὸ διάφορον were the feeling felt by Sparta, I should be inclined to propose Ἀργείων for Ἀθηναίων to explain why Thyrea was chosen: see v. 41. 2.

The statements about the position of Thyrea and the reasons for

87

Spartan action in placing the Aiginetans there are repeated in iv. 56. 2, which was clearly not written at the same time. ὑπὸ τὸν σεισμόν: i. 102. 1.

28. νουμηνίᾳ κατὰ σελήνην: inevitably with months of 29 and 30 days alternately, the official νουμηνία did not always coincide with the astronomical new moon; but besides this it is possible that there was already a more serious disturbance of the calendar, such as Aristophanes says occurred a few years later (*Nub.* 615–26; perhaps *Peace*, 406–15). See vol. i, p. 5, n. 2; Pritchett and Neugebauer, *Attic Calendars*, 12–13. On some fourth-century inscriptions (discussed in *Attic Calendars*) dates are given both κατὰ θεόν and κατ' ἄρχοντα.

I cannot agree with Dinsmoor, *Archons of Athens*, 1931, pp. 314–17, that Thucydides' expression here means that the Attic month began at the true conjunction, as astronomically determined, and not on the first evening after visual observation of the new moon. See for what is surely the right view, Meritt, *Att. Cal.* 104. The words ὥσπερ καὶ μόνον δοκεῖ, κ.τ.λ., can only refer to the astronomical cause of the eclipse, as lately determined or learnt by Greek philosophers, not to a rule about the calendar.

ὥσπερ καὶ μόνον δοκεῖ, κ.τ.λ.: this implies that Thucydides is accepting views put forward by philosophers, including Anaxagoras (Plut. *Nik.* 23. 3), who was perhaps still in Athens (see below, pp. 185–6), he himself not being a philosopher in this sense. It is a correct view, and shows that the immediate cause of an eclipse of the sun had been divined, but not that so much was known of the cycles of the earth and moon that both future eclipses could be accurately foretold and past ones accurately dated. On a later occasion, iv. 52. 1, Thucydides says simply that an eclipse took place κατὰ νουμηνίαν; and vii. 50. 4, of the eclipse of the moon, ἐτύγχανε γὰρ πασσέληνος οὖσα. Herodotos, i. 74, tells the well-known story of Thales' prophecy of the eclipse of 585 B.C. (which the Lydian and Median armies took to be a portent of supernatural meaning), but without hinting that he himself knew how it was done or that Thales knew any more than the year in which it would take place; if he calculated it from the records of eclipses which the Babylonians had kept, one would suppose that the Medes would be more familiar with them than the Ionians.

Thucydides shows no sign here, nor in iv. 52. 1 nor vii. 50. 4, that he would accept any but natural causes, governed by natural laws, for eclipses, nor that he regarded them as portents, as might be inferred from i. 23. 3 (see n. there). He does not even suggest, here and iv. 52. 1, that the masses had any superstitious awe, though Nikias and his soldiers were fearful enough of the moon's eclipse in 413; just as he seldom suggests that a general regularly consulted the auspices before beginning a march or making an attack. But he does record eclipses—as events of the war, or for their own interest? Plutarch, *Per.* 35. 2 (giving the wrong year for this eclipse), tells us of the fears of the multitude and how Perikles dispelled them; a story also told earlier by Cicero, *de Rep.* i. 16. 25.

The date of this eclipse was August 3, at about 5.22 p.m. at Athens. According to Ginzel, *Spezieller Kanon der Sonnen- u. Mondfinsternisse* (1899), 24–25, 58, 176–7, its central path lay through Odessa to Trebizond; it was annular, and not total at Athens; so that it was not dark enough to make stars visible there. (See Bolk, in *R.E.*, s.v. 'Finsternisse'.) Basing his arguments on this, J. A. R. Munro, *C.Q.* xiii, 1919, 127–8, thought that Thucydides must have been in Thrace this August, not Athens: he may have been in Athens during the Peloponnesian invasion and perhaps have returned for the funeral of the dead of the first year, but not in between; hence the very dry record of the events (with the Brasidas incident probably put in later). Moreover, he may have been in inland Thrace acting as Athens' representative in the negotiations with Sitalkes (c. 29), at the latter's capital, perhaps near Adrianople. Here stars would have been visible; and hence, all the detail, about Teres and Tereus, and the rest, and Thucydides' "triumphant satisfaction at the success of the mission (29. 7)".

If this exactness about the path of the eclipse is to be trusted, Munro's suggestion about Thucydides' movements at this time may well be right, and he was an obvious man for the Athenians to choose as negotiator in Thrace; but we may accept it only if we do not couple it with speculations about Thucydides' method of narration or his state of mind over the alliance with Sitalkes. But in fact astronomers do not seem to be agreed on the matter; for others say that during the eclipse it may have been dark enough at Athens for two, perhaps three stars (or rather planets) to be visible: see, e.g., J. K. Fotheringham, 'A Solution of Ancient Eclipses of the Sun', in *Monthly Notices*, Roy. Astron. Soc. lxxxi, 1920, 104–26.

29. 1. Νυμφόδωρον: mentioned by Herodotos, vii. 137, in connexion with the capture of Peloponnesian ambassadors in Thrace next year (below, c. 67), but not mentioned again by Thucydides. Abdera was a tributary member of the Delian League; its territory marched with that of Sitalkes (97. 1).

Σιτάλκης: the logical order of this whole sentence is reversed, and we do not learn who Sitalkes is, nor why Athens courted Nymphodoros, till the end of it. Similarly, on a larger scale, the brief reference in § 2 to the extent of his rule is not explained till cc. 95–97, when the first important action by Sitalkes in this war is related. Compare Hammond's interesting article on the arrangement of thought in i. 1–23 and elsewhere, *C.Q.* ii, 1952, 127–41 (though I do not accept all his conclusions about i. 1–23). Note τὴν μεγάλην βασιλείαν: it was common knowledge (Ar. *Ach.* 134–72). The death of Sitalkes is noted in iv. 101. 5.

2. ἐπὶ πλέον τῆς ἄλλης Θρᾴκης: 'over a larger part of the rest of Thrace (i.e. other than his own Odrysai) than his predecessors'; or, as we should put it (a little more logically), 'was the first *to extend* the kingdom over much of Thrace'. Herodotos, iv. 92, had mentioned the Odrysai, but as one of many Thracian tribes without suggesting that they were especially powerful.

3. Τηρεῖ δέ, κ.τ.λ.: σημείωσαι ὅτι ἐνταῦθα μόνον μῦθον εἰσάγει ἐν τῇ συγγραφῇ, καὶ τοῦτον διστάζων—schol., a characteristically empty comment. Thucydides once more shows his interest in past history, his (apparently) uncritical acceptance of all the main features of the 'myth'—the Thracians in Phokis, the marriage alliance with Athens, all the names of the characters—and his critical attitude to certain details (and to contemporary writers)[1] and an 'enlightened' interpretation. The new interpretation, here as in i. 1–18, is based on τὸ εἰκός, not on research (vol. i, pp. 40–41). In this case he was especially interested owing to his own possession of property in Thrace (but outside the Odrysian Kingdom, to the west).

For the story to which Thucydides refers, see Apollodoros, iii. 14. 8.

προσήκει - - - οὐδέν: I am inclined to adopt προσῆκεν, the reading of CG, 'was not connected with (by blood)' (as i. 128. 5), rather than προσήκει, which most edd. read, 'has nothing to do with' (as i. 126. 5).

ἐν Δαυλίᾳ: Strabo, ix. 3. 13, p. 423; Paus. x. 4. 8–9 (in i. 41. 8–9 Pausanias reports the Megarian tradition that Tereus was King in Pagai, where his tomb was shown). Leake, ii. 98; Bursian, i. 168–9.

[ὁ Τηρεύς]: bracketed by most edd., who say that the scholiast, who explains ὁ μέν by ὁ Τ. ὁ ἀρχαῖος, did not have it in his text. But there is no reason to suppose this (cf. i. 90. 3 n.), and I agree with Classen that Thucydides may well have written ὁ Τηρεύς. Cf. ὁ μὲν - - - ὁ Ἀριστογείτων, vi. 57. 4); it is in fact very like the Homeric idiom, e.g. ἡ μὲν ἄρ' ὣς εἰποῦσ' ἀπέβη πόδας ὠκέα Ἶρις (*Il.* xxiv. 188).

τότε ὑπὸ Θρᾳκῶν οἰκουμένης: for Thracians in Phokis and elsewhere in central Greece, see B. Lenk in *R.E.* vi A (1936), 416.

πολλοῖς δὲ καὶ τῶν ποιητῶν: curiously, no instance of this in Greek poets has been preserved, but several in Latin (Catull. lxv. 14; Ovid *Her.* xv. 154, etc.) borrowed from Greek.

εἰκός τε καί, κ.τ.λ.: a characteristic piece of reasoning, based on common sense—the distance and ἐπ' ὠφελίᾳ τῇ πρὸς ἀλλήλους. (I should prefer to read εἰκὸς δέ here, with ABEFM.)

---

[1] It has been conjectured, plausibly enough, that the story which Thucydides combats had been given in a tragedy, the motive being to compliment Sitalkes. I should suppose that Hellanikos also had given it currency.

Τήρης δέ, κ.τ.λ.: in order both to explain the MSS. readings and to give a clearer reasoning, I believe we should read here οὔτε τὸ αὐτὸ ὄνομα ἔχων βασιλεύς τε ⟨ἐν Θρᾴκῃ καὶ οὐκ ἐν Φωκίδι ὢν⟩ πρῶτος, κ.τ.λ. It seems probable that Thucydides had an οὔτε - - - τε construction, and he gives in fact two reasons for his own conclusion. The reading adopted by most edd., including Stuart Jones, from Classen is unsatisfactory in meaning, as Krüger saw: he conjectured οὔτε τὸ αὐτὸ ὅ. ἔ. ⟨οὔτε τῆς αὐτῆς γῆς ὢν⟩, βασιλεύς [τε], κ.τ.λ.; which is on the right lines, but my suggestion is simpler. 'Οδρυσῶν is genitive after ἐν κράτει: 'he became the first powerful ruler of the Odrysai.'

4. τὰ ἐπὶ Θρᾴκης χωρία: Χαλκιδέας, Βοττιαίους, schol.; many of whom were still in revolt after the siege of Poteidaia had begun, i. 65. 2. For the inclusion of Chalkidike in τὰ ἐπὶ Θρᾴκης, see i. 56. 2.

5. Σάδοκον - - - Ἀθηναῖον: five or six years later Aristophanes could still make play with this barbarian Athenian, Ach. 145-7.

6. Θέρμην αὐτῷ - - - ἀποδοῦναι: see i. 61. 2 n., and C. Edson's valuable article, C.P. xlii, 1947, 88-105. This entirely confirms my suggestion that no Macedonian cities, except Methone, a special case, were within the Delian League, and that Therme is not to be identified with the Serme of the tribute-lists. (Note that Therme is here to be *restored* to Perdikkas, as his by right.) Edson also shows that in all probability the site of Therme was in or very near Thessalonike itself, not at the hot springs of Sédes, two to three miles to the south-east.

Φορμίωνος: i. 65. 2 ad fin., ii. 31. 2.

7. οὕτω μὲν Σιτάλκης, κ.τ.λ.: a formal summary, with full names and titles of men just mentioned. Cf. 19. 1 n. Thucydides is saying, as it were, 'add the Thracian kingdom to the list of Athenian allies given in c. 9'. Contrast 22. 3.

30. 1. Σόλλιον - - - Παλαιρεῦσιν - - - Ἀστακόν: their positions are not explained here (indeed one might suppose from the context, ἔτι ὄντες περὶ Πελοπόννησον, that the former was in the Peloponnese, and perhaps Astakos as well), or elsewhere (iii. 95. 1, v. 30. 2—Sollion; ii. 33. 1, 102. 1—Astakos); and the scholia are not very helpful. The position of Kephallenia (§ 2) is roughly given; yet it must have been better known: cf. 66. 1 (Zakynthos). See R.E. s.vv.; Oberhummer, *Akarnanien*, pp. 30, 35, 37. Astakos is mentioned by Ps.-Skylax, and Strabo, x. 1. 21, p. 459, who places it near the Echinades Is. and not far from Oiniadai, on the south-west coast, therefore, of Akarnania. The sites of Sollion and Palairos (the latter also mentioned by Strabo) are unknown; Oberhummer puts the former in the Leukadian *peraia* (the NW. peninsula of Akarnania opposite the isthmus of Leukas), Palairos some 4 km. to the north-east, but within Akarnanian boundaries.

For a summary of Corinthian interests in this region (cf. c. 33), see Beaumont's article cited below, 80. 3 n., esp. p. 63.

Εὔαρχος: nothing is known of him but what we are told here and 33. 1.

2. Κεφαλληνίαν: see 9. 5 n. This added considerably to Athenian strength in the west, and was specially opportune for connexions with Kerkyra. Athens never won Leukas, the most northerly (except Kerkyra itself) of the larger islands in the Ionian Sea. τετράπολις οὖσα, κ.τ.λ.: but this detail has no significance for the *History*. Cf. 22. 3. Each of these cities issued its own coinage, on the same standard and with similar, but not identical, types, from about 500 B.C. (Bürchner in *R.E.*, s.v. 'Kephallenia', 203–11.)

31. 1. περὶ δὲ τὸ φθινόπωρον τοῦ θέρους τούτου: see 1. 1, 2. 1 (ἅμα ἦρι ἀρχομένῳ) nn. Thucydides has not said that he would date by spring and autumn as well as by summer and winter; but he makes it clear that his autumn is a subdivision of summer. Since the eclipse of c. 28 was on August 3, and the later activities and the return of the Athenian fleet were subsequent to it, we could not here put the autumn much before the end of September. The next subsequent event is dated τοῦ θέρους τούτου τελευτῶντος, and all of those recently related (24–32) are dated ἐν τῷ θέρει τούτῳ (c. 32); the event after that, which belongs to the same series, occurs τοῦ ἐπιγιγνομένου χειμῶνος. It is clear that summer does not end till the end of autumn, and secondly, it would seem that Thucydides had a precise date in mind for the division between summer and winter. See iv. 2. 1 and Appendix.

2. στρατόπεδόν τε μέγιστον: 'the largest combined armament', heavy-armed (citizen and metic), light-armed of all sorts, and a large fleet. Cf. iii. 17 nn.

μυρίων γὰρ ὁπλιτῶν, κ.τ.λ.: see 13. 6 n. They include the 1,000 who went with the fleet (23. 2).

οἱ ἐν Ποτειδαίᾳ τρισχίλιοι ἦσαν: a parenthesis to explain the figures as agreeing with the total Athenian hoplite force.

But, as so often, Thucydides has not been careful to say precisely what he means by the 3,000 hoplites at Poteidaia. In i. 61. 4 he says that this was the number of the combined forces sent out under Archestratos and Kallias in 432; in 64. 2 that another 1,600 were sent under Phormion. These were last heard of, except for the brief reference above (29. 6), as ravaging Chalkidike and Bottike after Poteidaia had been successfully invested (i. 65. 2). It was usual when a long siege was to be expected, for the majority of the besieging troops to be withdrawn after the investment (vol. i, p. 18); but we are not told that this had happened in this case, and we are told only later, 58. 2 below, that about midsummer of the following year,

Phormion and his 1,600 were no longer in Chalkidike. It is generally supposed that in fact his force had been withdrawn in 431 (after the treaties with Sitalkes and Perdikkas, 29. 6); but if so it is certainly curious that Thucydides does not say so here, where the fact is so clearly pertinent. We should have expected, as normal procedure, that about half the original force of 3,000 had been withdrawn soon after the investment of Poteidaia was complete, 1,500 men, properly entrenched, being ample to maintain a siege, and that Hagnon's force in 430 was sent, to attempt an assault (which required a much stronger force), because Phormion's 1,600—who had been laying waste the enemy's land, not besieging Poteidaia—had *recently* been withdrawn. The 3,000 mentioned here would then consist of the 1,500 besiegers and Phormion's force. This, however, would mean not only somewhat careless writing on Thucydides' part, for these 3,000 certainly look like the 3,000 of i. 61. 4 (casualties, as usual, unless they were particularly heavy, being ignored), but is apparently contradicted by iii. 17. 4. See n. there.

μέτοικοι: this was the first occasion, so far as we know, on which metic hoplites served on a foreign campaign (if this can be so called), and the experiment was not often repeated. As suggested above, p. 36 n., they may have been intended to replace the 3,000 citizen troops who were in Chalkidike.

ὁ ἄλλος ὅμιλος ψιλῶν οὐκ ὀλίγος: as usual, Thucydides gives no figures for these troops (cf. above, p. 42, and iii. 87. 3 n.), because, although the number of thetes at Athens was known, or could be inferred from the total citizen lists, many of them were serving in the fleet, and there would be many foreigners, and doubtless some slaves, among the light-armed with the army.

3. ἄλλαι ὕστερον - - - ἐσβολαί: twice a year according to iv. 66. 1 and Plut. *Per.* 30. 3, who gives an embroidered story of a special decree (part of Charinos' decree, i. 139. 2 n.) and an oath taken by the strategoi. See also Pausanias, i. 40. 3. As Classen says, the vague ἄλλαι here (and καὶ ἱππέων καὶ πανστρατιᾷ) suggests that the regular twice-yearly invasion was instituted later. Everyone knows from *The Acharnians* how much Megara suffered from them, and how cruel Aristophanes in his youth could be in his mockery.

Νίσαια ἑάλω: seven years later, in 424 B.C., iv. 66–69.

32. Ἀταλάντη: a small uninhabited islet just off Opous; see iii. 89. 3. The garrison there included, at least at the later date, two triremes, to stop raiding.

ταῦτα μέν, κ.τ.λ.: the Athenians in this year pursue a steady policy, making good use of their sea-power, both for defensive and for offensive purposes—hemming in the enemy, hindering his movements, and threatening raids at unexpected times and places.

33. 1. Εὔαρχος: see 30. 1.

Εὐφαμίδας τε, κ.τ.λ.: another case of names given which have no significance; clearly from information given and a note made at the time. Thucydides is specially well informed about the names of Corinthian commanders; cf. i. 29. 2, 47. 1 n.

3. βιαιότερον ἀναγαγόμενοι: 'got away not without a struggle', under considerable pressure from the enemy; as iii. 23. 4, διαβάντες τὴν τάφρον χαλεπῶς δὲ καὶ βιαίως, iv. 31. 2, v. 73. 4.

The narrative of events in cc. 19–33 might seem to illustrate well Aristotle's thesis that history has only to report τὰ γενόμενα, events, and to report them as they occur in time, and all that occur within a given period of time, whether they have logical connexion or no—by contrast with a narrative poem which is an organic whole and deals with οἷα ἂν γένοιτο. Yet Thucydides has a purpose in his selection: these chapters show clearly what the war, between a land-power and a sea-power, would be like, how non-Greek powers on the fringe of it would be affected (i. 1. 2), and one incident, Brasidas at Methone, forebodes the future. See my *Greek Attitude to Poetry and History*, pp. 127–32.

34–46. *The Funeral of the Dead*

34. 1. τῷ πατρίῳ νόμῳ χρώμενοι, κ.τ.λ.: the almost universal Greek custom was to bury those killed in war on the battlefield. So after Thermopylai (Hdt. vii. 228), Salamis (*I.G.* i.² 927 = Tod, 16), Plataia (Hdt. ix. 85); and the Spartans at Athens in 510 (Hdt. v. 63. 4) and in 403 (Xen. *Hell.* ii. 4. 33, and the tomb itself, *Arch. Anz.*, 1930, 90 ff., 102). This Athenian νόμος was a singularity (cf. Dem. xx. 141): after Chaironeia, for example, the Athenian dead were brought home, but the Thebans and Macedonians buried theirs where they fell (Dem. xviii. 285–8; Paus. i. 29. 13, ix. 40. 10; Plut. *Dem.* 21. 2; *Alex.* 9. 3).

Thucydides' statement that it was a πάτριος νόμος, i.e. one dating from at least as early as Solon, if not earlier, has been disputed by Jacoby in an important article, *J.H.S.* lxiv, 1944, 37–66; who argues that it was first introduced, by a new law, in 465–464 B.C. after the disaster at Drabeskos (i. 100. 3). His arguments are briefly as follows: (1) There had been important occasions besides Marathon (§ 5, below) on which the Athenian dead were buried on the battlefield, in accordance with the general Greek custom, notably Plataia (Hdt. ix. 85; cf. Thuc. iii. 58. 4;¹ Paus. ix. 2. 5–6),² and probably the war with

---

¹ The Plataian speaker mentions only the Spartan dead, but he is addressing his Spartan judges.

² Pausanias is not altogether in agreement with Herodotos, for he says that there were three graves only, for the Spartans, the Athenians, and the rest of

Chalkis in 506 B.C. (the epigram attributed to Simonides, No. 87 Diehl). Besides these, three individuals killed in battle were not buried in the Kerameikos, Tellos (Hdt. i. 30. 3–5), Tettichos (*I.G.* i.² 976: mid-6th cent. B.C.) and Hermolykos (Hdt. ix. 105: at Karystos, *c.* 474 B.C.); of them Tettichos was buried in a private grave at his home, the other two on or near the battlefield. (2) Pausanias, who in his account of the Kerameikos is following a good authority, in all probability Diodoros Periegetes (*F. Gr. Hist.* 372), says πρῶτοι ἐτάφησαν οὓς ἐν Θρᾴκῃ ποτὲ ἐπικρατοῦντας μεχρὶ Δραβησκοῦ τῆς χώρας Ἠδωνοὶ φονεύουσιν ἀνέλπιστοι ἐπιθέμενοι (i. 29. 4). (3) There have survived a number of inscriptions recording the names of men fallen in battle and buried in the Kerameikos, and none probably is earlier than *c.* 465.¹ Thucydides, writing after 404 B.C. (Jacoby is convinced that the Epitaphios, and therefore this chapter introducing it, was composed after the end of the war), may well have made a mistake about legislation sixty years earlier; and when Aeschylus, in *Agam.* 441–2, speaks of the ashes of the dead being brought home from Troy, "nobody will seriously doubt that the singularity is due to a typical and deliberate anachronism after the Athenian custom which had been introduced a few years earlier".

A.T.L. iii. 109–10, accepts Jacoby's main conclusions; but I am not convinced by his arguments, and not yet of the truth of the conclusion. We may leave Aeschylus out of account: I do not believe that he was given to deliberate anachronism of this kind; and his words—

ἀντὶ δὲ φωτῶν
τεύχη καὶ σποδὸς εἰς ἑκάστου δόμους ἀφικνεῖται—

do not suggest any public burial at home of all citizens killed in war, which is the essential of the Athenian custom, but a private homecoming of a man's ashes. (Headlam, ap. G. Thomson, *Oresteia*, was right in referring to *Cho.* 679–81 as a parallel.)² For Thucydides, we must remember that 464 B.C. was not long before his birth, and that he was already prepared to be a historian in the thirties; we cannot lightly assume that he would make a mistake of this kind, even granted that this chapter was written after 404. We might expect also, if Diodoros Periegetes at the end of the fourth century knew that the custom was introduced in or shortly before 465–464,

the Greeks; but he is not necessarily inaccurate, for there may have been changes in the course of six centuries.

¹ I agree with Jacoby (p. 48, n. 57) that no weight in this argument can be given to the small fragment from the agora which Raubitschek would attribute to a monument to the dead in Ionia in 498 B.C. (*Hesp.* iv, 1935, p. 53, xii, 1943, p. 23).

² Aeschylus may, as Jacoby suggests, have had *Il.* vii. 334–5, lines certainly interpolated, in his copy of Homer.

that some reference to the legislation (carried by Ephialtes and his party, according to Jacoby)[1] would have come down to us.

Nor, I think, need we consider the monuments of individuals. Tellos received a special honour akin to that of the Marathonomachai, as Jacoby recognizes ($\kappa\alpha i \ \mu\iota\nu \ A\theta\eta\nu\alpha\hat{\iota}o\iota \ \delta\eta\mu o\sigma i\eta \ \tau\epsilon \ \check{\epsilon}\theta\alpha\psi\alpha\nu$ $\alpha\dot{v}\tau o\hat{v} \ \tau\hat{\eta} \ \pi\epsilon\rho \ \check{\epsilon}\pi\epsilon\sigma\epsilon \ \kappa\alpha i \ \dot{\epsilon}\tau i\mu\eta\sigma\alpha\nu \ \mu\epsilon\gamma\dot{\alpha}\lambda\omega s$—did Herodotos make the same mistake as Thucydides?); we do not know that Tettichos died in an Athenian war, and, even if he did, Kimon also was buried in the family vault, not in the Kerameikos (Plut. *Kim.* 19. 5; Jacoby doubts this, but without sufficient reason; the statement may well come from Diodoros, $\pi\epsilon\rho i \ \mu\nu\eta\mu\dot{\alpha}\tau\omega\nu$); and any special circumstance may account for Hermolykos—he was clearly not buried on the battlefield with the rest of the dead in the Karystos campaign.

Secondly, Pausanias' description of the tombs is apparently haphazard and incomplete; but we cannot say anything precise about his relationship to earlier writers. Diodoros' account may well have been systematic and complete; but if Pausanias borrowed from him, and at second or third hand, carelessly, we cannot be sure what particular statements are accurately taken from him; we can only, as Jacoby himself agrees, take his account as it stands at present.[2] In that he makes one notable mistake: $\sigma\tau\hat{\eta}\lambda\alpha\iota \ \tau\dot{\alpha} \ \dot{o}\nu\dot{o}\mu\alpha\tau\alpha \ \kappa\alpha i \ \tau\dot{o}\nu$

[1] But I would not agree with Jacoby that there is anything specially democratic about the $\nu\dot{o}\mu os$, in the sense that it could only have been introduced in a democracy like the Athenian, and by the popular party in Athens.

[2] He mentions two earlier than 465-464 B.C. (for which see below), 6 from 465 to 446, 10 to 13 from the Peloponnesian war, 3 (perhaps 5) only from the fourth century, 4 from 306 to 287, and 2 from the second century. But the area had been devastated before Pausanias' day by both Philip V and Sulla, and we know nothing of its state in the second century A.D. except what we learn from him. Jacoby (p. 40, n. 12) points out, after Domaszewski, that § 11 in Pausanias suggests a restoration of the monument, but there is no ground for supposing that this was complete (*ex hypothesi* it was not a restoration "to its original state", for the argument from § 11 is that what had been four original monuments were amalgamated into one; and what became of the originals, which were there to be copied?). Pausanias himself says nothing of destruction or restoration; but I cannot agree that he "is professing to describe the original cemetery". Two at least of the monuments which he mentions are later than Diodoros Periegetes (§ 14). Jacoby notes that no monument of the Chremonidean war is in Pausanias' list. This may be accidental or due to carelessness; or the monument had been destroyed. Or there had never been one, and is this significant of conditions after 262 B.C.?

We must, moreover, remember that Pausanias' selection of monuments to be mentioned in his book is anyhow arbitrary (above, p. 54, n.2). This is not the place to discuss the methods of Pausanias, whether he described (carefully or carelessly) what he saw, or copied (carefully or carelessly) what he had read. For my part I prefer the sober judgement of Frazer, *Pausanias*, i, pp. lxxvii-xcvi. I have never been able to understand why, when we prove a mistake or assume negligence, it is taken for granted that the mistake or the negligence is more likely to have occurred in reading a book than in travelling in town and country.

δῆμον ἑκάστου λέγουσαι (§ 4); for only the *phylai* were given on the public monuments, and these not always, never the demes (cf. Pausanias himself on the monument at Marathon, i. 32. 3). This statement does not presumably come from the careful Diodoros; why then should one assume that the statement that the Drabeskos dead were the first to be buried in the Kerameikos is a careful record of what he had said? It is in any case contradicted by Pausanias himself, first by his mention of the *special* honour paid to the dead of Marathon (which is straight from Thucydides) and then by his record of monuments to the dead of the pre-Persian Aiginetan wars (§ 7)[1] and to those of Eurymedon (§ 14).[2] There is indeed nothing unreasonable in Jacoby's argument that these were exceptional cases, if his general thesis is right, just as Chalkis, Marathon, and Plataia were exceptional, if Thucydides' statement is right; but they are none the less inconsistent with Pausanias' own statement that the dead at Drabeskos were the first to be buried publicly in the Kerameikos. We cannot therefore accept that as a careful statement of the truth. Further, I incline towards the view that Pausanias meant by this to give not a temporal, but a topographical indication. He begins his list of monuments of *individuals* with the words Θρασυβούλου μὲν πρῶτον - - - πρῶτος μέν ἐστιν οὗτος τάφος, and the monument of Drabeskos is the first in his list of *polyandria*; the lists have no chronological order, but may be roughly topographical; the aorist ἐτάφησαν, where κεῖνται or the like would be 'correct', can be paralleled in §§ 8 and 13. The statement in that case does not, in its present form, come from Diodoros at all. If it does come from him, and has a temporal meaning, it is not accurate or not accurately recorded, and its value is not very great.[3]

But whatever the date of the institution of public burial of Athens'

---

[1] Jacoby, p. 48, thinks that Pausanias' dating of this war—οἱ πρὶν ἢ στρατεῦσαι τὸν Μῆδον ἐπολέμησαν πρὸς Αἰγινήτας—is deliberate because the event was long before 465–464. But it is only to differentiate it from the war of 458–457; cf. § 6, Θεσσαλῶν τάφος ἱππέων - - - ἐλθόντων, ὅτε σὺν Ἀρχιδάμῳ Πελοποννήσιοι πρῶτον ἐσέβαλον ἐς τὴν Ἀττικὴν στρατιᾷ, and other instances in this chapter.

[2] Jacoby, p. 48, n. 58, is inclined to doubt whether κεῖνται δὲ καὶ οἱ σὺν Κίμωνι τὸ μέγα ἔργον πεζῇ καὶ ναυσὶν αὐθήμερον κρατήσαντες refers to Eurymedon. There can be no doubt; and the monument for the later Cyprus campaign has already been mentioned, οἱ πλεύσαντες ἐς Κύπρον ὁμοῦ Κίμωνι (§ 13).
It is possible too that the monument ἱππεῦσιν ἀποθανοῦσιν ἡνίκα συνεπελάβοντο οἱ Θεσσαλοὶ τοῦ κινδύνου belonged to 506 (§ 6: Hdt. v. 63. 3–4); for Pausanias mentions it immediately after the μνήματα of Kleisthenes (Jacoby, n. 57); or at least that Pausanias thought it did. But the general opinion is probably right that it refers back to the cavalry engagement of 431, which he has mentioned just before Kleisthenes' tomb (above, p. 77).

[3] Perhaps not the public burial, but the custom of inscribing the names of the dead on the tombstone was introduced in 465–464, or after Eurymedon? This might help to explain why there are so few remains of, or references to, earlier monuments.

war dead in the Kerameikos, whether it was of unknown age or was introduced in 465–464, Thucydides is guilty of a blunder; for Plataia was as clearly an exception (on his view) as Marathon; and perhaps Chalkis as well. The latter he might have forgotten or not known, and it would be unimportant; but Plataia stands out. It is, of course, quite easy to see why Athens made an exception to her own custom in this case, if it was already her custom: not simply that the battle was of Panhellenic significance—so were Artemision and Salamis, and so would Athens like to consider Eurymedon—but that a Panhellenic cult of the dead was instituted at Plataia with a yearly festival, and the graves especially tended by the Plataians; it was scarcely possible for Athens to refuse her part. But that does not excuse Thucydides' failure to mention it.

Our choice, however, is not simply between two blunders. If Thucydides is right that the νόμος was πάτριος, he was wrong in thinking, or implying, that Marathon was the only exception; but if he is wrong about the law, if the Kerameikos burial was introduced in 465–464, he is not only guilty of a bad and (to my mind) barely credible blunder, but of the other mistake as well; for in any case, on his own hypothesis he should have mentioned Plataia. On the whole (I think) we must believe Thucydides that the custom was an old one, a good deal older than the Persian wars.

A word may be added about the 'Marathon' epigrams ($I.G.$ i.^{2} 763 and the new fr. published by Oliver, $Hesp.$ ii, 1933, 480–94), which have also been discussed by Jacoby, $Hesp.$ xiv, 1945, 157–85. He maintains (1) that they certainly celebrate Marathon, and (2) that they are epigrams from a victory memorial, not epitaphs to the dead. I am in doubt about both propositions. Jacoby (like most others) thinks that the words of the second poem,

$$h\acute{o}\tau' \ a\mathring{\iota}\chi\mu\acute{e}\nu$$
$$\sigma\tau\hat{\epsilon}\sigma a\nu \ \pi\rho\acute{o}\sigma\theta\epsilon \ \pi\upsilon\lambda\hat{o}\nu \ \mathring{a}\nu[\tau\acute{\iota}a \ \tau o\chi\sigma o\phi\acute{o}\rho o\nu],$$

must refer to a land-battle, fought outside the city walls but within Attica; and that the next line,

$$\mathring{a}\gamma\chi\acute{\iota}a\lambda o\nu \ \pi\rho\hat{\epsilon}\sigma a\iota \ \beta[o\lambda\epsilon\upsilon\sigma a\mu\acute{e}\nu o\nu \ \delta' \ \mathring{e}\sigma\acute{a}o\sigma a\nu]$$
$$\mathring{a}\sigma\tau\upsilon,^{1}$$

must imply a campaign in which the city was not burnt by the enemy. The battle, therefore, since the inscription belongs to the period $c.$ 490–480, must be Marathon; and consequently the first epigram is for Marathon too. This interpretation ignores $\mathring{a}\gamma\chi\acute{\iota}a\lambda o\nu$, which is in a remarkably emphatic position: "but it was a city near the sea that they sought to burn." What has that to do with

¹ This is Wilhelm's restoration, which Jacoby adopts, though hesitatingly. I am quite sure that $\beta[o\lambda\epsilon\upsilon\sigma a\mu\acute{e}\nu o\nu]$ will not stand. (The B on the stone is very doubtful; P is possible.) See $S.E.G.$ x. 404.

Marathon? It is surely Salamis that is in view, fought 'in sight of' the gates of the city which the enemy had burnt.[1] For $α\dot{ι}χμ\dot{η}ν$ $στ\^{η}σαν$ used of a battle mainly fought at sea, cf. the Eurymedon epigram, *Anth. Pal.* vii. 258 (Simonides, No. 115, Diehl),

$$α\dot{ι}χμηταί, πεζοί τε καὶ ὠκυπόρων ἐπὶ νη\^{ω}ν.$$

If both epigrams, as they surely must, refer to the same battle, we can of course restore l. 3 of the first as Hiller proposed—

$$ἔσχον γὰρ πεζοί τε [καὶ ὀκυπόρον ἐπὶ νεὸ]ν$$

(which the author of the Eurymedon epigram will then have copied), rather more easily than as Wilhelm—

$$ἔσχον γὰρ πεζοὶ τὲ[ν ἄλκιμον Ἀσίδος ἵππο]ν—$$

which requires a double construction for $ἔσχον$, the direct accusative in this and the infinitive clause in the next line. The $πεζοί$ at Salamis were Aristeides' company which landed on Psyttaleia.

Secondly, I do not believe with Jacoby that $οἵδε$ (which occurs in the first line of each poem) can be simply the demonstrative antecedent to the relatives, $οἵ$ (restored) in the first and $ὅτε$ in the second poem. They must refer to persons already mentioned in a prose inscription on another part of the monument; and the natural reference is to the dead, and probably a list of the dead, of the campaign; and the poems are in consequence epitaphs. Jacoby objected that an epitaph should contain a statement of the death. True; but Bowra found no difficulty in thus restoring l. 2 of the first poem,

$$[ἀντίον hοὶ Πε]ρ[σ\^{ω}ν ἐμ Μαραθ\^{ω}νι θάνον];$$

for there is only one, disputed, letter left of that line. To be sure, we should prefer $Μαραθ\^{ω}νι$ to $ἐμ$ $Μαραθ\^{ω}νι$ (cf. Thuc. i. 73. 4; Ar. *Equit.* 781); but $ἐ'$ $Σαλαμ\^{ι}νι$ can be as easily restored.

If this argument is sound, and these poems are epitaphs on the monument of the dead of Salamis, it would be further disproof of Jacoby's case that the public burial of the war dead in Athens was first instituted in 465–464. Jacoby remarks on the scarcity, "one might say the almost complete absence", of Athenian epitaphs of the fallen at Artemision, Salamis, and Mykale—nothing in Pausanias, nothing (which is much more surprising) in the literary tradition. But we may at least remember that Athens itself was thoroughly sacked by Sulla's army, and many monuments destroyed; had the monument to the dead of Salamis been set up on Salamis island, as Jacoby's theory demands (there is nothing about it in *this* part of Pausanias, i. 35–36. 2, either), there would have been more chance for its survival, at least to late classical times, than a monument in

[1] Cf. $πρὸ$ $πόληος$ in the Tegea epigram, Simonides 123 D., which surely means 'in front of the city', not 'in defence of'.

Athens, just as the memorial there to the Corinthian dead ($I.G.$ i.²
927 = Tod, 16) was not only remembered in antiquity, but has survived to our day.¹

Jacoby would also link this state burial of men killed in war with
the peculiar Attic festival of the dead, the Genesia, which he has
discussed in an illuminating manner in $C.Q.$ xxxviii, 1944, 65–75.
Again I am not convinced; but in this (for Thucydides) comparatively unimportant problem, I will only give my reasons briefly.
First, and most important, the Genesia was a yearly festival, the
burial in the Kerameikos and its accompanying ceremonies, including
the Epitaphios, occurred only $\delta\pi\delta\tau\epsilon$ $\xi\upsilon\mu\beta\alpha\iota\eta$ $\alpha\upsilon\tau\circ\hat{\iota}s$ (§ 7 below).
Secondly, the date of the Genesia, 5th Boedromion (in September
in most years), is much too early for a funeral for all those fallen
in a year's campaign. I agree with Jacoby that we should not set
too much store by the relative position in Thucydides' narrative of
the Akarnanian incident of c. 33 and the state funeral in Athens, not
because Thucydides, writing after 404, would have forgotten it (for
he had his notes, and the Genesia was on the same day every year),
but because it is of no significance for the narrative; but both are
clearly $\epsilon\nu$ $\tau\hat{\omega}$ $\chi\epsilon\iota\mu\hat{\omega}\nu\iota$, and for Thucydides September certainly belongs
to $\tau\grave{\circ}$ $\phi\theta\iota\nu\acute{o}\pi\omega\rho\circ\nu$, which is part of the summer, if not to summer in
its restricted sense. Events in these chapters are clearly dated—see
31. 1 n.: how could $\epsilon\nu$ $\tau\hat{\omega}$ $\alpha\upsilon\tau\hat{\omega}$ $\chi\epsilon\iota\mu\hat{\omega}\nu\iota$ in 34. 1 be September? A date
for such a ceremony would certainly have been fixed when, normally,
campaigning was at an end; and, particularly if the ceremony was
first instituted in 465–464, by which time most of the recent cam-

¹ The disappearance of these 'Marathon' epigrams from the literary tradition
is yet more remarkable, if they are for Marathon, and particularly if, with Oliver
loc. cit., and Bowra ($Gk.$ $Lyric$ $Poetry$, p. 355), we attribute them to Simonides
and Aeschylus. No destruction by the Persians would account for it; for, if the
Athenians had got so famous a man as Simonides to write the first, and thought
so highly of Aeschylus' poem as to have it inscribed as number two, they would
certainly have restored the monument after 479.

I put forward these doubts about the epigrams with great hesitation. They
are meant to be doubts only. It may be that $\dot{\alpha}\gamma\chi\acute{\iota}\alpha\lambda\circ\nu$ is a conventional epithet
and no more, though I think it unlikely. In an interesting article on the dedication
of Kallimachos the polemarch (i.² 609 = Tod, 13), $B.S.A.$ xlv, 1950, 140–64, in
the last section, B. B. Shefton upholds the traditional view that the epigrams are
for Marathon and are earlier than 480, and that the monument was destroyed then.
(In passing: Raubitschek's restoration of the first hexameter of the Kallimachos
dedication (ibid., p. 164) is metrically impossible. The writer may have varied an
original prose inscription—J. M. Cook's ingenious suggestion, ap. Shefton, n. 12;
he clearly meant to scan $A\phi\iota\delta\nu\alpha\hat{\iota}\circ s$ $\tau\acute{\alpha}\theta\epsilon\nu\alpha\acute{\iota}\alpha\iota$ $\cup-\cup\cup---$, which has only one
false quantity (cf. the less excusable $\Phi\epsilon\iota\delta\acute{\iota}\alpha s$ $X\alpha\rho\mu\acute{\iota}\delta\circ\upsilon$ $\upsilon\iota\grave{o}s$ $A\theta\eta\nu\alpha\hat{\iota}\acute{o}s$ μ' $\dot{\epsilon}\pi\circ\acute{\iota}\eta\sigma\epsilon$—
less excusable because the last syllable of $\Phi\epsilon\iota\delta\acute{\iota}\alpha s$ is by nature long; but some
licence had to be given for these awkward names); Raubitschek's $A\phi\iota\delta\nu\alpha\hat{\iota}\circ\nu$
(gen. plur.) $\tau\acute{\alpha}\theta\epsilon\nu\alpha\acute{\iota}\alpha\iota$ could only be $\cup----\cup\cup--$, which no Athenian, however
uncultivated, could have intended.)

paigns in which Athens was engaged had lasted well into late autumn, it is highly improbable that the funeral was held in late summer. Lastly, Thucydides certainly implies that it was a special festival, not part of a general one for all the dead.

τῶν ἐν τῷδε τῷ πολέμῳ πρώτων ἀποθανόντων: as stated above, 26. 2 n., I.G. i.² 944 is thought by Wilhelm and by Raubitschek to be part of the casualty list for this year, and the latter publishes another small fragment which from the lettering he claims to be from the same stele (see S.E.G. x. 415, with further references). He also thinks that I.G. i.² 946, which is a fragment of the epigram Anth. Pal. vii. 254, headed the whole monument and refers to all the losses in the many small engagements of this year. The lettering of I.G. i.² 944 is especially fine, and larger than that of most other casualty lists, especially suitable (it is suggested) to the solemn occasion, the burial of those who had died first in this decisive war, which was adorned also by Perikles in his Funeral Speech.

There are, however, difficulties in the way of this attractive proposal. (1) The epigram runs:

Χαίρετ᾽ ἀριστῆες πολέμου μέγα κῦδος ἔχοντες,
κοῦροι Ἀθηναίων, ἔξοχοι ἱπποσύνῃ,
οἵ ποτε καλλιχόρου περὶ πατρίδος ὠλέσαθ᾽ ἥβην
πλείστοις Ἑλλήνων ἀντία μαρνάμενοι.

"If the epigram", says Raubitschek, "is understood as referring to all the casualties, the phrase πλείστοις Ἑλλήνων ἀντία μαρνάμενοι becomes much more significant." Not much more significant, for the phrase means "fighting against heavy odds", whether in one or more engagements; and it is impossible to believe that the second line can include foot soldiers (for example, those who died at Poteidaia) as well as cavalry. If, then, I.G. i.² 946 is to be dated from its lettering later than the battle of Tanagra, and if there were no cavalry at Koroneia, this will be the epigram on those who fell 'in face of the whole Peloponnesian force' in the cavalry engagement in the Athenian plain, 22. 2. In that case it may have been on the monument seen by Pausanias, or on one set up elsewhere than the Kerameikos; but it cannot belong with I.G. i.² 944.¹ (2) I have already (26. 2 n.) expressed my doubts whether that inscription is to be placed in 431–430 B.C.; and (3) there is at least one reason for supposing that the new fragment found in the agora and published by Raubitschek does not belong with it: namely, that, whereas in

¹ Bergk attributed the epigram to an engagement against Kleomenes and his allies in 507–506, and so allowed it to be by Simonides (cf. my suggestion about the monument seen by Pausanias, 22. 2 n. above). In that case the inscription would be a renewal of an old one destroyed by the Persians, like I.G. i.² 394 (Tod, 12 and 43). This is by no means impossible.

i.[2] 944 the caption is set off by one space, in the new fragment the captions are set back one space, producing a quite different effect. True, the lettering of the two fragments is very similar, and is probably by the same hand; but so, according to Raubitschek and others, are *I.G.* i.[2] 96 and 149, both of which belong to 416 B.C. Arguments from letter-forms can clearly be too closely pressed.

Unfortunately the agora fragment is too much broken to be of much significance in itself; it may or may not belong to 431–430.

2. τῶν ἀπογενομένων: Marchant suggests that this word for the dead was specially used in ritual. But its use in 51. 5, 98. 3, and v. 74. 3 seems literary only. Souidas, s.v. ἀπεγένετο, notes that Antiphon also used it.

πρότριτα: two days before the actual burial. So Ar. *Lys.* 611. Later, in private burials, the burial took place on the day after the πρόθεσις: Dem. xliii. 62. For pictorial representations of the πρόθεσις, see Zschietzschmann, *Ath. Mitt.* liii, 1928, 17–47.

σκηνήν: "not a scaffolding, but a tent—that is, a building without a solid wall (Frickenhaus in *R.E.* iii A. 470) which represents the private houses of the mourners"—Jacoby (above, p. 94), n. 117.

This part of the ceremony may have taken place in the agora, as edd. have suggested.

3. φυλῆς ἑκάστης μίαν: because not only the civil but the military organization at Athens was based on the *phyle*.

τῶν ἀφανῶν: particularly in naval battles there must have been many missing. Marchant compares, for general Greek custom, Eur. *Hel.* 1241–2.

4. ὀλοφυρόμεναι: singing the dirge or lament. Cf. 46. 2.

5. ἐπὶ τοῦ καλλίστου προαστείου τῆς πόλεως: i.e. Kerameikos without the Walls, on the road from the Dipylon to the Academy— Paus. i. 29. 3; Judeich, pp. 175–6, 400–4.

πλήν γε τοὺς ἐν Μαραθῶνι, κ.τ.λ.: see note on § 1 above. Jacoby, p. 47, says "the burial of the Marathonomachoi on the battlefield is not an exception, but the rule. . . . The special honour conferred on the fallen Marathonomachoi did not consist in the place where they were buried, but in the cult which the state established at their grave." (We should perhaps bracket ἐν: above, p. 99.)

6. ἀνὴρ ᾑρημένος ὑπὸ τῆς πόλεως: he was chosen by the boule. Jacoby points out that not many *epitaphioi* were delivered by distinguished men nor were themselves distinguished. This, however, is what we should expect, in an almost annual ceremony; it does not follow that the choice of the speaker could not be significant on certain occasions, as that of Perikles in 440 or 439, Demosthenes in 338, Hypereides in 322. The present occasion, the first year of what was expected to be a long war, fought for the existence of the empire, was clearly a special one. The adverse judgement of Dionysios, *de*

Thuc. iud., pp. 849–51, condemns him, not Thucydides, or Perikles. See Grote, v. 74–75.

Cicero, *de legibus*, ii. 26, notes the Athenian custom with approval.

7. ὧδε μὲν θάπτουσιν: a clear instance to show that Thucydides is writing for a Greek, not an exclusively or predominantly Athenian audience.

35–46. *The Epitaphios*

35. 1. τὸν προσθέντα τῷ νόμῳ τὸν λόγον τόνδε: said by Anaximenes, F 24, to be Solon, and this is repeated by the scholiast here. Doubtless Jacoby (p. 39, nn. 8, 10: see above, p. 94) and others before him, are right that the originator was unknown, and the ascription to Solon is worthless.

κινδυνεύεσθαι: there was a 'risk' to the reputation of the fallen; it is not βέβαιον (see below). See i. 78. 2 n. For the exact interpretation and wording of the sentence see Stahl's adequate note.

How different is the ironical tone of Sokrates in *Menexenos*, 234 C–235 C: οὕτως ἡμῖν οἱ ῥήτορες δεξιοί εἰσιν, κ.τ.λ. (Steup is inclined to think that the opening paragraph of the speech in *Menexenos*, 236 D–E, is a polemic against the opinion about *epitaphioi* here attributed to Perikles. Not a polemic; but there are phrases which recall this speech, though they may be commonplaces. What we might say is that, if Plato had Thucydides in mind, he was determined to make his *epitaphios* as trite as that of Perikles was distinguished: hence the paradoxical or satirical attribution to Aspasia.)

2. ἡ δόκησις: a favourite word with Thucydides, but rare in other prose-writers. With μόλις - - - βεβαιοῦται cf. esp. iii. 43. 1, τῆς οὐ βεβαίου δοκήσεως.

ὅ τε γὰρ ξυνειδὼς καὶ εὔνους: corresponding, chiastically, with βούλεταί τε καὶ ἐπίσταται below, and with ὑμῶν τῆς ἑκάστου βουλήσεώς τε καὶ δόξης in § 3, though the latter logically includes the feelings of ὁ ἄπειρος as well.

ὅ τε ἄπειρος - - - διὰ φθόνον: according to Stahl, this is κατὰ μεταβολήν for ὅ τε ἄπειρος καὶ φθονερός. This is true in effect, for Thucydides cannot mean that everyone who is ἄπειρος feels envy any more than that everyone who ξύνοιδε is εὔνους.

It is always dangerous to generalize about a people, but no body of men has ever been so *conscious* of envy and its workings as the Greeks. κρέσσων οἰκτιρμοῦ φθόνος (Pind. *Pyth.* i. 85) and Herodotos' σὺ δὲ μαθὼν ὅσῳ φθονέεσθαι κρέσσον ἐστὶ ἢ οἰκτίρεσθαι (iii. 52. 5) are sayings that could be matched elsewhere (especially that of Herodotos, in its context); but, though Perikles is consciously avoiding the obvious and the trite, to what other people, on such an occasion as this, could these words of his have been addressed? Sallust, indeed, *Cat.* 3. 2, imitates the sentence μέχρι γὰρ τοῦδε, κ.τ.λ: but that is only literary reminiscence. (Cf. Lucian, de Imag. 2—Stahl.) Later in this speech itself (45. 1) it is said that envy is only felt for the living; cf. Plat. Legg. vii. 801 E–802 A; and no one could say that in cc. 42–44. 1 Perikles is careful to keep within the limits he here says are necessary to satisfy each man's βούλησις καὶ δόξα. But the Greeks, and Thucydides in particular, had a passion for covering all the ground in their generalizations, not always relevantly. Cf. i. 77. 5 n.

Professor Kakridés, in his valuable Ἑρμηνευτικὰ Σχόλια στὸν Ἐπιτάφιο τοῦ Θουκυδίδου, pp. 4–9, takes this chapter to be a particular proof of the view of Ed. Meyer, Schwartz, and others that the epitaphios is not at all what Perikles said or could have said in 431; but Thucydides' own thoughts after 404, written expressly for a humbled, incredulous, and envious generation of his countrymen, who doubted not only the wisdom of Perikles' imperial policy but the value of Athenian civilization itself as it had been created by the men of an earlier age. What Athenian, it is asked, was not ξυνειδὼς καὶ εὔνους in 431? Who was ἄπειρος καὶ φθονερός but the Athenian of 404? And how could Perikles hope to reach τῆς ἑκάστου βουλήσεώς τε καὶ δόξης ὡς ἐπὶ πλεῖστον by speaking in this manner? I shall touch on the general question again later (pp. 126, 129–30, 136); here I will only say this. Kakridés contrasts the more commonplace beginnings of other epitaphioi: the Lysian πᾶσιν ἀνθρώποις ὁ πᾶς χρόνος οὐχ ἱκανὸς λόγον ἴσον παρασκευάσαι τοῖς τούτων ἔργοις, Hypereides, vi. 2, Ps.-Demosthenes, lx. 1, Isokrates, Panegyrikos 36, and the irony of Menexenos; where there is no mention of this ignorant jealousy. The contrast is a just one; but these more ordinary orations belong to the later, disillusioned age; the unusual, the almost paradoxical sophistic of this chapter, the love of generalization, finds its place more easily in that of Euripides, Protagoras, and Prodikos.

36. 1. ἄρξομαι δὲ ἀπὸ τῶν προγόνων: so did all other speakers of epitaphioi; but in a different spirit. See n. on μακρηγορεῖν, § 4, below.

καὶ πρέπον δὲ ἅμα ἐν τῷ τοιῷδε: it is not only right in itself, but especially fitting on such an occasion as this. The next two sentences explain why it is fitting.

οἱ αὐτοὶ αἰεὶ οἰκοῦντες: see i. 2. 5–6 nn.

2. οἱ πατέρες ἡμῶν: the generation of the period of the Persian wars, say 490 to 465 B.C. They won what became the Athenian empire.

οὐκ ἀπόνως: cf. i. 70. 8 n. (esp. Eur. Suppl. 576–7 there quoted), and cc. 38, 39 below; also 62. 3, 64. 3. Aristophanes, Ach. 693–6. See Ehrenberg, J.H.S. lxvii, 1947, 47–56, who traces the idea of Herakles and Theseus, as heroes of πόνοι, from the vase-drawings of the sixth and fifth centuries to Demosthenes and Alexander.

3. ἡμεῖς οἵδε οἱ νῦν ἔτι ὄντες μάλιστα ἐν τῇ καθεστηκυίᾳ ἡλικίᾳ:
Perikles' own generation (he was now not much over 60), say of 465
to 440 B.C. "The most vigorous and resilient generation that Athens
ever produced"—Meiggs, *J.H.S.* lxiii, 1943, 33. (I would praise the
previous one and that of 430 to 400 as highly.)

The Greeks normally divided human life into three divisions only,
children, the young, and the old, and had no commonly used word
for the middle-aged. In tragedy and comedy, the contrast is between
the young and the old, two generations only, and the γέροντες may
be anything from 50 upwards (it is seldom relevant to inquire). Here
a special term is required: ἡ καθεστηκυῖα ἡλικία, the settled period
of life, say from 50 or more probably 40 (active service in the army
ending at some time between these ages: above, p. 37), to 60 or 65;
Plat. *Ep.* iii. 316 C, ἐν ἡλικίᾳ ὄντος μέσῃ τε καὶ καθεστηκυίᾳ (opposed
to σφόδρα νέου); translated by Cicero, *de Sen.* 20. 76, *constans aetas,
quae media dicitur,* by Tacitus, *Ann.* vi. 46. 2, *composita aetate.*
Hippokrates, *Aph.* i. 13, has οἱ καθεστηκότες for men of this period
of life. Plato, *Legg.* vii. 802 C, ἐκ παίδων μέχρι τῆς ἑστηκυίας τε καὶ
ἔμφρονος ἡλικίας, is vaguer; while Shakespeare's

> Youth no less becomes
> The light and careless livery that it wears
> Than settled age his sables and his weeds

(*Hamlet,* iv. 7. 79, quoted by Shilleto here) is the conventional contrast between youth and age. Cf. *Cymbeline,* iv. 2. 198–200,

> I had rather
> Have slipped from sixteen years of age to sixty,
> To have turned my leaping age into a crutch,
> Than to have seen this.

The men of Perikles' generation τὰ πλείω αὐτῆς - - - ἐπηυξήσαμεν:
which means not that they had increased the extent of Athenian
rule (except to a small degree as by the conquest of Aigina and
Naύpaktos), which would contradict ὅσην ἔχομεν ἀρχήν above, as
well as the facts, but that they had strengthened and consolidated
it and so made the city ἐς πόλεμον καὶ ἐς εἰρήνην αὐταρκεστάτην, by
the increase of the army and the navy and the various measures of
organization referred to in vol. i, pp. 470–85. Cf. above, 11. 1, 6 nn.
In i. 89. 1 the whole effort of both generations is described in the
words ἐν οἷς ηὐξήθησαν.

Note also that 'our fathers' generation' is Kimon's; their actions
and policy were in no way different from that of Perikles' own day.
All alike contributed to build the empire. See below, pp. 128–9.

αὐταρκεστάτην: this does not imply any degree of 'self-sufficiency',
in the sense of Athens, or even the empire, supplying all its own
needs. On the contrary, Athens imported freely from abroad, and

was proud of the fact (38. 2), and was particularly dependent on wheat and timber from outside the empire (from Egypt, the Kimmerian Bosporos, and Macedonia). But it was in a position to get all that it needed, both by its industry and commerce and its military power; especially the latter, according to Ps.-Xen. 2. 11. See below, 41. 4 n.

4. μακρηγορεῖν ἐν εἰδόσιν οὐ βουλόμενος ἐάσω: it is obvious that Thucydides would not wish to repeat either the story of the Persian wars which Herodotos had given and which he therefore passes over in i. 89–118 or the later events which he has himself there recounted (cf., with Classen, ἤλθομεν ἐπ᾽ αὐτά here and ἦλθον ἐπὶ τὰ πράγματα, i. 89. 1); but it is also in accordance with the tone of the speech that Perikles should omit them, just as he omits the glories of Athens in the mythical period which play a prominent part in other epitaphioi, and in Isokrates' *Panegyrikos*. Thucydides allows other Athenian speakers to boast of Marathon and Salamis (i. 73. 2–3, vi. 82–83).

Bodin, in his article on Isokrates and Thucydides in *Mélanges Glotz*, p. 94, would go much farther: he says that what is omitted here is, firstly, the heroic age (Herakleidai, Adrastos, etc.), "domaine des poètes, qui doit rester interdit à l'histoire", and, secondly, the Persian and subsequent wars which he has already given in the Athenian speech at Sparta in book i; add these and we should have the conventional *epitaphios* of *Menexenos*, of Lysias, Ps.-Demosthenes, and, in part, Hypereides. "Cet épitaphios que Thucydide ne nous a pas donné, mais qu'il exquissait tout en le démembrant, il semble bien qu'Isocrate s'en soit inspiré et assez fortement en composant la première partie de son *Panégyrique*." On which, however, one must remark (1) that Thucydides did not reject the heroic age as mythical; and (2) that the *result* in him is not at all like the conventional funeral speech. The 'dismemberment', and the giving of so important a part to the Athenian speech at Sparta, spoken as it was in that context and in that tone, make all the difference.

Of course ὧν τὰ κατὰ πολέμους ἔργα refers to the whole previous history of Athens, or as much of it as we may suppose that Thucydides thought relevant (the Amazons? Kodros? etc.); but so also do the ἐπιτήδευσις, the πολιτεία, and the τρόποι belong to the past of Athens, as well as to the present—they do not represent only the particular contribution of 450 to 430, as Kakridés argues. Certainly Solon, perhaps Theseus as well, are in mind. So in *Menexenos*, 238 C-D. ἀπὸ δὲ οἵας τε ἐπιτηδεύσεως, κ.τ.λ.: ἐπιτήδευσις means the principles underlying Athenian life public and private, πολιτεία the constitution and the methods of public life generally, τρόποι the Athenian character as shown both in personal manners and the professional life of trade, industry, art, and so forth (Steup). I agree with Steup that the difference in the prepositions here used is due to a desire for variation in expression, and has no special significance; cf. 39. 4, μὴ μετὰ νόμων τὸ πλέον ἢ τρόπων, and 41. 2, ἀπὸ τῶνδε τῶν τρόπων. Marchant contrasts Plato's denial that there were any general principles underlying Athenian public life, esp. *Phaed.* 82 A, and the famous picture of Demos' ship in *Rep.* vi. 488. We should also have in mind the fine description of the free and democratic state in *Rep.* viii. 557–8.

ταῦτα δηλώσας πρῶτον εἶμι καὶ ἐπὶ τὸν τῶνδε ἔπαινον: cc. 37–41 and 42–43 respectively.

ἐπί τε τῷ παρόντι οὐκ ἂν ἀπρεπῆ λεχθῆναι αὐτά: cf. i. 22. 1, ὡς δ' ἂν ἐδόκουν μοι ἕκαστοι περὶ τῶν αἰεὶ παρόντων τὰ δέοντα μάλιστ' εἰπεῖν. According to many scholars the following paragraphs should be more properly described as οὐκ ἀπρεπῆ only to the years following the surrender in 404 B.C.; see above, p. 104, and below, p. 129.

37. 1. οὐ ζηλούσῃ τοὺς τῶν πέλας νόμους: 'not emulating our neighbours.' This has no reference to the story that the Spartan constitution was borrowed from Crete. There are, of course, comparisons between Sparta and Athens in this speech, but not at every turn; they are to be found in cc. 39 and 40. (Cf. Π⁸ on 39. 1: ἀκ[ροβο]λίζει Λακεδαιμονίους.) Even if Thucydides was thinking of this story (which is referred to in Hdt. i. 65. 4), he knew also that the borrowing had taken place over 400 years before, and that Sparta had enjoyed ordered government ever since (i. 18. 1). If anything, he is referring to other states emulating the long-established order at Sparta.

Sparta, in her different way, also boasted that she was unique: Xen. *Const. Lac.* 1. 2, ἐκεῖνος γὰρ (Lykourgos) οὐ μιμησάμενος τὰς ἄλλας πόλεις, ἀλλὰ καὶ ἐναντία γνοὺς τοῖς πλείστοις, προέχουσαν εὐδαιμονίᾳ τὴν πατρίδα ἀπέδειξεν.

παράδειγμα δὲ μᾶλλον: I find it difficult to believe that we have any reference here to the picturesque story of the Roman embassy to Athens in 454 B.C. to study her laws (Livy iii. 31), which, if it really took place (Stuart Jones, in *C.A.H.* vii. 459, 461, accepts it), seems to have left no memories in Athenian history.

ὄνομα μὲν - - - δημοκρατία κέκληται, κ.τ.λ.: edd. have in general misunderstood this section because they have not properly analysed it, and because they believe that a contrast with Sparta is intended (cf. 39. 1, 42. 1 nn.). The main δέ-clause (μέτεστι δέ, κ.τ.λ.) must either qualify or more closely define the μέν-clause, such qualification or definition being necessary because of the inevitable ambiguity of the word δημοκρατία. This ambiguity arises from the two common meanings of δῆμος, *the whole people, the state, populus,* and *the masses,* in effect *the poor, populares* (as in 65. 2); so that δημοκρατία can mean either simply majority rule in a state where all citizens have the vote (cf. Athenagoras' statement, vi. 39. 1, ἐγὼ δέ φημι πρῶτα μὲν δῆμον ξύμπαν ὠνομάσθαι, ὀλιγαρχίαν δὲ μέρος; and Alkibiades, v. 89. 6, ἡμεῖς δὲ τοῦ ξύμπαντος προέστημεν), or the consistent domination of the state by the masses—the vulgar and ill educated, as, for example, the Old Oligarch understood democracy. This last again might be secured either by united and consistent action by the poor majority, without alteration of the laws of the normal Greek democratic state, or by an extension to the extreme limit of the use of the lot in elections to office (Arist. Rhet. i. 8, 1365 b 31, ἔστι δὲ δημοκρατία μὲν πολιτεία ἐν ᾗ κλήρῳ διανέμονται τὰς ἀρχάς. Cf. below, p. 109): instead of the principle 'everyone must have equal opportunity to prove himself worthy of office, or of giving advice to the state', we should have 'everyone is as good as his neighbour, and therefore anyone can advise and everyone should hold office in his turn'. That this distinction is what Perikles is referring to is shown by the structure of the defining μέτεστι δέ sentence, which itself is divided into μέν and δέ-clauses (for the position of μέν in such clauses see Denniston, p. 372, and G. Thomson's note on Aesch. Ag. 259–66; cf. vii. 44. 1, where it is the principal μέν-clause, which is subdivided into μέν and δέ-clauses): the former gives the general democratic principle of equality before the law of all citizens as individuals, the second, κατὰ δὲ τὴν ἀξίωσιν, gives the modification that for public affairs there is not complete equality (since in fact everyone is not as good as his neighbour), but ἀξίωσις, ἀρετή determines election to office; and Perikles then adds, as a necessary reminder, since ἀξίωσις, if not ἀρετή, so often accompanies wealth, that no poor man is barred from serving the state by his obscurity. οὐκ ἀπὸ μέρους, therefore, means, as the Oxyrhynchos commentator says, 'not in rotation' (οὐ κατὰ τὸ μέρος ἐπίβαλλον ἴσον αὐτῷ τῆς πολιτείας πρὸς τὸ κοινὸν τιμᾶται), i.e. amongst other things, 'we do not use the lot for election to important office'; it does not mean 'not from a section of the citizen body only, as at Sparta', as the scholiast here (see J. E. Powell, C.Q. xxx, 1936, 85) and nearly all edd. have supposed; which would not be a qualification of κατὰ μὲν τοὺς νόμους - - - πᾶσι τὸ ἴσον, nor of δημοκρατία κέκληται (except as in Arist. Pol. iv. 4, 1291 b 39). No one would write, 'it is in name a democracy, but office-holding is not confined to a class'. Compare again Athenagoras, βουλεῦσαι δ' ἂν βέλτιστα τοὺς ξυνετούς, κ.τ.λ., and καὶ ἴσον καὶ πλέον οἱ ἀγαθοὶ ὑμῶν μετασχεῖν (vi. 40. 1). Further, though ἀπὸ μέρους for κατὰ μέρος or ἐν μέρει may be unusual, it is not so difficult as to suppose that Thucydides wrote οὐκ ἀπὸ μέρους τὸ πλέον ἢ ἀπ' ἀρετῆς to mean 'not from a section of the citizens but from all according to merit'. See C.Q. xlii, 1948, 10–11; and, for the different kinds of democracy, compare the dry discussion in Aristotle, Pol. iii. 8, iv. 4.

ἐς πλείονας οἰκεῖν means the distribution, as it were, not so much of power, as of political activity; hence the emphasis on μέτεστι, the share of each citizen. For the use of $oἰκεῖν$ in the sense, not of 'living in a place', simply (as in ii. 17. 3), but of 'being a citizen', cf. iii. 48. 1, and 44. 2 n. Elsewhere it is something between the two, with a qualifying adjective or adverb, ii. 71. 2, vi. 18. 7, 92. 5.

A comparison with Sparta is ruled out by the simple fact that a more exact definition of the kind of democracy that prevailed in Athens is what Perikles gives; for Sparta was not, in Athenian eyes, a democracy at all.

Kakridés, pp. 24–26, agrees with this interpretation in every respect except one—he thinks that $δημοκρατία$ necessarily means 'government by the masses', by $δῆμος$ in the narrower sense, and that Athenagoras' maxim is intended to be personal to him and peculiar. I feel sure this is wrong: beside its normal use for 'the people' of any state (for Sparta, see below, p. 110), compare particularly the passage from Euripides' *Suppliants* quoted below; and both the Old Oligarch and Aristotle called Athens a democracy during that long period in which, as they assert, $oἱ ἐπιεικεῖς$ held the principal offices. Kakridés notes the 'displacement' of $μέτεστι$, as though it were to be the verb of both the $μέν$ and the $δέ$-clauses; so it is, in effect: 'the share is equal for all in civil right, before the law, but unequal in the administration of public affairs'—'we prefer that the best shall rule'.

It is to be remembered that when Plato (*Menex.* 238 C–D), and Isokrates (*Panath.* 131, 153) speak of an *aristocratic* element in the Athenian democracy, or of Athens being truly an aristocracy, and when Aristotle says that election to office $κατ' ἀρετήν$ is 'aristocratic' (*Pol.* iv. 7.1293 b 1, 8.1294 a 9), they mean strictly 'government by the best', not an aristocracy in the modern sense, which is government by $oἱ εὐγενεῖς$. Any form of government could be 'aristocratic' in the Greek sense: a democracy, if in fact the masses elected the most suitable men to office; an oligarchy, if the governing class consisted of the most suitable men to govern (also if they elected to office their own best men); a monarchy, if the monarch was the best man in the state. $ἀριστοκρατία$, that is, was not itself a form of government, an $εἶδος πολιτείας$. That $oἱ εὐγενεῖς$ thought themselves to be, by nature, $ἄριστοι$, and the rich did the same, and that none of these three writers, Plato, Isokrates, and Aristotle, thought that in practice a democracy would elect the best men (except Isokrates when he was sentimentalizing the past) makes no difference to the theory. Perikles is here speaking of the *theory* of Athenian democracy, which was also, he says, its practice. In the *Menexenos* passage Plato says expressly that at Athens the poor and obscure may be $τῶν ἀρίστων$ and are therefore eligible to office.

With $πᾶσι τὸ ἴσον$ cf. the use of $ἰσονομία$, Hdt. iii. 80 (in Otanes' speech in defence of democracy). J. A. O. Larsen, in his paper in

Essays in Political Theory presented to George H. Sabine (Cornell, 1948), pp. 8–11, notes the early use of the word by the democrats, after the overthrow of the tyranny; it was, however, as he recognizes, also used by the oligarchic party, equally the enemy of tyranny and (the more honest of them) the advocates of constitutional government, the kind of government which includes the principle, κατὰ τοὺς νόμους πρὸς τὰ ἴδια διάφορα πᾶσι τὸ ἴσον: cf. the Harmodios skolia, 10 and 13 D., Thuc. iii. 62. 3 and iv. 78. 2–3, and perhaps, Hdt. iii. 142. 3, v. 37. 2. And there is no reason to suppose that δημοκρατία was a word first created by the opponents of democratic government (R. Hirzel, *Themis Dike u. Verwandtes*, Leipzig, 1907, p. 263, n. 8; V. Ehrenberg, *R.E.* art. 'Isonomia', Supplb. vii. 297; Larsen, p. 13), or that Perikles in his use of it 'is on the defensive'; for δῆμος was a very respectable word in all manner of states, including Sparta.

It is worth noting as well that there is no reference to a 'just distribution of material goods' here (whether this justice would mean *equal* distribution or not), nothing, that is, about economic justice or economic equality. Solon, the founder of Athenian democracy, had refused a redistribution of land.

ἀξίωσιν: there is in effect very little distinction between ἀξίωσις (ὡς ἕκαστος ἔν τῳ εὐδοκιμεῖ) and ἀξίωμα below—the estimation in which a man is held and the position he occupies in his own world. Cf. 65. 8, and καταφρόνημα and καταφρόνησις, 62. 3–4.

οὐδ' αὖ κατὰ πενίαν: a further explanatory point is added, because the previous clause with its emphasis on ἀξίωσις and εὐδοκιμεῖν might be misinterpreted to imply that a poor man was handicapped.

I do not feel that there is need to alter the MSS. reading, ἔχων δέ, to ἔχων γε, as Reiske, followed by Stuart Jones and others; κατὰ πενίαν, ἔχων δέ for πένης μὲν ὤν, ἔχων δέ is in Thucydides' manner. vi. 78. 1, οὐ προδιεφθαρμένου ἐμοῦ, ἔχων δὲ ξύμμαχον ἐμέ, is not essentially different. Cf. also iii. 26. 2 n. and 40. 7, γιγνόμενοι - - - καὶ ὡς - - - ἂν ἐτιμήσατε.

For the whole of this section compare not only *Menexenos*, but, with de Romilly, p. 119, very aptly, from the nearly contemporary play of Euripides, *Suppl.* 404–8 (Theseus speaking):

οὐ γὰρ ἄρχεται
ἑνὸς πρὸς ἀνδρός, ἀλλ' ἐλευθέρα πόλις·
δῆμος δ' ἀνάσσει διαδοχαῖσιν ἐν μέρει
ἐνιαυσίαισιν, οὐχὶ τῷ πλούτῳ διδοὺς
τὸ πλεῖστον, ἀλλὰ χὠ πένης ἔχων ἴσον,

though there is a difference of emphasis in the second sentence, the meaning of which is found rather in § 3 below. See also n. on 65. 9.

2. ἐλευθέρως δέ, κ.τ.λ.: 'like free men', as Herodotos' ἡ ὑπόκρισις ἐλευθερωτάτη εἶναι (i. 116. 1, 'very much the reply of a free man, not

of a slave', though in that case the action and the reply of the young Cyrus was that of a king, not of a free citizen of a republic). See L. and S., s.v. II, $\dot{\epsilon}\lambda\epsilon\dot{\upsilon}\theta\epsilon\rho\sigma\varsigma = \dot{\epsilon}\lambda\epsilon\upsilon\theta\dot{\epsilon}\rho\iota\sigma\varsigma$; and cf. below, 65. 8 n. Perikles asserts that in Athens the important principle was observed that, though there was majority rule, there was no tyranny by the majority over individuals, either in public or in private affairs. There may be some reference to the rigidity of Spartan life here, but I doubt it; the contrast is rather with other less confident and so more oppressive democracies. See also Kleon, iii. 37. 2, $\tau\dot{\sigma}$ $\kappa\alpha\theta$' $\dot{\eta}\mu\dot{\epsilon}\rho\alpha\nu$ $\dot{\alpha}\delta\epsilon\dot{\epsilon}\varsigma$ $\kappa\alpha\dot{\iota}$ $\dot{\alpha}\nu\epsilon\pi\iota\beta\sigma\dot{\upsilon}\lambda\epsilon\upsilon\tau\sigma\nu$, and Nikias, vii. 69. 2, $\tau\hat{\eta}\varsigma$ $\dot{\epsilon}\nu$ $\alpha\dot{\upsilon}\tau\hat{\eta}$ $\dot{\alpha}\nu\epsilon\pi\iota\tau\dot{\alpha}\kappa\tau\sigma\upsilon$ $\pi\hat{\alpha}\sigma\iota\nu$ $\dot{\epsilon}\varsigma$ $\tau\dot{\eta}\nu$ $\delta\dot{\iota}\alpha\iota\tau\alpha\nu$ $\dot{\epsilon}\xi\sigma\upsilon\sigma\dot{\iota}\alpha\varsigma$; and contrast, with Stahl, vi. 15. 4, $\ddot{\epsilon}\kappa\alpha\sigma\tau\sigma\iota$ $\tau\sigma\hat{\iota}\varsigma$ $\dot{\epsilon}\pi\iota\tau\eta\delta\epsilon\dot{\upsilon}\mu\alpha\sigma\iota\nu$ $\alpha\dot{\upsilon}\tau\sigma\hat{\upsilon}$ (Alkibiades) $\dot{\alpha}\chi\theta\epsilon\sigma\theta\dot{\epsilon}\nu\tau\epsilon\varsigma$. For an obvious example we can instance the freedom which the eccentric Sokrates enjoyed; and may recall that, in this very political society, Timon was a fifth-century Athenian.

$\dot{\epsilon}\varsigma$ $\tau\dot{\eta}\nu$ $\pi\rho\dot{\sigma}\varsigma$ $\dot{\alpha}\lambda\lambda\dot{\eta}\lambda\sigma\upsilon\varsigma$ - - - $\dot{\upsilon}\pi\sigma\psi\dot{\iota}\alpha\nu$: "frustra Reifferscheid. *Coniect. in Th.*, p. 6 sq. (1876), $\dot{\alpha}\nu\upsilon\pi\sigma\psi\dot{\iota}\alpha\nu$ coniecit. Nam integram esse codd. scripturam similitudo verborum vii. 69. 2, $\sigma\dot{\upsilon}$ $\pi\rho\dot{\sigma}\varsigma$ $\tau\dot{\sigma}$ $\delta\sigma\kappa\epsilon\hat{\iota}\nu$ $\tau\iota\nu\dot{\iota}$ $\dot{\alpha}\rho\chi\alpha\iota\sigma\lambda\sigma\gamma\epsilon\hat{\iota}\nu$ $\phi\upsilon\lambda\alpha\xi\dot{\alpha}\mu\epsilon\nu\sigma\iota$ ostendit"—Stahl. This, however, is not parallel, because $\phi\upsilon\lambda\dot{\alpha}\xi\alpha\sigma\theta\alpha\iota$ by its meaning may carry a different construction from $\pi\sigma\lambda\iota\tau\epsilon\dot{\upsilon}\epsilon\iota\nu$. I think Reifferscheid was right; but Schwartz's $\langle\sigma\dot{\upsilon}\chi\rangle$ $\dot{\upsilon}\pi\sigma\psi\dot{\iota}\alpha\nu$ (cf. i. 137. 4) is better; cf. Π^8, $\pi[\rho\dot{\sigma}]\varsigma$ $\dot{\alpha}\lambda\lambda\dot{\eta}[\lambda\sigma\upsilon\varsigma$ $\dot{\epsilon}\nu$ $\tau\sigma\hat{\iota}\varsigma$ $\kappa]\alpha\theta$' $\dot{\eta}\mu\dot{\epsilon}\rho\alpha\nu$ $\dot{\epsilon}\pi\iota\tau\eta[\delta\epsilon\dot{\upsilon}\mu\alpha\sigma\iota\nu$ $\sigma\dot{\upsilon}]\chi$ $\dot{\upsilon}\pi\sigma\pi\tau\epsilon\dot{\upsilon}\sigma\nu\tau\epsilon\varsigma$, though probably it had no negative in the lemma.

$\epsilon\dot{\iota}$ $\kappa\alpha\theta$' $\dot{\eta}\delta\sigma\nu\dot{\eta}\nu$ $\tau\iota$ $\delta\rho\hat{\alpha}$: cf. 53. 1 n. Great variety in dress, however, except for a few exquisites, seems not to have been among the 'personal pleasures' of Athenians, but not because "the democracy had recently levelled the dress of Athenians to the $\mu\epsilon\tau\rho\dot{\iota}\alpha$ $\dot{\epsilon}\sigma\theta\dot{\eta}\varsigma$ mentioned by Thucydides, i. 6. 4" (Neil on *Equit.* 967–9), for the 'sober style' was a Dorian fashion. See my note, vol. i, pp. 105–6.

$\lambda\upsilon\pi\eta\rho\dot{\alpha}\varsigma$ $\delta\dot{\epsilon}$ $\tau\hat{\eta}$ $\ddot{\sigma}\psi\epsilon\iota$ $\dot{\alpha}\chi\theta\eta\delta\dot{\sigma}\nu\alpha\varsigma$ $\pi\rho\sigma\sigma\tau\iota\theta\dot{\epsilon}\mu\epsilon\nu\sigma\iota$: there can be no thought here of legal enactments ('as at Sparta'); as Steup points out, $\dot{\alpha}\zeta\eta\mu\dot{\iota}\sigma\upsilon\varsigma$ alone makes this impossible. Literally, 'bring on ourselves pains which are $\lambda\upsilon\pi\eta\rho\alpha\dot{\iota}$ $\tau\hat{\eta}$ $\ddot{\sigma}\psi\epsilon\iota$', mutually: it might happen to any citizen. $\pi\rho\sigma\sigma\tau\dot{\iota}\theta\epsilon\sigma\theta\alpha\iota$ as in i. 78. 1, 144. 1. "Il s'agit ici de ces humiliations qui, pour n'entraîner aucun dommage matériel, n'en sont pas moins douloureuses par le spectacle qu'elles présentent à celui qui en est l'objet, comme par exemple de rencontrer partout des regards chargés de blâme, et de voir les gens s'éloigner de lui" (Croiset). Π^8 again has a lucid explanation.

3. $\delta\iota\dot{\alpha}$ $\delta\dot{\epsilon}\sigma\varsigma$ $\mu\dot{\alpha}\lambda\iota\sigma\tau\alpha$ $\sigma\dot{\upsilon}$ $\pi\alpha\rho\alpha\nu\sigma\mu\sigma\hat{\upsilon}\mu\epsilon\nu$: such thoroughgoing freedom, it might be thought, would lead to anarchy; but the Athenians were saved from this by their respect both for their laws and for their freely chosen officers. Cf. Archidamos' claim for Sparta, i. 84. 3, which is more modest and (he would have said) more realistic; and another passage which comes readily to mind is Hdt. vii. 104. 4, ἔπεστι γάρ σφι δεσπότης νόμος, τὸν ὑποδειμαίνουσι πολλῷ ἔτι μᾶλλον ἢ οἱ σοὶ σέ.

This statement by Perikles is what Plato expressly denies: τὸ δὲ δὴ κεφάλαιον - - - ἐννοεῖς ὡς ἀπαλὴν τὴν ψυχὴν τῶν πολιτῶν ποιεῖ, ὥστε κἂν ὁτιοῦν δουλείας τις προσφέρηται, ἀγανακτεῖν καὶ μὴ ἀνέχεσθαι; τελευτῶντες γάρ που οἶσθ' ὅτι οὐδὲ τῶν νόμων φροντίζουσιν γεγραμμένων ἢ ἀγράφων, ἵνα δὴ μηδαμῇ μηδεὶς αὐτοῖς ᾖ δεσπότης (Rep. viii. 563 D). Aristotle, Pol. iv. 4. 1291 b 14, admits that in a democracy the law may prevail, theoretically at least, but he clearly thought that it was practically impossible in a large state like Athens, συμβαίνει δὲ τοῦτο διὰ τοὺς δημαγωγούς (1292 a 7; see 1293 a 1). Yet it was in the fourth century particularly, in the democracy that Aristotle knew (which he regarded as extreme and therefore irresponsible and depraved; and we follow him), that Athens adopted these measures, such as the institution of the new νομοθέται and the strengthening of the γραφὴ παρανόμων, which were designed to secure the rule of law, and were, as far as we know, reasonably successful. See also n. on ἢ καλῶς ἔχουσιν ἀκύροις, iii. 37. 3.

Similarly he says that the principle of election κατ' ἀρετήν (κατ' ἀξίωσιν, above, § 1) is an aristocratic one (above, p. 109); but he regards it as inevitable that the masses will not elect, in fact, κατ' ἀρετήν, and therefore law will not prevail (1293 a 10); just as Ps.-Xenophon says that naturally οἱ πονηροί will choose men of their own kind as their leaders (1. 4–6), in this contradicting Perikles on what happened in Athens. In Ἀθπ. 28. 1 Aristotle makes the conventional distinction in Athenian choice of leaders before and after Perikles (in 41. 2 the change is dated by the attack on the powers of the Areiopagos in 461); but in fact throughout the fifth and fourth centuries the men 'of good families' were ready to serve the state, most of them loyally enough, and were frequently elected to office: cf. my essay in Ath. Studies, 237–45.

δέος does not occur elsewhere in Thucydides in this sense of 'proper fear', 'respect' = αἰδώς, αἰσχύνη (cf. i. 36. 1, 84. 3 nn.); but there is no difficulty, any more than in αἰδὼς καὶ δέος, Il. xv. 657–8: Aesch. Eumen. 520–8, 693–709 (see Headlam ap. G. Thomson on 706); Soph. Aj. 1073–6; Hdt. vii. 104. 4 (above). Cf. Soph. O.T. 885, δίκας ἀφόβητος. If you break laws which you should respect, it brings (in cases where there is no punishment) αἰσχύνη. By way of linguistic contrast, easily understood, cf. Kleon's τὸ καθ' ἡμέραν ἀδεές, quoted above.

ὅσοι τε ἐπ' ὠφελίᾳ τῶν ἀδικουμένων κεῖνται: a well-known Athenian principle. Among the three most democratic elements in Solon's legislation, according to Aristotle, Ἀθπ. 9. 4, was τὸ ἐξεῖναι τῷ βουλομένῳ τιμωρεῖν ὑπὲρ τῶν ἀδικουμένων. Cf. Plut. Sol. 18. 3–8, especially the last sentence: ἐρωτηθεὶς γάρ, ὡς ἔοικε, ἥτις οἰκεῖται κάλλιστα τῶν πόλεων, ἐκείνη, εἶπεν, ἐν ᾗ τῶν ἀδικουμένων οὐχ ἧττον οἱ μὴ ἀδικούμενοι προβάλλονται καὶ κολάζουσι τοὺς ἀδικοῦντας (a principle, it is interesting to observe, adopted by Plato for his ideal state: *Rep.* v. 462 D). The purpose of Solon's law was both to end the old family and tribal system of judicial process, by which only the injured party or his kin could prosecute, and to protect the individual from misuse of power by the magistrate. In effect, ὁ βουλόμενος took the place of the public prosecutor and the police in modern states. The reverse side of the medal was the growth of πολυπραγμοσύνη and συκοφαντία; but a man who was called συκοφάντης by his enemies was called the watchdog of the people by his friends, and the honest Aristeides and Kimon, in attacking 'corruption in the state' (Plut. *Arist.* 4; *Them.* 24. 6) were equally πολυπράγμονες with Kleon and Aristogeiton. See also Plat. Com., fr. 186, the need for an Iolaos to help kill the many-headed hydra, the politicians.

ἐπ' ὠφελίᾳ τῶν ἀδικουμένων may have reference as well to the help traditionally given by Athens to the oppressed foreigner (Isokr. iv. 52; Xen. *Hell.* vi. 5. 45: *The Suppliants, Herakleidai*, etc.). If so, Perikles here touches on it without boasting, just as he passed over in silence the earlier history of which other orators made so much (36. 4 n.).

ὅσοι ἄγραφοι ὄντες: Sophokles has a wonderful stanza on the unwritten law, *O.T.* 863–70, which for him, but hardly for Perikles, was divine law; so *Ant.* 450–61. See Plato, *Legg.* vii. 793 A; Xen. *Mem.* iv. 4. 21; Arist. *Rhet.* i. 13. 2 (quoted by Jebb on *O.T.*); Isokrates, xii. 169. G. Thomson, on *Eumen.* 269–72, has an illuminating note. Another difference between Sophokles and Thucydides is that for the former the unwritten law is universal; the latter is probably thinking of Greek νόμιμα only. In this connexion compare the contrast between φύσις and νόμος as expressed for example by Antiphon the sophist, fr. 4 (Gernet's Budé edition, p. 173), though τὰ τῇ φύσει ξύμφυτα, which are opposed to τὰ νόμιμα, human custom, are not identical with νόμοι ἄγραφοι.

In Lysias, vi. 10 (where Perikles is quoted), the ἄγραφοι νόμοι are something quite different, for they are those καθ' οὓς Εὐμολπίδαι ἐξηγοῦνται. See Jacoby, *Atthis*, pp. 13, 19, and n. 46 on pp. 244–6; but I do not follow him entirely. It is perhaps worth recalling a third very different, but equally notable, meaning of 'law that is not written down'—that of the laws of 403 B.C. quoted by Andokides, i. 84–85, τοὺς δὲ κυρουμένους τῶν νόμων ἀναγράφειν εἰς τὸν τοῖχον ἵναπερ πρότερον ἀνεγράφησαν, σκοπεῖν τῷ βουλομένῳ, and ἀγράφῳ δὲ νόμῳ τὰς ἀρχὰς μὴ χρῆσθαι, μηδὲ περὶ ἑνός.

In his recent *Sophocles and Pericles* (1954), pp. 28–44, V. Ehrenberg draws two distinctions between the unwritten laws of *Antigone* and

113

those of the epitaphios, which seem to me unreal. (1) "They are not opposed, as are the unwritten laws in *Antigone*, to the decisions of the state authorities; on the contrary, magistrates and laws, including the unwritten laws, work hand in hand." But Sophokles' unwritten laws would not always be opposed by the state, only by such a ruler as Kreon and on such an occasion. (2) The unwritten laws of Perikles are Athenian. "It is the Athenian claim to have a monopoly of such laws. However general they may have been in theory, for the speaker here they are the laws of Athenian society. They, and the use made of them, are one of the things that distinguish Athens from any other state or society." This is to mistake the run of Perikles' argument, as can be seen by a comparison with c. 39: there he does not deny courage, or military skill, to Spartans, nor to anyone else; what distinguishes Athens is the combination of this courage and skill with $\dot{\rho}\dot{q}\theta\upsilon\mu\acute{\iota}a$ ($\dot{a}\nu\epsilon\iota\mu\acute{\epsilon}\nu\omega\varsigma$ $\delta\iota a\iota\tau\acute{\omega}\mu\epsilon\nu\iota$) instead of $\pi\acute{o}\nu\omega\nu$ $\mu\epsilon\lambda\acute{\epsilon}\tau\eta$; here Perikles says that Athens combines freedom for the individual to live his own life with $\epsilon\dot{\upsilon}\nu\iota\mu\acute{\iota}a$—he is not denying that other states have $\epsilon\dot{\upsilon}\nu\iota\mu\acute{\iota}a$, only that it was not the monopoly of oligarchies as was often claimed and sometimes even conceded. $\epsilon\dot{\upsilon}\nu\iota\mu\acute{\iota}a$ of course implies obedience to magistrates and to both written and unwritten laws; but magistracies may be, and were in Greece, much alike in different states, and laws, written and unwritten, might be universal in the Greek world.

In this chapter Perikles is asserting three things, the key words being $\dot{\epsilon}\lambda\epsilon\upsilon\theta\acute{\epsilon}\rho\omega\varsigma$ $\pi\iota\lambda\iota\tau\epsilon\acute{\upsilon}\iota\mu\epsilon\nu$, 'we live here in Athens as free men':[1] first, in § 1, there is no political control of the many by the few (that would be oligarchy), nor tyranny over the few by the many (that would not be our kind of democracy—*we* give men preference $\kappa a\tau'$ $\dot{a}\xi\acute{\iota}\omega\sigma\iota\nu$). Second, in § 2, there is no tyranny of the majority over individuals: there was, and is, a real danger that, as much by constitutional, lawful methods, by orderly process of debate, as by the force of a revolutionary party, the majority may be persuaded to suppress individual liberties—the right of association, of free speech, of learning, of living generally ($\epsilon\dot{\iota}$ $\kappa a\theta'$ $\dot{\eta}\delta\iota\nu\acute{\eta}\nu$ $\tau\iota$ $\delta\rho\hat{q}$), the danger that J. S. Mill spoke of: "there is a limit to the legitimate interference of collective opinion with individual independence. And to find that limit and maintain it against encroachments is as indispensable to a good condition of human affairs as protection against political despotism";

[1] I believe that in *Rep.* viii. 569 C, $\kappa a\acute{\iota}$, $\tau\grave{o}$ $\lambda\epsilon\gamma\acute{o}\mu\epsilon\nu\iota\nu$, $\dot{o}$ $\delta\hat{\eta}\mu\iota\varsigma$ $\phi\epsilon\acute{\upsilon}\gamma\omega\nu$ $\ddot{a}\nu$ $\kappa a\pi\nu\grave{o}\nu$ $\delta\iota\upsilon\lambda\epsilon\acute{\iota}a\varsigma$ $\dot{\epsilon}\lambda\epsilon\upsilon\theta\acute{\epsilon}\rho\omega\nu$ $\epsilon\dot{\iota}\varsigma$ $\pi\hat{\upsilon}\rho$ $\delta\iota\upsilon\lambda\omega\nu$ $\delta\epsilon\sigma\pi\iota\tau\epsilon\acute{\iota}a\varsigma$ $\ddot{a}\nu$ $\dot{\epsilon}\mu\pi\epsilon\pi\tau\omega\kappa\grave{\omega}\varsigma$ $\epsilon\ddot{\iota}\eta$, $\dot{\epsilon}\lambda\epsilon\upsilon\theta\acute{\epsilon}\rho\omega\nu$ is a subjective genitive, 'the slavery *of* free men', not 'to free men', as Adam and Cornford take it (the opposite of 'slavery to slaves' in 569 A); and that we have therefore the contradiction of what Perikles says here: they, the free men of Athens (or other democracy), who call all obedience, even to $\nu\acute{o}\mu\iota\varsigma$ and to $\iota\iota$ $\ddot{a}\rho\chi\iota\nu\tau\epsilon\varsigma$, $\delta\iota\upsilon\lambda\epsilon\acute{\iota}a$ ("$\ddot{\epsilon}\pi\epsilon\sigma\tau\iota$ $\gamma\acute{a}\rho$ $\sigma\phi\iota$ $\delta\epsilon\sigma\pi\acute{o}\tau\eta\varsigma$ $\nu\acute{o}\mu\iota\varsigma$", as Herodotos had said), will have fallen from that smoke into the fire of a slave's despotism.

the danger of which, more recently, de Jouvenel has reminded us. Thirdly, in § 3, we respect the laws, our freedom does not mean lawlessness, does not lead to the breakdown of the state, of society. Compare Mill again (though he is thinking of a people not ripe for such freedom rather than of freedom rotting away to violence): "a rude people, though in some degree alive to the benefits of civilized society, may be unable to practise the forbearance which it demands [Perikles' forbearance in private affairs, § 2; in public, § 3]: their passions may be too violent, or their personal pride too exacting, to forego private conflict, to leave to the laws the avenging of their real or supposed wrongs."

It matters not so much to what degree we regard this as a true picture of Athens or flattery. We must, indeed, keep in mind not only other passages in Thucydides—41. 1 below, Kleon's words and, more important, Nikias', quoted above, p. 111—not only the lives, the activities of his contemporaries, Aristophanes and Sokrates, but Plato's eloquent description of the free ways of Athens, where, like Dikaiopolis, a citizen need not be at war because the city is and a man condemned to death or exile, in a most forgiving and gentle spirit, walks the streets as though invisible (*Rep.* 558 A and 562 D–563 D especially); and the last part of *Kriton* (as eloquent in praise of Athens as are this epitaphios and Demosthenes *On the Crown*), where the city is exalted but with the important proviso, not only that the citizen whose duty it is to obey is a free citizen, with the right of speech in assembly and law-court, but that at any time he is free to leave his city, take his property, and live where he chooses. But, anyhow, the degree of flattery in Perikles is not so important: what is remarkable is the insight into the nature of political problems, and the observation, which seems to be made without effort, as though easy and natural, that those problems are not automatically solved when a democracy is established. I cannot in any way agree with the view first systematically put forward by Benjamin Constant, adopted by Fustel de Coulanges, and often repeated up to our own day,[1] that 'in antiquity' (as though 'antiquity' in all times and places was uniform) the concept of individual liberty was unknown, that the state was everywhere supreme. It was not so clearly formulated by any Greek writer as by Constant and Mill; but that is because the danger of state supremacy was not so great as in the modern world (for example, there was no danger from bureaucracy), and men were therefore less conscious of it. The other great problem of today—is it the duty of the state to provide the maximum physical and spiritual welfare for the greatest number of its citizens

---

[1] See, for example, Momigliano's criticism of Grote in his excellent paper, *George Grote and the Study of Greek History* (University College, London, 1952), p. 18. In my view Grote came nearer to the truth than Constant. (Addenda.)

with but little regard to the effect on individual freedom (and therefore on the sense of responsibility) of the means employed in the attainment of that aim?—was not present in Athenian minds in the fifth and fourth centuries; so little was the state supreme as we understand that supremacy today.[1] Indeed, as already noted, Perikles says nothing of economic equality; the problem does not seem to have been urgent; and the example of Sparta was not encouraging.

38. 1. τῶν πόνων πλείστας ἀναπαύλας: for τῶν πόνων, cf. 36. 2 n.; with the whole sentence contrast i. 70. 8, ἀπολαύουσιν ἐλάχιστα τῶν ὑπαρχόντων. Perikles, though, is speaking of recreations for the mind, the Corinthians in i. 70 of physical rest.

ἀγῶσι μέν γε καὶ θυσίαις διετησίοις: festivals from one year's end to the other, at all seasons of the year, as Ar. Nub. 298–313. Cf. Ps.-Xen. 3. 2, 8, ἑορτάσαι ἑορτὰς ὅσας οὐδεμία τῶν Ἑλληνίδων πόλεων; Isokrates, iv. 43 ff., who expands this chapter at great length. The common talk, especially in later writers, of the exceptional 'piety' of the Athenians has its origin in the number of festivals; but piety is not what Perikles has in mind. Indeed, it has been said that for him (or for Thucydides) the festivals and sacrifices only afford a rest for men's minds, and are no mark of any religious feeling; as Kakridés puts it (p. 37), απο τον ίδιο τον ιστορικό λείπει ολωσδιόλου η θρησκευτική πίστη. Είναι αλήθεια, ότι την επεμβάση του θεού στ' ανθρώπινα δέν την επολέμησε με όσην άλλοι οξύτητα· ' άθεο ηρέμα ' τον χαραχτηρίζει πολύ σωστά ο βιογράφος-του (Μαρκελλ. 22)· μιά φορά όμως στο έργο-του δεν παρουσιάζεται καθόλου το θείο. I am not so sure: ii. 53. 4 and iii. 82. 6, passages written with strong feeling, are at least very near.

ἰδίαις δὲ κατασκευαῖς: as Steup remarks, κατασκευαί may include houses as well as their furnishings; cf. 65. 2 and Hell. Oxyrh. 12. 5 quoted on 40. 1 below; but some writers at least did not think much of the private houses and streets of Athens itself—cf. Ps.-Dikaiarchos, 1, κακῶς ἐρρυμοτομημένη - - -· αἱ μὲν πολλαὶ τῶν οἰκιῶν εὐτελεῖς, ὀλίγαι δὲ χρήσιμαι. Dem. iii. 25 gives a conventional picture of the simplicity of the houses in the days of Miltiades and Aristeides (which may of course be true of that generation, though not of the later fifth century; but τὸ ἀβροδίαιτον was already known: vol. i, p. 104).

W. Schmid, Rh. Mus. xliii, 1888, 629 ff., noted the absence of any

---

[1] A good deal of the interest in reading Constant and de Coulanges today, especially the latter, is their utter unawareness of the inroads on individual liberty which the modern democratic state was about to make; e.g. the latter in his c. xviii on the omnipotence of the ancient state: "L'État voulait diriger seul l'éducation, et Platon dit le motif de cette exigence (Lois, vii): 'Les parents ne doivent pas être libres d'envoyer ou de ne pas envoyer leurs enfants chez les maîtres que la cité a choisis; car les enfants sont moins à leurs parents qu'à la cité.' "

reference to the new temples and other public buildings, and proposed to read ἱεροῖς δὲ καὶ κατασκευαῖς (cf. i. 10. 2), which he would translate "Heiligtümer und Profanbauten". This emendation Steup rejects (rightly I think), and suggests ἰδίαις δὲ ⟨καὶ δημοσίαις⟩ κ. This is better; perhaps ὧν καθ' ἡμέραν ἡ τέρψις, κ.τ.λ., more readily refers to private enjoyments; but see 43. 1, καθ' ἡμέραν ἔργῳ θεωμένους. What we might have had is a separate clause mentioning the temples and other new building.

With this expression of the *pleasure* derived from the beauty of everyday things, we may compare Plato's exposition of its value in *Rep.* iii. 400 D–401 B.

2. ἐκ πάσης γῆς τὰ πάντα: so Ps.-Xen. 2. 7; Hermippos, fr. 43; Isokr. iv. 42, 45; and elsewhere.

οἰκειοτέρᾳ τῇ ἀπολαύσει: 'we enjoy goods from abroad as though they were our own as much as our home products'; 'we make them as much our own'. Cf. iv. 98. 3, οἰκεῖα νῦν κεκτῆσθαι, 128. 4, οἰκείωσιν ἐποιοῦντο. Classen thinks this includes intellectual goods as well as products of the soil and manufacture; but I doubt this.

39. 1. διαφέρομεν δὲ καί, κ.τ.λ.: in cc. 37–38 Perikles has been emphasizing the distinction of Athens among Greek states generally; now he points to certain special differences from Sparta. See 37. 1, 42. 1 nn.

ξενηλασίαις: for the Spartan manner, cf. i. 144. 2, Ar. *Av.* 1012–13; Xen. *Const. Lac.* 14. 4; Plat. *Prot.* 342 A–D. For the opposite ideal to Perikles', see *Legg.* xii. 950–3, a passage full of interest (Plato admits that ξενηλασίαι have a harsh and barbarous sound).

ὃ μὴ κρυφθέν: Thucydides illustrates the secrecy which prevailed at Sparta more than once: iv. 80. 4, v. 68. 2.

πιστεύοντες οὐ ταῖς παρασκευαῖς, κ.τ.λ.: this might well have been a Spartan boast. Cf. Perikles himself, i. 141. 5, 142. 1, etc.; and for τῷ εὐψύχῳ, i. 84. 3.

ἐπιπόνῳ ἀσκήσει: cf. 36. 2 n. on οὐκ ἀπόνως. For Spartan rigour, cf. Xen. *Resp. Lac.* 4. 7.

ἀνειμένως διαιτώμενοι: so i. 6. 3. Contrast Archidamos' claim for Sparta, i. 84. 4 ad fin.

οὐδὲν ἧσσον ἐπὶ τοὺς ἰσοπαλεῖς κινδύνους χωροῦμεν: there is little doubt that ἰσοπαλεῖς κίνδυνοι must mean here not dangers equal to those which the Spartans encounter, but those which our forces are strong enough to meet—"les dangers contre lesquels nous sommes en état de lutter (par opposition aux dangers qu'il y a folie à affronter de gaîté de cœur)" (Croiset). Cf. iv. 73. 4, μὴ ἀντίπαλον εἶναι σφίσι τὸν κίνδυνον. So of numbers, *well-matched*, iv. 94. 1, or of the fighting itself, Hdt. i. 82. 4, v. 49. 8. Moreover, the next sentence instances such ἰσοπαλεῖς κίνδυνοι—met by the Peloponnesians in invading

Attica (where, indeed, they are in overwhelming strength—much more than safe), and by Athenians in invading their neighbours' country. It is quite true, as Stahl says, that the courage of the Athenians is here matched with the Spartan; but that is expressed by οὐδὲν ἧσσον not by ἰσοπαλεῖς. Nor is there any special hint of caution, as though 'we *only* run safe risks': simply, in ordinary neighbour-wars, we are as good as the enemy.

2. τεκμήριον δέ: 'for instance'. τεκμήριον here comes near to meaning 'proof', a *sure* inference from known facts. See i. 20. 1 n.

καθ' ἑαυτούς: this emendation (suggested by Valla's translation, *per se tantum*) seems necessary for the MSS. καθ' ἑκάστους. Shilleto adopts Arnold's argument that "Thucydides chose to say Λακεδαιμόνιοι rather than Πελοποννήσιοι because the Lacedaemonians were particularly the objects of his comparison"; and adds, "precisely as in the late war [1870–1] we should say 'the Prussians' used their contingents of Bavaria, Saxony, etc., and not 'the Germans' ". But it is because Sparta, not the Peloponnesians generally, is the special object of comparison (ξενηλασίαις, μὴ κρυφθέν, οἱ μὲν ἐπιπόνῳ ἀσκήσει εὐθὺς νέοι ὄντες, which do not apply to other Peloponnesian states), that Λακεδαιμόνιοι cannot here *stand for* the Peloponnesians. Besides, as Stahl points out, the opposite of καθ' ἑκάστους is ξύμπαντες, not μεθ' ἁπάντων.

αὐτοί: 'we ourselves', rather than 'we without allied help' (so Steup).

4. καίτοι: the rhetorical use, connecting with the end of § 1, the intervening sections being only the proof of the statement in § 1.

ῥᾳθυμία: in its original sense, 'ease of mind', 'without anxiety and a deal of trouble' (= ἀνειμένως διαιτώμενοι above); a not uncommon use of ῥᾴθυμος, etc., in both fifth and fourth centuries: Arist. *Eth. Nic.* vi. 1, 1138 b 28; Isokr. ix. 42. See L. and S. But ease of mind can in certain circumstances become carelessness, remissness, frivolity: Demosthenes often accused the Athenians of ῥᾳθυμία, which was by no means fitted to meet the restless activity of Philip; Kleon might have used it in iii. 37, and the Corinthians could have said it of Sparta in contrast to the *Athenians* who (like Philip) μετὰ πόνων πάντα καὶ κινδύνων δι' ὅλου τοῦ αἰῶνος μοχθοῦσι (i. 70. 2–9: cf. πόνων μελέτῃ and τῶν αἰεὶ μοχθούντων here and ἐπιπόνῳ ἀσκήσει above). Thucydides liked both to experiment in the use of words, and to show the different sides of the Athenian character, or the same side as it appeared to different men or in differing contexts.

τοῖς τε μέλλουσιν ἀλγεινοῖς μὴ προκάμνειν: cf. Aesch. *Ag.* 251—

τὸ μέλλον δ'
ἐπεὶ γένοιτ' ἂν κλύοις· πρὸ χαιρέτω·
ἴσον δὲ τῷ προστένειν,

and *Trag. fr. adesp.* 324, quoted by G. Thomson there. The meaning here, however, is not so much 'anticipate trouble', as to have all the hardships of a military life before as well as on a campaign.

καὶ ἔν τε τούτοις, κ.τ.λ.: we must surely punctuate with a full stop before this, as Stahl, Shilleto, and Weidner (ap. Steup), not with a comma (or nothing), as Steup and Stuart Jones. Not only is it clear that with καὶ ἔν τε τούτοις the speaker is going on to a new line of thought, which requires a longer pause before it, but ἀξίαν εἶναι θαυμάζεσθαι is not in any real sense dependent on περιγίγνεται, still less θαυμάζεσθαι ἐν ἄλλοις. I would begin the new paragraph here, as Crawley does in his translation, and insert φημί (Steup's suggestion) before θαυμάζεσθαι. Finley, however, pp. 260-1, would keep the text, which he regards as characteristic, in one respect, of Thucydides' antithetic style—"the comparative insecurity of the whole as against the parts" (of the sentence); "Thucydides not uncommonly makes such lapses in construction"; and Kakridés agrees, p. 45. But I know no close parallel to this; and I am not convinced.

40. 1. φιλοκαλοῦμέν τε γὰρ μετ' εὐτελείας: it is difficult to be happy about this clause. εὐτελής means either 'cheap because economical, inexpensive', of persons 'frugal', or 'cheap, because of poor quality'. For the former, cf. I.G. i.² 44, ὅπως ἄριστα καὶ εὐτελέστατα σκευάσαι (of a fencing of the Akropolis, or the Pelargikon, against slaves and thieves, who would, presumably, be seeking sanctuary); Thuc. viii. 1. 3, τῶν κατὰ τὴν πόλιν τι ἐς εὐτέλειαν σωφρονίσαι, 46. 2, 86. 6; Plat. Kriton, 45 A (sykophantai can be cheaply bought); Menander, fr. 800 ('thrifty', opp. to ἄσωτος, πολυτελής, θρασὺς σφόδρα: not, as L. and S., 'paltry'), Perinth. fr. 2; Xen. Mem. i. 3. 5, οὕτω γὰρ εὐτελὴς ἦν (ἡ δίαιτα, of Sokrates); Plut. Alkib. 23. 5, ἐν Σπάρτῃ γυμναστικός, εὐτελής, σκυθρωπός, ἐν Ἰωνίᾳ χλιδανός, ἐπιτερπής, ῥάθυμος; Eupolis, fr. 189; Trag. fr. adesp. 522, διδάσκαλος γὰρ ηὐτέλεια τῶν σοφῶν (which I should suppose rather to be from a comedy; at the least to be an adaptation of a tragic line); Krates of Thebes, 12 (ap. L. and S.), Εὐτελίη κλεινῆς ἔκγονε Σωφροσύνης; and cf. Isokr. vii. 30, οὐ γὰρ ἐν ταῖς πολυτελείαις ἐνόμιζον εἶναι τὴν εὐσέβειαν, ἀλλ' ἐν τῷ μηδὲν κινεῖν ὧν αὐτοῖς οἱ πρόγονοι παρέδοσαν (cf. Lysias, xxx. 21, εὐσέβειαν καὶ οὐκ εὐτέλειαν ὑμῖν ἀνέγραψε; and Sokrates' 'economy' in Xenophon was partly illustrated by his θυσίαι, Mem. i. 3. 3). These last are in praise of εὐτέλεια, but are not like anything that we have here. For the other meaning, 'cheap because of poor quality', see Ar. Av. 805, εἰς εὐτέλειαν χηνὶ συγγεγραμμένῳ; Arist. Pol. ii. 1272 b 41; Poet. 4. 1448 b 26, οἱ εὐτελέστεροι τῶν ποιητῶν, opp. to οἱ σεμνότεροι; Epinikos, fr. 1. 4-5, κἂν τὸ τυχὸν ᾖ πραγμάτιον ἢ σφόδρ' εὐτελές; above, n. on 38. 1.

But τὸ φιλόκαλον was not pursued in Athens with an eye to economy. Perikles will not have had only the new marble temples and the gold and ivory statue in mind; but they were prominent, and anything but inexpensive, as Thucydides has already pointed out in 13. 3–5; and other features of τὸ φιλόκαλον, the πομπαί and ἀγῶνες, both dramatic and athletic, and θυσίαι, were equally noted for their splendour; nor do the private κατασκευαὶ εὐπρεπεῖς of 38. 1 and the οἰκοδομίαι καὶ πολυτελεῖς κατασκευαί of 65. 2 suggest a strict economy; cf. too *Hell. Oxyrh.* 12. 5, τότε δὲ τῶν Ἀθηναίων ἡ χώρα πολυτελέστατα τῆς Ἑλλάδος κατεσκεύαστο - - - καθ' ὑπερβολήν. Splendour in fact (μεγαλοπρέπεια in Aristotle's sense, *Eth. Nic.* iv. 2, 1122 a 18), was one of the special characteristics of Athens at this time—ἡ Ἑλλὰς - - - ὁρῶσα - - - ἡμᾶς τὴν πόλιν καταχρυσοῦντας καὶ καλλωπίζοντας ὥσπερ ἀλαζόνα γυναῖκα, περιαπτομένην λίθους πολυτελεῖς καὶ ἀγάλματα καὶ ναοὺς χιλιοταλάντους, as Perikles' opponents had said (Plut. *Per.* 12. 2); and when Thucydides wished expressly to contrast Athens with Sparta, he said of the *latter*, οὔτε ἱεροῖς καὶ κατασκευαῖς πολυτελέσι χρησαμένης (i. 10. 2).[1] εὐτέλεια ('economy') in fact seems to be just the wrong word; and it is not made easier by its other meaning, 'cheap and nasty' (cf. esp. the line from *The Birds*, which describes a picture). Edd. have tried to persuade themselves and their readers that Perikles is contrasting the good taste and simplicity of Greek art with the extravagance of the East ("avoidance of the gorgeous ornamentation that *afterwards* characterized Asianism" (my italics), according to Marchant); but τὸ εὐτελές does not mean this kind of simplicity (Stahl's reference to Plat. *Legg.* i. 650 B is misleading; it means 'inexpensive' there as elsewhere). A man who only liked a vulgar extravagance in art might be called ἀπειρόκαλος, οὐ φιλόκαλος, or ἄμουσος;[2] but his opposite was not εὐτελής. Besides, a contrast with barbaric splendour is out of place here; and those Greeks who were then acquainted with 'barbarian' art, Persian or Egyptian, had the curiosity to look at it and the good taste to admire it. In the complementary phrase, φιλοσοφοῦμεν ἄνευ μαλακίας ('without loss of vitality, or vigour'), the comparison is with other Greeks, Boeotians and Peloponnesians,

---

[1] For this reason, though τὸ εὐτελές was excellent in a fencing (*I.G.* i.² 44, quoted above), I doubt the restoration εὐτελέστατα in *I.G.* i.² 92. 10 (Tod, 51 B) proposed in *A.T.L.* ii, p. 161.

We might compare perhaps Maecenas' speech to Augustus in Dio C. lii. 30. 1 ('money no object in a *ruling* city'—after a recommendation of frugality), for the imitation of classical models is clear from 30. 3 and 5–6. Cf. also n. on 63. 2 below.

[2] The chapter in the *Ethics* referred to above (iv. 2) is worth reading in this context, but the βάναυσος καὶ ἀπειρόκαλος, who spends too much on the wrong things, is different: he is extravagant οὐ τοῦ καλοῦ ἕνεκα, ἀλλὰ τὸν πλοῦτον ἐπιδεικνύμενος: which is more closely related to what Perikles says of the use of wealth in the next sentence. The μεγαλοπρεπής is the one who knows πῶς κάλλιστον καὶ πρεπωδέστατον σκέψαιτ' ἂν μᾶλλον ἢ πόσου καὶ πῶς ἐλαχίστου; and Perikles is here, as in §§ 4–5, below, illustrating Athenian μεγαλοπρέπεια.

who would think a love of learning to be as inconsistent with courage as political discussion with decisiveness of action.

Plato's discussion of $\mu o \upsilon \sigma \iota \kappa \dot{\eta}$ and $\mu a \lambda a \kappa \iota a$, *Rep*. iii. 410–11, should be compared, and, with Shilleto, the passage in *Gorgias*, 484 C–486 C, where Kallikles attacks the study of philosophy by grown men, because it unfits them, not so much for fighting ($\ddot{a}\nu \epsilon \upsilon \mu a \lambda a \kappa \iota a s$) as for an active public life; also the outburst of Adeimantos, *Rep*. vi. 487 B–D, against Sokrates' arguments for the philosopher as statesman. It is interesting to bear in mind two of the opponents of Perikles' ideal democracy, Kallikles and Sokrates.

As Kakridés, p. 47, points out, $\phi \iota \lambda o \kappa a \lambda \epsilon \hat{\iota} \nu$ is perhaps a verb first used by Thucydides (Gorgias had $\phi \iota \lambda o \kappa a \lambda o s$, fr. 6), and $\phi \iota \lambda o \sigma o \phi \epsilon \hat{\iota} \nu$ was not old (cf. Hdt. i. 30. 3, though Pythagoras called himself $\phi \iota \lambda o \sigma o \phi o s$); so that each word may have its original significance.

2. $\ddot{\epsilon} \nu \iota \tau \epsilon \tau o \hat{\iota} s$ a$\mathring{\upsilon} \tau o \hat{\iota} s$: ABEF and Π^8 have $\ddot{\epsilon} \nu$ for $\ddot{\epsilon} \nu \iota$; and as Steup says, the additional evidence from Ox. Comm. gives a preference to this reading.

$\acute{\epsilon} \tau \acute{\epsilon} \rho o \iota s$ $\pi \rho \grave{o} s$ $\ddot{\epsilon} \rho \gamma a$ $\tau \epsilon \tau \rho a \mu \mu \acute{\epsilon} \nu o \iota s$: so MSS. and Π^8; but I agree with most edd. that this cannot stand. $\tau o \hat{\iota} s$ a$\mathring{\upsilon} \tau o \hat{\iota} s$ in the first clause means the Athenians generally, and there is no 'other class' of Athenians to oppose to them. Classen conjectured $\ddot{\epsilon} \tau \epsilon \rho a$, which is adequate; but Richards's $\acute{\epsilon} \tau \acute{\epsilon} \rho o \iota s$ $\langle \ddot{\epsilon} \tau \epsilon \rho a \rangle$, adopted by Steup and Hude, is more attractive, 'notwithstanding our varied occupations'; for the combination cf. (in spite of Steup) 51. 1, 64. 5, and vii. 64. 2.

It was one of Plato's serious arguments against democracy that statesmanship was a craft which should only be undertaken by a man specially trained, and that those busy with other things had no opportunity to learn it.

o$\mathring{\upsilon} \kappa$ a$\mathring{\alpha} \pi \rho \acute{a} \gamma \mu o \nu a$, a$\mathring{\lambda} \lambda$' a$\mathring{\chi} \rho \epsilon \hat{\iota} o \nu$ $\nu o \mu \acute{\iota} \zeta o \mu \epsilon \nu$: Hobbes translates: "for we only think one that is utterly ignorant therein, to be a man not that meddles with nothing, but that is good for nothing". It is to be remembered that $\dot{a} \pi \rho \acute{a} \gamma \mu \omega \nu$ is a complimentary term, in Athens as elsewhere, the opposite of $\pi o \lambda \upsilon \pi \rho \acute{a} \gamma \mu \omega \nu$ and (a stronger word of abuse) $\sigma \upsilon \kappa o \phi \acute{a} \nu \tau \eta s$. Perikles is saying that in Athens and in Athens alone, this compliment is not paid, simply and without further thought, to a man who abstains from political life. In 63. 3 he uses it in the ordinary way; and on other occasions Athenians did pay this compliment: Antiphon, iii. 2. 1; Dem. xl. 32, $\nu \grave{\eta}$ $\Delta \acute{\iota}$', $\dot{a} \pi \rho \acute{a} \gamma \mu \omega \nu$ $\gamma \acute{a} \rho$ $\tau \iota s$ $\ddot{\iota} \sigma \omega s$ $\acute{\epsilon} \sigma \tau \grave{\iota} \nu$ $\ddot{a} \nu \theta \rho \omega \pi o s$ $\kappa a \grave{\iota}$ $o \mathring{\upsilon}$ $\phi \iota \lambda \acute{o} \delta \iota \kappa o s$, and xlvii. 82, $\dot{a} \kappa \acute{a} \kappa o \upsilon s$ $\kappa a \grave{\iota}$ $\dot{a} \pi \rho \acute{a} \gamma \mu o \nu a s$; Plat. *Rep*. viii. 565 A, a$\mathring{\upsilon} \tau o \upsilon \rho \gamma o \acute{\iota}$ $\tau \epsilon$ $\kappa a \grave{\iota}$ $\dot{a} \pi \rho \acute{a} \gamma \mu o \nu \epsilon s$; and the Knights say to Kleon, $\ddot{a} \nu$ $\tau \iota \nu$' a$\mathring{\upsilon} \tau \hat{\omega} \nu$ $\gamma \nu \hat{\omega} s$ $\dot{a} \pi \rho \acute{a} \gamma \mu o \nu$' $\ddot{o} \nu \tau a$ $\kappa a \grave{\iota}$ $\kappa \epsilon \chi \eta \nu \acute{o} \tau a$, Ar. *Eq*. 261; which show the normal Greek, including the Athenian, usage. In ordinary parlance, that is, Nikias wanted to be $\dot{a} \pi \rho \acute{a} \gamma \mu \omega \nu$; his enemies might have mockingly said that he succeeded when he tried to shed his responsibility in the Pylos campaign; Perikles here says, almost, that in Athens Timon only was the true $\mathring{a}\pi\rho\acute{a}\gamma\mu\omega\nu$. In vi. 18. 6 and 7, Alkibiades uses the same word in speaking about Athens as a state, which is, by its nature, not $\mathring{a}\pi\rho\acute{a}\gamma\mu\omega\nu$ (cf. the Corinthians' phrase, i. 70. 9); cf. also vi. 87. 3. See below, n. on § 5. The adverb $\mathring{a}\pi\rho\alpha\gamma\mu\acute{o}\nu\omega\varsigma$ is used to mean 'without trouble', iv. 61. 7, vi. 87. 4; but in the former case, at least, with the idea 'without civil troubles' in mind, and in the latter (from Euphemos' speech at Kamarina) with a direct contrast to Athenian $\pi o \lambda v \pi \rho a \gamma \mu o \sigma \acute{v} \nu \eta$.

V. Ehrenberg has discussed the use of the words in the fifth and fourth centuries in an interesting article, *J.H.S.* lxvii, 1947, 46–67 (though I do not agree with all his conclusions about the political life of Athens). I would add two warnings: because $\mathring{a}\pi\rho\acute{a}\gamma\mu\omega\nu$ is a complimentary word,[1] it does not follow that a man could not be called $\mathring{a}\pi\rho\acute{a}\gamma\mu\omega\nu$ by his friends (or his flatterers)[2] and $\mathring{a}\rho\gamma\acute{o}\varsigma$ by his enemies (or his candid friends: see Plutarch on how to distinguish a flatterer from a friend); and, as I have said (above, p. 113), the same politician might be $\pi o\lambda v\pi\rho\acute{a}\gamma\mu\omega\nu$ and $\sigma v\kappa o\phi\acute{a}\nu\tau\eta\varsigma$ to his victims and the watchdog of the people to his followers. Secondly, $\mathring{a}\pi\rho\alpha\gamma\mu o$-$\sigma\acute{v}\nu\eta$ does not in itself mean a life of cultured leisure (as the quotation from *Republic*, above, is sufficient to show), though doubtless a man who lived such a life would, if he was inclined to defend himself, call it $\mathring{a}\pi\rho\alpha\gamma\mu o\sigma\acute{v}\nu\eta$.

With $\mathring{a}\chi\rho\epsilon\hat{\iota}o\varsigma$ here we may also compare its use in *Medea* (produced in 431 B.C.), 299, for many $\sigma o\phi o\acute{\iota}$ claimed to be $\mathring{a}\pi\rho\acute{a}\gamma\mu o\nu\epsilon\varsigma$; and Plato may actually have had this whole passage in mind in *Rep.* vi, not only 487 B, $\tauo\grave{v}\varsigma\ \delta\grave{\epsilon}\ \mathring{\epsilon}\pi\iota\epsilon\iota\kappa\epsilon\sigma\tau\acute{a}\tauo v\varsigma\ \deltao\kappao\hat{v}\nu\tau\alpha\varsigma\ \text{- - -}\ \mathring{a}\chi\rho\acute{\eta}\sigma\tauo v\varsigma\ \tau\alpha\hat{\iota}\varsigma\ \pi\acute{o}\lambda\epsilon\sigma\iota\ \gamma\iota\gamma\nuo\mu\acute{\epsilon}\nuo v\varsigma$, but in the account of the ship and its crew, 488 A–E.

$o\mathring{\iota}\ a\mathring{v}\tauo\grave{\iota}\ \mathring{\eta}\tauo\iota\ \kappa\rho\acute{\iota}\nuo\mu\acute{\epsilon}\nu\ \gamma\epsilon\ \mathring{\eta}\ \mathring{\epsilon}\nu\theta v\muo\acute{v}\mu\epsilon\theta\alpha$: here too, as at $\mathring{\epsilon}\nu\iota\ \tau\epsilon$ above, Π^8 supports the reading of ABEF, $a\mathring{v}\tauo\acute{\iota}$, against $o\mathring{\iota}\ a\mathring{v}\tauo\acute{\iota}$ of CGM, and the former is to be preferred (though the value of the papyrus's support is lessened by the fact that it omits $o\mathring{\iota}$ before $a\mathring{v}\tauo\acute{\iota}$ again in § 3 below); as Stahl says, "quod eosdem duas diversas res simul agere significaret (cf. supra $\tauo\hat{\iota}\varsigma\ a\mathring{v}\tauo\hat{\iota}\varsigma$). Nam cum hoc sensu $o\mathring{\iota}\ a\mathring{v}\tauo\acute{\iota}$ neque ad $\mathring{\eta}\tauo\iota\ \kappa\rho\acute{\iota}\nuo\mu\acute{\epsilon}\nu\ \gamma\epsilon\ \mathring{\eta}\ \mathring{\epsilon}\nu\theta v\muo\acute{v}\mu\epsilon\theta\alpha,\ \kappa.\tau.\lambda.$, pertinere potest, cum distinctione indicetur non utrumque, sed alterutrum eos facere, neque respicere ad proxime praegressa, cum quod de homine publici negotii experte iudicant adeo non differat

---

[1] Ehrenberg, p. 48, n. 9, says that in our present passage it is derogatory; of course it is not: "we do not *flatter* him, as others would." It would be more excusable to take it as derogatory in 64. 4; where, however, it is used, as in 63. 2, with a fine scorn, which would be lost if the word were not a term of praise.

[2] Cf. e.g. the gay irony of Eupolis, $\mathring{a}\pi\rho\acute{a}\gamma\mu o\nu\epsilon\varsigma\ \pi\acute{o}\rho\nuo\iota$, fr. 40. 24 (Page, *Greek Literary Papyri*, p. 208; Demiańczuk, p. 43), a passage also misunderstood by Ehrenberg, *People of Aristophanes*,[2] 109. 3: "unpolitical pansies", Page; rather, "quiet, decent sort of pansies", and *pansies* is too delicate a word.

ab eo quod ipsi faciunt ut alterum alteri plane consentaneum sit."
ἐνθυμούμεθα must here be used of those who originate proposals, distinct from those who only judge them, as 60. 6 and, probably, viii. 68. 1 (said of Antiphon). In 62. 1 it is used of the generality of citizens, like κρίνομεν here, and means 'to think of' ("which has never yet suggested itself to you", Crawley). It is a word often found in Thucydides, especially in the speeches, generally with the sense 'reflect on' or 'reflect deeply on'. Cf. Soph. O.T. 739.

οὐ τοὺς λόγους, κ.τ.λ.: in contrast, of course, to the Spartan dislike of speeches; cf. Sthenelaïdas, i. 86. Cf. iii. 42. 2; and for due praise of πειθώ and Ζεὺς ἀγοραῖος, Aesch. Eumen. 970–5. The Athenians were accused of στωμυλία, and were well aware of it (Aristophanes, passim); and Plato particularly accused Perikles of encouraging it. There were occasions also when Athenians recognized that argument was unsuitable: iv. 10. 1.

3. ὁ τοῖς ἄλλοις ἀμαθία μὲν θράσος, κ.τ.λ.: 'whereas for others it is ignorance which brings confidence.' See i. 84. 3 n., though there and in Kleon's speech, iii. 37. 3, the advantage of ἀμαθία is that it leads to discipline, rather than to courage. Plato would have, in theory, supported Perikles here, especially the next sentence, κράτιστοι δ' ἂν τὴν ψυχὴν δικαίως κριθεῖεν οἱ τά τε δεινὰ καὶ ἡδέα σαφέστατα γιγνώσκοντες. Cf. e.g. Rep. iv. 429–30. True courage is thus defined (cf. 43. 5 n.); but this does not mean that θράσος here means 'rashness' (the opposite extreme to δειλία, ἀνδρεία being the virtue which is the mean between the two, Arist. Eth. Nic. ii. 2. 7, iii. 7. 11–12), as Marchant explains it. ἀμαθία is useful (to other states); and no one would accuse Sparta, or Greek states generally other than Athens, of 'rashness'. With κράτιστοι δ' ἂν τὴν ψυχήν, κ.τ.λ., cf. 43. 1, τολμῶντες καὶ γιγνώσκοντες τὰ δέοντα.

As Kakridés notes, p. 55, this union of speech and action had been for the Greeks a goal for which a man might strive, since Homer's time, Il. ix. 443, though it was not often attained, xiii. 726–34.

διὰ ταῦτα: 'on account of this knowledge.' (Classen would have preferred διὰ τοῦτο = τὸ γιγνώσκειν; but the plural is easy, even though it is not to mean, 'on account of these pains and pleasures'.) As Steup says, this sums up the paragraph beginning φιλοσοφοῦμεν ἄνευ μαλακίας; a new idea begins in the next sentence.

4. τὰ ἐς ἀρετήν: 'goodness', a restricted sense of the word (contrast 37. 1 above); which is a little surprising here, as another and more common meaning is 'courage'. Cf. i. 33. 1–2, iii. 56. 7, both close parallels to this passage ('a reputation for goodness' in the former), and iv. 19. 2–3. In ii. 51. 5 ἀρετή perhaps means, or at least includes, courage. Arist. Rhet. i. 9. 2, 1366 a 39, ἀρετὴ - - - δύναμις εὐεργετικὴ πολλῶν καὶ μεγάλων. In view of Eth. Nic. ix. 7. 1, 1167 b 16, Plut. Flam. 1. 1–3, and similar passages, ἐνηντιώμεθα τοῖς πολλοῖς probably

means that they differ from the generality of mankind not in the belief that conferring benefits is the better way of securing friendship, but in not being afraid to act freely in accordance with that belief; or, perhaps, the somewhat frigidly written sentence that follows ($\beta\epsilon\beta\alpha\iota\delta\tau\epsilon\rho\sigma\varsigma$ $\delta\epsilon$, $\kappa.\tau.\lambda.$) was the first, or among the first, to express what became later an agreed sentiment among philosophers. $\dot{\alpha}\mu\beta\lambda\dot{\upsilon}\tau\epsilon\rho\sigma\varsigma$: 'the friendship of the debtor has a blunter edge.' $\dot{\epsilon}\varsigma$ $\chi\dot{\alpha}\rho\iota\nu$: "in gratiam, i.e. ita ut inde gratia sibi habeatur—cf. iii. 37. 2"—Stahl.

5. $\tau\hat{\eta}\varsigma$ $\dot{\epsilon}\lambda\epsilon\upsilon\theta\epsilon\rho\dot{\iota}\alpha\varsigma$ $\tau\hat{\omega}$ $\pi\iota\sigma\tau\hat{\omega}$: 'with the confidence that belongs to us as free men.' $\dot{\alpha}\delta\epsilon\hat{\omega}\varsigma$ means 'freely' in another sense: 'without being anxious always about the result, whether we reap the benefit of gratitude or not.' Note the use of $\lambda\sigma\gamma\iota\sigma\mu\hat{\omega}$ here so soon after the same word has been used to describe something fundamental to Athenian principles (§ 3).

No sentence in the Funeral Speech is loftier in tone than this, and none was more often contradicted, not only by Athenian deeds, but by Athenian words as recorded by Thucydides, including Perikles' next speech. It expresses the ideal, or one ideal, of state action, as 37. 3, $\ddot{\delta}\sigma\sigma\iota$ $\tau\epsilon$ $\dot{\epsilon}\pi$' $\dot{\omega}\phi\epsilon\lambda\dot{\iota}\alpha$ $\tau\hat{\omega}\nu$ $\dot{\alpha}\delta\iota\kappa\sigma\upsilon\mu\dot{\epsilon}\nu\omega\nu$, $\kappa.\tau.\lambda.$, expressed one ideal for the citizens within the state. Euripides, in the lines already quoted on i. 70. 8 (*Suppl.* 576–7),

> $K\rho.$ $\pi\rho\dot{\alpha}\sigma\sigma\epsilon\iota\nu$ $\sigma\dot{\upsilon}$ $\pi\dot{\omicron}\lambda\lambda$' $\epsilon\ddot{\iota}\omega\theta\alpha\varsigma$ $\ddot{\eta}$ $\tau\epsilon$ $\sigma\dot{\eta}$ $\pi\dot{\omicron}\lambda\iota\varsigma.$
> $\Theta\eta.$ $\tau\sigma\dot{\iota}\gamma\alpha\rho$ $\pi\sigma\nu\sigma\hat{\upsilon}\sigma\alpha$ $\pi\sigma\lambda\lambda\dot{\alpha}$ $\pi\dot{\omicron}\lambda\lambda$' $\epsilon\dot{\upsilon}\delta\alpha\iota\mu\sigma\nu\epsilon\hat{\iota},$

expresses this ideal as an element in $\epsilon\dot{\upsilon}\delta\alpha\iota\mu\sigma\nu\dot{\iota}\alpha$; and boldly adopts the enemy's language, the charge of $\pi\sigma\lambda\upsilon\pi\rho\alpha\gamma\mu\sigma\sigma\dot{\upsilon}\nu\eta$ (as Archidamos adopts the charge of $\beta\rho\alpha\delta\upsilon\tau\dot{\eta}\varsigma$ brought against Sparta, i. 84. 1); and it is represented in contemporary drama by the stories of the suppliant Argives and the Herakleidai (see esp. *Herakleidai*, 329–32, with 197–8 and 305–6: de Romilly, p. 121). Note also how in *Acharnians*, 541 ff., Athens, ridiculed for readiness to go to war for a trifle, is said to be so touchy on behalf of the humblest of her subject cities. And just as within the state the defence of the victims of wrongdoing so easily develops into $\pi\sigma\lambda\upsilon\pi\rho\alpha\gamma\mu\sigma\sigma\dot{\upsilon}\nu\eta$ and $\sigma\upsilon\kappa\sigma\phi\alpha\nu\tau\dot{\iota}\alpha$, so does Athens' readiness to help the oppressed anywhere become $\pi\sigma\lambda\upsilon\pi\rho\alpha\gamma\mu\sigma\sigma\dot{\upsilon}\nu\eta$ and naked aggression everywhere, $\pi\lambda\epsilon\sigma\nu\epsilon\xi\dot{\iota}\alpha$. Both Perikles and Alkibiades, in rejecting $\dot{\alpha}\pi\rho\alpha\gamma\mu\sigma\sigma\dot{\upsilon}\nu\eta$ for Athens (ii. 63. 3, vi. 18. 7), implicitly accept $\pi\sigma\lambda\upsilon\pi\rho\alpha\gamma\mu\sigma\sigma\dot{\upsilon}\nu\eta$; but Alkibiades' variation on $\mu\dot{\omicron}\nu\sigma\iota$ $\sigma\dot{\upsilon}$ $\tau\sigma\hat{\upsilon}$ $\xi\upsilon\mu\phi\dot{\epsilon}\rho\sigma\nu\tau\sigma\varsigma$ $\mu\hat{\alpha}\lambda\lambda\sigma\nu$ $\lambda\sigma\gamma\iota\sigma\mu\hat{\omega}$, $\kappa.\tau.\lambda.$, is more narrowly thought, well expressed though it is: $\tau\dot{\eta}\nu$ $\dot{\alpha}\rho\chi\dot{\eta}\nu$ $\sigma\ddot{\upsilon}\tau\omega\varsigma$ $\dot{\epsilon}\kappa\tau\eta\sigma\dot{\alpha}\mu\epsilon\theta\alpha$, $\kappa.\tau.\lambda.$ (vi. 18. 2–3), which recalls Perikles' words in his last speech (ii. 63. 2–3). Even so, this was for Athenian ears; abroad, Athens could not get away with this doctrine of willing help, and at Sparta in 432, at Melos, and at Kamarina a cynicism based on contemporary *sophistry* is adopted (though again, note the difference between i. 73. 1, 76, and vi. 87. 3-4). We may compare, too, Alkibiades' description of democracy, when talking at Sparta, with what he had said in Athens (e.g. vi. 18. 6).

There is yet a third stage, the more brutal form of the same cynicism to be seen in Kleon's speech about Mytilene. This is not inserted by Thucydides for our admiration.

41. 1. τῆς Ἑλλάδος παίδευσιν εἶναι: a yet prouder boast, but this time a true one. Hippias of Elis, in *Protagoras* 337 D (where his character is as happily hit as anyone's in Plato), is made to say that all men of science and learning are by nature akin and fellow citizens, and here in Athens they were συνεληλυθότας τῆς Ἑλλάδος εἰς αὐτὸ τὸ πρυτανεῖον τῆς σοφίας. In the epigram on Euripides attributed by many to Thucydides himself occurs the famous Ἑλλάδος Ἑλλὰς Ἀθῆναι (*Anth. Pal.* vii. 45).

καθ' ἕκαστον δοκεῖν ἄν μοι, κ.τ.λ.: 'each man individually can combine in his own person a wider activity than men elsewhere, and is quicker witted (more flexible), and knows more of the graces of life.' ἄν is said three times to mark each distinctive feature. There is government by majority, but no heavy-handed majority; each man may develop his own personality freely, and has the opportunity to do so in more favourable surroundings than elsewhere; and this development is both varied (not only has each man various attainments, but one man differs from another) and humane (μετὰ χαρίτων; without crude self-assertion): the highest of which man is capable— Perikles', or Thucydides', variation on one theme in *Eumenides*. See the fine appreciation of Perikles by Wade-Gery, summarized in *Proceedings of the Classical Association*, xlii, 1945, 7-9. The quick wits and the flexibility of Athenian minds were what Aristophanes so often spoke of. It is the ideal which Plato, because he saw, as clearly as Thucydides did, that Athenians fell in practice so far short of it, not only said was impossible, but opposed as undesirable: and though his criticism of Athens is as sympathetic as it is profound, there is only one passage, I think, in his writings, in which he allows himself and Sokrates to pay tribute to the beloved city—that in *Kriton* which begins, φέρε γάρ, τί ἐγκαλῶν ἡμῖν καὶ τῇ πόλει ἐπιχειρεῖς ἡμᾶς ἀπολλύναι; (50 C), and contains words which may well be compared with the Funeral Speech (esp. cc. 37 and 40-41. 1): ἡμεῖς γάρ σε γεννήσαντες, ἐκθρέψαντες, παιδεύσαντες, μεταδόντες ἁπάντων ὧν οἷοί τ' ἦμεν καλῶν σοὶ καὶ τοῖς ἄλλοις πολίταις, ὅμως προαγορεύομεν τῷ ἐξουσίαν πεποιηκέναι Ἀθηναίων τῷ βουλομένῳ, ἐπειδὰν δοκιμασθῇ καὶ ἴδῃ τὰ ἐν τῇ πόλει πράγματα καὶ ἡμᾶς τοὺς νόμους, ᾧ ἂν μὴ ἀρέσκωμεν ἡμεῖς, ἐξεῖναι λαβόντα τὰ αὐτοῦ ἀπιέναι ὅποι ἂν βούληται· κ.τ.λ. In *Republic* Plato confines his discussion of right and wrong almost to political virtue (esp. in iv. 428); Perikles here, though he is praising Athens, not the Athenians, does not.

There are two other great works which are brought to our minds by Perikles' words, the one contemporary—the Parthenon frieze ("In the union of common aims and individual freedom, in an order which never breaks down although constantly looking as if it would, the frieze of the Parthenon is a perfect illustration of that ideal of democracy which is expressed in the funeral speech of Pericles"— Beazley, in *C.A.H.* v. 440-1); the other, referred to above, of almost a generation earlier, the end of *The Oresteia* (noted also by Beazley in this connexion): τὸ μήτ' ἄναρχον μήτε δεσποτούμενον (696); and the words of the Furies when they have been won over to civilization,

> δέξομαι Παλλάδος ξυνοικίαν,
> οὐδ' ἀτιμάσω πόλιν,
> τὰν καὶ Ζεὺς ὁ παγκρατὴς Ἄρης τε
> φρούριον θεῶν νέμει,
> ῥυσίβωμον Ἑλλάνων ἄγαλμα δαιμόνων (916-20);

Athena's στέργω δ' ὄμματα Πειθοῦς (970); and finally,

> χαίρετε, χαίρετ' ἐν αἰσιμίαισι πλούτου
> χαίρετ' ἀστικὸς λεώς,
> ἵκταρ ἥμενοι Διός
> Παρθένου φίλας φίλοι
> σωφρονοῦντες ἐν χρόνῳ (996-1000).

The Epitaphios in fact is closer to the early fifties than to the end of the century, where so many have placed it (see below, p. 129); ἐραστὰς γιγνομένους αὐτῆς is near to Παρθένου φίλας φίλοι. But the Periklean variation lies in the aristocratic expression of the ideal: rule over others because worthy to rule (but he says nothing of the sense of duty, of responsibility, which imperialism should give rise to), courage to be both free and generous, and to face the facts of defeat as well as of victory, a determination to live more intensely than others even if, like Achilles, it means living for but a short time (ἦν καὶ νῦν ὑπενδῶμέν ποτε, 64. 3), content to leave behind an imperishable name; like Aristotle's μεγαλόψυχος, ὁ μεγάλων αὐτὸν ἀξιῶν ἄξιος ὤν (*Eth.* iv, 3. 3, 1123 b 2), to whom τὸ μεγαλοπρεπές (see n. on 40. 1) comes naturally. It is remarkable, this aristocratic ideal for the very democratic Athenians—ennobled *petits bourgeois*, a whole people of aristocrats, more impressive even than 'the Senate of Kings' (and therefore denied by the aristocrat Plato?). The contrast with the reality is seen most clearly not in what her enemies said of Athens, nor even in Thucydides' story of her words and deeds, but in Aristophanes' pictures of the *petit bourgeois*, Dikaiopolis,

Strepsiades, Trygaios, and especially Philokleon (ἆρ' οὐ μεγάλην ἀρχὴν ἄρχω;). Demosthenes' magnificently romanticized recall of the ideal will also be remembered (xviii. 203, 208), especially τοὺς ἐν τοῖς δημοσίοις μνήμασι κειμένους, ἀγαθοὺς ἄνδρας, οὓς ἅπαντας ὁμοίως ἡ πόλις τῆς αὐτῆς ἀξιώσασα τιμῆς ἔθαψεν, Αἰσχίνη, οὐχὶ τοὺς κατορθώσαντας αὐτῶν οὐδὲ τοὺς κρατήσαντας μόνους.

παρ' ἡμῶν, I think, with Stahl and Classen, means that the individual's development is an effect of the spirit which informs the whole city; but others translate 'from among our fellow-countrymen'. τὸ σῶμα is here for ἑαυτόν (contrast i. 70. 6, where τὰ σώματα and ἡ γνώμη are distinguished); and αὔταρκες is used of the individual in the same sense in which it was used of the state in 36. 3—it does not of course mean that the individual does not give anything to, nor receive anything from, another, but that he is in a position to do both. (Cf. 51. 3, where τὸ σῶμα is the physical body and αὔταρκες means 'to stand by itself'. For the strict use of αὐτάρκης = selfsufficient, see Hdt. i. 32. 8: ὥσπερ χώρη οὐδεμία καταρκέει πάντα ἑωυτῇ παρέχουσα, ἀλλὰ ἄλλο μὲν ἔχει, ἑτέρου δὲ ἐπιδέεται· - - -ὧς δὲ καὶ ἀνθρώπου σῶμα ἓν οὐδὲν αὔταρκές ἐστι· τὸ μὲν γὰρ ἔχει, ἄλλου δὲ ἐνδεές ἐστι.)

2. ἡ δύναμις τῆς πόλεως: the present power of Athens proves not only the courage, energy, and political ability of her citizens, but that their enjoyment of leisure, their pre-eminence in art and learning, their versatility and their insistence on government by discussion and democratic discussion, had not impeded, but helped the exercise of those virtues. This sums up cc. 37–41. 1.

λόγων ἐν τῷ παρόντι κόμπος - - - ἔργων - - - ἀλήθεια: cf. § 4 below, τὸ αὐτίκα τέρψει, τῶν δ' ἔργων - - - ἡ ἀλήθεια; and for κόμπος, 62. 1 n.

3. τῷ πολεμίῳ ἐπελθόντι: there is much to be said for Classen's bracketing of ἐπελθόντι, not only because there is no reason to restrict Athenian success to defensive wars, but because it is Athenian initiative and energy that is in question, not her courage in selfdefence; and κακοπαθεῖ suggests 'rough treatment' of an enemy in his own country. We expect in fact that the attack would be Athenian, as in 39. 2, and as it is in the second half of this sentence, οὔτε τῷ ὑπηκόῳ, κ.τ.λ. Certainly we must not refer ἐπελθόντι particularly to the Peloponnesian invasions of Attica (Schwartz, Kakridés): it would be a mockery to allude to Peloponnesian sufferings on these occasions.

ὡς οὐχ ὑπ' ἀξίων ἄρχεται: one, perhaps the only, justification of empire, or at least an indispensable condition of it, without which it is intolerable. It is characteristic of Perikles that he understood this, that he had that understanding of political principles which Sokrates denied him. It is once more the aristocratic standpoint.

Cf. i. 75. 1, where the statement is much the same, and the effect of it very different.

4. καὶ οὐδὲν προσδεόμενοι: as Steup points out, this use of καί with a participle after the principal verb, 'and in particular', is paralleled in vii. 79. 5; and he is surely right, against Classen and Stahl (the latter of whom follows Krüger in bracketing καί), in the view that ἀλλὰ πᾶσαν μὲν θάλασσαν - - - ξυγκατοικίσαντες is the positive complement of οὐδὲν προσδεόμενοι οὔτε Ὁμήρου, κ.τ.λ., not of οὐκ ἀμάρτυρον only—'we need no Homer, our deeds speak for themselves'. For the idea, see also 43. 2–3.

τὸ αὐτίκα τέρψει: the same idea in essence as is expressed in i. 22. 4, ἀτερπέστερον, ἀγώνισμα ἐς τὸ παραχρῆμα ἀκούειν.

Kakridés, p. 73, takes ἔπεσι to mean not 'verses' ('no Homer or other poet'), but 'words', 'fine words', as iii. 67. 6, so that λογοποιοί will be included. This is probably right (though I do not agree that Thucydides scorns either Homer or his predecessors in history). It is interesting that just below, 42. 2, Perikles says τὴν πόλιν ὕμνησα, a word normally used of poets, later of eulogists in prose: Plato, Rep. i. 364 A; Aischin. i. 133.

τῶν δ' ἔργων τὴν ὑπόνοιαν ἡ ἀλήθεια βλάψει: ὑπόνοια is 'suspicion' or 'conjecture' about the facts (cf. v. 87), ἡ ἀλήθεια 'the truth' (rather than vera earum cognitio, as Stahl translates, comparing Plat. Men. 86 A). In the case of Athens, however, the truth even surpasses report (§ 3 and 42. 2); and I cannot help thinking that Thucydides wrote ἡ ὑπόνοια τὴν ἀλήθειαν βλάψει, or τῇ ὑπονοίᾳ ἡ ἀλήθεια βλάψεται (for the middle form of the future in passive sense, see i. 81. 4, vi. 64. 1): 'the suspicion naturally aroused by poetic narrative will in our case injure the true facts.' If the MSS. reading is right, the sentence is pure generalization about poetic narrative, without relevance to the particular case of Athens and not only irrelevant, but inconsistent, for it will mean, 'but whose interpretation of the deeds (which will be extravagant) will be injured by the truth'; which is, it has just been said, untrue of Athenian deeds. Cf. vi. 16. 2, ἐκ δὲ τοῦ δρωμένου καὶ δύναμις ἅμα ὑπονοεῖται, where again the truth would weaken the conception. The use of the future rather than the present is also against taking the sentence as pure generalization. Crawley's picturesque translation ("whose verses might charm for the moment only for the impression which they gave to melt at the touch of fact") does not hide the inconsistency.

πανταχοῦ δὲ μνημεῖα κακῶν τε κἀγαθῶν ἀίδια: not 'memorials of harm done to our enemies and of good done to our friends', even with the help of the assertion that the greatest compliment that could be paid to a Greek was to say that he was able to do most harm to the one and most good to the other; nor 'of benefits and wrongs done to the original inhabitants of a country where we have settled' (in cleruchies and the like); but 'both of success and failure', as Steup, who quotes Wilamowitz: "dass die Athener bei Memphis untergegangen sind, beweist Athens Grosse nicht weniger, als dass sie am Eurymedon gesiegt haben." Cf. 43. 1, καὶ ὁπότε καὶ πείρᾳ του σφαλεῖεν; and Demosthenes' words quoted above, and Phokion's, quoted below. After πᾶσαν θάλασσαν καὶ γῆν ἐσβατὸν τῇ ἡμετέρᾳ τόλμῃ καταναγκάσαντες γενέσθαι (with which compare 62. 2), the memory of the Egyptian expedition, Athens' most ambitious and far-flung attempt at empire before 431, is almost inevitably called up.

As Dr. O. Luschnat has pointed out to me, we should print κακῶν τε καὶ ἀγαθῶν.

ξυγκατοικίσαντες: 'settled in company with our citizens;' but there is no need to restrict the reference to permanent settlements by Athens in other lands, as Classen and Steup. κατοικίσαι belongs only to the μνημεῖα, which are permanent; certainly Eurymedon, Cyprus, Phoenicia, Egypt (see vol. i, pp. 310–11) are not excluded.

In cc. 37–41 "primo loco Atheniensium civitatis instituta ita describuntur ut primum civitatis forma et vitae publicae et privatae libertas cum legum oboedientia coniuncta (c. 37), tum publicae et privatae animi relaxationes atque omnia quibus ibi frui liceat bona (c. 38), postremum rei militaris studia, quae palam ac libere exerceantur (c. 39), laudentur; deinde ipsorum Atheniensium mores atque indoles denotantur (c. 40); denique superiores laudes summatim comprehenduntur easque veras esse rerum eventu demonstratur (c. 41)"—Stahl. I would modify this by saying that in c. 39 the argument is rather that our openness and freedom, and our democratic manner, are extended as well into the military field without loss of efficiency.

Those who maintain that Thucydides composed the Funeral Speech after 404, and as an Epitaphios for the fall of Athens rather than for the dead of the year 431, as a speech which, though it is Thucydides who is speaking to us, is in Perikles' vein, in the sense that it is one which 'he would have spoken had he been able to survey the whole situation, that is, the development up to the year 404' (as Meyer wrote of Perikles' last speech: see vol. i, p. 145, n. 2), should bear this section particularly in mind: τοῖς τε νῦν καὶ τοῖς ἔπειτα θαυμασθησόμεθα—was that not only written after 404, but by a man thinking especially of the position of Athens at that time? μνημεῖα κακῶν τε καὶ ἀγαθῶν, 'memorials of failure and of success'—that must have been written in great bitterness of spirit if after Aigospotamoi, the lingering and hopeless siege, and the tyranny.[1]

---

[1] It may be noted that modern historians who think that the speech was composed after 404, yet give their account of it, whether long or short, in the

The whole tone, so proud and so confident, of this chapter particularly, as of the similar passage in Perikles' last speech (63. 1, 64. 2–6), surely belongs to the thirties of the fifth century when the Athenian land was yet ἀπόρθητος (see above on § 1); and if the speech is Thucydides' own composition and written after 404, it is a remarkable projection back to the spirit of the earlier generation. Perikles could repeat the prophecy of everlasting fame after the pestilence, when he was trying to restore the spirit of his fellow countrymen (and Nikias on a desperate occasion could echo his sentiments, vii. 63, 69. 2); but he could hardly have spoken as he does here after 413 B.C. had he lived so long. Demosthenes, indeed, could speak as proudly; and we have the fine words of Phokion after Chaironeia: 'You agreed to attend the Congress of Corinth, and you must abide by that. But do not be resentful nor despondent; remember that our ancestors too were sometimes rulers, and sometimes ruled, καλῶς δὲ ἀμφότερα ταῦτα ποιοῦντες καὶ τὴν πόλιν ἔσωσαν καὶ τὴν Ἑλλάδα.' But that was two generations after 404, when there had been recovery, and when the immediate feelings caused by the disastrous defeat had long passed.

For (though Thucydides is in part thinking of Athens as παίδευσις Ἑλλάδος) it is a singular error that Athens' fame would rest on her imperial deeds; she left no everlasting memories of her successes and failures in Egypt or Asia or Thrace or Sicily, nor of the empire whose subjects could not complain that she was unworthy of it, but in her poets, artists, and thinkers, her politicians, and, if not in a Homer, to praise her, yet in Thucydides himself: in the record of her τρόποι, her ἐπιτήδευσις, her πολιτεία. Perikles' words would suit Alexander better, and, still better, Rome, whose empire, and with it the spread of her language, law, and the concept of a common European civilization, was also the result of military conquest.

5. περὶ τοιαύτης οὖν πόλεως: the new paragraph should surely begin here.

42. 1. οἷς τῶνδε μηδὲν ὑπάρχει ὁμοίως: τῶνδε refers not simply to what precedes, as Marchant and Steup, but is 'these good things we enjoy here in Athens'. μηδέν for οὐδέν, partly through the influence of μή in the principal clause (so Stahl), partly because it helps the generalization. Perikles is thinking of the world in general, or the Greek world, which was so different from Athens, not of Sparta particularly. See 37. 1, 39. 1 nn. The μή of the principal clause is to be rendered as an imperative: 'a lesson not to think that the contest is an equal one.'

τὴν εὐλογίαν: the use of this rare word, and of ὕμνησα and ἡ κατα-

context of 431–430 (e.g. Adcock in *C.A.H.* v. 199 and 483). Their instinct is better than their reasoning.

130

στροφή below, all with a poetical colour (for εὐλογία cf. esp. Simonides' epigram on the Athenians at Plataia—if it is genuine—No. 118, Diehl; ὑμνεῖν is used elsewhere by Thucydides especially of poets: i. 21. 2), introduces one of the most elaborate, carefully phrased, and difficult passages in Thucydides. He was doubtless much influenced by Gorgias, especially in his younger years; but the general effect is different. Gorgias is rich and flowing; the river of Thucydides' eloquence is equally abundant, but is obstructed by rocks, and curious eddies are formed. Unlike the other he had something to say. Like the finest passage of all in this manner (iii. 82–83), it was not approved by Dionysios of Halikarnassos: see de Art. rhet. 299. 13, Ep. ad Amm. ii. 806. 14.

2. ἰσόρροπος - - - ὁ λόγος τῶν ἔργων: cf. 41. 3, and contrast what the Corinthians said of Sparta, i. 69. 5. ("Quodsi τοῦ λόγου τὰ ἔργα expectes, cogita in exaequandi et commutandi verbis et apud Graecos et apud Latinos nihil referre utrum uti exaequari vel utrum utri commutari dicatur"—Stahl. So μὴ περὶ ἴσου, above; and see vi. 34. 7 n.)

πρώτη τε μηνύουσα καὶ τελευταία βεβαιοῦσα: "it is a proof both when it is the first to give us information of their worth and when it comes at the last to confirm the testimony already borne by a life of virtue"—Arnold. For τελευταία βεβαιοῦσα, cf. 44. 1 n. The first half of the sentence refers to those who have fallen in their first campaign; but in καὶ γὰρ τοῖς τἆλλα χείροσι the idea is extended to those who have hitherto led not very satisfactory lives.

4. πενίας ἐλπίδι: 'hopes concerned with poverty', defined by the following clause, πενίας being used in antithesis to πλούτου. So most edd., and this may be right; there is no difficulty in the genitive of reference, for which Classen cites a number of examples from Thucydides; see e.g. i. 61. 1, 129. 3, 140. 3 (τὸ Μεγαρέων ψήφισμα), v. 74. 3, viii. 15. 1, and esp. iv. 84. 2, τοῦ καρποῦ τὸ δέος. But in those cases in which the genitive depends on ἐλπίς, 44. 3 below, i. 138. 2, ii. 89. 10, and vi. 104. 1 (of these the second is most like the present passage in construction—τοῦ Ἑλληνικοῦ ἐλπίδα ἣν ὑπετίθει αὐτῷ δουλώσειν), it always expresses the object of the hopes—of other children, of winning an empire over Greece, of having a serviceable fleet, of saving Sicily—never anything to be avoided; and there is much to be said for Göller's and Krüger's explanation, τῶν πενήτων ἐλπίδι, 'the poor man's hope' (Solon, 1. 41–42,

εἰ δέ τις ἀχρήμων, πενίης δέ μιν ἔργα βιᾶται,
κτήσεσθαι πάντως χρήματα πολλὰ δοκεῖ).

The consequent variatio in the antithesis, that is, in the meanings of the two genitives, would be as much in Thucydides' manner as other forms of variatio (cf. the two datives below, ἐλπίδι - - - ἔργῳ;

and θεῶν φόβος ἢ ἀνθρώπων νόμος, 53. 4). The difficulty in this is αὐτήν in the next clause, as Steup points out (we might have had αὐτό, if Thucydides had written τῶν πενήτων; αὐτῶν below is probably neuter); but this is not decisive. 'Poverty's hope' is a vivid phrase that we might expect in this speech.

Ἐλπίς was often to the Greeks something which led men astray, into wrong paths: cf. e.g. iii. 45. 5. But not always: not, for example, just below and i. 43. 6; nor in Eur. Herakles, 105–6.

διαφυγὼν αὐτήν: cf. μὴ διαφεύγειν ἔργῳ αἴσχιον, 40. 1.

ποθεινοτέραν αὐτῶν λαβόντες: ποθεινός is a strong word, with a poetical colouring, 'something to be longed for'. λαβόντες for ὑπολαβόντες.

μετ' αὐτοῦ τοὺς μὲν τιμωρεῖσθαι τῶν δὲ ἐφίεσθαι: so MSS. and Dion. Hal., and of recent editors Steup and Stuart Jones; ἀφίεσθαι conj. Poppo, and this was adopted by Stahl, Croiset, and Hude. I believe the conjecture to be right. First, when we have μέν - - - δέ-clauses, either the two are of equal weight, or, if one is subordinate to the other, it is the μέν-clause, almost always, which is subordinate to the δέ-clause, not vice versa (Solon, 1. 7–8, χρήματα δ' ἱμείρω μὲν ἔχειν, ἀδίκως δὲ πεπᾶσθαι οὐκ ἐθέλω, and cf. e.g. the closely parallel ἀσφαλεστέραν μὲν εὔχεσθαι, κ.τ.λ., 43. 1, with n. there; iv. 126. 4 n.; and Jebb's note on O.T. 673–4); we cannot therefore translate 'though they aim at the retention or gaining of wealth, they determined to resist the enemy', nor as if we had τοὺς πολεμίους τιμωρησάμενοι τούτων ἐφίεσθαι, which is what Marchant does. Secondly, the order of the words makes it clear that μετ' αὐτοῦ (μετὰ τοῦδε τοῦ καλλίστου κινδύνου) is to be taken with the second clause as with the first; which has little sense if we read ἐφίεσθαι. In any case it would be contradictory as well as tasteless, after asserting that both rich and poor have abjured the charms of wealth, to add that in their last fight it was still their aim. Steup argues that Perikles does not say that they had absolutely abjured wealth, but only preferred a brave stand on the battlefield (which they might have survived). True: but what difference does that make? For ἀφίεσθαι, cf. 60. 4 and Dem. xxxvii. 1.

τὸ ἀφανὲς τοῦ κατορθώσειν: this, it is necessary to explain, is success in the battle with the enemy and their own survival, not in becoming rich in private life. Cf. Plat. Gorgias, 512 E, οὐ φιλοψυχητέον, ἀλλ' ἐπιτρέψαντα περὶ τούτων τῷ θεῷ - - - τὸ ἐπὶ τούτῳ σκεπτέον; and for κατορθώσειν, Dem. xviii. 208 quoted above, p. 127.

καὶ ἐν αὐτῷ, κ.τ.λ.; the general sense is clear; but the MSS. readings differ, and edd. are not agreed on the construction of the sentence. τῷ before ἀμύνεσθαι CG¹ and Dion. Hal. in his quotation; τό cett. τό before ἐνδόντες codd.; om. Dion. Hal. (the latter also omits καί before παθεῖν, which is probably only a slip by the copyist; that is, the

MSS. of Diónysios are no better evidence of what *he* wrote than those of Thucydides for *him*). If we keep the majority readings, $\tau\grave{o}$ - - - $\tau\grave{o}$, and take $\dot{\epsilon}\nu\ a\dot{v}\tau\hat{\wp} = \dot{\epsilon}\nu\ \tau\hat{\wp}\ \kappa\iota\nu\delta\acute{v}\nu\wp$, we have an awkward combination of present and aorist in $\dot{a}\mu\acute{v}\nu\epsilon\sigma\theta a\iota\ \kappa a\grave{\iota}\ \pi a\theta\epsilon\hat{\iota}\nu$ (emended by Herwerden to $\dot{a}\mu\acute{v}\nu a\sigma\theta a\iota$, apparently after one MS. of Dion. Hal.); and a difficult construction after $\dot{\eta}\gamma\eta\sigma\acute{a}\mu\epsilon\nu o\iota$. The latter may perhaps have a 'pregnant' meaning, as $o\check{\iota}\epsilon\sigma\theta a\iota$ and $\nu o\mu\acute{\iota}\zeta\epsilon\iota\nu$ often have, 'think it right to' (see Stahl's note); but $\tau\acute{o}$ with the infinitive after $\dot{\eta}\gamma\epsilon\hat{\iota}\sigma\theta a\iota$ in this sense seems impossible—Arnold's comparison of 53. 3 below, $\tau\grave{o}\ \pi\rho o\sigma\tau a\lambda a\iota\pi\omega\rho\epsilon\hat{\iota}\nu$ - - - $o\dot{v}\delta\epsilon\grave{\iota}s\ \pi\rho\acute{o}\theta\nu\mu os\ \mathring{\eta}\nu$, is clearly irrelevant. Hence the conjectures $\kappa\acute{a}\lambda\lambda\iota o\nu$ for $\mu\hat{a}\lambda\lambda o\nu$ (Dobree, adopted by Classen, Steup, and Croiset), and $\mathring{\eta}\rho\eta\mu\acute{\epsilon}\nu o\iota$ for $\dot{\eta}\gamma\eta\sigma\acute{a}\mu\epsilon\nu o\iota$ (Weil). If we accept $\dot{\epsilon}\nu\ a\dot{v}\tau\hat{\wp}\ \tau\hat{\wp}\ \dot{a}\mu\acute{v}\nu\epsilon\sigma\theta a\iota$ and bracket the second $\tau\acute{o}$, either of these conjectures, or $\langle\delta\epsilon\hat{\iota}\nu\rangle$ after $\pi a\theta\epsilon\hat{\iota}\nu$ (suggested by Classen and adopted by Hude), is possible; or we must take $\dot{\eta}\gamma\eta\sigma\acute{a}\mu\epsilon\nu o\iota$ in its pregnant sense (Stahl, Stuart Jones), which is preferable. There would appear to be some weight in Steup's objection that Thucydides, who immediately below writes $\ddot{o}\sigma a\ \dot{\epsilon}\nu\ \tau\hat{\wp}\ \tau o\grave{v}s\ \pi o\lambda\epsilon\mu\acute{\iota}o\nu s\ \dot{a}\mu\acute{v}\nu\epsilon\sigma\theta a\iota\ \dot{a}\gamma a\theta\grave{a}\ \check{\epsilon}\nu\epsilon\sigma\tau\iota\nu$, is unlikely to have included $\dot{\epsilon}\nu\delta\acute{o}\nu\tau\epsilon s\ \sigma\acute{\wp}\zeta\epsilon\sigma\theta a\iota$ as a possibility within the sphere of $\tau\grave{o}\ \dot{a}\mu\acute{v}\nu\epsilon\sigma\theta a\iota$—cf. v. 10. 9, where $\dot{a}\mu\acute{v}\nu\epsilon\sigma\theta a\iota$ and $\dot{\epsilon}\nu\delta o\hat{\nu}\nu a\iota$ are opposed to one another. But $\dot{\epsilon}\nu\ a\dot{v}\tau\hat{\wp}\ \tau\hat{\wp}\ \dot{a}$. may mean 'in the moment of action'.

Classen makes clear the direction of ideas in this paragraph: (1) $o\dot{v}\kappa$ - - - $\dot{a}\nu a\beta o\lambda\dot{\eta}\nu\ \tau o\hat{v}\ \delta\epsilon\iota\nu o\hat{v}\ \dot{\epsilon}\pi o\iota\acute{\eta}\sigma a\nu\tau o$, (2) $\dot{\epsilon}\beta o\nu\lambda\acute{\eta}\theta\eta\sigma a\nu\ \mu\epsilon\tau\grave{a}\ \tau o\hat{v}\ \kappa\iota\nu\delta\acute{v}\nu o\nu\ \tau o\grave{v}s\ \dot{\epsilon}\nu a\nu\tau\acute{\iota}o\nu s\ \tau\iota\mu\omega\rho\epsilon\hat{\iota}\sigma\theta a\iota$, (3) $\dot{\epsilon}\nu\ a\dot{v}\tau\hat{\wp}\ (\tau\hat{\wp}\ \kappa\iota\nu\delta\acute{v}\nu\wp$, or $\dot{\epsilon}\nu\ a.\ \tau.\ \dot{a}\mu\acute{v}\nu\epsilon\sigma\theta a\iota)$ - - - $\tau\grave{o}\ a\check{\iota}\sigma\chi\rho\grave{o}\nu\ \check{\epsilon}\phi\nu\gamma o\nu,\ \tau\grave{o}\ \delta'\ \check{\epsilon}\rho\gamma o\nu\ \dot{v}\pi\acute{\epsilon}\mu\epsilon\iota\nu a\nu$, and (4) $\delta\iota'\ \dot{\epsilon}\lambda a\chi\acute{\iota}\sigma\tau o\nu\ \kappa a\iota\rho o\hat{v}$ - - - $\dot{a}\pi\eta\lambda\lambda\acute{a}\gamma\eta\sigma a\nu$.

$\tau\grave{o}\ \mu\grave{\epsilon}\nu\ a\check{\iota}\sigma\chi\rho\grave{o}\nu\ \tau o\hat{v}\ \lambda\acute{o}\gamma o\nu\ \check{\epsilon}\phi\nu\gamma o\nu,\ \tau\grave{o}\ \delta'\ \check{\epsilon}\rho\gamma o\nu\ \tau\hat{\wp}\ \sigma\acute{\omega}\mu a\tau\iota\ \dot{v}\pi\acute{\epsilon}\mu\epsilon\iota\nu a\nu$ is a conceit typical of Gorgias' manner. Cf. above, n. on § 1. It is certainly on the whole more likely that Gorgias' direct influence on Thucydides' style was strong in the twenties rather than later; and so far this is an argument for early composition of the Epitaphios. Without the mannerism Demosthenes, vi. 8, has $\tau\dot{\eta}\nu\ \pi\rho o\sigma o\hat{v}\sigma a\nu\ \dot{a}\delta o\xi\acute{\iota}a\nu\ \tau\hat{\wp}\ \pi\rho\acute{a}\gamma\mu a\tau\iota\ \phi\epsilon\acute{v}\gamma o\nu\tau\epsilon s$.

$\delta\iota'\ \dot{\epsilon}\lambda a\chi\acute{\iota}\sigma\tau o\nu\ \kappa a\iota\rho o\hat{v},\ \kappa.\tau.\lambda.$: most edd. take $\tau\acute{v}\chi\eta s$ with $\kappa a\iota\rho o\hat{v}$ (e.g. *brevissimo fortunae momento*, Stahl), $\ddot{a}\mu a\ \dot{a}\kappa\mu\hat{\eta}$ with $\tau\hat{\eta}s\ \delta\acute{o}\xi\eta s\ \mu\hat{a}\lambda\lambda o\nu\ \mathring{\eta}\ \tau o\hat{v}\ \delta\acute{\epsilon}o\nu s$, and $\dot{a}\pi\eta\lambda\lambda\acute{a}\gamma\eta\sigma a\nu$ absolutely, with an effective poetical use of the word, without $\tau o\hat{v}\ \beta\acute{\iota}o\nu$, as Eur. *Herakleid*. 1000 (cf. n. on $\tau\dot{\eta}\nu\ \epsilon\dot{v}\lambda o\gamma\acute{\iota}a\nu$, § 1, above), to close the period. If this is right, $\ddot{a}\mu a\ \dot{a}\kappa\mu\hat{\eta},\ \kappa.\tau.\lambda.$, must mean 'at the height of their glory and not of their fear', as in the imitations of Dio Cassius, lxvi. 18. 5, $\dot{\epsilon}\nu\ \dot{a}\kappa\mu\hat{\eta}\ \tau\hat{\eta}s\ \delta\acute{o}\xi\eta s\ \dot{a}\pi\acute{\epsilon}\theta a\nu o\nu$, and of Arrian, *Anab*. vii. 16. 11, $\dot{\epsilon}\nu\ \dot{a}\kappa\mu\hat{\eta}\ \tau\hat{\eta}s\ \tau\epsilon\ \ddot{a}\lambda\lambda\eta s\ \delta\acute{o}\xi\eta s\ \kappa a\grave{\iota}\ \tau o\hat{v}\ \pi\acute{o}\theta o\nu\ \tau o\hat{v}\ \pi a\rho'\ \dot{a}\nu\theta\rho\acute{\omega}\pi\omega\nu\ \dot{a}\pi\eta\lambda\lambda\acute{a}\chi\theta a\iota$, cited by Stahl (as he says "eo tantum Thucydides ab imitatoribus differt quod $\dot{a}\kappa\mu\dot{\eta}\nu\ \tau\hat{\eta}s\ \delta\acute{o}\xi\eta s$ non dicit maximam quam habent, sed maximam quam fortiter mortem obeuntes sibi parant gloriam"); not, as Marchant, "at the crisis not of fear but of glory"; nor 'at the height of their expectations, hopes'. I am, however, very doubtful about this. (1) The rhythm of the sentence seems to demand a pause at καιροῦ and that τύχης ἅμα ἀκμῇ be taken together, and therefore τῆς δόξης and τοῦ δέους with ἀπηλλάγησαν. (2) I can see no real sense in ἐλάχιστος καιρὸς τύχης: 'a brief opportunity for fortune to seize'? cf. ἔργου καιρός in 40. 1, 43. 2. Apart from other objections, fortune can at any time destroy a man at the shortest notice (cf. Hdt. i. 32. 4). Croiset's interpretation—τύχης governed by διά and καιροῦ dependent on it, "par le hasard d'un instant"—is hardly in the Greek. (3) It is a very poor compliment to a man who has chosen to stand against the enemy, who trusts to his own valour in the moment of fighting, who prefers death to surrender and has 'run away from' τὸ αἰσχρὸν τοῦ λόγου, to say that he was not at the extreme point of fear when he died. Herwerden, in adopting the easy solution of bracketing μᾶλλον ἢ τοῦ δέους, at least perceived a major difficulty; and Dio Cassius and Arrian carefully avoided it. If a contrast to τῆς δόξης is required, it should be 'their good fortune' or 'their hopes', not their fears (cf. ἀσφαλεστέραν μὲν εὔχεσθαι, 43. 1, and μετὰ κοινῆς ἐλπίδος, 43. 6). On the other hand, if my analysis of the sentence is right, with τύχης ἅμα ἀκμῇ meaning 'at the turning point of fortune', we should have to transpose τῆς δόξης and τοῦ δέους, 'they rid themselves of their fear though not of their glory'. Cf. the Lysian epitaphios, 15, τὰ μὲν σώματα εἰς ἄδειαν κατέστησαν, ἀπαλλάξαντες δὲ τοῦ δέους καὶ τὰς ψυχὰς ἠλευθέρωσαν. ἀπαλλαγῆναι is consistently used with a genitive by Thucydides in the sense 'get quit of' something undesirable; for a close parallel to this passage, see viii. 106. 2, ἀπηλλάγησαν τοῦ σφᾶς τε αὐτοὺς καταμέμφεσθαι καὶ τοὺς πολεμίους ἔτι ἀξίους του ἐς τὰ ναυτικὰ νομίζειν; or iv. 61. 7, τάχιστα δ' ἂν ἀπαλλαγὴ αὐτοῦ (sc. τοῦ κοινῶς φοβεροῦ) γένοιτο; cf. Soph. El. 783, ἀπηλλάγην φόβου. In the perfect, i. 143. 3, ὧνπερ ἐκείνοις ἐμεμψάμην ἀπηλλάχθαι (cf. i. 138. 3; and Hdt. i. 60. 3, εὐηθίης ἠλιθίου ἀπηλλαγμένον), iii. 63. 4, αἰσχύνης ἀπηλλαγμένην. With more concrete objects it is of course common: δουλείας, iv. 87. 3, ξυμφορῶν, i. 122. 4, τοῦ κινδύνου, vii. 53. 4, Κλέωνος, iv. 28. 5. The only certain instance of the verb being used absolutely in Thucydides is, I think, viii. 83. 3, ἀπαλλάξεται ὅθεν τροφὴν ἕξει, 'get away from here to where they will find supplies'. But it must be admitted that, with the MSS. of Dionysios supporting those of Thucydides, and with the later imitators taking ἀκμῇ with δόξης, the difficulties in the way of the suggestion to transpose τῆς δόξης and τοῦ δέους are obvious.

My interpretation is in general accord with Arnold's, who, however, thought it could be maintained without any alteration of the text such as would seem to me necessary: " 'were taken away from what was their glory rather than their fear'; i.e. 'Death found them not dreading his approach, fearful and miserable, but in the height of their glory; for the battlefield was not their terror but their glory'." 'They have gone from their field of glory, not of fear.' So also L. and S. But I am doubtful if this is possible. Crawley's more faithful translation shows the difficulty very clearly: "escaped, not from their fear, but from their glory."

L. Pearson, in his discussion of this whole passage, $A.J.P.$ lxiv, 1943, 399–404, takes the last sentence in the main as I do, and for ἀκμή compares vii. 14. 1, βραχεῖα ἀκμὴ πληρώματος, and Soph. $El.$ 22,

$$ἵν' οὐκέτ' ὀκνεῖν καιρός, ἀλλ' ἔργων ἀκμή$$

and 1337–8,

$$τὸ μὲν μέλλειν κακὸν$$
$$ἐν τοῖς τοιούτοις ἔστ', ἀπηλλάχθαι δ' ἀκμή.$$

But though he says, rightly, that ἀπαλλάττεσθαι with the genitive means 'ridding oneself of something unpleasant', and compares the Lysian phrase ἀπαλλάξαντες τοῦ δέους, he thinks the MSS. text can stand and be given the meaning 'they escaped ill-repute rather than the terror of death'. This I cannot understand (apart from the quite unexampled use of δόξα); for they did escape the terror of death.[1]

43. 1. προσηκόντως τῇ πόλει: still continuing the combined praise of men and city begun in 41. 5 and developed in 42. 1–2.
ἀσφαλεστέραν: boldly used, though only in anticipation, with τὴν διάνοιαν—'that the spirit in which they face the enemy may not be so fatal in its result'. With ἀσφαλεστέραν μὲν εὔχεσθαι, ἀτολμοτέραν δὲ μηδὲν - - - τὴν - - - διάνοιαν ἔχειν, cf. Soph. $Ajax$, 550–1:

$$ὦ παῖ, γένοιο πατρὸς εὐτυχέστερος,$$
$$τὰ δ' ἄλλ' ὁμοῖος· καὶ γένοι' ἂν οὐ κακός.$$

With this contrast $O.T.$ 1512–4:

$$νῦν δὲ τοῦτ' εὔχεσθέ μοι,$$
$$οὗ καιρὸς αἰεὶ ζῆν, βίου δὲ λῴονος$$
$$ὑμᾶς κυρῆσαι τοῦ φυτεύσαντος πατρός.$$

In $Oedipus$ (after such misfortune as his) a more fortunate life than their father's is the important thing for Antigone and Ismene; in $Ajax$, as here in Perikles' speech, it is less important than the courage with which life's incidents must be borne. (Cf. n. on μετ' αὐτοῦ, κ.τ.λ., 42. 4.)

The exhortation begins: first of the citizens in general, which is

---

[1] Line 3 of the epigram on the dead at Chaironeia, quoted by Demosthenes, xviii. 289, is corrupt (Wilamowitz, $Sappho\ u.\ Simonides$, 214); or it might have helped us, with its mention of ἀρετή and δεῖμα, to an understanding of this passage.

closely linked with the praise of the city and of the fallen which has preceded, then (cc. 44–45) of the relatives.

σκοποῦντας μὴ λόγῳ μόνῳ - - -, ἀλλὰ - - - ἔργῳ θεωμένους: another variation of the so frequently used antithesis of λόγος and ἔργον. ἔργῳ here = οἷα ἔργῳ ἐστὶν ἡ τῆς πόλεως δύναμις, not action by the citizens themselves. "Il ne s'agit pas de *comprendre* seulement d'une manière abstraîte, grâce à des discours et à des raisonnements, l'utilité de défendre sa patrie; il faut que le spectacle quotidien de cette patrie vivante et concrète fasse passer cette conviction de l'esprit dans les entrailles et dans le cœur, et la transforme en un véritable amour"—Croiset.

I should prefer to read τίς ἄν for ἄν τις, rather than τί ἄν τις or ἄν τί τις, as some have conjectured.

This idealistic passage, καθ' ἡμέραν θεωμένους καὶ ἐραστὰς γιγνο-μένους αὐτῆς, is illustrated by the ode in *Medea*, 824 ff.,

> Ἐρεχθεῖδαι τὸ παλαιὸν ὄλβιοι
> καὶ θεῶν παῖδες μακάρων, ἱερᾶς
> χώρας ἀπορθήτου τ' ἄπο, κ.τ.λ.

(where, however, χώρας ἀπορθήτου, in a play produced in the spring of 431 B.C., when men were preparing the great migration from the country to safety within the walls, is ominous), by the famous Kolonos ode in *O.C.*, and, perhaps best of all, by Aristophanes in *The Clouds*, 299–313, παρθένοι ὀμβροφόροι, which recalls much in cc. 37 and 38 as well. Perikles is indeed here lauding the power of Athens rather than her beauty and wisdom; but that power is accompanied by, and in part dependent on, her love of beauty and wisdom. And, with its note on δύναμις, was this passage also written after 404 B.C. and with the conditions of that time in mind? Remember, too, that Aristophanes mocks the use of ἐραστής in politics, *Ach.* 143, *Equit.* 732, 1340–4; the last is particularly interesting,

> πρῶτον μέν, ὁπότ' εἴποι τις ἐν τἠκκλησίᾳ,
> ὦ Δῆμ', ἐραστής τ' εἰμι σὸς φιλῶ τέ σε,
> καὶ κήδομαί σου καὶ προβουλεύω μόνος,
> τούτοις ὁπότε χρήσαιτό τις προοιμίοις,
> ἀνωρτάλιζες κἀκερουτίας,

for it is on all fours with the ἰοστέφανοι and λιπαραί passage in *Acharnians*, 637–40, and suggests, as Neil pointed out, that someone had made the use popular; and who more likely than Perikles? If it was not Perikles, was Thucydides guilty of attributing to him what belonged to someone else; and was he thinking out in 404 what had already been uttered about 430? If it was Perikles, then it was a phrase that was remembered, and Thucydides, keeping as closely

136

as possible to the general sense of what had actually been said, was able to incorporate it within his own rewriting of the speech.

Aeschylus, *Eumen.* 851–2, had perhaps given the first impetus (Athena to the Furies):

$$\text{ὑμεῖς δ' ἐς ἀλλόφυλον ἐλθοῦσαι χθόνα}$$
$$\text{γῆς τῆσδ' ἐρασθήσεσθε.}$$

Plato later refers to the phrase, *Alkib.* 132 A, τοῦτο γὰρ δὴ μάλιστα ἐγὼ φοβοῦμαι μὴ δημεραστὴς ἡμῖν γενόμενος διαφθαρῇς· πολλοὶ γὰρ ἤδη καὶ ἀγαθοὶ αὐτὸ πεπόνθασιν Ἀθηναίων. εὐπρόσωπος γὰρ ὁ τοῦ μεγαλήτορος δῆμος Ἐρεχθέως.

καὶ γιγνώσκοντες: true Athenians, they did not dare only, without knowing the reason why.

αἰσχυνόμενοι: cf. i. 84. 3 n.

ὁπότε καὶ - - - σφαλεῖεν: cf. κακῶν τε καὶ ἀγαθῶν, 41. 4. One wonders whether Thucydides remembered that *Kleon* was among those who lost their lives in a battle which was a defeat for Athens, and that his name was recorded on the stele (Paus. i. 29. 13).

στερίσκειν: cf. i. 40. 2 n., iii. 42. 4. Thucydides is fonder of the simple form of this verb, which is by comparison scarce in other prose writers, than of the compound ἀποστερεῖν.

ἔρανον: a contribution due to an association (of any form) from its members. προϊέμενοι 'offering freely', a more lively word than the normal εἰσφέροντες (Poppo). Shilleto compares Ar. *Lys.* 651–5 (the women's chorus speaking):

$$\text{τοὐράνου γάρ μοι μέτεστι· καὶ γὰρ ἄνδρας ἐσφέρω,}$$
$$\text{τοῖς δὲ δυστήνοις γέρουσιν οὐ μέτεσθ' ὑμῖν, ἐπεὶ}$$
$$\text{τὸν ἔρανον τὸν λεγόμενον παππῷον ἐκ τῶν Μηδικῶν}$$
$$\text{εἶτ' ἀναλώσαντες οὐκ ἀντεσφέρετε τὰς ἐσφοράς,}$$
$$\text{ἀλλ' ὑφ' ὑμῶν διαλυθῆναι προσέτι κινδυνεύομεν.}$$

2. τὸν ἀγήρων ἔπαινον: there seems little point in this position of the adjective ('their enduring praise'); and I should prefer to transpose it to make it predicative, ἀγήρων τὸν ἔπαινον, corresponding to τὸν τάφον ἐπισημότατον.

2–3. οὐκ ἐν ᾧ κεῖνται μόνον, κ.τ.λ.: the same idea as in 41. 4. We have a fresh collocation of λόγος and ἔργον: first an ordinary contrast in λόγου καὶ ἔργου καιρῷ, where λόγος is an epitaphios (future epitaphioi will also remember the dead of today), ἔργον a commemorative festival, as in 35. 1 (or, perhaps, as Steup renders: "bei jedem sich darbietenden Anlass, mag dieser dem Gebiete des Redens oder des Tuns angehören, immer erwahnt. λόγου ist auf die Preisung in festlichen Reden, ἔργου auf die Heranziehung als Vorbilder bei der Gelegenheit zu ähnlichem Tun zu beziehen"); and secondly, ἔργον is the actual grave with its stele and the name engraved on it of everyone who had fallen in the campaign, and the funeral rites, while

137

λόγος is represented by ἄγραφος μνήμη, undying memory in men's hearts, and, unlike the stele, preserved through all the world.

Thrasyboulos, before the fight on the slopes of Mounichia Hill, said to his men: ὦ μακάριοι δῆτα οἳ ἂν ἡμῶν νικήσαντες ἐπίδωσι τὴν πασῶν ἡδίστην ἡμέραν. εὐδαίμων δὲ καὶ ἄν τις ἀποθάνῃ· μνημείου γὰρ οὐδεὶς οὕτω πλούσιος ὢν καλοῦ τεύξεται (Xen. Hell. ii. 4. 17; a passage misunderstood by Ehrenberg, People of Aristophanes,[2] 238). In fact for Athens it is the material monument, the work of art, that has endured; witness the Mourning Athena stele. So has one from Sparta, the early Lakonian cup with the men bringing back the body of a former comrade.

τῆς γνώμης μᾶλλον ἢ τοῦ ἔργου: "memoria animi magis quam monumenti, i.e. in animis magis quam in cippis inscripta"—Stahl, following Dobree and Classen; and so Steup, except that he suggests του for τοῦ to get over the obvious difficulty of the article. "Le souvenir de leur valeur encore plus que du résultat effectif de leur action (vainqueurs ou vaincus, ils sont dignes de la même estime)"—Croiset, after Krüger and Böhme; so also Kakridés, 98–99; cf. Dem. xviii. 208, quoted above, p. 127. I incline to the latter, in spite of Steup's objection that we should want τῶν ἔργων; if it is right, a new idea is introduced with these words, or rather a repetition of the idea found in κακῶν τε καὶ ἀγαθῶν and ὁπότε καὶ - - - σφαλεῖεν above. But see B. B. Shefton in B.S.A. xlv, 1950, 154, n. 38, who compares I.G. i.[2] 945 (Tod, 59), the Poteidaia epigram,

ἀθάνατόμ με θα[νῦσι πολῖται σὲμ᾿ ἀνέθεκαν]
σημαίνεν ἀρετ[ὲν τόνδε καὶ ἐσσομένοις]
καὶ προγόνο᾿ σθέν(ο)ς [ἐσθλόν, ℎοὶ ἐνορέες ἀρετὲς τε]
νίκεν εὐπόλεμομ μνὲμ᾿ ἔλαβον [σ]φ[ετέρας],

"with its bold transference of νίκη into something concrete", the stone monument.

A closer parallel to this passage (and to 44. 1) is to be found in Simonides' noble enkomion of those who fell at Thermopylai (5 Diehl), doubtful though the text is here and there:

εὐκλεὴς μὲν ἁ τύχα, καλὸς δ᾿ ὁ πότμος,
βωμὸς δ᾿ ὁ τάφος, πρὸ γόων δὲ μνᾶστις, ὁ δ᾿ οἶκτος ἔπαινος.
ἐντάφιον δὲ τοιοῦτον
εὐρὼς οὔθ᾿ ὁ πανδαμάτωρ ἀμαυρώσει χρόνος
ἀνδρῶν ἀγαθῶν, ὁ δὲ σηκὸς οἰκέταν εὐδοξίαν
Ἑλλάδος εἵλετο.

With ἀνδρῶν ἐπιφανῶν πᾶσα γῆ τάφος (another phrase which may well be Perikles' own) compare the beginning of the epigram on Euripides attributed to Thucydides himself:

μνῆμα μὲν Ἑλλὰς ἅπασ᾿ Εὐριπίδου, ὀστέα δ᾿ ἴσχει
γῆ Μακεδών.

138

4. τὸ εὔδαιμον τὸ ἐλεύθερον: this is boldly expressed—'happiness *is* freedom, and freedom courage'; more strictly, 'happiness depends on freedom, freedom on courage'. (Cf. 36. 1; and χώρας - - - αἰεὶ διὰ τὸ εὔψυχον ἐλευθέρας, v. 9. 1.)

μὴ περιορᾶσθε: 'do not be nervous of'; lit. 'look around with anxiety' (cf. vi. 93. 1, 103. 2, etc.; and ἐκλογιζόμενος ἅπαν τὸ περιεστὸς ἡμᾶς δεινόν, iv. 10. 1).

5. οὐ γὰρ οἱ κακοπραγοῦντες, κ.τ.λ.: a generalization about all men, not with any reference to the Spartans, who could not be described as κακοπραγοῦντες (see iv. 55. 4, ἐκ τῆς πρὶν ἀηθείας τοῦ κακοπραγεῖν— the whole context is worth comparing with this passage). As the scholiast remarks, τὸ νόημα παράδοξον καὶ ἐναντίον τῇ κοινῇ συνηθείᾳ· Θέογνις γὰρ ὁ ποιήσας τὰς ὑποθήκας φησί (ll. 175–6)

$$\chi\rho\grave{\eta}\ \pi\epsilon\nu\acute{\iota}\eta\nu\ \phi\epsilon\acute{\upsilon}\gamma o\nu\tau a\ \kappa a\grave{\iota}\ \grave{\epsilon}\varsigma\ \mu\epsilon\gamma a\kappa\acute{\eta}\tau\epsilon a\ \pi\acute{o}\nu\tau o\nu$$
$$\acute{\rho}\acute{\iota}\pi\tau\epsilon\iota\nu\ \kappa a\grave{\iota}\ \pi\epsilon\tau\rho\^{\omega}\nu,\ K\acute{\upsilon}\rho\nu\epsilon,\ \kappa a\tau'\ \acute{\eta}\lambda\iota\beta\acute{a}\tau\omega\nu.$$

The unthinking courage of desperate men was not what Perikles was looking for in his Athens. Cf. above, 40. 2–3, 62. 5, and i. 144. 4.

Steup would insert τ' between οἷς and ἐλπίς, for not all unfortunates have no hope, and in order to get a better-balanced sentence, so that in the antithesis οἷς ἐλπίς - - - ἀγαθοῦ is contrasted with οἷς ἡ ἐναντία μεταβολή, κ.τ.λ., and οἱ κακοπραγοῦντες with ἐν οἷς μάλιστα - - - πταίσωσιν. But the change is hardly necessary; and strictly we should have οὐδ' οἷς ἐλπίς.

ἐν τῷ ζῆν ἔτι: to be taken together (Classen), rather than ἔτι κινδυνεύεται (Stahl).

μεγάλα τὰ διαφέροντα: cf. 42. 1.

6. ἀλγεινοτέρα: 'more painful', the word chosen to contrast with ἀναίσθητος θάνατος below.

κάκωσις: i.e. ἡ ἐναντία μεταβολή, *condicionis in deterius mutatio* (Haacke): 'if, through (or, together with) μαλακία, instead of being free and proud citizens of a great city, we were to become subject to another or citizens of a humbled and impoverished Athens'. ἀνδρί γε φρόνημα ἔχοντι is only an additional point: citizens of Athens should φρόνημα ἔχειν. (Steup, taking this as the important phrase, and translating κάκωσις as the shame which follows cowardice, remarks on the lack of logical connexion with the previous sentence, and reads ⟨ἀλλ'⟩ ἀλγεινοτέρα γάρ. Unnecessarily; and the logic is not thereby greatly improved. Nor can I agree with Marchant that κάκωσις means 'cowardice' here—"= ἡ ἐναντία μεταβολή, according to the doctrine that cowardice is misery, and therefore to the prosperous involves degradation".)

μετὰ ῥώμης καὶ κοινῆς ἐλπίδος: that death which, 'accompanied by courage and hope for your country's victory', is almost unfelt.

44. 1. οὐκ ὀλοφύρομαι μᾶλλον, κ.τ.λ.: once more Plato in *Menexenos* (247 C–D) seems to have had Thucydides particularly in mind.

ἐπίστανται: I would write ἐπίστασθε, as Herwerden, and suppose that this was misspelled ἐπίστασθαι, and then corrected to our MSS. reading.

τὸ δ' εὐτυχές, κ.τ.λ.: I believe that we should insert εὖ before ἐντελευτῆσαι, and that there is no difficulty in interpretation. 'Good fortune is theirs who meet with the noblest end as these men have done or, as you, with the noblest sorrow, and whose years of happiness in life only end with their happy death.' With ξυνεμετρήθη compare Soph. *O.T.* 963, καὶ τῷ μακρῷ γε συμμετρούμενος χρόνῳ, and *Ant.* 387. This extraordinarily vivid sentence is exactly illustrated by Solon's words to Kroisos in Herodotos, i. 32, by the story of Tellos and the warning 'call no man happy till he has died' (not, it is perhaps still necessary to say, because the Greeks thought death preferable to life, but, as Solon makes clear in giving the palm of happiness to Tellos, not to Kleobis and Biton, because during life disaster may come to the most prosperous at any time):[1] ἐκεῖνο δὲ τὸ εἴρεό με οὔ κώ σε ἐγὼ λέγω, πρὶν τελευτήσαντα καλῶς τὸν αἰῶνα πύθωμαι. οὐ γάρ τι ὁ μέγα πλούσιος μᾶλλον τοῦ ἐπ' ἡμέρην ἔχοντος ὀλβιώτερός ἐστι, εἰ μή οἱ τύχη ἐπίσποιτο πάντα καλὰ ἔχοντα εὖ τελευτῆσαι τὸν βίον. - - - εἰ δὲ πρὸς τούτοισι ἔτι τελευτήσει τὸν βιον εὖ, οὗτος ἐκεῖνος τὸν σὺ ζητέεις, ὁ ὄλβιος κεκλῆσθαι ἄξιός ἐστι. - - - ὃς δ' ἂν αὐτῶν πλεῖστα ἔχων διατελέῃ καὶ ἔπειτα τελευτήσῃ εὐχαρίστως τὸν βίον, οὗτος παρ' ἐμοὶ τὸ οὔνομα τοῦτο, ὦ βασιλεῦ, δίκαιός ἐστι φέρεσθαι. The repeated καλῶς, εὖ, εὖ, εὐχαρίστως τελευτῆσαι shows clearly that a good death, whether on the battlefield as Tellos, or in their sleep as the two Argives, is *part* of a happy life: it is not simply a matter of death before disaster falls (the contrast to Queen Margaret's prayer, "Long die thy happy days before thy death", in *Richard III*, I. iii. 208). Hence ἐν τελευτῆσαι, which besides corresponds with ἐνευδαιμονῆσαι, must be kept; and there is no need, and much disadvantage, in Reifferscheid's emendation ⟨ἡ εὐδαιμονία⟩ before ξυνεμετρήθη, which is adopted by Stahl ("vitam non morte, sed in vita finiri absurdum est"). The expression is rhetorical, but none the worse for that; Shakespeare too had a similar idea—

> Nothing in his life
> Became him like the leaving it.

Death is "the culmination" of men's lives, as Lord David Cecil puts it, in *Hardy as Novelist*, p. 150. The parallel in Herodotos shows as

[1] There is no need to suppose for Herodotos, with G. Thomson, *Oresteia*, ii. 40, that the Greeks avoided calling a *man* εὐδαίμων (till he was dead and beyond the reach of fortune) because the gods were εὐδαίμονες. It is only that life is not yet completed.

well that $\epsilon \tilde{v}$ is required, as Poppo saw, conjecturing $\epsilon \tilde{v}$ $\tau \epsilon \lambda \epsilon v \tau \hat{\eta} \sigma a \iota$; but $\epsilon \tilde{v}$ $\dot{\epsilon} v \tau \epsilon \lambda \epsilon v \tau \hat{\eta} \sigma a \iota$ is better, in sense and in style—'whose life has been closely measured—alike to live well and to die well in it'. For the style, cf. vi. 23. 3, $\pi o \lambda \lambda \grave{a}$ $\mu \grave{\epsilon} v$ $\dot{\eta} \mu \hat{a} s$ $\delta \acute{\epsilon} o v$ $\epsilon \tilde{v}$ $\beta o v \lambda \epsilon \acute{v} \sigma a \sigma \theta a \iota$, $\ddot{\epsilon} \tau \iota$ $\delta \grave{\epsilon}$ $\pi \lambda \epsilon \acute{\iota} \omega$ $\epsilon \dot{v} \tau v \chi \hat{\eta} \sigma a \iota$. Cf. also Hdt. v. 92 ϵ-ζ, the career of Kypselos (Loxias does not mind foretelling that he will be $\ddot{o} \lambda \beta \iota o s$). Miltiades, on the other hand, did not die well, nor Nikias (though he so much wanted to, v. 16. 1).

Herwerden's $\dot{\epsilon} v \tau a \lambda a \iota \pi \omega \rho \hat{\eta} \sigma a \iota$, which is foreign to the context, and as tasteless as it is irrelevant, has found a curious assent with some editors, culminating in Steup's $\kappa a \grave{\iota}$ $\dot{o} \lambda \acute{\iota} \gamma o \iota s$ $\dot{\epsilon} v \epsilon v \delta a \iota \mu o v \hat{\eta} \sigma a \acute{\iota}$ $\tau \epsilon$ - - - $\kappa a \grave{\iota}$ $\dot{\epsilon} v \tau a \lambda a \iota \pi \omega \rho \hat{\eta} \sigma a \iota$ $\xi v v \epsilon \mu \epsilon \tau \rho \acute{\eta} \theta \eta$, after $\tau \grave{o}$ δ' $\epsilon \dot{v} \tau v \chi \acute{\epsilon} s$, - - - $\dot{v} \mu \epsilon \hat{\iota} s$ $\delta \grave{\epsilon}$ $\lambda \acute{v} \pi \eta s$ in parenthesis. To few indeed! (Steup takes the strongest objection to the indicative $\xi v v \epsilon \mu \epsilon \tau \rho \acute{\eta} \theta \eta$, if this sentence is to be taken as part of the explanation of $\tau \grave{o}$ $\epsilon \dot{v} \tau v \chi \acute{\epsilon} s$, denying that iv. 92. 1, $\epsilon \dot{\iota} \sigma \grave{\iota}$ $\delta \acute{\eta} \pi o v$ $\pi o \lambda \acute{\epsilon} \mu \iota o \iota$ $\dot{\epsilon} v$ $\hat{\dot{\omega}}$ $\tau \epsilon$ $\ddot{a} v$ $\chi \omega \rho \acute{\iota} \omega$ $\kappa a \tau a \lambda \eta \phi \theta \hat{\omega} \sigma \iota$ $\kappa a \grave{\iota}$ $\ddot{o} \theta \epsilon v$ $\dot{\epsilon} \pi \epsilon \lambda \theta \acute{o} v \tau \epsilon s$ $\pi o \lambda \acute{\epsilon} \mu \iota a$ $\ddot{\epsilon} \delta \rho a \sigma a v$, is parallel. But the comparison seems close; and if it were not, and if the indicative is here impossible, we should emend by inserting $\ddot{a} v$ after $o \hat{\iota} s$ and reading $\xi v \mu \mu \epsilon \tau \rho \eta \theta \hat{\eta}$.)

$\dot{\epsilon} v$ $\pi o \lambda v \tau \rho \acute{o} \pi o \iota s$ $\xi v \mu \phi o \rho a \hat{\iota} s$ $\tau \rho a \phi \acute{\epsilon} v \tau \epsilon s$ is close to Herodotos' $o \ddot{v} \tau \omega$ $\ddot{\omega} v$, $\hat{\dot{\omega}}$ $K \rho o \hat{\iota} \sigma \epsilon$, $\pi \hat{a} v$ $\dot{\epsilon} \sigma \tau \iota$ $\ddot{a} v \theta \rho \omega \pi o s$ $\sigma v \mu \phi o \rho \acute{\eta}$;[1] but note that Thucydides' use of $\tau \grave{o}$ $\epsilon \dot{v} \tau v \chi \acute{\epsilon} s$ is different: Herodotos says, the man who has been happy in his life and dies well, can be called $\ddot{o} \lambda \beta \iota o s$· $\pi \rho \grave{\iota} v$ δ' $\ddot{a} v$ $\tau \epsilon \lambda \epsilon v \tau \acute{\eta} \sigma \eta$, $\dot{\epsilon} \pi \iota \sigma \chi \epsilon \hat{\iota} v$ $\mu \eta \delta \grave{\epsilon}$ $\kappa a \lambda \acute{\epsilon} \epsilon \iota v$ $\kappa \omega$ $\ddot{o} \lambda \beta \iota o v$, $\dot{a} \lambda \lambda$' $\epsilon \dot{v} \tau v \chi \acute{\epsilon} a$. Cf. Sophocles, fr. 646,

> $o \dot{v}$ $\chi \rho \acute{\eta}$ $\pi o \tau$' $\epsilon \tilde{v}$ $\pi \rho \acute{a} \sigma \sigma o v \tau o s$ $\dot{o} \lambda \beta \acute{\iota} \sigma a \iota$ $\tau \acute{v} \chi a s$
> $\dot{a} v \delta \rho \acute{o} s$, $\pi \rho \grave{\iota} v$ $a \dot{v} \tau \hat{\dot{\omega}}$ $\pi a v \tau \epsilon \lambda \hat{\omega} s$ $\ddot{\eta} \delta \eta$ $\beta \acute{\iota} o s$
> $\delta \iota \epsilon \kappa \pi \epsilon \rho a \theta \hat{\eta}$ $\kappa a \grave{\iota}$ $\tau \epsilon \lambda \epsilon v \tau \acute{\eta} \sigma \eta$ †$\beta \acute{\iota} o v$.†

Below § 2, $\epsilon \dot{v} \tau v \chi \acute{\iota} a \iota s$ is near to Herodotos' use (the good fortune of having sons living, which may be destroyed at any time).

2. $\pi \epsilon \acute{\iota} \theta \epsilon \iota v$: there is no valid objection to this. However well men may know in general that they are $\dot{\epsilon} v$ $\pi o \lambda v \tau \rho \acute{o} \pi o \iota s$ $\xi v \mu \phi o \rho a \hat{\iota} s$ $\tau \rho a \phi \acute{\epsilon} v \tau \epsilon s$, and however eloquently they are urged to remember that their present sorrow is $\epsilon \dot{v} \pi \rho \epsilon \pi \epsilon \sigma \tau \acute{a} \tau \eta$, persuasion is difficult.

$\mu \grave{\eta}$ $\pi \epsilon \iota \rho a \sigma \acute{a} \mu \epsilon v o s$ $\dot{a} \gamma a \theta \hat{\omega} v$ $\sigma \tau \epsilon \rho \acute{\iota} \sigma \kappa \eta \tau a \iota$: cf. v. 69. 1. "$\sigma \tau \epsilon \rho \acute{\iota} \sigma \kappa \epsilon \sigma \theta a \iota$ hat nicht notwendig einen vorhergehenden Besitz zur Voraussetzung, vgl. iii. 39. 8, iv. 20. 1, 64. 5"—Classen. True; but it is a strange expression here, "to lose good things which they have not experienced", or "before experiencing them". The examples quoted by Classen (esp. iii. 39. 8) are much easier.

$\dot{\epsilon} \theta \acute{a} s$ is not apparently used elsewhere in Attic, and is rare everywhere except in the Hippokratic *corpus* (cf. 49. 2 n.).

---

[1] i.e. 'with every man it is a question of what *happens*' (the issue of events), not, as it is so often translated, 'man is the victim of chance'. It was not chance which overthrew Kroisos' good fortune.

3. ἄλλων παίδων ἐλπίδι: it is extraordinary that this should mean, as it must, 'hopes of having other sons', not 'from younger (or, indeed, elder) sons'; for not only would very few parents of sons killed in war be likely to have more, however philoprogenitive the Greeks were, but many must actually have had other sons who would help forgetfulness of the loss, and these are ignored; though the other sons, as brothers of the fallen, are mentioned in 45. 1.

ἀσφαλείᾳ: explained by what follows—as valuable or as just counsel is only to be expected from those who are, equally with others, risking the lives of their children by their speeches or votes in the assembly. Compare, in its very different context, i. 91. 7, and my note there. Perikles recurs to the advantages to the city, with which those of the individual Athenian were so closely bound.

4. τόνδε βραχὺν ἔσεσθαι: chill comfort. Cf. Eur. Alk. 649–50.

τῇ τῶνδε εὐκλείᾳ: cf. Soph. Ant. 703–4—Classen.

ὥσπερ τινές φασι: Simonides among others, according to Plut. Mor. 786 B; Ar. Pax, 697–9. Shilleto also compares Arist. Eth. N. iv. 1. 37, 1121 b 14, δοκεῖ δὲ τὸ γῆρας καὶ πᾶσα ἀδυναμία ἀνελευθέρους ποιεῖν.

Simonides is said to have been the first to make money out of poetry; but see Solon, 1. 41–42 (above on πενίας ἐλπίδι, 42. 4), 51–52.

45. 1. παισὶ δ' αὖ, κ.τ.λ.: cf. Menex. 246 D–247 B.

τὸν γὰρ οὐκ ὄντα ἅπας εἴωθεν ἐπαινεῖν: so they would have to overcome a certain envy of the dead, besides finding it hard to be thought their equal. See 35. 2 n. Wilamowitz and Steup would bracket the sentence, as an intrusion from a marginal note which quoted an aphorism; unnecessarily. For another case of interruption of a statement and its more precise definition (καὶ μόλις ἄν, κ.τ.λ.) by a general statement, compare, with Stahl, i. 8. 2–4, where we have similarly two explanations introduced by γάρ.[1] Steup would also bracket τοῖς ζῶσι: "sed fallitur. Nam . . . contraria sunt πρὸς τὸ ἀντίπαλον et ἀνανταγωνίστῳ εὐνοίᾳ [immo ἀνανταγωνίστῳ tantum], τοῖς ζῶσι et τὸ μὴ ἐμποδών, φθόνος et τετίμηται [immo εὐνοίᾳ τετίμηται]. Exempto igitur τοῖς ζῶσι mutilata est oppositio" (Stahl). οἱ ζῶντες are of course the envied, not those who envy; and πρὸς τὸ ἀντίπαλον is probably to be taken as Stahl takes it, propter aemulationem, 'in rivalry'.

For the general sentiment, cf. vi. 16. 5; Dem. xviii. 315. Shilleto quotes from Bacon's essay Of Death: "Death hath this also; that it openeth the gate to good fame, and extinguisheth envy."

2. ἐν χηρείᾳ: this is used only of widows, not of mothers who have lost their children; so that mothers must be included in the parents

---

[1] I would not, however, put τὸν γὰρ - - - ἐπαινεῖν in parenthesis as Stahl and Stuart Jones do; for μόλις ἄν - - - κριθεῖτε is as much a closer definition of that sentence as of μέγαν τὸν ἀγῶνα.

142

who have been consoled in the previous chapter, and γυναικεία ἀρετή is 'a wife's virtue', not 'a woman's'.

βραχείᾳ παραινέσει ἅπαν σημανῶ: his explanation of the whole matter is not only brief and priggish, but advice, not consolation, and advice that is most of it not called for by the occasion. τῆς ὑπαρχούσης φύσεως μὴ χείροσι γενέσθαι is in effect to be taken, I think, with Haacke, "vult ut ne sint abjecto prorsus animo"; and for the expression, cf. 61. 4, τῆς ὑπαρχούσης δόξης - - - ὅστις μαλακίᾳ ἐλλείπει. In both passages the φύσις and the δόξα are noble, something to be proud of. Perhaps Lysistrate's fine lines are the best comment:

ἡμεῖς τὸν μὲν πρότερον πόλεμον - - - ἠνεσχόμεθ᾽ ὑμῶν
ὑπὸ σωφροσύνης τῆς ἡμετέρας τῶν ἀνδρῶν ἅττ᾽ ἐποιεῖτε.
οὐ γὰρ γρύζειν εἴαθ᾽ ἡμᾶς. καίτοὐκ ἠρέσκετέ γ᾽ ἡμᾶς.
ἀλλ᾽ ᾐσθανόμεσθα καλῶς ὑμῶν, καὶ πολλάκις ἔνδον ἂν οὖσαι
ἠκούσαμεν ἄν τι κακῶς ὑμᾶς βουλευσαμένους μέγα πρᾶγμα·
εἶτ᾽ ἀλγοῦσαι τἄνδοθεν ὑμᾶς ἐπανηρόμεθ᾽ ἂν γελάσασαι,
' τί βεβούλευται περὶ τῶν σπονδῶν ἐν τῇ στήλῃ παραγράψαι
ἐν τῷ δήμῳ τήμερον ὑμῖν;' ' τί δὲ σοὶ ταῦτ᾽;' ἦ δ᾽ ὃς ἂν ἀνήρ·
' οὐ σιγήσει;' κἀγὼ 'σίγων (507–15).

When the other woman here intervenes, ἀλλ᾽ οὐκ ἂν ἐγώ ποτ᾽ ἐσίγων, we are back at the lively realism of the *petite bourgeoisie* that Aristophanes loved to portray.

For the sentiment in general, and its place in Greek social history, see my *Essays*, ch. 5 (pp. 89–115). Perikles was at this time married to Aspasia.

There is a bleakness in the *personal* consolation of the parents, children, and widows of the fallen (from 44. 3 to 45) which is in marked contrast to the warmth and splendour of all the rest of the speech in which the greatness of the city and the opportunities and qualities of the citizens are lauded. But this is in accordance with Perikles' character, at any rate as many of his contemporaries saw him; he was, unlike Peisistratos whom in other respects he was said to resemble, not at all δημοτικός in manner, nor, like Kimon, generous and hospitable, but unsociable, reserved, even haughty: Plut. *Per.* cc. 5 and 7.

46. 1. εἴρηται καὶ ἐμοὶ λόγῳ, κ.τ.λ.: "ob alterum membrum proprie καὶ λόγῳ ἐμοὶ εἴρηται scribendum erat, sed ut contionem ad finem properare indicaret, scriptor εἴρηται, quo verbo finiri orationes solent, anteposuit, deinde orationem mutavit"—Stahl. The absence of a connective also marks the end. 'I have done. I have said my part and the ceremonies are now over.' Similarly οἱ θαπτόμενοι is loosely placed before τὰ μέν.

ἡ πόλις μέχρι ἥβης θρέψει: cf., with Stahl, Plat. *Menex.* 249 B.

143

τοῖς δέ: Thucydides occasionally uses δέ in apodosis, ὁ δέ, ii. 65. 5, οἱ δέ, iii. 98. 1, τόσῳ δέ, i. 37. 5; and i. 11. 1, where see n. It is difficult to see what in Greek writing and speech would be the difference between τοῖς δέ and τοῖσδε; there would be little between ὁ δέ and ὅδε, οἱ δέ and οἵδε; more between τόσῳ δέ and τοσῷδε.

2. ἀπολοφυράμενοι: after completing the funeral dirge, that is, the lament fixed by custom for the occasion, as 34. 4.

ἄπιτε: on the whole I would prefer the alternative reading (of ABEFM), ἀποχωρεῖτε. In a similar conventional ending Menexenos, 249 C, and Ps.-Demosthenes, 37, have ἄπιτε, a fact which, as Kakridés says, may explain the variant here.

If, after the eloquence of philosophical politics that we read in the Epitaphios, we turn back to the sections immediately preceding it, especially, say, cc. 30, 32, and 33, which seem to contain apparently nothing but the narrative of particulars, and trivial particulars at that, without special connexion with each other, we cannot but ask ourselves what was Thucydides' aim? And what was Aristotle's view of the place of the Epitaphios in the History, in the light of his statement that history only told the story of events related to each other in time, not by logic, and so was less philosophical, and less important, than poetry? But see above, my note at the end of c. 33, and, at more length, my Greek Attitude to Poetry and History, there referred to.

A contrast of quite a different kind is that between the picture of Athens as Perikles wished it to be and what she was in reality in a great disaster, as described in the pages which follow.

47. 1. πρῶτον ἔτος τοῦ πολέμου τοῦδε ἐτελεύτα: for the various forms adopted for this formula by Thucydides, see Classen's note here; and Appendix.

Expenditure from the Reserve Fund in the First Year of the War

Below, in nn. on iii. 116. 3 and v. 20. 3, I have given a brief account of the important inscription *I.G.* i.² 324, the accounts of the logistai for the quadrennium 426 to 422 B.C., including that part of it which gives a summary of the expenditure during the previous seven years, 433 to 426. We have no corresponding inscription giving the detailed expenses for those seven years or for the previous quadrennium, 430 to 426 (though *I.G.* i.² 300—*S.E.G.* x. 226 init.—may be a fragment of the latter, *A.F.D.*, p. 68; but it is a tamiai-, not a logistai-record; it has no figures preserved); but i.² 295 gives the expenditure for the Kerkyra expedition in 433 B.C., and 296 that for the campaigns against Macedonia and Poteidaia from midsummer 432 to midsummer 431 (see vol. i, pp. 188, 196–7; 224, 423); of the latter the four payments made in the eighth, ninth, and tenth prytanies and those for the naval expedition round the Peloponnese in the ninth and tenth prytanies (above, 23. 2–3 nn.) fall within the first Thucydidean year of the war. Further, *I.G.* i.² 294+299+308 (Wade-Gery, *J.H.S.* l, 1930, 288–93, and liii. 136; West, *T.A.P.A.* lxi, 1930, 217–39; Meritt, *A.F.D.* 83–86; *S.E.G.* x. 226) is a record of the tamiai of Athena similar to i.² 293 (Samos campaign: vol. i, p. 356), 295, and 296, and probably belongs to 431–430 (more probably, I think, than to 428–427, where *S.E.G.* puts it, and Wade-Gery in 1933—see below); if it does, the payments in the first two-thirds of the account will have belonged to Thucydides' first year. Unfortunately, only very small fragments of this inscription are preserved, and the only details known are two payments of 50 tal. each, one of which certainly and the other possibly, were for new triremes; but the impressive total for the archon-year (exclusive of this 100 tal.) is preserved, 1,267 tal.+. Of this more than half presumably belongs to the Thucydidean year 431–430. Of the 432–431 accounts (i.² 296) not more than 80 tal.+in the last four payments for Macedonia and Poteidaia and an unknown amount for the naval expedition fall within our year.

It is mainly because the sum spent is so large that the inscription should be placed in 431–430 and the cost attributed mainly to the siege of Poteidaia, rather than in 428–427 for the campaign against Mytilene. The statement of the Mytilenean envoys at Olympia that Athens was financially as well as physically exhausted, iii. 13. 3, was the result of wishful thinking and greatly exaggerated; but it must be allowed to have some truth. Athens did not send a very large force under Paches. There is also some force in A. B. West's argument that the amount of interest accumulated by 426 B.C. is better explained by assuming that this large expenditure was incurred as early as 431–430 (see *A.F.D.* 86).

YEAR 2: 430–429 B.C. (CC. 47–70)

47–54. *Second Invasion of Attica. The Pestilence*

2. τοῦ δὲ θέρους εὐθὺς ἀρχομένου: in spite of the fact that elsewhere the spring appears as part of the summer (ii. 2. 1 n., iv. 2. 1) we must take this phrase here to mean the first days of summer, in the narrow sense, not long before θέρους καὶ τοῦ σίτου ἀκμάζοντος (19. 1), about the beginning of May. Thucydides cannot be excused a confusion of terms which ought not to be confused.

ἡγεῖτο δὲ Ἀρχίδαμος, κ.τ.λ.: the same formal title as in 19. 1, 71. 1. We are not told this time by which route they entered Attica (cf. nn. on 18. 1, 19. 1), nor in 57 that by which they left it: they presumably entered direct by Eleusis, and very likely went back through

Oropia and Boeotia, as in 431 (23. 3), since they went last to the north-east corner of Attica (Classen).

3. ἡ νόσος: the well-known pestilence. Stahl cites the many imitations of Thucydides: Lucretius, vi. 1138–1286 (describing this outbreak, much of it in direct translation); Prokopios, *Bell. Pers.* ii. 22–23 (the plague of A.D. 542 and 543); Kantakouzenos, iv. 8 (that of A.D. 1347). "Nec sine fructu comparabuntur Verg. *Georg.* iii. 478 sqq., Ovid. *Met.* vii. 523 sqq." If one wishes to compare a vigorous copy with an original, to observe how they differ, perhaps the most interesting passages in Lucretius are 1219–21, 1252–5, and 1259–63; he makes no mention of the war and the consequent crowding in temporary shelters within the walls, and on the other hand has details which are not in Thucydides, and which seem to be taken from Hippokratic treatises (see C. Bailey, ad loc.). Prokopios' account (of bubonic plague) has more originality than he is generally given credit for, though there is some dull imitation of Thucydides and some yet duller exaggeration (e.g. in his absurd introduction, 22. 1–5); and where he differs he is not always credible, as when he says that doctors and others who attended the sick were themselves not attacked by the plague (22. 23);[1] but in essentials his narrative is independent, and particularly when superstition plays a part.

λεγόμενον: interpreted by most edd. as though τὸ νόσημα had preceded (so the schol., who compares *Od.* xii. 74–75), or, more generally, 'a thing which was said'; by some, e.g. Krüger, as an accusative absolute, with αὐτήν understood with ἐγκατασκῆψαι. Classen, however, points out not only the grammatical difficulties but that Thucydides does not apparently mean that *this outbreak* was observed previously at Lemnos and elsewhere, for it appeared first in Ethiopia, then in Egypt and Libya (48. 1), but other cases of a similar disease elsewhere (and probably of an earlier period) were remembered. He proposed to insert something like πλεῖστα δὴ βλάψασα τῶν γεγενημένων ἀνθρώποις, followed by λεγομένων μὲν καὶ προτέρων. The inserted words seem to me unnecessary; but there is something to be said for his argument and his λεγομένων, κ.τ.λ., except that ⟨ἄλλων⟩ πρότερον would be preferable.

4. ἀγνοίᾳ: εἰ γὰρ ᾔδεισαν ὅτι λοιμὸς ἦν, οὐκ ἂν ἐπεχείρουν, says the scholiast; which is not flattering to the doctors of *his* time and place, whatever they were. τὸ πρῶτον may mean simply that they treated it in its beginning in ignorance of its nature; though, even when later they had learned something about it, they could discover no certain cure (51. 2). Classen, however, translates 'treating the disease as they were for the first time, they could do little to help, owing to their ignorance'; and this is perhaps preferable.

[1] This, however, is meant to distinguish that plague from the epidemic in Thucydides: see § 4, with n. there.

146

αὐτοὶ μάλιστα ἔθνῃσκον: for the possible significance of this, see below, p. 153.

ἄλλη ἀνθρωπεία τέχνη: the scholiast interprets this, οἷον μαντική, ἐπῳδή; and this is accepted by Stahl. But μαντική is described in the next sentence; 'other human skill' means looking after the sick, amateur efforts, etc.

μαντείοις καὶ τοῖς τοιούτοις: Grote, v, p. 81, n. 1, refers to Sophokles, *Trach.* 1000–2,

$$\text{τίς γὰρ ἀοιδός, τίς ὁ χειροτέχνης}$$
$$\text{ἰατορίας, ὃς τήνδ' ἄτην}$$
$$\text{χωρὶς Ζηνὸς κατακηλήσει;}$$

where we have the physician, the supplication of the gods, and the use of incantations. See, too, n. on 54. 4 below. Grote also remarks (what was worth remarking; and is worth repeating, for we often take it for granted) "that amidst all the melancholy accompaniments of the time, there are no human sacrifices, such as those offered up at Carthage during pestilence to appease the anger of the gods— there are no cruel persecutions against imaginary authors of the disease, such as those against the Untori (anointers of doors) in the plague of Milan in 1630" (though the attacks on Anaxagoras and Aspasia, below, pp. 184 ff., were doubtless aided by such superstitions). τελευτῶντές τε: a colon should be placed before this, for here we have a further fact and almost a summing up, αὐτῶν, as the scholiast says, including both τῶν θείων and τῶν ἀνθρωπίνων.

It is characteristic of Thucydides' method of writing that he gives here a brief summary of the effects of the pestilence (the heavy death-roll, the uselessness alike of medicine and care and of the superstitious practices that men resorted to, the despair), though he is about to describe it all in detail and from the beginning.

48. 1. Αἰθιοπίας: Upper Egypt, the Sudan. Note Thucydides' cautious ὡς λέγεται, which is not repeated by Galen, Plutarch, and others (see Stahl here), who refer to this passage. Strabo, xvii. 3. 10, p. 830, quotes Poseidonios for a reason why plagues began in Egypt.

2. ἐσβεβλήκοιεν ἐς τὰ φρέατα: 'that there was poison in the wells and cisterns, put there by the Peloponnesians.' On the meaning of φρέαρ (either wells or cisterns, here both are included) and of κρήνη, see Hitzig–Blümner on Pausanias, i. 14. 1; in 49. 5 the meaning will be cisterns, or even reservoirs, as in Plat. *Lach.* 193 C.

κρῆναι γὰρ οὔπω ἦσαν αὐτόθι: unlike Athens itself, which had several (15. 5 n.). Schol. Ar. *Av.* 997 (Μέτων, ὃν οἶδεν Ἑλλὰς χὠ Κολωνός) quotes from Phrynichos' *Monotropos* (fr. 376 K),

$$\text{Α. τίς δ' ἐστιν ὁ μετὰ ταῦτα φροντίζων; Β. Μέτων}$$
$$\text{ὁ Λευκονοεύς. Α. ἐγῷδ', ὁ τὰς κρήνας ἄγων.}$$

Another note, ibid., has: ἄλλως· ἴσως ἐν τῷ Κολωνῷ κρήνην τινὰ κατεσκευάσατο (this reading confirmed by D. Mervyn Jones). From this Ullrichs conjectured that Meton had constructed fountains in the Peiraeus, shortly before 414 B.C., and this has been amiably accepted by many edd.; but there is no ancient authority for it. There is some archaeological evidence that water was taken from the Ilissos (from 'Kallirroe' spring: above, p. 53) to Peiraeus in classical times; see Judeich, pp. 202, 203.

Whatever the date, and whoever the designer of the work of supplying Peiraeus with water, this is a particularly interesting passage in its relation to the problem of the construction of Thucydides' *History*. The detailed description of the pestilence is clearly one which he might have written immediately after his own recovery, and is certainly from notes made at the time; but equally clearly this sentence, from the introduction to the description, was written some time after—though how long after we do not know: for aqueducts and fountains may have been constructed soon after the pestilence, because the existing cisterns and wells were fouled (49. 5) and to avoid other disasters in the future.

ἔθνῃσκον πολλῷ μᾶλλον ἤδη: simply 'the number of deaths was at once greatly increased'.

3. λεγέτω μὲν οὖν, κ.τ.λ.: Thucydides displays a certain impatience with the opinions, both professional and lay, about the probable origin of the pestilence and the cause of the violent changes it produced; presumably because many wild and mutually inconsistent, but confident, theories were propounded, and even those of professional doctors seemed to him little more than guesses (something perhaps like the causes given by Lucretius, vi. 1095–1137). He therefore contents himself with a description of its symptoms, and of its moral and political effects. This is in apparent contrast with the way in which he deals with the causes of the war, which occupy the greater part of book i (i. 23. 3 n.); but see n. on ἀπ' οὐδεμιᾶς προφάσεως below, 49. 2. The careful description of what occurred (οἷον ἐγίγνετο λέξω, below) and the outlook towards the future recall i. 22. 2–4; here the possible practical benefits of description are obvious.

The 'probable origin' means presumably, 'how do such pestilences arise at all?' (cf. e.g. Poseidonios' view referred to in n. on § 1 above), and includes the nature of contagion and infection, why the disease spread, yet spread only, or mainly, in Athens (54. 5); and 'the causes of the violent changes produced by it', mean primarily the physical make-up of human beings and their material conditions at this time and place, why they fell victims to it and why they suffered in the particular ways they did; in particular perhaps also why there was so great a change from a previous unusually healthy condition (49. 1). Diodoros, xii. 45. 2, 58. 3–5, presumably from Ephoros, does relate the immediate causes—the crowding, a very wet winter, which left much stagnant water lying till the summer, poor food owing to crop failures, and absence that summer of the usual cooling etesian winds. It would be interesting to know if Ephoros had any evidence for this; Thucydides' silence suggests that he had not, and the failure of the crops, when they were anyhow destroyed by the enemy, and when there had probably been but little sowing, suggests purely *a priori* reasoning. Those symptoms which are described in Diodoros, 58. 5, come from Thucydides (49. 5); and this makes it probable that the 'causes' are theories after the event rather than observations made at the time.

If the superficial treatise in the Hippokratic corpus, *Airs, Waters, Places*, which is so different from such works as the *Epidemiai* in that it is largely a description of climatic causes of physical character-istics, assumed *a priori*, belongs to the fifth century (see W. H. S. Jones, *Hippocrates*, Loeb edition, 1948, vol. i, p. xxi), and is at all typical, it would account for Thucydides' impatience with those who expounded the causes of the epidemic at Athens. The much more scientific *Epidemiai* lays much stress on weather conditions during epidemics (cf. i. 2–3); and such speculations may account for Ephoros' theories as related by Diodoros. Thucydides' refusal to discuss causes seems a reflection of, or at least to be influenced by, another principle found in some of the Hippokratic treatises—that of the importance of prognostic, as stated at the beginning of the *Prognostikon*: see Cochrane's *Thucydides and the Science of History*, 1929, who has been followed by Finley, pp. 69–70, and recently by D. L. Page in the article which is discussed below.

The peculiar care which Thucydides gives to the description of the symptoms has often been noted. Grote, v, p. 80 n., quotes an interesting passage from Littré (*Œuvres d'Hippocrate*, iv, p. 646) on the rarity, outside the Hippokratic school, of such publication of the results of clinical experience by Greek medical writers; at the same time Thucydides and Hippokrates must be remembered when we assert, too loosely, the Greek incapacity for particular observation in the fields of biological science. See particularly 50. 2 n.

Later writers (see, e.g., Pliny, *N.H.* vii. 37) asserted that Hippo-krates came to Athens and helped to stay the pestilence, or sent his sons and an assistant. Thucydides shows a knowledge of medical terms (see below); but he does not hint that any one doctor was more efficient than another in practice or wiser in theory. Among the genuine writings of Hippokrates, and other fifth-century writings by members of his school, there is no description of this pestilence; and all the stories of his presence in Athens are probably false. (That, if he were there, Thucydides should not mention him by name is, however, as Poppo says, not remarkable; there were others whose names he had opportunity to give, had he desired, as Pheidias, Gorgias, or Meton; but he refrained.)

Page's article, $C.Q.$ iii, 1953, 97–119, contains much the most important discussion of cc. 48 and 49 of Thucydides ii that has yet appeared; and to him I owe most of what is stated below on the meaning of the medical terms. He shows that Thucydides was familiar with medical writings by his strict use not only of technical words for the symptoms of the disease (e.g. $\theta\acute{\epsilon}\rho\mu\alpha\iota$, $\dot{\epsilon}\rho\upsilon\theta\acute{\eta}\mu\alpha\tau\alpha$, $\phi\lambda\acute{\upsilon}$-$\kappa\tau\alpha\iota\nu\alpha\iota$), but of other words which can have a special medical significance ($i\sigma\chi\upsilon\rho\acute{o}s$, $\dot{\epsilon}\pi\iota\kappa\alpha\tau\iota\acute{\epsilon}\nu\alpha\iota$, $\sigma\tau\eta\rho\acute{\iota}\zeta\epsilon\iota\nu$, $\dot{\epsilon}\pi\iota\sigma\eta\mu\alpha\acute{\iota}\nu\epsilon\iota\nu$); that the great majority of the words he has considered (77 out of 94) occur as standard terms in the medical writers; some of them are seldom or never found except there and in these chapters, and none of Thucydides' technical terms, and only two of his general terms ($\tau\alpha\lambda\alpha\iota\pi\omega\rho\acute{\iota}\alpha$ and $\dot{\alpha}\sigma\theta\acute{\epsilon}\nu\epsilon\iota\alpha$), conflict with medical usage.

For Professor Page's support of the new theory that the pestilence was an epidemic of measles, see below, n. on $\dot{\alpha}\phi'$ $\dot{\omega}\nu$ $\ddot{\alpha}\nu$ $\tau\iota s$ $\sigma\kappa o\pi\hat{\omega}\nu$.

$i\kappa\alpha\nu\dot{\alpha}s$ $\epsilon\hat{i}\nu\alpha\iota$ $\delta\acute{\upsilon}\nu\alpha\mu\iota\nu$ $\dot{\epsilon}s$ $\tau\dot{o}$ $\mu\epsilon\tau\alpha\sigma\tau\hat{\eta}\sigma\alpha\iota$ $\sigma\chi\epsilon\hat{i}\nu$: I agree with those who find the verbosity not tolerable; but the words I would bracket are $i\kappa\alpha\nu\dot{\alpha}s$ $\epsilon\hat{i}\nu\alpha\iota$, both because they are the kind of words to be found in scholia as an explanation of $\delta\acute{\upsilon}\nu\alpha\mu\iota\nu$ $\sigma\chi\epsilon\hat{i}\nu$, while the reverse is quite improbable, and because this tautology is much less bearable than that of $\mu\epsilon\tau\alpha\beta o\lambda\hat{\eta}s$ and $\dot{\epsilon}s$ $\tau\dot{o}$ $\mu\epsilon\tau\alpha\sigma\tau\hat{\eta}\sigma\alpha\iota$ (cf. for this, with Poppo, vi. 20. 2, and Stahl's comment). Classen objects that a scholiast would not explain the past tense, $\sigma\chi\epsilon\hat{i}\nu$, by a present, $\epsilon\hat{i}\nu\alpha\iota$; but this is unconvincing.

$\dot{\alpha}\phi'$ $\dot{\omega}\nu$ $\ddot{\alpha}\nu$ $\tau\iota s$ $\sigma\kappa o\pi\hat{\omega}\nu$, $\kappa.\tau.\lambda.$: a particular instance of the general principle laid down in i. 22. 4, and in i. 23. 5 ($\tau o\hat{\upsilon}$ $\mu\acute{\eta}$ $\tau\iota\nu\alpha$ $\zeta\eta\tau\hat{\eta}\sigma\alpha\iota$, $\kappa.\tau.\lambda.$). It may be noted that even here, where the future practical benefits of an accurate description are obvious, Thucydides confines himself to the hope, or the expectation, that it will result in knowledge ($\mu\dot{\eta}$ $\dot{\alpha}\gamma\nu o\epsilon\hat{i}\nu$); he does not necessarily expect a cure, he is not giving practical advice. His expectation, however, has not been fulfilled; there has been much dispute by modern medical writers, though we may now be nearer to agreement, on the true nature of this pestilence. Two recent theories should be mentioned: first, that the disease was really ergotism, which is a severe poisoning induced by a fungus growth on rye, but is non-infectious. This suggestion was first made, it seems, by Kobert, as reported in Böhme-Widmann, n. on 51. 6; for a clear account, see Finley, p. 158, n. 2. Rye was not used for bread in classical Greece, but may have been in Thrace; and Finley thinks that it could have been imported from Thrace to make up the deficiency caused by the Peloponnesian invasions of Attica.[1] That

---

[1] Page, p. 116, n. 1, reports that according to some the fungus may attack other grains, including wheat.

Thucydides thought the illness infectious may not be so important as the similarity of the symptoms he describes to those of ergotism; but we should have to give up the Egyptian origin, and Thucydides' conviction that it spread to other places as well. Two other questions also suggest themselves to the layman: is ergotism likely to have attacked so large a part of the population, because *some* rye had been imported? (The cereal normally imported, from South Russia or Egypt or Sicily, was wheat.) And, secondly, is it probable that all classes would have been similarly affected? The rich, in the cavalry, who would probably not be eating rye bread, had heavy losses (iii. 87. 3). Cf. 51. 3, τὰ πάσῃ διαίτῃ θεραπευόμενα. One would suppose, too, that if rye bread was eaten in Attica, it would, as a Thracian food, have been eaten by the troops before Poteidaia; and it would be an unexpected accident that the latter did not get ergotism, a non-infectious disease, before the arrival of fresh troops from Athens (58. 2). We must assume, too, that similarly affected rye was imported again in 427 (iii. 87), but not thereafter. We have, in fact, to assume too much to make this theory a probable one.

The other recent theory is that of Professor J. F. D. Shrewsbury, that it was measles, attacking with severity a population which came into contact with it for the first time (*Bull. of the History of Medicine*, xxiv, 1950, 1–25).[1] He points out that we cannot be certain of the exact meaning of certain terms used by Thucydides, especially in his account of the exanthem, for the meaning may depend on whether he is using technical medical, or popular terminology (but see Page's article, noted above); and he gives an account of an epidemic of measles in the Fiji Islands in 1875 (this visitation being to a "virgin field") which had very severe effects and many symptoms that were remarkably like those described here (esp. in 49. 5). He adds that even in its mild form to which modern peoples, long accustomed to it, are subjected, it is more like Thucydides' account than is any other known disease. Admittedly, however, though some symptoms, in one or two modern cases, are strikingly similar, there is no overall identity; and the case for typhus must again be considered. Shrewsbury objects that epidemic typhus is carried only by the black rat, which was unknown, it seems, in Greece in the fifth century B.C.; or by the body louse, on which Page comments (p. 114, n. 2) that there is no reason to suppose that the Athenians had already sunk so low in 430 B.C. But conditions cannot have been good even in 431; and the case for typhus has been given to me by Professor T. Ferguson of Glasgow, to whom I showed Page's article, and who was good enough to allow me to quote from his letter. He writes as follows:

"Certain symptoms occur in all febrile illnesses, their appearance

1 I have to thank Professor Meritt for drawing my attention to this article.

or their severity depending largely on the height of the temperature. Other symptoms are common to two or more febrile illnesses so that the presence of such symptoms may be little guide in distinguishing one illness from the other. Furthermore, the chief characteristics of a disease in one epidemic are not necessarily the same as those of a disease with the same label in another. Take the modern conception of influenza. In one epidemic the mortality is high; in another almost negligible. One epidemic is characterized by pulmonary complications, another by gastro-enteritis, a third by severe headache, and so on. So it was in earlier days with typhus fever and some other continued fevers resembling it. In the past 500 years many infectious diseases have died out, to be superseded by others, or have changed their clinical picture; there must have been many such changes over a period of 2,000 years.

"The epidemic described by Thucydides may have been measles; but it seems a little unnecessary to bring forward this possibility when the illness as described bore so much resemblance to typhus fever (or another 'continued fever')—an ill-defined group of fevers, endemic and of slight severity in times of peace and plenty, but becoming epidemic and of enhanced severity with high case mortality in times of war, poverty, crowding, and famine. These typhus fevers attacked chiefly young adults between the ages of 20 and 30, whereas measles, except in special circumstances—as in the famous Fiji outbreak—is a disease chiefly affecting children. The modern conception of typhus is of a disease carried by the body louse. Whether all the modifications of continued fever described in the past were in fact conveyed in this way must now remain uncertain, but the story of their having been conveyed in many instances by clothing and blankets is certainly suggestive that they often were conveyed in this way. There seems to be no reason for introducing the black rat into the argument, as is done by Shrewsbury and Page. Page makes the point in a footnote (on page 114) that the Athenians in 430 B.C. were not a dirty people; but in the circumstances of war anyone can acquire infection with body lice. At the present day in this country the head louse (which fortunately does not carry typhus) is of widespread distribution, even in peace time. Typhus is still endemic in the Balkans and was a source of trouble in both the Great Wars of the present century.

"Another obstacle mentioned by Page to the acceptance of the theory that the epidemic was one of typhus is that Thucydides made no mention of the occurrence of mental symptoms. From the descriptions by medical men of the symptoms in outbreaks of typhus-like fevers occurring in this country in the 19th century it is obvious that severe mental symptoms were not invariably present. Medical experience suggests that the loss of memory from which some of the

Athenian cases suffered in convalescence may have followed some affection of the brain during the acute stage of the disease.

"Page (on page 114) recognizes that the similarity in symptoms between typhus fever and the epidemic described by Thucydides is strong. In further corroboration, it may be mentioned that many cases of typhus fever occurring in this country in the 17th and 18th centuries had a putrid stench: a surgeon who attended cases in Carlisle in 1781, for example, reported that the smell was so offensive that it was with difficulty that he could stay in the house of a patient. There is no comparable odour associated with measles.

"By way of summary, I should say that while it is not possible to deny that the Athenian outbreak may have been measles, there is so much to be said in favour of the diagnosis of typhus that I should accept a diagnosis of measles with great reserve."

This view was put forward some years ago in medical journals by Sir W. P. MacArthur,[1] who has also written a reply to Page in $C.Q.$ iv, 1954, of which the author and editors kindly allowed me to see a copy in proof; Page has a brief rejoinder. The case for typhus is clearly very strong; and where Thucydides' description differs from a modern one, I would rely on Ferguson's judgement that particular characteristics of diseases do vary from one epidemic to another. In a letter to me Sir Wm. MacArthur made the interesting point that Thucydides says (47. 4) that doctors were among the most frequent victims, and "typhus is unique as the *morbus medicorum*, and from the earliest times until the present it has remained the one infectious disease from which doctors die"; and he mentioned some remarkable figures of mortality in epidemics of the nineteenth century (in Ireland), and even during the last war, in spite of modern knowledge and means of protection. Sir William added three other things: typhus is no respecter of the rich and well-fed (cf. 51. 3, and iii. 87 for the mortality among the better-off citizens); sleeplessness and intolerable restlessness (49. 6) are outstandingly characteristic of typhus; and "if Thucydides had said no more than that the disease was a severe infectious fever with gangrene of the extremities as a character, that alone would be a diagnostic of typhus". Two colleagues to whom he showed Thucydides' account, with great experience of typhus, but innocent of all knowledge of the Athenian epidemic, said 'Typhus, of course'. I am by nature sceptical when experts say 'of course' (or 'we now know'); but it seems that the solution of this problem has now been reached.

---

[1] 'Old-time Typhus in Britain', *Trans. R.S. Trop. Med.* xx, 1927, 487 ff. ad fin., and *Trop. Diseases Bulletin*, xxiv, 1927, 335 ff.; and 'A Medical Survey of the Irish Famine of 1846' in *Ulster Medical Journal*, May 1951. I owe my knowledge of these to the kindness of Sir William MacArthur. In the former the layman will find an illuminating account of typhus epidemics in this country, which throws much light on the description in Thucydides.

εἴ ποτε καὶ αὖθις ἐπιπέσοι: cf. the similar thought in i. 22. 4 and iii. 82. 2. I do not believe, with Finley, pp. 159–71, and others, that Thucydides had a cyclical view of history, that is, that he thought events repeated themselves in such a way that an accurate knowledge of the past (such as he was providing for future readers) would enable men to foretell what was to come, except in so far as we all believe this, and act on the belief, from our own experience and our knowledge of history ('if we behave in such and such a way, the consequence will surely be so and so'); and this passage supports my view. Ἄδηλα τὰ τῶν πολέμων, says Archidamos (11. 4; cf. i. 84. 3), not at all to be foretold; Perikles had put the same thought in a livelier way, i. 140. 1;[1] and the event of the war which was above all unforeseeable, incalculable, was the pestilence (61. 3, 64. 1). This might recur; but Thucydides' description did not make it any the more foreseeable, even though certain steps (such as the provision of an adequate supply of good water) could be taken which might lessen its effects, and though a cure might some time be discovered. αὐτός τε νοσήσας καὶ αὐτὸς ἰδὼν ἄλλους πάσχοντας: the only event in the war, except his own strategia, for which Thucydides gives the source of his knowledge (i. 22. 2; vol. i, p. 28). (By a strange lapse for such a scholar, Cobet bracketed the second αὐτός, on the ground that Greek said αὐτός τε καὶ ἄλλους; but not only would this require the order καὶ ἄλλους ἰδὼν πάσχοντας, or καὶ ἄ. π. ἰ., but the repeated αὐτός has its special purpose: 'my own illness and my own observations of the experience of others'. So Classen.)

49. 1. ἐκ πάντων: to be taken preferably with ὡμολογεῖτο, as Madvig and most edd., not with μάλιστα δὴ ἄνοσον, as Stuart Jones. See Classen.

εἰ δέ τις καὶ προύκαμνέ τι, κ.τ.λ.: see 51. 1 n.

2. ἀπ' οὐδεμιᾶς προφάσεως: 'from no visible cause.' Cf. Hippokrates, i, p. 588 Kühn. Thucydides may have known a special medical use of the common word πρόφασις, as most scholars think (see L. and S.), including Page. If it had such a special use, Thucydides would be familiar with it; but it may not have it here any more than 'cause without' in Hamlet (IV. iv. 28–30):

> This is the imposthume of much wealth and peace,
> That inward breaks, and shows no cause without
> Why the man dies.

For a general discussion of the meanings of αἰτία and πρόφασις in Thucydides, see i. 23. 6 n. and, in the light of G. M. Kirkwood's

[1] See my note; and iv. 17–18. We may perhaps compare Plato's πλανωμένη αἰτία, "a real cause which is non-rational. . . . That element of 'cussedness' in Nature which is familiar to every farmer and every engineer" (Dodds, J.H.S. lxv, 1945, 20; who refers to Cornford's full discussion in Plato's Cosmology, 162 ff.). 'Cussedness' is very like Thucydides' ἀμαθῶς χωρῆσαι, i. 140. 1.

article in $A.J.P.$ lxxiii, 1952, 37–60, and L. C. Pearson's in $T.A.P.A.$ lxxxiii, 1952, 205–23, my further n. on προφάσεις καὶ αἰτίας, iii. 13. 1, and on iv. 80. 2. Suffice it to say here that $O.T.$ 1235–6,

τέθνηκε θεῖον Ἰοκάστης κάρα.
Χο. ὦ δυστάλαινα, πρὸς τίνος ποτ' αἰτίας;

suggests that there need not be, at all times, much distinction in meaning between the two words; and I doubt the special medical use of πρόφασις. In *Airs, Waters, Places*, for example (above, p. 149), we have in c. 4, ἔμπνοί τε πολλοὶ γίνονται ἀπὸ πάσης προφάσιος· τούτου δὲ αἴτιόν ἐστι τοῦ σώματος ἡ ἔντασις, κ.τ.λ., a similar distinction to that between πρόφασις and αἰτία here in Thucydides; so cc. 6, 12 (αἴτιον), 10 (πρόφασις); but in c. 15 we have πρόφασις used in the same way as αἴτιον, and in 16 αἰτίαι and προφάσεις referring to the same causes, ultimate, not immediate causes, of physical character in men. I prefer the meaning here 'no explanation', 'no apparent cause'; and I think the doctors took the word, with its ordinary meaning, from ordinary usage.

3. ὁπότε ἐς τὴν καρδίαν στηρίξειεν: 'when the disorder settled in the heart.' Page, p. 100, has shown that in all probability καρδία means 'heart', as generally in the medical writers, not τὸ στόμα τῆς γαστρός, as Galen (v. 275 Kühn) thought, and the scholiast here. στηρίζειν in this sense is a special medical use.

ἀποκαθάρσεις χολῆς: here apparently by vomiting only (Page, p. 108). The later effect on the bowels is mentioned below, § 6.

4. λύγξ - - - κενή: λύγξ appears normally to mean 'hiccuping'; but the addition of κενή requires the meaning 'ineffectual retching' (see L. and S.; Page, 101); ἔστι γὰρ καὶ λὺγξ πλήρης, ὡς καὶ Ἱπποκράτης διδάσκει (*Aphor.* vi. 39), schol. Lucretius gives *singultus frequens* (vi. 1160), which, however, Bailey translates 'retching'. See also his interesting n. on 1151–9.

σπασμὸν - - - ἰσχυρόν: 'violent convulsions' arising from mental disturbance, according to MacArthur (above, p. 153); 'the strong muscular reaction which occurs in vomiting rather than a subsequent convulsion', according to a medical opinion quoted by Page (ibid.). Certainly in the *Epidemiai*, as the former pointed out to me, σπασμός is independent of retching (see e.g. pp. 164, 192, 206, 226, 266, and 276 of Jones's Loeb edition, vol. i); the only case that, to a layman, seems to favour Page's view is the second on p. 164.

μετὰ ταῦτα λωφήσαντα: surely to be taken together—'after these symptoms (ἀποκαθάρσεις χολῆς) had abated'.

5. ἐξηνθηκός: already a medical term: see L. and S.

ἥδιστά τε ἄν, κ.τ.λ.: "a plunge into cold water would give the greatest relief", Page. Surely 'the sick *liked* most to plunge into cold water'.

καθειστήκει: 'it was a fixed, regular symptom', or 'feeling, desire'.

155

6. ἢ διεφθείροντο οἱ πλεῖστοι: i.e. the majority of those who were attacked by the disease (the significant words being ἔτι ἔχοντές τι δυνάμεως); similarly οἱ πολλοί below means the majority of those who died after surviving the first 6 or 8 days. But clearly we would do better without this ἤ, for ὥστε does not continue its effect on ἢ εἰ διαφύγοιεν, κ.τ.λ. This second ἤ means 'or else', with a stop before it, as Page translates.

ἔτι ἔχοντες τι δυνάμεως: 'while still comparatively strong', rather than 'before their strength was entirely exhausted' (Page; cf. his p. 111 (i)).

ἀκράτου: 'uniformly fluid', and applicable to diarrhoea only, not to dysentery (Page, 102–3).

ἀσθενείᾳ διεφθείροντο: 'succumbed from weakness.' I prefer ἀπεφθείροντο, the reading of ABEFM (διεφθ. C ⟨G⟩). It is not found elsewhere in Attic prose; but is fairly frequent in tragedy. (Stahl says it occurs in Aristophanes too; but only in phrases like οὐκ ἐς κόρακας ἀποφθερεῖ, Eq. 892.) It seems a clear case of *lectio difficilior*.

7. τὸ - - - ἱδρυθὲν κακόν: I would put a stop after κακόν, and a colon only after ἐπεσήμαινεν (so Page translates), and perhaps after διεφθείροντο (ἀπεφθ.) of the previous sentence. Editors dispute whether αὐτοῦ is subjective genitive with ἀντίληψις and means τοῦ κακοῦ, or possessive with τῶν ἀκρωτηρίων (= τινός); the latter seems to make better sense, but one might expect αὐτῷ. ἐπεσήμαινεν, 'symptoms appeared', was a special medical use.

8. στερισκόμενοι τούτων: Lucretius (vi. 1208–10) understood this to mean 'loss by amputation' ('self-amputation', apparently), and Maas, as reported by Bailey on vv. 1205–12 of Lucretius, thinks that Thucydides meant this too. I do not believe this.

παραυτίκα ἀναστάντας: 'immediately after recovery', thought by most edd., but not by Steup, to imply that the loss of memory was but temporary.

50. 1. τῶν ξυντρόφων: Classen compares Hdt. vii. 102. 1, τῇ Ἑλλάδι πενίη μὲν αἰεί κοτε σύντροφός ἐστι.

2. τεκμήριον δέ: this argument is very carefully expressed—'for, while we have only negative evidence about birds of prey, who, very remarkably, kept away from the neighbourhood of Athens and none was seen devouring corpses or otherwise engaged, the dogs, being domestic animals and so unable to stay away (as the birds could), afforded opportunity for observing the results of their action—they either would not touch the dead (unless ἢ οὐ προσῄει is to be taken to refer only to the birds), or if they did, they died'. "Here (vv. 1215–24) Lucretius follows Thucydides closely and carefully" (Bailey). I would rather say that Lucretius' rhetorical method and lack of scientific interest, his difference from the historian, are illustrated perhaps more clearly in this passage than elsewhere.

51. 1. ὡς ἑκάστῳ ἐτύγχανέ τι - - - γιγνόμενον: cf. iii. 82. 2, τοῖς εἴδεσι διηλλαγμένα, another close parallel between these two passages.

καὶ ἄλλο - - - ἐς τοῦτο ἐτελεύτα: "haec ideo quod similia 49. 1 legantur delenda non esse inde apparet quod ibi de morbis pestilentia prioribus, hic de eodem tempore exsistentibus sermo est"—Stahl; see also Steup here. This is true; but for all that we can be confident that the two sentences were not written in one draft, and perhaps that these chapters, carefully composed though they are, lack final revision. Cf. § 5, n. ad fin.

2-3. As Steup says, these three clauses ('no nursing, no medicine, no strength of body was sufficient') belong closely together, and should have only light punctuation (perhaps colons) between them.

οὐδὲ ἓν κατέστη ἴαμα: 'no one cure *established* itself'; cf. καθειστήκει 49. 5.

σῶμά τε αὔταρκες ὂν οὐδὲν διεφάνη, κ.τ.λ.: 'no one was distinguished from the rest by bodily strength or weakness so as to be capable of resistance.' "As far as strength or weakness were concerned, all constitutions fell alike the victims of the disorder", Arnold.

For σῶμα αὔταρκες, cf. 41. 1 n.

4. ἥ τε ἀθυμία: note the distinction—great or little bodily strength and much or no medical care made little difference; but weakness of will, despair, was the truly fatal symptom.

5. ἀρετῆς: virtue in general, perhaps, but primarily courage and a sense of duty, not kindliness.

ἐπεὶ καί: like γάρ often, ἐπεί here gives not so much the reason for the action just mentioned, as the reason, or rather an additional reason, for the author's statement: 'I mention the very great courage of some, as others went to the opposite extreme, growing weary even of the customary offices to the dead.' Cf. vii. 30. 2.

τὰς ὀλοφύρσεις τῶν ἀπογιγνομένων: 'funeral dirges for the dead' (see 34. 4), with the participle taken as imperfect, 'those who were dying one after the other'. So most edd., I feel rightly. 'Grew weary even of lamenting the dying (or the dead)', in the sense of 'expressing sorrow for', seems out of place in this context; and 'grew tired even of the laments and cries of the dying' (cf. the use of ὀλοφυρμός, vii. 71. 3, 75. 4), which would otherwise fit well, is inconsistent with the normal use of ἐκκάμνω and similar verbs, which mean to grow weary of what one is doing oneself. Further, τὸν θνήσκοντα just below, which, coupled as it is with τὸν πονούμενον, presumably means the dead, not the dying, is a variation only of οἱ ἀπογιγνόμενοι. Livy, xxv. 26, and Lucretius, vi. 1246, seem to combine meanings one and two above (but see Bailey, ad loc., for the latter).

157

ἐξέκαμον, the reading of ABEFM, seems here preferable to ἐξέκαμνον; like ἀπέστησαν, 47. 4. (The repetition of ὑπὸ τοῦ κακοῦ νικώμενοι too suggests that the narrative lacks final revision: § 1 n.)

6. οἱ διαπεφευγότες: we must remember that Thucydides was himself one of them. The words διὰ τὸ προειδέναι τε, κ.τ.λ., anticipate somewhat; for they must refer to later experience. They were written later; but when? See Page, 118.

52. 1. ἐπίεσε δ' αὐτοὺς μᾶλλον: the crowding added to the general distress. Thucydides does not here mean that it was a contributory cause of the great and rapid spread of the disease (as Diodoros explicitly says, xii. 45. 2) though, since he states that the disease was contagious and infectious (51. 4–5), he must have thought that it was. Nor does he say that better provision should have been made for the reception of the people evacuated from the countryside, either here or in c. 59 when Perikles was attacked for the disaster; nor do we know that any improvement was made in later years: see Ar. Eq. 792–3, quoted above on 17. 3. We should, of course, remember that the crowding in the city was compelled only during the short period each year when the Peloponnesians were in Attica; but, since so much of domestic equipment was removed, or destroyed by the enemy, and corn was not sown, doubtless large numbers did in fact remain in the city all the year round.

2. ὥρᾳ ἔτους: in vi. 70. 1 this phrase has a quite general meaning, 'the season of the year' (in fact, the beginning of winter, when thunderstorms are to be expected); so ἡ ὥρα τοῦ ἐνιαυτοῦ, vii. 47. 2; and this may be its meaning here; in which case it is to be taken with πνιγηραῖς. But since some later writers, as Galen, vii. 290, and Arrian, Anab. v. 9. 6, explain it as having the specific meaning 'the height of summer' (about the summer solstice, Arrian), this is perhaps to be preferred.

νεκροὶ ἐπ' ἀλλήλοις ἀποθνῄσκοντες ἔκειντο: I do not believe that this can stand. The participle can of course be iterative imperfect, as τῶν ἀπογιγνομένων, 51. 5, and ἐναποθνῃσκόντων, below; but the simple participle can hardly here mean 'just as they died, one after another' (ἐναποθνῃσκόντων is a genitive absolute, or to be taken with νεκρῶν—'bodies of men who died there'). The objection to Oncken's transposition of ἀποθνῄσκοντες before ἐν ταῖς ὁδοῖς is that it leaves ἡμιθνῆτες without purpose. Steup inserts τε before ἔκειντο joining the participle with νεκροί, 'they lay on top of one another, both dead and dying'. This probably gives the right meaning; but I should prefer καί (which is just as likely or as unlikely to have dropped out) before ἀποθνῄσκοντες; of Steup's instances in Thucydides of the joining of single ideas by τε (i. 12. 4, 29. 1, 37. 2, iii. 36. 6, vi. 72. 4) only i. 29. 1 is at all parallel, and even that is much easier. νεκροί and

158

ἀποθνήσκοντες will be predicates, and an indefinite 'they' the subject of both ἔκειντο and ἐκαλινδοῦντο. (Marchant's bracketing of ἀποθνήσκοντες—so easy and improbable a correction—is also wrong in that we need something besides νεκροί as subject to ἐκαλινδοῦντο; an objection which applies as well to the text as it stands.)

3. τά τε ἱερά: see 17. 1. Deaths within sacred precincts were avoided if possible: i. 126. 4, 134. 3; iii. 104.

καὶ ἱερῶν καὶ ὁσίων: divine and human laws, or customs, both normally compelling. So 53. 4, with a wider context.

4. θήκας: here 'modes', not 'places' of burial, as τάφος for ταφή, 47. 1; cf. Plat. *Rep.* iv. 427 B (see Stahl).

53. 1. πρῶτόν τε ἦρξε - - - ἀνομίας: this implies that lawlessness (contrast 37. 3) survived the pestilence—'the later lawlessness had its origin in the pestilence'. It is by no means obvious from Thucydides, or from Aristophanes, that this is a correct inference, that Athens did not recover her general morale as she did her fighting spirit and self-confidence.

μὴ καθ' ἡδονὴν ποιεῖν: contrast the use of the phrase in 37. 2; and iii. 82. 8. A simple instance of Thucydides' love of illustrating different aspects of words in different contexts: cf. iii. 37. 3 n.

3. προσταλαιπωρεῖν: 'to persevere in', 'to hold out yet longer', as L. and S. (coll. Ar. *Lys.* 766), is the right rendering here. The reading προταλαιπωρεῖν of CE, adopted by Stahl, Classen, Steup, and Hude, is attractive, but (I think) wrong: "ad assequendum id quod honestum visum est antea labores suscipere" (Stahl). This is what would be predicated in normal times—'few are willing to submit to the prolonged training necessary to obtain virtue'; it would not be special to this crisis; whereas 'to persevere in good conduct' (when there was every temptation to give way) is just what we want. πρὶν ἐπ' αὐτὸ ἐλθεῖν is suitable to either compound.

τῷ δοξάντι καλῷ: 'what *had* been thought honourable'?

οὐδεὶς πρόθυμος ἦν: an exaggeration; see 51. 5–6.

ὅτι δὲ ἤδη τε ἡδύ, κ.τ.λ.: Stahl objected to πανταχόθεν taken with κερδαλέον on the ground that "qui voluntatem sectantur, eis, cum quovis modo ea frui contendant, non ea tantum placent quae omni modo, sed quae ullo modo eo conducunt"; Steup followed him in this (though rightly objecting to Stahl's remedy, τό τ' ἐς αὐτό, by which πανταχόθεν goes with ἡδύ), and added that men are described as wanting two things, the immediately pleasant, and what will conduce to the immediately pleasant, yet we have only a singular, τοῦτο, to follow. He therefore proposed a more drastic change, ὅ τι δὲ ἤδη τε ἡδὺ καὶ τὸ ἐφ' αὐτὸ κερδαλέον ('what is in itself advantageous, without considering consequences'), πανταχόθεν τοῦτο, κ.τ.λ. I do not see how this better explains the singular τοῦτο, and πανταχόθεν is left

halting. No change from CG's text (except καί before καλόν) is necessary. For πᾶς and its compounds in the sense of 'any and every', cf.
πᾶν ποιεῖν μᾶλλον ἤ.

4. νόμος οὐδεὶς ἀπεῖργε, τὸ μὲν κρίνοντες: perhaps the most remarkable of such anacolutha in Thucydides, especially with οὐδείς following, which in sound echoes οὐδείς before ἀπεῖργε. It does not belong
to the common type, such as we see illustrated in iii. 36. 2, ἔδοξεν
αὐτοῖς - - -, ἐπικαλοῦντες, or iv. 108. 4, ἄδεια ἐφαίνετο αὐτοῖς - - -,
κρίνοντες, or Eur. Hek. 971, αἰδώς μ' ἔχει - - - τυγχάνουσα; for in those
there is only a *grammatical* change of subject, here there is rhetorical
purpose in writing φόβος ἤ - - - νόμος οὐδεὶς ἀπεῖργε instead of φόβῳ
ἤ - - - νόμῳ οὐδεὶς ἀπείργετο. The scholiasts have not preserved any
ancient comment.

This chapter has a variety of other interesting anacolutha: the
common ἐτόλμα τις - - - ὁρῶντες, οὐδεὶς πρόθυμος ἦν - - - νομίζων, κρίνοντες
- - - οὐδεὶς ἐλπίζων, οὐδεὶς ἐλπίζων - - - πολὺ δὲ μείζω, κ.τ.λ. (as though
πάντες or πᾶς τις had been inserted).

54. 3. ἐγένετο μὲν οὖν ἔρις, κ.τ.λ.: 'there *had* been a dispute whether
the word was (ὠνομάσθαι, perfect) λοιμός or λιμός.' The irony is kept
to the end, τὴν μνήμην ἐποιοῦντο: men's *memories* were affected by
their experiences. Cf. i. 22. 4 and below, p. 161.

There has also been a dispute, equally ineffectual, between scholars
as to whether these doubts show that the diphthong οι was or was
not pronounced the same as single iota in the fifth century in Athens.
4. τοῦ Λακεδαιμονίων χρηστηρίου: see i. 118. 3; and cf. iv. 118. 1–2 nn.
The repetition here of the actual words does not suggest that Thucydides had the former passage in mind when he wrote this one. Apollo,
of course, is the god who would send the pestilence, as in the *Iliad*.
The statue of Apollo Alexikakos in the agora at Athens, by Kalamis,
is said by Pausanias, i. 3. 3, to have been set up on the occasion of
this pestilence; but this is rejected by modern scholars, who put
Kalamis a generation earlier. The festival of Bendis, however, may
have been now instituted: W. F. Ferguson, *Hesp.* Suppl. viii. 130–63.
5. ἐσβεβληκότων δέ, κ.τ.λ.: giving the date—'however that may be,
it was during the first days of the invasion that the pestilence broke
out'.

τῶν ἄλλων χωρίων τὰ πολυανθρωπότατα: "perhaps Chios, but hardly
Lesbos, otherwise the fact would have been noticed when the revolt
of the island occurs", Grote, v. 85. 2. Ephesos, Byzantion, and others
are also possible; but the important conclusion to draw is that in
none of them was the epidemic so severe as in Athens.

For the further story of the pestilence, see iii. 87. 1–3; from that
passage we learn that the first visitation lasted two years.

There can be no doubt that Thucydides was conscious of the deep contrast between the sunlit description of Athens in the Funeral Speech and this of the sufferings and demoralization of the very next summer, as he was of that between the Funeral Speech and the realism of Perikles' last speech, which he is soon to give; as he was of the effect produced by the Mytilenean debate being followed by the speeches at the trial of the Plataians, and of the presage in the Melian war of the disaster at Syracuse. This does not prove that the speeches and events did not take place, and in the order in which he gives them. Moreover, the narrative of the pestilence, in its essentials, is contemporary with the events; the moral of the juxtaposition of the epitaphios may have been conceived early too. Curiously, Cornford, who in his *Thucydides Mythistoricus* was looking everywhere for 'dramatic' composition in the historian, missed this juxtaposition; indeed, he thought the careful description of the pestilence to be in Thucydides' earlier manner, when he was writing 'scientifically' (more or less), relating the truth as he saw it, by contrast with the dramatic narrative of so much of the rest of the book.

Ullrich, *Beiträge*, 70–72, 72–78, maintained that §§ 2–3 and § 4 of this chapter must both of them have been written before 404, the former because Thucydides could not have said ἦν δέ γε οἶμαί ποτε ἄλλος πόλεμος καταλάβῃ Δωρικὸς τοῦδε ὕστερος καὶ ξυμβῇ γενέσθαι λιμόν after the siege of Athens in 405–404, during which many had died of hunger, and the final surrender, and the latter because in v. 26. 3–4 (written after 404) it is said that the only oracle which had come true was the one which said that the war would last twenty-seven years: clearly, argues Ullrich, he could not at the same time have been thinking of Apollo's promise to aid the Peloponnesians in the war which also by that time had proved true, but not by 414 (vii. 18. 2). See Grundy, *Thucydides*, i.² 471–2. The second of these I find very unconvincing: Apollo only said he would *help* Sparta, not bring victory, and he did; it was not a prophecy that victory would be theirs, however *they* behaved, nor anything like so precise as that of the twenty-seven years' fighting—hence in § 5, ἤκαζον ὁμοῖα εἶναι. The first, however, is a stronger argument; if true, then τοῦδε here means the ten years' war only.

ταῦτα μὲν τὰ κατὰ τὴν νόσον γενόμενα: that part of Thucydides' story of the great pestilence which is a detailed account of the *symptoms* is, essentially, a digression in the *History* (for they have little to do with politics or war); it is there primarily because he was interested, scientifically, in the disease besides being the recorder of a great disaster which had much to do with politics and the war. It is in this way parallel to other digressions—the character and last years of Themistokles and Pausanias, or the overthrow of the Peisistratidai.

It is to be remarked that neither Diodoros (so presumably not Ephoros) nor Plutarch says anything about the nature of the disease itself, though the former has something about its immediate causes (see 48. 3 n.); they do not even repeat Thucydides. Either no attempt was made by later medical writers to elaborate or explain Thucydides' account, or the historians were not aware of any. It is also characteristic of the Byzantine age that, as has been said, when the historians had occasion to record plagues as disastrous as that of the Peloponnesian war, they did repeat much from Thucydides, and there was not much that was fresh in their descriptions of events which might, one supposes, have moved contemporaries to some genuine expression.

55–58. *The Peloponnesian Invasion. Athenian Counter-measures*

55. 1. ἐς τὴν Πάραλον γῆν καλουμένην: i.e. the whole of the coastal belt of Attica from Aixone to Sounion and from Sounion to Rhamnous (where it looks towards Euboea), which is not the same as the area of all the coastal trittyes of Kleisthenes' organization (this included all the land west of Aigaleos as well); just as τὸ πεδίον seems to mean here, as in 20. 1, 4, not the area of the inland-trittyes, but the basin of the Kephissos (the southern half of which comprised the town-trittyes). The Peloponnesians presumably went by the Mesogeia, past the demes Paiania and Lamptrai, east of Hymettos, down to the coast near Aixone, or Anagyrous.

μέχρι Λαυρείου: but we are not told how destructive the visitation was. The silver-mines were of the first importance to Athens, producing as they did one of the most valuable articles of export; but the tools of the trade were simple, and most of them removable, and it is probable that in a short visit the Peloponnesians did but little harm, and that for the greater part of the year the mines were worked as usual. Nor can many of the slave-workmen have escaped into the Peloponnesian lines (though some did, 57. 1) or been killed; for we hear nothing of any special effect of the invasions on Athenian finance during the Archidamian war; and a particular value of the occupation of Dekeleia in 413 was said to be that, by such a permanent hold on Attica, the production of the mines would be stopped (vi. 91. 7; cf. vii. 27. 3–5).

τὴν πρὸς Εὔβοιαν, κ.τ.λ.: contrast Diodoros, xii. 45. 1, who says the Peloponnesians spared the Tetrapolis (Marathon and other ancient townships in that region), out of gratitude for the help given to the Herakleidai against Eurystheus; a story which it would be unnecessary to refer to—Thucydides believed in the historical truth of Eurystheus and the sons of Herakles, but not in this childish and sentimental attitude to history—but that it recalls the similar story of the sparing of Dekeleia in Herodotos, ix. 73. The Peloponnesians *may* have ravaged one deme and spared another, in order to create jealousies and mutual suspicions among the enemy (cf. 13. 1); but since Thucydides suggests no such thing (cf. 57. 2, $\tau\grave{\eta}\nu$ $\gamma\hat{\eta}\nu$ $\pi\hat{a}\sigma a\nu$ $\H{\epsilon}\tau\epsilon\mu o\nu$), we have no reason to believe that they did, at least not on this occasion.

56. 1. $\H{\epsilon}\tau\iota$ δ' $a\dot{v}\tau\hat{\omega}\nu$, $\kappa.\tau.\lambda.$: here and in § 3 this expedition is very precisely dated, rather more vaguely in § 6. Unfortunately we have not any official inscription, as we have of the naval expedition of the previous year (23. 2 n.) which might have helped us in estimating the time between the first payment of money direct to the strategoi and the later payments through the Hellenotamiai, and the meaning of the different formulae used.

2. $\acute{o}\pi\lambda\acute{\iota}\tau a\varsigma$ - - - $\tau\epsilon\tau\rho a\kappa\iota\sigma\chi\iota\lambda\acute{\iota}ov\varsigma$, $\kappa.\tau.\lambda.$: cf. vi. 31. 2, where these numbers are recalled by way of comparison with the Sicilian expedition. From that passage also we learn expressly what we ought to believe from this one that $\acute{o}\pi\lambda\acute{\iota}\tau a\varsigma$ $A\theta\eta\nu a\acute{\iota}\omega\nu$ did not include metics (see p. 36, above).

$\nu a\upsilon\sigma\grave{\iota}\nu$ $\acute{\iota}\pi\pi a\gamma\omega\gamma o\hat{\iota}\varsigma$ $\pi\rho\hat{\omega}\tau o\nu$ $\tau\acute{o}\tau\epsilon$ $\acute{\epsilon}\kappa$ $\tau\hat{\omega}\nu$ $\pi a\lambda a\iota\hat{\omega}\nu$ $\nu\epsilon\hat{\omega}\nu$ $\pi o\iota\eta\theta\epsilon\acute{\iota}\sigma a\iota\varsigma$: either 'for the first time in this war' (cf. iv. 42. 1, vi. 43 ad fin.), or 'for the first time in Athens (or in Greece)', or, 'for the first time made out of reconstructed triremes'; for, as edd. point out, the Persians had used horse-transports, Hdt. vi. 48. 2, vii. 97. Cf. iii. 19. 1, where there is a similar ambiguity about $\epsilon\acute{\iota}\sigma\phi o\rho\acute{a}$. Since $\tau\acute{o}\tau\epsilon$ $\pi\rho\hat{\omega}\tau o\nu$ generally means 'then and not till then', and this was only the second year of the war, the first interpretation is probably wrong, and the third is the best.

Aristophanes makes fun of such transport-vessels (*Eq.* 599–603).

4. $\acute{\epsilon}\varsigma$ '$E\pi\acute{\iota}\delta a\upsilon\rho o\nu$: the strongest city in the Argolic peninsula after Argos itself; generally at enmity with Argos, and so friendly to Sparta. Its capture by Perikles would not only have been important in itself, as a severe blow to Peloponnesian confidence, but would have provided a way of direct access to Argos, neutral, but at odds generally with the Peloponnese dominated by Sparta.

5. $\tau\grave{\eta}\nu$ $T\rho o\iota\zeta\eta\nu\acute{\iota}\delta a$ $\gamma\hat{\eta}\nu$, $\kappa.\tau.\lambda.$: see i. 115. 1 n. For earlier Athenian relations with Halieis and Hermione, see vol. i, pp. 311, 367; and for the later alliance with the former (*I.G.* i.² 87), below, iv. 45. 2 n. Troizen was on the north-east coast of the Akte, south-east of Epidauros, Hermione and Halieis on the east coast.

6. $\acute{\epsilon}\varsigma$ $\Pi\rho a\sigma\iota\grave{a}\varsigma$ $\tau\hat{\eta}\varsigma$ $\Lambda a\kappa\omega\nu\iota\kappa\hat{\eta}\varsigma$: on the coast south of the Gulf of Argos and south of Thyrea (above, 27. 2) and, like Thyrea, sometimes within the domain of Argos; see Polyb. iv. 36. 5; Strabo, viii. 6. 1–2, p. 368; Paus. iii. 24. 2–3. It has been located at some ruins near H. Andréas (e.g. by Leake, ii. 498), and, with more probability, near

Leonídi, farther south: see Frazer and Hitzig and Blümner on Pausanias.

There was another Prasiai in Attica, mentioned viii. 95. 1.

εἷλον καὶ ἐπόρθησαν: but they did not attempt to hold it, as they later held Pylos. It suffered severely (perhaps in other raids as well, which Thucydides does not mention): Ar. Peace, 242, ἰὼ Πρασιαὶ τρισάθλιοι καὶ πεντάκις, κ.τ.λ.; and again later in the war, vi. 105. 2, vii. 18. 3.

ἐπ' οἴκου ἀνεχώρησαν: Telekleides, fr. 43 (above, 27. 1 n.), was thought by Bergk to refer to Perikles; if so, possibly on this occasion.

F. E. Adcock, Cambridge Historical Journal, i, 1923–5, 319–22, has argued that the debatable chapter, iii. 17, was intended by Thucydides to be inserted here. See the n. ad loc.

57. 1. τῶν αὐτομόλων: the definite article because desertion was to be expected (mainly of slaves) and was normal in war-time.

2. πλεῖστόν τε χρόνον: edd. have pointed out that there is here no true comparison between the invasions of the Archidamian war and the permanent occupation of Dekeleia; but I agree with Ullrich (Beiträge, 80–83; Grundy, Thucydides, i.² 472) that Thucydides probably only had the Archidamian war in mind when he wrote this. This was also the severest, as well as the longest, of those invasions, iii. 26. 3; but the author of Hellenika Oxyrhynchika (12. 5) said that no very great damage was done in Attica before the occupation of Dekeleia. We must remember that destruction, especially of trees— olive-trees and vines in Attica—would be a slow business. See, however, n. on iii. 26. 2.

58. 1. τοῦ δ' αὐτοῦ θέρους: not further defined; but since the expedition against the Peloponnese returned after the invasion of Attica was over (56. 6), and there must have been an interval between then and the sailing of the new one, and since the invasion will have lasted well into June (47. 2 n., 56. 2), Hagnon and Kleopompos cannot have started much before the end of the month, and more probably left in July. This, however, would still be before the end of the archon-year, which in 430 was on July 23 (the bouleutic year ended on July 1), according to Meritt, A.F.D. 176. Their return to Athens forty days later (§ 3) must have occurred in the new archon-year.

Ἄγνων ὁ Νικίου: strategos also in 440–439, i. 117. 2; again in 429–428, ii. 95. 3 (unless he was only ambassador then; see n. ad loc.). Oikistes of Amphipolis, 437 B.C., iv. 102. 3, v. 11. 1; one of the 'signatories' of the Peace of Nikias and of the alliance with Sparta, v. 19. 2, 24. 1; and at an advanced age one of the ten πρόβουλοι elected in 413, viii. 1. 3, Lysias, xii. 65; almost certainly the father of the famous Theramenes (cf. viii. 68. 4), and a man, according to Xenophon,

Hell. ii. 3. 30, held in much honour by the people. He took some part in the attacks made on Perikles (65. 1–3 nn.), attempting compromise in Perikles' interest, Plut. *Per.* 32. 3. His deme was Steiria (if he was Theramenes' father); it is not known if he was any relation to Nikias, the well-known statesman (who was of the deme Kydantidai), as his father's name might suggest. See, for recent notes, Kratinos, *Ploutoi*, fr. ap. Page, *Greek Literary Papyri* (Loeb), No. 38 (below, 65. 4 n., pp. 188–9); *A.T.L.* iii. 308, n. 41.

Κλεόπομπος: see 26. 1 n.

ξυστράτηγοι ὄντες Περικλέους: this implies not only that they had been elected at the same time as Perikles, but probably that they had also been his colleagues on the previous expedition. If this last is correct, we should note Thucydides' mode of expression in 56. 1–2: παρεσκευάζετο, ἀνήγετο, ἦγε, as though Perikles were alone responsible (cf. vol. i, p. 70, n. 2). (Diodoros, xii. 46. 1–2, not only dates this expedition in 429, and in the year after the expedition to the Peloponnese under Perikles, but specifically after Perikles' death, apparently through a careless misunderstanding of Thucydides' words here, λαβόντες τὴν στρατιὰν ἧπερ ἐκεῖνος ἐχρήσατο. He, that is, Ephoros, *may* have had evidence that the expedition to Poteidaia started, or was mainly active, in the *archon-year* subsequent to that of the expedition to the Peloponnese, and it may be only Diodoros' error to put them, as he does, in different campaigning seasons; but even so the archon-years are wrong (430–429 and 429–428, instead of 431–430 and 430–429); which shows how little reliance we can have on any date in Diodoros. See vol. i, pp. 4–5, 411–12.)

ἐπὶ Χαλκιδέας - - - καὶ Ποτείδαιαν: a double objective like that of Archestratos and Kallias, i. 57, 61. 2; *I.G.* i.² 276 (*C.R.* lv, 1941, 59–67).

μηχανάς τε, κ.τ.λ.: another failure to take a place by storm (cf. 18. 1–2), though here there are special reasons as well (vol. i, pp. 16–19).

2. Φορμίων δέ, κ.τ.λ.: a remarkable piece of careless writing by Thucydides, for the information, or something of the kind, was badly needed in 31. 2. In itself this sentence would suggest that the withdrawal of Phormion's force had taken place not long before Hagnon's arrival, earlier in the same campaigning season; and I believe this to be possible (see 31. 2 n.). As usual, in such statements casualties are ignored, both those in Phormion's and those in Perikles' force, unless we are to suppose that losses were regularly made up by new drafts; the words mean rather 'the force of 1,600 under Phormion, the force of 4,000 under Perikles, which I have previously mentioned', as we might say 'General A's army-corps' or 'his two divisions' without any statement about their present strength.

3. χιλίους καὶ πεντήκοντα: nearly the same proportion as the total

losses of hoplites by the pestilence (iii. 57. 3). It is possible that Eupolis, fr. 191, ὃς θυμήνας τοῖς στρατιώταις λοιμὸν καὶ ψῶζαν ἔπεμψεν, from *Marikas*, though written ten years later, may refer to this.

οἱ δὲ πρότεροι στρατιῶται: this implies that the same units, made up of the same individual soldiers, stayed behind, who had been there since the summer of 432, and that none were relieved. This may be pressing the words too closely, though Hagnon may have felt himself responsible particularly for the force with which he had set out, and it was no use leaving behind men who might still succumb to the pestilence.

59–65. 4. *Attacks on Perikles. His Last Speech*

59. 1. μετὰ δὲ τὴν δευτέραν ἐσβολήν: by this dating Thucydides would appear to make the change of heart in Athens contemporary with Hagnon's expedition, and this is probably correct; Perikles' own return from a not very successful expedition will have encouraged his enemies, who may, besides, have begun the attacks on his friends during his absence. Hence the pluperfect ἠλλοίωντο ("mutatas fuisse et aliquamdiu mansisse eorum sententias", Stahl); yet after ὡς ἥ τε γῆ αὐτῶν, κ.τ.λ., and without ἤδη, we might have expected an imperfect, ἠλλοιοῦντο.

On this change, both in opinion and will-power, Classen says, "im Gegensatz zu der c. 8. 1 geschilderten Stimmung wozu der Übergang schon c. 16 u. 21–22 angedeutet ist". A contrast with 8. 1, certainly; and 16 in a sense marks a transition; but not 21–22: there the city ἀνηρέθιστο and τὸν Περικλέα ἐν ὀργῇ εἶχον, because he would not lead them out to battle; here they are in despair and τὸν Π. ἐν αἰτίᾳ εἶχον because they had gone to war at all.

2. πρέσβεις τινάς: τινάς has no purpose unless it is to indicate that more than one attempt was made by sending embassies to Sparta to make peace; and if this is meant, we should perhaps read πρεσβείας (the reading of M), with Stahl.[1]

Perhaps nothing makes more clear the reality of democracy in Athens, of the *control of policy* by the ekklesia, than this incident: the ekklesia rejects the advice of its most powerful statesman and most persuasive orator, but the latter remains in office, subordinate to the people's will, till the people choose to get rid of him. The latter action equally well shows the ekklesia's control of the executive. See my paper in *History*, xxxvi, 1951, 23–24.

ἄπρακτοι ἐγένοντο: we may perhaps note that there is no expressed condemnation of Sparta here, that they τοῦ πλέονος ὠρέγοντο, as there is of Athens in 425 (iv. 21. 2, 41. 4; and of both in Aristophanes, *Peace*, 211–19). Was this because Spartan intransigence did not so

---

[1] That Diodoros, xii. 45. 5, has πρεσβείας is not significant.

obviously turn out wrong? Or because Thucydides was less interested in Sparta? The latter, surely; or something of both.

ἐνέκειντο τῷ Περικλεῖ: for the stories about these attacks, see 65. 4 n.

3. ξύλλογον ποιήσας: see 22. 1 n. It is characteristic of Perikles and of Athens, that when he found his fellow countrymen unduly excited and confident, and critical of his *strategy*, he refused to call a special meeting; when he found them in despair and ready to find fault with his whole policy, when his own position was in danger, he called one.

ἔτι δ' ἐστρατήγει: i.e. he had not yet been dismissed from office (65. 3–4). As strategos, or rather as one of the ten strategoi (cf. 22. 1 n.), he could request the prytaneis to call a special meeting of the ekklesia. It is not clear whether the prytaneis were bound to accede to the request; but little men were in any case not likely to oppose a popular politician.

ἐβούλετο θαρσῦναί τε, κ.τ.λ.: cf. 65. 9.

60. 2. πόλιν πλείω ξύμπασαν, κ.τ.λ.: a sentiment already expressed by Sophokles, *Ant.* 184–90 (spoken by Kreon, of course), and very likely by others as well (cf. τῆς πόλεως εὖ ἠκούσης, Hdt. i. 30. 4). It was certainly repeated later: e.g. Xen. *Mem.* iii. 7. 9.

4. οἳ ξυνέγνωτε: so 61. 2, 64. 1. Perikles does not fail to point out to his hearers their share of the responsibility, a share they were often inclined to forget; cf. viii. 1. 1.

5–6. καίτοι ἐμοί, κ.τ.λ.: the answer to the first half of the previous sentence (ἐμέ τε τὸν παραινέσαντα πολεμεῖν); that to the second half (καὶ ὑμᾶς αὐτούς) is given in different form, not antithetically, in 61. 2.

γνῶναί τε τὰ δέοντα, κ.τ.λ.: cf. i. 138. 3 and my notes there. As I said, it is remarkable that in this generalized statement nothing is said of will-power and executive ability. The weakness of the people's will is shown in 61. 2, and his own strength implied; but we might have had something about it here. This passage, in fact, is not pure generalization, though it comes near to being so: the particular context ('the argument, which *persuaded* you', § 7) is much in mind.

I find these two sections, however, perhaps the most artificial thing in all Thucydides' speeches, the farthest removed from actuality, and therefore, apparently, devised by Thucydides himself, not 'as Perikles would have said τὰ τότε δέοντα'; yet we may be misled in this. The Athenians, just at this time, certainly had a passion for generalization in rhetoric such as we find it difficult to appreciate, as can be seen most easily in Euripides, nearly as well in Antiphon, and, in his own way, in the 'Old Oligarch'. The antithetical style is its suitable vehicle (Finley, pp. 250–84).

167

γνῶναί τε τὰ δέοντα καὶ ἑρμηνεῦσαι ταῦτα: virtues possessed to an exceptional degree by Themistokles (i. 138. 3), and, in a sense, by Antiphon (viii. 68. 1). The idea was often expressed by later writers, and some add the necessary practical ability, as Ps.-Lysias, *Epitaphios*, 42 (of Themistokles: cf. Thuc. i. 74. 1); Plat. *Laches*, 178 B; Polybios, iv. 8. 2, etc. For the use of ἐνθυμηθῆναι, see 40. 2 n.

φιλόπολις: this includes not only patriotism in the ordinary sense, conspicuously lacking, for example, in Alkibiades (cf. especially the words attributed to him, vi. 92. 2–4), but loyalty to the constitution, which meant, for example, at Athens a readiness by aristocrats to work with the demos, a quality so notable in Kimon, Perikles, Kleinias, Nikias, and many another, and lacking in Antiphon and the few extremists, and, when he was crossed, in Alkibiades (τό τε φιλόπολι οὐκ ἐν ᾧ ἀδικοῦμαι ἔχω, ἀλλ' ἐν ᾧ ἀσφαλῶς ἐπολιτεύθην). With these latter cf. Plato, *Kriton*, 50 B–C; and for the general picture, Ps.-Xen. *Const. Ath.* i. 7, 3. 12–13 (*Ath. Studies*, pp. 237–44). See also, Ar. *Vesp.* 411, ἄνδρα μισόπολιν; Arist. *Rhet.* ii. 1. 3, 1378 a 7.

χρημάτων κρείσσων: not simply 'not open to bribery', but 'superior to the temptations of money': one who would not make wealth one of his aims in politics, even one who would sacrifice his wealth, or his opportunities for wealth, for the sake of politics. Themistokles may be in mind here, for stories of the great wealth he had amassed were already current; if he had intrigued with Persia, if dreams of wealth had accompanied dreams of power, that is what would be meant by saying he was χρημάτων ἥσσων, not necessarily that he had been directly bribed by Persia with a sum of money to do this or that. Alkibiades, again, was not χρημάτων κρείσσων, or was said not to be, for he needed money to pay for his extravagances, and his public policy was in part guided by this (vi. 12. 2, 15. 2–3).

6. οἰκείως: " 'as a loyal citizen', who regards himself as much bound to the state as to his family", Marchant; 'suitably to his fellow citizens (as though they were members of his own family)'. Cf. 38. 2.

προσόντος δὲ καὶ τοῦδε, κ.τ.λ.: a characteristic but not difficult sentence—τοῦδε is neuter, τὸ εὔνουν or τὸ φιλόπολι, understood from the context; this quality of loyalty may itself be defeated by love of money; and τούτου is again a neuter, but strictly not 'love of money' but money itself, for it is a genitive of price. πωλεῖσθαι, as usual, means 'to be offered for sale', 'to be up for sale'. Dobree's and Cobet's νικώμενος and ἀπόδοιτο (adopted by Hude in 1898, but in his 1913 edition he returned to the MSS. reading), though very ingenious, is nothing like so characteristic.

7. καὶ μέσως - - - μᾶλλον ἑτέρων: cf. διαφερόντως τι - - - μᾶλλον ἑτέρου, i. 138. 3 n.

τοῦ γε ἀδικεῖν: in the most general sense, 'being guilty' of whatever charges are brought, or 'being guilty of ἀδικία towards the state';

cf. Hdt. vi. 136. 3 (of the trial of Miltiades), τοῦ δήμου - - - ζημιώσαντος κατὰ τὴν ἀδικίην πεντήκοντα ταλάντοισι.

61. 1. οἶς μὲν αἴρεσις, κ.τ.λ.: cf. iv. 62. 2, and Hdt. i. 87. 4, οὐδεὶς γὰρ οὕτω ἀνόητός ἐστι ὅστις πόλεμον πρὸ εἰρήνης αἰρέεται, κ.τ.λ.

ἢ εἴξαντας εὐθύς: cf. i. 141. 1, from Perikles' first speech.

2. ἐγὼ μὲν ὁ αὐτός εἰμι: cf. i. 140. 1, the opening words of the first speech. They were imitated later by Kleon, iii. 38. 1. Sophocles, O.T. 557, has a similar phrase.

The sense of this section must be made clear: 'You and I both voted for war when our minds and our resolution were strong, that is, when we were best fitted to make a wise decision; but whereas I have remained the same, you have changed your opinion, when your minds are weak, unfitted to take a proper view of the situation.'

Stahl gives this as one of the cases in which γνώμη means the will as well as the intelligence, his others in Thucydides being i. 70. 6, 71. 1, ii. 20. 4. Of these I think only i. 71. 1 is certain (or rather it means 'will' there, not 'intelligence') ; i. 70. 6, γνώμη is simply 'mind', in a general sense, opposed to body. Here I believe it means the intelligence.

ἡ δήλωσις ἅπασι: according to Krüger, who is followed by most edd., these words are to be taken together in the sense of 'general understanding'. I am doubtful of this. The objection to taking ἅπασι with ἄπεστιν ἔτι—'the advantages are not yet clear to anyone' ('are still obscured to all')—is that Perikles would not thus exaggerate; but this is a weak argument.

ἐγκαρτερεῖν ἃ ἔγνωτε: not, of course, 'in patiently abiding the change' (Marchant), but 'to persevere in the policy you decided on'.

3. δουλοῖ γὰρ φρόνημα τὸ αἰφνίδιον: see iv. 34. 1 n.

4. ἐν ἤθεσιν ἀντιπάλοις αὐτῇ τεθραμμένους: as explained in the Epitaphios, 37–42.

τῆς ὑπαρχούσης δόξης: cf. 45. 2 n.

καὶ τῆς μὴ προσηκούσης: this half of the sentence is irrelevant here and only added for the rhetorical generalization. 'It is not for every city, but only those worthy of it, to aim at empire.' Cf. 41. 3; and for the wording, 65. 8, ἐξ οὗ προσηκόντων.

62. 1. ἐκεῖνα ἐν οἶς - - - ἀπέδειξα: i. 140–4 and ii. 13; cf. esp. the last sentence in 13. 9.

δηλώσω δὲ καὶ τόδε: because his previous expositions have in fact not sufficed; so that ἀρκείτω μέν is put for εἰκὸς μὲν ἦν ἀρκεῖν.

ἐνθυμηθῆναι: 'realized', 'got it fixed in your minds', like ἐντεθύμηται, i. 120. 4; perhaps 'an advantage which has never yet suggested itself to you' (Crawley). Contrast its use in 40. 2 and 60. 6.

169

μεγέθους πέρι ἐς τὴν ἀρχήν: "de magnitudine ad imperium obtinendum (i.e. et tuendum et augendum, id quod ex § 2 apparet)"—Stahl. Cf. de Romilly, p. 110, n. 1, who takes ἐς τὴν ἀρχήν grammatically with ὑπάρχον: " 'la force que vous avez, relativement à l'importance, *pour* votre domination': ἐς implique nettement l'idée que cette domination est un but traité ici pour lui-même, et non une circonstance."

οὔτ' ἐγὼ ἐν τοῖς πρὶν λόγοις: we cannot supply ἐνεθυμήθην, in either sense of the word, for Perikles has had it very much in mind, and had initiated the idea. ἐδήλωσα or ἐδίδαξα or ἀπέδειξα is what is required, but the supplement (rather, of δοκῶ δηλῶσαι) is too harsh; and I believe Arnold was right in 'understanding' ἐχρησάμην, and therefore would put no stop, or only a comma, after λόγοις; so that, κομπωδεστέραν - - - προσποίησιν belongs in effect both to οὔτ' ἐν τοῖς πρὶν λόγοις and to οὐδ' ἂν νῦν. Cf. iii. 40. 2, καὶ τότε πρῶτον καὶ νῦν διαμάχομαι, where a past tense is understood with τότε πρῶτον. So in effect Jebb, to judge by his translation: "a special advantage . . .—one, I think, which has never occurred to you, and which I should not have noticed now", etc. (*Speeches of Thuc.*, in Abbott's *Hellenica*, p. 283).

With κομπωδεστέραν cf. the different tone of the Epitaphios, 41. 2.

καταπεπληγμένους: cf. 65. 9, where, however, by a nice *variatio*, we have δεδιότας of the Athenians and κατέπλησσεν of Perikles' own action on the contrary occasion.

2. τοῦ ἑτέρου ὑμᾶς παντὸς κυριωτάτους ὄντας: 'you are absolute masters of the entire sea', a statement that is certainly κομπωδέστερον. As Classen says, it goes well beyond what Perikles had said in i. 143. 4–5 (and ii. 13. 2); and it is an exaggeration, like that of Ps.-Xen. 2. 5, 11–12 (*Ath. Stud.*, p. 225), though of course an intended and purposeful exaggeration. It has always been difficult to persuade others, whether allies or enemies, and especially the former, of the value of sea-power; and even the citizens of the country which exercises it have often to be reminded of its importance. Athens, in her present mood, needed the reminder, in a forceful and exaggerated form. At other times Athens was ready to think of the sea as her exclusive territory: cf. iv. 121. 2, n. on ὡς ἐς νῆσον, and v. 56. 2.

οὔτε βασιλεὺς οὔτε ἄλλο οὐδὲν ἔθνος: since these words must be closely connected with οὐκ ἔστιν ὅστις (= οὐδείς) Classen argues that βασιλεύς must be generic and cannot be taken as the Persian king; and since "other peoples" are contrasted with kingdoms, they must here be understood as "independent peoples", not ruled by kings. This is quite unnecessary; I am sure every hearer in Athens would think of the Great King only, and many other ἔθνη, as the Macedonians, the Thracians, the Molossians, were ruled by kings. We could have said in English, 'No Tsar, no people will stay our passage', even though there was only one Tsar in the world, and many peoples besides the Russians had kings.

3. οὐ κατά: either 'incomparable', 'not to be compared with', and in Greek, like ἴσος and οὐκ ἴσος, either incomparably greater or incomparably less; or 'not relevant to'.

χαλεπῶς φέρειν αὐτῶν: cf. i. 77. 3, τοῦ ἐνδεοῦς χαλεπώτερον φέρειν, with my n., and ii. 65. 4, ὧν ἤλγει.

κηπίον καὶ ἐγκαλλώπισμα πλούτου: 'a garden, an adornment of our wealth'; i.e. a pleasure garden, or a park rather than a farm. A vivid expression, much in the style of Perikles' recorded sayings ('the spring has been taken out of the year', 'the eyesore of the Peiraeus'), and of others given him by Thucydides (43. 3, 63. 3). What is more remarkable is the boldness of the statesman who could, on such an occasion, thus address his fellow citizens who were so proud of their country homes (c. 16, above; and the notable passage already referred to, *Hell. Ox.* 12. 5): 'think little of your farms in relation to this great power of ours (in time of war, be it understood)'; many of the farmers, including the bellicose Acharnians, will have had little idea of the meaning of sea-power. Note particularly κηπίον instead of κῆπος, a colloquial use; such a use was becoming common at this time, as can be seen in Aristophanes; but this particular word is not elsewhere found in literature before Polybios. 'Park', therefore, is too grand a word; and 'pleasure garden' not sufficiently colloquial. Very different is the feeling expressed by Dikaiopolis and Trygaios; yet Aristophanes was born a townsman, as Perikles and Thucydides were probably not.

καὶ γνῶναι: I should prefer a colon before this sentence, and before τῶν τε πατέρων below.

καὶ τὰ προκεκτημένα: there should, as Steup points out, be some contrast with ταῦτα; yet the latter clearly means the farms and homes of Attica, and if they are not included in τὰ προκεκτημένα, what is? Steup proposes to insert ἅπαντα after καί (so that καί will then mean 'indeed', not 'as well'), which is not convincing. It looks like careless writing; ταῦτα might mean the good buildings and equipment recently acquired, after the Persian destruction; but the distinction seems forced; and the language would more properly belong to a distinction between the old Attica and the empire, as in 36. 1–2, and as the next sentence suggests.

μετὰ πόνων: cf. 36. 2, and i. 70. 8, ii. 39. 4 nn.

αἴσχιον δέ, κ.τ.λ.: the inevitable generalization, inevitably copied by later writers, as Sallust, *Jug.* 31. 17.

μὴ φρονήματι μόνον, ἀλλὰ καὶ καταφρονήματι: this elaborate conceit is also another instance of Thucydides' fondness for playing with possible meanings of words in different contexts; cf. the different colouring of καταφρονεῖν in i. 122. 4, ii. 11. 4, v. 9. 3–4, and vi. 34. 9; and see v. 8. 3 n.

It is difficult to give any adequate rendering in English which would preserve the paronomasia: φρονήματι may be translated 'with spirit' (cf. 61. 3) and καταφρονήματι by 'in a spirit of superiority'; but this misses the purely intellectual element in καταφρόνησις below, a conviction of superiority based on reason, φρόνησις. A free, and wordy rendering might be: 'get to grips with the enemy confident not only that you are strong, but that you are stronger than he'. Similarly, in Herodotos, viii. 10. 2, καταφρονήσαντες ταῦτα: J. E. Powell translates, "having formed this conviction" simply; but it is a conviction based on a feeling of superiority. (For καταφρόνημα followed by καταφρόνησις, cf. ἀξίωμα and ἀξίωσις, 37. 1.)

4–5. αὔχημα μὲν γάρ, κ.τ.λ.: 'boasting indeed will often arise from stupidity when good luck attends it, and is found in the coward; but this confidence means reliance on *reason* for a man's trust in his superiority over his enemy; which is our position. Further, intelligence combined with (*or*, based on) this superior feeling, provided that fortune is equal, makes boldness also much stronger; for it does not trust to hope (which is the comfort of the desperate), but to reason based on facts, whose foresight is much more reliable.' It is all very elaborate, but not so obscure as Dionysios, *Thuc. iud.* 928, thinks and as some modern editors have made it. αὔχημα, says Marchant, "is not *identified* with φρόνημα [as the schol. says it is, just *variatio*], but is substituted as the natural result of it". True, that this is not a case of *variatio*; but the word for which it might have been supposed to be substituted is καταφρόνημα, not φρόνημα; and it is not "the natural result of" καταφρόνημα, but often or generally accompanies a contemptuous attitude—the attitude which in other contexts and in normal thought, is folly (i. 122. 4, etc.). Here Perikles says, 'there is no boasting in καταφρόνησις in the sense in which I am using the latter word'. τὸ ὕπερφρον, on the other hand, is *variatio* for καταφρόνησις; it is a word not found elsewhere in classical prose, but is borrowed from tragedy, where it means 'arrogant'; purposely borrowed for this unique context, because folly and arrogance are the usual accompaniments of contempt. But it is not folly and arrogance to say 'I see, ἐκ τῶν ὑπαρχόντων, that my resources (both material and spiritual) are, in the long run, stronger than the enemy's, and I must therefore hold out under this temporary reverse, confident, under Heaven, that I will win in the end'.

Similarly ἡ τόλμα is often the result of a foolish contempt for difficulties and only leads to defeat; but an intelligent self-confidence of the kind now explained will make it a reliable asset, ἀπὸ τῆς ὁμοίας τύχης, i.e. τῶν θεῶν ἴσα νεμόντων, 'under Heaven' (no man can be *sure* of success, whatever his superiority of strength; for fortune

172

may intervene: that is all that this phrase means; see below). Bloomfield well compares 89. 3, τῷ δὲ ἑκάτεροί τι εἶναι ἐμπειρότεροι θρασύτεροί ἐσμεν, and vi. 72. 4, τὴν δ' εὐψυχίαν - - - μετὰ τοῦ πιστοῦ τῆς ἐπιστήμης θαρσαλεωτέραν ἔσεσθαι; and for a more general expression of this, compare ii. 40. 3, and for particular instances of τὸ θαρσεῖν and καταφρόνησις justified by the visible facts, ii. 88. 2 and iv. 34. 1.

I do not believe that Marchant is right in seeing in καὶ ἀπ' ἀμαθίας εὐτυχοῦς καὶ δειλῷ τινι any reference to Kleon; it is all quite general. Even if Thucydides composed this speech, quite freely, in later years when he was familiar with Kleon's achievements (especially his ἀμαθία and his boasting about Sphakteria), he was too good a writer to expect his readers to look ahead to what he has not yet related, to a man he has not yet mentioned.

5. ἧς ἐν τῷ ἀπόρῳ ἡ ἰσχύς: cf. v. 103, for a more generalized statement; and for the phrase ἰσχὺς τῆς ἐλπίδος, iv. 65. 4, where, however, the hope is the result of present *success* (notice the first sentence in v. 103: the Athenians are the speakers, as they are the ones who rely on hope in iv. 65. 4). Cf. also the use of εὔελπις, iv. 10. 1 (above, 40. 3 n.), and i. 70. 3, and ἀντελπίσαντες, i. 70. 7.

Perikles' fellow countrymen must have felt, at the moment at least, that they *were* in a difficulty from which there was no escape, with only hope to comfort them; cf. 59. 2, πανταχόθεν τῇ γνώμῃ ἄποροι καθεστηκότες. Perikles is stressing, and exaggerating, Athens' continued strength for this very reason.

Steup and Marchant adopt Döderlein's transposition of ἀπὸ τῆς ὁμοίας τύχης after ἐλπίδι, comparing v. 102 to justify this, failing to observe not only that the words have a very good meaning where the MSS. have them (τόλμα will not always be ἐχυρά, even in those intelligently confident of their strength, if fortune is contrary: for it is possible for τὰς ξυμφορὰς - - - ἀμαθῶς χωρῆσαι, i. 140. 1), but that the transposition makes nonsense of ἐν τῷ ἀπόρῳ: no man in a position from which he could see no escape, certainly not the Athenians at this moment, would say that fortune had been fair. Nor is γνώμη here contrasted with τύχη, as Marchant says, but with ἐλπίς.

γνώμῃ δὲ ἀπὸ τῶν ὑπαρχόντων: Arnold well compares iv. 18. 2, esp. ἀπὸ δὲ τῶν αἰεὶ ὑπαρχόντων γνώμῃ σφαλέντες. "For even τὰ ὑπάρχοντα, although βεβαιοτέρα ἡ ἐξ αὐτῶν πρόνοια, are yet not infallible." ἡ πρόνοια was amongst the most conspicuous of Perikles' qualities (65. 13), as of Themistokles too (i. 138. 3); but he could not foresee everything.

63. 1. τῷ τιμωμένῳ ἀπὸ τοῦ ἄρχειν: Perikles insists on this often, both in the calm of the Epitaphios (41. 4) and in this dangerous hour, here and at 64. 3.

173

ᾧπερ ἄπαντες ἀγάλλεσθε: this is surely the right reading; Perikles' point is that *all* Athenians, including οἱ ἀπράγμονες, and all those who have now, from different motives, combined to attack him, take pride in the empire. Cf. Dem. xxii. 13, τὰ προπύλαια καὶ τὸν παρθε- νῶνα - - - καὶ τἆλλ' ἀπὸ τῶν βαρβάρων ἱερὰ κοσμήσαντες, ἐφ' οἷς φιλοτι- μούμεθα πάντες εἰκότως.

ἀλλὰ καὶ ἀρχῆς στερήσεως: other states, Aigina, Mytilene, those in the Thraceward parts (v. 9. 9), or Mantineia, might be at war for δουλεία ἢ ἐλευθερία; but defeat, for an Athenian, would be so much greater than for the citizen of an ordinary state; and much more dangerous too, because of the unpopularity already incurred. For this latter, cf. i. 75. 4 and v. 91. 1; and 64. 5, below. It is the one sentence in this speech which might reasonably be thought to have been written after 404 B.C.; and even here an earlier date is by no means excluded. Thucydides has already stated that the Peloponnesian was the generally popular cause (8. 4); ὧν ἀπήχθεσθε will mean unpopularity in Greece generally as well as in the subject cities.

Mme de Romilly, pp. 74–75, notes the close association of ἐλευθερία and ἄλλων ἀρχή, and the use of this by Ps.-Xenophon (1. 8) to explain the position of the δῆμος within the state. But it is not very different from the exhortation to Britannia to rule the waves coupled with the assertion that her sons will never be slaves. The difficulty for Athens (in a bad world, where she may be 'compelled to fight'— 61. 1, above) was that, in order to be strong enough to preserve com- plete independence of Sparta—as Corinth, for example, was not— she must have some resources outside Attica; and these could only be got by rule over others and command of the sea: which in part, though in part only, explains the empire. 'We must hold Megara for the sake of security against Sparta, Plataia against Thebes, and all the islands of the Aegean and the Chersonese and Byzantion so that we may control the seas and assure the supplies of food and timber by which we live.' Sparta, of course, with equal reason, said 'we must possess Messenia and look after Corinth and Sikyon to secure ourselves against the ambitions of Argos'.

In the course of the war there developed in Athens a cynicism about their unloved rule which knew no limits; but I do not feel that there is much here, nor in 64. 5, below. It would have been an enlightened rather than a cynical Roman who had said in the third century B.C., 'we cannot expect to be anything but unpopular with the Samnites, and we can only hope that Pyrrhus and the Carthaginians will be yet more unpopular'; nor would the English- man who said we were not liked by the Boers in 1902, or the French- man who said that France was not liked in Morocco about the same time, necessarily have been cynically non-moral.

2. εἴ τις καὶ τόδε - - - ἀνδραγαθίζεται: imitated by Kleon, iii. 40. 4, with which again compare the description of Nikias' political attitude in v. 16. 1. 'If there are some who, from their present craven fears, would play this noble part from love of peace.' 'Pacifism', 'love of peace', is not an adequate or exact translation of ἀπραγμοσύνη, though the word is here applied to state policy, not to the conduct of the individual citizen, as in 40. 2; but it comes closest. 'Quietism' has a different colouring. It must be insisted again that ἀπράγμων is a complimentary term (and 'no one is so foolish as to prefer war to peace'); the vigour and irony of this whole passage depend upon that. See above, 41. 4 n.

ὡς τυραννίδα γὰρ ἤδη ἔχετε αὐτήν: 'it is now like a tyranny, which we know it is a crime in popular opinion to seize, but which it is very dangerous to let go.' Also imitated, with a characteristic difference, by Kleon, iii. 37. 2, who omits ὡς, essential here ('it is *like* a tyranny'), though bracketed by Dobree and Hude, and ignored by many others.

We have had the word τύραννος applied to Athens by her enemies (i. 122. 3, 124. 3); this is the first time we have it from an Athenian. Later, Euphemos, vi. 85. 1, is more cynical even than Kleon. Aristophanes gives charming expression to the pride of the average *petit-bourgeois* Athenian, in words which recall Perikles', however different the tone:

> ὦ Δῆμε, καλήν γ' ἔχεις
> ἀρχήν, ὅτε πάντες ἄν-
> θρωποι δεδίασί σ', ὥσ-
> περ ἄνδρα τύραννον (*Eq.* 1111–14);

cf. 1330, 1333; and *Vesp.* 620; above, 41. 1 n.

ἀφεῖναι δὲ ἐπικίνδυνον: cf. i. 75. 4; and iv. 61. 5 n. This, and δουλείας ἀντ' ἐλευθερίας above, are not only rhetorical and demagogic commonplaces, but, for all that Perikles could see, the truth at that time. For example, if Mytilene had won her war with Athens (which means in effect, if Athens had been made much weaker by the pestilence than in fact she was—it is part of Perikles' argument in this speech that she is still strong—or, if her enemies had had more strength or more enterprise), other cities would have revolted, and Athens would probably have been defeated soon in the whole war, and have become at once subject to Sparta: as in fact she became in 404.

We in this country have expressed ourselves in a similar fashion: e.g. *The Times* of March 20, 1849—"Time, therefore, which has so rapidly given us this widespread dominion, may as rapidly take it away [πάντα γὰρ πέφυκε καὶ ἐλασσοῦσθαι, below, 64. 3]. But a natural and an honourable instinct abhors the idea of a political collapse. It is an old legal maxim, *Cave de resignationibus*. We cannot make up our minds to the effort of resigning half a dozen of the least useful and most costly colonies.' (Cf. Alkibiades' οὐκ ἔστιν ἡμῖν ταμιεύεσθαι ἐς ὅσον βουλόμεθα ἄρχειν, vi. 18. 3.) As Mme de Romilly says of the Melian dialogue (p. 257), if Thucydides is condemning anything, it is human nature rather than Athenian imperialism in particular.

3. ἑτέρους τε πείσαντες, κ.τ.λ.: 'if they persuaded the rest of us, or if they formed a state of their own.' Chios was one state noted for its ἀπραγμοσύνη, and it was subject to Athens (cf. viii. 24. 4–5); Melos was another, and it was destroyed, though Thucydides was not so cynical as to have this instance in mind here. For Alkibiades' adaptation of this argument, that τὸ ἡσυχάζειν would be a positive danger to Athens, see vi. 18. 3–6. See also Plato, Politikos, 306 E–308 A, esp. 307 E.

τὸ γὰρ ἄπραγμον - - - τεταγμένον: we might almost translate 'the luxury of pacifist opinion', only to be allowed in a strong and active state, where the majority are prepared to fight. τεταγμένον is a military metaphor, 'in the ranks with'. See my article in J.H.S. lxxi, 1951, 78–79; and Ehrenberg, J.H.S. lxvii, 1947, 46–67.

οὐδὲ ἐν ἀρχούσῃ πόλει, κ.τ.λ.: 'and pacifism is no advantage in an imperial city, but in a vassal, to be safe and a slave.' See Eur. Suppl. 321–5, 576–7, quoted on i. 70. 8, for praise, in effect, of πολυπραγμοσύνη; and Alkibiades, vi. 18. 6–7; Nikias, vi. 9. 3 (τοὺς τρόπους τοὺς ὑμετέρους), and Euphemos (vi. 87. 3). At a later time, on a different but equally noteworthy occasion, Demosthenes spoke the famous passage: ἀλλ' οὐκ ἦν ταῦθ', ὡς ἔοικε, τοῖς Ἀθηναίοις πάτρια οὐδ' ἀνεκτὰ οὐδ' ἔμφυτα, οὐδ' ἐδυνήθη πώποτε τὴν πόλιν οὐδεὶς ἐκ παντὸς τοῦ χρόνου πεῖσαι τοῖς ἰσχύουσι μὲν μὴ δίκαια δὲ πράττουσι προσθεμένην ἀσφαλῶς δουλεύειν (xviii. 203; Shilleto notes that we have had ἀσφάλειαν ἄδοξον and τὸ κελευόμενον ποιεῖν just before, 201, 202).

τὸ ἄπραγμον is the subject of ξυμφέρει, and ἀσφαλῶς δουλεύειν is epexegetic (not consecutive for ὥστε δουλεύειν). Both the order of words and the sense make this clear; and it is surprising that so many editors, and de Romilly, p. 111. 2, have misunderstood this. No one would suggest that τὸ δουλεύειν is advantageous for an imperial city, and there is no need to contradict it; for (of course) it is not disadvantageous, but a contradiction. Nor, indeed, would anyone say that subjection in itself is advantageous for any state; but a safe subjection, peace and material prosperity at the cost of independence, might attract; for freedom, in the state as in the individual, implies danger. Perikles declares that ἀπραγμοσύνη, the much vaunted policy, is nothing better than ἀσφαλῶς δουλεύειν, just as in the Epitaphios he had said that in the individual it was equivalent, in Athens, to τὸ ἀχρεῖον.

For a variation of this theme, cf. vi. 87. 4, where, according to Euphemos, owing to the activity of Athens others ἀναγκάζονται ὁ μὲν ἄκων σωφρονεῖν, ὁ δ' ἀπραγμόνως σῴζεσθαι.

176

δουλεία is commonly used by Thucydides (and by later writers in a more conventional way) to express the subjection of one state to another, as i. 98. 4 of the subject cities of the empire, or i. 141. 1 and just above ii. 63. 1 of possible domination of Athens by Sparta; see n. on v. 9. 9.

The vigour and liveliness of this speech by Perikles is unsurpassed in Thucydides; it does indeed 'leave its sting behind'. Kleon's speech in book iii matches it for vigour, but it is on a lower intellectual plane; to Alkibiades are given vigorous and vivid sentences; but Perikles stands alone, as Thucydides portrays him and as Aristophanes and Eupolis, and Plato afterwards, bear equal witness. But it is Perikles the realist in this speech, not the lofty idealist of the Epitaphios; and the contrast is intended. The tragedy of the war, as Thucydides saw it, was in part just this—the contrast between the two speeches, or rather that implied by them, and by the Epitaphios and the account of Athens during the pestilence, between the ideal and the real city in 431 and 430, and between Perikles on the one hand, and Kleon and Alkibiades on the other; for, as he indicates, they, not Nikias, are the true successors of Perikles, the inheritors and corrupters of his policy (*J.H.S.* lxxi, 1951, 78–80, and below, p. 186).

I do not think, with e.g. de Romilly, pp. 113–14, that the ἀπράγμονες of this passage are the small party of extreme oligarchs who (it is said) were for peace at any price and were prepared for subordination to Sparta (ἀσφαλῶς δουλεύειν) in order to obtain the overthrow of the democracy, in accordance with the usual practice of Spartan domination (i. 19). I do not in general agree with the picture of Athens divided between two main groups, the moderate imperialists who were also moderate democrats and prepared for war with the barbarian only and for peace and a share of power with Sparta (the 'Kimon ideal'), and the extreme imperialists and democrats who were for war with everyone, but especially with Sparta; with these few extremist oligarchs in the background. As I have argued elsewhere (in *Athenian Studies*, 238–42; see below, 65. 2 n.), this is all too much simplified. And apart from that, Perikles has not here, I think, any specific political group or party in mind, but those who, to whichever group they traditionally belonged, were at this moment in a nervous state (ἐν τῷ παρόντι δεδιώς), and said, 'we are all for ἀπραγμοσύνη; let us make peace, for peace is much better than war'. 'As if we did not all know', says Perikles, 'that peace is better; but is it possible, without too great a sacrifice?' Of course there were some who liked to consider themselves οἱ ἀπράγμονες—a class, almost a class apart—and they would use the word of themselves as a label, needing no further comment, like 'the peace-loving nations' of to-day; and εἴ που ἐπὶ σφῶν αὐτῶν αὐτόνομοι οἰκήσειαν suggests perhaps a group of doctrinaire pacifists different from, or thinking themselves different from, those who were merely ἐν τῷ παρόντι δεδιότες; but they are not to be identified with the few extremists among the oligarchs, who were neither ἀπράγμονες nor distinguished for ἀνδραγαθία.

64. 1. ἐλπίδος κρεῖσσον γεγενημένον: the pestilence was an event beyond all expectation, something that *could* not be foreseen. Thucydides, though he will describe its symptoms so that it may be recognized if (as is possible enough) it should recur, does not mean that its recurrence can be foreseen. It is the same with στάσις (iii. 82. 2) and war, or war occasioned by imperialism (i. 22. 4): given similar circumstances, they will almost certainly recur; but this is not a 'cyclical' view of history, and not only pestilences, but the course of war in particular is quite unpredictable (i. 122. 1, 140. 1, iv. 18).

Xenophon, *Hipparchikos*, 9. 1–2, puts Perikles' argument well; 'to prepare for every event is as impossible as to know the whole future; you can only do what you know to be prudent.' It might, however, be said that Perikles here in part begs the question; for it could be argued that better precautions should at least have been taken against diseases in general when the people were crowded within the walls.

2. τά τε δαιμόνια ἀναγκαίως: a not uncommon sentiment. Edd. compare Soph. *Phil.* 1316–17; Eur. *Phoen.* 382, 1763. Perikles had himself been a victim of this blow 'from heaven', in himself, his two sons, and other friends. Did Thucydides have this in mind? He may have done, for the expression would be characteristic of Perikles.

3. ταῖς ξυμφοραῖς μὴ εἴκειν: cf. i. 70. 5, 7; and with πλεῖστα δὲ - - - πολέμῳ, i. 70. 8.

ἧς ἐς ἀίδιον τοῖς ἐπιγιγνομένοις, κ.τ.λ.: cf. 41. 4, with the n. there. I find it difficult to believe that this is what Perikles would have said had he been able to survey all that happened between 430 and 404. See below, § 5 n. Again we note that success, for Perikles, is not the final test.

ὑπενδῶμεν: 'give ground', as 80. 6, 65. 12. Many have said that the commonplace which follows, πάντα γὰρ πέφυκε καὶ ἐλασσοῦσθαι, must have been written after 404 B.C.; foolishly, for it is something that all know. Cf. Dem. xviii. 200; Scipio at Carthage (e.g. Appian, *Punica*, 132: whether the story is true or not, it is earlier than the fall of Rome); or Swift, "the fate of empires is grown a commonplace". Even Plato's Republic will decay (viii. 546 A). See iv. 18. 5 n.

ἤρξαμεν, - - - ἀντέσχομεν, - - - ᾠκήσαμεν: historic aorists, whereby Perikles speaks from the point of view of posterity. Just above, with ἀνηλωκέναι and κεκτημένην (as well as ἦν καὶ νῦν ὑπενδῶμέν ποτε), he has spoken as a contemporary. So Croiset.

πόλιν τε τοῖς πᾶσιν εὐπορωτάτην καὶ μεγίστην: as eloquently explained in the Epitaphios, but here with material power and resources only in mind. Cf. 43. 1 n.

4. καίτοι ταῦτα, κ.τ.λ.: for the first two words Reifferscheid conjectured καὶ τὰ τοιαῦτα; which Stahl rejected because καίτοι is often used in rhetoric without adversative force. Yet I believe the conjecture needs further consideration. The only contrast in this sentence with what has preceded is (I feel sure) in its first clause, ὁ μὲν ἀπράγμων μέμψαιτ' ἄν: the other two, the ζῆλος and the φθόνος of others, help to confirm the greatness of Athens; and, according to the laws of μέν - - - δέ clauses, καίτοι should go not with the first ('while the pacifist will find fault'), but with the subsequent clauses. καίτοι in iii. 39. 2, compared by Stahl,[1] and in ii. 39. 4, to which Classen refers, are both different. καὶ τὰ τοιαῦτα would make excellent sense: 'we have fought the greatest wars, our city is the most powerful. And, though the pacifist will find fault, *that* is what those who share our ambition will admire and those without it will envy'— that is, it is a further point in our favour.

If καίτοι ταῦτα is kept, translate: 'True, the pacifist will find fault with that; but', etc. It will be one of those cases (otherwise confined to Plato?) in which "καίτοι covers the μέν-clause only: so that δέ, while formally balancing μέν, really goes behind μέν to answer καίτοι" (R. W. Chapman, ap. Denniston, p. 558; contrast, however, *Philebos*, 26 c, cited by Denniston, p. 561). "There is usually a certain combative tone in καίτοι. For this reason it is not common in unimpassioned cold-blooded exposition. It is significant that out of 24 Thucydidean examples all except i. 10. 2 are from speeches" (Denniston, p. 556).

ὁ μὲν ἀπράγμων μέμψαιτ' ἄν: Nikias would, for example; for his hope was καταλιπεῖν ὄνομα (cf. ὄνομα μέγιστον above) ὡς οὐδὲν σφήλας τὴν πόλιν διεγένετο, νομίζων ἐκ τοῦ ἀκινδύνου τοῦτο ξυμβαίνειν, κ.τ.λ. (v. 16. 1). Aristophanes, on the other hand, would not, or not always, nor the aristocrats of Athens whom he depicted: *Equit.* 565–85.

ὁ δὲ δρᾶν τι - - - βουλόμενος: cf. τοῦ δραστηρίου, 63. 3.

5. τὸ δὲ μισεῖσθαι, κ.τ.λ.: a generalization of the particular case of Athens (63. 2, iii. 40. 3, ἐξ ἀνάγκης καθεστῶτας αἰεὶ πολεμίους; see nn. on ii. 8. 5, iv. 108. 3–4). See the excellent analysis in de Romilly, 262–8, who quotes both contemporary generalizations, such as Ps.-Xen. 1. 14 and Eur. *Ion*, 596–7, and later references to Athenian

---

[1] Reifferscheid conjectured καὶ τοῦτο for καίτοι there; but I agree with Stahl, who compared Soph. *Trach.* 719, that this is poor and based on a misunderstanding.

unpopularity, Xen. *Hell.* iii. 5. 10 and Isokr. *Peace*, 79, 84. These last suggest that Perikles was too optimistic in asserting that the hatred would last but a short time, while the immediate splendour would be for ever remembered.

In vi. 16. 5 Alkibiades borrows this sentiment, and uses it, characteristically, not, like Perikles, of the city, but of individuals and particularly of himself.

ὅστις δὲ ἐπὶ μεγίστοις, κ.τ.λ.: edd. compare Eur. *Phoen.* 524–5,

εἴπερ γὰρ ἀδικεῖν χρή, τυραννίδος πέρι
κάλλιστον ἀδικεῖν,

said to be Julius Caesar's favourite lines; but this is different from Perikles' meaning, which is more clearly expressed in 41. 3, οὔτε τῷ ὑπηκόῳ κατάμεμψιν ὡς οὐχ ὑπ' ἀξίων ἄρχεται. It is still the aristocratic ideal, proper to Athens: above, 41. 1, 3; but here, as in 63. 1, urged, not taken for granted, as in the Epitaphios.

ἡ δὲ παραυτίκα τε λαμπρότης, κ.τ.λ.: most edd., but not Hude nor Stuart Jones, have bracketed τε. "Si etiam λαμπρότης dicitur αἰείμνηστος καταλείπεσθαι, non perspicitur quid intersit inter λαμπρότητα αἰείμνηστον καταλειπομένην et δόξαν eodem modo notatam, cum haec nulla alia esse possit nisi τῆς παραυτίκα λαμπρότητος δόξα. . . . Itaque τε deleto . . . ἡ παρ. λ. praesens dignitatis splendor quem ex aliorum imperio obtinent relinquitur ut sempiterna in posterum tempus fiat gloria" (Stahl). In this way we get an easier sentence; but I do not believe it is what Thucydides meant, which was, *both* present glory and future fame are to be balanced against temporary unpopularity; just as he says below, ἔς τε τὸ μέλλον καλὸν προγνόντες ἔς τε τὸ αὐτίκα μὴ αἰσχρόν, where προγνόντες does not properly fit the second object. It is, however, as Stahl says, not very logically expressed.

Perikles' insistence on the glory of Athenian deeds of the last two generations, so characteristic of him, is to be noticed once more: cf. i. 144. 3; ii. 41. 4 with n., 63. 1, 64. 3. It is echoed by Nikias, on a desperate occasion, vii. 64. 2 (cf. 63. 3); and by Demosthenes in more than one passage in *De Corona*. And the thought was shared by some others at least of Perikles' contemporaries: cf. Eur. *Suppl.* 320–5 and the oracle often referred to by Aristophanes (both quoted in n. on i. 70. 8); cf. with them the general truth of Pindar, *Nem.* iii. 82 and *Parthen.*, fr. 104 c (Schr.),

παντὶ δ' ἐπὶ φθόνος ἀνδρὶ κεῖται
ἀρετᾶς, ὁ δὲ μηδὲν ἔχων ὑπὸ σι-
γᾷ μελαίνᾳ κάρα κέκρυπται.

6. ὑμεῖς δέ, κ.τ.λ.: 'it is *your* duty', with a strong emphasis—the application of the general rule given in § 5 to the present case.

τὸ αὐτίκα μὴ αἰσχρόν corresponds, as edd. say, to ἡ παραυτίκα λαμπρότης; and cannot therefore mean, as many translate, 'your present escape from disgrace', but 'the immediate situation which, however difficult as a result of the pestilence and the consequent break in morale, is the reverse of disgraceful'. τὸ μὴ αἰσχρόν is the usual *litotes* for τὸ καλόν. Athens is still a great city. τῷ ἤδη προθύμῳ: 'by your courage *now*.'

πρὸς τὰς ξυμφοράς, κ.τ.λ.: as § 3, above.

It is interesting to read Dionysios' criticism of this speech, *de Thuc. iud.* 44–47 (pp. 923–7): in such a situation, he says, Perikles should have been given a speech which was humble and begged for mercy. He not only does not ask himself the question: Was Perikles that sort of man?—that is, he does not, for example, consider the meaning of Thucydides' words in 65. 9; nor does he consider what sort of people the Athenians were, that is, what the situation was at that particular moment (τὰ τότε παρόντα). He can only think of set speeches of types suitable to certain typical, and really quite artificial situations—victory, defeat, arguments for war or for peace, or for and against democracy, and so forth: that is how he interpreted Thucydides' words, ὡς δ' ἂν ἐδόκουν μοι ἕκαστοι περὶ τῶν αἰεὶ παρόντων τὰ δέοντα μάλιστ' εἰπεῖν; an attitude highly characteristic both of his criticism and of his own work as historian. He also demands a full account of the embassies sent to Sparta (59. 2), and long speeches on their occasion, on the blessings of peace and the miseries of war. He liked rhetorical embellishments inserted in narrative, no more. Many modern criticisms of Thucydides' speeches have been in essentials based on Dionysios' criterion. Thucydides may have composed this speech freely, out of his own head; but he surely intended it to illustrate what Perikles, and not any other man, was like, and what he was like just on that occasion, in that situation, and not on other occasions, as the autumn of 432 or the spring of 431, or the winter of 431–430; nor, as it seems to me, is the speech at all what he would have said had he been able to view the whole course of events till the defeat in 404.

65. 2. ὁ μὲν δῆμος - - - οἱ δὲ δυνατοί: the masses and the rich, quite simply, not parties. Contrast Ps.-Xen. 2. 14, who, in his fashion, pretends to believe that the demos suffered nothing, and furthermore, uses ὁ δῆμος of the town population only, as though the peasant-farmers did not belong (cf. Ar. *Peace*, 632–6); then that the farmers (and the rich) were ready to kowtow to Sparta to save their lands, and many modern scholars have repeated this in spite of Thuc. ii. 21–22 and *The Acharnians* (Marchant actually in a comment on ii. 22. 1). Now, as on other and different occasions, e.g. in the enthusiasm for the Sicilian expedition, the few and the many in Athens feel and act alike.

This is not to deny the truth of the other side of the picture, the eager politicians and their followers who tried, with some success, to form cliques and run affairs themselves, both in the fifth century (*Acharnians*, esp. 595–8; *Peace*, 615–18) and in the fourth (*Republic*, viii. 564 C–565 C); but Plato uses $\delta\hat{\eta}\mu o s$ in the same way as Thucydides, ὅσοι αὐτουργοί τε καὶ ἀπράγμονες, οὐ πάνυ πολλὰ κεκτημένοι· ὃ δὴ πλεῖστόν τε καὶ κυριώτατον ἐν δημοκρατίᾳ ὅτανπερ ἀθροισθῇ (where the αὐτουργοί comprise all craftsmen, not only "the peasantry who work their own farms", as Cornford translates, unconsciously misled by modern conditions). And he follows both historian and comic poet closely when he describes the politicians denouncing the rich ὡς ἐπιβουλεύουσι τῷ δήμῳ καί εἰσιν ὀλιγαρχικοί, and the demos οὐχ ἑκόντα, ἀλλ' ἀγνοήσαντά τε καὶ ἐξαπατηθέντα ὑπὸ τῶν διαβαλλόντων.

καλὰ κτήματα - - - πολυτελέσι κατασκευαῖς: cf. 38. 1 (and 40. 1 n.); *Hell. Ox.* 12. 5.

τὸ δὲ μέγιστον, κ.τ.λ.: applicable to both groups, the rich and the poor.

3. οὐ μέντοι, κ.τ.λ.: somewhat awkwardly expressed, for the sentence is in contrast with the first part of § 2, yet in its present position ought to be in contrast with the second part; i.e. the logical order would have been οἱ δὲ δημοσίᾳ μὲν τοῖς μὲν λόγοις - - -, οὐ μέντοι - - - πρὶν ἐζημίωσαν· ἰδίᾳ δέ, κ.τ.λ.

ἐζημίωσαν χρήμασιν: according to Plutarch, *Per.* 35. 4–5, ancient historians differed both as to the amount of the fine, 15 tal. being the lowest figure, 50 the highest (Diodoros, xii. 45. 4, says 80, which was hardly in Ephoros—it is perhaps a MS. error—and dates the trial before the embassies to Sparta: 59. 2, above), and as to the name of Perikles' accuser—Kleon according to Idomeneus, Simmias according to Theophrastos, and Lakratidas according to Herakleides Pontikos: all three poor authorities, but if such obscure names as Simmias and Lakratidas survived in the tradition, men of these names may have played some part (whether in the law-courts, as prosecutors, or in the ekklesia in urging a prosecution). But it does not look as though later writers had any authority for their statements other than Thucydides and comedy. (Simmias is a rare name for an Athenian; but it is found (see *P.A.*). It is also possible that he was a foreigner acting as μηνυτής: cf. vi. 27. 2, 28. 1; and below, p. 187).

Nor do we know for certain the nature of the charge against Perikles, which may have been one of 'deceiving the people', or of having mismanaged the expedition to the Argolid. Plato, *Gorg.* 516 A, says he was accused of κλοπή, i.e. embezzlement of public funds; which may be true enough, for it was a common mode of attack on public men; but in this case may be doubted, for it looks like an echo of the charge against Pheidias, in which Perikles was involved,

and Plutarch does not suggest anything of the kind in his narrative
of the events of 430 (*Per.* 35. 5; see below, p. 187). On the other hand,
Plutarch tells us earlier, c. 32. 1–3, of an accusation regarding the
public accounts, which, if we could be at all sure of his chronology,
should have occurred in 432, and did not result in a trial. It was
normal in Athens to fine a public man heavily as a way of expressing
disagreement with his policy or his administration or command.

4. ὕστερον δὲ αὖθις: the fine meant that Perikles was at the same
time dismissed from office; and this presumably occurred in the
summer of 430, not later than the event narrated in c. 66, and earlier
than that in c. 67 (though in such an episode as this, we should not
press Thucydides to too close a sequence in his narrative). But
how long he was out of office we do not know; all we can say is that
Thucydides' words do not suggest that he had to wait till the following spring, 429 B.C., the seventh prytany at the earliest (about the
middle of February), for the normal annual elections (Ἀθπ. 44. 4),
still less till midsummer, the end of the civil year, before resuming
office. He had probably been accused at an ordinary ἐπιχειροτονία,
which was held every prytany (Ἀθπ. 61. 2); and it is possible that
no successor was elected to fill his place, and that he was back in
office only a few weeks after his dismissal. He will have paid the
fine, and so got rid of the technical ἀτιμία. So Wilamowitz, ii. 247–8;
for the other view, that he was not re-elected till the following spring,
see Busolt, iii. 955. 2, 963. 2 (but some of his arguments are very
weak). See also below, p. 201. It is worth while drawing attention
to Xenophon, *Resp. Lac.* 8. 4; for if we could take Xenophon
seriously we should have to conclude that no high official in Athens,
certainly no strategos, could be dismissed from office.

For the further stories of attacks on Perikles through his friends,
see below.

πάντα τὰ πράγματα ἐπέτρεψαν: cf. Telekleides, fr. 42, quoted vol. i,
p. 357, and Plut. *Per.* 15. 1, who gives the conventional picture.
Most historians take this to mean that Perikles was made *strategos
autokrator*, and suppose that he had regularly held this special office
before. I am doubtful of this, for I think these 'full powers' were only
granted for a special duty on a special occasion (i. 126. 8 n.); and
Thucydides here probably means no more than that the Athenians
'entrusted him with everything', as before, in the sense of being
prepared always to follow his advice. He was πιθανώτατος, as, on
occasion, was Kleon (iii. 36. 6, iv. 21. 3); so were Kleon and his
successor said to have 'all power in their hands' (*Eq.* 836–40).

ἡ ξύμπασα πόλις: so CG and edd. (ξύμπασα ἡ πόλις ABEFM); 'the
city as opposed to the individuals', 'the state'. But why ξύμπασα at
all (cf. 60. 3–4)? Rather 'the whole city', i.e. all the parties and
groups in it.

The Prosecutions of Perikles and His Friends

It will be as well to give here some account of the attacks on Perikles and his friends, as related by ancient writers and interpreted
by modern scholars, whether they belong to the time just before
the outbreak of the war or to the summer of 430, or to the period
between them; about all of which Thucydides is deliberately silent.[1]

The only hint which Thucydides himself gives of personal attacks
on Perikles shortly before the war, in 432 or the winter of 432–431,
is in i. 127. 2–3, where he relates that the Spartans bade the Athenians
"drive out the curse", not so much expecting that Perikles would
be driven out (if for no other reason, he was not an Alkmeonid),
as hoping to disparage him with his fellow citizens who might
regard the war as in part due to his unfortunate connexion with the
Alkmeonidai; ὧν γὰρ δυνατώτατος τῶν καθ' ἑαυτὸν καὶ ἄγων τὴν πολιτείαν he was consistently opposed to Sparta and was urging Athens
to fight. Whether anyone in Athens took this sufficiently seriously
to use it in order to weaken Perikles' position, we do not know;
Ephoros says nothing of it in his narrative of the attacks on him;
Plutarch says simply that his position was strengthened by it.
Thucydides' silence about these attacks is not in itself surprising:
biographical detail was foreign to his purpose, especially about persons not directly concerned with the war—Pheidias, Aspasia, Anaxagoras—and idle stories he would anyhow not repeat; but we can
infer something from his silence, that in his opinion Perikles was not
seriously involved in the prosecution of Pheidias for peculation,
whether Pheidias was guilty or innocent (to this we may add his
statement that Perikles' great influence was largely due to his having
been χρημάτων διαφανῶς ἀδωρότατος: § 8, below), that Perikles had
no base personal motives for urging Athens into war, and, above all,
that his position in 432–431 was not shaken by attacks on him or his
policy. There was considerable difference of opinion in Sparta over
policy in 432; hence Thucydides gives space to speeches by the
Corinthians, by Archidamos, and by Sthenelaïdas, and he follows
the same principle to show opinion in Athens about Mytilene and
even about the Syracusan expedition, though opinion then was
nearly unanimous, and in Syracuse in 415 (Hermokrates, Athenagoras, and one of the strategoi: as at Sparta in 432). In Athens in
432 only a speech by Perikles is reported, and but the briefest mention made of doubts and hesitations (i. 139. 4, and in the speech).

---

[1] It is a nice question whether this note should be inserted here or at 59. 2 (τὸν
Περικλέα ἐν αἰτίᾳ εἶχον ὡς πείσαντα σφᾶς πολεμεῖν, κ.τ.λ.). This place seems the
more obvious; yet a note at 59. 2 might seem to prepare better for Perikles'
speech which is to follow. My decision was made on consideration of Thucydides'
own silence; he did not thus prepare the way for the speech.

Thucydides is in this interpretation in conflict with Ephoros, who (according to Diodoros, at least, xii. 38–41. 1) attributed to Perikles the base motives but made him easily successful in hoodwinking the Athenians, and with Plutarch's account, consistent and credible enough in itself (*Per.* 29–33. 2), according to which attacks were made on Perikles' friends in order to injure him, and, as a result, Pheidias was, in effect, condemned after his death in prison,[1] Anaxagoras was "sent away" from Athens by Perikles to avoid prosecution (or, according to others, was put on trial, and escaped death by a few votes, and was exiled), and Aspasia was only acquitted after a moving personal appeal by Perikles himself. All this is dated, by Ephoros and by Plutarch, to the time shortly before the outbreak of the war, and is given as a cause, or a possible cause, of the war, because it influenced, or may have influenced, Perikles' conduct. But it is inconsistent with Thucydides, for it implies that there was a deep cleavage within the state and that Perikles' position was much shaken, whether or no we accept the base motive, the view that he caused the war because of his difficulties. Those modern scholars who prefer the evidence of Ephoros to that of Thucydides do not mind this, and accept the former's story; some confess the difficulties, as Plutarch did; wiser men prefer the better authority, but without always seeing where the inconsistency lies. Plutarch gives a clue at the end of his narrative (33. 1–2): he returns to Thucydides for the story of the Spartan demand to drive out the curse, and says that this had the opposite effect from what they expected; Perikles was re-established in his old authority. But Thucydides implies that no such re-establishment was necessary. The only real evidence for any deep rift in Athens at this time is Aristophanes, *Peace*, 619–24:

$$\kappa \hat{a} \tau' \; \epsilon \pi \epsilon \iota \delta \grave{\eta} \; ' \gamma \nu \omega \sigma a \nu \; \dot{\upsilon} \mu \hat{a} s \; a \dot{\iota} \; \pi \acute{o} \lambda \epsilon \iota s \; \mathring{\omega} \nu \; \mathring{\eta} \rho \chi \epsilon \tau \epsilon$$
$$\mathring{\eta} \gamma \rho \iota \omega \mu \acute{\epsilon} \nu o \upsilon s \; \dot{\epsilon} \pi' \; \dot{a} \lambda \lambda \mathring{\eta} \lambda o \iota \sigma \iota \; \kappa a \grave{\iota} \; \sigma \epsilon \sigma \eta \rho \acute{o} \tau a s, \; \kappa. \tau. \lambda.,$$

written ten years later.

There are, as is well known, many other difficulties in the way of acceptance of either Ephoros or Plutarch, apart from the very many inconsistencies in the details (which are like those in the late accounts of the prosecution of Perikles himself: n. on § 3, above). I pass over that of the date of Anaxagoras' trial or departure from Athens, for I doubt whether there is much substance in A. E. Taylor's argument

---

[1] *Per.* 31. 7, τῷ δὲ μηνυτῇ Μένωνι γράψαντος Γλύκωνος ἀτέλειαν ὁ δῆμος ἔδωκε, καὶ προσέταξε τοῖς στρατηγοῖς ἐπιμελεῖσθαι τῆς ἀσφαλείας τοῦ ἀνθρώπου. I am, however, doubtful about this: the second clause is a common formula for the protection of informants; and I suspect that the decree only gave ἄδεια and protection to Menon (as in 31. 3), not ἀτέλεια (the mistake might be either Plutarch's or in his MSS., but anyhow he will have misunderstood the case), and was passed before formal charge of peculation had been made against Pheidias.

for putting it c. 450 B.C. ($C.Q.$ xi, 1917, 81: see J. S. Morrison, $C.Q.$ xxxv, 1941, 5); but the date of Pheidias' trial is another matter; for Philochoros (according to the scholia on Ar. $Peace$, 605: F 121) says that he was tried for peculation and exiled in 438–437, went to Elis and made the statue of Zeus for Olympia, and was put to death there, also for peculation.[1] This account is obviously very suspect; but it shows that Philochoros rejected the story of Pheidias' trial in Athens in 432–431; and since Ephoros (and, as far as we know, later writers) depended on Aristophanes, $Peace$, 605 ff., for it, it has little authority.[2] It has indeed been argued that, though Aristophanes' story of Perikles' starting the war because he was involved in Pheidias' misfortune had not been heard of before 421 (vv. 615–18), he would not have invented it (or others would not have invented it, and he laughed at them for it) unless the trial of Pheidias had taken place in 432–431 or very shortly before; but how good were people's memories, or how much would they mind this difficulty? There was a special point in this slander about Perikles just at this time; for Kleon was charged with just such conduct, with wanting to prolong the war so that he might hide his wrongdoing, and charged not only in the streets of Athens (as reflected, $passim$, in Aristophanes), but in the pages of Thucydides himself, v. 16. 1: there were those who said that Kleon was only following in the footsteps of his master. (The other story in Ephoros, more childish, about the youthful Alkibiades' advice to the distraught Perikles, how not to give an account of public money in his charge—Diod. xii. 38. 2–4— may also belong to this time, the last two or three years before the peace of 421, when Alkibiades was making himself notorious.) However, I would not deny that Philochoros, in the absence of direct evidence of any trial of Pheidias in 432, may only have $inferred$ that since the Parthenos statue was dedicated in 438–437, the charge of peculation was brought then, and, since the Zeus statue at Olympia was made later (if he had, or thought he had, independent evidence for this), that the punishment must have been exile. There is nothing in itself improbable in the suggestion that, if Pheidias returned to Athens in 432 or 431, information was laid against him for a crime committed six or seven years before; and Plutarch's

[1] There is little or no doubt about the date, 438–437, in Philochoros, for it is given as 6 years before the Megarian decree or 7 years before the beginning of the war; the MSS. corruption, therefore, of the names of the archons, which in any case has been satisfactorily corrected, is unimportant.

[2] I would not myself lay much stress on the improbability of Pheidias being given the work of making the statue of Zeus just after he had been exiled for peculation in making the statue of Athena; nor on the honour shown later to Pheidias and his descendants at Olympia (Pausanias, v. 14. 5; cf. 11. 9). Politics may have played its part (e.g. the treaty between Athens and Elis, Mantineia, and Argos in 420).

account (much the most sensible and coherent) may be correct that he died in prison before the charge was heard, so that the only official record of the proceedings that was preserved may have been the decree of the ekklesia about Menon.[1]

Aspasia is said to have been prosecuted, for impiety, by Hermippos the comic poet, who made the additional accusation against her of procuring. There was nothing to prevent Hermippos being the prosecutor; but there is a natural suspicion that this is a misunderstanding of a statement that Hermippos attacked her in a comedy—perhaps in the same one in which Perikles was attacked for not prosecuting the war vigorously enough, in 431 (21. 3 n.). Besides this, two other decrees are mentioned (both are in Plutarch, c. 32), one moved by Diopeithes demanding impeachment for atheism (or unorthodoxy in religion—τοὺς τὰ θεῖα μὴ νομίζοντας) and for teaching about celestial phenomena—this was aimed especially at Anaxagoras; the other moved by Drakontides that Perikles be required to submit accounts of public money spent to the *prytaneis* and that the dicasts vote openly and on the altar on the Akropolis (a rider by Hagnon—see below, p. 189—changed this last provision to an ordinary trial before 1,500 dikastai). There is clearly something missing in this account of the second decree—some procedure between the first action by the prytaneis and the trial; but both decrees seem clearly to be authentic. Plato says that Perikles was charged (at some time) with κλοπή (above, § 3 n.); Plutarch here adds εἴτε κλοπῆς καὶ δώρων εἴτ' ἀδικίου βούλοιτό τις ὀνομάζειν τὴν δίωξιν. There was only one *trial* of Perikles (when he was fined), and that was in the late summer of 430, here mentioned by Thucydides; and Drakontides' decree must belong to this time; but Plutarch brings it expressly into connexion with the attacks on Perikles' friends in 432: with Pheidias out of the way, Aspasia about to be tried and Diopeithes' decree carried, οὕτως ἤδη ψήφισμα κυροῦται, Δρακοντίδου γράψαντος, κ.τ.λ. It is possible enough that this, the wrong dating of this last decree, is the only error in Plutarch; but it gives cause for doubt; and I follow Adcock (in *C.A.H.* v. 577–80) in putting the decree of Diopeithes and the attacks on Aspasia and Anaxagoras, and perhaps that on Pheidias as well, in 430, when hostility to Perikles was at its height and superstition excited by the terrors of the pestilence. This is in much better accord with Thucydides; we can readily believe that at that time Perikles only saved his mistress and his friend with difficulty. It does not, of course, mean that Perikles had not for many years

[1] Above, p. 185 n. I do not think there is anything in Praschniker's view ('Επιτύμβιον Swoboda, 210–14: see Lenschau in *Bursian*, ccxliv, 1934, p. 56) that Plato, *Protag.* 311 B–C, is evidence that Pheidias was alive and in Athens in 433–432, which is perhaps the dramatic date of the dialogue. Lenschau thought that it was evidence that he was alive then; but Plato is not to be so pressed for his dates.

187

been the victim of scurrility and slander. His eldest son's mockery may have been going on for some time; the ostracism of Damon ($Ἀθπ$. 27. 4; E. Vanderpool, *Hesp.* Suppl. viii, 1949, 407–12) may have been earlier, though Plat. *Alkib.* i. 118 C would suit 430 better; but it would be as well to distinguish between attacks on him in 430 as the author of the war ($τὸ μέγιστον, πόλεμον ἀντ' εἰρήνης ἔχοντες$) and those in 431 for not prosecuting it with more energy.

For the more commonly held views see Busolt, iii. 818–29 (who, in my view, was wrong in thinking his version reconcilable with Thucydides), and Beloch, ii.² 1. 294–8.[1]

There is perhaps one more piece of evidence for these attacks on Perikles' friends and their date, the new fragments of Kratinos' *Ploutoi* (Goossens, *Rev. Ét. Anc.* xxxvii, 1935, 405–34; Körte, *Archiv f. Papyrusf.* xi, 1935, 260–2; Page, *Gk. Lit. Pap.*, No. 38, who gives further bibliography). So little remains of the play that any speculation is hazardous, and we are warned by previous speculation made when even less was known; but this much may be said. In a passage near the beginning of the play the chorus, or part of it, say, with reference presumably to hopes of victory in the theatre,

$$ἀλλ' ἀξιόνικον [τὴν γνώμην$$
$$ἀποφαινόμεν[οι πειρώμεθ' ὅμως$$
$$τὸ τυχὸν στέργει[ν. ἀλλὰ φοβούμεθα$$
$$μὴ συντυχίαισι βαρυνόμενοι$$
$$μενετοὶ κριταὶ οὐ δ[$$

(the last word may be restored $δικάσωσι$, as Körte proposed; anyhow $δικαίως δικάσωσι$ presumably would give the meaning required). Assuming that $συντυχίαισι βαρυνόμενοι$ refers to an historical event, not to something (perhaps a jest) in the play itself, no better occasion could be found than the summer and winter of 430–429. A few lines later the chorus announce who they are, the Ploutoi of the good days when Kronos ruled. But Zeus drove Kronos out; then, after five missing lines,

$$ὡς δὲ τυραννίδος ἀρχῆς [στέρεται,$$
$$δῆμος δὲ κρατεῖ,$$
$$δεῦρ' ἐσύθημεν πρὸς ὄμ[αιμόν τ' ὄντ'$$
$$αὐτοκασίγνητόν τε παλαιὸν$$
$$ζητοῦντες κεἰ σαθρὸν ἤδη.$$

As Goossens conjectures (pp. 415–16), Zeus may here be Perikles, the tyrant, as in Kratinos' *Cheirones*, frr. 240, 241 (quoted in part in

---

[1] Busolt, as usual, writes with good sense generally; but on p. 821, n. 1, he combines without analysing the evidence of Ps.-Xenophon, Thucydides (ii. 65. 2, ignoring ii. 21–22 which is here relevant), and Aristophanes, and from the latter quoting confusedly from *Knights*, *Peace*, and *Ekklesiazousai* as though we had not the inestimable advantage of knowing when these plays were written.

vol. i, p. 104); and if Beazley's restoration στέρεται is right (as it surely is), and if we have reference to a contemporary event, the play was written soon after Perikles was dismissed from office, and democracy ('the true democracy of the olden days') restored.[1] The 'poor old kinsman' of the Ploutoi may well be Thoukydides, son of Melesias, returned from ostracism, as in *Acharnians*, 703. If this is right, then the mockery of Hagnon of Steiria and his wealth (58. 1 n., above) has special relevance, for he was not only prominent as strategos in 430, but took some part in the prosecution of Perikles, probably, as is generally thought, as a friend, modifying the harshness of the original decree of Drakontides (above, p. 187).

Ploutoi was dated by Geissler not later than 436 because it was the earliest of the group of comedies cited by Athenaios, vi. 267 E ff., which included pictures of the golden age of old (see above, vol. i, p. 104); but since the dates of the other plays are all unknown, this argument is weak.

For other frr. of comedy with possible reference to these attacks on Perikles, see Kratinos, 111 (from *Nemesis*: ὦ Ζεῦ ξένιε may, as Zündel suggested, hint at the grant of citizenship to Aspasia's son); Telekleides, 1, 2, 17; Eupolis, 123 (from the later *Demoi*), 249 (from *Prospaltioi*—above, p. 76), 274. In Kratinos' *Dionysalexandros*, we are told, there was a general attack on Perikles (Demiańczuk, 31–33); but we do not know the date of the play or the occasion.

65. 5–13. *Summary of Perikles' Character and Influence*

5. ἀσφαλῶς διεφύλαξεν αὐτήν: note the change of tense—'always led it with a moderate policy and thus kept it in safety', the aorist denoting the result. We may contrast iv. 65. 4.

We all know that the description of the restless Athenians (as seen by their enemies) in i. 70 was the *democratic* ideal, shared by Perikles, even though in his strategy he was so cautious; and that Kimon was the opponent of Perikles and his opposite in every way. But it was Kimon who, not content with Salamis, Plataia, and Mykale, went on to Eurymedon, and not content with that great victory, wanted (we are told) to conquer Egypt: παρὰ δύναμιν τολμηταὶ καὶ παρὰ γνώμην κινδυνευταί, ἄοκνοι καὶ ἀποδημηταί, κρατοῦντες τῶν ἐχθρῶν ἐπὶ πλεῖστον ἐξέρχονται; and it was he who, so resilient after that disaster—ἦν ἄρα του καὶ πείρᾳ σφαλῶσιν, ἀντελπίσαντες ἄλλα ἐπλήρωσαν τὴν χρείαν—was ready for another big expedition to Cyprus. Perikles, δημαγωγὸς ὤν, and the great defender of the empire and of seapower, for they brought glory, was the more prudent and withdrew, and in general ἀσφαλῶς διεφύλαξε τὴν πόλιν.

---

[1] Goossens read ὡς δὲ τυραννίδος ἀρχή 'σ[τι Διὸς] | δῆμος δὲ κρατεῖ, identifying the tyranny with Athenian democracy at the time, as some others have done. This is clearly wrong.

ἐγένετο ἐπ' ἐκείνου μεγίστη: see i. 19 n. There can be little doubt that Thucydides thought Athens stronger in 445–431 than she had ever been, in 460 or in 450, nor (to my mind) that he was right.

προγνοὺς τὴν δύναμιν: 'the power of the city', not 'the magnitude of the war' (as Classen, Stahl, and Steup); cf. § 13, ἀφ' ὧν προέγνω, κ.τ.λ. The phrase in the next sentence ἡ πρόνοια ἡ ἐς τὸν πόλεμον (to which Classen points) remains relevant, for ἡ δύναμις means the city's military power.

This foresight is the most important element in Perikles' military wisdom (it is mentioned again in §§ 6 and 13), as it had been in Themistokles (i. 138. 3). It does not mean prognostication: Perikles could not foresee the pestilence as the Pythian oracle 'foretold' the danger of occupying the Pelargikon, and others the plague or the hunger that would accompany a Dorian war, and yet others the length of the war, as Kalchas had been able to foretell the length and result of the Trojan war. Perikles' foresight was human.

6. ἐπεβίω δὲ δύο ἔτη καὶ ἓξ μῆνας: he died, that is, in the autumn of the following year; according to Plutarch, he had caught, but not succumbed to the pestilence, but the resulting weakness was fatal (Per. 38. 1).

Whether all this part of c. 65 was a later addition to an already published, or at least completed, history of the Archidamian war, or the whole history was written after 404 B.C. from the notes made continuously throughout the war, it is entirely characteristic of Thucydides that he does not mention the death of Perikles in its chronological place, any more than he does that of Phormion (see iii. 7. 1 n.) or any other man not killed in battle, even though Perikles' death had, he thought, so decisive an influence on the course of the war. For it moved him to make reflections on that course, and those reflections may appear at an appropriate place in the narrative which is not necessarily most accurate chronologically. The reflections on στάσις in book iii are another example of the same kind.

Thucydides comments on the deaths of only three Athenians: of Perikles, because it was so disastrous; of Kleon, because it removed an obstacle to peace; and of Nikias, for personal reasons, because he was an honest man. (We should perhaps add a fourth, Antiphon.)

7. ἡσυχάζοντας: 'keeping quiet', 'being patient', just what Athenians were incapable of doing (i. 70. 9 and ii. 21–22); what they called doing nothing, a policy which in another context Perikles and most other Athenians repudiated—it was glory they looked for: 63. 3, 64. 5 nn. And, incidentally, a difficult policy to carry out in war for any people, but especially for the Athenians: see vi. 18. 7. So difficult a policy, indeed, and not strictly that of Perikles (cf. 62. 2), that I believe we should insert here ⟨τῷ ὁπλιτικῷ⟩ (J.H.S. lxxi, 1951, 70, n. 4). In 72. 1 ἡσυχίαν ἄγειν actually means to be neutral.

ἀρχὴν μὴ ἐπικτωμένους ἐν τῷ πολέμῳ: the policy already enunciated in i. 144. 1. Plutarch tells us that the 'fatal passion' for Sicily held men's minds, and there were even dreams of conquering Carthage and Etruria, already in Perikles' day; but Perikles kept them in check (in the time of the peace as well), even though he was prepared to sail to Sinope on the Pontos (*Per.* 20; *Alk.* 17. 1; cf. Ar. *Ach.* 606, *Eq.* 1303). Plutarch may be wrong; but Perikles must have been aware that the Athenians thought one of the advantages of the alliance with Kerkyra to be that island's favourable position on the route to the Greek cities in the west (i. 44. 3), and Thucydides leaves us to suppose that he, Perikles, shared the view. He knew his fellow countrymen, and he was at least playing with fire: μᾶλλον γὰρ πεφό-βημαι τὰς οἰκείας ἡμῶν ἁμαρτίας ἢ τὰς τῶν ἐναντίων διανοίας.

οἱ δὲ ταὐτά τε πάντα ἐς τοὐναντίον ἔπραξαν, κ.τ.λ.: this is a sweeping statement, and it is a pity that Thucydides is not more precise; except for the Sicilian expedition mentioned below, § 11, he does not further define what subsequent action was quite contrary to Perikles' policy or was foreign to the war. And are τὰ ἔξω τοῦ πολέμου δοκοῦντα εἶναι military expeditions or internal rivalries? Editors have doubted. Most agree to put ταὐτά τε πάντα and καὶ ἄλλα both into the military sphere, and follow Arnold in citing the sending of a squadron to Crete (ii. 85. 5–6: which was doubtless a blunder, but was a trifle and had no serious consequences), the small expeditions to Sicily in 426, which wasted their own energies and tended to unite the Sikeliots against Athens, "the iniquitous attack on Melos" (which was made in time of peace, and was at least in accord with the general policy of dominating the islands), and perhaps the Delion campaign and the dispatch of νῆες ἀργυρολόγοι (iii. 19). Of these I would only include the expedition to Sicily and the Delion campaign; and I would certainly add to them Demosthenes' Aitolian and Akarnanian wars, and perhaps Alkibiades' Peloponnesian campaign in 418, which are good examples of fighting which brought loss to the state in failure and gain to the individual in success—though, at the same time, both Aitolia and Delion are intelligible as attempts, if not very well judged attempts, to end the deadlock, just as was Brasidas' (not Sparta's) invasion of Thrace; for it did not occur to men then, any more than it does now, to end a deadlock in war by making peace; nor did their failure mean the destruction of Athens. These are far from being enough to justify the condemnation ταῦτα πάντα ἐς τοὐναντίον ἔπραξαν; and it should be noted that in none of them was Kleon particularly involved (*his* two campaigns, Pylos and Amphipolis, were not at all ἔξω τοῦ πολέμου), and in two of them Demosthenes, generally thought to be a friend, and perhaps a relation, of Thucydides, was, both as planner and commander. If, on the other hand, the historian is in the main thinking of the great

Sicilian expedition (as I feel sure he was), then his expression is misleading; for this would mean that (in the main) Perikles' policy was followed during the whole of the Archidamian war, and his death in 429, when he was over 60, was not therefore as significant as Thucydides says. See below, § 11 n., and my article in *J.H.S.* lxxi. 70–71.

δοκοῦντα εἶναι: generally supposed to mean, 'were thought to be irrelevant to the issue of the war, but later proved disastrous' (σφαλέντα δέ, κ.τ.λ.); but it is only 'seemed generally to be foreign to the purpose of the war', and were therefore ill-judged actions. δοκεῖν is used as, e.g., 63. 2.

τοῖς ἰδιώταις: not the word one expects. ἰδιώτης means sometimes the individual as opposed to the state (see i. 124. 1, iii. 10. 1; Plat. *Symp.* 185 B; Xen. *Vectig.* 4. 18), though normally the private citizen as opposed to the official and the layman as opposed to the expert: vi. 72. 3 n.; but in all these other cases it definitely implies the private citizen acting on his own initiative—private as opposed to state action; here it must mean the state's own officers, strategoi, or at the very least the semi-official and altogether public προστάται τοῦ δήμου. I suspect that we should read αὐτοῖς ἰδίᾳ. The scholiast recognized the difficulty: ἰδιώτας καλεῖ τοὺς ῥήτορας καὶ τοὺς δημαγωγούς, οὐχ ὅτι ἰδιῶται κατὰ τὸ ἀληθές, ἀλλ' ὡς πρὸς ἀντιδιαστολὴν τοῦ κοινοῦ καὶ τῆς πόλεως.

For the sentiment here cf. Kleon's words, iii. 38. 3, and Nikias against Alkibiades, vi. 12. 2.

Mme de Romilly, pp. 164–5, notes that the refusal of peace in 425 is not here stated as one of the blunders committed after Perikles' death; but I do not interpret the silence quite as she does.

8. τῷ τε ἀξιώματι: Perikles was the conspicuous example to prove the truth of the statement in 37. 1 that in the Athenian democracy all men, the able and the commonplace, were not reduced to the same level, that ability was both recognized and made use of. See also n. on ἀξίωμα, ἀξίωσις there.

ἐλευθέρως: 'freely', i.e. without hesitation, 'as a free man should', rather than "eo modo qui cum singulorum libertate et ingenuorum dignitate congrueret", as Bloomfield renders it, giving ἐλευθέρως the same meaning as in 37. 2 in a very different context, and contrasting iii. 62. 4 (of the Theban oligarchy), κατέχοντες ἰσχύι τὸ πλῆθος. Cf. Solon, 24. 20–22 D,

> κέντρον δ' ἄλλος ὡς ἐγὼ λαβών,
> κακοφραδής τε καὶ φιλοκτήμων ἀνήρ,
> οὐκ ἂν κατέσχε δῆμον.

μὴ κτώμενος ἐξ οὐ προσηκόντων τὴν δύναμιν: his influence rested not so much on his incomparable eloquence, and not at all on any purely

192

demagogic arts, but on his known integrity of character and intellect. (Plut. *Per.* 15. 4, refers to this passage, but limits the cause of Perikles' influence to his superiority to money.) Note the present tense, $\kappa\tau\dot{\omega}\mu\epsilon\nu\sigma$, 'in the pursuit of power', the word contrasted with $\check{\epsilon}\chi\omega\nu$, 'when he had it', when he did not have to (or no longer had to) struggle for it. Plutarch divided Perikles' political career sharply into two halves, the first when he did use base demagogic arts to gain power, the second when he had gained it and used it nobly (see vol. i, pp. 66–67). Classen notes as well the present $\lambda\dot{\epsilon}\gamma\epsilon\iota\nu$ and the aorist $\dot{\alpha}\nu\tau\epsilon\iota\pi\epsilon\hat{\iota}\nu$; but the contrast 'he did not habitually speak to please' and 'he would on occasion speak $\pi\rho\dot{\sigma}s$ $\dot{\sigma}\rho\gamma\dot{\eta}\nu$' does not seem to have much point.

With $\dot{\epsilon}\xi$ $o\dot{v}$ $\pi\rho\sigma\sigma\eta\kappa\dot{\sigma}\nu\tau\omega\nu$ cf. 61. 4 and 45. 2 nn.

$\pi\rho\dot{\sigma}s$ $\dot{\sigma}\rho\gamma\dot{\eta}\nu$: 'angrily', as most edd., or 'so as to provoke their anger', in direct contrast with $\pi\rho\dot{\sigma}s$ $\dot{\eta}\delta\sigma\nu\dot{\eta}\nu$, 'to give them pleasure'? I do not doubt that the latter is correct, both because of the contrast intended, and because it was not in Perikles' manner to speak angrily, or even emotionally (certainly not as reported in his last speech). In Ar. *Ran.* 856, $\mu\dot{\eta}$ $\pi\rho\dot{\sigma}s$ $\dot{\sigma}\rho\gamma\dot{\eta}\nu$, $A\dot{\iota}\sigma\chi\dot{v}\lambda$', $\dot{\alpha}\lambda\lambda\dot{\alpha}$ $\pi\rho\alpha\dot{\sigma}\nu\omega s$ $\check{\epsilon}\lambda\epsilon\gamma\chi$' $\dot{\epsilon}\lambda\dot{\epsilon}\gamma\chi\sigma v$, 'in a manner to provoke anger' is certainly as appropriate to the first verb as 'angrily' is to the second.

9. $\kappa\alpha\tau\dot{\epsilon}\pi\lambda\eta\sigma\sigma\epsilon\nu$: "quare Athenae eius terrorem timuisse dicuntur a Cic. *Brut.* 11. 44" (Stahl). See 62. 1 n. on $\kappa\alpha\tau\alpha\pi\epsilon\pi\lambda\eta\gamma\mu\dot{\epsilon}\nu\sigma v s$; and Jaeger, *Demosthenes* (Sather Lectures, 1938), 158–9, with nn. 15 and 17, for a comparison in this respect of Perikles with Demosthenes.

All recognized his power as an orator, as Plutarch says; besides the well-known lines of Aristophanes and Eupolis, see Kratinos too, fr. 293.

$\dot{\epsilon}\gamma\dot{\iota}\gamma\nu\epsilon\tau\dot{\sigma}$ $\tau\epsilon$: the imperfect is noticeable, and means 'it was turning out, proving to be', not 'it was', or 'it had become'. In iii. 12. 1 $\dot{\epsilon}\gamma\dot{\iota}\gamma\nu\epsilon\tau\sigma$ is similarly used.[1]

What dangerous things words are! I have quoted Eur. *Suppl.* 404–8 above in the n. on 37. 1, to which they are very apt. But one might quote the first six words, $o\dot{v}$ $\gamma\dot{\alpha}\rho$ $\check{\alpha}\rho\chi\epsilon\tau\alpha\iota$ $\dot{\epsilon}\nu\dot{\sigma}s$ $\pi\rho\dot{\sigma}s$ $\dot{\alpha}\nu\delta\rho\dot{\sigma}s$, and suppose that Thucydides is here deliberately contradicting not only the general opinion about Athens, but the words he has recorded from, or composed for, Perikles himself. Nor can we in any case take him here too literally, or prosaically, unimaginatively: he has himself just told us how, smoothly, peacefully, in a constitutional manner, Perikles was dismissed from office and re-elected; and, what is even more significant if we would try to understand how the Athenian constitution really worked, what was the nature of Perikles' power, that on the one cardinal issue of war and peace, the demos had

---

[1] On the other hand, it is difficult to distinguish between the meanings of $\dot{\epsilon}\gamma\dot{\epsilon}\nu\epsilon\tau\sigma$ and $\dot{\epsilon}\gamma\dot{\iota}\gamma\nu\epsilon\tau\sigma$ in ii. 97. 1 and 2.

recently ignored his advice while he was still in office, and he remained in office to carry out its policy. Perikles wielded such influence, and for a long period, as has been given to few men to wield over their fellow countrymen; but his constitutional powers were small, and he could only continue to keep his position through his direct influence with the ekklesia—the ekklesia could not be ignored or circumvented, however much it might trust a leader and be wisely led or grossly misled by him. In another context Thucydides would say this was democracy: not only in 37. 1, but in vi. 89. 3–6 (Alkibiades' speech at Sparta), and viii. 68. 4. (*History*, xxxvi, 1951, 24.)

Another interesting example of verbal usage is Plutarch's Θουκυδίδης μὲν ἀριστοκρατικήν τινα τὴν τοῦ Περικλέους ὑπογράφει πολιτείαν (*Per.* 9. 1), whereas if *we* were to give an adjective, it would be monarchical. Plutarch is equating ὑπὸ τοῦ πρώτου ἀνδρὸς ἀρχή with ὑ. τ. ἀρίστου ἀ. ἀρχή, which theoretically is aristocracy (see above, p. 109). In other passages (16. 1, 39 ad fin.) he refers to current attacks on Perikles as τύραννος.

Although I follow Wade-Gery in his estimate of the Periklean democracy (above, p. 125), I do not think his choice of 'principate' as a translation of ὑπὸ τοῦ πρώτου ἀνδρὸς ἀρχή a happy one; for that word is proper to a very different form of administration. I do not agree at all with J. S. Morrison's view that Perikles' position could at that time in Athens be thought of as μοναρχία and that Herodotos had "the supporters of the Cleisthenic democracy, the oligarchic party . . . and the supporters of Pericles" respectively in mind in the speeches of Otanes, Megabyxos, and Dareios in the 'debate on the constitution of Persia', iii. 80–82 (*C.Q.* xxxv, 1941, 11–14; *J.H.S.* lxx, 1950, 76–77). Dareios' words describe the rise of a *tyrant* and are not at all descriptive of Perikles' rise to power in Athens; they are also a defence of monarchy in Persia, of the Persian type of kingship; for, while other Persian names might be substituted for Otanes and Megabyxos, no one but Dareios, the future Great King, could speak for monarchy. It is the Persian monarch, and the foolish Xerxes as well as the wise Dareios, whom Herodotos has in mind; and I am sure that no friend or admirer of Perikles called him, or thought of him, as μόναρχος. Plutarch, 16. 1, has it more accurately: καίτοι τὴν δύναμιν αὐτοῦ σαφῶς μὲν ὁ Θουκυδίδης διηγεῖται, κακοήθως δὲ παρεμφαίνουσιν οἱ κωμικοί, Πεισιστρατίδας μὲν νέους τοὺς περὶ αὐτὸν ἑταίρους καλοῦντες, αὐτὸν δὲ ἀπομόσαι μὴ τυραννήσειν κελεύοντες, ὡς ἀσυμμέτρου πρὸς δημοκρατίαν καὶ βαρυτέρας περὶ αὐτὸν οὔσης ὑπεροχῆς. ὁ δὲ Τηλεκλείδης, κ.τ.λ. (see i. 127 n.); and at the very end of the *Life*, with reference to the gap felt in Athens after his death, ἡ ἐπίφθονος ἰσχὺς ἐκείνη, μοναρχία λεγομένη καὶ τυραννὶς πρότερον, ἐφάνη τότε σωτήριον ἔρυμα τῆς πολιτείας γενομένη.

10. οἱ δὲ ὕστερον, κ.τ.λ.: it is important to keep in mind exactly what Thucydides here says—not that the policy of Kleon, Nikias, or Alkibiades was necessarily wrong, or contrary to that of Perikles (ταῦτα πάντα ἐς τοὐναντίον ἔπραξαν, § 7 n.), but that no one of them was strong enough, in character and intellect, or possessed enough influence with the ekklesia, to conceive and carry out a *consistent* policy; 'the conduct of affairs too was offered to the whims of the people', and policy *varied* from year to year, every politician vying for the popular favour. τὰ πράγματα ἐνδιδόναι (present tense): they were prepared to surrender leadership to the people, unlike Perikles. For the phrase in a different context ('to surrender control to a foreign power'), see v. 62. 2, vii. 48. 2.

11. ἄλλα τε πολλὰ - - - ἡμαρτήθη: it is again a pity that Thucydides does not further specify; we should have had a much clearer idea of his judgement if he had. See on § 7, above.

ὡς ἐν μεγάλῃ πόλει: 'as was to be expected in a great city ruling an empire.' This must certainly be the meaning of ὡς here, not 'many for a great city' which would not be many for a small one.

οὐ τοσοῦτον - - - ἐπῆσαν: not a mistake of judgement from the purely military point of view; the armament was strong enough to overcome the enemy, had other things not intervened. Cf. vi. 31. 6, vii. 42. 2–3. This is clear enough; yet in the context it is surprising, for the Sicilian expedition was the clearest case of divergence from Perikles' policy, his *strategy*, that is, of not attempting to extend the empire before the war with the Peloponnesians had been truly ended.

ἐπιγιγνώσκοντες: literally, 'by additional decisions', i.e. by the policy of those at home (οἱ ἐκπέμψαντες) after the expedition had sailed.

κατὰ τὰς ἰδίας διαβολάς: with a reference presumably to the attack on Alkibiades for the mutilation of the hermai and the profanation of the Mysteries; but not only to this. The affair of the hermai started the game of mutual recrimination, which then could not stop, till it ended, after the defeat in Sicily, with the first serious internal disturbances in Athens.

ἀμβλύτερα ἐποίουν: 'weakened the army in the field', 'blunted the edge of its power to attack the enemy'.

This judgement of Thucydides on the reasons for the Athenian failure in Sicily is interesting not only in itself, but because it is not borne out by his own narrative in books vi and vii, as I have tried to show in *J.H.S.* lxxi, 1951, 70–72. See also L. C. Pearson, *T.A.P.A.* lxxviii, 1943, 37–60. Of course Athens was weakened by the quarrels which began over the hermai affair and the advantage taken of that by factious and envious demagogues, rivals to Alkibiades and ἴσοι μᾶλλον αὐτοὶ πρὸς ἀλλήλους ὄντες καὶ ὀρεγόμενοι τοῦ πρώτος ἕκαστος γίγνεσθαι; and the decision to send Alkibiades with the expedition and to continue the inquiries into his conduct in his absence was both unjust to him and damaging to the efficiency of the armada (vi.

28–29). But no one would conclude from Thucydides' narrative that it was decisive. True, Alkibiades did his city untold harm when he deserted to the enemy; but, as Thucydides himself says, vii. 42. 3, the advice he gave Sparta to send Gylippos to Syracuse would not have been given or would have been given in vain, if only Nikias had carried on the campaign more intelligently and with more vigour after the recall of Alkibiades; and the other injuries he inflicted on Athens were only to take effect after the expedition had ended. Moreover, we cannot say that it was Alkibiades' recall that led at once to the weak-kneed plans of Nikias; for his own plans for conquering Sicily had not been much more intelligent—only Lamachos of the three had understood the military situation (vi. 47–49); at the most we can surmise that Alkibiades' diplomacy might have won some successes and that when he found he could delay the attack no longer he would have attacked with more vigour than Nikias. Nor can οἱ ἐκπέμψαντες οὐ τὰ πρόσφορα τοῖς οἰχομένοις ἐπιγιγνώσκοντες mean simply that the politicians at home neglected the army in the field, failing to send necessary supplies and reinforcements; or if it does mean that, it is inconsistent with Thucydides' own narrative; for, on each occasion that Nikias asked for them, supplies and reinforcements were sent, and in good measure, and, comparatively, with little or no delay. In fact οἱ ἐκπέμψαντες, after Alkibiades' recall, play little part in the expedition, and what they do, they apparently do well. The failure of the expedition was due, to judge from books vi and vii, almost entirely to military blunders by the men on the spot. (Sparta, indeed, was more open than Athens to such a charge of failing to support her armies in the field, and that owing to private jealousies, iv. 108. 7.)

This indicates that the present passage was written at a different time from the narrative in those books; and since it was written after 404, it would seem that vi and vii were finished considerably earlier. There is a similar conclusion, I think, to be drawn from ταὐτά τε πάντα ἐς τοὐναντίον ἔπραξαν in § 7; there is little in the narrative of iii, iv, and v. 1–24 to justify the statement; and, in fact, Thucydides is there, as I said, surely thinking of the Sicilian expedition as the great example of effort at variance with the strategic plan of Perikles. That passage too was written after 404, when the events of the years after 413 had made so deep an impression on Thucydides' mind, as on most men of the time, that the course of the ten years' war had been almost forgotten and he has telescoped events in his judgement. See also nn. on iv. 81. 3, 108. 4, and vi. 15. 4. The natural conclusion is that the narrative was written earlier than these comments.

12. τρία μὲν ἔτη ἀντεῖχον, κ.τ.λ.: it is difficult either to interpret the MSS. reading satisfactorily or to make a certain emendation. If, with most edd., we take Κύρῳ τε ὕστερον - - - προσγενομένῳ closely with what precedes ($\tau o\hat{\imath}\varsigma$ $\tau\epsilon$ $\pi\rho\acute{o}\tau\epsilon\rho o\nu$ - - - $\kappa\alpha\grave{\imath}$ $\tau o\hat{\imath}\varsigma$ - - - $\kappa\alpha\grave{\imath}$ $\tau\hat{\omega}\nu$ $\xi\nu\mu\mu\acute{\alpha}\chi\omega\nu$ $\check{\epsilon}\tau\iota$ $\tau o\hat{\imath}\varsigma$ - - - $K\acute{\nu}\rho\omega$ $\tau\epsilon$) and $\kappa\alpha\grave{\imath}$ $o\grave{\nu}$ $\pi\rho\acute{o}\tau\epsilon\rho o\nu$ $\grave{\epsilon}\nu\acute{\epsilon}\delta o\sigma\alpha\nu$ as the answer to - - - $\mu\grave{\epsilon}\nu$ $\check{\epsilon}\tau\eta$ $\grave{\alpha}\nu\tau\epsilon\hat{\imath}\chi o\nu$, we must read $\grave{o}\kappa\tau\grave{\omega}$ $\mu\grave{\epsilon}\nu$ $\check{\epsilon}\tau\eta$ (spring of 412 to spring of 404); Haacke's conjecture, $\delta\acute{\epsilon}\kappa\alpha$, based on Xen. *Hell.* ii. 4. 21 and Isokr. xii. 57 and xviii. 47, and accepted by many, is much less likely. (Xenophon and Isokrates are using a round number, seemingly for the period autumn 413 to spring 404.) But I am not convinced that this is right: - - - $\mu\grave{\epsilon}\nu$ $\check{\epsilon}\tau\eta$ suggests that another *period* is to be added, and that this is represented by $K\acute{\nu}\rho\omega$ $\tau\epsilon$ $\check{\nu}\sigma\tau\epsilon\rho o\nu$ ($\mu\acute{\epsilon}\nu$ answered by $\tau\epsilon$, uncommon in prose, but a little more common than $\mu\acute{\epsilon}\nu$ answered by $\kappa\alpha\acute{\imath}$), $\grave{\alpha}\nu\tau\epsilon\hat{\imath}\chi o\nu$ of course belonging to both periods. This was Bury's view; and it is supported by the fact that the Sicilians withdrew from the war in 409 B.C. Kyros, especially instructed to give all possible help to the Peloponnesians, reached Sardis in the autumn of 408 (Busolt, iii. 1569. 2) or the spring of 407 (*C.A.H.* v. 473); we should with this interpretation read $\pi\acute{\epsilon}\nu\tau\epsilon$ $\mu\grave{\epsilon}\nu$ $\check{\epsilon}\tau\eta$; or, with Bury, keep $\tau\rho\acute{\imath}\alpha$ $\mu\grave{\epsilon}\nu$ $\check{\epsilon}\tau\eta$ (411–410 to 408–407 B.C.), referring $\kappa\alpha\tau\grave{\alpha}$ $\tau\grave{\eta}\nu$ $\pi\acute{o}\lambda\iota\nu$ $\check{\eta}\delta\eta$ $\grave{\epsilon}\nu$ $\sigma\tau\acute{\alpha}\sigma\epsilon\iota$ $\check{o}\nu\tau\epsilon\varsigma$ to the revolution of 411. We should expect, however, another indication of time, i.e. another three (or four) years, with $K\acute{\nu}\rho\omega$ $\tau\epsilon$ $\check{\nu}\sigma\tau\epsilon\rho o\nu$, if $\grave{\alpha}\nu\tau\epsilon\hat{\imath}\chi o\nu$ is to belong here, unless Bury is right in his ingenious suggestion that here, as sometimes in Pindar, $\mu\acute{\epsilon}\nu$ - - - $\tau\epsilon$ is equivalent to anaphora with $\mu\acute{\epsilon}\nu$ - - - $\delta\acute{\epsilon}$, so that $K\acute{\nu}\rho\omega$ $\tau\epsilon$ = $\tau\rho\acute{\imath}\alpha$ $\delta\grave{\epsilon}$ $\check{\epsilon}\tau\eta$ $K\acute{\nu}\rho\omega$ (ed. *Isthmian Odes*, App. A; Denniston, p. 374, n. 2). Steup objects that, if this were the meaning, we must have $\check{\nu}\sigma\tau\epsilon\rho\acute{o}\nu$ $\tau\epsilon$—or better $\delta\acute{\epsilon}$—$K\acute{\nu}\rho\omega$; but $K\acute{\nu}\rho\omega$ is emphatic; and it is even more clear that if $\kappa\alpha\grave{\imath}$ $o\grave{\nu}$ $\pi\rho\acute{o}\tau\epsilon\rho o\nu$ $\grave{\epsilon}\nu\acute{\epsilon}\delta o\sigma\alpha\nu$ answers to - - - $\mu\grave{\epsilon}\nu$ $\check{\epsilon}\tau\eta$ $\grave{\alpha}\nu\tau\epsilon\hat{\imath}\chi o\nu$, we should, on Steup's argument, have had $\grave{\alpha}\nu\tau\epsilon\hat{\imath}\chi o\nu$ $\mu\grave{\epsilon}\nu$ $\grave{o}\kappa\tau\grave{\omega}$ $\check{\epsilon}\tau\eta$. Shilleto saw this, and suggested that $\mu\acute{\epsilon}\nu$ conceals a participle (cf. iii. 111. 2 n.), $\tau\rho\nu\chi\acute{o}\mu\epsilon\nu o\iota$ or $\tau\rho\iota\beta\acute{o}\mu\epsilon\nu o\iota$ $\check{\epsilon}\tau\eta$ $\check{\eta}$. I am sure neither of these participles will do; $\mu\alpha\chi\acute{o}\mu\epsilon\nu o\iota$ or $\pi o\lambda\epsilon\mu o\hat{\nu}\nu\tau\epsilon\varsigma$ would be better; and undoubtedly the *simplest* reading is $\check{o}\mu\omega\varsigma$ $\grave{o}\kappa\tau\grave{\omega}$ $\pi o\lambda\epsilon\mu o\hat{\nu}\nu\tau\epsilon\varsigma$ $\check{\epsilon}\tau\eta$ $\grave{\alpha}\nu\tau\epsilon\hat{\imath}\chi o\nu$.[1]

As Shilleto and others have noticed, it is a little surprising that the support, often considerable, given to the Peloponnesians by Tissaphernes and Pharnabazos, which is related in detail in book viii, is here ignored, because it did not prove decisive. It is another argument in favour of the view that this whole passage (§§ 5–13) was written at a different time from the narrative of events, though Thucydides must have been well aware of their course.

$\alpha\grave{\nu}\tau o\grave{\imath}$ $\grave{\epsilon}\nu$ $\sigma\phi\acute{\imath}\sigma\iota$, $\kappa.\tau.\lambda.$: $\pi\epsilon\rho\iota\pi\epsilon\sigma\epsilon\hat{\imath}\nu$ takes a dative (or $\pi\epsilon\rho\acute{\imath}$ and accusative as Hdt. viii. 16. 2), and Herwerden proposed to bracket $\grave{\epsilon}\nu$: 'fell foul

---

[1] For the discussion of the chronology of this period, with full references to earlier writers, see W. F. Ferguson in *C.A.H.* v. 483–5, and *Treasurers of Athena*, 38–45; Beloch, ii.² 2, 268, 274; A. Andrewes, *J.H.S.* lxxiii, 1953, 2–9. Other views in Busolt, iii. 1529–32; Kahrstedt, *Forschungen*, 162 ff.

of each other', as Hdt. loc. cit., or 'stumbled over themselves', like Hdt. i. 108. 4. If not, we must take $\pi\epsilon\rho\iota\pi\epsilon\sigma\acute{o}\nu\tau\epsilon\varsigma$ absolutely, as Steup, which in effect means understanding $\dot{\epsilon}\alpha\upsilon\tauο\hat{\iota}\varsigma$. Note that C⟨G⟩ have $\alpha\dot{\upsilon}\tauο\grave{\iota}\ \dot{\epsilon}\nu\ \sigma\phi\acute{\iota}\sigma\iota\nu\ \alpha\dot{\upsilon}\tauο\hat{\iota}\varsigma$. The internal quarrels here are those of the last years of the war, the dismissal of Alkibiades after Notion and his retirement to the Chersonesos, the Arginousai trial, and the last struggles between Kleophon and his political enemies. Observe how Thucydides emphasizes the effect of these internal quarrels on the issue of the war ($\tau\grave{\alpha}\ \pi\epsilon\rho\grave{\iota}\ \tau\grave{\eta}\nu\ \pi\acute{o}\lambda\iota\nu$ - - - $\dot{\epsilon}\tau\alpha\rho\acute{\alpha}\chi\theta\eta\sigma\alpha\nu$, § 11, $\dot{\epsilon}\nu\ \sigma\tau\acute{\alpha}\sigma\epsilon\iota\ \acute{o}\nu\tau\epsilon\varsigma$ just above, and here; Perikles was right—Athens would not be defeated by her enemies: de Romilly, 196); which is enough to justify the conventional $\tau\hat{\eta}\ \dot{\eta}\mu\epsilon\tau\acute{\epsilon}\rho\alpha\ \alpha\dot{\upsilon}\tau\hat{\omega}\nu\ \delta\iota\alpha\phi\rhoο\hat{\alpha}\ \dot{\epsilon}\kappa\rho\alpha\tau\acute{\eta}\theta\eta\mu\epsilon\nu,\ \dot{ο}\dot{\upsilon}\chi\ \dot{\upsilon}\pi\grave{ο}\ \tau\hat{\omega}\nu\ \ddot{\alpha}\lambda\lambda\omega\nu$ of Plat. *Menex.* 243 D (but in what a different world that is!). Perikles' argument was this: Athens was safe, for the walls could always be defended against a land-power, and, owing to her accumulation of wealth, her material resources, and her sea-power, she could not be starved (this had been understood by Archidamos); if then Athenian morale could survive the destruction in Attica, and it did, on the whole, triumphantly, and if they made no foolish blunders, political and military, they would win. But they made both; and all Perikles' $\pi\rhoό\nuο\iota\alpha$ came to nothing. Clearly Thucydides did not believe in a foreseeable future in any literal sense, even by the most intelligent of men.

If we keep $\alpha\dot{\upsilon}\tauό\varsigma$ in this sentence, there is in my view only one way to translate it—he saw that he himself, i.e. Athens if guided by him and no other, would defeat the enemy. This is just possible, without any more arrogance than is inherent in 'I know that I can save my country, and that no one else can'; and for the use of the person for the city, see i. 137. 4 n. But I agree with Classen that this is not the point here; we might, with him, read $\alpha\dot{\upsilon}\tauο\acute{\upsilon}\varsigma$, but we cannot just leave it at that, with $\alpha\dot{\upsilon}\tauο\acute{\upsilon}\varsigma$ in this emphatic position—we should have to transpose after $\dot{\rho}\alpha\delta\acute{\iota}\omega\varsigma$, and as well read $\tau\hat{\omega}\nu\ \Pi\epsilon\lambdaο\pi\omicron\nu\nu\eta\sigma\acute{\iota}\omega\nu$ (ABEFM), not $\tau\grave{\eta}\nu\ \pi\acute{ο}\lambda\iota\nu\ \Pi\epsilon\lambda$. (CG), even though the latter has the support of Π^{21} and the quotation in Aristeides. This latter reading ($\tau\hat{\omega}\nu\ \Pi\epsilon\lambda$.) seems required with either $\alpha\dot{\upsilon}\tauό\varsigma$ or $\alpha\dot{\upsilon}\tauο\acute{\upsilon}\varsigma$ (presumably in this case $\tau\grave{\eta}\nu\ \pi\acute{ο}\lambda\iota\nu$ was inserted because with $\alpha\dot{\upsilon}\tauό\varsigma$ taken only with $\pi\rhoο\acute{\epsilon}\gamma\nu\omega$ a subject to $\pi\epsilon\rho\iota\gamma\epsilon\nu\acute{\epsilon}\sigma\theta\alpha\iota$ seemed wanting); and I should much prefer to bracket $\alpha\dot{\upsilon}\tauό\varsigma$ and read $\tau\grave{\eta}\nu\ \pi\acute{ο}\lambda\iota\nu$.

Note once again how Thucydides confines himself to the war: we have here a review not of Perikles' whole career, not of his general policy and statesmanship—into which we get an insight from the Epitaphios—but of his career in relation to the Peloponnesian war only: his intellectual grasp of the strategic problems involved and ability to frame a strategy proper to Athenian needs, and his integrity and firmness of character which had enabled him to maintain for so long his influence over his fellow citizens, and which would have been decisive had he lived. Even this description is limited to the purely military sphere; nothing for example is here said of Perikles' administration of finance (though § 5 may be intended to include it), still less on the organization of the empire—on his success in 'keeping the allies in hand', and what that meant.

66. Peloponnesian Expedition against Zakynthos

66. 1. τοῦ αὐτοῦ θέρους: for a more exact date see n. on ναύαρχος, § 2.

ναυσὶν ἐκατόν: cf. 7. 2 n.

ἥ κεῖται ἀντιπέρας Ἤλιδος: cf. 30. 1 n.

Ἀχαιῶν τῶν ἐκ Πελοποννήσου ἄποικοι: Pausanias, viii. 24. 3, says that the *oikistes* of Zakynthos was from Psophis in Arkadia; which may point to a different tradition of the settlement.

Ἀθηναίοις ξυνεμάχουν: see 9. 4.

2. ἐπέπλεον: 'were on board'; but not as ἐπιβάται, or not only, but to serve as land troops, like the 1,000 Athenian hoplites of 23. 2, where see n. Cf. 102. 1 n.

Κνῆμος Σπαρτιάτης ναύαρχος: the Spartan nauarchos served for a year, and, it would appear, from autumn to autumn; for Knemos was still in command late next summer (80. 2 n.): Beloch, ii.² 2. 269–89. He must therefore have recently been appointed; and the date for this expedition is late in the summer of 430. M indeed here reads, according to Hude, τ. α. θέρους τελευτῶντος in § 1; but (if Hude is right) that will only be a copy from 67. 1 init. For the use of τὸ θέρος to include τὸ φθινόπωρον, see above, 31. 1 n.

The powers of the Spartan nauarchos at sea corresponded to those of the king in command of the army on land on an expedition abroad: Arist. *Pol.* ii. 6. 22, 1271 a 40, ἡ ναυαρχία σχεδὸν ἑτέρα βασιλεία καθέστηκε. A Spartan was normally in command of the combined Peloponnesian fleet, as Eurybiades had been of the allied fleet in 480.

67. Peloponnesian Embassy to Persia; arrested in Thrace

67. 1. Ἀριστεὺς Κορίνθιος: see i. 60–65.

Λακεδαιμονίων πρέσβεις: the story is told by Herodotos, vii. 137, in connexion with that of the fathers of two of these ambassadors (Aneristos and Nikolaos) who had offered themselves to be killed by Xerxes in expiation of the Spartan crime against the heralds of Dareios; but Xerxes had spared them and they returned to Sparta. The wrath of Talthybios, patron-hero of heralds, only ended with the death of the sons. Herodotos mentions the fate of Aristeus as well, but not Pratodamos, nor Timagoras and Pollis. Thucydides tells the tale in a different fashion.

Herodotos adds that Aneristos had captured Halieis, apparently by treachery: perhaps when Athens and Argos were allies (before 451 B.C.: vol. i, pp. 395–6—so How and Wells), perhaps shortly before 430, when Halieis was allied with Sparta (56. 5).

Ἀργεῖος ἰδίᾳ Πόλλις: for Argos was neutral (9. 2); but Pollis doubtless was intriguing for an alliance with Sparta. Argives might be well received in Persia for their neutrality fifty years before.

χρήματά τε παρασχεῖν: I agree with Classen that παρέχειν, the reading of AB^1EFM now perhaps supported by Π^{21}, is preferable to παρασχεῖν.

Σιτάλκην: see 29. 1.

οὗ ἦν στράτευμα, κ.τ.λ.: i. 64. 2; but the siege has been more recently mentioned, ii. 31. 2 and 58, and one expects a definite article here, as much as in § 2, τὸν Σάδοκον τὸν γεγενημένον Ἀθηναῖον.

Φαρνάκην τὸν Φαρναβάζου: satrap of the Daskylitis, on the Asiatic shore of the Propontis. He was still satrap in 422–421 (v. 1. 1); and his family seem to have had a hereditary interest in the office (i. 129. 1; viii. 6. 1, etc.).

2. Λέαρχος - - - Ἀμεινιάδης: neither is mentioned elsewhere in Thucydides, nor otherwise known.

τὸν Σάδοκον, κ.τ.λ.: see 29. 5, and Ar. Ach. 145–7:

> ὁ δ' υἱός, ὃν Ἀθηναῖον ἐπεποιήμεθα,
> ἦρα φαγεῖν ἀλλᾶντας ἐξ Ἀπατουρίων,
> καὶ τὸν πατέρ' ἠντεβόλει βοηθεῖν τῇ πάτρᾳ.

Herodotos says nothing of the intervention of Sadokos; but does mention Nymphodoros of Abdera (above, 29. 1, 5).

3. ᾧ ἔμελλον: Π^{21} reads ἔμελλε (omitting ᾧ in error), which Poppo had conjectured, reading ὃ ἔμελλε (ὅ being a reading of some recentiores). Perhaps ᾧ ἔμελλε should be read: 'by which he (Sadokos) was intending to convey them across the Hellespont', for it would preserve the transitive sense of περαιοῦν; we should then have the double accusative with περαιοῦν, as with διαβιβάζειν (Plat. Legg. x. 900 C; Polyb. iii. 113. 6 has it with both these verbs), or else read ⟨κατὰ⟩ τ. Ἑ.

τὸν Ἑλλήσποντον περαιώσειν: Herodotos says from the port of Bisanthe (the later Raidestos); 'Hellespont' anyhow here includes, as it often did, the Propontis.

4. μὴ αὖθις σφᾶς, κ.τ.λ.: Böhme compares the fears of the Corinthians about Nikias when he had been captured, vii. 86. 4.

ἀμύνεσθαι - - - ὑπῆρξαν: the proper terms for 'to defend oneself against an aggressor who has begun the attack' (cf. Isokr. ix. 28)—Croiset.

τοὺς ἐμπόρους οὓς ἔλαβον: "probably some special occasion is here referred too"—Marchant.

πάντας γὰρ δὴ κατ' ἀρχὰς τοῦ πολέμου, κ.τ.λ.: this, the action of the weaker naval power, is familiar to us of the present day. iii. 32. 1 gives another instance; and i. 30. 1 one of killing prisoners taken in battle. The Athenian threat to kill the Spartans taken on Sphakteria if the Peloponnesians invaded Attica was on the same level, morally.

Hermippos, fr. 63. 7 (see below, on iii. 71. 2), may refer to this episode: καὶ παρὰ Σιτάλκου ψώραν Λακεδαιμονίοισι. (So Meineke; Kock says: "ceterum scabiem non advectam ad Lac. dicere sed imprecari eis poeta videtur." Not if Hermippos is correctly quoted, for this is among the good things Dionysos *has* brought to Athens.)

For Peloponnesian privateering, cf. 69. 1, iii. 51. 2, v. 115. 2.

Marchant says that Kleon was "probably responsible" for the execution of the Peloponnesian ambassadors, who "should have been kept in prison as hostages"; for Perikles "had now no voice in the government, and Thucydides hints that he views this act as a blunder". Thucydides certainly implies a base motive in Athens (δείσαντες - - - δικαιοῦντες); but since we do not know the exact dates of Perikles' dismissal and reinstatement (65. 4 n.), we cannot say for certain that he was not now back in office. There is no evidence that Kleon was especially responsible; if he was, Thucydides misses an opportunity to say so, just as he says nothing of his attacks on Perikles in 431 (21. 3 n.). Cf. 70. 4 n.

Note the full details, with the names of envoys on both sides, of this episode—surely from 'notes' made at the time, and with but little added: indeed with perhaps more left out. We always assume that Thucydides 'expanded his notes'; but he may often have abbreviated.

68. *Amprakian Attack on Argos Amphilochikon*

68. 1. Ἀμπρακιῶται: see i. 26. 1, ii. 9. 2–3.

τῶν βαρβάρων: see § 9, below.

Ἄργος τὸ Ἀμφιλοχικόν: situated at the head of the bay at the south-east corner of the Amprakiot Gulf. See Hammond, *B.S.A.* xxxvii, 1936–7, 128–40; and iii. 105 nn.

3. οὐκ ἀρεσκόμενος τῇ ἐν Ἄργει καταστάσει Ἀμφίλοχος: εὗρε γὰρ τὴν μητέρα Ἐριφύλην ἀναιρεθεῖσαν ὑπὸ Ἀλκμέωνος τοῦ ἀδελφοῦ αὐτοῦ— schol. Note again how closely Thucydides follows the details of traditional history in the heroic age, and, by ignoring the personal element, interprets the past in the light of his own day (see i. 12. 2).

For some variation in the story of Eriphyle and of the foundation of this colony, see Strabo, vii. 7. 7, p. 326, x. 2. 25–26, p. 462; Apollod. iii. 95. Hdt. iii. 91. 1 tells of Amphilochos in Kilikia.

4. μεγίστη: smaller places in Amphilochia are mentioned in iii. 105 ff.

5. ἡλληνίσθησαν: Amprakia being a colony from Dorian Corinth.

See vol. i, p. 96, for the meaning of this in relation to Thucydides' belief about the spread of the Hellenic language. Looking again at this passage, I should naturally suppose that Amphilochos and his settlers are said to be βάρβαροι, i.e. that οἱ ἄλλοι Ἀμφίλοχοι who are here said still not to speak Greek were the descendants of settlers from Peloponnesian Argos in ἡ ἄλλη Ἀμφιλοχία, § 3 (note esp. § 4). Yet I still find it difficult to believe that Thucydides thought that Amphilochos, and with him Agamemnon, Achilles, or Odysseus, spoke 'Pelasgian', and that Homer only spoke Greek through contact with Dorians. Would he have rejected as spurious the inscriptions in Greek on objects said to have been dedicated in the temple at Lindos by Minos, Herakles, and several heroes who had taken part in the Trojan war (the *Lindian Anagraphe, F. Gr. Hist.* 532, §§ 4–14; cf. § 3)?

7. οἳ αὐτοῖς Φορμίωνά τε στρατηγὸν ἔπεμψαν, κ.τ.λ.: see vol. i, p. 367. Busolt, iii. 763. 6, argues that the expedition was later than the Samian war, for the Corinthians were then still friendly, at least diplomatically friendly, to Athens (i. 41. 2), and earlier than τὰ Κερκυραϊκά, for it would have influenced events in that episode and must have been mentioned; therefore *c.* 437 B.C. But see iii. 105. 1 n.

κοινῇ τε ᾤκισαν αὐτό: this is the reading of C, adopted by most editors. I prefer ᾤκησαν, with the other MSS., including G. Cf. κοινῷ δικαστηρίῳ ἐχρῶντο, iii. 105. 1 n.

8. ἡ ξυμμαχία: 9. 4. The Akarnanians renewed their friendship with Athens in the fourth century. See the summary in Tod, ii, p. 178.

9. Χαόνων: living in the Pindos mountains, east and north-east of the Amprakiot Gulf, and west of the Acheloos R.

For the further story of the war in this region see iii. 102, 105 ff.; that these peoples were involved in the Peloponnesian war is the reason for the insertion of this chapter.

69. *Athenian Naval Expeditions*

69. 1. τοῦ δ᾽ ἐπιγιγνομένου χειμῶνος: we are reminded that Greek triremes would sail round C. Malea and across the Aegean, and that Greek merchantmen would come from Phoenicia to the Aegean, in winter time.

ἐκ Ναυπάκτου: vol. i, pp. 304–5, 404–5.

τοῦ Κρισαίου κόλπου: i.e. the Corinthian Gulf, as it later came to be called. See 86. 3.

ἀργυρολογῶσι: cf. iii. 19, iv. 50. 1. The duties of these squadrons were not confined to collecting arrears of tribute, or tribute from cities which had not hitherto paid, but went regularly, in war-time at least, to escort the tribute-bringing ships. Thucydides only mentions them when some special task was allotted to them, or some noteworthy incident occurred. Meritt, however, *A.F.D.* 17–25, and now *A.T.L.* iii. 69–70, connect them particularly with the years of assessment of tribute, which in these three cases would be 430, 428, and 425. Of these the last is certain (*I.G.* i.² 63 = *A.T.L.* A 9 = Tod, 66), and 428, from the quota-list, highly probable; this makes 430 too seem probable; if it is correct, 431 cannot also have been a year of assessment (13. 3 n., p. 18; and *Historia* ii, p. 46). But the argument assumes that the νῆες ἀργυρολόγοι were sent to collect the tribute (in war-time) in the autumn or winter before the Dionysia at which it was due. This seems in itself doubtful; and, if true, why did the fleets go only to specified parts of the empire? And there are difficulties arising from the times mentioned in A 9: for which see n. on iv. 50. 1.

ἀπὸ Φασήλιδος καὶ Φοινίκης: see vol. i, p. 9, for Thucydides' general treatment of economic factors, and for details, the index to vol. i, s.v. For Phaselis as a city of the empire, vol. i, p. 290.

2. ὁ Μελήσανδρος ἀποθνῄσκει: nothing more is known of him but that his tomb in the Kerameikos was seen by Pausanias, i. 29. 7.

70. *Surrender of Poteidaia*

70. 1. αὐτόθι: Reiske conjectured ἄτοπα, and the conjecture is worth recording. ⟨καὶ⟩ ἄτοπα perhaps.

βρώσεως πέρι ἀναγκαίας: see J. Tate, *C.R.* lxii, 1948, 7–8, for this use of ἀναγκαῖος, 'the extreme paucity of food', 'the minimum necessary to keep body and soul together'. (I would not, however, agree with him that 'imposed by necessity' is an impossible meaning because "the besieged were not *compelled* to eat unnatural food". They might be said to be: cf. iii. 45. 4, ἡ πενία ἀνάγκῃ τὴν τόλμαν παρέχουσα.)

Ξενοφῶντί τε, κ.τ.λ.: Xenophon is named again, 79. 1 (the Athenian defeat at Spartolos); and as τρίτος αὐτός is there added, the other two may well have been Hestiodoros and Phanomachos. (Diodoros, xii. 47. 3, says that Xenophon and Phanomachos were in command at Spartolos; the omission of the third name is a slip by Diodoros or his MSS. Plutarch, *Nik.* 6. 3, gives Kalliades as the commander, clearly by confusion with Kallias son of Kalliades of i. 61. 1.) Xenophon had been (probably) hipparch c. 446 (*I.G.* i.² 400; see vol. i, p. 328. 1), and strategos against Samos in 441–440 (Androtion, F 38); and is well spoken of in Lysias, xix. 14. He may be the man attacked in Kratinos, fr. 53.

2. ὁρῶντες μέν, κ.τ.λ.: one expects ⟨καὶ σφίσι⟩, or the like.

ἐν χωρίῳ χειμερινῷ: apparently 'a place exposed to storms or great cold in winter' (it being winter at this time); but we are told that the word for 'stormy' is χειμέριος, not χειμερινός, which means only 'suitable to winter' or 'in winter-time', χειμεριναὶ ἡμέραι, etc. (see, e.g., Rennie, ed. Ar. *Ach.* 1141).

δισχίλια τάλαντα: see above, 13. 3 and 47. 1 nn., and below, iii. 116. 3. Compare with it the cost of the siege of Samos in 440–439, vol. i, pp. 335–6.

4. ἐπητιάσαντο: the Athenians could not complain that the generals had thrown away much military advantage, though the defenders lived to fight, presumably, with their allies in Chalkidike; but, had the city surrendered at discretion, they might perhaps have killed their prisoners or sold them as slaves; or at least threatened to do so, as a lesson to other subject cities that might think of revolting. Thucydides does not say that Kleon was responsible for these complaints (cf. 67. 4 n. ad fin.); and Xenophon was not recalled, nor, probably, his colleagues (§ 1 n.).

ἐποίκους: Diodoros, xii. 46. 7, says there were a thousand. In his account of the surrender of Poteidaia (and of Phormion's expedition, c. 69, in xii. 47. 1), he follows Thucydides closely, and characteristically misdates the events; and some have supposed that ἄ (χιλίους), or ἐς ἄ, has been dropped in error from the text of Thucydides. The settlers dedicated an offering on the Akropolis at Athens before leaving: *I.G.* i.² 397 (Tod, 60). For the term ἔποικοι (used on this inscription as well), see above, p. 34 n. 1.

The story of the campaign in Chalkidike is resumed in c. 79. It is perhaps surprising that Thucydides does not here say that the war there did not end with the surrender of Poteidaia.

Another document having connexion with this colony is an Athenian decree in favour of Aphytis, the town on the east coast of the Pallene peninsula which had served as a base of operations to Phormion (i. 64. 2): Meritt, *Hesp.* xiii, 1944, No. 2 (pp. 211–29), which joins with a fragment previously published as *I.G.* ii.² 55; see *S.E.G.* x. 67. In the decree certain privileges are granted to Aphytis similar to those given to Methone in 430–429 (*I.G.* i.² 57 = Tod, 61 = *A.T.L.* ii, D 3), freedom to import corn, and payment of the ἀπαρχή only for tribute; the Aphytaioi take an oath to support the colonists (ἔποικοι, as above) in Poteidaia. Cf. also *I.G.* i.² 58, a decree for Aphytis, c. 426 B.C.: Meritt, loc. cit., p. 218.

YEAR 3: 429–428 B.C. (CC. 71–103)

71–78. *Siege of Plataia begun.* (Cf. Dem. lix. 101–2)

71. 1. τοῦ δ' ἐπιγιγνομένου θέρους: a date fairly early in the summer, not later than the middle of May, the normal time for the invasions of Attica, seems to be intended. But see 78. 2, 79. 1 nn.

ἡγεῖτο δὲ Ἀρχίδαμος, κ.τ.λ.: for the formality, cf. 10. 3, 19. 1 nn. Demosthenes, lix. 101, heightens the tone.

2. Διὶ ἐλευθερίῳ: for the altar to Zeus as god of freedom, set up after the battle, presumably in the agora at Plataia, see Plut. *Aristeid.*

20. 4–6, Paus. ix. 2. 5–7; and for the verses said to have been inscribed on it, *Anth. Pal.* vi. 50 (see Stahl's n. here).

ἀπεδίδου: interpreted by most edd. as 'granted', rather than 'restored'; but the latter is preferable ("formally reinstated us in the independent possession of our city and territory"—Thirlwall, ap. Shilleto). The imperfect is generally described as that 'of lasting effect'; it is rather 'made the offer or suggestion of reinstatement', which was only made effective when all the representatives of states had taken the solemn oath. Compare the aorists, ἔδοσαν, παρέδωκεν, § 3, 72. 1. (The purpose of the different tenses, στρατεῦσαι and ἀμύνειν, is harder to see.)

3. ἀρετῆς ἔνεκα καὶ προθυμίας, κ.τ.λ.: so Hdt. viii. 1. 1, ὑπὸ δὲ ἀρετῆς τε καὶ προθυμίης Πλαταιέες (at Salamis). Note also Thuc. iii. 56. 5, 57. 2.

4. ἡμετέρους ἐγχωρίους: according to Stahl different from, according to Classen (because of the one definite article) the same as τοὺς ὑμετέρους πατρῴους. The former is probably right: cf. 74. 2, and Paus. ix. 2. 7, 4. 1.

τοὺς ὅρκους: the Plataians appear to be referring only to the promise made by Pausanias to them after the victory; but there was another famous oath said to have been taken before the battle of Plataia, the oath not only of mutual loyalty between all the allies, but to destroy Thebes and other medizing states (ξυνώμοσαν, 72. 1, iii. 64. 3). This is the one referred to by Herodotos, vii. 132. 2, but the hostility to Thebes shows that it was not taken before Thermopylai; it is quoted by Lykourgos, *Leokr.* 80–81, and Diodoros, xi. 29. 2–3; it was denounced as fictitious by Theopompos, F 153 (as an Athenian invention; but it was said to have been taken by all the Greeks who fought against Persia); and a fourth-century copy of it, together with a copy of the archaic oath of the Athenian epheboi, has been found inscribed on a marble stele at Acharnai (L. Robert, *Ét. épigr. et philol.* 302: Tod, ii. 204—add to Tod's bibliography, H. W. Parke, *Hermathena*, 1948, 106 ff.; G. Daux, *R.E.G.* lvii, 1949, 1, who makes some corrections in the text). But this copy is of the Athenian oath only, though it is clearly not Athenian only in scope, for the ἐνωμοτάρχης, a Spartan officer (Thuc. v. 66. 2), is mentioned as well as the ταξίαρχος.[1] Was it this or a similar fourth-century copy which Theopompos saw and said was an *Athenian* forgery, just as he denounced the Kallias treaty because, very likely, he saw a later copy in Ionic lettering (vol. i, pp. 332–4)?

For the general covenant agreed at Plataia see *A.T.L.* iii. 101–5; and for one clause of it, below, iii. 59. 3 n.

72. 1. ὅσοι μετασχόντες - - - εἰσὶ νῦν ὑπ' Ἀθηναίοις: not very many in fact (Chalkis, Tenos, Keos, Naxos, and half a dozen others), but

---

1 Tod, p. 307. Daux shows that ταξίαρχον is to be read in l. 25, not ταξίλοχον.

among them was Aigina, who had been awarded the prize of valour at Salamis (cf. iii. 64. 3).

πρότερον ἤδη: not mentioned by Thucydides; cf. iii. 68. 1, n. on τόν τε ἄλλον χρόνον.

καὶ τάδε ἡμῖν ἀρκέσει: Shilleto would put a comma only before this; certainly a full stop (edd.) is too much.

2. παῖδες γὰρ σφῶν, κ.τ.λ.: see 6. 4.

σφίσιν οὐκ ἐπιτρέπωσιν: ἐμμένειν τοῖς δόξασιν—schol.

3. αὐτοὶ δὲ μεταχωρήσατε ὅποι βούλεσθε: apparently a generous offer, for it would enable the Plataians to retire to Athens, to their wives and children, and there fight. But it is not surprising that Plataia had not much faith in Sparta, and none in Thebes. Thucydides himself did not believe in the honesty of the Spartan proposals (iii. 68. 1).

It is less easy to see why the Athenians set so much store by Plataian resistance to the end. Strategy dictated that they could not themselves send effective help, in spite of their fine words, 73. 3 (for if they might not defend their own land with their hoplites, still less could they march farther afield and risk all to defend Plataia: i.e. *Perikles'* strategy dictated this; later, unintentionally, they ran this kind of risk at Delion); but, that being so, the town ceased to be of much strategic value. Only if it could hold out till the end of hostilities would continued resistance be worth while.

73. 3. ἀφ' οὗ ξύμμαχοι ἐγενόμεθα: see iii. 68. 5 n.

74. 2. ἡρώων τῶν ἐγχωρίων: those, presumably, mentioned in the impressive list given by Plutarch, *Arist.* 11. 3 (Wasse ap. Arnold on iii. 24. 1). Cf. Brasidas at Akanthos, iv. 87. 2; and the excuses in the two cases are not dissimilar.

ξυνίστορές ἐστε: Stahl, Classen, and Steup prefer the imperative, ἔστε (with FM), as below, ξυγγνώμονες ἔστε.

75. 1. ἐπεξιέναι: 'to march out against them', as in 21. 3 (and ἐπεξάγειν, ibid.), and 55. 2. But ἐξιέναι (see crit. n.) is surely the better reading here ('to prevent any escape'); and I should prefer to bracket ἔτι. Steup defends ἔτι, by explaining ἐξιέναι as 'go out of the city to bring in food, etc.'.

χῶμα ἔχουν: cf. Hdt. i. 162. This was primarily a ramp, which (it was hoped) could be carried as far as, and to the height of, the city-wall, and would be broad enough to enable troops to march up it and effectively fight the defenders.

For a recent account of the site of Plataia, see E. Kirsten in *R.E.* xx (1950), s.v. He says, rightly I think, that this ramp must have been on the south side, where the outside level came to the foot of the city-wall. Northwards (in the direction of the Asopos river and Thebes) the ground outside slopes downwards, and the south wall was set at the top of a stone escarpment.

2. ξύλα: fir-trees mostly. The δένδρα for the fencing (§ 1) were fruit-trees growing near the city.

φορμηδὸν ἀντὶ τοίχων: 'wicker-work, in place of walls.' That is, the sides could not be perpendicular, but the timber was used, as stone is used in earth embankments, to prevent the spread of the earth (especially as the result of rain).

ὕλην: brushwood, of which, with earth and stones, the ramp consisted.

3. ἡμέρας δὲ ἔχουν ἐβδομήκοντα: this figure has given rise to serious doubts. The longest time spent in Attica in the ordinary invasions was 40 days (57. 2); supplies might run out before 40 days (23. 3, iv. 6. 1); the Boeotians indeed might supply the Peloponnesian forces with food for a longer period, but, since the attack on Plataia was in substitution for the invasion of Attica, and it was hoped to take the place quickly (§ 1), and so get the troops home to complete the harvest, we must suppose that a much shorter time than 70 days was expected for the building of the ramp, and the delays caused by the Plataian counter-measures could hardly have extended it this much (see nn. on 76. 1, 2). Secondly, a wall of a similar kind (in some respects more complicated) was built round the precinct of Delion in 2½ days (iv. 90); and though the relative length, height, and breadth of the two works and the numbers of workers employed on them (large in both cases) are not known, the difference between 2½ and 70 days is altogether too great. Cf. also iii. 18. 3–5. It is impossible to suggest any correction of ἐβδομήκοντα with confidence: Stahl conjectured ἐννέα (θ for ō), others ἑπτακαίδεκα. Busolt, iii. 965. 2, summarizes a rough calculation: the two-thirds muster of the Peloponnesian and Boeotian forces (10. 2, 12. 5 n.) amounted to some 27,000 men, a one-third muster to c. 14,000, not including helots and other attendants; at least 12,000 could have been employed— στρατεύματος τοσούτου ἐργαζομένου (§ 1).[1] Assuming an average height of 20 m. for the ramp (which is surely too high even for the maximum) and a breadth of 20 m. at the top and 40 m. at the base (this last figure probably too low) and a total length of 200 m., we should have 120,000 cubic m. of earth, etc., to be carried and deposited. If, he continues, one man in his daily shift completed 1 cubic m. only (a very small amount), 12,000 men would complete the work in ten

---

[1] We must exclude *all* the Spartiates, the cavalry, and, I suspect, a good many of the hoplites of Boeotia and perhaps other cities, though the Peloponnesians were most of them αὐτουργοί and Athenian hoplites were ready workers with their hands (iv. 4). At Delion over 10,000 were available for building the wall, not including the hoplites (iv. 94. 1, 93. 3).

days and nights; and the delay caused by the Plataians would not extend this beyond another ten. This argument, however, ignores possible difficulties of transport (which were negligible at Delion), and assumes that 6,000 men could work all at once on a 20×200 m. ramp (76. 2 n.); we may contrast Hdt. i. 189. 3, as well as Delion, both cases in which very large numbers could be at work together. For all that the figure 70 must be by a good deal too large. Diodoros (xii. 47. 2) does not on this occasion give us any help with Ephoros' figure (cf. i. 103. 1, ii. 13. 6 nn.).

For further argument, based on the dating of these events, see 78. 2, 79. 1 nn.

οἱ ξεναγοί - - - ξυνεφεστῶτες: the Spartan officers regularly attached to allied Peloponnesian contingents, in joint control with each city's own commanding officers. There is something to be said for Hude's οἱ ξ. καί (CG) ἐ. π. ⟨οἱ⟩ ἐφεστῶτες (CGP), though I should expect ξεναγοί ⟨τε⟩ καί, and would prefer ⟨οἱ⟩ ξυνεφεστῶτες.

The scholiast here takes ξεναγοί in the sense normal in other Greek states 'commanders of mercenaries'; and L. and S. follow this. But it is difficult to see who the mercenaries were.

4. ξυνθέντες καὶ ἐπιστήσαντες: they constructed a wooden framework and set it up on their wall.

5. ξύνδεσμος: that is, probably, the union with the existing wall, by sinking the upright timbers some depth into it; not, as generally assumed, the framework for the bricks, which has already been described.

6. ᾗ προσέπιπτε τὸ χῶμα: while the ramp was being built, its end, towards the city-wall, would slope down towards the foot of the wall, the bringing of the top of the ramp to a level with and right up against the wall being the last stage of the work. The Plataians could afford to make a way through their wall at the bottom, because it was there screened by the ramp, and the enemy could not attack by it.

76. 1. ἐν ταρσοῖς, κ.τ.λ.: a much more elaborate procedure, which would take some time.

τὸ διῃρημένον: the gap that had been (and was continually being) made in the ramp, rather than the hole in the city-wall, in spite of διελόντες above; otherwise διαχεόμενον ὥσπερ ἡ γῆ seems to explain nothing. So Stahl and Steup.

2. καὶ ξυντεκμηράμενοι: bracketed by Marchant—"as the χῶμα was close to the wall and touched it at the base, it is plain that the Plataeans would not need any τεκμήρια to discover how far to burrow. The edd. speak of calculating length and direction, but the Plataeans had nothing to do but to dig straight ahead, until the χῶμα began to subside". They had to calculate not only length, but depth; they must be neither too close to the original surface of the ground nor too far below it; and if they just went on digging till the earth began to subside, they would have been suffocated. It was in fact a delicate operation.

There is no need, with Classen, to suppose from $\xi\nu\nu\tau\epsilon\kappa\mu\eta\rho\acute{a}\mu\epsilon\nu o\iota$ that there was a gap (when the $\chi\hat{\omega}\mu a$ was finished) between it and the wall. How was the battering ram able to shake the wall (§ 4), if there was a gap large enough to demand calculation by these Plataians? See 77. 3 n.

καὶ ἐλάνθανον ἐπὶ πολὺ τοὺς ἔξω: and we are not told how the latter overcame this difficulty. Not many Plataians could have worked 'at the face' in removing the earth; and, since their labour was effective, not a very large number of men on the Peloponnesian side could have been bringing up earth at the same time. On the other hand, the surface of the ramp had to be reasonably level, in order that the heavy battering ram could be pushed up it; a settling of the earth a foot or two in one place would spoil their efforts.

3. ἔνθεν δὲ - - - ἐκ τοῦ ἐντός: 'on either side of the high building, beginning from the low, i.e. the original, city-wall on the inner side.' Elaborately careful description. $\beta\rho a\chi\acute{\epsilon}o s$, which normally means in such a context 'inconsiderable, unimportant' (cf. i. 14. 3, vii. 29. 3), is hardly the word we expect here.

I agree with Stahl, Classen, and Steup, against Hude and Stuart Jones, that $\pi\rho o\sigma\omega\kappa o\delta\acute{o}\mu o\nu\nu$ (ABEFM) is here clearly preferable to $\acute{\epsilon}\sigma\omega\kappa o\delta\acute{o}\mu o\nu\nu$ (CGP).

ἐν ἀμφιβόλῳ - - - γίγνεσθαι: ἀντὶ τοῦ ἑκατέρωθεν βάλλεσθαι—schol. We hear also of hides and skins as a special protection against flame-bearing arrows, but nothing of any *action* by arrow or javelin on the part of defenders or attackers.

4. μηχανάς: evidently rams ($\kappa\rho\iota o\acute{\iota}$), here perhaps for the first time mentioned in siege operations. The care with which Thucydides relates all the details proves at least a comparative novelty. See, however, i. 117. 3 n., especially the reference to Ar. *Nubes*, 478–81.

ἀνέκλων: "*break short off*, or more probably, *fend off*", L. and S. 'Turned them aside (upwards or sideways)', so as to weaken their impact against the wall, seems the right meaning here. Stahl compares Livy, xxxvi. 23. 2, and Vegetius, *de re militari*, iv. 23; and Arnold quotes an interesting passage from Tasso, *Gerus. Liber.* xviii. 80.

ἐγκαρσίας: at right angles, roughly, to the ram which it was intended to break. τὸ προῦχον τῆς ἐμβολῆς seems to imply that the ram had a pointed end, which would pierce rather than simply batter down a wall; but some have disputed this.

77. 1. τὸ ἀντιτείχισμα: both the upper 'story' to the wall (75. 4) and

the inside 'crescent' wall (76. 3), which together formed the Plataian counter-stroke to the ramp.

πρὸς τὴν περιτείχισιν: the definite article, because circumvallation was a well-known, and indeed the more usual, method of taking a walled town. See vol. i, pp. 16–19 (esp. 18–19, in connexion with ἄνευ δαπάνης καὶ πολιορκίας, § 2, below).

3. ἐς τὸ μεταξύ, κ.τ.λ.: the space between the ramp and the wall must have been very narrow, not more than 2–3 feet, for at least the width necessary to work the battering ram which shook, or shook down, part of the upper wall (76. 4). Nor would this space be very deep: all the lower part of the ramp will have been built up against the city-wall. See 76. 2 n. We cannot agree with Shilleto that τοῦ τείχους here means the inner 'crescent' wall, unless we are to suppose that the decision not to complete the upper 'story' (76. 3) and the damage done to the old wall by the ram had the effect of making the latter wall quite useless, so that Peloponnesian troops were free, though ἐν ἀμφιβόλῳ γιγνόμενοι, to move across it into the crescent.

τῆς ἄλλης πόλεως: Arnold, Böhme, Stahl, and Marchant say that this means that bundles of sticks were thrown over the wall inside the city; Dobree, Krüger, Classen, and Steup that the bundles were placed against the wall on either side of the ramp. There can be little doubt that the latter are right. "As far into the town as they could reach", says Arnold: how far can a man throw a bundle, a large bundle, of faggots? And why did the Plataians not remove them as they fell, into a safer place? Stahl asks, if ἐπιπαρένησαν means 'heaped additional faggots against the wall' (παρά as in παρέβαλον above), "quid ad hanc rem opus fuit τὸ μετέωρον?" The answer is, to make the heaps high enough. Working from the normal ground level the men could not make a fire at the base of a stone or mud-brick wall high enough to be of much effect; only from the top and the sides of the ramp could they heap up faggots to the height, or nearly to the height, of the wall, and hope that, with a favourable wind, the flames would cross the wall and catch the houses within, and the heat be so great that the Plataians could do little to stay them.

4. ὅσην οὐδείς πω, κ.τ.λ.: a somewhat childish instance of 'the largest ever'; the largest bonfire.

ἔς γε ἐκεῖνον τὸν χρόνον: see 48. 2 n. This phrase does not mean that Thucydides knew of another and larger bonfire later. See iv. 48. 5 n.

χειροποίητον: ἔστι γὰρ καὶ αὐτόματον—schol. But this does not mean that he did not read the next sentence in his text.

τριφθεῖσα ὑπ' ἀνέμων: edd. compare Lucretius, i. 897–900. I agree with Classen that ἀπ' αὐτοῦ below (bracketed by many) means ἀπὸ τοῦ πυρός: 'fire and from it very high flames.' It is the extent of the *flames* that Thucydides is emphasizing, not the (ultimate) spread of destruction, by fire or the like.

6. νῦν δὲ καὶ τόδε λέγεται ξυμβῆναι: 'as it was, not only did the wind not blow, but by a coincidence (so we are told) there was a heavy fall of rain.' Thucydides clearly gets all his material for his narrative of events in Plataia, here and in book iii, from eyewitnesses, probably from among those who got out of the city (iii. 22–24); but he did not at once believe all that he was told, including a story that Plataia was saved in much the same way as Croesus had been.

ὕδωρ [ἐξ οὐρανοῦ]: see crit. n. ἐξ οὐρανοῦ is "evidently a gloss" (G. Thomson on *Agamemnon*, 565–7). Possibly a gloss, I agree; but more likely genuine after ὕδωρ, which does not, as such, mean rain.

78. 1. μέρος μέν τι - - - ἀφέντες: normally an army stayed till circumvallation was complete and would only then depart leaving a small number as garrison for the besiegers' wall (§ 2; vol. i, Introd., pp. 18–19); but the joint Peloponnesian and Boeotian army was much larger than the usual force that set out to besiege a town (e.g. Poteidaia, Mytilene, Melos), and the Peloponnesians could certainly afford to send home, for the threshing, the olive-picking, and the vintage, the larger part of their troops, and would not willingly have kept them all away for the entire summer. The Boeotians may have stayed in larger numbers till the wall was built. No major attack by the Athenians was to be expected; and if it was made, the whole Boeotian army, as well as the remaining Peloponnesians, was there to meet it. So Steup defends the reading of the majority of MSS. here, against Classen and Stahl, who would bracket these clauses.

ἐξ ἧς ἐπλινθεύσαντο: 'from which they had taken the clay to make bricks.' Cf. the procedure at Delion, iv. 90. 2, though there no bricks were made, the Athenians, in a hurry, having to be content with a χοῦς, an earthwork.

2. πᾶν ἐξείργαστο: it was a very elaborate wall, as good as the average city-wall except that it was not intended to last long; but Thucydides reserves its description for that part of the story in which its character is most relevant, iii. 20–21.

περὶ ἀρκτούρου ἐπιτολάς: i.e. the heliacal rising of Arktouros when it first becomes visible after the period of forty days during which it has been invisible because it rises after the sun; this is a few days before the autumnal equinox. For this phenomenon as the beginning of autumn, in both scientific and popular usage, see below, Appendix, pp. 706–9.

If Archidamos and his army left the Isthmos at the latest in the second half of May (71. 1, 79. 1 nn.), some of his troops will have had over four months away from their homes and their fields. If the various attempts to take Plataia by storm had lasted till the end of

June (which seems a maximum: 75. 3 n.), the greater part of the Peloponnesians would be home for the threshing of the year's corn (most of which, except that in the uplands, will have been gathered, by the women and the men who had stayed behind); the remainder will have had rather more than $2\frac{1}{2}$ months for the building of the wall. This, since much skilled labour was required, and only a limited number of unskilled men could be employed in one place at one time, is not at all too long.

3. παῖδας μέν, κ.τ.λ.: see 6. 4.

πλῆθος τὸ ἀχρεῖον: I was too absolute in my statement, vol. i, p. 17, with n. 2, about the 'useless' elements in the population and the manning of walls. Compare, besides this passage, vii. 28. 2, viii. 69. 1. The ἀχρεῖοι served rather as a watch-guard, to give an alarm, than as defenders (Busolt, iii. 887 n.).

τετρακόσιοι - - - ὀγδοήκοντα: Aristeus had advised leaving 500 men only to defend Poteidaia, i. 65. 1.

γυναῖκες σιτοποιοί: perhaps slaves; note οὔτε δοῦλος οὔτε ἐλεύθερος below. But see n. on ἠνδραπόδισαν, iii. 68. 2.

The length of wall to be defended at Plataia is unfortunately not certain; no thorough archaeological examination has been made of the site, and the size of the walled town at this period has not been ascertained. Grundy, who studied the site thoroughly, estimates the circumference, in the fifth century, at some 1,300 to 1,500 metres (*The Topography of the Battle of Plataea*, London, 1894, pp. 53–72). Kirsten's article in *R.E.* (above, p. 206) cannot add anything that is certain to this. It would mean that each man of the garrison, if on duty for half of every day, had about 6 metres to watch (12 m. after the escape of half of them); and that is assuming no reserve.

The story of the siege of Plataia is resumed in iii. 20. It should be noted that in c. 78 Thucydides deserts his normally strict chronological order (for in c. 79 he goes back to the time of c. 71), in order to finish with Plataia for this year. This was the easier because no events occurred there during the months covered by c. 78 other than the building of the wall and the settling down of the Peloponnesians and Plataians to a long siege.

At this point the third volume of the thirteen-volume edition of Thucydides ended, according to the scholiast here.

79. *Athenian Defeat at Spartolos*

79. 1. τοῦ δ' αὐτοῦ θέρους - - - ἀκμάζοντος τοῦ σίτου: i.e. in the last ten days of May. See 19. 1 n. It is true that the harvest is about three weeks later in the Chalkidic peninsula than in Attica; but it is not probable that Thucydides is thinking of the Chalkidic harvest and not saying so. This enables us to date Archidamos' attack on Plataia too. But note that Thucydides is not exact in his language: in 19. 1 when ὁ σῖτος ἤκμαζε, τὸ θέρος ἤκμαζε as well; in 71. 1 the attack on Plataia begins τοῦ ἐπιγιγνομένου θέρους and though that means 'in the following summer' and not 'as the summer succeeded', it could mean a time somewhat earlier than the ἀκμή. That is, ἅμα τῇ - - - ἐπιστρατείᾳ does not mean that both expeditions started on the same day.

Χαλκιδέας - - - καὶ Βοττιαίους: see vol. i, pp. 203–8, 211, and map facing p. 222; and ii. 29. 5–7, 31. 2, 58.

Ξενοφῶν - - - τρίτος αὐτός: see 70. 1 n.

2. διέφθειραν: but there is a good case for the imperfect (ABEF) in preference to the aorist (CGM), in spite of Hude and Stuart Jones. See Steup's note.

4. εἶχον δέ, κ.τ.λ.: sc. the Athenians, who only had hoplites and cavalry from Athens. They had recruited some peltasts from the neighbouring cities.

ἐκ τῆς Κρουσίδος γῆς: see vol. i, p. 217, and A.T.L. i, Gazetteer, s.v. πόλεις Κροσσίδος.

5. καὶ ἀναχωροῦσι: οἱ Ἀθηναῖοι—schol. 'And so they retreated.' The change of subject is possible enough (cf. § 4, above); but I suspect that ἀναχωροῦσι is a participle and that another before it has been dropped from the MSS., as ⟨κεκμηκόσι τε τῇ μάχῃ⟩ καὶ ἀναχωροῦσι.

τὰς δύο τάξεις: presumably two of the phylai. In a force of 2,000 such as this, it was as likely as not that all ten phylai-regiments would be represented.

6. ἀναχωροῦσι δ' ἐνέκειντο: cf. iii. 97. 3, 98. 1. I believe, however, that here the weight of MS. authority, now reinforced by Π²⁵, justifies the reading ἀποχωροῦσι ('leaving the actual scene of fighting to reach the baggage-train'). There are three other instances of ἀναχωροῦσι in this chapter. Π²⁵ also reads ἐπέκειντο, which had been conjectured by Krüger, and seems better.

7. ἐς τὰς Ἀθήνας ἀναχωροῦσι: this had been a severe defeat for the Athenians, and presaged future events in the Chalkidic and Thracian regions, where in both the fifth and the fourth centuries Athens had little success, military or diplomatic.

The battle is also interesting as being the first in which an intelligent use was made of light-armed troops (including the peltasts) in combination with cavalry against a hoplite force. Other successes of light-armed, in Aitolia and on Sphakteria, differed from this in that they were won in mountain country where hoplites were always at a disadvantage; the Chalkidian victory was gained on comparatively level ground where cavalry could act as well. The battle of Amphipolis in 422 was like it in this respect. Thucydides, as always, is interested in military technique; and we could wish that he had given us rather more detail. It may be that Aristophanes' line about what the Thracians will do for Athens (*Ach.* 160), καταπελτάσονται τὴν Βοιωτίαν ὅλην, expresses some of the Athenian feeling of weakness before a peltast attack.

For the effect on the tribute from this region of the defeat at Spartolos, see *A.F.D.* 23–25, with the slight modification in *A.T.L.* ii, list 26.

80–92. *Land and Sea Campaigns in the North-west*

80–82. *Peloponnesian Attack in Akarnania*

80. 1. οὐ πολλῷ ὕστερον τούτων: about the end of June or early in July. Cf. § 2 n.

Ἀμπρακιῶται καὶ Χάονες: after the failure of the limited enterprise of the year before, 68. 1, 9.

πείθουσι Λακεδαιμονίους, κ.τ.λ.: cf. iii. 102. 6 n.

καὶ ὁ περίπλους, κ.τ.λ.: Zakynthos and Kephallenia were all-important stations on the sea-route round Peloponnese to Naupaktos and to Kerkyra and Italy (vol. i, p. 19). For their alliance with Athens, and Leukas' alliance with the Peloponnesians (§ 2), see 9. 2, 4; 30. 2 nn.

2. Κνῆμον μὲν ναύαρχον ἔτι ὄντα: generally taken to mean that his normal period of office had not yet run out (cf. ἔτι δ' ἐστρατήγει, 59. 3, which is only different in that it anticipates not a normal event—the end of the period of office—but an abnormal one, Perikles' dismissal); and that, if this period was from *c.* September to September, and because the Spartans dispatched him and his force at once, we may assume here a date not long after midsummer. But see 66. 2 n.

3. ἦσαν δὲ Κορίνθιοι ξυμπροθυμούμενοι μάλιστα: as in 432, i. 67. 5, etc. The Athenian occupation of Naupaktos hit them hardest: see 30. 1, 33, and R. L. Beaumont's postumously published article, *J.H.S.* lxxii, 1952, 64.

τὸ μὲν ναυτικόν, κ.τ.λ.: see 9. 3 n.

4. ἐπεραιώθησαν: in itself we might expect this to mean that Knemos and his force crossed the Gulf of Patras only, that is, to Oiniadai, which was friendly (82. 1); but in fact he sailed as far north as Leukas and perhaps farther to Amprakia (§ 8 n.).

Φορμίωνα: see 69. 1.

5. Ἀνακτόριοι: see i. 55. 1 n.

5–6. βάρβαροι δὲ Χάονες, κ.τ.λ.: a characteristic multitude of names and other details, obviously from notes made at the time. Cf. 22. 3 n. For the Thesprotoi see i. 46. 4 (vol. i, p. 181); and for the other tribes, besides the articles in *R.E.*, Beaumont's paper cited above.

Θάρυπος: Plutarch, *Pyrrhos*, 1. 2, says that he was the first of his line to be distinguished by his adoption of Greek customs and letters, and by his νόμοις φιλανθρώποις, the kings between his ancestor Neoptolemos, son of Achilles, and himself having been barbarized and, in consequence, obscure. He was the great-grandfather of Olympias, the mother of Alexander the Great. He was educated at Athens, and was made a citizen (I.G. ii.² 226 = Tod, 173; see Tod's note, ii, p. 216). The Molossoi occupied the country round Yánnina, the centre of all communications in this region, with Macedonia, Illyria, Kerkyra, and Amprakia (Beaumont, p. 65).

7. Περδίκκας κρύφα τῶν Ἀθηναίων: when last heard of, two years before, 29. 6, he had become an ally of Athens; and he observes the alliance in his fashion. Beaumont (above, § 3 n.) believed that his troops must have reached Amprakia not by Thessaly, the ordinary route (for his action would have been reported to Athens), but by the route so well known in modern times, by Kastória (western Macedonia), Koritsá (in Albania), and Yánnina; and that his purpose was to show to the Peloponnesians an alternative approach to Macedonia and Thrace, which would avoid Thessaly. I am sure that at least he would never have persuaded Peloponnesians to try so long and difficult a journey; they built a fortress in Trachinia, and Brasidas in fact preferred the hazards of Thessaly. For Athenian feelings about Perdikkas, see Hermippos, fr. 63. 8 (vol. i, p. 201, and below, p. 362).

8. διὰ τῆς Ἀργείας ἰόντες Λιμναίαν - - - ἐπόρθησαν. ἀφικνοῦνταί τε ἐπὶ Στράτον: almost due northwards from Stratos runs a road along a level valley, past two lakes, to the sea-shore at the eastern end of the Amprakiot Gulf, reaching it not far from Argos Amphilochikon. See Leake, iv. 178; Oberhummer, art. 'Stratos' in R.E. This would be the way taken (in the reverse direction) by the Amprakiotai and their barbarian allies, διὰ τῆς Ἀργείας; and it is generally supposed that the whole force, Knemos' as well, started from Amprakia. Classen, however, supposed that Leukas was the army's as well as the naval base and that Knemos marched along the southern shore of the gulf till he reached Argeia (to avoid the more difficult direct route to Stratos through the mountains), and then turned south: a roundabout way, especially for the Amprakiots. Limnaia is very likely to be placed at the northern end of the larger of the two lakes, or perhaps nearer the south-east corner of the gulf. See Hammond (above, 68. 1 n.), p. 132, and iii. 105 nn., with Map, below, opp. p. 428.

Stratos, which has some very imposing ruins, was situated on a low hill some 2 miles west of a ford over the Acheloos (where there is now a road bridge), just below where the river valley bends eastward and then north. The river is a large one and in winter and spring not always fordable. Stratos was later an important city of the Aitolian League (Livy, xxxvi. 11. 6).

ῥᾳδίως - - - προσχωρήσειν: in spite of the near-parallel of § 1 above I prefer to read here ῥᾳδίως ἄν (all MSS. except C) - - - προσχωρῆσαι (which G appears to have).

81. 1. οὔτε ξυνεβοήθουν: as expected, 80. 1. Diodoros, xii. 48. 5, says the opposite; but this is probably only his carelessness; or perhaps he assumed it from 83. 1.

2. τρία τέλη ποιήσαντες: οὐκ ἐπὶ μῆκος ἀλλ᾽ ἐπὶ πλάτος—schol. Doubtless one or two divisions marched to the west of the two lakes (above, 80. 8 n.), along the line of the modern road, the others to the east.

3. οἱ μετὰ τούτων: either perioikoi of Leukas and Anaktorion (Arnold, Stahl), which does not seem very likely, or undefined Akarnanians hostile to the Athenian cause. The Oiniadai seem not to have joined in till later (82).

4. οὔτε ἐπέσχον τὸ στρατόπεδον καταλαβεῖν: Stahl must be right in his interpretation of ἐπέσχον, i.e. sc. τὸν νοῦν, as Herodotos has it with the infinitive (i. 80. 4, 153. 4, vi. 96), even though the meaning here is slightly different; but I agree with Steup that this requires the bracketing of τό—there is no case for keeping it ('*their* camp', or 'the usual camp'); see § 7, below—or, with Steup, its correction to τοῦ.

5. προλοχίζουσι δή: "die Partikel δή (CG only) würde in unserem Zusammenhang nur stören"—Steup; a correct judgement.

8. ἐνέκειντο: as edd. note, used elsewhere of victors pursuing, not of fugitives; ἐσέπιπτον, as Arnold says, is expected.

ἄνευ ὅπλων κινηθῆναι: they were confined to their camp and, apart from the general discomfort, could not forage except in full armour and in line, 'marching to attention'. The Akarnanian light-armed could do what the Thessalian cavalry did (i. 111. 1 n.).

82. ἐπὶ τὸν Ἄναπον ποταμόν: it was presumably in the direction of Oiniadai from near Stratos, but it has not been identified.

Οἰνιαδῶν ξυμπαραγενομένων κατὰ φιλίαν: see i. 111. 3, and for the site, ii. 102. 2–6 nn.

κἀκεῖθεν ἐπ᾽ οἴκου: only the barbarians and the Amprakiots, Anaktorioi, and Leukadioi. Knemos and his men returned to their base in Leukas (84. 5). An inglorious affair, because they had not fought at all; but the sea-battles in the Corinthian Gulf now compelled Knemos' attention.

For further events in Akarnania, see c. 102 and iii. 100 ff.

83–92. *Phormion's Battles in the Gulf*

83. 1. τοῦ Κρισαίου κόλπου: 69. 1 n.

ὅπως μὴ ξυμβοηθῶσιν, κ.τ.λ.: 80. 1, etc.

2. ἐν τῇ εὐρυχωρίᾳ: in itself, this means simply 'in the open sea', as opposed to just off shore; and as such does not exclude the entrance to the Gulf of Corinth between Rion and Antirrion, 7 stades, or 1,400 yards wide (86. 2–3; see n. there). See 90. 5. This indeed is the natural interpretation of κατὰ μέσον τὸν πορθμόν, § 3 ad fin. But 86. 5 and 89. 8 show that Phormion liked as much space as possible; and since the Gulf of Patras widens very rapidly west of Rion, in effect ἐν τῇ εὐρυχωρίᾳ means outside the narrows, to the west. The morning breeze, moreover (84. 2), has more effect on the waters outside than within the narrows. The reason why the Peloponnesians did not attempt to cross in the narrowest part is presumably that Antirrion and the nearby coast was in Athenian hands (cf. below, ii. 84. 4 n. on Molykreion, and iii. 102. 2), and that the coast between Naupaktos and the Euenos valley is steep-to, and barely allows passage to an army.

3. στρατιωτικώτερον παρεσκευασμένοι: i.e. ὡς ἐπὶ στρατείαν παρ., the ships to be used more like transports than fighting vessels. An increase in the number of 'passengers' on board had a great effect on the speed of the trireme, and the Peloponnesian was already a slower vessel than the Athenian.

ἐκ Πατρῶν: they would sail nearly due west from here to reach, e.g., Oiniadai, and so get beyond the Athenians in the Euenos valley; more probably they intended to put in at the landing-place by Kryonéri: see next n. The Athenians by sailing *south*, would compel them to a fight. Patrai became a more important place in Roman and later times, up to the present day, with the increase of commerce with the west, and the unification of Greece.

τῆς Χαλκίδος καὶ τοῦ Εὐήνου ποταμοῦ: see i. 108. 5 n. (where for "Molykreion (to the west)" read "M. (to the east)"). The Euenos river, the modern Phídaris, is a considerable stream which flows through the heart of Aitolia, on a course roughly parallel with the Mórnos farther east (n. on iii. 95. 1); but after it has reached the coastal plain, near ancient Kalydon (n. on iii. 102. 5), it is easily fordable in summer: Woodhouse, *Aetolia*, 92–93. Chalkis, the last city to the east originally in Peloponnesian hands, may still have been Athenian since its capture by Tolmides in 456–455, or may have been given back by the Thirty Years' Peace; it lay east of the coastal plain in a small valley beyond the mountain of the same name (now Varássova) which allows no path by the coast (Woodhouse, p. 107). It seems likely that the Peloponnesians intended to land at Kryonéri (the terminus of the present railway to Agrinion and therefore of the ferry steamer from Patras), where there is abundant water, and to march thence by the easy road through the friendly Aitolian country of Kalydon and Pleuron, rather than to sail more than twice the distance to Oiniadai or, as Woodhouse thought, to land in the lagoons of Mesolónghi. They probably did not expect Phormion to appear west of Molykreion, certainly not west of Chalkis.

ἀφορμισάμενοι: this correction by Poppo, from Bloomfield (see app. crit.), of the MSS. reading ὑφ. seems necessary, unless we are to assume, a lacuna in the narrative such as is required, e.g. by Grote's ingenious but unconvincing explanation (v. 118–19 n.), and which, if assumed, might also explain the genitive διαβαλλόντων above (corr. Stahl, and most edd. since, except Steup, whose argument does not convince).

ἀναγκάζονται: 'they saw themselves compelled' (Stahl).

κατὰ μέσον τὸν πορθμόν: see n. on § 2, above. The Gulf of Patras must be here meant (ἐστὶ δὲ πορθμὸς ἀμφίγειος θάλασσα, schol.).

4. στρατηγοὶ δὲ ἦσαν, κ.τ.λ.: cf. i. 29. 2, 46. 2 nn.; and above, p. 94. Machaon and his colleagues are not elsewhere mentioned.

5. κύκλον τῶν νεῶν - - - μὴ διδόντες διέκπλουν: the oldest kind of sea-fighting had been as much like land-fighting as possible: the opposing ships drawn up in line (but not too closely, for oars must not clash), centre, right, and left flank (very few in reserve), attempts at outflanking, fighting between marines in boarding operations, and so forth (i. 49. 1). The διέκπλους, such as was tried at Lade and elsewhere, was an attempt by one of the two opposing fleets to attack in column (two columns generally), break through the enemy line and turn to attack in rear. This became a favourite method with those states which possessed the faster ships and the better trained crews; if it was successful, many of the enemy ships were disabled, by the breaking of their oars and the like, before any hand-to-hand fighting took place; hence the reduction in the number of *epibatai* to ten per ship in order to increase speed. The Peloponnesians now try to counter this by forming their ships, prows outwards, in a circle large enough to enable them to manoeuvre—especially the five best ships kept in the centre—but not so large as to give the Athenians an opportunity to sail through them by attacking in column. The device was a sensible one, and would have worked if the Peloponnesian seamen had been more skilled and more confident and their ships not overloaded; for they might have taken the initiative in attacking as soon as the Athenian ships drew near.

προσπίπτοιεν: for this reading (CG), as against προσπλέοιεν (cett., including G¹), see Classen's note. προσπλεῖν elsewhere means 'to approach' in Thucydides, not 'to attack'.

84. 1. ἐν χρῷ αἰεὶ παραπλέοντες: a vigorous phrase, not often used (unlike our 'within a hair's breadth'); cf. Soph. *Aj.* 786.

δόκησιν: 35. 2 n.

πρὶν ἂν αὐτὸς σημήνῃ: Phormion, it is implied, and we should expect

218

it of Athenian strategoi in general and of him in particular, was in the leading trireme.

2. ὥσπερ ἐν γῇ πεζήν: as hoplites would if confronted with such an attack (83. 5 n.); for they were better trained than rowers in the Peloponnesian forces, and not subject to the winds, as boats were. εἴ τ᾽ ἐκπνεύσειεν, κ.τ.λ.: it is not often that we hear of good seamanship in this manner in Greek warfare; yet Thucydides does not suggest that Phormion was unique.[1]

καλλίστην γίγνεσθαι: Classen compares i. 93. 3 for an infinitive present after νομίζειν with some future sense; but it will not do here and we should read κάλλιστ᾽ ἂν γίγνεσθαι, Krüger's conjecture.

3. αἱ νῆες - - - ἐταράσσοντο: winds arise suddenly in Greek waters, and make not rough, but choppy seas, just the kind to affect the comparatively lightly built trireme, and especially triremes trying to keep position. Amongst other things, it was difficult for all but the most skilled oarsmen to keep the blades clear of the water when coming forward (τὰς κώπας - - - ἀναφέρειν ἄνθρωποι ἄπειροι, below).

τῶν παραγγελλομένων: order passed from ship to ship, or from one officer to another. Cf. v. 66. 3–4, of the highly trained Spartan army.

τῶν κελευστῶν: the petty officers whose business it was to keep the rowers in time, an all-important matter, and to encourage them. According to schol. Ar. Ach. 554, he also had the duty of seeing to the fair distribution of rations and their proper consumption (e.g., to prevent·a man selling his own ration and consuming a share of the rest); but the general responsibility for supplies was the steward's (above, p. 35 n.).

τοῖς κυβερνήταις: the captains, those responsible for the navigation of the ships. The trierarch on board (who might, and generally did, know nothing of seamanship) was responsible for giving out the tactical orders received from the nauarchos or strategos.

Δύμην: the westernmost of the Achaian cities. The Peloponnesian fleet is dispersed, and sails part eastwards, part southwards.

4. ἀνελόμενοι: 'picked up' from waterlogged or otherwise disabled vessels (καταδύουσι, διέφθειρον above; i. 50. 1 n.).

Μολύκρειον: its site is uncertain; near the northern C. Rion according

[1] Plutarch tells us that Themistokles similarly waited for the wind at Salamis (Them. 14. 2); but, according to Lenschau, in Bursian, clxxx (1919), 136, wrongly, for there the wind would not affect the waters before 11 a.m., and the battle began at dawn according to both Herodotos and Aeschylus. This may not be a correct inference, for winds are not so constant, and it is just possible that Plutarch had some information from another source; but if Lenschau is right, we may have an interesting instance of a common error among the learned, the duplication of an action for another occasion—'for Themistokles would have acted as Phormion did'—without due observation of all the facts; and Plutarch would naturally have followed such learning. N. G. L. Hammond, however, uses his statement in a reconstruction of the battle of Salamis, which he has kindly allowed me to see. (This will appear shortly in J.H.S.)

to Strabo, x. 2. 21, p. 460. Woodhouse, pp. 64, 322-6, put it at a kástro near Velvína, about 2 hours north of the cape and 1,700 feet above sea-level. Oldfather, in *R.E.*, s.v. (1935), regards this as too far and too difficult of access, and would place Molykreion at the cape itself.

ἐπὶ τῷ 'Ρίῳ: i.e. τὸ 'Ρίον τὸ Μολυκρικόν, 86. 2, or Antirrion, as it is generally called. For the dedication of a captured ship (as in 92. 5), cf. Hdt. viii. 121. 1.

ἐς Ναύπακτον: they would have some 20 miles at least to go; but they must return to refit, to get rest, and probably for food.

5. ἐς Κυλλήνην: see i. 30. 2 n.

ἀπὸ Λευκάδος Κνῆμος: 80. 2-3 and 82. Leukas was the naval base, and Knemos must have retired there from Oiniadai to await the allied squadrons. Phormion was not able to prevent him from taking his forces to Kyllene; nor could such ships as Zakynthos and Kephallenia possessed; he may well have made a wide detour.

85. 1. τῷ Κνήμῳ: he had not himself been present at the naval battle, but was responsible for the whole campaign.

ξυμβούλους: not very uncommon in the history of Sparta's wars at sea, iii. 69. 1 (Brasidas again) and viii. 39. 2 (eleven of them); and not unknown when a king was in command on land (v. 63. 4: ten ξύμβουλοι for Agis; cf. Arist. *Pol.* ii. 6. 22, quoted above, 66. 2 n.). They were, however, subordinate to the nauarchos (iii. 79. 3).

This is the second mention of Brasidas in the *History*.

2. πρῶτον ναυμαχίας πειρασαμένοις: i.e. for the first time in this war (said especially of the Spartans, not of their allies, who had had at least some taste of Attic fighting in 433 B.C., i. 49), as noted by the scholiast. But there is something to be said for Classen's view that μετὰ πολὺν χρόνον has dropped out after πρῶτον, or better, ἐν τῷδε τῷ πολέμῳ, the more usual formula. A similar phrase is used in 87. 2, πρῶτον ναυμαχοῦντας; but clearly that would be easily understood if ἐν τῷδε τῷ πολέμῳ stood here. Cf. above, 56. 2, and iii. 19. 1 n.

μαλακίαν: want of vigour, energy, rather than cowardice (cf. v. 7. 2 n.); and therefore primarily a fault in the commanding officers, not in the men.

ἐμπειρίαν - - - μελέτης: the Corinthians (i. 121. 3-4) had been too confident; Perikles (i. 142. 6-9) had shown his usual foresight.

3. ὀργῇ οὖν ἀπέστελλον: one of the occasions on which Sparta acts excitedly; cf. iv. 108. 6 n.

προσπεριήγγειλαν: doubtless recent edd. are right to take from CG this double-compound verb; but the imperfect (περιήγγελλον, cett.) would be better, as 10. 1, etc. There is more to be said for ἀπέστειλαν just above (ἀπέστελλον, codd., edd.).

4. πέμπει δὲ καὶ ὁ Φορμίων: he might have tried landing one or two men near Aigosthena at the head of the Corinthian Gulf with instructions to make their way over the mountains to Attica—no very difficult feat; but more probably a ship was sent round the Peloponnese, which would take some days, and perhaps longer than usual if it had to keep well clear of the Peloponnesian fleet at Kyllene.

5. τῷ δὲ κομίζοντι: as Classen remarked, it is curious that he is not named (contrast 67. 2, 80. 5–6, 83. 4) either here or at 92. 7, especially as ὁ μὲν λαβών below should refer to him rather than to Nikias of Gortyn. Even Busolt, iii. 660. 1, thinks the suppression of the name due to personal or political reasons; but why? The main fault at least (according to Thucydides) lay with the ekklesia, not with the strategos (n. on § 6, below). Cf. 92. 7 n. In iii. 52. 2 the Spartan commander at the siege of Plataia has no name; but, though even this is unusual in Thucydides, and some Plataians are known by name (iii. 52. 5), it is more easily explicable.

ἐς Κρήτην πρῶτον ἀφικέσθαι: they would kill two birds with one stone, but unfortunately not with one throw. With no big naval expedition on hand, they could surely have managed two squadrons of twenty ships each at the same time.[1] It looks like a characteristic piece of misunderstanding by the Athenians at home, though not characteristic of them alone. Were they over-confident ('Phormion can do anything')? Or still oppressed by the effects of the pestilence (cf. Busolt, iii, p. 964)? The date is near that of Perikles' death; and it is possible enough that this particular folly was a consequence of his absence from the ekklesia (see below, 103 n.). But it is not unique; the orders given to Eurymedon and to Demosthenes in 425 (iv. 2. 3, 4) were not very different.

Thucydides gives us no hint of any special Athenian interest in Crete; but her concern for her trade with the Levant (69. 1), which might be interrupted by privateers based on Crete, was genuine. Kasos and Karpathos, the islands north-east of Crete, between it and Rhodes, were within the Athenian empire; Crete was not.

It is to be noted that no support for Phormion is expected from Kerkyra; that state interprets her ἐπιμαχία with Athens literally (i. 44. 1). Contrast ii. 25. 1.

Κρὴς Γορτύνιος: 'a Cretan (to explain ἐς Κρήτην, above) from Gortyn.' Gortyn was towards the eastern end of the island, a long way from Kydonia (800 stades according to Strabo, x. 4. 13, p. 479).

6. καὶ ὑπ' ἀνέμων καὶ ἀπλοίας: there is something to be gained by bracketing ἀνέμων καί, for, when the ships are triremes, ἄπλοια means stormy weather, not a calm (Krüger, Stahl, and Classen); that the

---

[1] Not long after, however, they ought to have had a large expeditionary force in Chalkidike (95. 3); and preparations for this may have been going on.

ABEFM group of MSS. has a second $\dot{v}\pi\dot{o}$ before $\dot{a}\pi\lambda o\acute{\iota}as$ supports the suggestion that $\dot{v}\pi$' $\dot{a}\nu\acute{\epsilon}\mu\omega\nu$ was an explanation of $\dot{v}\pi$' $\dot{a}\pi\lambda o\acute{\iota}as$.

I see no reason to suppose that Thucydides is here hinting at great fault in the commanding officer.

86. 1. παρεσκευασμένοι ὡς ἐπὶ ναυμαχίαν: they had been στρατιωτικώτερον παρεσκευασμένοι before, 83. 3.

ἐς Πάνορμον τὸν Ἀχαϊκόν: just east of Rion, 15 stades away, opposite Naupaktos, Paus. vii. 22. 10; Polyb. v. 102. 9.

τῶν Πελοποννησίων: not Achaians and Eleans only. Presumably all Achaia was now allied with the Peloponnesian League (9. 2).

3. ἦν δὲ τοῦτο μὲν τὸ Ῥίον, κ.τ.λ.: as so frequently, Thucydides inserts some geographical or other information not at the first mention of a place, but on a later occasion. A conspicuous instance of this habit is the account of Amphipolis, iv. 102 and 108. 1; see also ii. 93. 3 n.

σταδίους μάλιστα ἑπτά: Strabo, viii. 2. 3, p. 335, says five, Skylax ten (l. 35), and Pliny, *N.H.* iv. 2. 6, *minus mille passuum.* It is in fact between 10 and 11 stades; and so large a discrepancy is hardly to be accounted for by later changes of coastline. See also 90. 1, 4 nn.

4. ἐν ᾧ αὐτοῖς ὁ πεζὸς ἦν: hardly necessary so soon after § 1.

ἑπτὰ καὶ ἑβδομήκοντα: C (unsupported by the other MSS.) has ἑπτὰ καὶ πεντήκοντα, which Hude adopts, wrongly. The alarm of the Athenians (88. 1) would hardly have been caused by an increase in the number of the enemy from 47 (83. 3) to 57, even though they were now better prepared, after so signal a victory of skill and daring. Of the 47, 12 or more had been lost (84. 3–4); so more than 40 other ships had arrived from Leukas (84. 5) and by fresh contingents from the maritime states. See also 90. 2 n.

5. οἱ δὲ μὴ ἐσπλεῖν ἐς τὰ στενά: the Athenians are prepared to fight, however fearful of the opposing numbers. But it is not clear how they could prevent the enemy from entering the narrows. The latter had just come from Panormos, within the Gulf of Corinth, and they could return along the coast as far eastwards as they wished and threaten Naupaktos; and they could, if they wished, sail out from Rion and offer battle in the narrows themselves. All, it seems, that Phormion could do was to prevent them from landing, or maintaining themselves once they had landed, on the north coast anywhere to the east of Oiniadai, and so threatening the Akarnanians, and to refuse battle unless they moved westwards into the Gulf of Patras in order to reach Oiniadai; which they must do if they were to attack again in Akarnania. If the only aim of the Peloponnesians now was the destruction of the Athenian fleet, Phormion could refuse battle altogether and defend Naupaktos, if he wished; but he was still for battle—hence his preference for the open sea.

87. Speech of Peloponnesian Commanders

87. 1. οὐχὶ δικαίαν ἔχει τέκμαρσιν τὸ ἐκφοβῆσαι: if the text is sound, the natural way to construe this is to take τὸ ἐκφοβῆσαι as direct object and τέκμαρσιν as predicate, as Reiske did—"superius proelium navale habet τὸ ἐκφοβῆσαι non iustam argumentationem futuri; nempe quod superior pugna navalis vos terruerit, in eo non est satis firmum argumentum de futuro eventu male sperandi". I would only modify this by saying that τὸ ἐκφοβῆσαι has not in itself any future meaning, but is timeless. 'To let it frighten you is wrong', i.e. 'to think that it *rightly* frightens you is to draw a wrong inference'. Croiset, "n'entraîne pas à titre de conclusion légitime ceci, qu'elle doive vous effrayer". The future to which the inference relates is contained in the words, εἴ τις - - - φοβεῖται τὴν μέλλουσαν, and in οὐδὲ δίκαιον - - - ἀμβλύνεσθαι, § 3.

With ἔχει τέκμαρσιν, cf. ἀγανάκτησιν ἔχει, 41. 3, αἴσθησιν ἔχει, 61. 2, and iii. 44. 2 n. on ξυγγνώμην ἔχοντας.

3. προσεγένετο: here 'happened to us', 'befel us', as not infrequently in Sophocles, without the sense 'in addition to'; we can allow this to Thucydides, like his use of προσεῖναι (Steup).

τῆς γνώμης τὸ μὴ - - - νικηθέν: not a partitive, but a subjective genitive, as τὸ ὀργιζόμενον τῆς γνώμης, 59. 3 (Marchant). 'Our *spirit* was not then beaten, crushed, but has some answer yet within its power': the aorist νικηθέν, to which Classen took exception, does, as he says it must, refer to the recent battle. Cf. with Stahl, v. 75. 3, of Sparta, as the result of Mantineia, τύχῃ μὲν ὡς ἐδόκουν κακιζόμενοι, γνώμῃ δὲ οἱ αὐτοὶ ἔτι ὄντες (this is particularly apt, as we have here ταῖς μὲν τύχαις ἐνδέχεσθαι σφάλλεσθαι τοὺς ἀνθρώπους, ταῖς δὲ γνώμαις τοὺς αὐτοὺς αἰεὶ ὀρθῶς ἀνδρείους εἶναι just below); vi. 72. 3, Hermokrates encouraging the Syracusans after defeat, τὴν μὲν γὰρ γνώμην αὐτῶν οὐχ ἡσσῆσθαι, τὴν δὲ ἀταξίαν βλάψαι; also, vi. 11. 6, from Nikias' speech, χρὴ δὲ μὴ πρὸς τὰς τύχας τῶν ἐναντίων ἐπαίρεσθαι, ἀλλὰ τὰς διανοίας κρατήσαντας θαρσεῖν; and ii. 61. 3, δουλοῖ γὰρ φρόνημα.

Because B omits μή and because he could find no good sense in κατὰ κράτος ('with all one's might' with an active verb, or 'by storm') Classen dropped the negative, and Steup was inclined to adopt Herwerden's specious μέν for μή. But this gives just the wrong sense: Classen indeed says that is just what had happened, that the Peloponnesians κατὰ κράτος νικηθῆναι; but not their *spirit*; and this is the point. We might almost translate 'our spirit was not *stormed*'; cf. the phrase τὰς διανοίας κρατήσαντας from vi. 11. 6, quoted above. (Steup perversely would emend κατὰ κράτος to κατ' ἄκρας, as though the speaker wished to say that they were utterly crushed.)

τῆς γε ξυμφορᾶς τῷ ἀποβάντι: not 'the result of chance', but 'the issue of the event'. Cf. Jebb's note on Soph. *O.T.* 44-45; and

Herodotos' οὕτω ὢν, ὦ Κροῖσε, πᾶν ἐστι ἄνθρωπος συμφορή (i. 32. 4): which means not that man is the sport of chance, but that he depends on events, on what happens (the statement is independent, that is, of any theory of the cause of events, whether chance or something else).

ἀμβλύνεσθαι: Thucydides is fond of this metaphor—40. 4, 65. 4, 11; iii. 38. 1.

ταῖς μὲν τύχαις, κ.τ.λ.: cf. v. 75. 3, quoted above.

ὀρθῶς ἀνδρείους: Cobet's suggestion (after Badham) that we should bracket ἀνδρείους, and for τοὺς ἀνθρώπους above read τοὺς ἀνδρείους, so that τοὺς αὐτούς becomes the predicate, is tempting; but it leaves ὀρθῶς in the air. An alternative suggestion is ⟨τοὺς⟩ ὀρθῶς ἀνδρείους here ('truly brave men should remain the same', as οἱ αὐτοὶ ἔτι ὄντες, v. 75. 3); or, as we should perhaps not change the subject, τοὺς αὐτοὺς ⟨καὶ⟩ αἰεὶ ὀρθῶς ἀνδρείους εἶναι.

καὶ μὴ ἀπειρίαν, κ.τ.λ.: 'if courage is there, one cannot make inexperience a defence for cowardice'; i.e. 'no brave man (as you all are) will ever make inexperience the excuse for unworthy conduct'.

No one would say that the *language* of this speech is such as would be likely to appeal to the simple Peloponnesian sailor.

4. τόλμῃ προύχετε: 'daring' was rather the Athenian characteristic. By a notable instance of μεταβολή this word becomes in turn ἀνδρεία, εὐψυχία, and ἀλκή—the last used by no other Attic prose writer. (Contrast ἀνδρείους - - - τοῦ ἀνδρείου above.) εὐψυχία is expressly claimed for Sparta by Archidamos, i. 84. 3, for Athens by Perikles, ii. 43. 4; cf. 89. 3, below. Classen proposed to read ἄνευ αὐτῆς (sc. μνήμης) for ἄνευ ἀλκῆς; certainly the received text is only repetition.

ἀνδρείαν μὲν ἔχουσα, κ.τ.λ.: e.g., Spartan ἐπιστήμη in hoplite warfare. τέχνη: as in i. 142. 9, τὸ ναυτικὸν τέχνης ἐστίν.

5–6. πρὸς μὲν οὖν τὸ ἐμπειρότερον αὐτῶν - - - περιγίγνεται δὲ ὑμῖν, κ.τ.λ.: perhaps, as Arnold says, the last clause does not mean simply 'we have superiority in numbers'; but 'put our courage against their skill (cf. οὐκ ἀντιτιθέντες, κ.τ.λ., 85. 2) and our knowledge of our unpreparedness in the last battle against our fears arising from that defeat; and there is a balance in our favour of a superiority in numbers and tactical position'; πλῆθος by itself implying greater numbers. In that case we should print a colon before περιγίγνεται.

τὰ δὲ πολλὰ τῶν πλεόνων, κ.τ.λ.: true enough, and perhaps of greater appeal than the assurances about Peloponnesian τόλμα.

7. νῦν αὐτὰ ταῦτα προσγενόμενα: our very mistakes are an additional assurance, because we have learned by bitter experience (τὰ παθήματα μαθήματα). Classen takes προσγενόμενα as in § 3, above, less probably.

9. ἦν δέ τις ἄρα καὶ βουληθῇ: a strong hint that the new commanders did not believe the excuses made for the former defeat.

88–89. *Speech of Phormion*

88. 1. κατὰ σφᾶς αὐτοὺς ξυνιστάμενοι: as κατὰ ξυστάσεις or κατὰ ξυλλόγους γιγνόμενοι (21. 3, iii. 27. 3)—Classen. We must remember that the Athenians had a choice—they would be perfectly safe back in Naupaktos harbour, and one of their principal duties was to defend Naupaktos; but Phormion was deliberately proposing battle against very heavy odds, and more in order to frighten the enemy off the sea for a long time than for immediate strategic advantage (89. 10).

2. οὐδὲν αὐτοῖς - - - τοσοῦτον, κ.τ.λ.: cf. 62. 2, an equally vigorous and confident appeal. No one, ancient or modern, but applauds Perikles and Phormion; Aristophanes in particular felt the magic of the latter's name (*Eq.* 550–62: see below, 92. 7 n.); but in Kleon's mouth such words would be universally condemned. Cf. iv. 65. 4 n. True, the particular circumstances differ: Perikles, and Phormion now, δεδιότας ἀλόγως (but hardly ἀλόγως now!) ἀντικαθίστη πάλιν ἐπὶ τὸ θαρσεῖν, whereas after Sphakteria it was success that made the Athenians overwhelmingly confident, and Kleon did not, ὁπότε αἴσθοιτό τι αὐτοὺς παρὰ καιρὸν ὕβρει θαρσοῦντας λέγων κατέπλησσεν ἐπὶ τὸ φοβεῖσθαι. Yet Phormion can hardly plead this, for he πρότερον αἰεὶ αὐτοῖς ἔλεγε, κ.τ.λ.

Böhme's conjecture τοσοῦτον ἂν ἐπιπλέοι for τοσοῦτον, ἢν ἐπιπλέῃ, is easy (with οι and η pronounced alike) and attractive; but all his reasons—especially the fault found with αὐτοῖς (after οὐδέν)—not equally sound. αὐτοῖς means 'for them'; and its position early in the sentence gives some emphasis, a mark of their self-confidence.

μηδένα ὄχλον Ἀθηναῖοι ὄντες: much in the same vein as the Spartans in regard to other land troops, but with rather more justification (καταφρόνησις, ὃς ἂν καὶ γνώμῃ πιστεύῃ τῶν ἐναντίων προύχειν, 62. 4). ὄχλον, distinct from πλῆθος above and below, may be contemptuous here, 'crowd of ships'—the expression of the sailors rather than of Phormion. Cf. *Eq.* 569–70 (below, p. 233).

3. τοὺς Ἀθηναίους: secl. Cobet, Stahl; and with the ordinary punctuation the words are awkward, as though Phormion selected the Athenians among his sailors for exhortation; and marginal notes of the kind τοὺς Ἀθηναίους δηλονότι are so common in our MSS. that it may be right to bracket here; cf. e.g. 89. 4: αὐτῶν CG; τῶν ξυμμάχων ABEFM. But Classen keeps them, and places a full stop after θαρσεῖν; and this, or a colon, is an improvement.

89. 2. τὸ πλῆθος - - - καὶ οὐκ ἀπὸ τοῦ ἴσου: positive and negative rendering of the same idea, 'in superior numbers and not equally, i.e. more than equal'.

ὡς προσῆκον σφίσιν ἀνδρείοις εἶναι: 'namely, that it is in their *nature* to be brave.' This answers 87. 4–5 (as though Phormion had heard that). So εὐψυχίᾳ οὐδὲν προφέρουσιν and τὴν τόλμαν below.

σφίσι - - - ποιήσειν: the subject is ἡ ἐν τῷ πεζῷ ἐμπειρία, and σφίσι the normal dative of interest (Classen).

3. ἐκ τοῦ δικαίου: it is a *legitimate* confidence, as δικαίαν, 87. 1.

τῷ δὲ ἑκάτεροί τι - - - ἐσμεν: I agree with Stahl that, though we may defend the nominative ἑκάτεροι on the ground that οἱ Ἀθηναῖοι are included in it, and perhaps take τι as 'in one field or the other' (which is difficult: ABFM omit τι), we cannot, with the MSS. reading, assume ἡμεῖς οἱ Ἀθηναῖοι as subject to ἐσμέν, with Böhme, Classen, and Croiset. But I disagree with him in supposing that ἡμεῖς οἱ Ἀθ. *must* be the subject, still more, that we should get a satisfactory sentence by bracketing ἑκάτεροί τι. ἐσμέν here means 'both we and they are', or 'men are', and τι means, as usual, 'in some degree': 'in so far as we, Athenians and Peloponnesians, are either of us in some degree more experienced than the other, we are the bolder'. (English would be more likely to use the third person, 'one side more experienced than the other'.) It is not rare for Thucydides to insert in his speeches a generalization which has not a very strict application to the context. Cf. i. 78. 5, ii. 11. 4 (n. ad fin.), and perhaps 41. 4, τῶν δ' ἔργων, κ.τ.λ.

5. μὴ δὴ αὐτῶν τὴν τόλμαν δείσητε: i.e. in effect, do not expect τόλμα from *them*.

πιστότερον: paradoxically with φόβον (Croiset): 'their fear which *you* can rely on to help you'. Cf. 62. 4–5, where it is γνώμη that a man relies on, and τόλμα which is in consequence ἐχυρωτέρα, or πρόνοια which is βεβαιοτέρα. See below, too, τῇ δυνάμει τὸ πλέον πίσυνοι ἢ τῇ γνώμῃ ἐπέρχονται: all contrasted with the Athenians of ii. 62 and here, μέγα τι τῆς διανοίας τὸ βέβαιον ἔχοντες ἀντιτολμῶσιν.

ἄξιον τοῦ παρὰ πολύ: this phrase is surely not Greek (Bohme's comparison with τὸ παρ' ἐλπίδα, iv. 62. 3, is very unconvincing), nor can it stand for τοῦ παρὰ πολὺ προνενικηκέναι: nor is Stahl's too simple bracketing of τοῦ παρὰ πολύ at all probable. Steup's τοῦ παραλόγου is the most ingenious emendation yet proposed. A simple τῆς τόλμης, or better τῆς δόξης, is what we want; but where did the MSS. reading come from?

6. ἀντίπαλοι μὲν γὰρ οἱ πλείους: Hude adopts Madvig's conjecture ἢ πλείους; but we need the article, if this is to be the subject of the verb, and, with Madvig's interpretation, we should have rather ἀ. μὲν γὰρ ἢ πλ. ὄντες οἱ ἄνθρωποι. ἀντίπαλοι is answered by οἱ δ' ἐκ πολλῷ ὑποδεεστέρων (sc. ἐπιόντες), and gives a clear enough meaning; and οἱ πλείους is 'the majority of men'.

ἃ λογιζόμενοι, κ.τ.λ.: if they use their brains, the enemy will fear us all the more; cf. 40. 3, τοῖς ἄλλοις ἀμαθία μὲν θράσος, λογισμὸς δὲ ὄκνον φέρει.

226

Bohme compares vi. 34. 8 (Hermokrates recommending a bold attack on the Athenian forces as they sail from Kerkyra): εἰ δ' ἴδοιεν παρὰ γνώμην τολμήσαντας, τῷ ἀδοκήτῳ μᾶλλον ἂν καταπλαγεῖεν ἢ τῇ ἀπὸ τοῦ ἀληθοῦς δυνάμει, which is a close enough parallel for the general sense of the present passage ('they are in fear of us just because of our improbable—almost unnatural—daring'); but Steup points out the difference between ἀπὸ τοῦ ἀληθοῦς there ('our real strength') and the apparent meaning of τῇ κατὰ λόγον παρασκευῇ, 'the strength which they would have expected us to show', with perhaps, as Marchant says, a hint at the long-delayed reinforcements (85. 4–6); "to fear us more . . . than they would if our preparations were less out of proportion to their own" (C. F. Smith). Steup denies that this meaning is possible, and says τῇ κ. λ. παρασκευῇ must refer to the excellent build and equipment of the Athenian triremes (and the experience of the crews?). This seems to me forced, and the more common interpretation to be not beyond Thucydides' power of compression, in speeches, and especially in speeches by commanding officers to their men.

7. τῇ ἀπειρίᾳ - - - τῇ ἀτολμίᾳ: Classen contrasts 11. 4.

8. ἡ στενοχωρία οὐ ξυμφέρει: a commonplace; but how narrowly circumscribed must the waters be? The battles in the straits of Salamis and the Syracusan harbour are the classic instances of this truth in Greek history; but the gulf opposite Naupaktos, just within the narrows, is a good deal larger than either.

At Salamis also the narrow waters helped the smaller numbers as well as the slower movements of the Greek fleet. Here there is a contrast (which illustrates as well the revolution in naval warfare brought about by the Athenians in the last fifty years): Phormion wants the open waters both because he has the best ships and seamen, and because they are fewer in number.

ἐς ἐμβολήν: 'to ram', to attack head on, with τὸ ἔμβολον, the sides or the oars of the enemy ship. See vii. 36. 3, and 70. 4, as an illustration of this whole sentence.

πρόσοψιν - - - ἐκ πολλοῦ: 'a clear view, from a distance'; or πρόοψιν (coni. Bekker), 'a view for some time before the moment of attack'.

ἀναστροφαί: any kind of reverse-movement, by which a ship can disengage, whether by sudden turn to right or left, or by backing water, here of course for the purpose of counter-attack. The word is used as well of troops manœuvring on land, especially of cavalry; and of troops 'rallying'. See L. and S.

τὴν ναυμαχίαν πεζομαχίαν: cf. i. 49. 2, vii. 62. 2. All this explanation of the advantages of open waters to the Athenians seems out of place in an address immediately before a battle to well-trained sailors; it is Thucydides rather, reminding the reader. Cf. 60. 6 n. This section is also cold and academically rhetorical, like 60. 5–6.

227

9. παρὰ ταῖς ναυσὶ μένοντες: contrasted with ἐν τῷ ἔργῳ, below. The ships are not boarded till a definite movement by the enemy is observed (90. 3), in order not to tire the men unnecessarily. But they must stand by: no more foraging or wandering away—as happened later at Aigospotamoi.

τὰ παραγγελλόμενα ὀξέως δέχεσθε: see 84. 3 and 11. 9.

τῆς ἐφορμήσεως: rather the mutual watching by both sides than the enemy's watch, as the scholiast has it; or 'our stations are only a short distance apart'. So Arnold.

κόσμον καὶ σιγήν: qualities which the Dorians claimed for themselves (11. 9, v. 70. 1), but had not shown in the previous battle (84. 3). We, too, are inclined to forget Athenian self-discipline: which an Alkibiades could value (vi. 18. 6, τῷ εἰωθότι κόσμῳ), though he and his class did not perhaps practise it as well as the sailors (Xen. Mem. iii. 5. 19). Grote could appreciate it (in ugly words): "The idea of entire silence on board the Athenian ships while a sea-fight was going on is not only striking as a feature in the picture, but is also one of the most powerful evidences of the force of self-control and military habits among these citizen-seamen" (v, p. 125).

τῶν πολεμίων: all the good MSS. except C have τῶν πολεμικῶν, and this is preferable. Hude has reverted to it, though Stuart Jones follows C. (In iv. 80. 3 the latter adopts ἐν τοῖς πολέμοις against the MSS. rather than read ἐν τοῖς πολεμίοις.)

10. καταλῦσαι Πελοποννησίων τὴν ἐλπίδα τοῦ ναυτικοῦ: this was the great aim, for which it was worth running a great risk; see 88. 1 n.

11. οὐκ ἐθέλουσιν αἱ γνῶμαι - - - ὁμοῖαι εἶναι: the Peloponnesians had said that brave men would preserve the same courage (87. 3).

The two speeches here introduced do not seem to have any special aim other than to lend weight to the description of the most notable battle at sea of the Archidamian war, and to remind readers of the principal features of naval tactics.

90. 1. ἐπὶ τεσσάρων - - - ὥσπερ καὶ ὥρμουν: i.e. they had been drawn up at anchor (ὁρμοῦσαι) in line four deep, with the coast, as usual, behind them; when they weighed anchor (ἀναγαγόμενοι), they 'turned right' so to speak and sailed in column, four abreast, with their twenty fastest ships, which had been attached to their right wing, now in the lead. So far there is no difficulty; but ἐπὶ τὴν ἑαυτῶν γῆν is impossible, as Grote saw (v, pp. 136–41). What happened we can see from the sequel: the Peloponnesian fleet sailed sufficiently closely in the direction of Naupaktos, i.e. only a little east of north, to make Phormion hurry to its defence, but also near enough to the Peloponnesian shore for a 'left turn' and advance in line direct for the opposite shore to be described as ἐπιστροφὴ ἐς τὴν εὐρυχωρίαν (§ 5 n.:

Grote forgot this when he said that Thucydides says no word of any second movement by the Peloponnesians). Phormion, who started from west of Antirrion and had clearly supposed that the purpose of the Peloponnesians was still to carry out their attack on Akarnania, had to keep close in to shore in sailing back to Naupaktos; for that was the shortest way. Grote asks why, if the enemy kept close to their own shore and then started to cross $\dot{\epsilon}s$ $\tau\dot{\eta}\nu$ $\epsilon\dot{v}\rho\upsilon\chi\omega\rho\dot{\iota}a\nu$, Phormion did not there attack them, where he wanted them; the answer is, firstly, that they were attacking in line ($\dot{\epsilon}\pi\iota\sigma\tau\rho\dot{\epsilon}\psi a\nu\tau\epsilon s$ - - - $\mu\epsilon\tau\omega\pi\eta\delta\dot{o}\nu$ $\dot{\epsilon}\pi\lambda\epsilon o\nu$, § 4; cf. n. on $\ddot{a}\kappa\omega\nu$, § 3), and secondly, that in the race for Naupaktos he was barely more than level with them by the time they had crossed to the north coast, and he had no chance of putting them to confusion by superior tactics. Even if the main body, by clumsy action, had given him a successful chance of manœuvre, it would have left the fast right wing free to attack an undefended Naupaktos. The distance from C. Drepanon to Naupaktos is about two and a half times that between the two Capes Rion; if the Peloponnesians 'turned to the open sea' shortly before reaching Drepanon, they may have had 5 kilometres, or about half an hour or more, rowing in the open; less, if they waited longer before turning; Phormion, thinking their aim was Naupaktos, as indeed it would have been had they won a decisive victory, had to row hard to defend it. It is possible also that Thucydides, who under-estimates the width of the narrows (86. 3), may also have thought the distance from Drepanon to Naupaktos to be less than it is.

That being so, we must read $\pi a\rho\dot{a}$ $\tau\dot{\eta}\nu$ $\dot{\epsilon}a\upsilon\tau\hat{\omega}\nu$ $\gamma\hat{\eta}\nu$ with CG, not $\dot{\epsilon}\pi\dot{\iota}$ with ABEFM; the latter must be a slip caused by the presence of $\dot{\epsilon}\pi\dot{\iota}$ immediately before and after. $\pi a\rho\dot{a}$ $\tau\dot{\eta}\nu$ $\dot{\epsilon}a\upsilon\tau\hat{\omega}\nu$ $\gamma\hat{\eta}\nu$ is the necessary contrast with the later $\dot{\epsilon}\pi\iota\sigma\tau\rho\dot{\epsilon}\psi a\nu\tau\epsilon s$ $\dot{\epsilon}s$ $\tau\dot{\eta}\nu$ $\epsilon\dot{v}\rho\upsilon\chi\omega\rho\dot{\iota}a\nu$. Apart from this, it is absurd to suppose that $\dot{\epsilon}\pi\dot{\iota}$ τ. $\dot{\epsilon}$. γ. can mean 'in the direction of their own homes, i.e. Corinth and Sikyon' (the *direction* is given by $\dot{\epsilon}\sigma\omega$ $\dot{\epsilon}\pi\dot{\iota}$ $\tau o\hat{v}$ $\kappa\dot{o}\lambda\pi o\upsilon$), or should be taken with $\tau a\xi\dot{a}\mu\epsilon\nu o\iota$ in the sense 'who had drawn up their ships in line, four deep, with the shore behind them'. It is to be noted that by sailing 'along their own shore' from Panormos the Peloponnesians were going very nearly in a line for Naupaktos; they had in fact out-manœuvred Phormion, first by compelling his hurried return within the narrows along his shore, and then by their sudden attack. We can surely see Brasidas behind this. But they were not equal to following up their temporary victory.

Busolt, iii, p. 979. 1, also asks why Phormion did not attack the Peloponnesians on their way from Kyllene, while they were still in the open east of Rion, where he wanted them to be. The answer is that they were hugging the shore, and that they were 77 to 20. He had no hope unless he could get them as they were crossing the wide gulf to Akarnania, and then only if he could huddle them together into a confusion or get at small units separately. Phormion was, in all other circumstances, hopelessly outnumbered (the enemy fleet was now equipped for battle); he was a good commander if ever there was one, but he was not invincible and neither Thucydides nor he himself thought he was. It would really be more pertinent to ask, why did he not retire to Naupaktos earlier instead of risking his whole squadron? He had indeed to prevent his reinforcements, also of twenty ships, being overwhelmed before they joined him; but he could watch for that. See below, pp. 234-7.

2. εἴκοσιν ἔταξαν: i.e. as Classen thought, not to form the right wing, but in addition to it, like cavalry to aid a right wing on land. This is an additional reason for the number 77 for the Peloponnesian fleet (86. 4 n.).

πλέοντα τὸν ἐπίπλουν: Böhme and Stahl adduce viii. 102. 2 and ii. 17. 4 for the concrete sense of ἐπίπλουν (and the former compares πόλεμον ἐπιόντα, 36. 4, above, where see n.). They are, however, very different; and even if we could translate ἐπίπλους 'fleet', πλέοντα is ridiculously otiose. (Stahl compares ἔπλεον in § 4; but that has μετωπηδόν and ὡς εἶχε τάχους ἕκαστος to define it, which is just the point.) Dobree's πλέοντες (accepted by Hude) is no better in sense, and Böhme's πλέω ὄντα rather worse. Croiset's view that πλέοντα is the relic of some such note on τὸν ἐπίπλουν σφῶν as πλέοντας ἑαυτούς is the only reasonable one until a convincing emendation can be found.

3. ἐρήμῳ ὄντι: with no garrison. Cf. 25. 1 n. on ἀνθρώπων οὐκ ἐνόντων; and perhaps iv. 3. 3.

ἄκων καὶ κατὰ σπουδήν: he had hoped to the last that the enemy were adhering to their original plan of attacking Akarnania, for which they would have been compelled to pass out of the narrows somewhere, in a westerly direction. Now Phormion has to *avoid* a fight, at least till he gets back to Naupaktos; for, at the very least, the leading Peloponnesian ships would be able to attack Naupaktos if he attempted to engage any section of the enemy on his way. Contrast Diodoros, xii. 48. 2-3; for which see 92. 7 n.

καὶ ὁ πεζὸς ἅμα τῶν Μεσσηνίων: they have not been mentioned before. They were especially necessary as land support for so small a squadron as Phormion's as soon as it left its base; apart from a possible attack by Aitolians from the inland on a temporary camp at Molykreion or elsewhere, a *partial* success by the numerous Peloponnesian navy at least was to be reckoned with and steps taken to minimize it in the way illustrated in § 6, below.

4. ἀπὸ σημείου ἑνός: i.e. it did not have to be passed from squadron to squadron and ship to ship, but was a signal that all could see; the manœuvre had, that is, been pre-arranged.

230

ἐπιστρέψαντες - - - μετωπηδόν: i.e. they formed into line again, turning left, and advanced, four deep, towards the northern shore. I suspect that Thucydides had not accurately envisaged the coast between Drepanon and Rion, and imagined that the Peloponnesians had been going more nearly in an easterly direction than was the case and so had had to change direction almost by 90 degrees to attack the opposite coast; just as he may have underestimated the distance between the coasts (86. 3, 90. 1 nn.).

ὡς εἶχε τάχους ἕκαστος: at the most half an hour's fast rowing, less, if they had been gradually getting farther from their own shore.

5. ἕνδεκα μέν τινες: Classen rejects τινες (the reading of C⟨G⟩ only) because of the precise τὰς ἕνδεκα in 91. 1; which is insufficient reason (in 91. 1 it is 'the eleven I have mentioned'). But we could do without it.

ἐς τὴν εὐρυχωρίαν: the open waters between the two fleets, ἔσω τοῦ κόλπου; which is very awkward, a careless piece of writing, after the use of the word expressly to mean the waters outside the narrows, 83. 2, 86. 5. So 91. 1, below. I do not agree with editors, and historians, that ἐς τὴν εὐρυχωρίαν here and at 91. 1 is to be taken with ὑπεκφεύγουσι; rather with τὴν ἐπιστροφήν. Phormion's purpose is to avoid battle and get to Naupaktos; unless compelled he would not go out of his way, southward, and what Thucydides says is that the eleven ships just got past the line of the enemy's attack. It was the Peloponnesians, who had kept more or less closely to their own shore, who turn and enter the open waters.

6. καὶ ἐπιβάντες: as edd. point out, καί connects ἐπεσβαίνοντες with μαχόμενοι, two present participles, and the aorist shows the manner of fighting, dependent on μαχόμενοι, 'from on board'.

For this episode in the struggle, which shows so clearly one factor in Greek naval warfare, cf. iv. 14. 2–3 n.

91.1. διέφθειραν: see Powell's crit. n. (which corrects a misstatement by Grenfell & Hunt, Ox. Pap. ii, No. 225 = Π⁴, which misled Hude); I incline to the imperfect, διέφθειρον, to indicate that the 'destruction' mentioned in 90. 5 had to some degree been undone by the Messenians in 90. 6; it would fit with the other imperfects.

τὴν ἐπιστροφὴν ἐς τὴν εὐρυχωρίαν: see 90. 5 n.

σχοῦσαι ἀντίπρῳροι: i.e. they took up new stations, prows facing the enemy, ready to fight if they were compelled, in order to defend Naupaktos, or if opportunity offered. σχοῦσαι (or ἴσγουσαι) does not, however, mean that they rode at anchor: that would have delayed an attack.

3. καὶ περιπλεύσασα: this, though omitted by AB and by many edd., is to be kept. Without it περὶ ἦν might mean 'near which', as it does in 92. 3, and both in clarity and in vividness the narrative

231

would lose much. The oarsmen on one side of the trireme must have stayed the boat while those on the other rowed, in order to get round three-quarters of a circle in as narrow a compass as possible; otherwise the Leukadian would have had time to observe and alter course.

Who gave this intrepid order—the trierarch or the $\kappa \upsilon \beta \epsilon \rho \nu \acute{\eta} \tau \eta s$? and what was his name? Was he directly or indirectly rewarded with thanks or promotion? This is the sort of thing we often miss in Attic history. It would be pleasant to think that he was the Amynias of *Equit.* 570 (below, p. 233).

4. καθεῖσαι τὰς κώπας, κ.τ.λ.: they dropped their oars in the water and so stopped the boat. Edd. compare Livy xxxvi. 44. 8, 'demittere remos in aquam ab utroque latere stabiliendae navis causa'. It was a wrong thing to do so near the enemy, for it would take some time for the ships to get up speed again to attack or to avoid attack.

92. 1. θάρσος ἔλαβε: Homeric expression, a use of $\lambda \alpha \mu \beta \acute{\alpha} \nu \epsilon \iota \nu$ found only here in Thucydides, and once each in Herodotos, Xenophon, and Plato (Classen).

ἀπὸ ἑνὸς κελεύσματος: cf. 90. 4; but here there is no assumption of a pre-arranged signal; there were only eleven vessels, and the order was a simple one.

ἐτράποντο: the whole Peloponnesian fleet, as appears from the sequel. A sorry end to an action well thought out and so successfully begun.

2. τὰς ἑαυτῶν ἀφείλοντο: either the retreating fleet abandoned them, or the vessels towing them naturally lagged behind the rest and were caught.

3. ἐξέπεσεν: his body was washed up on shore; and hence the suicide became known. Or else the sinking of the Leukadian had taken place just outside the harbour, and all was seen.

4. τροπαῖον ἔστησαν: it is possible also that the Athenians on this occasion made a dedication at Dodone; for a bronze plaque has been found there with the inscription (in letters which may belong to this time): $Ἀθηναῖοι \ ἀπὸ \ Πελοποννεσίον· \ ναυμαχίαι \ νικέσαντες \ ἀ[νέθε-σαν]$ (*S.I.G.*[3] 73, Hicks-Hill, 57; Busolt, iii. 981. 2). Pausanias, x. 11. 6, mentions Athenian dedications of war-booty ($πλοίων \ τὰ \ ἄκρα \ καὶ \ ἀσπίδες \ χαλκαῖ$) from many Peloponnesian cities at Delphi, which he thinks were made after Phormion's victories.

τὰ ναυάγια: this includes ships' oars and other valuable property, besides waterlogged and damaged hulls.

6. ἐσέπλευσαν ἐς τὸν κόλπον, κ.τ.λ.: Phormion was not in any position to prevent this (so large a fleet could always sail along its own shore); nor would he especially have wished to, since he could not destroy it.

7. οἱ ἐκ τῆς Κρήτης Ἀθηναῖοι: 85. 5–6.

αἷς ἔδει - - - παραγενέσθαι: literally, 'with which they should have been present at the battle'. Here also I can discern no particular criticism of the commander, only of the whole episode.

καὶ τὸ θέρος ἐτελεύτα: that is, not before the beginning of autumn, but before the beginning of winter, early in November, as is to be seen from 93. 1.

These two brilliant episodes illustrate vividly those qualities of the Athenians at war which so much impressed their contemporaries (the Corinthians, i. 70), and the value of which Perikles and a few others of the leading men in Athens (Aristophanes among them) well understood (ii. 36. 2–3, 41. 4, 62. 2–3, 64. 3; *Equit.* 565–73), and all were proud of: their inventiveness and readiness to act on novel ideas, their daring and even rashness (παρὰ γνώμην κινδυνευταί) (i. 70. 3) and their optimism in a crisis; quickness of perception and of movement in action; κρατοῦντές τε τῶν ἐχθρῶν ἐπὶ πλεῖστον ἐξέρχονται καὶ νικώμενοι ἐπ' ἐλάχιστον ἀναπίπτουσιν. - - - ἢν δ' ἄρα του καὶ πείρᾳ σφαλῶσιν, ἀντελπίσαντες ἄλλα ἐπλήρωσαν τὴν χρείαν (i. 70. 5–7). Or, as Aristophanes puts it,

> οὐ γὰρ οὐδεὶς πώποτ' αὐτῶν τοὺς ἐναντίους ἰδὼν
> ἠρίθμησεν, ἀλλ' ὁ θυμὸς εὐθὺς ἦν Ἀμυνίας·
> εἰ δέ που πέσοιεν ἐς τὸν ὦμον ἐν μάχῃ τινί,
> τοῦτ' ἀπεψήσαντ' ἄν, εἶτ' ἠρνοῦντο μὴ πεπτωκέναι,
> ἀλλὰ διεπάλαιον αὖθις.[1]

You could not have better words to illustrate the spirit of Phormion and his men (88. 2, and the daring action that follows an apparently hopeless defeat).

The Spartans' answer to this daring spirit was an occasional counter-daring (when Brasidas was about, as in the next chapter), generally hampered by an inability κρατοῦντες τῶν ἐχθρῶν ἐπὶ πλεῖστον ἐξιέναι, except when Brasidas could act alone, as in Thrace; but properly it was their slowness, praised by Archidamos (i. 84. 1) and so well displayed at Mantineia: Ἀργεῖοι μὲν καὶ οἱ ξύμμαχοι ἐντόνως καὶ ὀργῇ χωροῦντες, Λακεδαιμόνιοι δὲ βραδέως, κ.τ.λ (v. 70). Both Athenian and Spartan had their fine qualities, and Thucydides could appreciate them both, just as he could see the defects of these

[1] It is of the previous generation (τοὺς πατέρας ἡμῶν and καὶ στρατηγὸς οὐδ' ἂν εἷς | τῶν πρὸ τοῦ σίτησιν ᾔτησ' ἐρόμενος Κλεαίνετον) that this is expressly said, as Perikles, ii. 36. 2–3, 62. 3; but Phormion is in mind (l. 562) and the spirit is as much his as Kimon's. So Müller-Strübing, p. 652. Neil in his edition of *The Knights* argued that Poseidon was the Tory god of Athens, the god of the conservatives and the rich, Athena of the industrials and the radicals; but this will not do for this passage; for not only is Poseidon the god of the sailors as much as of the cavalry, of the democratic sailor crowd, but the fathers of these knights ἄνδρες ἦσαν τῆσδε τῆς γῆς ἄξιοι καὶ τοῦ πέπλου.

233

qualities and the disasters that resulted from them (iv. 65. 4; viii. 96. 4–5; or indeed ii. 93. 4, 94. 1, below, Peloponnesian hesitations, and 94. 2, κατὰ σπουδὴν καὶ πολλῷ θορύβῳ, Athenian haste).

Phormion and his Athenians stayed the winter out, campaigning in Akarnania (yet no amount of reading Thucydides will persuade some scholars that Greek ships, triremes or merchantmen, ever left harbour between October and April), and returned early in the spring of 428. After that Thucydides does not mention him, except to say that in the summer of that same year, 428, the Athenians sent a force to Naupaktos and Akarnania under the command of his son Asopios, the Akarnanians having expressly asked for Asopios or for some other relative of Phormion (iii. 7. 1). The implication is that Phormion was not available; but Thucydides gives no hint why he was not—sickness, death, deposition from office? any one is possible, but we expect Thucydides to tell us, because the clause τῶν Φορμίωνός τινα σφίσι πέμψαι ἢ υἱὸν ἢ ξυγγενῆ ἄρχοντα demands explanation, i.e. why did they not ask for Phormion himself? quite apart from the interest that Thucydides obviously felt, and arouses in his readers, in his personality. It is not enough in this case to say that Thucydides is normally silent about the personal life of any character (except Perikles, Brasidas, Nikias, and Alkibiades, and Themistokles in a digression), and does not mention their deaths unless in battle, even if the interest in Phormion does not equal that in any of the others.

To help fill the gap left by Thucydides in the later history of Phormion (though not to explain why there is this gap), historians quote the story which the scholiast on Ar. *Peace*, 347, on the authority of Androtion (F 8), and Pausanias, i. 23. 10, tell about the Akarnanians asking for Phormion to be sent again to their help, but he could not go because he was under the ban of ἀτιμία (he had, at his εὔθυνα, been fined 100 minae and could not pay it); whereupon the Athenians, by a legal fiction (because a fine once imposed by a dikastery could not be simply remitted—there was no higher court, not even the ekklesia itself, which could do this), gave him a minor public service to perform and paid him 100 minae for doing it.[1]

This, however, as told, can have nothing to do with the strategia of 428 as related in Thuc. iii. 7; for the whole point of Androtion's story is that the fine was (in effect) remitted, and therefore Phormion enabled to sail. If there is truth in the story, it must refer to an earlier expedition to Akarnania (for none later is recorded), that is,

[1] Neither the scholiast nor Pausanias understands the legal side to this action; but doubtless Androtion did, for in his generation the device was used again to relieve Demosthenes of a fine (Plut. *Demosth.* 27. 9). The variations between the scholiast and Pausanias are not important for our purpose.

to Phormion's command of the year before, which has just ended—
to Thuc. ii. 69. 1, not to iii. 7. 1. If that is true, Phormion may have
been sick or may have died before the early summer of 428; and the
only wonder then will be Thucydides' silence. Whether the passage
in *The Knights* implies that he was alive and well in 424, as Müller–
Strübing asserted, I would not say; certainly he was not again on
active service.

The scholiast's words (from Androtion), however, Ἀκαρνᾶνες
στρατηγὸν αὐτὸν ᾔτουν, look like a reflection of iii. 7. 1, and it is
possible, though not more than possible, that we should pay more
attention to his next words, ὁ δὲ οὐκ ὑπήκουσε, and Pausanias'
ναύαρχον αὐτὸν Ἀθηναίων αἱρουμένων, ἐκπλεύσεσθαι οὐκ ἔφασκεν: that
is to say, that we should attribute the *refusal* to Phormion himself,
and suppose that the Athenians were ready to 'remit' the fine, but
that he would not, for whatever reason, accept the command. For,
quite apart from Androtion's story of his being fined at his εὔθυνα
(if this refers to the spring of 428, though he might, and with more
reason, have been fined after his campaign in Chalkidike), there is
some hint of controversy in Athens about his conduct of the campaign of 429. This is how Diodoros, xii. 48. 3, tells the story of the
second battle (Thuc. ii. 90–92): Φορμίων δὲ τῇ προγεγενημένῃ νίκῃ
φρονηματισθεὶς ἐτόλμησεν ἐπιθέσθαι ταῖς πολεμίαις ναυσὶν οὔσαις
πολλαπλασίαις, and won a doubtful victory, with losses on both sides;
and the Athenians sent a second squadron of twenty ships, and the
Peloponnesiaris thereupon returned to Corinth. Diodoros is capable
of any misunderstanding; but if this is something like what Ephoros
wrote, and if Ephoros here reflects Comedy (or rather one aspect
of Comedy), Comedy may be reflecting criticism of Phormion made
at the time. Phormion had, after all, taken a great, perhaps an un-
justifiable risk in challenging the large enemy fleet to battle outside
the narrow straits, instead of retiring to the safety of Naupaktos
till reinforcements arrived, and had been out-generalled—by a simple,
almost obvious manœuvre—and lost a large part of his small
squadron in consequence; the brilliant recovery does not alter that,
nor does the long delay of the reinforcing squadron excuse him,
whether that delay was due in the main to the ekklesia or its commander or to the bad, perhaps foreseeable weather. There may well
have been people in Athens, men of cautious minds, grave, experienced counsellors, or envious enemies, who attacked Phormion on
his return to Athens for the excessive confidence which led him to
endanger both his ships and, more important, the hold on Naupaktos
itself; and perhaps an action against Phormion was brought[1]—at

---

[1] But at his εὔθυνα, as Androtion says? We can hardly reject this too, and still
trust Androtion; but when was the εὔθυνα held—in March or July? If the latter,
Phormion was still strategos when his son set out.

which doubtless the officer in command of the second squadron was denounced for his delay.

Eupolis' comedy, *Taxiarchoi*, gave Phormion a part, perhaps a prominent one. The scholiast on *The Peace* who quotes Androtion also quotes this play; there was something in it of the hardships of a sailor's lot on service, the rough conditions, and the poor food. So rigid and inhibited are our minds that we are convinced that Phormion was held up for our admiration as the man of the older generation who could bear hardships and willingly did so with his men (as in Aristophanes' hints). Perhaps; but the picture may have been more like that of another stout warrior and brave man, Lamachos, in *The Acharnians*. We know nothing of the date of *The Taxiarchs* (and little of its purpose); but it may belong about 426 or 425, and Ephoros *may* have got something from it for a less flattering portrait of Phormion than Thucydides gives us.[1] Eupolis mentioned him again in *Astrateutoi*, fr. 40, as Aristophanes in *The Babylonians*, fr. 86, and in one edition of *The Clouds* (fr. 382).

This, however, though possible as an account of what happened, would do nothing to explain Thucydides' silence. Vituperation, even actions in the courts, Thucydides would ignore, as he does those against Perikles and his friends, if he thought them both baseless and ineffective; but if their consequence was the sudden and premature end of a brilliant naval career, we cannot understand why he did not mention it. Certainly we cannot accept the easy solution that he would deliberately conceal either the attacks of oligarchic and pro-Spartan enemies of the popular Phormion (if any such took place) or the envious action of an ungrateful and unstable multitude. He does not do this sort of thing elsewhere: why should he here? It is on the whole easiest to suppose that Phormion was getting old and that he retired voluntarily (which is not sufficient reason for Thucydides' omission to say so; but is less unlikely than an omission to say that he had died, and than a deliberate suppression) ;[2] and that, if there is some truth in Androtion's story, the remittance of the fine belongs to 429 rather than to 428. Phormion was certainly popular enough in 424, when *The Knights* was produced; and though that proves nothing about his popularity in the spring of 428 with the Ἀθηναῖοι μετάβουλοι, it does indicate that, if he was alive, he was no longer young; for he was not again to be in command. He may well have been a man of Perikles' generation, perhaps ten years or

---

[1] I am not questioning Meineke's ingenious suggestion (i. 144) that in one scene of the play Phormion was shown explaining the arts and the hardships of war to the effeminate and unskilful Dionysos. This could be quite consistent with what I have said above.

[2] The way in which he implies the death of Archidamos of Sparta is very similar, though the context is not quite the same: iii. 1. 1, 26. 2, 89. 1. So also Philippos of Macedonia, ii. 95. 3 n., and Derdas, i. 59. 2.

so younger; that would fit *The Knights* very well. His fame lived on as the great seaman and captain, beloved of his crews, popular with the sailor crowd—he was both daring and he shared their hardships (*Peace*, 347, and two other scholia ad loc.); in 424, in the hey-day of Athenian success, the aristocratic cavalry were ready to pay their tribute to him too; in 421 he is mentioned again as a typical figure of the war (*Peace*, 347), and in 411, with Myronides, as a hero of the older generation—

$$\kappa\alpha\grave{\iota} \ M\nu\rho\omega\nu\acute{\iota}\delta\eta\varsigma \ \gamma\grave{\alpha}\rho \ \mathring{\eta}\nu$$
$$\tau\rho\alpha\chi\grave{\upsilon}\varsigma \ \mathring{\epsilon}\nu\tau\epsilon\hat{\upsilon}\theta\epsilon\nu \ \mu\epsilon\lambda\acute{\alpha}\mu\pi\upsilon-$$
$$\gamma\acute{o}\varsigma \ \tau\epsilon \ \tauo\hat{\iota}\varsigma \ \mathring{\epsilon}\chi\theta\rhoo\hat{\iota}\varsigma \ \mathring{\alpha}\pi\alpha\sigma\iota\nu\cdot$$
$$\mathring{\omega}\varsigma \ \delta\grave{\epsilon} \ \kappa\alpha\grave{\iota} \ \Phi o\rho\mu\acute{\iota}\omega\nu \ (Lys. \ 801\text{-}4).$$

His tomb was to be seen still in Pausanias' day (i. 29. 3) on the road to the Academy, near those of Perikles and the fourth-century sailor, Chabrias.

93–94. *The Peloponnesians think of attacking Peiraeus*

93. 1. ἀρχομένου τοῦ χειμῶνος: about the beginning of November, and not long after the recent engagement off Naupaktos.

τοῦ λιμένος τῶν Ἀθηναίων: a perhaps surprising addition, but not therefore to be bracketed; for τῶν Ἀθ. is required to enable us to supply the subject to ἐπικρατεῖν. A warning against the 'adscript' theory, and a reminder that Thucydides did not write with Athenian readers always in mind. (The words are not of course added to distinguish the Athenian post from the obscure Corinthian Peiraios or Speiraion, viii. 10. 3, *al.*, as Stahl and Classen supposed.)

ἦν δὲ ἀφύλακτος, κ.τ.λ.: yet in the summer of 431 B.C. the Athenians φυλακὰς κατεστήσαντο κατὰ γῆν καὶ κατὰ θάλασσαν, ὥσπερ δὴ ἔμελλον διὰ παντὸς τοῦ πολέμου φυλάξειν (ii. 24. 1). The ships of course were there; but they had not always at Peiraeus triremes manned and ready for sea. Long immunity, and perhaps the effects of the pestilence as well, had made them careless. And it was winter, and, all things considered, an attack by *Peloponnesians*, just after Phormion's victories, was the last thing to be expected. The sentence does not (I think) mean that it was Athenian policy not to have ships ready to defend Peiraeus at all times; but that they were not strict in the observance.

2. ἕκαστον τὴν κώπην: as Arnold observes, this implies that in the Greek trireme there was only one man to the oar. The Megarian vessels had long been out of use—probably from long before the war, most of them (only twelve went with the Corinthians against Kerkyra in 433—i. 46. 1), certainly since its beginning—and it was likely enough that much of their movable equipment would have

237

been moved, with and without authority, or have become unserviceable (cf. 94. 3).

τὸ ὑπηρέσιον: some kind of mat on the rower's seat, needed not so much διὰ τὸ μὴ συντρίβεσθαι αὐτῶν τὰς πυγάς, as the scholiast says (which reminds us of much in Aristophanes), as to prevent him from slipping on the bench especially when rowing with particular energy; see Bishop quoted by Arnold in his Appendix III.

τὸν τροπωτῆρα: explained as the twisted leather thong with which the oar was fastened to the thole, the Homeric τροπός (Od. iv. 782; Aesch. Pers. 376; Ar. Ach. 549, 553), and still used in Greek boats and called τροπωτῆρι. But, again as Bishop pointed out, ap. Arnold, while this is true of the ships in the Odyssey and in modern times, it has little meaning in a trireme, in which two-thirds of the oars at least, and probably all, used no thole (which was a peg fixed in the gunwale against which the oar was pulled), but a rowlock bored through the side of the vessel, and no peg nor thong was required. Bishop suggested that it was a length of strap—rope or leather— wound round the oar-handle for a length required to give a compensating weight to the loom (the part of the handle which was within-board) and of a thickness sufficient to prevent the oar slipping through the rowlock into the sea. Each one may have had as well, he said, a loop enabling the oar-handles to be fastened back to the side of the ship, all parallel to each other, during a rest.

κατὰ τάχος ἐς Μέγαρα: they could not use the Corinthian port of Kenchreai (which would have been a better starting-point for an attack on Peiraeus and had no triremes watching it from a fort just opposite) because there were no triremes, even old ones, ready for them. To have dragged their good triremes across the isthmus from Lechaion on the Gulf of Corinth would have advertised the plan; see iii. 15. 1, 16. 1, and n. below on § 3, ἀπὸ τοῦ προφανοῦς.

3. οὔτε γὰρ ναυτικὸν ἦν, κ.τ.λ.: this belongs with ἦν δὲ ἀφύλακτος in § 1, above, and is considerably modified (in effect) by § 4, below, where we are told that the Athenians kept a watch on Nisaia from C. Boudoron opposite. It is remarkable that Thucydides should not have put all this into one sentence. (86. 3, where see n., 93. 4, n. on καί τις καὶ ἄνεμος, κ.τ.λ., and 94. 3 are of a different kind.)

ἐξαπιναίως οὕτως: 'to attack suddenly' might be said either in reference to the enemy, 'when they do not expect it', or in reference to the attacker—'after so little preparation'. Here οὕτως shows that the latter is meant. (There is some advantage in this method of attack, for the enemy will be even less prepared; just as there is some disadvantage in long preparation, which gives time to the enemy as well.)

ἐπεὶ οὐδ' ἀπὸ τοῦ προφανοῦς, κ.τ.λ.: the interpretation of this sentence, anyhow difficult, has been obscured because the meaning of ἐξαπιναίως above has not been properly understood. The sentence beginning ἐπεὶ οὐδέ must give a contrast with ἐξαπιναίως; and this is given by καθ' ἡσυχίαν, 'after quiet and careful preparation'; cf. i. 85. 1 and iv. 117. 1 n. That being so, the first οὐδέ is correct ('for, they were sure, they would not make the attempt after much preparation either', or 'even after much preparation'); and therefore the second is too ('nor, if they had been planning, i.e. such a well-prepared attack, was there any fear that they themselves would have failed to observe it in time'). διενοοῦντο carries further the idea already implicit in καθ' ἡσυχίαν. Nor is there any difficulty in the imperfect indicative: it *is* an unfulfilled condition, because such a well-prepared attack had not been made; it is part of the Athenian excuse for their unreadiness for the attack which did take place, and the indicative is kept by the usual 'vivid' construction.

This, I feel confident, is right, but there is a difficulty, namely ἀπὸ τοῦ προφανοῦς, in the emphatic position: it suggests that an open (and well-prepared) attack was, as such, more likely to succeed than a secret one (cf. viii. 8. 4), whereas the meaning is that a well-prepared (and therefore open) attack was more to be expected than an unpremeditated one. (We must remember that, as stated above, there are certain advantages and disadvantages in either method, if you have to choose: the enemy will be less prepared to meet the sudden attack, and careful preparation will both be seen by him and will give him time to prepare as well.) We can only take ἀπὸ τοῦ προφανοῦς closely with καθ' ἡσυχίαν, and take it to mean an attack which would be for all to see, once it was made, even if the preparations for it were not so open to the world as, for example, those of the Peloponnesians for the invasion of Attica in 431, or of the Athenians for the expedition to Sicily. It probably also refers to the fact that the actual attack was by night, though we only learn this in the next sentence. For a variation in this meaning of ἀπὸ τοῦ προφανοῦς see v. 9. 4.

Steup saw the true meaning of the sentence, and the mistakes of the various emendations, but because of a certain harshness in the construction (μὴ οὐ following an understood προσδοκία οὐδεμία, and the absence of any expressed subject to προαισθέσθαι) and the difficulty of the implied 'a secret attack is less likely to succeed than an open', gave up the sentence in despair, as the addition *von einem unkundigen Erklärer*. As if this sort of harshness in construction were not much more characteristic of Thucydides than of any of his ancient commentators; and as if an ignorant one would not take refuge in the commonplace that a sudden attack was more likely to succeed. The essential thing in this attack on the Peiraeus is not only that it was sudden, but that it was quite unprepared, and failed largely for that reason.

4. καταδείσαντες τὸν κίνδυνον: 'fearing the risk', thinking the chances of real success not worth the risk run. We presumably see Knemos in this, not Brasidas; but was he so certainly wrong? How much harm could they have done to Athens? But Thucydides is all for the daring Brasidas, though he may appreciate extreme caution in others (Perikles; Nikias, perhaps, in vi. 9–14, and Chios, viii. 24. 4). His criticism here and in 94. 1 looks to me like criticism of the moment; but when a similar, though for Athens much more dangerous, situation recurs, his opinion is nearly the same (viii. 96. 1–5).

καί τις καὶ ἄνεμος, κ.τ.λ.: again Thucydides separates by narrative the special reasons for this hesitation: the supposed contrary wind here and the poor condition of the ships, 94. 3. There is, however, point in this separation: the leaking in the ships was only noticed and thought dangerous towards the end of the raid. This is characteristic of Thucydides' very direct method of narration, as though he wrote down everything just as it occurred. See below, on Brasidas' march to Thrace, p. 546.

καὶ φρούριον ἐπ' αὐτοῦ ἦν: it is given its name, Boudoron, below, 94. 3. Another curious division of information; and in this case editors have suggested a lacuna here, which may be right. If so, Steup's conjecture is the best, ὃ καλεῖται Βούδορον after ὁρῶν, with in consequence καὶ φρούριον, κ.τ.λ., as the second member of the relative clause.

Bölte and Weicke, Ath. Mitt. xxix, 1904, 79–100, give the name Boudoron not to the promontory just north of Teichó peninsula, as most scholars have done (see e.g. the map in Frazer's Pausanias), but to that south of Teichó, opposite the islet of Trýpika. See the n. on the topography of Megara, below, iii. 51. 4.

νεῶν τριῶν φυλακή: cf. § 3, above, n. on οὔτε γὰρ ναυτικὸν ἦν. We are not told the name of the officer responsible for this negligence, nor what his punishment was. Cf. 91. 3 n.

ἀπροσδοκήτοις: there is something to be said for Hude's conjecture ἀπροσδοκήτως (dropped in the 1913 edition), and more for ἀπροσδόκητοι.

94. 1. φρυκτοί τε - - - πολέμιοι: according to the scholiast here, torches held aloft, from high places, and held still to indicate friends, shaken to indicate a hostile attack and to summon aid. These of course would only have been of use at night time; and they must have been more complex than this: see iii. 22. 7, 80. 2 nn.

οὐδεμιᾶς τῶν κατὰ τὸν πόλεμον ἐλάσσων: clearly, one would say, referring to the Archidamian war only and written before 415 B.C. Cf. vii. 71. 7, viii. 1, 96. 1.

ὅπερ ἂν . . . ἐγένετο: exactly what? They could have sailed into one or more of the Peiraeus harbours (and burnt an arsenal)? Thucydides thinks nothing of their caution (see 93. 4 n.).

2. κατὰ σπουδὴν καὶ πολλῷ θορύβῳ: see 92. 7 n., pp. 233–4. The Athenians might have launched, but presumably did not, the hundred best ships of the reserve (24. 2). Cf. iii. 16.

4. λιμένων τε κλήσει: a better watch at Boudoron or elsewhere in Salamis would also seem to be demanded. Diodoros, xii. 49. 5, whose narrative is in other respects but a dull version of Thucydides (except that it is misdated), says expressly that a better guard on Salamis was kept henceforward.

The Mytileneans chose a rather different method of defence, τῶν λιμένων τὴν χῶσιν (iii. 2. 2).

95–101. Sitalkes and his Thracian Kingdom. Macedonia

Most of this is digression, and the whole of it might almost be so described; for the event narrated, Sitalkes' invasion of Macedonia and Chalkidike, is of very little importance. Thucydides had much information to give about the Thracians, from his own knowledge (iv. 105. 1), and he thought it worth while recording it. For a n. on this see 96. 3, below.

95. 1. Σιτάλκης ὁ Τήρεω, κ.τ.λ.: see 29 and 67. 1–3.

ἐπὶ Περδίκκαν: an ally of Athens, reconciled by Sitalkes' friend Nymphodoros, 29. 4, 6–7; but a doubtful one, 80. 7.

ἐπὶ Χαλκιδέας: the Athenians had been recently badly defeated there, 79.

δύο ὑποσχέσεις, κ.τ.λ.: 'of two promises, anxious to exact the one and fulfil the other.'

2. εἰ Ἀθηναίοις, κ.τ.λ.: 29. 6–7.

Φίλιππον τὸν ἀδελφὸν αὐτοῦ: see i. 57. 3, with n. there on the division of Macedonia by Alexandros the Philhellene. Philippos was in alliance with Athens against his brother Perdikkas at that time; and fled to Sitalkes' court later when Perdikkas patched up his quarrel with Athens.

ἐπὶ βασιλείᾳ: i.e. either to his own kingdom of part of Macedonia (100. 3) or to seize the throne from Perdikkas.

αὐτὸς ὡμολογήκει: 29. 5.

3. τόν τε Φιλίππου υἱὸν Ἀμύνταν: presumably Philippos was dead, though Thucydides does not say so. Cf. above, 92. 7 n., p. 236.

ἡγεμόνα Ἅγνωνα: for Hagnon, the oikistes of Amphipolis and well known in these parts, see 58. 1, iv. 102. 3. ἡγεμών implies that he was to lead the Athenian army when it arrived ἔδει γὰρ καὶ τοὺς Ἀθηναίους, κ.τ.λ.), and perhaps also that he was adviser to Sitalkes. Classen compares iii. 105. 3.

ἔδει γὰρ καὶ τοὺς Ἀθηναίους, κ.τ.λ.: see 101. 1 n.

96. 1. ἐντὸς τοῦ Αἵμου τε ὄρους καὶ τῆς Ῥοδόπης: within, that is, to

the south of, the Balkan and Rodope ranges, as Stahl takes it. The two ranges run roughly parallel, west to east (to the Euxine) and east-south-east (to the Hellespont), through what is now Bulgaria and western (Greek) and eastern (Turkish) Thrace; but Sitalkes' kingdom must also have included the northern, inland parts of the present Greek province of eastern Macedonia, between the Hebros and the Strymon.

[ἐς τὸν Εὔξεινόν τε πόντον καὶ τὸν Ἑλλήσποντον]: bracketed by Stahl, Krüger, Hude, and Stuart Jones on the ground that the scholiast (who says ἕως τοῦ Εὐξ. π. καὶ τοῦ Ἑλλ.) did not have it; and Stuart Jones's brackets remain in Powell's edition, though without any critical note. But the scholion is a late note, without authority for the text (Powell, in C.Q. xxx, 1936, 148); another, apparently late note in the Laurentian on 92. 3 has ἡ περὶ τὴν ὁλκάδα καταδῦσα; but that has not yet persuaded anyone to bracket ἦ περὶ τὴν ὁλκάδα κατέδυ; see also a scholion on ἐρῆμοι, 51. 5; and i. 90. 3 n. The words are necessary to explain that two regions, divided by mountains, are meant, stretching the one to the Euxine, the other to the Helles- pont. (I would prefer, if anything, with Croiset, to bracket τὴν τοῦ Εὐξείνου πόντου, below.) The Thracian kingdom reached the Helles- pont at and about Raidestos (67. 3 n.; 'Hellespont' as usual including the Propontis) and the Euxine at the coast of Bulgaria.

3. μέχρι γὰρ Λαιαίων, κ.τ.λ.: recent editors accept γάρ from C and γρ ABFM and, in consequence, Arnold's bracketing of οὗ. I do not feel that the result of the latter is satisfactory; and should prefer to keep οὗ and assume that a word, e.g. ἦρχεν, has dropped out after ποταμοῦ. We also need Παίονας ⟨τοὺς⟩ αὐτονόμους, because some Paionian tribes were within Sitalkes' rule.

Very little is known of the Thracian peoples and of the Odrysian kingdom in the fifth century beyond what Herodotos and Thucy- dides tell us, though archaeology has given us something of the con- tact of their princes with Greece—the masses, however, were never hellenized. The fragments of Hekataios on Thrace (F 146–83) are too scanty to inform us how much he knew. See S. Casson, *Macedonia, Thrace, and Illyria* (Oxford, 1926), and R.E., art. 'Thrake', by Oberhummer, B. Lenk, and W. Brandenstein (1937), cols. 393–452. As stated above, the power of the Odrysai extended practically over the territory of present-day Bulgaria, Turkish Thrace (east of the Hebros), and Greece between the Hebros and the Strymon except for the coastal strip occupied by Greek cities then within the Athenian empire; that is, from the Danube in the north to the Hellespont and the Greek fringe in the south and from Constanti- nople to the sources of the Strymon in south-west Bulgaria. Of the places named in c. 96, the Haimos range is the Balkan, Stara Planina,

242

Rodope the southern, parallel range from Rila and Pirin Dagh eastwards, along whose southern slopes runs the present boundary between Bulgaria and Greece. Many of the mountain tribes in the Rodope were autonomous, though to the north and south of them, even between the Balkan mountains and the Danube, the Odrysai had extended their rule (§ 1). Mt. Skombros (§ 3) is Vitosha, the highest point of Rila Dagh, south of Sofia, from which come many of the streams that form the Strymon; west of the upper Strymon the Paionian Thracians were independent. North of Rila Dagh and the Rodope, as far west as the river Oskios were the Treres and Tilataioi; the Oskios is the Isker, which flows northwards from the northern slopes of Rila near Sofia to the Danube. The Hebros and the Nestos flow, the one from the north-east, the other from the south-east slopes of Rila. (The Mygdonians, Krestones, and Bisaltai, west of the Strymon, were Thracian tribes which had been already absorbed in Macedonia: see c. 99.) Thucydides may have got his geographical information from Thracians; but it looks as though he had travelled much in Thrace himself. As Lenk observes, it is noteworthy that no capital city is mentioned.

97. 1. ἀπὸ Ἀβδήρων πόλεως: this does not mean that Abdera was one of the Greek cities which paid tribute to Sitalkes (§ 3, below), but that its boundaries were the starting-point of Thucydides' calculation; it was a regularly paying member of the Athenian empire. Cf. § 2, ἀπὸ Βυζαντίου. There was doubtless some arrangement made in the treaty between Athens and Sitalkes about Greek cities east of Abdera which were subject to Athens; but what it was—whether they were to be free from any interference from the Thracian or were to pay so much, and no more, to him—we have no means of knowing. Some Greek cities paid Sitalkes, or at least his successor Seuthes, tribute (§ 3); but there were Greek cities in the region which were not within the Athenian empire.

The site of Abdera is known, with traces of the city-wall, 7 km. south-east of the village now called by the ancient name: *J.H.S.* lxxi, 1951, 245.

τεσσάρων ἡμερῶν καὶ ἴσων νυκτῶν: by Herodotos' reckoning, iv. 86. 1, a merchant vessel, ναῦς στρογγύλη, would sail 700 stades by day and 600 by night; and if Thucydides adopts this, he makes the distance by the shortest route (τὰ ξυντομώτατα) 5,200 stades, or about 560 miles. This is in fact the distance by direct route; allow for a little deviation from this, but add a little to the normal speed, for there is assumed a favourable wind all the way, and the calculation in the text is right. This is indeed to ignore the strong currents in the Hellespont and the Bosporos which would lengthen the journey into the Euxine considerably (see the interesting article by Rhys Carpenter,

$A.J.A.$ xlii, 1948, 1–10); but the 700 stades a day is a conventional figure. See next n.

ὁδῷ δὲ - - - ἀνὴρ εὔζωνος ἑνδεκαταῖος: an 'unencumbered man' on foot would cover 200 stades a day according to Hdt. iv. 101. 2, c. 37 km., or 22 to 23 miles; with this Ps.-Dikaiarchos, 6, agrees, when he says that from Athens to Oropos is ὁδὸς ἐλευθέρῳ βαδίζοντι σχεδὸν ἡμέρας, for the distance is c. 35 km. by the direct but more hilly route by Dekeleia, nearly 40 by Aphidnai.[1] If Thucydides is using the same measures, he underestimates somewhat the distance from Abdera to the mouth of the Danube, which is about 260 miles. Much of this, moreover, is across mountainous country, whereas Herodotos is speaking of the flat lands of South Russia; but if 200 stades is a conventional, average figure for a day's march, the use of it would be unaffected by the nature of the country described: that is, ἑνδεκα-ταῖος means '2,000 stades or more' ('arrival on the eleventh day', after ten days' travel) by the conventional reckoning, rather than 'a man would actually take ten days to do this journey'. Similarly above, 'four days and four nights sailing' is rather a measure of distance than of time.

2. ἀπὸ Βυζαντίου: i.e. from its western borders, for Byzantion was not itself in the Thracian empire.

ἐς Λαιαίους - - - ἡμερῶν - - - τριῶν καὶ δέκα: this reckoning, to the source of the Strymon (see 96. 3 n.), is about right, taking the natural route via the later Adrianople and Philippopolis.

It is highly characteristic of our scholia on Thucydides that they contain no comment on anything in the geography of these chapters (except that 'Doberos is now called Gebres' and the Axios R. the Vardar), though Thrace was a good deal better known both in early and late Byzantine days than in the fifth century B.C. There is a little more on 102. 2.

3. τῶν Ἑλληνίδων πόλεων: we do not know which these were; most probably those on the Euxine coast, north of Mesembria. But, in Seuthes' day, they had been included in the Athenian empire—certainly assessed in 425, and some at least paid tribute later; perhaps by arrangement with Seuthes (but see next n.). $A.T.L.$ i, p. 539, and A 9.

ὅσον προσῆξαν: this can hardly be accepted as what Thucydides wrote. ἦξα is a dubious rarity; προσάγειν is equally rare for 'paying' money in any way; and the aorist is strange. (For the supposed scholiast reading, see J. E. Powell, $C.Q.$ xxx, 1936, 90.) Since, moreover,

---

[1] In v. 53 (when Aristagoras is explaining to Kleomenes the distance from Sardeis to Sousa) Herodotos reckons 150 stades to the day's march. This may mean for an army, which would be good going, and indeed should mean it; but Herodotos does not always remember to make these fine distinctions. Here he may mean that Aristagoras is making the Persian empire as large as possible.

the good MSS. all have ὅσων, Dobree's ὁσωνπερ ἦρξαν has been generally adopted (cf. Böhme's correction of ὅθεν πρὸς Σικελίαν, vii. 50. 2). It is not entirely satisfactory, for we should expect ὅσων ἦρξε Σεύθης, if not ὅσος γε προσῇει ἐπὶ Σεύθου.

Note that if ἦρξαν, or some other form of ἄρχω, is right, Seuthes definitely ruled Greek cities; he did not simply get some revenue from them (in return for not molesting them) by arrangement with Athens. See above.

ἐπὶ Σεύθου: cf. 101. 5–6. He succeeded his uncle (displacing Sitalkes' son Sadokos, the 'Athenian', 29. 5, 67. 2, perhaps because his policy was more nationalist and less friendly to Athens, 101. 5) in late summer, 424, iv. 101. 5. It is not known how long he reigned; but my impression from this sentence is that the whole of this digression on Thrace was written not long after Seuthes came to the throne, not later, certainly, than c. 418–417. See Grundy, i, p. 473.

τετρακοσίων ταλάντων, κ.τ.λ.: this must be read in the light of the figures for Athens and her empire in c. 13. The Thracian royal revenue, though less than the Athenian, was of the same order of magnitude; but there was, as far as we know, no reserve. The area of Thrace was of course many times that of the land-area of the Athenian empire.

τοῖς παραδυναστεύουσι: the minor kings of the regions now comprised within the Odrysian empire, rather than persons of influence at court.
4. τοὐναντίον τῆς Περσῶν: cf. Xen. Cyrop. viii. 2. 7, διαμένει ἔτι καὶ νῦν τοῖς βασιλεῦσιν ἡ πολυδωρία.

ὅμως δέ: by contrast not only with ὄντα μὲν καὶ τοῖς ἄλλοις Θρᾳξί, but, in effect, with κατεστήσαντο. 'They, the Odrysian kings, established, or had established, the custom of demanding gifts; more accurately, this was an old custom universal among Thracian princes, but the Odrysai, for all that, had carried it to much greater lengths because of their great power.'
5. τῶν γὰρ ἐν τῇ Εὐρώπῃ, κ.τ.λ.: the Macedonian, and the smaller principalities in Epeiros and Illyria (cf. 80. 5–6).
6. ἔθνος ἓν πρὸς ἕν: meaning presumably that the Persians, for example, as a nation could not compare in strength and numbers with the Scythians, though the whole Persian empire might.

Σκύθαις ὁμογνωμονοῦσι πᾶσιν ἀντιστῆναι: the might of the innumerable inhabitants of Russia, especially in defence, has been illustrated throughout recorded time. It has been suggested that Thucydides is here intentionally contradicting Herodotos, who said that the Thracians were the largest single people (after the Indians) and would be the strongest if they were united into one kingdom.[1]

---

[1] Hdt. v. 3. This must have been written before the rise of the Odrysian kingdom, though he has already mentioned Sitalkes (iv. 80) and late in life knew of the episode of the Peloponnesian ambassadors: see above, c. 67 nn.

Perhaps; but Thucydides too is emphasizing the great strength of a Thracian empire at this time, even though he adds that they would be inferior to a united Scythia; and the strength of the Scythians is shown clearly enough by Herodotos in his account of the expedition of Dareios.

οὐ μὴν οὐδέ, κ.τ.λ.: this denial of general good sense (political sense, that is) to the Scythians has also been thought to be in reference to Herodotos' praise of them, iv. 46; but it is very guarded praise, and Herodotos would in general have agreed with Thucydides (τὰ μέντοι ἄλλα οὐκ ἄγαμαι, and his account of Scythian invasions of Asia). The conventional Airs, Waters, Places of the Hippokratic corpus, which may be of the fifth century (above, p. 149), has a different account of the Scythians (cc. 19–22), but one which is hardly based on observation.

ὁμοιοῦνται: one expects ὡμοίωνται.

98. 1. διὰ Κερκίνης: they kept well to the interior of the country, and did not arrange with the Athenians to cross the Strymon by the bridge at Amphipolis (iv. 108. 1 n.). See 99. 1.

ὅτε ἐπὶ Παίονας ἐστράτευσεν: the date of this is unknown. It is interesting to find the Thracian king a road-builder and a Greek historian noting it as a natural thing (cf. 100. 2).

2. Δόβηρον τὴν Παιονικήν: the epithet serves not only to define more accurately the direction taken by the army, but to distinguish the town from Doberes north-east of Amphipolis mentioned by Herodotos, vii. 113. 1; where, however, a people of Paionian race lived.

3. οὐκ ἔλασσον πέντε καὶ δέκα μυριάδων: a fairly modest figure, and not guaranteed by Thucydides. Diodoros, xii. 50. 3, in a narrative based almost entirely on Thucydides, has slightly varying figures, 120,000 foot and 50,000 horse; but it is doubtful if this has any significance.

4. τριτημόριον δὲ μάλιστα ἱππικόν: a truly formidable force, if they could be kept together. But fodder must have been a difficulty, even in winter when there would be some grazing on the lower hills and in such plains as were not marshy: cf. 101. 5.

99. 1. ὅπως κατὰ κορυφὴν ἐσβαλοῦσιν ἐς τὴν κάτω Μακεδονίαν: see 98. 1 n.

2. τῶν γὰρ Μακεδόνων, κ.τ.λ.: here a second digression begins, to explain the presence of Macedonians, under the Temenid dynasty, in the low country between the mouths of the Haliakmon and the Axios rivers, and farther east along the line of the lakes to the Strymon valley. In this last part, however, the coastline was not theirs (iv. 102–3); where the boundaries with the Greek cities lay is not known.

'Upper Macedonia' is to the west and south-west of the Axios valley and of the plain immediately to the west of that river, extending to the northern boundaries of Thessaly, and westwards to Epeiros. These upper Macedonians, in the original Macedonian home, with their separate but subordinate kingships, hardly come into the present picture; but this is digression on past history. Philippos' 'kingdom', however, was not one of these in the west (100. 3 n.).

ξύμμαχα μέν ἐστι τούτοις καὶ ὑπήκοα: the Greeks, since the beginning of the fifth century at least, mainly thought of Pella and the low country when they spoke of Macedon (§ 3, init.), though this was not their early home and had been comparatively recently acquired.

3. Ἀλέξανδρος ὁ Περδίκκου πατήρ: the 'Philhellene', i. 137. 1. Two events are here referred to, closely connected with one another: the conquest of the low country and the emergence of the Temenids to the headship of all the Macedonian tribes, though many kept their own kings.

Τημενίδαι - - - ἐξ Ἄργους: cf. Hdt. vii. 137. 1. Thucydides says later of Perdikkas, ἦν δὲ καὶ αὐτὸς τὸ ἀρχαῖον ἐξ Ἄργους, v. 80. 2, to help explain a political manœuvre.

4. τῆς δὲ Παιονίας - - - Ἠδῶνας: for these and other Thracian tribes mentioned below, who had lived west of the Strymon, see 96. 3 n.

5. τῆς νῦν Ἐορδίας: we expect here ⟨ἔτι καὶ⟩ νῦν, whereas in § 3, καὶ ἔτι καὶ νῦν Πιερικὸς κόλπος καλεῖται, we might delete ἔτι καί. Here the name must be old; there it was, comparatively, new.

6. οἱ Μακεδόνες οὗτοι: i.e. that section of them whose immediate chiefs were the Temenidai; other Macedonian tribes are those called M. αὐτῶν below, to distinguish them from non-Macedonian peoples now absorbed in Macedonia.

τόν τε Ἀνθεμοῦντα: see vol. i, pp. 216–18.

Γρηστωνίαν καὶ Βισαλτίαν: see iv. 109. 4; Hdt. vii. 115, 124, 127. (In these the spelling is Κρηστωνικόν, Κρηστωναῖοι.)

καὶ Περδίκκας Ἀλεξάνδρου, κ.τ.λ.: although there is a formality in this which makes it comparable with Ἀρχίδαμος ὁ Ζευξιδάμου, κ.τ.λ., 19. 1, al., that is, makes it independent of previous mention of the same person, yet this sentence was not, I think, written at the same time as i. 57–65 or ii. 29. 4–6 or 80. 7.

100. 1. οἱ μὲν Μακεδόνες οὗτοι: at first sight, one would say, not the M. οὗτοι of 99. 6, but 'all these Macedonians under Perdikkas'. But he may mean only those of the plains, the immediate object of the Thracian attack.

2. Ἀρχέλαος ὁ Περδίκκου υἱός: he reigned from 413 to 399 B.C.; and it is generally assumed that Thucydides would not have written this till after his death, because it is his manner to sum up an individual's career only after his death (e.g. Ullrich, Beitr. (1846), 145–8). This is

247

a mechanical argument; he could have written this sentence immediately after Archelaos' achievement, which, for all we know, may have been early in his reign.

It is, however, in any case, an addition to the rest of the narrative if I am right in surmising from ἐπὶ Σεύθου, 97. 3, that that was written not long after 421. (Ullrich, p. 148, noted that § 2 could be omitted and the syntax remain sound. This is true, but unimportant—Thucydides knew how to adapt, if he wanted to insert a new sentence in a narrative already composed.)

οἱ ἄλλοι βασιλῆς ὀκτώ: Herodotos, viii. 139, gives their names, back to Perdikkas I, ὁ κτησάμενος τὴν ἀρχήν (137–8); Thucydides once more agrees with him. See vol. i, p. 201, n. 2.

3. ἐς τὴν Φιλίππου πρότερον οὖσαν ἀρχήν: this was, as we learn here, in the Axios valley, from near the present Greek–Yugoslav border southwards; perhaps on both sides of the river, rather than as stated in vol. i, p. 202.

Ἀμύντου: see 95. 3.

4. Κύρρου: an unknown site, not elsewhere mentioned.

ἔσω δὲ τούτων: i.e. farther westward into upper Macedonia. Bottiaia is the Bottia of 99. 3, not Bottike in Chalkidike, the later home of the tribe, where they are mentioned, 101. 1, 5.

5. τῶν ἄνω ξυμμάχων: generally interpreted as the Macedonians of 99. 2; but since these were already subject to Perdikkas (though described there as ξύμμαχα), it is possible that the allies here mentioned are independent peoples from the north.

101. 1. ἐπειδὴ οἱ Ἀθηναῖοι - - - ἀπιστοῦντες αὐτὸν μὴ ἥξειν: a not at all surprising mistrust, not perhaps because Sitalkes had waited two years since the alliance (95. 1), but because this year he had not moved till the winter—an inconvenience for his own troops (§ 5, below) and a greater one for Athenians. No aid came from him when the Athenians were in Chalkidike this summer (79); but perhaps none had then been asked and this present arrangement was an immediate consequence of the Athenian defeat.

δῶρα δὲ καὶ πρέσβεις ἔπεμψαν αὐτῷ: Poppo's conjecture δέ for τε of the MSS. has been everywhere accepted. If we keep τε, we must alter to ἔπεμψεν—Sitalkes sent gifts (contrary to the Thracian custom, 97. 4, but perhaps wisely) and ambassadors to Perdikkas. This has in general already been said in λόγους ἐποιεῖτο; but for all that I incline to this correction. As an example of scholiast's folly, the note here may be mentioned, ἔπεμψαν: οἱ Μακεδόνες.

Βοττιαίους: see 99. 3 n.

5. ὁ δὲ τήν τε Χαλκιδικήν, κ.τ.λ.: the Thessalians were frightened and the whole of the Greek world beginning to be anxious about this monster of a barbarian army; but all Sitalkes' did more was to raid

248

Chalkidike for a week. No wonder Aristophanes made comedy out of the alliance between Athens and this great king.

ὑπὸ Σεύθου: see 97. 3 n.

6. ὥσπερ ὑπέσχετο: for once, Perdikkas kept his word.

102-3. *The Athenians in Akarnania*

102. 1. ἐπ' Ἀστακοῦ: see 30. 1, 33. 1–2, where Euarchos, a collaborator with the enemy, had been restored in the winter of 431–430. He must have been driven out again and Astakos restored to the rest of Akarnania and to the alliance with Athens; Knemos had not attempted to take it the previous summer (80. 2–4), and Oiniadai was alone in her enmity to her fellow Akarnanians and so to Athens, or to Athens and so to Akarnania (§ 2, below).

τετρακοσίοις μὲν ὁπλίταις Ἀθηναίων τῶν ἀπὸ τῶν νεῶν: since no special body of hoplites had been sent from Athens, for land operations, either with Phormion's first squadron or with the second (69. 1, 85. 5), and because no opposition at sea is expected, these hoplites will be the epibatai from the forty ships of the two squadrons, the normal 10 per ship. Note that during the naval campaign in the gulf (83–92) only the Messenian hoplites are on shore. Cf. 23. 2, 86. 2 nn. But one ship had been lost to the enemy with all its crew and others had been killed (90. 5–6, 92. 5); if then 10 was the normal complement of epibatai to a trireme, there must have been fewer than 400 now landed at Astakos, though perhaps not many fewer. Thucydides often ignores casualties when speaking of the continuing activities of a force: cf. 31. 2. (The genitive τῶν ἀπὸ τῶν νεῶν is not, of course, a partitive of *hoplites* on board, but of all Athenians on board. Perhaps we should read τοῖς.)

Κύνητα τὸν Θεολύτου ἐς Κόροντα: he and his father and his city, all unknown, an even obscurer man than Euarchos of Astakos. See 33. 2 n.

2. ἐς γὰρ Οἰνιάδας, κ.τ.λ.: there are considerable remains of Oiniadai still in existence, though much overgrown. It lies immediately to the west of the Acheloos, here a considerable river and difficult to cross, except by boat or swimming, even in summer. It has, as Thucydides says, a long course mainly from north to south, and for most of it between the steep slopes of the Pindos range; largely owing to the snows of Pindos it is the largest river of continental Greece. It comes out into the more level region of Akarnania just above Stratos (near which there is a fordable passage, 80. 8 n.). Owing to the large amount of earth, stones, and brushwood that it brings down, it has formed an alluvial mouth, which causes both marsh land round Oiniadai, to south and west, and the phenomenon of the Echinades Is. which Thucydides describes.

249

διὰ Δολοπίας, κ.τ.λ., must mean, if Thucydides is at all accurate, between Dolopia on the east and Amphilochia and Agraiis on the west, and between Akarnania on the west, and Aitolia (for here the Acheloos seems to have been the boundary between them); and even so there is lack of precision, for Amphilochia did not extend as far east as the river. Woodhouse, pp. 81–84; and see below, iii. 106. 1, 113. 6 nn.

3. ἐλπὶς δὲ καὶ πάσας - - - τοῦτο παθεῖν: it has happened to many, but not to all, owing to the depth of the water not far from the shore.

4. [τῷ μὴ σκεδάννυσθαι]: 'by reason of their soil not being scattered'; or, with Poppo, we should read τοῦ, 'to prevent their being scattered'. The islands tend to be tied with each other, as timber beams 'tie' brick or rubble in a building (75. 5). There is no good reason for bracketing the words (though see Powell, C.Q. xxx, p. 80).

παραλλὰξ καὶ οὐ κατὰ στοῖχον κείμεναι: not in regular columns, one behind the other (from near the shore out to sea), so as to leave a clear passage between them. Thucydides has here in mind two things; that the silt brought down by the Acheloos was not quickly carried out to deep waters in 'lanes' between the islands; and the difficulty of attacking Oiniadai from the sea, with the help of the navy: which could hardly approach the town. And on land, in winter, there was much marsh.

With this interesting geological observation and speculation, cf. Plato's on the steep-to coast of Attica, *Kritias*, 111 A–B. It will be remembered that wide alluvial lands, at river mouths, are rare in mainland Greece and the Aegean islands, and that the Greeks knew of them chiefly from Macedonia, the coast of Ionia and (above all) from the Nile; hence, partly, the interest taken.

5–6. λέγεται δὲ καὶ Ἀλκμέωνι, κ.τ.λ.: once more Thucydides shows his interest in ancient history, and in what we call the mythical period; but here his main concern is with an exceptional natural phenomenon.

One would suppose from the detail of this story that it was not well known in Thucydides' day, or not everywhere known.

ἀπὸ Ἀκαρνᾶνος παιδὸς ἑαυτοῦ: Thucydides does not say that the Akarnanians, like the Amphilochoi (ii. 68. 5), did not at this time speak Greek.

103. 1–2. ἅμα ἦρι - - - καὶ ὁ χειμὼν ἐτελεύτα: it might be argued from this sentence alone that spring was counted part of the winter, or at least began before winter ended. But we should not be pedantic. Thucydides closes the episode, the year's events, with Phormion's return home; which actually overlapped the beginning of the following year. He anticipates a little. The next season's *campaigns* begin later.

250

Naupaktos could be left to be guarded from the land only for the time being, with the enemy fleet dispersed (102. 1). It was not easy to keep up supplies from Athens to so distant a place.

Busolt, iii, pp. 964, 984, notes the absence of any major offensive by Athens at sea in 429, the third year of the war—no attacks on the Peloponnesian coast; and explains it by the continuing effects of the pestilence and the illness of Perikles. Perikles died in the autumn of this year, about the time of the sailing of the squadron that was to reinforce Phormion's and spent some precious time in Crete (85. 5, with n. there).

BOOK III

YEAR 4: 428–427 B.C. (CC. 1–25)

1. *Peloponnesian Invasion of Attica*

1. 1. ἅμα τῷ σίτῳ ἀκμάζοντι: perhaps a little earlier, at least a little more precise, than τοῦ σίτου ἀκμάζοντος, ii. 19. 1, 79. 1 (71. 1 n.); about the middle of May.

Ἀρχίδαμος ὁ Ζευξιδάμου: see ii. 19. 1 n.

2–6, 8–18. *Revolt of Mytilene*

2. 1. μετὰ δὲ τὴν ἐσβολὴν --- εὐθύς: the length of the Peloponnesians' stay in Attica will have been some 30–35 days (ii. 57. 2 n.); so the revolt of Mytilene took place at the end of June. The event here dated is not, probably, the negotiations and preparations immediately to be related, but the outbreak of war (4. 1; or 5. 1, see n. there), or the dispatch of the fleet under Kleippides (3. 2).

Λέσβος πλὴν Μηθύμνης: there were five states in the island, Mytilene the largest of them; three others, Antissa, Pyrra, and Eresos (18. 1), were sympathetic with Mytilene. Methymna, with a democratic form of government, was on the north coast; Mytilene was oligarchic and nationalist. These cities and Chios were the only states which were still autonomous members of the Delian League, contributing each its own squadron of ships, under their own officers, and no tribute (cf. vii. 57. 5).

καὶ πρὸ τοῦ πολέμου: exactly when, we do not know; perhaps when Samos revolted in 440, as Classen suggests, more probably in 433 or 432, when Sparta was preparing for war, but was not at all ready to send help across the Aegean, nor willing to see war started before she herself decided: cf. 13. 1 (Busolt, iii. 836, n. 3).

ἀλλ' οἱ Λακεδαιμόνιοι, κ.τ.λ.: both this clause and ἀναγκασθέντες δέ, κ.τ.λ., in effect answer βουληθέντες μέν with a neat construction— 'they had wanted to revolt before, but had been discouraged', and 'they had long been wanting to revolt, but now, when they did, they acted too soon'. It is wrong, therefore, to put ἀλλ' οἱ Λ. οὐ προσεδέξαντο in parenthesis, as Classen and Hude; compare the way the first contrast is expressed in 13. 1.

2. τῶν --- λιμένων τὴν χῶσιν: cf. ii. 94. 4 n. Mytilene had to guard against an enemy much stronger at sea than herself.

καὶ ἅ: ἃ καί would give a better, because a more precise, clause— 'which they were, indeed, in the act of sending for'.

3. ἰδίᾳ ἄνδρες κατὰ στάσιν: Aristotle, *Pol.* v. 3. 3, p. 1304 a, as an example of small things leading to big events, tells a story of a purely private quarrel, in which a certain Dexandros, proxenos of Athens,

252

piqued at not getting the two heiresses of the rich and aristocratic Timophanes as brides for his sons, stirred the Athenians to war. There will have been more to it than this; and it was natural to Thucydides to pass over even this.

ξυνοικίζουσι: there is no reason to suppose that any removal of the inhabitants of the other cities to Mytilene was intended. Cf. 18. 1, below; and cf. ii. 15. 2 on the synoikismos of Attica.

τὴν παρασκευὴν ἅπασαν: i.e. 'all the preparations which the Athenians could see were being made'. As an autonomous city, Mytilene could secure her food-supplies, and get in some Scythian bowmen, if she wished; but, her enemies said, this was being done in conjunction with Sparta and Boeotia with the intention of seceding from the League.

ξυγγενῶν ὄντων: with Βοιωτῶν only; as Αἰολεῖς, vii. 57. 5, viii. 5. 2, 100. 3.

3. 1. τοῦ πολέμου ἄρτι καθισταμένου καὶ ἀκμάζοντος: Steup argued that καθίστασθαι here, and in 68. 4, could not mean what it means in i. 1. 1 and v. 25. 1, 'come into being', or 'take shape', because, first, this could not be said of a war now in its fourth year, and, secondly, because it contradicts ἀκμάζοντος. The second argument is weak; for a war, like a pestilence (ii. 49. 6), can, and often does, reach its peak very soon after its beginning, while enthusiasm on both sides is still strong—unlike σῖτος, which ἀκμάζει slowly, as it becomes ripe and ready to cut; but the first has some weight. Steup thinks the meaning here must be like that in ἡ καθεστηκυῖα ἡλικία (ii. 36. 3), 'settled, middle age', and so 'as the war was reaching its settled, middle period, some time after its beginning, but before the end could be foreseen'; as, e.g., in Il. xiv. 96; but I prefer to think that καθίστασθαι means here nearly what it does in i. 1. 1, but is modified by καὶ ἀκμάζοντος, and that Thucydides, writing later, is in thought telescoping somewhat the events of the early years of the war. Cf. J.H.S. lxxi, 1951, 71–74, for other and more striking instances of such telescoping.

μέγα μὲν ἔργον, κ.τ.λ.: the Athenians, immediately after the plague, were in a very different mood from what they were later, in 415–413, vii. 28. 3. (We need not say, with Busolt, iii. 1005, that they did not believe that Mytilene was mending her walls, and that this shows how poor were communications at the time. What Athens would have liked not to believe was the Mytilenean intention to revolt.)

2. Κλεϊππίδης: of the deme Acharnai (see below). Nothing further is known of him, except that he had been a candidate for ostracism in the forties, perhaps in 443 (I.G. i.² 911–12; Tod, 45; E. Vanderpool, Hesp. Suppl. vol. viii, 1949, pp. 405–12: many ostraka with his name

253

have, accidentally, survived), so he was now an oldish man; nor of his father Deinias. But we now know that Kleophon was his son (or at least that Kleophon's father's name was Kleïppides Acharneus: Vanderpool, *Hesp.* xxi, 1952, 114–15); it seems that the demagogue was one of Aristophanes' lusty Acharnians. Nothing more is known of Kleïppides' two colleagues either.

3. πολεμεῖν: an infinitive dependent not so much, like εἰπεῖν, on the orders given to Kleïppides, as on εἰπεῖν itself—'with orders to tell them to hand over their fleet, and to say that, if they refused, it meant war', 'that they were at war'.

4. κατὰ τὸ ξυμμαχικόν: we have not been told of this obligation before. Presumably every year, in the spring, a squadron left Mytilene, and another Chios, for Peiraeus, to be sent on whatever expedition the Athenians decided. Cf. viii. 15. 2.

5. διαβὰς ἐς Εὔβοιαν, κ.τ.λ.: the string of participles indicates perhaps the haste of the man; the presence and absence of a copula between any two of them are supposed to be explained by saying that the first two give the stages of the carefully chosen land-route, the last two the manner of the sea-journey, after ὁλκάδος ἀναγομένης ἐπιτυχών has given the fortunate means of accomplishing the latter (Classen). This is unsatisfactory, principally because only πλῷ χρησάμενος shows the manner of the sea-journey; τριταῖος ἀφικόμενος gives the result. What we want is to read καὶ πλῷ χρησάμενος τριταῖος - - - ἀφικόμενος: 'having both found a boat about to sail and had good weather, he reached Mytilene on the third day.' We could translate the whole sentence, 'but the news was brought to Mytilene by a man who crossed from Attica to Euboea, went to Geraistos, and, finding a boat there ready to sail and a favourable wind, reached Mytilene after two days' travelling'.

It is possible to go almost in a straight line from Athens, via Araphen or Brauron, to Geraistos, a distance of about 42 miles, of which 18 are by land; but this man was presumably landed at Karystos (or even farther west), and made his way to Geraistos. From Geraistos to Mytilene is about 140 miles. So the traveller was active as well as fortunate (cf. ii. 97. 1–2 nn.).

τά τε ἄλλα τῶν τειχῶν, κ.τ.λ.: I agree with Steup that the text can stand, as explained by Haacke, and that the change of περί to πέρι (Haase's conjecture, adopted by Stahl) is decidedly for the worse. 'For the rest, they kept guard around the unfinished walls and harbour-works, having palisaded the gaps (literally, sc. αὐτά, the unfinished sections).' But it is not entirely satisfactory; for, whatever Steup may say, it reads naturally that only the unfinished sections of the walls and harbour-works were guarded. We might perhaps construe, 'having palisaded the rest around the unfinished parts of the walls and harbours, they kept watch'.

4. 1. καὶ οἱ Ἀθηναῖοι - - - ὡς ἑώρων: not a case of ὡς *postpositum*, as 5. 1, but the subject, οἱ Ἀθηναῖοι, is resumed in a restricted form, οἱ στρατηγοί; this is clear, because οἱ Ἀθ., not οἱ στρατηγοί, is the subject καθίσταντο. A simple case in fact of a subordinate μέν-clause; and a comma therefore should be placed before ὡς ἑώρων. Cf. 15. 1.

2. τοῦ λιμένος: Mytilene had two harbours, 6. 1 n.; Steup therefore suggested reading τοῦ ἑτέρου λιμένος here; but even with this we should not know which of the two harbours is meant.

4. τῶν τε διαβαλλόντων ἕνα: Dexandros? and was he reconciled to the loss of the rich daughters-in-law? See 2. 3 n.

5. ἐν τῇ Μαλέᾳ: see 6. 2 n., for the discussion of the geographical difficulty. Here suffice it to say that the scholiast, with a characteristic ἀκρωτήριον Λέσβου, does not help; and that Stahl's solution, a comma after Μαλέᾳ and πρὸς βορέαν τῆς πόλεως taken with ἀποστέλλουσι, is not tolerable. Apart from the awkwardness of the order, ἀποστέλλουσι καὶ ἐς τ. Λ. πρ. τριήρει πρὸς βορέαν τῆς πόλεως has no good sense; we should want at least λαθόντες τὸ τ. Ἀθ. ναυτικὸν - - - πρὸς βορέαν τ. π. ⟨ἐξιόντες⟩. Stahl compares for the order of words, 81. 2, τὰς ναῦς περιπλεῦσαι κελεύσαντες ἃς ἐπλήρωσαν ἐς τὸν Ὑλλαϊκὸν λιμένα; we should say, contrast, rather than compare.

6. ταλαιπώρως διὰ τοῦ πελάγους: 'with some distress', not because they were afraid of the open sea, but it was a long journey for a trireme to the Peloponnesian coast (perhaps near Thyrea) without a landing for rest. Cf. 3. 5, and 49. 3–4.

αὐτοῖς ἔπρασσον: αὐτοῖς must be the Spartans, as Classen saw (by contrast with οἱ ἐκ τῶν Ἀθηνῶν, below), not the Lesbians (a *dativus commodi*: which would be αὑτοῖς). What would be the point of 'acted for themselves'? In iv. 106. 2 and v. 76. 3 πράσσειν with the dative means 'acting, or intriguing, on the side of, in the interests of'; iv. 110. 2, οἱ πράσσοντες αὐτῷ, may be more like this passage, 'those who were negotiating with him'; viii. 5. 4 is an exact parallel (Agis was not simply working in the interests of Lesbos).

5. 1. ἐς πόλεμον καθίσταντο: on their side the Athenians were already at war (4. 1). A slight carelessness in expression; Mytilene had tried to avoid war.

Ἴμβριοι καὶ Λήμνιοι: see iv. 28. 4, v. 8. 2, vii. 57. 2. The authors of *A.T.L.*, iii. 293, say that the Imbrioi and Lemnioi "appear again and again as a kind of mobile unit at the disposal of Athenian generals"; and A. H. M. Jones argues that their presence on these four occasions shows that the full hoplite forces of the two islands and of all other cleruchies were regularly sent to Athens during the war and were included in Thucydides' 13,000 hoplites in the ranks (ii. 13. 6, where see n., esp. pp. 37–38). On the contrary, I think the Imbrioi and

255

Lemnioi were seen at Mytilene and in Thrace (v. 8. 2) because their homes were near at hand, and in Sicily because that was a very special occasion and all kinds of troops were engaged; only for the Sphakteria landing (iv. 28. 4) was their presence a chance one, and this is the only passage which might suggest, or support a suggestion, that they were sent to Athens regularly.

If the argument in $A.T.L.$, ibid., is valid that $\H{\alpha}\pi o\iota\kappa o\iota$ (or $\H{\epsilon}\pi o\iota\kappa o\iota$) and $\kappa\lambda\eta\rho o\hat{\upsilon}\chi o\iota$ mean two different kinds of Athenian settlers, in Thucydides and elsewhere (see above, p. 34 n. 1), the authors are doubtless right that the pre-480 settlements in Lemnos and Imbros were $\H{\alpha}\pi o\iota\kappa\acute{\iota}\alpha\iota$ and therefore separate $\pi\acute{o}\lambda\epsilon\iota s$, and for that reason assessed for tribute from the beginning of the Delian League; and that the second settlement in Lemnos c. 450 B.C. was of $\kappa\lambda\eta\rho o\hat{\upsilon}\chi o\iota$, when in accordance with practice elsewhere, the tribute of the island was halved to compensate for the loss of land to the new-comers—the $\kappa\lambda\eta\rho o\hat{\upsilon}\chi o\iota$ being always liable to military service, but not paying tribute. We should have to understand that the $\H{\iota}\mu\beta\rho\iota o\iota$ and $\Lambda\acute{\eta}\mu\nu\iota o\iota$ of the four passages cited above were all from this second settlement. We have mention of them in casualty lists separately from Athenians, but distributed amongst the phylai in the Attic fashion, and the phylai having their Athenian names ($I.G.$ i.² 947–8); but this does not prove that these men were $\kappa\lambda\eta\rho o\hat{\upsilon}\chi o\iota$, for $\H{\alpha}\pi o\iota\kappa o\iota$ also might have the same institutions as Athens, as, for example, those in Aigina (ii. 27. 1, $\H{\epsilon}\pi o\iota\kappa o\iota$, and vii. 57. 2) and at Notion (iii. 34. 4); and in these institutions the phylai would certainly be included. Moreover, Aigina paid no tribute after 431, though an $\H{\alpha}\pi o\iota\kappa\acute{\iota}\alpha$.

2. ἐπὶ τὸ τῶν Ἀθ. στρατόπεδον: that is, the *land* station, which served both the crews of the ships and the land-forces, from Athens, Imbros, etc.; it was presumably at Malea (4. 5).

ἔπειτα οἱ μὲν ἡσύχαζον, κ.τ.λ.: 'from now on, they remained quiet', answered by οἱ δὲ Ἀθηναῖοι in 6. 1; the sentence, καὶ γὰρ αὐτοῖς - - - καὶ ἐκπέμπουσιν, is inserted parenthetically to explain their hopes of aid from the Peloponnese. So Classen. On the other hand, he was perhaps wrong to put only a colon after the parenthesis; for in the next sentence διὰ τὴν τῶν M. ἡσυχίαν is a recognition of the long intervening sentence.

ἐκ Πελοποννήσου - - - κινδυνεύειν: 'wishing to try their fortunes with Peloponnesian help and with other reinforcements'; i.e. 'after further preparations (such as getting food and mercenaries from Scythia, 2. 2) and particularly with help from Peloponnese'. A roughly made, but not very difficult sentence. εἰ προσγένοιτό τι expresses hope rather than expectation.

Μελέας - - - Ἑρμαιώνδας: not otherwise known. They were not very helpful; and seem to have been anxious to get out of Mytilene themselves as soon as possible. No wonder Lesbian hopes were unfulfilled.

6. 1. πολὺ θᾶσσον παρῆσαν: it seems clear from this that the subject allies of Athens still had some say in the matter; in sending land forces, they might or might not at least hurry.

περιορμισάμενοι τὸ πρὸς νότον: 'changed their station and took up position to watch the south side'; they then prepared the necessary camps on land so that they could have a permanent watch (τοὺς ἐφόρμους ποιεῖσθαι), amounting to a blockade, over both harbours. The accusative after περιορμισάμενοι, however, is not easy; ἐπὶ τὸ πρὸς νότον would be easier. Steup, because the Athenians, moving from the north, keep a watch over the northern harbour as well, suggests ⟨καὶ⟩ τὸ πρὸς ν.; but this involves the geographical problem, on which see n. on ἡ Μαλέα, below.

ἐπ᾿ ἀμφοτέροις τοῖς λιμέσιν: cf. Strabo, xiii. 2. 2, p. 617: ἔχει δ᾿ ἡ Μιτυλήνη λιμένας δύο, ὧν ὁ νότιος κλειστὸς τριηρικὸς ναυσὶ πεντήκοντα, ὁ δὲ βόρειος μέγας καὶ βαθύς, χώματι σκεπαζόμενος· πρόκειται δ᾿ ἀμφοῖν νησίον, μέρος τῆς πόλεως ἔχον αὐτόθι συνοικούμενον· κατεσκεύασται δὲ τοῖς πᾶσι καλῶς. That is to say, the two harbours of Mytilene are formed, like those of Syracuse, by a peninsula which was at one time (probably in Thucydides' time) an island and formed the akropolis of the city. The neck of land now connecting the 'akropolis' with the mainland is today called Κουμιδιά, which means a shallow arm of the sea full of sea-weed (D. P. Mantzouránes, Οἱ πρῶτες ἐγκαταστάσεις τῶν Ἑλλήνων στὴ Λέσβο, Mytilene, 1949, p. 19, n. 2).

2. τὸ δὲ περὶ τὰ στρατόπεδα: the Athenians had only a small force with them, and that mainly naval (though since it was all ready for a *periplous* of the Peloponnese, 3. 2, it may have had some land troops, for raiding-parties, on board).

μᾶλλον ἦν: more than what? Perhaps 'more than the other one': i.e. Malea is the site of one of the two camps. But, more probably, a station was maintained at Malea, separate from both camps, and this was used for the import of supplies; i.e. 'rather as a ναύσταθμον πλοίων καὶ ἀγορά than as a camp'.

ἀγορά: soldiers and sailors got some part of their food, when on shore, not as rations, but by purchase, in a permanent or a temporary market; or some officers, as the ταμίαι on the triremes, purchased supplies in bulk from such a local market (cf. vi. 44. 2–3; Ar. *Vesp.* 556–7). On this occasion, however, all supplies will have reached the Athenian forces by sea; Thucydides leaves us to suppose that they had no land communication even with Methymna, which was 30 miles away to the north-west.

ἡ Μαλέα: Thucydides' topography is consistent in itself. The Athenians station themselves 'in Malea to the north of the city' (4. 5), then move to the south of the city, but in such a way as to blockade both harbours (6. 1 : see n.), keeping Malea as a supply base.

Since Thucydides does not tell us the distance of Malea from the city (which is clearly relevant : οὐ πολὺ κατεῖχον οἱ Ἀθηναῖοι), we may perhaps suppose that he took it to be well known. But his account is inconsistent with that of all other writers who mention Malea : Strabo, xiii. 2. 2, pp. 616–17, who says it is the southernmost point of the island (more correct would be the south-easterly point), 70 stades from Mytilene; Xen. *Hell.* i. 6. 26–27; Arist. *Hist. An.* v. 16, 548 b 25; and Ptolemy, v. 2. 29. True, neither Xenophon nor Aristotle gives the position relative to the city of Mytilene;[1] but both say it is a cape, and imply that it was well known, recognizable, and not one of the many headlands, not easily distinguishable from each other, to the north of Mytilene. Thucydides, indeed, does not call it a cape, and implies rather that it was a bay. To get over the difficulty it has been argued, (1) by Stahl, that Thucydides does mean the well-known cape to the south (see 4. 5 n.) and that in 6. 1, περιορμισά-μενοι, κ.τ.λ., means that the fleet moved up from Malea to the south side of the city; apart from other difficulties, it has been objected that C. Malea is too far off to be used as a ναύσταθμον by a force that could only command the land near their own camps. (2) That Thucy-dides was ignorant of the geography of Lesbos and mistook some information given him by others. (3) That there were two places with names somewhat similar and that our MSS., either of Thucy-dides, or of the other writers, have confused the reading; this is Steup's argument, who points out that Μαλία is the reading in Strabo and Μανία in Ptolemy. The second of these three solutions seems the most probable; and, if it is correct, we should conclude that the first Athenian camp was north of the city, as Thucydides says, at one of the small bays there, but that he gives the wrong name to its site.

See also Arrian, *Anab.* ii. 1–3, who describes the siege of Mytilene by Memnon (and mentions another Malea!).[2]

καὶ τὰ μέν, κ.τ.λ.: a pause in the action (the Athenians and Myti-leneans settle down to a quiet and partial blockade), which as often gives Thucydides the opportunity to interrupt the narrative in the interests of chronology. A notable instance of this practice is ii. 78

---

[1] Xenophon's text is corrupt : Kallikratidas' fleet - - - ἐδειπνοποιεῖτο τῆς Λέσβου ἐπὶ τῇ Μαλέᾳ ἄκρᾳ ἀντίον τῆς Μυτιλήνης - - - οἱ Ἀθηναῖοι δειπνοποιούμενοι ἐν ταῖς Ἀργινούσαις· αὗται δ' εἰσὶν ἀντίον τῆς Λέσβου ἐπὶ τῇ Μαλέᾳ ἄκρᾳ ἀντίον τῆς Μυτιλήνης. Marchant follows Krüger in bracketing the first ἀντίον τῆς Μυτιλήνης and the second ἀντίον τῆς Λέσβου ἐπὶ τῇ Μαλέᾳ ἄκρᾳ; but there are clearly other possi-bilities linguistically, for example, to leave the first sentence as it stands and to bracket ἐπὶ τῇ M. ἄ. ἀ. τῆς M. in the second; and this might be thought to be nearer Thucydides' topography.

[2] The Malea mentioned in *I.G.* xii.[2] 74. 16 is perhaps yet another, near Plomarion according to Mantzouránes, *Byz. Zeitschr.* xliv, 1951, 411.

ad fin. He is not of course at all pedantic in this: he carries Asopios' expedition in c. 7 to its conclusion, which was later than the Olympian festival (cc. 8–15), just as in cc. 2–3. 1 he goes back to a time before the Peloponnesian invasion of c. 1.

7. *Asopios in Akarnania and Leukas*

7. 1. περὶ Πελοπόννησον: this had been the first purpose of Kleïppides' squadron (3. 2). The original intention may have been to send Asopios, with fewer ships, to Naupaktos and to help Akarnania; he was given more ships and instructions to raid the Peloponnese after Kleïppides had been diverted.

τῶν Φορμίωνός τινα σφίσι πέμψαι: see n. on ii. 92. 7, p. 234. The popularity of Phormion in Akarnania doubtless began with his first expedition there (ii. 68. 7; for the date see iii. 105. 1 n.). An Akarnanian about this time called his son Phormion; who became grandfather to another Phormion, honoured at Athens in 337 B.C. (*I.G.* ii.² 237 = Tod, 178).

3. ἐπ' Οἰνιάδας: ii. 102. 2 n.

κατὰ τὸν Ἀχελῷον ἔπλευσε: κατά as in κατὰ θάλασσαν and κατὰ γῆν, 'by river', not 'down stream'. Π²² (5th–6th century A.D.) had ἀνέπλευσε, probably a reading which was derived from an explanatory note.

4. ἐς Νήρικον: mentioned in the *Odyssey*, xxiv. 377 (which is all that the scholiast can tell us). Strabo, x. 2. 8, p. 452.

φρουρῶν τινῶν: perhaps foreign troops (e.g. Corinthians) in contrast to οἱ αὐτόθεν ξυμβοηθήσαντες (Classen).

8–15. *Mytilenean Envoys at Olympia*

8. 1. οἱ δὲ ἐπὶ τῆς πρώτης νεώς: the second embassy (5. 2 ad fin.) had indeed little to do.

εἶπον Ὀλυμπίαζε παρεῖναι: one would like to know whether this caused any delay. The various actions related in c. 4 should not have taken more than a week to ten days, and if Kleïppides left Athens at the end of June (2. 1 n.), the Mytilenean envoys should have arrived at Sparta somewhere about the middle of July. (They may have taken a circuitous route to avoid Athenian triremes; but they must travel as quickly as possible, as they got very little rest διὰ τοῦ πελάγους κομιζόμενοι, 4. 6 n.) According to Busolt, iii. 912 n., who followed Mommsen and Nissen, the Olympic festival took place in 428 during the five days August 11–15. If all these assumptions are correct, there was considerable delay, offset in part by a hoped-for delay in the negotiations in Athens; but that Sparta wanted the envoys to get first into touch with her allies, and persuade them, is sufficient evidence that she was not acting in haste. After the meeting at Olympia, however, she is very eager.

259

καὶ οἱ ἄλλοι ξύμμαχοι: neutrals as well, and indeed enemies, if the Olympic truce held. Presumably Sparta sent word to her allies to send suitable delegates to Olympia: 'combine politics with a visit to the races'.

ἦν δὲ 'Ολυμπιὰς ᾗ Δωριεὺς 'Ρόδιος τὸ δεύτερον ἐνίκα: Dorieus won the pankration at Olympia at three successive festivals (432, 428, 424). In later times at least it was the name of the victor in the stadion which served to date the Olympiad (cf. Diodoros on this year, Ἠλεῖοι ἤγαγον 'Ολυμπιάδα ὀγδόην πρὸς ταῖς ὀγδοήκοντα, καθ' ἣν ἐνίκα στάδιον Σύμμαχος Μεσσήνιος ἀπὸ Σικελίας, xii. 49. 1);[1] and this reference to Dorieus' victory may not therefore be another date, but only a record of a celebrated event (as 'this was the year in which the Prime Minister won the Derby'). In v. 49. 1, however, where also the Olympic festival is the scene of an event, the victor in the pankration is again mentioned; it may be therefore that a method of identifying Olympiads had not yet been settled.

For Dorieus, see viii. 35. 1; Xen. Hell. i. 5. 19; Paus. vi. 7. 1–6; S.I.G.³ 82 (he won 8 Isthmian, 7 Nemean, and 4 Pythian victories, besides his 3 at Olympia: Tod, C.Q. xliii, 1949, 106). His name became proverbial of the successful athlete (Arist. Rhet. i. 2. 13; Cic. Tusc. i. 46. 111). He was driven out of his own city of Ialysos in Rhodes, in a στάσις, and became a citizen of Thourioi; but when, is quite uncertain. Beloch, iii. 1. 43, n. 2, argues that he must already have migrated by 428, for, as a citizen of Ialysos, within the Delian League, he could not have competed at Olympia during the war; Thourioi, it is true, was an Athenian foundation, but, according to Beloch, already on no very friendly terms. If Beloch is right, it is another reason for thinking that Thucydides is not mentioning his victory as a means of dating; for officially Dorieus would have been called Θούριος. And indeed 'Ρόδιος would hardly have been officially used for 'Ιαλύσιος in 428; on the basis of his statue at Delphi, which has been found, 'Ρόδιος has been restored (S.I.G.³ 82), but this inscription was cut in the fourth century. Pausanias, commenting on the companion statue at Olympia, says ἀνηγορεύοντο δὲ οὗτός τε καὶ Πεισίροδος Θούριοι.

The inscription records as well four victories of Dorieus at the Panathenaia and others at the Asklepieia (Epidauros), Hekatombaia (Argos), and Lykaia (Arkadia), which Pausanias omits. If Beloch's view is right, we should have to suppose that all his Panathenaic contests were won before 428 (429–428 being the latest date for his exile from Ialysos), and his Peloponnesian and Delphic contests before 431 and after 429. This on the whole seems reasonable; the alternative would be to suppose that the Olympic truce, and perhaps the

[1] But Diodoros succeeds in dating the Mytilenean revolt to the next year, 427, xii. 55. 1.

Nemean and Isthmian, were observed even for enemy contestants (which is possible: see e.g. viii. 10. 1), and to put the other Peloponnesian victories before 431.

9. 1. τοὺς γὰρ ἀφισταμένους: we should, I think, translate strictly, 'those who secede' or 'withdraw from an alliance', not 'rebel' or 'revolt', as from a master. It is used of Plataia 'breaking away' from Athens, 55. 3, of Kerkyra, iii. 70. 1, of Corinth and Tegea from Sparta, v. 30. 1, 32. 3, 14. 4, etc.

ἐν ἡδονῇ ἔχουσι: 'are glad to see them.' "Man liebt den Verrat, man hasst den Verräter"—Böhme. Stahl compares Dem. xviii. 47; Liv. xxvii. 17; Tac. *Ann.* i. 58; the comparison is interesting, for Demosthenes is alive, the others only repeat a commonplace.

3. μηδέ τῷ χείρους, κ.τ.λ.: the negative here follows grammatically on οὐκ ἦν; and we should perhaps place the full stop after ἀποστάσεως and the colon after ἦν.

The anxiety of the Mytileneans about their reception is natural enough; for it is true that all suspect the turncoat, and tend to think little of the help he is likely to bring. (At this time, indeed, Sparta was actually engaged in 'liberating Greece', and might expect the support of the subjects of Athens (cf. iv. 85); but Mytilene, ἐν τῇ εἰρήνῃ τιμώμενοι, was rather a special case—see 10. 5 especially.) But in a different society, we should not expect to see this so frankly avowed in the course of diplomatic negotiations for a change of sides; nor perhaps the confessions of the Mytileneans in c. 10 of how far they had gone with Athens.

10. 1. μετ' ἀρετῆς δοκούσης: 'with apparent honesty'; "cum conspicua honestate, i.e. societas ita fieri debet, ut honestas in ea appareat"—Stahl (rather than 'with what is generally reputed to be honesty', as L. and S.). But I agree with Classen that the subject of γίγνοιντο, as obviously that of εἶεν, is ἰδιῶται καὶ πόλεις. Böhme conjectured γίγνοιτο.

Note the meaning of ἀρετή here, 'honesty', 'sincerity'. In the first line of the chapter it might have meant something like courage (corresponding to the last sentence of c. 9, 'do not think the worse of us for deserting Athens in her hour of danger'); but this clause makes the meaning clear.

ὁμοιότροποι: not with any special reference to the oligarchic government of Mytilene, which, if intended, must have been more explicit (Classen); for all that there is a hint of 'you and we know what the canaille is like'.

τῷ διαλλάσσοντι τῆς γνώμης: 'with different ways of thought', or 'with a conflict of fundamental principles'.

2. ξυμμαχία ἐγένετο, κ.τ.λ.: Hdt. ix. 106 and Thuc. i. 95. 1. There is no need to look for inaccuracies of detail here, or inconsistencies between the two historians.

3. ξύμμαχοι - - - Ἀθηναίοις - - - τοῖς Ἕλλησιν: most edd. take the two datives with $\xi\acute{\upsilon}\mu\mu\alpha\chi o\iota$ because 13. 1, $\delta\iota\pi\lambda\grave{\eta}\nu$ $\mathring{a}\pi\acute{o}\sigma\tau\alpha\sigma\iota\nu$, $\kappa.\tau.\lambda.$, gives, rhetorically, the dissolution of this alliance. See, however, the n. there; and $\mathring{A}\theta\eta\nu\alpha\acute{\iota}o\iota s$ would more easily perhaps be taken as dative with $\kappa\alpha\tau\alpha\delta o\acute{\upsilon}\lambda\omega\sigma\iota s$, as in vi. 76. 4, or, better, as a *dativus commodi*, with $\tau o\hat{\iota}s$ $\mathring{E}\lambda\lambda\eta\sigma\iota\nu$ in rhetorical antithesis ('liberation from Persia in the interests of Greece', 'for Greece'); a simpler writer would have had $\mathring{\epsilon}\lambda\epsilon\upsilon\theta\epsilon\rho\acute{\omega}\sigma\epsilon\iota$ $\alpha\mathring{\upsilon}\tau\hat{\omega}\nu$ $\mathring{a}\pi\grave{o}$ $\tau o\hat{\upsilon}$ $M\acute{\eta}\delta o\upsilon$. Since the Delian League was specifically an alliance against Persia, the members of it were $o\acute{\iota}$ $\mathring{E}\lambda\lambda\eta\nu\epsilon s$ and their first officers $\mathring{E}\lambda\lambda\eta\nu o\tau\alpha\mu\acute{\iota}\alpha\iota$ ($A.T.L.$ iii. 97, n. 12; Larsen, $Harv.$ $Stud.$ li, 1940, 202: where Thuc. i. 109. 4, 110. 1 would be perhaps better instances; and see above, p. 31).

Brasidas' speech at Akanthos, iv. 85–87, makes an interesting comparison with this one; and 87. 6, $\tau o\hat{\iota}s$ $\mathring{E}\lambda\lambda\eta\sigma\iota\nu$ $\mathring{a}\rho\xi\alpha\iota$ $\pi\rho\hat{\omega}\tau o\iota$ $\mathring{\epsilon}\lambda\epsilon\upsilon\theta\epsilon\rho\acute{\iota}\alpha s$, a parallel to the use of the dative. Cf. also Xen. $Hell.$ ii. 2. 23 (above, p. 15).

4. ἐπαγομένους: 'supplying for themselves'; but Ross's $\mathring{\epsilon}\pi\epsilon\iota\gamma o\mu\acute{\epsilon}\nu o\upsilon s$, a better contrast to $\mathring{a}\nu\iota\acute{\epsilon}\nu\tau\alpha s$, is to be preferred. Brasidas used the more obvious word $\mathring{\epsilon}\pi\iota\phi\acute{\epsilon}\rho\epsilon\iota\nu$, but not in an obvious way: see iv. 87. 6 n. (It is perhaps worth recording the schol.: $\mu\epsilon\tau\hat{\eta}\kappa\tau\alpha\iota$ $\delta\grave{\epsilon}$ $\mathring{a}\mu\phi\acute{o}\tau\epsilon\rho\alpha$ $\mathring{a}\pi\grave{o}$ $\tau\hat{\omega}\nu$ $\tau o\grave{\upsilon}s$ $\delta\epsilon\sigma\mu o\grave{\upsilon}s$ $\mathring{a}\nu\iota\acute{\epsilon}\nu\tau\omega\nu$ $\tau\epsilon$ $\kappa\alpha\grave{\iota}$ $\mathring{\epsilon}\pi\alpha\gamma\acute{o}\nu\tau\omega\nu$, $\mathring{o}\pi\epsilon\rho$ $\mathring{\epsilon}\sigma\tau\grave{\iota}$ $\sigma\phi\iota\gamma\gamma\acute{o}\nu\tau\omega\nu$, i.e. not 'supplying', but 'applying', in their own interests.)

5. διὰ πολυψηφίαν: this was doubtless one of the reasons—the difficulty, natural enough in a large body, of getting a sufficient number to agree (see below, 11. 4, n. on the meetings of members of the League); but another reason was that very many of the states of the League were small, and would rally behind Athens as a protection against more powerful neighbours—not to mention much pro-Athenian feeling of the masses in all the larger states, especially those with a ruling class of the rich (11. 4 n.).

ἀμύνασθαι: the present tense (with ABEFM suprascr. G) seems preferable; the subjection, $\mathring{\epsilon}\delta o\upsilon\lambda\acute{\omega}\theta\eta\sigma\alpha\nu$, is seen as one action, but it took place because 'we were never able, on the several occasions, to unite in self-defence'.

ἡμεῖς δέ: throughout this passage there is a variation, almost a vagueness, in the use of 'we' for the Greek allies of Athens in general, and for Lesbos and Chios, distinct from the rest, and for Lesbos only. Cf. 11. 1.

6. ἐδυνήθησαν, κ.τ.λ.: 'they would have enslaved us like the rest had they had the power; hence our mistrust of their leadership. And this independence of ours, such as it is, will be more and more irksome to them, the greater their power and the more isolated we

262

become (11. 1).' So Böhme. The MSS. reading is preferable to Dobree's δυνηθεῖεν, adopted by Hude. 40. 5 gives a similar construction: ἃ εἰκὸς ἦν αὐτοὺς ποιῆσαι κρατήσαντας ὑμῶν (= εἰ ἐκράτησαν).

11. 1. χαλεπώτερον εἰκότως ἔμελλον οἴσειν, κ.τ.λ.: 'the very fact that (καὶ πρός) the majority had yielded made our isolation more difficult for Athens to put up with'; referring to the natural distaste of the arrogant Athenians for Mytilene's pretensions to independence. καί, which Dobree bracketed, is needed; πρός means 'in relation to' or 'compared with'. "Genetivus absolutus est, non ex χαλεπώτερον οἴσειν pendet (cf. i. 77. 3, ii. 62. 3, 65. 4), cuius obiectum ex ἡμῖν ὁμιλοῦντες repetendum est" (Stahl). i. 77. 3 gives the Athenian attitude to this 'equality', and applies the equality to all the allies (οἱ δὲ εἰθισμένοι πρὸς ἡμᾶς ἀπὸ τοῦ ἴσου ὁμιλεῖν, κ.τ.λ.).

Though the words καὶ πρός - - - ἀντισουμένου add nothing to the *fact* stated in ὑποχειρίους δὲ - - - ὁμιλοῦντες, they have considerable rhetorical force, and there is no case for Steup's deletion of them. Note that μόνου ἀντισουμένου formally at least, ignores Chios, which, with Methymna, was the last of the independent allies (vii. 57. 4–5).

The size of the independent fleets was considerable, even though no match for that of Athens at full strength (ii. 13. 8, iii. 16. 1): Samos had 70 triremes in 440 (20 of them used mainly for transport), Mytilene and Chios sent 55 between them to help subdue her (i. 116. 1–2, 117. 2), and they doubtless had many others. In 413–412 Chios had 60 triremes, after considerable losses in Sicily (viii. 6. 4; vi. 43, vii. 20. 2).

2. τὸ δὲ ἀντίπαλον δέος: Steup is right that this follows closely on the foregoing sentence (ὁ δέ ἀντὶ τοῦ γάρ, schol.), which should end with a colon rather than a full stop.

ἀντίπαλον δέος is "mutui metus aequalitas" (Stahl), if by that is meant 'fear based on equal power', as the schol. (Böhme and others). Steup regards this as forced; and because the resulting generalization is quite out of keeping with 10. 1 and 12. 1, which postulate εὔνοια and ἀρετὴ δοκοῦσα as the necessary basis for alliance, he would bracket δέος. But this hardly helps; for 'equal strength is the *only* guarantee for an alliance' is also quite different in tone from 10. 1 and 12. 1. In 9. 2 equal strength is stated to be necessary, but combined with εὔνοια. Thucydides in fact represents the Mytileneans as maintaining different views in different contexts: 'virtue' would be necessary when they were asking for an alliance with Sparta; but between Athens and Mytilene there can only be fear, on each side, and an alliance is possible only if strength on each side also is equal (cf. i. 91. 7). But we might have expected this point to have been made more explicit; generalized as it is, it would hardly appeal to Sparta. Cf. i. 77. 5 n.

263

3. γνώμης μᾶλλον ἐφόδῳ ἢ ἰσχύος: the rhetorical use of ἔφοδος ('attack') with γνώμης must not be missed. Not "vielmehr mit kluger Berechnung, als mit offner Gewalt: ἐφόδῳ, μεθόδῳ" (Classen), still less "ἔφοδος in weaker sense, 'aditus', with γνώμης, in stronger, 'impetus', with ἰσχύος", "by diplomatic approach rather than by armed aggression" (Spratt); but something like 'by moral pressure', or 'moral rather than armed force', explained by ἐν τῷ αὐτῷ, κ.τ.λ., below, as εὐπρεπείᾳ λόγου is explained by μὴ ἂν τούς γε ἰσοψήφους, κ.τ.λ.

4. τούς γε ἰσοψήφους: the power of independent action still possessed by Mytilene and Chios may not have been great in practice; but they not only had their own navies, built and manned by themselves, but formally must agree, in their own constitutional manner, to send squadrons for particular campaigns to the assistance of the League, i.e. the Athenian, forces. This freedom was modified by the obligation to send a squadron of ten ships every year of the war to Peiraeus (3. 4).

The authors of *A.T.L.* (iii. 138–41) take ἰσοψήφους here and πολυψηφίαν in 10. 5 to refer to voting in the *synodoi* of the League (i. 96. 2–97. 1). They suppose that these meetings continued to take place after the transfer of the treasury from Delos to Athens, but in Athens at the time of the Panathenaia; and that at them every state, large and small, including Athens, had but one vote. Hence, Mytilene was ἰσόψηφος with Athens, and the larger states would find difficulty in getting a majority because the many small ones would vote with Athens (διὰ πολυψηφίαν). Such procedure may have lasted till the Samian war of 440–439, for the Mytileneans doubtless have here in mind the awkward question, 'why did you and Chios join Athens in subduing Samos (i. 116. 1–2)?' but they had ceased, even as a formality, before the Peloponnesian war began. This view may be correct, but I doubt the last point, that these *synodoi* ceased after 439; for Mytilene would surely have used it to strengthen their case now: 'even this small right has now been taken from us'; and if this doubt is just, it weakens somewhat the rest of the argument. Perhaps the *synodoi* were held, after 454, at the time of the Dionysia, when delegates from all the tribute-paying cities were present, and the few autonomous states, invited to Athens, could be impressed by the number of dutiful subjects, and also by the grandeur of the festival of Dionysos. But see Meiggs, *J.H.S.* lxiii, 1943, 33.

Larsen regrets that the voting in the *synodoi* was not secret (*C.P.* xliv, 1949, 177): "a secret vote might have been an advantage. With it the smaller states might not have been intimidated and might actually have dared to vote contrary to the interests of Athens. It would be claiming too much to say that secret voting in the symmachies (Delian, Peloponnesian, and Achaian) would have saved the causes of Greek freedom and Panhellenic unity and co-operation, but it might have helped considerably." Or have led to their immediate break-up, if, for example, many states had sided with Naxos in 468? The alternative would have been Athens' taking even more high-handed action than in fact she did.

ἄκοντας: one scholiast read ἑκόντας, which Steup prefers. It is obvious that either will do, and that with ἄκοντας the sentence means: 'Athens argues that she could not have compelled us against our will to join in an attack on an innocent city; so, since we did join in, the city was not innocent, and we were willing allies.'

ἐπί τε τοὺς ὑποδεεστέρους πρώτους: not historically true; for the earliest secessions had been, naturally, made by the more powerful states, Naxos and Thasos. Nor could Mytilene very easily excuse herself for helping to reduce Aigina (i. 105. 2) and Samos (i. 116. 1–2).

τὰ τελευταῖα λιπόντες: whether we keep the article or not, τελευταῖα is predicative: 'leaving them, τὰ κράτιστα, to the last.' Cf. 23. 3, οἱ τελευταῖοι.

6. τό τε ναυτικόν, κ.τ.λ.: for this third reason why Athens refrained from suppressing Lesbian independence (again a false argument, for Naxos, Thasos, and Samos had fleets), cf. i. 44. 2.

καθ' ἓν γενόμενον: there is a slight difficulty here, for γενόμενον appears to be dependent on προσθέμενον (or vice versa?), and there is little point in emphasizing the uniting of the entire Lesbian fleet (Steup). A better meaning would be the uniting of all the remaining independent squadrons (in fact only the Lesbian and Chian), if we may take ἡμεῖς to refer not to Mytilene only in the sentences beginning with § 3.

7. τὰ δὲ καὶ ἀπὸ θεραπείας: this amounts to a damaging admission—they had courted the Athenian public and leading Athenians—though they put the best face on it; cf. 12. 1. Müller–Strübing, *Arist. u. d. hist. Kritik*, 366, compares *Wasps*, 672–9; more to the point is *Acharnians*, 633–45—especially perhaps, καὶ τοὺς δήμους ἐν ταῖς πόλεσιν δείξας ὡς δημοκρατοῦνται; for, though Mytilene had been conquered two years before *The Acharnians* was produced, and one year before *The Babylonians*, doubtless Mytilenean envoys in Athens, whatever the effective constitution of Mytilene was, had, like others, paid lip-service to democracy. This pretence Aristophanes, who was hardly a stout defender of 'the cities', saw through ('I pointed out what sort of democratic government they had'; for the meaning of δημοκρατοῦνται, see Lysias, xii. 4). Add *Equit.* 801–2, ἵνα μᾶλλον σὺ μὲν ἁρπάζῃς καὶ δωροδοκῇς παρὰ τῶν πόλεων, and Ps.-Xen. i. 16–18.

Isokrates in his *Panegyrikos* (iv), 104, went far in the opposite direction: οὐ γὰρ ἐφθονοῦμεν ταῖς αὐξανομέναις αὐτῶν οὐδὲ ταραχὰς ἐνεποιοῦμεν πολιτείας ἐναντίας παρακαθίσταντες, ἵν' ἀλλήλοις μὲν στασιάζοιεν ἡμᾶς δὲ ἀμφότεροι θεραπεύοιεν. The whole of this passage is interesting for those who believe both in the harshness of Athenian rule and in the political acumen of Isokrates. Cf. 38. 1, n. on τὰς μὲν Μυτιληναίων ἀδικίας.

12. 1. τίς οὖν αὕτη, κ.τ.λ.: it is characteristic of many speeches in Thucydides that much sophistic argument is suddenly broken by a rhetorical outburst which seems very much to belong to the speeches and the occasion. Cf. i. 85 (Archidamos), iv. 64 (Hermokrates).

ἐγίγνετο: 'was becoming', 'was proving to be', very much as in ii. 65. 9.

παρὰ γνώμην: 'insincerely', against our true feelings or judgements. ὑποδέχεσθαι is the regular word, from Homer onwards, for friendly reception; so here, of states, 'friendly intercourse'. See Classen's n.

οἱ μὲν ἡμᾶς - - - ἐθεράπευον: we have not had this stated explicitly before, but it serves admirably to screen their own θεραπεία of Athens (11. 7 n.). 9. 3 puts the same matter rather differently.

ὅ τε τοῖς ἄλλοις, κ.τ.λ.: I can only say with Classen ,"je öfter ich diese Stelle lese und erwäge, desto weniger kann ich glauben, daβ sie so, wie sie in den Hss. steht, von Th. geschrieben sei"; and I agree that the only solution is to bracket πίστιν, as an inaccurate marginal note to ὅ and its antecedent τοῦτο—inaccurate, for what *fear* strengthens for us and goodwill for others, is not πίστις but the alliance, as the next sentence makes clear.

κατεχόμενοι ξύμμαχοι: 'held down as allies' (for κατέχεσθαι cf. Hdt. i. 59. 1), a form of expression similar to ἐλευθερίαν ἐπιφέρειν (iv. 87. 6 n.).

παράσχοι ἀσφάλεια θάρσος: in other circumstances or cases it is ἀμαθία which makes for boldness, ii. 40. 3, or hope, iv. 10. 1, or an intelligent understanding of facts, ii. 62. 4–5.

παραβήσεσθαι ἔμελλον: cf. 11. 2.

3. εἰ γὰρ δυνατοὶ ἦμεν, κ.τ.λ.: another much vexed sentence. Certain things seem to be clear: (1) we cannot have ἐπ' ἐκείνοις εἶναι in the sense 'to be at their mercy' (if it can ever mean this: see Antiphon, v. 3) followed by ἐπ' ἐκείνοις ὄντος, 'because it is in their power' to do something (the normal meaning: ii. 84. 2); (2) even if we could, 'why should we be in their power?' is not the required antithesis to προαμύνασθαι; and (3) ἐκ τοῦ ὁμοίου, which answers to ἐκ τοῦ ἴσου, would have no meaning. There is nothing wrong in itself with the MSS. reading, καὶ ἀντεπιβουλεῦσαι καὶ ἀντιμελλῆσαι (they have ἀντεπιμελλῆσαι, for which see below): 'if it were equally within our power both to take action against Athens and to bide our time'—a power which Athens has and has displayed by not yet subduing Mytilene (τὴν ἐκείνων μέλλησιν)—makes excellent sense; but in view of the other difficulties, I feel that Krüger's ἐπ' ἐκείνους ἰέναι gives the meaning we need, and that therefore Heilmann's ingenious ἀντεπιβουλεῦσαι, καὶ ἀντιμελλῆσαί τι is to be adopted (so Stahl, Böhme, Classen, Steup, and Hude, except that the first two would simply delete ἐπ' ἐκείνοις εἶναι, producing an awkward order): 'if it were equally in our power to move against them in our turn, then, we agree, we ought similarly to have waited before attacking them; but since the initiative is always with them, you must concede to us the right to anticipate an attack by measures of self-defence.' For καί - - - καί in subordinate and principal clauses, cf. i. 83. 3, though there there can be no ambiguity. Stahl's objection to ἐπ' ἐκείνους ἰέναι that it must mean *invade*, in the literal sense, which Mytilene cannot do, is pedantic; but another possibility is ὁμόσε ἐκείνοις ἰέναι, 'get to grips with them'—cf. ii. 62. 3, where also there was no question of either invasion or even a battle in open field.

All our good MSS. have ἀντεπιμελλῆσαι (except that, by an obvious slip, AB have ἀντεπιμελῆσαι—corr. B¹). No recent editor prints this, but I do not feel certain that Thucydides could not have coined the word for rhetorical effect—he was fond of such compounds, especially those using ἀντεπι-, and he could coin κακοξύνετος, vi. 76. 4; it gives excellent sense, 'to wait with hostile intent in our turn'; and it certainly does not look like an ordinary copyist's mistake. It is doubtful, however, whether it would be used other than absolutely (i.e. with it we should have to keep the old punctuation, ἀντεπιμελλῆσαι, τί, not Heilmann's).

13. 1. προφάσεις καὶ αἰτίας: see i. 23. 6 n., and above on ii. 49. 2. The meanings of these words need further discussion, particularly in the light of G. M. Kirkwood's article in *A.J.P.* lxxiii, 1952, 37–61, and L. C. Pearson's excellent paper, *T.A.P.A.* lxxxiii, 1952, 205–23; who, I think, is right in giving 'explanation' as the fundamental meaning of πρόφασις, explanation of conduct that needs explaining, and which may be an external event (an αἰτία), a motive of the person whose conduct is in question (another kind of αἰτία), or an excuse made by him. In this passage, however, I differ in thinking that the combination προφάσεις καὶ αἰτίας is rhetorical; and that, if we are to distinguish between them, αἰτίαι are 'our complaints' (which are σαφεῖς τοῖς ἀκούουσι, κ.τ.λ.: cf. Dem. xviii. 12, xxii. 21–22— though in the latter αἰτία falls short of producing full conviction), and προφάσεις are external causes (Athens' behaviour towards her allies generally), ἱκανὰς ἡμᾶς ἐκφοβῆσαι, as in i. 23. 6; but I doubt whether such precision is intended.

βουλομένους μέν, κ.τ.λ.: see 2. 1.

εὐθὺς ὑπηκούσαμεν: as though they were the most willing and self-sacrificing of allies, who therefore deserve some support. 2. 3 and 5. 4 do not support the claim; nor does the rest of this speech. § 2 below gives the consequence of this eagerness to help a good cause.

ἀποστήσεσθαι διπλῆν ἀπόστασιν: 'we thought that we should be making a double secession'; a conceit in the sophistic manner (and not unlike those of the Elizabethans). It will help if we remember that every ἀπόστασις from the Athenian empire was in form, and to some extent genuinely, a 'withdrawal' from the League, a secession, not a revolt of subjects (9. 1 n.). See 10. 3 n.; we should observe that ἀπὸ τῶν Ἑλλήνων here is not a dissolution, rhetorically so described, of the alliance there mentioned: that was for the purpose of freeing Greek states from Persia, this was to subject Greek states to Athens. ξὺν κακῶς ποιεῖν is explained by ξυνεστρατεύσαμεν (against seceding states), 10. 5, and ξυστρατεύειν, 11. 4; and I believe that αὐτοῖς is implied with ξὺν κακῶς ποιεῖν—'hitherto we have joined with them (i.e. we have all been members of the same league) in helping Athens to do them harm; we are now withdrawing'. In ξυνελευθεροῦν the compound is used only for rhetorical effect; for their fellow liberators are the Peloponnesian Alliance; or does this also mean 'join with other members of the league in a battle for freedom'?

προποιῆσαι: not, I think, 'to destroy them first', a precise meaning being given to ποιῆσαι from διαφθαρῆναι, but quite generally, 'to take action first', 'to forestall' (= προαμύνασθαι, 12. 3).

2. ᾗ καὶ μᾶλλον χρὴ ξυμμάχους δεξαμένους ἡμᾶς: we badly need ὑμᾶς to mark the change of subject—'we have done our part, and we are not fully prepared; you must therefore help us'; and the scholiast may have had it in his text—τὸ ἑξῆς· ξυμμάχους ἡμᾶς δεξαμένους ὑμᾶς τοὺς Λακεδαιμονίους. I would insert it before or after χρή. Steup saw this need, and besides assumed a larger lacuna in order to explain both the absence of any specific appeal for help in Lesbos and the sudden introduction in § 4 of the new theme, a second invasion of Attica that summer, and with a fleet as well as the army.

ἵνα φαίνησθε, κ.τ.λ.: as Classen says in his n. on 10. 1, the Mytileneans divide their arguments for Peloponnesian support into two main divisions—a moral claim and the strategic advantage. These are here summed up, and the second now developed in some detail.

3. νόσῳ τε γὰρ ἐφθάραται Ἀθηναῖοι: the fierce Athenian reaction to this confident assumption (36. 2) is not so surprising.

χρημάτων δαπάνῃ: though ἐφθάραται was a great exaggeration, Athens had certainly already spent much of her reserve fund: see below, n. on 102.

4. οὐκ εἰκὸς αὐτοὺς περιουσίαν νεῶν ἔχειν: the Athenians at this time, owing to the pestilence, had difficulty in keeping their ships in good trim and in manning them; but of course they had the 100 best in special reserve (ii. 24. 2), and more than 70 (3. 2, 7. 1) besides. The Mytileneans knew this well enough; but they are saying ἐφολκὰ καὶ οὐ τὰ ὄντα, and they also deceived themselves about the strength

268

of Athens, as did so many of the subject states later (iv. 108. 4–5, vii. 28. 3). The Peloponnesians had had some warning, but perhaps a misleading one, the previous winter (ii. 93–94). The consequence is related in 16. 2.

ναυσί τε καὶ πεζῷ ἅμα: ναυσί is the important word. The Athenian allies at least will have begun to realize by now that land-invasions of Attica would not by themselves be decisive.

5. ἀλλοτρίας γῆς πέρι οἰκεῖον κίνδυνον: the Athenians in 432 had said that this was what the Peloponnesians would be doing if they decided on war (i. 78. 1), and Archidamos had in effect agreed (i. 83. 3); the Corinthians had in general denied it (i. 120. 2). The argument, ever necessary, was common: cf. vi. 78. 1. Hude's conjecture ⟨οὐκ⟩ οἰκεῖον is unnecessary; it is clear that you might put the matter either way, as with ἄκοντας and ἔκοντας in 11. 4.

οὐ γὰρ ἐν τῇ Ἀττικῇ ἔσται ὁ πόλεμος, κ.τ.λ.: again compare Archidamos' words, i. 81. 2, 83. 2. As Classen pointed out, ἐν τῇ Ἀ. here is not used in a strictly geographical sense ('the war will not be fought in Attica'—the Mytileneans have just asked that it should be), but 'the issue of the war will not depend only on the resources of Attica (which you might destroy)'.

6. τῶν χρημάτων - - - ἡ πρόσοδος: i. 80. 3–4, ii. 13. 2. (I would punctuate with a colon only before ἔστι δὲ τῶν χρημάτων.)

ἔτι μείζων ἔσται, εἰ ἡμᾶς καταστρέψονται: but see 39. 8, 46. 3. πάθοιμέν τ' ἂν δεινότερα proved true.

7. βοηθησάντων δὲ ὑμῶν: the most remarkable case of a genitive absolute in Thucydides where the noun is also the subject of the main verb; most of the other cases are easy enough, and only viii. 76. 4 is comparable. As Classen says, the clause describes the second major alternative, and the genitive brings this into greater prominence: 'if we are left to ourselves and defeated, Athens will be stronger than before; if you help us, victory will be nearer.' ὑμῶν is 'you' seen from a somewhat different angle from the subject of προσλήψεσθε. Cf. Plat. Rep. v. 458 D, with Adam's n.

τήν τε αἰτίαν - - - ἣν εἴχετε: cf. i. 69. 5, and, for examples, i. 101, 114. The opening words of the next chapter (τάς τε - - - ἐλπίδας) also recall αἵ γε ὑμέτεραι ἐλπίδες in i. 69. 5. εἴχετε, read by most edd., is rather more diplomatic than ἔχετε, the reading of BG.

14. 1. ἐν οὗ τῷ ἱερῷ, κ.τ.λ.: 'we are virtually suppliants within his precinct'; the meeting was not in fact being held there.

κοινοτέραν: a purely rhetorical comparative (for 'common' can hardly have one), but very effective; and it means 'common to a larger number of states', 'more widely spread'.

μὴ πεισθέντων ὑμῶν: 'we shall do more widespread harm if we are conquered because you have not been persuaded by us', a flattering way of assuming the responsibility, while saying that their security depends on Spartan help.

15–16, 18. Failure of Attempt at Second Invasion of Attica. Mytilene besieged

15. 1. καὶ τὴν ἐς τὴν Ἀττικὴν ἐσβολήν, κ.τ.λ.: though the order of words is a natural one (cf. ii. 62. 1), the resulting sentence, to express a simple idea, is unnecessarily complex. We need not, however, make too much of the change of subject from οἱ Λ. καὶ οἱ ξύμμαχοι to οἱ Λ. only, for the former were, in a sense, also the subject of ἔφραζον: that is, it was a common decision, taken before they separated on leaving Olympia; and οἱ Λ. only becomes distinctively the subject with αὐτοὶ ἀφίκοντο. The subject of ὁλκοὺς παρεσκεύαζον is also Sparta and some of her allies, e.g. the Corinthians at least.

παροῦσι: "verbinde mit ἰέναι", Böhme. But to what purpose? Steup rightly objects; but it does not solve the problem to say, "π. wird aus einer Randbemerkung in den Text eingedrungen sein". ἔτι παροῦσι is possible, "they decided before leaving Olympia" (see above); or emend to παρασκευασαμένοις (as in 16. 1), to be taken with ἰέναι.

τοῖς δύο μέρεσιν: see ii. 10. 2 n.

ὁλκούς: some kind of chain and pulley arrangement, or, more simply, rollers. The line of the Isthmos (not far south of the present canal) over which ships were drawn came later to be known as δίολκος, Strab. viii. 6. 22, p. 380. Cf. viii. 7, and for similar action over the isthmus which joins Leukas to the mainland, iii. 81. 1, iv. 8. 2. There, however, the passage is over a low and narrow stretch of sand; at Corinth the distance is 5 miles, and the land rises to 250 feet.

ἐκ τῆς Κορίνθου: the territory of Corinth extended to both seas; but the city was just in shore of the Corinthian Gulf, and the δίολκος started at Lechaion, the port on the gulf.

2. οἱ μὲν προθύμως: it was not often that the Spartans were eager; and they soon despaired. Brasidas and Knemos again (ii. 94. 3 n.)? And were the Corinthians on this occasion slow (Busolt, iii. 1013)?

ἐν καρποῦ ξυγκομιδῇ: since this is the second half of August (see 8. 1 n.), the harvest will be of grapes and olives; perhaps threshing is included. Even in the upland plains of Arkadia, the cutting of wheat and barley is over by the middle of July.

ἀρρωστίᾳ τοῦ στρατεύειν: just as Perikles had foretold, i. 141. 3–7.

16. 1. δηλῶσαι βουλόμενοι, κ.τ.λ.: the Athenians had observed the preparations which were being made, and were in a more confident mood and more efficient than they had been the previous autumn, ii. 94. 1–2.

τὸ ἐπὶ Λέσβῳ ναυτικόν: we certainly expect a reference to the other Athenian squadron as well, the one which had sailed round the Peloponnese under Asopios and the greater part of which was sent back to Athens while he attacked Oiniadai (7. 1–3), for it had been mentioned in the relevant passage by the Mytileneans (13. 3); e.g. ⟨μηδὲ τὸ μετ' Ἀσωπίου⟩ after ναυτικόν. (Note that if Thucydides composed the speech freely out of his own head, the omission here is the more remarkable; it becomes even more difficult to say, with Steup, 'we must suppose that in the meantime it had returned home'.) See below on αἱ περὶ τὴν Π. τριάκοντα νῆες, § 2.

ναῦς ἑκατόν: not, obviously, *the* hundred of the special reserve, ii. 24. 2, but probably some of them, for an attack from the sea was expected. See n. on 17. 2. It is, however, curious that there is no reference to the special reserve; nor to the measures taken the previous year to guard Peiraeus (ii. 94. 4). We might indeed suggest ⟨τὰς⟩ ἑκατὸν ναῦς; but I am sure that Thucydides would have defined them more precisely.

αὐτοί τε - - - καὶ οἱ μέτοικοι: i.e. without calling on any of their allies, or any of the foreigners who normally volunteered for service in the Athenian fleet; many were engaged elsewhere, and there was no time to summon more. This is an argument in favour of supposing that Asopios' squadron had not returned. It was, however, a sign of the difficulties at Athens at this time that there was no reserve force of sailors present.

We may suppose that the ten Mytilenean ships, but not their crews (3. 4), were used by the Athenians; and that the contingent of Chios was elsewhere.

πλὴν ἱππέων καὶ πεντακοσιομεδίμνων: it is not often that we have references to these old Solonian classes as still effectively surviving, in fifth- and fourth-century literature. Their members will have had no training for the sea, though many will have served as trierarchs, and a hundred of these will have been aboard. What training the hoplites had had as *rowers* is unknown; not much, we would suppose from our other sources, such as Ἀθ. πολ., and untrained rowers would be worse than useless; and it may be that these hoplites, or the greater part of them, served only as ἐπιβάται, an ἐπιβάτης being normally of the thetic class supplied with his hoplite armour by the state. But in 18. 4 the hoplites can row triremes to Mytilene—helped by the wind perhaps, but they could not rely on it. That would be a simpler business than rowing in battle; but they must have had considerable training.

The happier cavalry must be retained in Attica for their proper duties when the enemy invaded (ii. 22. 2, iii. 1. 2). At another time they were to go aboard to raid the Peloponnese (iv. 42. 1).

2. τά τε ὑπὸ τῶν Λεσβίων ῥηθέντα: see 13. 4.

271

καὶ αἱ περὶ τὴν Πελοπόννησον τριάκοντα νῆες: because there is no mention of this squadron in § 1 (see n. on τὸ ἐπὶ Λέσβῳ ναυτικόν), and because the raiding of the Peloponnese by Asopios' squadron (7. 2) must have been finished some time before (though it was still continuing during the Olympic festival: 13. 3) and was certainly well known to the Spartans and so would not now be reported, Steup deletes τριάκοντα, and takes this as a reference to the activities of the fleet of 100 ships which ἀποβάσεις ἐποιοῦντο τῆς Πελοποννήσου ᾗ δοκοίη αὐτοῖς. This has been accepted by Stahl and by Busolt, iii. 1013, n. 6. But the argument ignores the logic of the speech and the narrative in relation to it: there was no reason for the mention of Asopios' squadron in the *speech* (whether it was invented by Thucydides or reported to him) unless it had some relevance. We must at least have had a statement that it had returned. And, for the facts themselves, we do not know exactly when Asopios sailed, perhaps not many days before the Olympic festival, and, as stated above, if the eighteen ships which he sent back (7. 3) had returned to Athens, the formation of the fleet of 100 would not have been so abnormal as we are evidently meant to believe that it was. Nor do I believe that this fleet would be described as αἱ περὶ τὴν Π. νῆες when αἱ ἑκατὸν νῆες is its natural title, and αἱ περὶ τὴν Π. νῆες (without τριάκοντα) would naturally refer back to 13. 3, even if we assume, with Steup, that the descents of the hundred on the Peloponnese ᾗ δοκοίη αὐτοῖς must have been in Lakonia rather than on the northern and eastern coasts of the Argolid; we should anyhow in that case expect καί not before αἱ περὶ τὴν Π., but before τὴν περιοικίδα. I prefer to think that there is a lacuna in § 1 after τὸ ἐπὶ Λέσβῳ ναυτικόν, perhaps an accidental omission by Thucydides; and that the eighteen ships, on their return voyage, were raiding the Lakonian coast again. (Busolt thinks that their return was ordered when the naval preparations of the Peloponnesians were known in Athens.) Since the number should be 18, not 30, perhaps τριάκοντα should still be bracketed.

The solution of the problem of c. 17 to some degree affects the answer to our present question; see n. on καὶ περὶ Πελοπόννησον ἕτεραι ἑκατὸν ἦσαν, 17. 2.

3. ναυτικὸν παρεσκεύαζον ὅτι πέμψουσιν - - - τεσσαράκοντα νεῶν: compare this with the number hoped for at the beginning of the war, ii. 7. 2, and the n. there. Even these forty took a long time to get ready (25. 1, 27. 1, 29. 1).

4. ἀνεχώρησαν δὲ καί, κ.τ.λ.: retreat to home quarters on both sides, especially necessary after such an exceptional muster as this.

17. This much discussed chapter has been (1) accepted as genuine, and the figures in §§ 2–4 taken to refer to the first year of the war (Arnold, Böhme); (2) accepted as genuine, and, with the necessary adoption of Campe's $\langle \ddot{\eta} \rangle$ before $\dot{\alpha}\rho\chi o\mu\acute{\epsilon}\nu ov$, and some other changes, the figures taken to refer to the current year, 428 B.C. (Stahl); (3) accepted as genuine but out of place, the figures, with Campe's emendation, being taken to refer to 430 B.C. (Adcock: above, ii. 56. 6 n.); (4) rejected as spurious, the work of an ignorant interpolator (Steup, Busolt, iii. 870. 2, Stuart Jones, Hude). Of these, Adcock's, though not without difficulty, seems to me the most probable as a solution of the problem, which will be briefly discussed below and yet another suggestion made; notes on particular points are given first.

1. κατὰ τὸν χρόνον τοῦτον ὃν αἱ νῆες ἔπλεον: 'during the time at which the ships were at sea', i.e. during the summer. Apart from Steup's doubt about this absolute use of $\pi\lambda\epsilon\hat{\iota}\nu$, 'to be at sea', this is not Thucydidean for the simple $\dot{\epsilon}\nu$ $\tau o\acute{\upsilon}\tau\omega$ $\tau\hat{\omega}$ $\theta\acute{\epsilon}\rho\epsilon\iota$. We must, I believe, either read $\langle a\ddot{\upsilon}\tau a\iota \rangle$ $a\dot{\iota}$ $\nu\hat{\eta}\epsilon s$, which will mean that a particular naval expedition, and a large one (such as that of c. 16), is referred to, or bracket $\ddot{o}\nu$ $a\dot{\iota}$ $\nu\hat{\eta}\epsilon s$ $\ddot{\epsilon}\pi\lambda\epsilon o\nu$.

ἐν τοῖς πλεῖσται: most scholars, including L. and S.[9], maintain that this means 'the very largest number', not 'among the largest'; cf., in Thucydides, i. 6. 3, iii. 82. 1, vii. 19. 4. If this is correct, $\kappa a\dot{\iota}$ $\ddot{\epsilon}\tau\iota$ $\pi\lambda\epsilon\acute{\iota}o\upsilon s$ in the next clause makes Campe's emendation $\langle \ddot{\eta} \rangle$ $\dot{\alpha}\rho\chi o\mu\acute{\epsilon}\nu o\upsilon$ $\tau o\hat{\upsilon}$ $\pi o\lambda\acute{\epsilon}\mu o\upsilon$ necessary, and the figures in §§ 2–4 cannot refer to 431 B.C. (If, however, a later writer compiled the chapter, he may have misunderstood the phrase, and have meant by it, 'among the largest'.) See also n. on $\tau o\sigma a\hat{\upsilon}\tau a\iota$ $\delta\dot{\eta}$ $\pi\lambda\epsilon\hat{\iota}\sigma\tau a\iota$, § 4.

ἐνεργοὶ †κάλλει: ἐνεργοί means 'in commission', and would, for example, expressly exclude, not only old ships no longer to be used though not yet broken up, but the 100 $\dot{\epsilon}\xi a\acute{\iota}\rho\epsilon\tau o\iota$ $\tau\rho\iota\acute{\eta}\rho\epsilon\iota s$ of ii. 24. 2 (if 100 were still kept in dock).

The combination ἐνεργοὶ κάλλει is clearly corrupt (and corrupt, as Steup admitted, whether Thucydides or an interpolator wrote the sentence). κάλλος itself is not out of place in a description of ships; Aristophanes could use καλός of the older Attic coinage (*Frogs*, 722–3),

καλλίστοις ἁπάντων, ὡς δοκεῖ, νομισμάτων
καὶ μόνοις ὀρθῶς κοπεῖσι καὶ κεκωδωνισμένοις,

where καλλίστοις does not mean aesthetically beautiful (though I would not altogether agree with J. G. Milne, *C.R.* lxiv, 1950, 150, that its meaning is *only* that of the next line, 'correctly struck and of good sound metal'; this line adds something); and $\epsilon\dot{\upsilon}\pi\rho\epsilon\pi\epsilon\acute{\iota}\alpha$ $\tau\epsilon$ - - - $\kappa a\dot{\iota}$ $\tau\hat{\omega}$ $\tau a\chi\upsilon\nu a\upsilon\tau\epsilon\hat{\iota}\nu$ of the fine fleet sailing for Sicily, vi. 31. 3, might together make up κάλλος. But such a description would be unsuitable to the hastily manned fleet of c. 16, and to the general conditions of 428 B.C. Of emendations Bergk's νῆες ἅμα καὶ κάλλισται αὐτοῖς ἐνεργοί

273

ἐγένοντο (Philol. xxix, 1870, 320) deserves recording. Of those which reject κάλλος altogether, Herwerden's ἄλλαι ἄλλῃ is the best; and this is consistent with a reference to 428 B.C.

2. τήν τε γὰρ Ἀττικὴν - - - ἐφύλασσον: we have not heard before, and we do not hear again, of any such provision; and it would appear to be inconsistent with the disposition of the fleet both in 431 (see ii. 26. 1, the squadron of thirty ships sent against Lokris καὶ Εὐβοίας ἅμα φυλακήν) and in 428—at least in the late autumn of 429 there was no fleet guarding the entrance to Peiraeus (ii. 93. 3), and the creation of a fleet 100 strong to defend Attica, Salamis, and Euboea is hardly implied by the description of the measures taken after the scare of that time (ii. 94. 4: this is independent of the question whether the absence of ships to guard Peiraeus was due to over-confidence that no attack would ever be made by sea, or to exhaustion, moral and physical, caused by the pestilence). Stahl thinks that these hundred were in fact the ἐξαίρετοι νῆες of ii. 24. 2, now put into commission because a naval attack was expected (see 16. 1 n.); but this does not help us out of this difficulty. See also next n.

If this and the following sentences refer to the year 431 and were written by Thucydides, we should have had, I am sure, τότε γὰρ τήν τε Ἀττικήν, or τήν τε γὰρ Ἀ. τότε.

καὶ περὶ Πελοπόννησον ἕτεραι ἑκατὸν ἦσαν: according to Stahl the fleet hurriedly got together in 16. 1, an improbable description (even if we accept, as Stahl does, the bracketing of τριάκοντα in 16. 2) of a fleet just mentioned. Besides, as Steup and others have pointed out, if a hundred vessels were regularly on guard off Attica, Salamis, and Euboea, (a) the Peloponnesians would not have ventured to attack, (b) the Mytilenean envoys would hardly have implied so clearly that there was no squadron near Attica (13. 3), and (c) the Athenians would have had no need to man another hundred to threaten the Peloponnese 'without disturbing the fleet at Lesbos'.

For those who think that the year in question is 431 (whether so meant by Thucydides, or by the interpolator) the reference is to ii. 23. 2.

αἱ περὶ Ποτείδαιαν καὶ ἐν τοῖς ἄλλοις χωρίοις: Stahl, preferring the reference to the current year, must bracket περὶ Ποτ. καί. On the whole, however, μετὰ Ποτειδαίας in § 3 supports the MSS. reading here, and is against supposing the year to be 428.

The 'ships elsewhere' Stahl takes to be the 40 at Mytilene (3. 2) and the 12 at Naupaktos (7. 3), i.e. 252 in all. But this is to suppose that there were no ships at Byzantion, Sestos, Thasos, Rhodes, and other strategically important places.

We do not know how many of the original seventy ships (i. 57. 6, 61. 1) stayed for the siege of Poteidaia; probably not many, for neither Poteidaia nor her allies in Chalkidike possessed a fleet.

3. τὰ χρήματα - - - μετὰ Ποτειδαίας: see ii. 70. 2.

4. δίδραχμοι ὁπλῖται: clearly a special rate of pay, for those engaged, summer and winter, in the siege, 3,000 in number (a larger number than would usually be left to conduct a siege which was intended to reduce a town by hunger; see ii. 31. 2 n.; but in this case the besiegers had to be prepared for attack by land from Olynthos and Spartolos). We have no precise information about normal rates at this time (see Böckh–Frankel, Staatshaushaltung, i.³ 340–2); but some indication is to be got from special cases, as the sailors in the fleet for Sicily (vi. 31. 3) and the Thracian mercenaries of 413 (vii. 27. 2). Cf. also v. 47. 6. A. H. M. Jones, in his article in Past and Present (1952), p. 16, n. 33, assumes from this passage and vi. 8. 1 that 1 dr. a day was the normal pay for hoplite and sailor, until it was reduced by half in 413 (viii. 45. 2, a passage referring to the sailors in the Peloponnesian fleet).

καὶ ὑπηρέτῃ: one would naturally suppose from this passage that, like the Spartans (iv. 16. 1), every Athenian hoplite had his servant; yet such servants are seldom mentioned, and they would not fit into every picture, e.g. that of the soldiers building the wall at Pylos (iv. 4: the presence of ταξίαρχοι there shows that hoplites as well as sailors are included)—why not leave such banausic work to the servants? At Delion, too, there would have been little need of the specially mentioned force of light-armed, if every hoplite had his servant with him (iv. 90). Nikias mentions the desertion of θεράποντες at Syracuse (vii. 13. 2), and in so expensive an expedition doubtless there were many of them; but they are not stated to be the hoplites' servants, still less is it implied that every hoplite had one.

τρισχίλιοι μὲν οἱ πρῶτοι: i. 57. 6 and 61. 1, ii. 31. 2.

ὧν οὐκ ἐλάσσους διεπολιόρκησαν: Steup, as one of his arguments for the interpolator, objects that there had been heavy casualties (i. 63. 3 and ii. 58. 2 esp.) and no drafts had been sent to replace them; he even suggests that the 2,000 men under Xenophon who fought at Spartolos six months after the fall of Poteidaia (ii. 79. 1) were the same as those who had endured two and a half years of siege, and that therefore there had been some 1,000 casualties. This is to mistake Thucydides' method (see above, p. 165; a method which Steup recognizes at ii. 31. 2 and 58. 2); and we do not know that no drafts were sent.

ἑξακόσιοι δὲ καὶ χίλιοι μετὰ Φορμίωνος: i. 64. 2, ii. 29. 6, 31. 2 (where see n.), 58. 2.

Edd. note that no mention is made of Hagnon's force of 4,000 hoplites and 300 cavalry (ii. 56. 2, 58. 1) that made the unsuccessful attempt to take Poteidaia by storm. This was a short campaign and hardly counted as part of the siege of Poteidaia.

τὸν αὐτὸν μισθόν: that is, one drachme a day, for sailors had no servants. Again we are in some doubt, for a drachme a day was exceptional pay in 415, vi. 31. 3 (cf. vi. 8. 1), double the ordinary rate, viii. 45. 2 (see Böckh-Fränkel, i.³ 342–5). We can understand why the soldiers at Poteidaia received special 'hardship' money, not why all of the sailors did, in 431 or 430 or 428.

τοσαῦται δὴ πλεῖσται: as Steup says, this is sufficient to show that the naval forces described were the largest ever in commission at one time, not simply among the largest.

Sufficient has been said in the notes to make it clear that (in my view) the reference of the figures to the summer of 428 is impossible. The year 431 is no easier: in the account of the general strategy of the Athenians a fleet of a hundred in home waters must surely have been mentioned, such a fleet seems inconsistent with the squadron of 30 ships of ii. 26, and, above all, if there were 250 ships in commission, there were 350 in all, including the 100 ἐξαίρετοι, not 300, the figure given in ii. 13. 8.

Against Steup's view that the chapter is a late interpolation and inaccurate is the argument that, apart from the corruption in § 1, there is nothing in the language which would cause suspicion; it looks like Thucydides' own. If this is so, we must fall back on Adcock's ingenious suggestion that the chapter is genuine, but misplaced, and belongs in the narrative of the second year of the war; that the editor of the *History* after Thucydides' death found it separate and inserted it here in error (in an unsuitable place, it must be admitted); and I agree with Adcock that on the facts the year 430 is the most suited to the figures which are given. We may suppose that 50 more ships had been built in the winter of 431 to 430; it is a little easier to admit that mention of the 100 ships in home waters might have been reserved for this place; there were some ships at Poteidaia, and if these numbered 15–20, it leaves 30–35 for duties elsewhere in the empire; and there was an expedition of 100 ships to the Peloponnese (ii. 56). Further, this was the time when the first effects of the very heavy expenditure were likely to be felt—the large reserve was not now looking so large after all. If this is correct, the proper place for the chapter is between ii. 56 and 57 (or perhaps between 58 and 59); and it will be necessary to read ⟨ἦ⟩ ἀρχομένου τοῦ πολέμου and, as I think, ⟨αὗται⟩ αἱ νῆες in § 1. It can be removed from where it now stands without affecting the connexion between cc. 16 and 18.

There are, however, two difficulties in addition to those already suggested (of which perhaps the greatest is the unexplained rate of pay in the fleet): first, that ἀρχομένου τοῦ πολέμου is an unnatural phrase to describe the first year of the war by contrast with the second (contrasted with the fourth or any later year, it is much

276

easier); and second, that the *implication* in the chapter is of Athenian success, great energy and vigour, and abundant resources, and for this a place in the narrative where the story of the pestilence still dominates is unsuitable. The question of genuineness is an important one; for on it depends the reliability of the figures, especially the financial figures, of the chapter. I have indicated some doubts; and if these doubts were justified, it would support Steup's view; which otherwise relies only on the hundred ships on guard around Attica, not otherwise attested, a statement which, if by an interpolator, could be interpreted as a misunderstanding of the hundred ships in reserve. Between these views the balance of the argument seems in favour of Adcock.

But there is one other possibility: that the chapter is in place, that ἀρχομένου τοῦ πολέμου refers, more loosely, to the first two years of the war, or, more specifically, to 430, not 431, and that, in consequence, παραπλήσιαι δὲ καὶ ἔτι πλείους is a modification or correction of ἐν τοῖς πλεῖσται: in effect, 'more ships were at sea than at any other time except that there were slightly more in 430'. We should then read, not only ⟨αὗται⟩ αἱ νῆες ἔπλεον, but τήν τε γὰρ Ἀττικὴν ⟨τότε⟩, or the like; no other change of the text is necessary (apart from some correction of ἐνεργοὶ κάλλει), but τοσαῦται δὴ πλεῖσται at the end will refer to παραπλήσιαι καὶ ἔτι πλείους, not to ἐν τοῖς πλεῖσται. If this is right, it becomes more significant that on another occasion of great confidence at Athens and a great armament, reference is made to the very great numbers of troops and ships engaged in 430: vi. 31. 2, by comparison with the Sicilian expedition. It gets rid of the great difficulty in Adcock's view, that the chapter implies present confidence and vigour.

18. 1. Μυτιληναῖοι δέ: by contrast with Peloponnesian and Athenian actions, c. 16, and resuming the narrative of events in Lesbos from 6. 2. **οἱ ἐπίκουροι:** here and in § 2, perhaps the archers mentioned in 2. 2, possibly including men from Mytilenean territory on the opposite mainland; in any case very much in the service of the men then in power. **ἐπ' Ἀντίσσης καὶ Πύρρας καὶ Ἐρέσου:** independent states, like Methymna, but those in power in each of them, strengthened now by Mytilene (doubtless the ἐπίκουροι of § 2 were part of the strengthening), were ready for synoecism (2. 3) and for independence of Athens. **τείχη κρατύναντες:** we should surely read ⟨τὰ⟩ τείχη κρ. Classen compares 3. 3; but as he says in his n., the absence of the article there belongs to the formula of surrender (i. 101. 3, 108. 4, 117. 3).

3. περὶ τὸ φθινόπωρον ἤδη ἀρχόμενον: see ii. 31. 1 n., and Appendix. **4. αὐτερέται:** see 16. 1 n., and i. 10. 4. Busolt, iii. 1015, says it was lack of money which made Athens dispense with regular rowers; much more probably it was, as in c. 16, shortage of men.

ἁπλῷ τείχει: contrast the double wall round Plataia described in c. 21. The Athenians did not fear any big attack from the land side by Mytilene's allies.

ἐγκατῳκοδόμηται: the tense is defended by Stahl, Böhme, and Marchant ("they make a wall (hist. present), and by the time it is finished there are forts built into it", as though they woke up to find the forts there); others have conjectured the present, the imperfect, the aorist, and the pluperfect, and the aorist active. Of these the aorist passive would be 'correct'. The forts of course went up at the same time as the wall; for their purpose compare the more elaborate wall round Plataia (c. 21).

For the very similar siege operations of Memnon in 333, see Arrian, *Anab.* ii. 1. Then, too, the cities of the island were divided politically.

5. ὁ χειμών: see Appendix. This wall took four to five weeks to build; cf. ii. 75. 3, 78. 1 nn.

19. *Eisphora at Athens. Tribute collecting in Karia*

19. 1. προσδεόμενοι - - - χρημάτων: see *A.T.L.* iii. 343, with n. 84; and for a note on Athens' financial position, pp. 432 ff., below.

τότε πρῶτον ἐσφοράν: for the εἰσφορά, a special property tax levied on Athenian citizens and metoikoi, assessed not on income but on capital, see Böckh-Frankel, i. 555–8; Busolt, ii.² 266 n.

One would naturally suppose, from the words here used, that Thucydides means that this was the first occasion in Athenian history that the εἰσφορά was levied, not simply the first occasion in this war. Yet this can hardly be true; for the reference to it in the second Kallias decree (*I.G.* i.² 92 = *A.T.L.* D 2 = Tod, 51 B), ll. 17–20, is to something familiar, something whose procedure can be used as a precedent. See my article in *Historia*, ii. 1953, 59. Antiphon, ii a 12, πολλὰς καὶ μεγάλας εἰσφορὰς εἰσφέροντα, is unfortunately of doubtful value as evidence; for the date of the tetralogies (whether by Antiphon or another) is uncertain: see the discussion by K. J. Dover in *C.Q.* xliv, 1950, 58–59.

Kleon, who may have been a member of the *boule* in this year, 428–427 (Ar. *Eq.* 774; Busolt, iii. 998. 1), is generally held to have been responsible for this special tax on the well-to-do; certainly he was charged with a brutal exactness in its enforcement. See West, *C.P.* xix, 1924, 139 (who, however, misunderstands the nature of Athenian administration in calling him "director of the finances of the state"): Ar. *Eq.* 773–6 (Kleon speaking),

> καὶ πῶς ἂν ἐμοῦ μᾶλλόν σε φιλῶν ὦ Δῆμε γένοιτο πολίτης;
> ὃς πρῶτα μὲν ἡνίκ᾽ ἐβούλευον σοὶ χρήματα πλεῖστ᾽ ἀπέδειξα
> ἐν τῷ κοινῷ, τοὺς μὲν στρεβλῶν τοὺς δ᾽ ἄγχων τοὺς δὲ μεταιτῶν,
> οὐ φροντίζων τῶν ἰδιωτῶν οὐδενός, εἰ σοὶ χαριοίμην·

Eq. 923–6; *Vesp.* 31–41 (but see v. Leeuwen and Starkie, ad loc.); perhaps Eupolis, fr. 278. If Kleon did take a leading part in proposing the tax, note the silence of Thucydides.

He is silent as well on another matter: the number of times during the war that the εἰσφορά was repeated and the amounts raised, or aimed at, each time. I cannot agree with *A.T.L.* iii. 345, that it was not levied after the increase of the tribute in 425 (which would make the mockery in *The Knights* almost pointless), nor with Dover, loc. cit., that because there were only two εἰσφοραί between 411 and 404 (Lysias, xxi. 1–4), at a time of great financial stress, there were probably not more than four or five throughout the war; Lysias' πολλαὶ εἰσφοραί (xii. 20, xxv. 12, xxx. 26) might of course mean anything from six to a dozen or more. Still less can I believe that Kleon, who harried the rich by the εἰσφορά, and is presumed to have been the initiator of the increase of tribute in 425 (below, p. 500), intended the latter mainly to relieve the Athenian rich of paying the special tax.

διακόσια τάλαντα: the amount should be considered by comparison with the total tribute of the League (ii. 13. 3; above, pp. 19, 33), and with the highest amount paid annually by any state, which was at this time 30 tal. paid by Aigina and Thasos. We are indeed in want of the information about the frequency of εἰσφορά and the amounts levied.

ἀργυρολόγους ναῦς: cf. ii. 69. 1, iv. 50. 1. One would certainly suppose that on this occasion at least they were to make a special levy, comparable to the εἰσφορά in Athens itself, not simply to collect arrears or escort the normal tribute, nor just sent out because there was a new assessment (above, pp. 202–3).

Λυσικλέα: very likely the politician who was said to have risen to power by becoming the protector of Aspasia after the death of Perikles (schol. Ar. *Equit.* 132 and 765, and schol. Plat. *Menex.* 235 E, on the authority of Aischines the Socratic and probably Kallias the comic poet, fr. 15: see Meineke, i. 182. 4 and *P.A.* 9417). If the story has truth in it (and it is partly the result of ingenious modern combination),[1] he did not enjoy his ascendancy long, nor choose a comfortable post (cf. ii. 69. 1–2).

πέμπτον αὐτόν: although there were only twelve ships, they had to visit many cities; hence the number of strategoi. Also the Athenians were careful and suspicious where collection of public money had to be made.

2. ἐκ Μυοῦντος: not mentioned elsewhere by Thucydides, except

[1] Mr. Mervyn Jones tells me that the mention of Aspasia in connexion with Lysikles in these schol. is to be found in Θ only of the MSS., and may be a comment on Lysikles' name given in the older scholia; and that the schol. on 765 only reproduces a fragment of schol. on 132.

i. 138. 5 as one of the places given to Themistokles by the King of Persia. See vol. i, pp. 290–2.

τοῦ Σανδίου λόφου: a detail of geography preserved, but not explained. The hill is not apparently mentioned elsewhere in classical authors (Bürchner in *R.E.*, s.v.).

Ἀναιτῶν: doubtless the community of Samians (with others perhaps) who had left Samos in 439 to settle in Anaia on the mainland opposite, and who had continued in irreconcilable hostility to Athens: 32. 2, iv. 75. 1 (where some detail is given), and viii. 19. 1. They even furnished and perhaps manned a ship in the Ionian war, viii. 61. 2.

The mainland opposite islands which were politically disturbed was often a source of further disturbance, as Antandros and Mytilene (iv. 52, 75), and the coastland opposite Kerkyra (iii. 85. 2).

20–24. *Escape of half the Garrison of Plataia*

20. 1. οἱ Πλαταιῆς: the story of the siege of Plataia is resumed from ii. 78. Cf. Dem. lix. 103.

Θεαινέτου - - - Εὐπομπίδου: both probably, the second certainly, Plataian. Daïmachos is known as a Boeotian and Plataian name; and Eupompidas was strategos in Plataia.

2. ἐθελονταί: if the original resolution had been carried out, all would have been under the orders of the strategos to go. Demosthenes, or Ps.-Dem., has the more conventional διακληρωσάμενοι (but see 22. 5 n.). There is something to be said for Hude's ingenious ἐνέμειναν τῇ ἐξόδῳ· ἐξῆλθον δὲ τρόπῳ τοιῷδε; which, however, he does not record in his 1913 edition.

3. ἐξαληλιμμένον: it is common in Greece still to see cottages built of mud-brick both whitewashed and not (also plastered; but that is a more elaborate process which is not in question here). Generally, if my memory is correct, owing to the dark colour soon taken by the clay, the layers of bricks in a wall would be more easily distinguishable from a distance if the wall had been whitewashed, unless the wash had been laid on very thick. Here the reverse is implied; but it was clearly not easy to count the layers, in spite of ῥᾳδίως καθορωμένου, below.

ἀπέχοντες: Didot's ἀπέχοντος, adopted by Hude (in 1898; the 1913 ed. is here confused), though easy, is unnecessary.

ἐς ὃ ἐβούλοντο: both Stahl's ἐς ὅσον and, still more, Steup's deletion of these words (as the usual 'Randbemerkung') miss the point. The whole elaborate description of the counting and calculating recognizes the fact that exactness was necessary: the ladders must be short of the top of the wall, or the defenders will be able to push them over, but only just short, or it will be difficult to get from the

top rung on to the wall; and they must be put against it at an angle
not so steep that it may fall backward, or, with a very slight effort,
be pushed over, and not so wide that, with many men mounting
at a time, it may break. See how the wordy Polybios explains that,
for this very purpose, a general should have a sound knowledge of
mathematics: ix. 19. 5–9. So Grundy, *Topography of Plataea* (*R.G.S.
Suppl. Pap.* iii), 1894, p. 68. (Thucydides was content to leave the
calculation to the ordinary citizen. When he says above, by the way,
that the ladders were ἴσαι τῷ τείχει, this does not necessarily mean
"of exactly the same height as the walls", as though he did not know
that ladders have to lean, as Müller–Strubing and Steup thought.
Polybios calculates the proportion of ladder to wall to be 12 to 10.)
Further, the land immediately outside the walls of Plataia is not
particularly level, and to secure a level top to the wall (which was
clearly done: see c. 21) a different number of layers of brick would
be required at different points. The Plataians, therefore, in planning
their escape had to think not only of the best direction to take once
they were over the wall and the outer ditch (after consideration of
the paths outside, the Peloponnesian defences, etc.), but also to discover a section of the Peloponnesian wall where the layers were, all
of them, countable, and calculate a length of ladder which would
fit that part of the wall and perhaps no other. Hence both ᾗ ἔτυχε
πρὸς σφᾶς οὐκ ἐξαληλιμμένον above and here ἐς ὃ ἐβούλοντο are required (sc. ἀνιέναι, or the like—'in the direction they wanted'). τοῦ
τείχους is the subject of καθορωμένου: 'was easily visible.'

Edd. quote the parallel case of the single Roman soldier calculating
the height of the Syracusan walls, Livy, xxv. 23 (it is a pity we have
not Polybios to describe the same incident).

Grundy conjectured that the north side of the city-wall of Plataia
at this time ran along the top of a steep and nearly precipitous cliff,
and that the Plataians must have escaped on this side. It is noticeable, if so, that Thucydides says nothing of this feature. More probably, however, the men escaped on the west side, which presented
no difficulty of this kind, and from which the Thebes road (24. 1)
was easily reached.

21. 1. τὸ δὲ τεῖχος ἦν - - - τοιόνδε: this description of the wall is
given here, not in ii. 78, because there the fact of the building, the
establishment of the siege, was alone relevant; here the design of the
wall is all-important. See my Sather lectures, pp. 132–3. We may compare the full description of Achilles' hut in the *Iliad*, xxiv. 448–56:
it might have been given in the first book when Thetis goes to see
her son; or in the ninth, on the occasion of the embassy; but it is
most relevant, and so most effective in the last book, in the story of
Priam's visit to Achilles, when Hektor's body lay there too.

πρός τε Πλαταιῶν, κ.τ.λ.: in effect, two *defensive* walls, serving the same purpose for the besiegers as the city-wall for the defenders; but the former have two possible enemies. Cf. Livy, v. 1.

2. οἰκήματα: a simple predicate, 'the intervening space was so built as to form quarters distributed among the garrison'. These οἰκήματα served as rest quarters for those of the garrison who from time to time were not on duty.

3. καὶ οἱ αὐτοὶ καὶ τὸ ἔξω: other instances of this predicative use of οἱ αὐτοί in Thucydides (i. 23. 3, ii. 40. 3, iv. 17. 1) suggest that we should either delete the first καί, as L. Herbst, or emend the second to ἐς.

ὥστε πάροδον μὴ εἶναι: the broad and flat top of the wall was formed by the roofing of the rooms for the garrison, which reached from inner to outer wall. This was furnished with parapets, and the garrison normally watched here; and could only pass from one section of the wall, on the top, to another through a tower, not alongside it, because the tower walls were flush with the main walls.

4. ὄντων δι' ὀλίγου: but he does not say how long, i.e. what was the width of each ἔπαλξις and the distance between them.

22. 1. τὴν τάφρον διέβησαν: we are not told the distance they had to cover between their own and the Peloponnesian wall. The τάφρος was briefly mentioned in ii. 78. 1; the outer ditch was in such weather difficult to cross, full of water and ice (below, 23. 4–5), but no difficulty is implied here. Grundy (op. cit., above, p. 281), p. 69, explained: "if the ground below the depression, where this escape evidently took place (since the fugitives subsequently took the Thebes road), be noticed, it will be seen that the outer ditch would be at a considerably lower level than the inner, and the water would naturally drain into the former." But not through the heavy soil which surrounds Plataia, and not through the Peloponnesian wall, unless the Peloponnesians had constructed a drain for that special purpose; which is unlikely. We must suppose that the inner ditch, at least at this point, was in fact shallow and offered no difficulty, and that therefore Thucydides' informant made no mention of it to him. All round the city-wall, except on the north side towards the Oeroe valley, there is in fact no great depth of soil above the natural rock.

ἀνὰ τὸ σκοτεινόν: "in dem überall herrschenden Dunkel" (Classen, who compares iv. 72. 2, the only other place where Thucydides uses the preposition ἀνά).

οὐ κατακουσάντων: the compound verb is used just as in ii. 84. 3 (to hear through noise); but I suspect, partly because the words are not necessary, partly because of the unusual μὲν οὐ - - -, δέ - - - οὐ, that we should bracket οὐ κατακουσάντων. It is a likely adscript; and ἀντιπαταγοῦντος τοῦ ἀνέμου makes a good Thucydidean antithesis to οὐ προϊδόντων.

2. ἀσφαλείας ἕνεκα: it is the naked right foot that prevents them slipping in the clay, not, as some have thought, the shod left foot (see Marchant). It would be normal to wear shoes of some kind for this purpose and in this weather; one was left off, for a special reason. Arnold aptly quotes from Scott, *Last Minstrel*, canto iv. 18,

> Each better knee was bared, to aid
> The warriors in the escalade.

3. κατὰ οὖν μεταπύργιον: they only attempted to cross by one section of the wall between two towers (23. 1 ad fin.) ; and there is much to be said for Gertz's conjecture μεταπύργιόν τι.

πρὸς τὰς ἐπάλξεις: not only because they would not be manned in such bad weather, but their ladders had been made of a length proper for this point.

ὧν ἡγεῖτο Ἀμμέας, κ.τ.λ.: the best punctuation is, I think, a colon before these words, and a comma only (as Poppo and Hude) after ἀνέβη. ἀνέβαινον after τῶν πύργων might well be omitted, and ἀνέβησαν (not ἀνέβαινον) understood after οἱ ἑπόμενοι: 'then six making for each of the two towers.'

Some have disputed whether Ammeas was the *thirteenth*, or belonged to one or other of the two groups of six.

4. ὡς δὲ ἄνω πλείους ἐγένοντο: the men of these two groups who first went to the towers, did not attack the guard at once, but kept silent; they were not out to provoke the defence.

κεραμίδα: used collectively, 'tiling', not a single roof-tile, which would not make much noise. And baked, not unbaked like the bricks; the Peloponnesians could have got what they wanted from houses outside the city-walls.

5. τὸ δὲ στρατόπεδον ἐπὶ τὸ τεῖχος ὥρμησεν: that is, the greater part of the besieging army, who had been asleep in their quarters, went up on to the walls, presumably by inside ladders to the towers and hence to their several sections of the wall (§ 6). They did not know what the trouble was when the alarm was given, and therefore did not concentrate at the point of danger. Steup, who supposed that the whole στρατόπεδον was every night in the towers or on the walls, had to suggest οὐδ' ὧς before ἐπὶ τὸ τεῖχος.

προσέβαλον τῷ τείχει: but what would such an attack, without even scaling ladders, amount to? What sort of diversion would it make? It might, of course, have been sufficient to make a great deal of noise. In any case it seems to have been a brave action by men whose nerve had failed them when they first thought of escaping from the town (20. 2) ; perhaps there is more truth in the statement of Demosthenes (n. on 20. 2) that the besieged drew lots, the plan being that half should escape, so that the food might last longer. Probably also, if all had tried, a second μεταπύργιον would have had to be scaled, and this would have increased the danger of detection and earlier counter-attack. There was a natural limit of numbers in the interests of safety.

The aorist here is preferable to the imperfect, the reading of C only, adopted by Hude and Steup.

6. ἐθορυβοῦντο: this means, primarily, 'they became confused', the Plataians producing just the effect that they wanted.

ἐκ τῆς ἑαυτῶν φυλακῆς: each party moved to its own section of the wall except those who should have been on the section now occupied by the Plataians. They are confined to the towers at either end by units of the Plataians (§ 3), and their fortunes are related below, c. 23.

7. οἱ τριακόσιοι αὐτῶν: as the scholiast remarks, these are introduced as though they had been mentioned before; but the explanation of their purpose, οἷς ἐτέτακτο, κ.τ.λ., is inserted because they have not been. Arnold compares 3. 4.

ἐχώρουν ἔξω τοῦ τείχους πρὸς τὴν βοήν: Thucydides may mean that this picked body encamped outside the walls, ready for any danger, from within or from without the city, every night in all weathers; but I doubt it. More probably they slept within, like the rest; to get quickly to any threatened point they must go outside, for the rooms and corridors inside the walls (if there were any corridors; the space between the inner and outer walls was only 16 ft.) would be congested with the ordinary soldiers trying to find their arms, grumbling, and going to their several posts.

φρυκτοί τε - - - πολέμιοι: see ii. 94. 1 for the expression. A late scholiast, in his simple way, says that to signal the approach of a friend, in the dark, lighted torches were held aloft and kept steady, to signal an enemy, they were waved about; κίνησις γὰρ ὁ πόλεμος, he adds. And Polybios, x. 43–47, implies nothing more complicated for times earlier than his own, when science had perfected so much. Yet that cannot be the whole picture; for, as Arnold points out here, if agitated lights meant simply 'enemies approaching; help!', further confusing signals by the Plataians could only have made them look more agitated and therefore more urgent. In 80. 2 ἐφρυκτωρήθησαν ἑξήκοντα νῆες Ἀθηναίων may mean exactly that: 'sixty Athenian ships approaching', not simply 'enemy sighted'; and maybe here the besiegers of Plataia were trying to signal 'attack from within the city' (so far as they themselves understood what was happening), and the besieged could confuse that sufficiently to leave the Thebans guessing where they were asked to go, and, therefore, hesitating; and every delay helped the escapers. As Grote observed, v, pp. 155–6, the besiegers had probably been using such signals for some time, for different messages, which the Plataians had observed and therefore expected on this occasion.

284

23. 1. οἱ δ' ὑπερβαίνοντες τῶν Πλαταιῶν: the whole escaping party (σφῶν οἱ ἄνδρες οἱ ἐξιόντες of the previous sentence), by contrast with those staying behind. The subject is later in the sentence divided into parts, with the final verb ὑπερέβαινον belonging, almost, to the whole again. There is a certain confusion, though it is not misleading, perhaps characteristic of the confusion prevailing in the dark.

διαφθείραντες: once the alarm has been given, the Plataians attack; there is no further need for silence (22. 4 n.). So τὰς ἐπάλξεις ἀπώσαντες below; they get rid of every hindrance possible.

2. ὁ δὲ διακομιζόμενος αἰεί: if these words are sound and there is no lacuna, I cannot construe them to mean other than 'each man as he was getting over the wall' (as ὑπερέβαινον, above); and believe therefore that ἐπὶ τοῦ χείλους τῆς τάφρου is wrong, and that we should read simply ἐπὶ τοῦ χείλους, if χεῖλος may be used of the top edge of a wall (which is perhaps doubtful; I can find no other case of it, nor a very close parallel),[1] or ἐπὶ τοῦ τείχους. The late scholiast, c_2, may have had ἐπὶ τοῦ χείλους only in his text: τοῦ ἔξωθεν δηλονότι· ἤδη γὰρ εἶπε περὶ τοῦ ἔνδον; at least it is difficult to see why he did not say τῆς ἔξωθεν if he meant the ditch; but his value is small. (In Thucydides' text, too, we should have expected τῆς ἔξω τάφρου, to distinguish it from the inner ditch mentioned in 22. 1.) See below, on § 4.

It will then mean that each man in his turn watched for a few moments at the head of the ladders to send javelins or arrows against any enemy he saw running along the foot of the wall who could attack men temporarily helpless as they descended the ladders. (They must of course have used ladders for the descent on the outer side of the wall; they hauled many to the top in order to mount the towers, and they could as easily haul up the rest, or as many as they needed.)

4. ἐπὶ τοῦ χείλους τῆς τάφρου: a clumsy repetition, in our MSS., of the same words in § 2, and not only of the locality but of the action, ἐτόξευόν τε καὶ ἐσηκόντιζον; and I cannot believe that this is right. Besides, it is not till § 3 that the whole party is over the wall and the last of them then approach the ditch. I have therefore suggested that in § 2 the outer edge of the wall is meant, and that we read ἐπὶ τοῦ τείχους there; here the edge of the ditch may be the nearer, not the farther edge—a covering party, changing in personnel perhaps, who protect those actually crossing the ditch. They shoot ἐς τὰ γυμνά; from which we should suppose that the enemy had his right towards them. If, that is, the Plataians had crossed the wall on the west side of the city (above, 20. 3 n.), the enemy approached them from the north, between the wall and the outer ditch.

διὰ τὰς λαμπάδας: once within bowshot of the Plataians the torches

---

[1] L. and S.⁹ cite Polyb. x. 44. 11; but this is a misprint for τεύχους. The 'lip' of a cup, or of a ship (Eupol., fr. 324), is different.

285

were a positive hindrance to the 300—they threw light on themselves and prevented them seeing exactly where their enemies stood.

5. οἷος ἀπηλιώτου [ἢ βορέου]: in C.Q. xlii, 1948, 11–12, I have argued that βορέου must be kept, both because northerly winds do in fact bring cold stormy weather in winter in Boeotia, with snow, sleet, and wet but not firm ice, and because they are so described by other Greek writers, especially Homer and Aristotle. (To the passages cited, we might add Ar. Vesp. 264–5. But in Iliad, xxi. 346–7, Boreas in autumn is a drying wind, welcome to farmers.) ἀπηλιώτου ἤ is perhaps more doubtful; but since Apeliotes can be the ENE. wind, which brings storms from the Hellespont at least to Euboea, and Boreas (generally NNE. wind rather than N.) can apparently be substituted for it (or, as a god, can take offerings on its behalf), as in Hdt. vii. 188. 2, 189, there is no reason why we should not keep the MSS. reading here, translating 'as with a wind from the north-east, Boreas or Apeliotes'. (Catullus, 26. 3, has the same combination.)[1]

ἐγένετο δὲ καί, κ.τ.λ.: one expects ὅμως; for the meaning is, the stormy weather made the passage of the outer ditch very difficult; but for all that the success of their flight was due primarily to this same storm.

24. 1. τὴν ἐς Θήβας φέρουσαν ὁδόν: the way leading north-east and then north from Plataia. The pursuers took the road up hill south-east and east from Plataia, which joined the Thebes–Eleusis–Athens road north of the Dryoskephalai pass. See Hdt. ix. 39. As J. L. Myres points out, C.R. lxiv, 1950, 11–12, τοῖς ζεύγεσι in Herodotos means wheeled vehicles, and the main road was a wagon-road.

τὸ τοῦ Ἀνδροκράτους ἡρῷον: the site has not been identified, and the topography of the great battle of Plataia is in consequence still uncertain. Cf. Hdt. ix. 25. 3; Plut. Arist. 11. 3; Grundy, Plataea, 17–18.

2. Ἐρύθρας καὶ Ὑσιάς: their sites are doubtful, but appear to have been at a short distance to the east of the Thebes–Athens road, and in the foothills of Kithairon. They were Boeotian townships, but claimed to be, like Plataia, in alliance with Athens. See, however, Grundy, 10–11, who puts both to the west of the main road: which is consistent with Herodotos (ix. 15), but hardly with Thucydides.

From here the party would go directly over the mountains (λαβό-μενοι τῶν ὀρῶν), i.e. in an ESE. direction towards Phyle and Athens, not south-east to Eleusis.

δώδεκα καὶ διακόσιοι: out of about 220 (20. 2); and none was killed—only one was captured and a few turned back; a most successful sally.

[1] Chambry and Widmann also defended ἢ βορέου: see Bursian, Jahresb. c, 1899, 197.

3. ἀπαγγειλάντων ὡς οὐδεὶς περίεστι: note the vivid tense—'no one has got away'; but from what source did Thucydides have this detail? Cf. 59. 4 n.

οἱ μὲν· δὴ τῶν Πλαταιῶν ἄνδρες οὕτως ὑπερβάντες ἐσώθησαν: 'this was the way the men from Plataia got across the encircling walls and ditches and reached safety.'

This lively narrative of the escape from Plataia gives rise to the same questions about the composition of the *History* as is suggested by the narrative of the pestilence, ii. 49–53. The facts were surely told to Thucydides by one or more of the men who escaped, on their arrival in Athens; and this means that he knew at once every detail that they themselves remembered, the measuring for the ladders, the noise made by the storm and also by the falling of the tiles, the first man up, the crossing of the second ditch, the enemy with their torches offering an easy mark and later seen disappearing up the glens of Kithairon, the one man captured—everything in the narrative was known to him except the last incident, the half-dozen turning back with the story that all were lost and the men in the town next day asking for leave to collect their dead. Did Thucydides leave all this in the form of disconnected jottings from 427 to about 400 B.C., before writing a connected narrative? That is to say, those who maintain the unity of the *History* in the sense of believing that Thucydides started to write it after 404 and went on with it continuously till he died (and they have reasons for their belief), should state more clearly what they believe Thucydides' 'notes' (which of course they agree that he made through the course of the war and used later) consisted of; for 'notes', as here, in ii. 49–53 and often elsewhere, might be virtually equivalent to the final narrative.

25, 27–35. *Mytilene. The City Surrenders. Peloponnesian Squadron in Eastern Aegean*

25. 1. τοῦ αὐτοῦ χειμῶνος τελευτῶντος: towards the end of February, 427 B.C.

Σάλαιθος: the Spartans had great belief in the ability of single Spartans to sway the course of events, not always unreasonably: Meleas, 5. 2; Tantalos, iv. 57. 3, above all, Gylippos. They were not all Spartiates, by any means.

ἐς Πύρραν: see 18. 1 n.

κατὰ χαράδραν τινά: i.e. a rocky gully, dry for most of the year, but full from time to time immediately after rain. If the Athenian περιτείχισμα was continuous, it must have been carried over the χαράδρα by a bridge; more probably, a place where it was narrow and rocky was chosen for the line of the wall, and a gap left in it—a gap which would be scarcely vulnerable to any hoplite attack from the

287

city, but which would give passage to a single man bold enough to risk being seen. There is no difficulty in ὑπερβατόν (for which Herwerden conjectured ὑποβατόν, accepted by Hude)—it means simply the spot where the wall, as a continuous defensive work, could be crossed, by whatever means were most suitable.

αἱ τεσσαράκοντα νῆες: 16. 3.

YEAR 5: 427–426 B.C. (CC. 26–88)

26. Peloponnesian Invasion of Attica

26. 1. τοῦ δ' ἐπιγιγνομένου θέρους: this is not said to be before the usual time for such invasions, about the middle of May; but, as there was a special urgency in this case, we may assume that it was earlier.

τὰς - - - δύο καὶ τεσσαράκοντα ναῦς: both before, 16. 3 and 25. 1 (which is immediately before), and afterwards, 29. 1, 69. 1 (cf. 76), this squadron is said to have consisted of forty ships; edd. have therefore deleted δύο καί, or the whole numeral (Steup), as the usual explanation of a commentator; not just a stupid commentator this time, but one painstakingly exact who added the two Mytilenean triremes (4. 5 and 5. 2), which indeed may have accompanied Alkidas' squadron but which Thucydides clearly ignored. This is the most unlikely supposition—why should the commentator, if Thucydides wrote τὰς ἐς τὴν M. ναῦς, not insert τεσσαράκοντα simply, which he could get from the foregoing chapter? or why should he correct τεσσαράκοντα, if at all, here only? I prefer to believe that Thucydides did hear at one time that Alkidas had forty-two ships under him (cf. 31. 1, οἱ Λέσβιοι οἱ ξυμπλέοντες), and that in 29. 1, if at any of these places, the commentator has added the figure, τεσσαράκοντα (μ̄—for the numeral—being written very like ν in minuscule, may have been inserted before ναυσί, as Mervyn Jones reminds me); if the extra two were the Mytilenean, they would of course not be included in the other passages. Thucydides would then be guilty of forgetting here to explain the two extra ships, and of not revising his history thoroughly.

M. Boas, *Phil. Woch.* 1927, 700–3, defends with some reason the MSS. reading ἔχοντα (ἄρχοντα Stephanus, edd.), Ἀλκίδαν being the object of ἀπέστειλαν and ναῦς of the participle; cf. Xen. *Hell.* ii. 2. 5; Dem. iii. 5. This would carry with it the bracketing of προστάξαντες (as Boas admitted was possible); which is perhaps right.

ἀπέστειλαν: 'had dispatched.' But they had not got very far (§ 4, 27. 1).

Ἀλκίδαν, ὃς ἦν αὐτοῖς ναύαρχος: for a Spartan ἄρχων or στρατηγός of a naval force was not necessarily the ναύαρχος (ii. 86. 6, 93. 1).

Knemos was nauarchos for 430–429 (ii. 66. 2, 80. 2); his successor is unknown, for Alkidas is in command for 428–427, apparently, autumn to autumn (iii. 69, 76, 80). See ii. 93. 1 n.

ταῖς ναυσὶν - - - καταπλεούσαις ἐπιβοηθήσωσιν: if, as Steup maintains, ἐπιβοηθεῖν must here have the meaning it has elsewhere in Thucydides (and in other writers), 'send to the aid of', ταῖς ναυσίν must mean 'with their fleet'. To this there is no objection; cf. 29. 1, τοὺς μὲν ἐκ τῆς πόλεως Ἀθηναίους λανθάνουσι, a new Athenian fleet sailing from Athens being taken for granted. But in that case ἐς τὴν M. goes naturally with the main verb and καταπλεούσαις is otiose. Steup brackets it; but it does not really help to say that a word confuses the meaning and therefore is an *explanatory* addition from the margin. If ἐπιβοηθεῖν can mean 'to send an expedition against' (cf. the frequent neutral meaning of βοήθεια and βοηθεῖν, and the hostile meaning of ἐπί in ἐπιπλεῖν or ἐπιέναι), there is no difficulty: 'against their, the Peloponnesian, fleet as it was approaching Mytilene.' Another possibility is ταῖς ναυσὶ ⟨σφίσιν⟩ ἐς τὴν M. καταπλέουσιν ἐ.; for it seems easier to understand ταῖς ναυσίν to be the Athenian fleet.

2. Κλεομένης: Pleistoanax and Kleomenes were sons of Pausanias the regent; Pleistoanax had been in exile since 445 (ii. 21. 1), and did not return before the autumn of this year, 427 (v. 16. 3 n.). The younger Pausanias resumed his reign on his father's death in 408. Unless he was born after his father's exile, and yet had been accepted as king, he was over 18 at this time, though Kleomenes acts for him on the campaign.

Since Archidamos had led all previous invasions of Attica and his son Agis, already king, led the next (and last of the ten years' war), 89. 1, it is reasonable to suppose that Archidamos was at this time, May 427, still alive, but too ill to serve abroad, and Agis not yet king. See vol. i, p. 405.

For Thucydides' silence about the death of Archidamos, cf. his silence about Phormion, 7. 1 n.

πατρὸς δὲ ἀδελφὸς ὤν: as though he had written αὐτὸς μὲν οὐ βασιλεὺς ὤν, ἀλλ' ὑπερ Πλ., κ.τ.λ. (Steup). This seems to me sound; cf. ii. 37. 1, κατὰ πενίαν, ἔχων δέ, and n. there; and Stahl's πατρὸς δή (adopted by Hude) most unlikely, and not made more probable by his other instances of δή in participial clauses.

3. εἴ τι ἐβεβλαστήκει: yet according to the author of *Hellenica Oxyrhynchia*, 12. 5, the well-appointed and prosperous land of Attica did not suffer much before the occupation of Dekeleia. We must suppose that olive-trees were not uprooted, only their expected fruit as completely as possible destroyed; and the fertile plain near the city was protected by the Athenian cavalry. Busolt, indeed, iii. 994. 6, following up a suggestion by Gilbert based on Theopompos,

F 93 and 94 (from schol. Ar. *Eq.* 226, and *Ach.* 6), thinks that in this year the cavalry did not defend the plain, and that Kleon accused them of λιποστρατία and tried to bring pressure on them by withholding 5 tal. due to them—the famous five which the cavalry compelled him to disgorge. This he is said to have done either as bouleutes (in 428–427, towards the end of his term of office), or, according to the older view, in 427–426, as hellenotamias (if he held that office in 427–426; but this is not accepted in *A.T.L.* i. 567). This is an ingenious and possible explanation of Aristophanes' jesting; but clearly we cannot conclude, as Busolt does, p. 1021, that the plain near Athens *was* ravaged.

μετὰ τὴν δευτέραν: see ii. 57. 2.

4. ἐπεξῆλθον τὰ πολλὰ τέμνοντες: 'they carried through to the end their destruction of nearly everything they saw', to express it at length. ἐπεξιέναι as in i. 70. 7, 120. 5, v. 100.

27. 1. ὡς αἵ τε νῆες αὐτοῖς οὐχ ἧκον: this is the second time that Alkidas' delay is referred to (see 26. 4); but it is not related till c. 29. ἐπελελοίπει: the pluperfect should certainly mean 'was now exhausted'; but apparently there was some food still (§ 3)—unless we are to suppose that demagogues demanded 'distribution of the food which the rich are hoarding', which was in fact no longer there.

2. ὁπλίζει: the authorities had at least been storing arms—a special supply brought in before the revolt (2. 2)?

3. κατὰ ξυλλόγους τε γιγνόμενοι: κατὰ ξυστάσεις in ii. 21. 3. Cf. also ii. 22. 1 n.

τοὺς δυνατούς: this phrase, and οἱ ἐν τοῖς πράγμασιν below, do not in themselves necessarily imply an oligarchic form of government, any more than does τῶν ἀρχόντων just above; but as the masses do not take action till they are armed, and then threaten independent, not constitutional, action, it is clear that Mytilene was in fact an oligarchy.

28. 1. ποιοῦνται κοινῇ: 'both parties together.' One would guess that, till the crisis was come, they had not been widely separated in policy.

πρός τε Πάχητα καὶ τὸ στρατόπεδον: Paches also consults his soldiers about a *military* truce. Cf. *I.G.* i.² 60 (Tod, 63: see below, p. 330), ὑπὸ τῶν στρατηγῶν καὶ τῶν στρατιωτῶν.

Ἀθηναίοις μὲν ἐξεῖναι, κ.τ.λ.: i.e. Paches had been given no powers to conclude *peace*, or to guarantee any terms of peace.

πρεσβείαν δὲ ἀποστέλλειν: see 36. 5 n.

2. ὥστε μὴ ἀδικῆσαι: i.e. he and his army will not break the truce by harming them; it is no promise for the peace treaty (Ἀθηναίοις μὲν ἐξεῖναι, κ.τ.λ., above).

3. Ἄντισσαν: Antissa had been the most active against Athens, or at least against a neighbour who chanced to be Athens' ally (18. 2); Eresos and Pyrrha could wait a little (35. 1).

29. 1. ταῖς τεσσαράκοντα ναυσί: see 26. 1 n.

ἐνδιέτριψαν: there is no such difficulty in the construction as Steup sees, who would delete this, or read ἐνδιατρίψαντες. 'On their voyage they had spent much time off the Peloponnesian coast and, crossing the Aegean in leisurely fashion, had indeed escaped the attention of the Athenians till they at last reached Delos, but, by the time they reached Ikaros, heard that Mytilene had fallen.'

τοὺς μὲν ἐκ τῆς πόλεως Ἀθηναίους: some edd. have made heavy weather of this: it means only the Athenians in Athens ('the authorities at home') who might be expected to take action from Athens. No special squadron is implied, though see 26. 1, n. on ταῖς ναυσίν. The Athenians (to whom the fall of Mytilene may already have been signalled—see below) in fact leave Alkidas to Paches.

πρὶν δὴ τῇ Δήλῳ ἔσχον: protected, they might suppose or hope, by the sanctity of the island. At least there would be no Athenian garrison there. But, we may conjecture, the arrival of a Peloponnesian squadron of forty ships was signalled at once to Athens, by beacons, via Tenos, Andros, and Karystos. (Müller-Strübing suggested Μήλῳ; which is not impossible—see the map; and n. on 32. 2.)

2. Ἔμβατον τῆς Ἐρυθραίας: the site of Embaton is not known; Erythraia is the mainland peninsula opposite Chios, separated from the island by a strait sufficiently narrow for them to be observed from Chios at once, though they may have been mistaken for an Athenian squadron (32. 3). What exactly made them temporarily secure at Embaton we do not know.

Τευτίαπλος: not otherwise known.

τάδε: this is the only speech prefaced by τάδε, instead of τοιάδε (vol. i, p. 144; the short speech of Sthenelaïdas is prefaced by ὧδε).

30. Speech of Teutiaplos

30. 1. πρὶν ἐκπύστους γενέσθαι: I have suggested that the presence of the Peloponnesians at Delos was signalled at once to Athens; but I do not mean that there were efficient means of communication generally; the news was not flashed back to Paches at Mytilene. See 33. 2 for the way the news did reach the latter.

2. ἡμῶν ἡ ἀλκή, κ.τ.λ.: as Böhme and Stahl saw, there is no difficulty here. On *this* occasion (τυγχάνει) the Peloponnesian strength lay principally in their ships; and it was at sea that there was the greatest hope of success from a surprise attack.

3. εἴ τις ἄρα, κ.τ.λ.: a fine touch of sarcasm—either 'our slowness will turn friends into enemies' (32. 2); or, perhaps, 'we have given the Athenians time to destroy all our friends'.

4. τὸ κενὸν τοῦ πολέμου: as between κενόν and καινόν (both pronounced alike from about the second century B.C.) the MSS. authority here, and in the other authors where the proverbial phrase is quoted (Arist., *Eth. Nic.* iii. 8. 6, 1116 b 7; Polyb. xxix. 16; Diod. xx. 30, 67; Cicero, *ad Att.* v. 20. 3), is of no weight; and unfortunately the context is nowhere decisive. Here neither fits easily, whatever the meaning of τὸ τοιοῦτον. If we take the relative clause by itself, it is clear that τὸ τοιοῦτον is a defect or an error, something to be avoided: 'that which a successful commander will guard against in himself and as soon as he observes it in the enemy will attack'; cf. v. 9. 3-4. τὸ τοιοῦτον then should not be τὸ ἄφνω προσπεσεῖν, which is not the error itself but the way one takes advantage of the error in the enemy; but it might be τὸ ἀφύλακτον. This, however, seems to limit it too much, and I prefer to take it, quite generally, with a forward reference: 'τὸ κ. τοῦ πολέμου is just this and nothing else, namely what we should avoid in ourselves', etc. If that is correct, we must read τὸ κενόν. See for example Stahl who, reading τὸ καινόν, has to render τὸ τοιοῦτον as τὸ ἄφνω προσπεσεῖν, and ὅ "sic intellegendum esset ut cum verbo φυλάσσοιτο iunctum significaret τὸ ἄλλους ἑαυτῷ προσπεσεῖν ἄφνω, cum verbo ἐνορῶν contra τὴν δύναμιν τοῦ τοῖς πολεμίοις προσπεσεῖν ἄφνω". Stahl recognizes the *durities* of this, but not its improbability. If we do read τὸ καινόν, the meaning must be 'the so-called novelties of war amount only to this sort of thing, namely, avoiding being taken by surprise yourself and taking the enemy by surprise'; that is, the 'enterprising general' is no more than one who takes precautions and seizes his chances (at v. 9. 3-4 the language is very similar). This is hardly in the Greek. But, though τὸ κενόν seems right, an exact interpretation of 'the empty, or the fruitless thing in war' is not easy. Polybios' instance of it, for example, is quite different: an eclipse of the moon, which was thought to portend the 'eclipse' of Perseus, and so discouraged the Macedonians and encouraged the Romans; οὕτως ἀληθές ἐστι τὸ περιφερόμενον ὅτι πολλὰ ⟨τὰ⟩ κενὰ τοῦ πολέμου; here καινά might do equally well.

I can see no reason for Steup's acceptance of τὸ κοινόν, the reading of some *recentiores* (ξυνὸς Ἐννάλιος, *communis Mars*; Arist. *Rhet.* ii. 21), which he supports by reference to v. 102; for it means the impartiality of war, likely to favour the weak side as well as the strong; and how can this be something to be avoided in oneself and looked for in an opponent?

This short speech provides a test for those who believe that all the speeches in Thucydides are 'free inventions'; for if we reject it as unhistorical, the whole episode of the advice given to Alkidas goes. Was Teutiaplos himself invented? Or did he exist, but give no such advice? We cannot, that is, reject the speech, yet believe that such advice was given. We are misled by the Greek use of direct speech, which for us suggests a verbatim report, but clearly did not for them. If Thucydides had put this into oblique oration (as, for example, 32. 2, below), I believe all would have accepted it, without further thought; yet from whom did Thucydides get his information about Teutiaplos? Perhaps from Ionian Greeks. See my *Essays*, pp. 173–4.

31. 1. οἱ Λέσβιοι οἱ ξυμπλέοντες: for these Lesbian fellow-travellers, cf. 26. 1, n. on δύο καὶ τεσσαράκοντα.

Κύμην: a city of some fame, but with little history. It plays some part in the Ionian war (bk. viii). It paid the comparatively high tribute of 9 tal. regularly, after having paid 12 tal. in 451 and 450.

ὅπως - - - ἀποστήσωσιν - - - ὑφέλωσι - - - γίγνηται: I do not doubt that Herwerden's deletion of ἤν before ὑφέλωσι and punctuation of the whole sentence, adopted by Stuart Jones, is both reasonable in itself and much the best correction yet made: 'that they may get Ionia to revolt and so drain away from Athens a large revenue, and at the same time, if [as might easily happen] Athens blockaded them in the city which was their base, [they could easily hold out with the help of Ionia and probably of Pissouthnes, and] it would cause her great expense [at a time when she was financially embarrassed, 13. 3, 19. 1].' That such a blockade was indeed something which Paches at least wished to avoid is stated below, 33. 3, as Poppo noted. There is some emphasis on αὐτοῖς: '*they* would have the expense' (not 'they alone', without Ionia, as Herwerden); but Thucydides, to help the reader, might have written δαπάνη αὐτοῖς. Steup agrees to the last part of this interpretation, but thinks that ἤν ὑφέλωσι may be kept, and καὶ ἄμα translated "auch zugleich" (with a comma therefore after ἐλπίδα - - - ἀφῖχθαι); but 'if we deprive Athens of a large revenue' is not a condition of Athens' blockading Alkidas at great expense, and "auch zugleich" has no good meaning here either.

ἐκ πόλεως ὁρμώμενοι: 'with a city as base of operations'; a city with all its resources and its political chances, not simply a useful harbour somewhere.

οὐδενὶ γὰρ ἀκουσίως ἀφῖχθαι: see ii. 8. 4–5, and n. there. Lindau's conjecture ἀκουσίῳ is attractive.

τὴν πρόσοδον ταύτην μεγίστην οὖσαν: officially 'Ionian tribute' included 'Karian tribute' (from the R. Maiandros southwards) since 438, and Thucydides may have had this in mind.

Πισσούθνην: satrap of Lydia, at least since 440 (i. 115. 4). As his father's name was Hystaspes, he had doubtless royal connexions.

32. 1. Μυοννήσῳ τῇ Τηΐων: a headland forming a peninsula, between Teos and Lebedos (Strabo, xiv. 1. 29, p. 643 ad fin.); not to be confused with Myous, the city ENE. of Miletos.

οὓς κατὰ πλοῦν εἰλήφει ἀπέσφαξε: as was the Spartan practice, ii. 67. 4.

2. τῶν ἐξ Ἀναίων: see 19. 2 n.

οὐ καλῶς τὴν Ἑλλάδα ἐλευθεροῦν: 'that that was not the right way to liberate Greece.' There was little to be said for Alkidas: his delay lost him all friends in Mytilene (30. 3, εἴ τις ἄρα, κ.τ.λ.), and his perverted cruelty would lose him all others.

There is a Lakonian inscription, *I.G.* v (1). 1 (Tod, 62), containing a list of contributions to a war-fund, by individuals and groups, Peloponnesians and others; mention is made of triremes; and, as it probably belongs to the period of the Archidamian war, not later, and since τοὶ Ἐφέσιοι and τῶν Χίων τοὶ φίλοι (pro-Peloponnesians among the Chians) are among the donors, it has been connected with the revolt of Mytilene. M. Cary thought of 428 B.C. (*J.H.S.* xlv, 1925, 245. 9), Adcock (in *Mélanges Glotz*, 1932, 1–6) of 427 and Alkidas' expedition. Unless the Ephesian and Chian gifts were made under duress, they are not likely to have been given to Alkidas, and Cary's view is perhaps to be preferred (their friends encouraging Sparta to send a fleet). If Adcock is right, the presence of Melians in the list may support the reading Μήλῳ in 29. 1.

3. ὁρῶντες γὰρ τὰς ναῦς, κ.τ.λ.: γάρ does not explain the previous statement, but the fact that Alkidas had made many prisoners (from merchantmen, κατὰ πλοῦν, above, not by landing anywhere, which he avoided doing). Thucydides gives an explanation which he might well have given before; and, as Steup says, he might have altered this chapter in a final revision. He had, however, time to revise between 421 and 415.

33. 1. ὑπὸ τῆς Σαλαμινίας καὶ Παράλου: the first time Thucydides has mentioned these specially fast Athenian vessels; who sight the enemy fleet by chance, and at once take the news to Paches.

ἔτι περὶ Κλάρον ὁρμῶν: Klaros was between Kolophon and Ephesos, so that Alkidas had been seen before he reached the latter (as indeed ἔτι implies). His putting into Ephesos, therefore, must have been imposed on him by necessity (for water, if he could not get it outside the city, or a rest) before his hurried retreat to the Peloponnese. But Thucydides has not put this in the natural way.

αἱ δ' ἀπ' Ἀθηνῶν ἔτυχον πλέουσαι: 'they had just arrived in those waters after a journey from Athens', on some business which is not told us; perhaps, however, they had been sent when the news reached Athens that an enemy fleet was crossing the Aegean.

2. ἀτειχίστου γὰρ οὔσης: perhaps since the Persian victory in 495.

Athens would not want them walled, against her, on the sea side (cf. i. 56. 2 n.); but might have wanted walls against a Persian attack. That they did not build them suggests a peaceful time for the Ionians under the tyrant city, and not much enmity between Athens and Persia. At Teos, perhaps much later, the Athenians built a wall on the land side; and when the city revolted, the citizens, with the help of the Persians, pulled it down (viii. 16. 3). Wade-Gery, in his study of the Peace of Kallias, *Ath. Stud.* 141, thinks that by the treaty Athens agreed not to fortify any city on the mainland of Asia as a reciprocal concession to Persia, as the latter was not to approach the coast with her land-forces.

μὴ - - - πορθῶσιν: there was a danger of this; but even of this Alkidas was incapable.

καὶ ὥς: 'even with this advantage' (because the cities were unwalled).

3. μέχρι μὲν Πάτμου: an ancient correction found in the scholia and *recentiores* for Λάτμου. Latmos is only known as a mountain in Karia.

κέρδος δὲ ἐνόμισεν: it would have been expensive, and, in the ordinary way, a long-drawn-out business (cf. 31. 1 n.); and Paches had much to do still at Mytilene (35. 1). The ensuing passives, especially ἠναγκάσθησαν, are notable, particularly with αἱ νῆες (Alkidas' fleet) the unexpressed subject: Greek is more chary generally of the passive than English, and here, if there was to be a passive, we should expect Paches to be the subject: 'he was glad he was not compelled to a long blockade.' I think the use here is intentional and ironic: Alkidas and his fleet might cause Paches to waste a lot of time and money, but not of their own volition, only if they were compelled—if, that is, they were caught (by storm, or by the Athenians) and shut themselves up in a harbour; they would be purely passive agents. This all depends, of course, on a city being willing, in the circumstances, to side with Alkidas.

We must remember the strength of the defensive in Greek siege warfare, and a fleet's need of a camp on land (above, p. 257, and vol. i, p. 19, init.).

34. 1. ἐς Νότιον τὸ Κολοφωνίων: the implication is that Notion and Kolophon properly formed one community, called Kolophonioi, which had been divided since the seizure of the upper town by Itamanes and his Persians; when the bulk of the inhabitants of the upper town migrated to Notion. But the two cities had been regularly, since 454 at least, assessed separately for their tribute to the League, Notion paying 2,000 dr., Kolophon 3 tal. or $1\frac{1}{2}$ tal., down to the beginning of the war.

There had been trouble at Kolophon earlier, as at Miletos and Erythrai (vol. i, pp. 350, 380: see now *A.T.L.* iii. 252–3), probably between 449 and 446, for she had paid her tribute regularly in the first period, 453–450, but her name is missing in the next (*A.T.L.* iii. 58–59). Fragments of a treaty with Athens exist, showing not only interference and settlement of political questions by Athens, including the establishment or restoration of democracy, and an oath of loyalty by the Kolophonians, but a colony as well (*I.G.* i. 14–15 = *A.T.L.* ii, D 15; *S.E.G.* x. 17); see R. Meiggs's article in *J.H.S.* lxiii, 1943, 'The Growth of Athenian Imperialism', p. 28, and *A.T.L.* iii. 282–4. The colony at this date shows that there cannot have been a clause in the Treaty of Kallias by which Athens agreed not to send new settlers to the mainland of Asia Minor (cf. vol. i, p. 335).

ὑπὸ 'Ιταμάνους: not otherwise known. It is also not known whether he was at the beginning acting under orders of Pissouthnes.

κατὰ στάσιν ἰδίαν: "ἰδίᾳ is a necessary correction of Krüger's, which Göller has adopted [and nearly all later edd.]; for στάσις ἰδία must be nonsense, there being no such thing as στάσις κοινή"—Arnold. The argument is not decisive; but Krüger's correction is probable. Aristotle, *Pol.* v. 2. 12, p. 1303 b 10, gives the distance of the two towns, Kolophon and Notion, from one another, as one cause of the strife; but he may be thinking of later times. The distance is eight miles only: see the Gazetteer in *A.T.L.* i.

ἡ δευτέρα Π. ἐσβολή: in the early summer of 430 B.C., ii. 47. 2, 55, 57. Thucydides might have said 'when the pestilence was first ravaging Athens'; which was doubtless the cause of Athenian ἡσυχία, ἀπραγμοσύνη, in the quarrel at Kolophon.

Kolophon and Notion are both missing from quota-lists 25 (430–429) and 26 (429–428); but the lists are fragmentary, and not much survives of the Ionian panel. For later years, see n. on § 4, below.

2. ἐπικούρους Ἀρκάδων: cf. Hdt. viii. 26 (in Xerxes' army), Hermippos, fr. 63. 18 (below, 71. 2 n.), ἀπὸ δ' Ἀρκαδίας ἐπικούρους, and Thuc. vii. 57. 9, where, however, a motive other than poverty at home and love of military adventure is mentioned.

ἐν διατειχίσματι: "in parte urbis, quae a reliqua muro separata et castelli instar erat. Ita Polybii verba διατειχίζειν τὴν πόλιν ἀπὸ τῆς ἄκρας (viii. 32. 2) a Bloomfieldio allata Livius xxi 11 expressit Latinis vallo urbem ab arce intersaepire. Cf. vii. 60. 2" (Stahl).

ξυνεσελθόντες ἐπολίτευον: Gertz's conjecture, ἐσελθόντες ξυνεπολίτευον, which makes this addition to the pro-Persian and anti-Athenian forces (dignified by the title of the aristocratical party) subsequent to the defeat of the pro-Athenians ('the democratic party') in Notion, is attractive.

τὸν Πάχητα ἐπάγονται: doubtless Apollophanes of Kolophon, whose services were recognized by an honorary decree in Athens, was one of these (*I.G.* i.² 59; some subsequent literaturė, *S.E.G.* x. 70).

4. οἰκιστάς: 'founders', meaning that the new Kolophon at Notion was to be an ἀποικία from Athens, though not consisting of Athenian citizens (Thourioi and Amphipolis had a minority only of Athenians among their first citizens). It was, of course, to be an independent community, within the Delian League, with its own constitution, modelled on that of Athens, as had been that of the original Kolophon, and of other cities, many years before (n. on § 1, above).

Both places continued to be assessed separately as members of the League, but with very small payments, Kolophon 500 dr. and Notion 100 dr. in 428–427; in 425 Kolophon was assessed at an unknown figure, Notion at 1 tal.; later, in 421–420 and 420–419 (in the intervening years, their names are missing), Kolophon again paid 500 dr., Notion returned to its old figure of 2,000 dr. See list 27 in *A.T.L.* ii, and ibid. iii. 289. It is not easy to understand the purpose or the meaning of this separate assessment in 427. It was Old Kolophon, presumably, which was recovered by Athens in 410 (Xen. *Hell.* i. 2. 4).

This episode well illustrates the strife of parties in these little states (their freedom to quarrel had at least not been stifled by Athens) and the way they got involved in greater struggles: cf. 82. 1–2. It also shows how to overcome an enemy with the saving of many lives, and how to punish war-crimes; but a hundred years ago Grote was shocked (v, pp. 163–4).

35. 1. τήν τε Πύρραν καὶ Ἔρεσον: 18. 1; for the third city, Antissa, see 28. 2.

τοὺς ἐκ τῆς Τενέδου: 28. 2. Presumably a decree had been passed by the Athenians to send them, with Salaithos and any other presumed ringleader of the revolt, to Athens; otherwise Paches would have been breaking his word (Classen). It is not, however, impossible that Paches did break his word.

36–48. *Debate at Athens on the Terms for Mytilene: Speeches of Kleon and Diodotos*

36. 1. τὸν μὲν Σάλαιθον εὐθὺς ἀπέκτειναν: cf. iv. 57. 3, 4. Salaithos was in a different position from Tantalos.

2. τήν τε ἄλλην ἀπόστασιν ὅτι, κ.τ.λ.: there is much in favour of Classen's insertion of καί before ὅτι—'the revolt in general, and because Mytilene had been privileged, and in addition (προσξυνελάβοντο) because the Peloponnesians had dared to cross the Aegean'; but it is not essential.

προσξυνελάβοντο: I believe the reading προσξυνεβάλετο (AEGM), or προσξυνεβάλοντο, is to be preferred. ξυμβάλλεσθαι, 'contribute towards', gives a more exact meaning; for ξυλλαμβάνεσθαι is rather 'to

297

have a part in', e.g. in iv. 47. 2, where the ambition of the Athenian strategoi 'contributed to' a policy in which they shared (see n. there); whereas the Peloponnesian fleet has no share in this ὁρμή. Cf. 45. 6, below, ἡ τύχη - - - ξυμβάλλεται ἐς τὸ ἐπαίρειν. If the remarkable singular, προσξυνεβάλετο, cannot be justified by αἴτιον ἦν οἱ Λακεδαιμόνιοι, iv. 26. 5, and viii. 9. 3, I would read προσξυνεβάλοντο. προσξυνελάβοντο is, however, preferred by Powell (ed. Hdt. viii, n. on 90. 5).

3. κατὰ τάχος: Stuart Jones's suggestion to join this with πέμπουσιν, by putting the comma after it, rather than with διαχρήσασθαι, is surely right.

4. ὠμὸν καὶ μέγα: see 49. 4, n. on πρᾶγμα ἀλλόκοτον.

5. οἱ παρόντες πρέσβεις: see 28. 1. (Classen thought that these could not be the same delegation, because the Athenians, according to him, must already have sent orders to Paches in answer to its requests, 35. 1 n. But there was nothing to prevent the delegation staying on.)

παρεσκεύασαν τοὺς ἐν τέλει: 'got the authorities to.' There are many ways of 'getting' people; but bribery or promises are not suggested here, as explained below.

The authorities are the strategoi, who might demand that the prytaneis summon a special meeting of the ekklesia (ii. 22. 1, 59. 3, iv. 118. 14). Arnold, in the light of vi. 14, discusses the problem whether, after a resolution had properly passed the ekklesia, it could again be put to the vote; and points out that Kleon says nothing of any illegal procedure. This sentence shows that ἀναψηφίσαι was not illegal; but perhaps a preliminary resolution was carried that discussion be reopened. See an article by A. R. W. Harrison in *J.H.S.* lxxv, 1955, 26–35.

αὖθίς τινας σφίσιν ἀποδοῦναι: in spite of the passages noted by Böhme and others, iv. 69. 1, vi. 41. 2, and the *v.l.* in vii. 29. 3 (which are not all parallel; in vi. 41. 2 it means 'certain persons'), I believe we should read τινα here, as Reiske conjectured.

6. ἀφ' ἑκάστων: not ἀφ' ἑκατέρων, so there were more than two 'sides' to the question.

Κλέων ὁ Κλεαινέτου: his first mention in Thucydides (though he had had at least one earlier opportunity: see ii. 21. 3, n. on ἐκάκιζον, and iii. 19. 1 n.); and he is at once judged, βιαιότατος τῶν πολιτῶν. However, both this and τῷ δήμῳ πιθανώτατος are well witnessed in the speech which is now given to him. See Ar. *Eq.* 626 ff.; indeed, the whole play. Kleon is seen as the typical product of the war (cf. v. 16. 1): βίαιος διδάσκαλος ὁ πόλεμος; but see n. on v. 16. 1.

τὴν προτέραν: Classen pointed to the awkwardness of understanding γνώμην here in the sense of 'decision' from ἄλλαι γνῶμαι, where it means 'opinions', 'views'; and suggested τῇ προτέρᾳ, 'at the previous sitting' (cf. 41). But 'view' will surely serve as the meaning in both places.

ἐν τῷ τότε: not written till some time afterwards, perhaps not before Kleon's death; but not necessarily later than 418 or 417, in a work not designed especially for Athenian readers, nor only for contemporaries. Mme de Romilly, p. 146, n. 4, with 162 and n. 4, denies that τότε has special significance, so that, as far as that is concerned, these words could have been written the day after the debate; but I am not convinced that all the cases, i. 139. 4, iv. 12. 3, and 21. 3, can be thus dismissed.

37. 1. δημοκρατίαν ὅτι ἀδύνατον, κ.τ.λ.: from the start there is no flattery of the demos by this persuasive demagogue, no letting himself be led by the people (cf. Grote, v, pp. 394–5 nn.). ἔγωγε at once marks his self-assertion.

2. διὰ γὰρ τὸ καθ' ἡμέραν ἀδεές, κ.τ.λ.: cf. ii. 37. 2 and 39. 1 (Perikles), and vii. 69. 2 (Nikias). The Corinthians had said something very like this of Sparta, i. 68. 1. It is a quality in fact not confined to democracies, and not to be found in every democracy; but one of which Athens was proud. As the scholiast says, τὸ καθ' ἡμέραν ἀδεές is just what the tyrant lacks, who is ever anxious and cannot sleep for thinking of the conspirator's dagger (cf. O.T. 584–6); and the phrase points forward to τυραννίδα, below.

λόγῳ πεισθέντες ὑπ' αὐτῶν: Aristophanes agreed (Ach. 634–7)! He had not much pity either, at least not in his youthful plays.

οὐκ ἐπικινδύνως ἡγεῖσθε, κ.τ.λ: 'you do not realize that such weakness is dangerous to yourselves and wins no gratitude from the allies.' The first οὐ governs, of course, both clauses, and so negatives the second: 'you think it safe and that it wins gratitude.'

τυραννίδα ἔχετε τὴν ἀρχήν: Kleon imitates and strengthens Perikles' words (ii. 63. 2—see n. there); but here too the word is qualified— Athenian rule is a tyranny because it is a rule over unwilling subjects who are always conspiring against it (so that there can be no καθ' ἡμέραν ἀδεές καὶ ἀνεπιβούλευτον between them and Athens). Compare Plato's description of the very rich man finding himself on a desert island surrounded by all his servants: Rep. ix. 578 D–E.

οἳ οὐκ ἐξ ὧν: οἳ is from the recentiores only, and is probably a reader's correction; it is a stopgap. But some such stopgap is necessary (Gertz's οὐ ⟨γὰρ⟩ ἐξ ὧν is as good), as can be seen from the scholiast's and Spratt's attempts to explain the existing text, from Stahl's vain emendation, or Classen's defence of the asyndeton.

βλαπτόμενοι αὐτοί: 'to your own hurt', with χαρίζησθε.

ἰσχύι μᾶλλον ἢ τῇ ἐκείνων εὐνοίᾳ: cf. the Mytileneans' words, 9. 2, 12. 1.

3. πάντων δὲ δεινότατον, κ.τ.λ.: not really in logical sequence with

299

the last sentences; but it has this in common with them, that it is a fault in democracy.

νόμοις ἀκινήτοις: ἀκινήτοις here means not 'unchanged', but 'undisturbed', that is 'valid', 'always obeyed', the opposite simply of ἀκύροις, below. Cf. i. 18. 1 (vol. i, p. 128); also G. Thomson on *Eumen.* 696; above, ii. 37. 3; and Arist. *Pol.* iv. 4. 3, 1292 a 1, and 6. 3, 1294 a 1, for a later view. 'Content with inferior ἤθη καὶ νόμοι' in vi. 18. 7 has a different colouring. Cf. Plat. Com., fr. 220, for frequent changes of law in Athens: 'go away for three months, and it is no longer the same city.'

Kleon, as has often been pointed out, is confusing ψηφίσματα with νόμοι; the laws of Athens would not be affected by the rescinding of an executive decree. He does so of set purpose; it is one of his ways of bullying and confusing the issue. He has, however, a case: he is attacking his countrymen's instability of purpose.

ἀμαθία τε μετὰ σωφροσύνης: see i. 84. 3, Archidamos' way of putting the same thought (vol. i, pp. 249–50). Kleon is here repudiating Perikles' claim, ii. 40. 2–3, 62. 5. Naturally such demagogues as Kleon were also called ἀμαθεῖς by their enemies: Ar. *Eq.* 188–93, with 228 and 233 for the other side. Σωφροσύνη, besides, was the virtue especially claimed by the oligarchic parties (82. 8).

δεξιότης μετὰ ἀκολασίας: just the qualities of an Alkibiades, whom Kleon feared and hated equally. Kleon would have no patience with the brilliant, sophist-trained youth of Athens, as Aristophanes makes clear; his own ἀκολασία was of a different aspect. Aristophanes himself was another of these brilliant younger men (cf. *Nub.* 545–9) whom Kleon, with good reason, disliked and feared.

οἵ τε φαυλότεροι τῶν ἀνθρώπων: 'inferior men', 'men of second-rate intellect'. Cf. 83. 3. Euripides has something like this in *Andromache* (probably written about this time (iii. 68. 1, n.; but see below, p. 425)), 479–82, though the moral is different, namely the disadvantages of democracy when in opposition to a monarch:

> πνοαὶ δ' ὅταν φέρωσι ναυτίλους θοαί,
> κατὰ πηδαλίων δίδυμαι πραπίδων γνῶμαι,
> σοφῶν τε πλῆθος ἀθρόον ἀσθενέστερον
> φαυλοτέρας φρενὸς αὐτοκρατοῦς.

Cf. Plato, *Rep.* vi. 503 c–d (how rare is the combination of quick wits with steadiness of character).

ἄμεινον οἰκοῦσι τὰς πόλεις: 'run their cities better', or 'make better citizens'.

4. τῶν τε νόμων σοφώτεροι, κ.τ.λ: again echoed from Archidamos of Sparta, i. 84. 3 (noted by the scholiast in this case). Sokrates, in *Kriton*, would also have agreed; and cf. Arist. *Rhet.* i. 15. 12. These good conservative sentiments, here and in the next chapter, proper to Archidamos and the Just Argument of *The Clouds*, should not surprise us on the lips of Kleon (any more than we should object that he confuses law and decree, above, as though Thucydides were writing an essay on politics) ; Aristophanes as usual gives us a picture of the man complementary to that drawn here—part of the picture being that Kleon's followers were, typically, the older generation, the conservatives and Marathon-men, who liked the old songs of Phrynichos. Particularly interesting would be the passage in *Equit.* 985 ff., if Kleon's admiration for good Dorian sentiment had been noted:

$$\begin{aligned}
&\text{ἀλλὰ καὶ τόδ' ἔγωγε θαυ-}\\
&\text{μάζω τῆς ὑομουσίας}\\
&\text{αὐτοῦ· φασὶ γὰρ αὐτὸν οἱ}\\
&\text{παῖδες οἳ ξυνεφοίτων,}\\
&\text{τὴν Δωριστὶ μόνην ἂν ἁρ-}\\
&\text{μόττεσθαι θαμὰ τὴν λύραν,}\\
&\text{ἄλλην δ' οὐκ ἐθέλειν μαθεῖν.}
\end{aligned}$$

(With this we may compare the *pretended* ἀμαθία of Sparta in Plato, *Protagoras*, 342.)

It was also especially characteristic of Thucydides' generation at Athens that men should experiment with the meanings of words, the same words in different contexts (cf. Eur. *Hipp.* 380–7) ; and more particularly of Thucydides himself that he should be so much concerned with the ideas behind the words, apparently similar ideas held by such different men as Archidamos and Kleon, the imitations and as well the contradictions of Perikles by Kleon, or by Alkibiades (vi. 18 nn.), or different ideas expressed by the same man, or similar men, on different occasions (for this, see iv. 10. 1 n.). Every belief, every faith, every argument, was turned inside out for criticism and analysis.

περιγίγνεσθαι: 'to get the best of', whatever is said, on all occasions, in the public assembly.

ὡς ἐν ἄλλοις μείζοσιν: 'as though there could be no more important occasion for them to display their views' ; i.e. every occasion is for them the most important, so they must speak ; but the point of this is not too clear. Because of 40. 3 Bloomfield conjectured μείοσιν, 'as though they could not display their cleverness more suitably on less important occasions' than those of public debate ; but μείων is not found in Attic prose outside Xenophon, nor in Herodotos.

τοῦ καλῶς εἰπόντος μέμψασθαι λόγον: against the opinion of most edd., I believe τοῦ κ. εἰπόντος is genitive of comparison, not possessive with λόγον. It must surely mean 'the clever speaker', not 'the wise adviser' (cf. 38. 2, 4: τῷ λέγειν πιστεύσας, τὸ εὐπρεπὲς τοῦ λόγου, τῶν εὖ εἰπόντων, and especially τῶν λόγῳ καλῶς ἐπιτιμησάντων) ; and, if the genitive is possessive, that is weak in logic—'not so well able to criticize the clever orator's speech'; for as good judges, this is just what they have to do. Better is 'not so well able as the clever orator to pull a speech to pieces'; and the second half of the sentence is thus closely parallel with the first, ἀμαθέστεροι τῶν νόμων. Stobaios, in his quotation (*Ecl.* iv. 1. 59 H.), however, has τὸν τοῦ καλῶς εἰπόντος; and for καλῶς εἰπεῖν meaning 'speak honourably', cf. 82. 7. κριταὶ δὲ ὄντες: 'good judges' of the effect of a speech, as opposed to clever critics of its style.

ἀπὸ τοῦ ἴσου: either 'impartial', unlike the ἀγωνισταί, or, perhaps, 'on level terms' with the clever speakers (or with each other), not at a disadvantage. With ἀγωνισταί cf. 38. 6, below, αὐτὸς εἰπεῖν ἕκαστος βουλόμενος δύνασθαι.

Perikles, ii. 40. 2, αὐτοὶ ἤτοι κρίνομέν γε ἢ ἐνθυμούμεθα ὀρθῶς τὰ πράγματα, says apparently much the same; but he does not repudiate the good speaker (ii. 60. 5), and does not regard good judgement, any more than courage, as a likely result of ἀμαθία. Kleon gets near to saying that the ekklesia should only be an organ of control, not of legislative and executive action: the masses can only *judge* well, and then only when not misled by clever speakers, or when they are too stupid to be misled by them. Contrast the truer judgement of Demosthenes, λόγους εὐπροσώπους καὶ μύθους - - - συνθεὶς καὶ διεξελθὼν ἀνθρώπους ἀπείρους λόγων - - - πείθει (xviii. 149).

5. καὶ ἡμᾶς: apparently 'we', the leading politicians, not 'we here in Athens', as would at first be expected.

ξυνέσεως ἀγῶνι: cf. 82. 7.

παρὰ δόξαν: all edd. agree that this should mean 'contrary to their real opinion'; but normally in Thucydides the phrase means 'contrary to expectation', παρὰ γνώμην being his invariable phrase elsewhere for 'contrary to their opinion' (cf. 12. 1, 42. 6). Hence some have adopted Reiske's παρὰ τὸ δόξαν, 'contrary to what has been decided' (generally, rather than 'what was decided yesterday'). It is possible to take παρὰ δόξαν in its normal sense, 'unexpectedly', here equivalent to 'paradoxically'; but it seems unlikely, for this point is not taken up till 38. 2 and 5. Plato uses παρὰ δόξαν in the sense 'against their true opinion', e.g. *Kriton*, 49 D (see Burnet's n. on 49 A), *Protag.* 337 B; and Thucydides may be so using it here.

38. 1. ὁ αὐτός εἰμι τῇ γνώμῃ: so Perikles, ii. 61. 2.

ὁ γὰρ παθών, κ.τ.λ.: a direct, but not quite an open, claim that in such circumstances at least ὀργή and not λογισμός should guide our actions. Cf. 82. 2, ὁ πόλεμος - - - πρὸς τὰ παρόντα τὰς ὀργὰς τῶν πολλῶν ὁμοιοῖ.

In the next clause we not only have ἀμύνεσθαι without definite article as subject to the verb, but there is no real distinction of meaning between subject and verb. This is an additional reason for bracketing ὄν with Haase and many edd., in order to put the emphasis on ἀντίπαλον as predicative adjective with τὴν τιμωρίαν: 'the avenger gets an *adequate* revenge'; "quo propius acceptam iniuriam vindicatio sequatur, eo magis par iniuriae supplicium sumitur" (Stahl). A notable case of μεταβολή, of which there are others in this elaborately phrased chapter.

ἀμβλυτέρᾳ τῇ ὀργῇ: see ii. 87. 3 n.

τὰς μὲν Μυτιληναίων ἀδικίας: 'that Mytilene's crimes are an advantage to us, and that our misfortunes do harm to our allies.' The second part means, not exactly as Arnold puts it, "when we suffer all our allies suffer with us", which, as he said, requires ⟨καὶ⟩ τοῖς ξ.; but 'our misfortunes are really theirs', or 'are their loss, not ours' (βλάβας is another case of μεταβολή). Both are equally paradoxical, particularly in Kleon's eyes, who has insisted that the subjects are unwilling subjects, as in a tyranny (37. 2).

Of course he *calls* the subjects ξύμμαχοι; cf. 39. 8 n., and contrast again Isokr. iv. 104-5 (see 11. 7 n.): ἀλλὰ τὴν τῶν συμμάχων ὁμόνοιαν κοινὴν ὠφέλειαν νομίζοντες τοῖς αὐτοῖς νόμοις ἁπάσας τὰς πόλεις διῳκοῦμεν, συμμαχικῶς ἀλλ' οὐ δεσποτικῶς βουλευόμενοι περὶ αὐτῶν, etc., only instituting democratic governments in the interests of peace and justice.

2. ἢ τῷ λέγειν πιστεύσας - - - ἢ κέρδει ἐπαιρόμενος: the alternatives lie in the two participial clauses only, 'either confident in his powers of oratory or excited by selfish ambition', not in the main verbs, the second of which, παράγειν πειράσεται, is only a generalized form of the first; for to prove that something that is is not, is an example of deceiving. As Steup says, there is some weakness in the rhetoric, in that confidence in oratory in effect reappears in the second clause in τὸ εὐπρεπὲς τοῦ λόγου ἐκπονήσας; later Kleon classifies his opponents more simply, 40. 1, ἐλπίδα οὔτε λόγῳ πιστὴν οὔτε χρήμασιν ὠνητήν.

τὸ πάνυ δοκοῦν - - - ὡς οὐκ ἔγνωσται: the use of ἔγνωσται here, especially after ἐγνῶσθαι in 36. 4, makes it, to me at least, almost certain that τὸ πάνυ δοκοῦν = ὃ πάνυ ἐδόκει: 'what was altogether our view yesterday was not decided at all'—the complete paradox. So Classen; Stahl's view, adopted by Steup, "id quod omnibus probatum est non constat", besides being much less forceful in itself, gives a weaker sense to ἔγνωσται. The perfect tense gives the meaning 'our resolution is recorded, for all to see'.

κέρδει ἐπαιρόμενος: the words do not necessarily imply bribery, or more than selfish ambitions; but Kleon doubtless meant the former.

τὸ εὐπρεπὲς τοῦ λόγου ἐκπονήσας: in *Knights*, 346-50, Kleon laughs at the sausage-monger who thinks he can easily become a good

303

speaker like Kleon himself: one little success will give him confidence in his powers. Demosthenes had told him it would be easy—

$$\tau\grave{o}\nu\ \delta\hat{\eta}\mu o\nu\ \mathring{a}\epsilon\grave{\iota}\ \pi\rho o\sigma\pi o\iota o\hat{v}$$
$$\mathring{v}\pi o\gamma\lambda\upsilon\kappa a\acute{\iota}\nu\omega\nu\ \mathring{\rho}\eta\mu a\tau\acute{\iota}o\iota s\ \mu a\gamma\epsilon\iota\rho\iota\kappa o\hat{\iota}s\ (215\text{--}16).$$

See also ll. 461–3, with Neil's n.

This was the period when the influence of Protagoras and Gorgias was at its height—Kleon feared it; he preferred to bully his opponents into silence (42. 2, ἐκπλῆξαι τούς τε ἀντερoῦντας καὶ τοὺς ἀκουσομένους); but this speech given him by Thucydides is itself a fine example of the elaborate style—Kleon joins in the ἀγών with a will. But I cannot agree with Stahl that τῷ λέγειν πιστεύσας refers specifically to Protagoras' skill in argument, and, by contrast, τὸ εὐπρεπὲς τοῦ λόγου ἐκπονήσας, to Gorgias' flowery rhetoric.

3. τὰ μὲν ἆθλα ἑτέροις δίδωσιν, κ.τ.λ.: cf. Thucydides' own words, ii. 65. 7, ἃ κατορθούμενα μὲν τοῖς ἰδιώταις τιμὴ καὶ ὠφελία μᾶλλον ἦν, κ.τ.λ.; and below, 40. 3 and 82. 8.

4. αἴτιοι δ' ὑμεῖς: 'and you are to blame', with a pause after it. Cf. Dem. xviii. 50, αἴτιος δ' οὗτος, κ.τ.λ., in one of his most effective passages. Elsewhere in Thucydides a similar phrase is less emphatic: i. 69. 1, iii. 55. 1.

κακῶς ἀγωνοθετοῦντες: κακῶς just as οὐ καλῶς 32. 2; but here the very act, ἀγωνοθετεῖν, 'to hold a festival of oratory', is a mistake. The Athenians, so to speak, had called for an *encore* of yesterday's debate, not in order, gravely and with more circumspection, to reconsider the merits of the case, but only to enjoy more and wittier speeches, a longer festival (not at all, by the way, what Thucydides says in 36. 4; see 40. 2 n.). This picture of a whole people enjoying the festival is elaborated in a most complex series of lively and vivid phrases to the end of this chapter, as remarkable a picture of the Athenian people as that in i. 70, and as anything in Aristophanes. Like Aristophanes, though in his different way, Thucydides had sympathy with the faults of his countrymen. Compare, too, Demosthenes, xviii. 226, xix. 217.

θεαταὶ μὲν τῶν λόγων, κ.τ.λ.: 'You are the spectators at a speech-festival', as though *it* were the whole performance, and no action were related to it; 'you merely hear tell of the actions' as though they concerned someone else, as in a story. Besides, they ought to *listen* to words and to *see* deeds with their eyes (as the Athenian soldiers often did, as Nikias knew, vii. 48. 4, soldiers who came home and voted against their generals for their mismanagement of a campaign). The rhetoric is effective; but the distinction is, of course, false (for in a theatre there is no difference between θεαταί and ἀκροαταί), and disappears in the next clause, where they listen to words (ἀπὸ τῶν εὖ εἰπόντων). This is very much in Gorgias' manner, parisosis, homoioteleuton, and the rest (just what Kleon professes to be attacking), with always this difference, the quality of the thought behind the words.

ἀπὸ τῶν εὖ εἰπόντων σκοποῦντες: wise men ἀπὸ τῶν ὑπαρχόντων σκοποῦσι, ii. 62. 5, iv. 18. 2 nn.

ὡς δυνατὰ γίγνεσθαι: these are Kleon's words, rebuking Athens for her easy optimism. Cf. iv. 21. 2–3, 65. 4 n.; but also i. 70. 7, ἀντελπίσαντες, κ.τ.λ., said in praise of her.

τὰ δὲ πεπραγμένα ἤδη - - - ἀπὸ τῶν λόγῳ καλῶς ἐπιτιμησάντων: ἐπιτιμᾶν for the more general λέγειν is a fine touch; for denunciation was the special gift of the demagogues, especially of Kleon (cf. iv. 27. 3, for a ready instance). Cf. Diodotos' words, εὖ διαβαλὼν ἐκπλῆξαι, 42. 2, and Nikias, vii. 48. 3. Archidamos implied much the same of the Corinthians in 432, λόγῳ καλῶς μεμφόμενοι (i. 84. 3), in a different context.

5. μετὰ καινότητος, κ.τ.λ.: not only do they indulge their passion for oratory and therewith lose all sense of reality, but the oratory must be novel and abnormal (τῶν αἰεὶ ἀτόπων). Again compare this with Aristophanes, especially The Clouds, remembering at the same time what he says of himself—

ἀλλ' ἀεὶ καινὰς ἰδέας ἐσφέρων σοφίζομαι,
οὐδὲν ἀλλήλαισιν ὁμοίας καὶ πάσας δεξιάς (547–8).

With ἀπατᾶσθαι ἄριστοι ('winning the prize for being deceived') cf. Hdt. iii. 80. 4 of the tyrant, διαβολὰς ἄριστος ἐνδέκεσθαι.

6. αὐτὸς εἰπεῖν ἔκαστος: that is, each would be a contestant rather than a spectator, ἀγωνισταί as in 37. 4; then the word ἀγωνίζεσθαι is introduced in the second-best alternative—if they must be spectators, there will be an ἀγών among them still, or between them and the orators.

ὀξέως δέ τι λέγοντος προεπαινέσαι: we need τι, and Krüger's τοῦ λέγοντος is no improvement. In their rivalry with the speakers, they applaud a point (whether of argument or of style) even before it has been made. These are the θεαταὶ δεξιοί of Aristophanes.

καὶ προαισθέσθαι, κ.τ.λ.: 'and so show themselves eager in appreciation of the oratory and slow in foreseeing its consequences.' πρόνοια, it will be remembered, was one of Perikles' distinguishing qualities (ii. 65. 6, 13). We could do well without εἶναι (secl. Poppo).

The Knights make a similar reproach to Demos, though in a gentler tone than Kleon (and in what a different style from Thucydides):

ὦ Δῆμε, καλήν γ' ἔχεις
ἀρχήν, ὅτε πάντες ἄν-
θρωποι δεδίασί σ' ὥσ-
περ ἄνδρα τύραννον.

$$\mathring{a}\lambda\lambda' \ \epsilon \mathring{v}\pi a\rho\acute{a}\gamma\omega\gamma os \ \epsilon \mathring{\iota},$$
$$\theta\omega\pi\epsilon v\acute{o}\mu\epsilon v\acute{o}s \ \tau\epsilon \ \chi a\acute{\iota}-$$
$$\rho\epsilon\iota s \ \kappa\mathring{a}\xi a\pi a\tau\acute{\omega}\mu\epsilon vos$$

(cf. $\mathring{a}\pi a\tau\mathring{a}\sigma\theta a\iota \ \mathring{a}\rho\iota\sigma\tau o\iota$, above),

$$\pi\rho\grave{o}s \ \tau\acute{o}v \ \tau\epsilon \ \lambda\acute{\epsilon}\gamma ov\tau' \ \mathring{a}\epsilon\grave{\iota}$$
$$\kappa\acute{\epsilon}\chi\eta vas\cdot \ \acute{o} \ vo\mathring{v}s \ \delta\acute{\epsilon} \ \sigma ov$$
$$\pi a\rho\grave{\omega}v \ \mathring{a}\pi o\delta\eta\mu\epsilon\mathring{\iota}. \hspace{2cm} (Equit. \ \text{1111-20})$$

Only $\kappa\acute{\epsilon}\chi\eta vas$, that favourite word with Aristophanes, gives a different and less flattering picture.

7. $\zeta\eta\tau o\mathring{v}v\tau\acute{\epsilon}s \ \tau\epsilon \ \mathring{a}\lambda\lambda o \ \tau\iota, \ \kappa.\tau.\lambda.$: 'looking for a different world, practically, from that in which we live, with no intelligent thought for our actual surroundings ($\acute{o} \ vo\mathring{v}s \ \mathring{a}\pi o\delta\eta\mu\epsilon\mathring{\iota}$); overcome in fact by your love of listening to words, just like men sitting listening to a sophist's display rather than counsellors deliberating on affairs of state.' $\kappa a\theta\eta\mu\acute{\epsilon}vo\iota s$ may have the meaning, 'sitting idly', as so often in Demosthenes (ii. 23, 24, iv. 9, 44, viii. 77, cited by Classen); but if so, we can hardly take $\theta\epsilon a\tau a\mathring{\iota}s$ predicatively with it (as seems right); for $\beta ov\lambda\epsilon vo\mu\acute{\epsilon}vo\iota s$ presumably corresponds with $\theta\epsilon a\tau a\mathring{\iota}s$, not with $\kappa a\theta\eta\mu\acute{\epsilon}vo\iota s$.

I can find no good meaning to $o\mathring{v}\delta\acute{\epsilon}$, and would prefer $o\mathring{v}\delta\acute{\epsilon}v$. 'Not even about the present, let alone about the future' is not here effective. (According to Hude AM have $o\mathring{v}$ (corr. a^2).)

This is interesting as the only direct mention of the sophists in Thucydides. Edd. note that Gorgias is said to have arrived in Athens later this summer, as ambassador for Leontinoi, and to have struck all Athens dumb with his speech: Diodoros, xii. 53. 2-5, $\tau\mathring{\omega} \ \xi\epsilon v\acute{\iota}\zeta ov\tau\iota$ $\tau\mathring{\eta}s \ \lambda\acute{\epsilon}\xi\epsilon\omega s \ \mathring{\epsilon}\xi\acute{\epsilon}\pi\lambda\eta\xi\epsilon \ \tau o\grave{v}s \ A\theta\eta va\acute{\iota} ovs \ \mathring{o}v\tau as \ \epsilon\mathring{v}\phi v\epsilon\mathring{\iota}s \ \kappa a\grave{\iota} \ \phi\iota\lambda o\lambda\acute{o}\gamma ovs. \ \pi\rho\mathring{\omega}\tau os$ $\gamma\grave{a}\rho \ \mathring{\epsilon}\chi\rho\acute{\eta}\sigma a\tau o \ \tau o\mathring{\iota}s \ \tau\mathring{\eta}s \ \lambda\acute{\epsilon}\xi\epsilon\omega s \ \sigma\chi\eta\mu a\tau\iota\sigma\mu o\mathring{\iota}s \ \pi\epsilon\rho\iota\tau\tau o\tau\acute{\epsilon}\rho o\iota s \ \kappa a\grave{\iota} \ \tau\mathring{\eta} \ \phi\iota\lambda o$-$\tau\epsilon\chi v\acute{\iota}\mathring{a} \ \delta\iota a\phi\acute{\epsilon}\rho ov\sigma\iota v, \ \mathring{a}v\tau\iota\theta\acute{\epsilon}\tau o\iota s \ \kappa a\grave{\iota} \ \mathring{\iota}\sigma o\kappa\acute{\omega}\lambda o\iota s \ \kappa a\grave{\iota} \ \pi a\rho\acute{\iota}\sigma o\iota s \ \kappa a\grave{\iota} \ \acute{o}\mu o\iota o\tau\epsilon\lambda\epsilon\acute{v}$-$\tau o\iota s \ \kappa a\acute{\iota} \ \tau\iota\sigma\iota v \ \mathring{\epsilon}\tau\acute{\epsilon}\rho o\iota s \ \tau o\iota o\acute{v}\tau o\iota s, \ \mathring{a} \ \tau\acute{o}\tau\epsilon \ \mu\grave{\epsilon}v \ \delta\iota\grave{a} \ \tau\grave{o} \ \xi\acute{\epsilon}vov \ \tau\mathring{\eta}s \ \kappa a\tau a\sigma\kappa\epsilon v\mathring{\eta}s$ $\mathring{a}\pi o\delta o\chi\mathring{\eta}s \ \mathring{\eta}\xi\iota o\mathring{v}\tau o, \ v\mathring{v}v \ \delta\grave{\epsilon} \ \pi\epsilon\rho\iota\epsilon\rho\gamma\acute{\iota}av \ \mathring{\epsilon}\chi\epsilon\iota v \ \delta o\kappa\epsilon\mathring{\iota}$ ('seem fussy') $\kappa a\grave{\iota}$ $\phi a\acute{\iota}v\epsilon\tau a\iota \ \kappa a\tau a\gamma\acute{\epsilon}\lambda a\sigma\tau a \ \pi\lambda\epsilon ov\acute{a}\kappa\iota s \ \kappa a\grave{\iota} \ \kappa a\tau a\kappa\acute{o}\rho\omega s \ \tau\iota\theta\acute{\epsilon}\mu\epsilon va$. (This is very likely from Timaios, fr. 95, and, perhaps, was not in Ephoros—so Busolt, iii. 706. 4; cf. also Plat. $Hipp. \ Mai.$ 282 B, and Ar. $Ach.$ 633-5.) Thucydides, however, though this speech is full of $\mathring{a}v\tau\acute{\iota}\theta\epsilon\tau a$, $\mathring{\iota}\sigma\acute{o}\kappa\omega\lambda a, \ \pi\acute{a}\rho\iota\sigma a$, and $\acute{o}\mu o\iota o\tau\acute{\epsilon}\lambda\epsilon v\tau a$, but not in so 'extravagant and artificial' a manner as in Gorgias, passes the orator over in silence in his brief mention of the Leontinoi embassy, 86. 3; and certainly many of the new rhetorical devices and conceits were known in Athens before 427, for they can be seen already in the plays of Euripides ($Medeia, \ Hippolytos$: see J. H. Finley, 'The Origins of Thucydides' Style', $Harv. \ Stud.$ l, 1939, 35-84, and 'Euripides and Thucydides', ibid. xlix, 1938, 23-68).

For the tone of Kleon's reference here to the sophists, cf. Aristophanes once more, *Nub.* 331–4 (Sokrates to Strepsiades)—

οὐ γὰρ μὰ Δί' οἶσθ' ὁτιὴ πλείστους αὗται βόσκουσι σοφιστάς,
Θουριομάντεις ἰατροτέχνας σφραγιδονυχαργοκομήτας,
κυκλίων τε χορῶν ᾀσματοκάμπτας ἄνδρας μετεωροφένακας,
οὐδὲν δρῶντας βόσκουσ' ἀργούς, ὅτι ταύτας μουσοποιοῦσιν.

39. 2. ἐγὼ γάρ: this, following ἐγώ in § 1, again marks the egoism of Kleon (37. 1 n.).

αὐτόνομοί τε οἰκοῦντες καὶ τιμώμενοι ἐς τὰ πρῶτα: cf. the Mytileneans' own words, 9. 3, 11. 3.

ἐπανέστησαν μᾶλλον, κ.τ.λ.: a somewhat frigid conceit, with homoioteleuton. German translators suggest "sie haben eher einen Anfall als Abfall gemacht". ἀποστῆναι is 'to secede', 'withdraw' (cf. 13. 1 n.); but the definition of ἀπόστασις is very forced, as though it were something which could not be helped.

3. παράδειγμα δὲ αὐτοῖς οὔτε, κ.τ.λ.: in their own way, the Mytileneans argued, this is just what they had done, 10. 6, 11. 8. See also 40. 7.

οὔτε ἡ παροῦσα εὐδαιμονία: Chios was the ideal state: viii. 24. 4, μόνοι μετὰ Λακεδαιμονίους ὧν ἐγὼ ᾐσθόμην ηὐδαιμόνησάν τε ἅμα καὶ ἐσωφρόνησαν, κ.τ.λ. See Headlam, ap. G. Thomson on Aesch. *Cho.* 687–95. Kleon's indignation at the rashness, the lack of caution in Mytilene, is finely simulated.

ἐλπίσαντες: on the use of ἐλπίς in this debate see 45. 5 n.

μακρότερα μὲν τῆς δυνάμεως, κ.τ.λ.: another example of a rhetorical figure very much in Gorgias' manner, displaying ἀντίθετον, ἰσόκωλον, πάρισον, and ὁμοιοτέλευτον, all four.

ἰσχὺν ἀξιώσαντες τοῦ δικαίου προθεῖναι: this may have been true, and Mytilene felt uneasy (9–10); but it was hardly for the apostle of force (37. 2, 40. 7) to complain. See also 44. 4 n., for Kleon's use of τὸ δίκαιον.

ἐν ᾧ γὰρ ᾠήθησαν: they chose what they thought was the moment of Athenian weakness, 3. 1, 13. 3.

4. εἴωθε δέ, κ.τ.λ.: doubtless true, but not strictly relevant here; for the only thing unexpected about Mytilene's good fortune was the ill-fortune of Athens (the pestilence). It is another case of love of generalization making its way into a speech. Arnold quotes 'beggars mounted run their horses to death'. The further explanation of this wisdom, τὰ δὲ πολλά, κ.τ.λ., does not improve it. However, Philistos thought it worth while to imitate it (F 67).

μάλιστα καὶ δι' ἐλαχίστου: both these adverbial expressions may be taken with the verb, ἔλθῃ, or, less probably, with ἀπροσδόκητος—'to whom unexpected prosperity comes in a very great degree and at very short notice'; and the order found in the MSS. may stand.

307

Steup's objection that Mytilene's prosperity had not arrived suddenly has little weight: see previous n.; their opportunity had come suddenly, before indeed they were prepared for it (13. 2).

5. πέφυκε γὰρ καὶ ἄλλως, κ.τ.λ.: another wide generalization, but more to the point than the last. For θεραπεύειν, on both sides, see 12. 1.

6. κολασθέντων δὲ καὶ νῦν: a sudden turn to the immediate case before the speaker, away from the generalizations. Cf. 12. 1 n. καὶ νῦν follows πάλαι above: "ut antea non in maiore eos esse oportebat honore quam ceteros socios, ita nunc merita iniuriae poena afficiendi sunt" (Stahl). We might have had νῦν δὲ καί at the beginning of the sentence: 'so now, as it is.'

πάντες γὰρ ὑμῖν γε ὁμοίως ἐπέθεντο: 'they may have quarrelled among themselves, but all alike attacked us' (reading ἡμῖν with B). Kleon was probably right in this; there is no sign in Thucydides that the commons, at least in Mytilene (for the other states, see 18. 1), objected to what the ruling class was doing until defeat was certain. See, e.g., 25. 2. Antiphon, v. 76, also says that ἡ πόλις ὅλη was so ill-advised as to secede; but, in its context, that does not amount to much. οἷς γε ἐξῆν here means 'including those who might have'.

ἐν τῇ πόλει εἶναι: 'be citizens again in Mytilene.' Cf. 44. 2 n.

τὸν - - - κίνδυνον - - - βεβαιότερον: cf. v. 108; and ἀσφαλέστερα, § 4.

8. πόλιν ἐφθαρμένην: an argument against Kleon's own proposal. It is taken up by Diodotos, 46. 3.

τῆς ἔπειτα προσόδου, κ.τ.λ.: this is undoubtedly pleonastic, 'we shall in the future lose the subsequent revenue'; and, as Steup says, 'wherein lies our strength' is not specially apt to 'our *future* revenue'. Cf. 46. 3, where there is no such ambiguity. ἔπειτα has been emended to ἐκεῖθεν and to ἐπετείου, neither convincing. τῆς προσόδου δι' ἧν ἰσχύομεν, in different forms, was a trite phrase: see i. 122. 1, 143. 5, ii. 13. 2, iii. 46. 3 (cf., with τὸ ναυτικόν in place of ἡ πρόσοδος, i. 121. 3, ii. 13. 2, vi. 17. 7, vii. 66. 2; also i. 15. 1); perhaps Diodotos' answer was quoted in the margin and thence some words incorporated in the text.

It is perhaps worth noting that all these instances come from the first four books, only two of those with τὸ ναυτικόν coming from vi and vii.

τοῖς οἰκείοις ξυμμάχοις πολεμήσομεν: a paradox, but, for Kleon, hardly more than a verbal one; cf. 38. 1.

40. 1. οὔτε λόγῳ πιστὴν οὔτε χρήμασιν ὠνητήν: Stahl and Classen refer to 38. 2, ἢ τῷ λέγειν πιστεύσας - - - ἢ κέρδει ἐπαιρόμενος, rightly; but πιστήν must for all that surely be passive in sense, like ὠνητήν: 'made sure by fine words', not 'relying on' them, as though it were the orator's, and not the Mytileneans' hope.

ξυγγνώμην: 'ground for pardon', as in 44. 2, according to Widmann and Classen ('will get the verdict "human error" as ground for pardon'). This is not easy, for ξ. λήψονται is the natural Greek for 'will secure a pardon'; I prefer Stahl's way, to take ἁμαρτεῖν after ξυγγνώμην.

It is interesting that in viii. 24. 5, the words εἴ τι ἐν τοῖς ἀνθρωπείοις τοῦ βίου παραλόγοις ἐσφάλησαν are used of Chios and her revolt, so much later than Mytilene's and not isolated, as hers was, and are Thucydides' own reflections.

2. καὶ τότε πρῶτον: since τότε πρῶτον is the regular Greek for 'then for the first time', Krüger's suggestion [καὶ] τό τε πρῶτον has some probability.

Not only does the present tense διαμάχομαι belong strictly only to καὶ νῦν, but μὴ μεταγνῶναι as well. This presents, however, little difficulty; we should make a slight pause after διαμάχομαι, and treat μὴ μεταγνῶναι as imperative: 'do not unvote (as it were) your previous decision.'

μηδὲ τρισί, κ.τ.λ.: Kleon has used two kinds of argument—(1) do not be for ever changing your moods and so your decisions, which is a sign of weakness, whatever the merit of the decisions (cf. Aristophanes' πρὸς Ἀθηναίους μεταβούλους, Ach. 632); and (2) your decision in this case was anyhow right, and my opponents wish to sway you by appeals to pity and humanity and your love of oratory. Up to this point, however, he has only discussed at length the argument from weakness (in c. 37) and ἡδονὴ λόγων (in c. 38; see n. on κακῶς ἀγωνοθετοῦντες); and the latter seems to have had little to do in fact with the Athenian change of mind as Thucydides understood it, while οἶκτος and ἐπιείκεια, or at least ἐπιείκεια, had (36. 4, 49. 4).

Arnold says of these two words: "οἶκτος or ἔλεος is a feeling, ἐπιείκεια a habit. The former, pity or compassion, may occasionally touch those who are generally far from being ἐπιεικεῖς, mild or gentle. Ἐπιείκεια relates to all persons, οἶκτος to particular individuals: we may be always mild and gentle, but pity is only awakened by the immediate presence of suffering." This is in general just, though I would translate ἐπιεικής 'humane', 'fair-minded' (as near as we can get to the meaning) and call it a quality of mind rather than a habit; but note that Kleon in the next sentence makes very little use of the distinction, the clause explaining ἡ ἐπιείκεια adding very little to what has already been said of ἔλεος.

Pity and humanity are virtues recognized by all, which Kleon is asserting to be only dangerous temptations; but only Greeks, and Athenians, would have included ἡδονὴ λόγων with them, in any context.

3. ἔλεός τε γάρ, κ.τ.λ.: an exceptionally restricted field to allow this virtue, about as different from the Christian concept as can be; a restriction, too, not general in classical Greece, and given here to Kleon. We may contrast Homer; but pity was not an outstanding Greek virtue. There was an altar to Pity in Athens (Paus. i. 17. 1); but when was it set up? Also to $A i\delta \omega s$, $\Phi \eta \mu \eta$, and $'O\rho \mu \eta$. See Frazer, ii. 143–4, and Hitzig-Blumner. For the wording contrast, too, Arist. *Poet.* 53 a 3–7.

τοὺς ὁμοίους: like ἴσοι μὲν τῇ γνώμῃ καὶ εὐνοίᾳ, 9. 2, 'like-minded', not natural enemies. Steup, following Krüger, said it must mean 'persons of similar station or position', not, e.g., subjects of those who are to feel pity, because τοὺς ἐξ ἀνάγκης καθεστῶτας αἰεὶ πολεμίους means 'those who, being our subjects, cannot help being our inveterate enemies'; but the argument is not sound, especially with τοὺς οὔτ' ἀντοικτιοῦντας intervening. τοὺς καθεστῶτας αἰεὶ πολεμίους goes farther than the last words of 39. 8.

ῥήτορες: 'politicians', spoken contemptuously, as though Kleon himself were not an example of the ῥήτωρ-politician.

ἐν ἄλλοις ἐλάσσοσιν ἀγῶνα: see 37. 4, n. on ὡς ἐν ἄλλοις μείζοσιν. ἀγών: cf. 37. 4, 38. 2, 6.

μὴ ἐν ᾧ: an imperative, 'let them not'; cf. μὴ μεταγνῶναι ὑμᾶς, § 2.

ἡ μὲν πόλις, κ.τ.λ.: cf. 38. 3, and ii. 65. 7.

τὸ παθεῖν εὖ: if Kleon is being logical (which is perhaps hard to grant), this should mean not, as most edd., 'will get the bribes' (38. 2, 40. 1), but 'will win applause or popularity'; for these orators are those who λόγῳ τέρπουσι, not κέρδει ἐπαίρονται.

πρὸς τοὺς ὁμοίους τε καὶ οὐδὲν ἧσσον πολεμίους ὑπολειπομένους: it is easy to say that ὁμοίους, to be taken predicatively, can mean 'the same as before' (cf. ii. 80. 1); but since there is both an initial ambiguity, especially after πρὸς τοὺς ὁμοίους at the beginning of this section, and ὁμοίους must have here a different meaning from what it has there, it is perverse not to accept the reading of the *recentiores*, ὁμοίως. In ii. 80. 1 there is a divergence of reading between ὁμοίως (F) and ὅμοιος (cett.); and the accent would make the confusion here a little more likely than the other.

4. τά τε δίκαια: Kleon emphasizes the justice of his cause, which in him includes and is confused with its legal correctness; see n. on δικαιότερος, 44. 4, and on τὸ εἰκός, below.

δικαιώσεσθε: 'you will be passing sentence on', or 'exacting justice from, yourselves'. This is a double contrast: if you reverse yesterday's decision, you will be exacting justice, not, as you think, acting kindly (χαρίζεσθαι), but not from Mytilene, which deserves justice not kindness, but from yourselves.

ὀρθῶς: 'correctly.' Cf. n. on τὰ δίκαια, above.

εἰ δὲ δή, κ.τ.λ.: a cynical and ruthless logic, which is, strictly, inconsistent with the bold assertion of the tyranny in 37. 2—'if you say that you are going to continue ruling them in spite of its not being proper, then, in Heaven's name punish them in your own interest too, though it be against the canons of equity; or give up your empire and play the honest man with no risk at all'. The particle τοι, rare in Thucydides, appears to give a vigorous and colloquial colour here, though not in the other two passages where it occurs (ii. 41. 4, vii. 77. 2). See Denniston, p. 537.

τὸ εἰκός is 'equity', often opposed to strict legal justice; see above, n. on τὰ δίκαια, and Arist. Eth. Nic. v. 10, 1137 a 31.

ἐκ τοῦ ἀκινδύνου ἀνδραγαθίζεσθαι: the third, and the most striking of Kleon's borrowings from Perikles in Thucydides (ii. 63. 2–3); and contrast ἐκ τοῦ ἀκινδύνου in the description of Nikias, v. 16. 1. Empire is attended always by risk, like freedom; only the slave, who has no responsibility, is safe. Mme de Romilly, p. 145, doubts whether Thucydides meant to indicate a close association in language between Perikles and Kleon; I think wrongly. When Aristophanes says of Kleon, in the boule, ἐλασίβροντ' ἀναρρηγνὺς ἔπη (Eq. 626), he is 'likening his oratory to Perikles', though, as Neil says ad loc., while Perikles is the Olympian, Kleon is rather the giant (and cf. Aeschylus, in Ran. 823). Kleon also appears to imitate Perikles in Eq. 732, ὅτιὴ φιλῶ σ', ὦ Δῆμ', ἐραστής τ' εἰμὶ σός (cf. 1341; Thuc. ii. 43. 1 n.).

(Steup finds a difficulty here because there is no proper logical connexion between the protasis, εἰ - - - ἀξιοῦτε τοῦτο δρᾶν and this part of the apodosis, παύεσθαι τῆς ἀρχῆς, κ.τ.λ.; and says that again we have an instance to show that Thucydides did not finally revise his work. But this is to show a lack of rhetorical sense; and the connexion is clear: 'if you won't act in the one way consistent with your own interests, equity or no equity, give up the empire.' It is the word ξυμφόρως which makes the connexion clear.)

There are good examples of Thucydides' love of variatio in this passage: οἶκτος, ἔλεος and ἐπιείκεια, εἰκός (vocabulary), ἡδονὴ λόγων, οἱ τέρποντες λόγῳ ῥήτορες (vocabulary and concrete for abstract), εὖ εἰπεῖν, παθεῖν εὖ (order), ὑμεῖς ἂν οὐ χρεὼν ἄρχοιτε, δεῖ κολάζεσθαι (grammatical form). On the other hand, he has no objection to repeating εἰκός below with a quite different meaning.

5. τῇ τε αὐτῇ ζημίᾳ: explained by most edd. as in the scholion, ἥπερ ἂν ἐτιμωρήσαντο καὶ αὐτοὶ ἡμᾶς περιγενόμενοι ἡμῶν, that is, as parallel in meaning to the next clause, καὶ μὴ ἀναλγητότεροι, κ.τ.λ., and explained only by the one after that. This is possible, but I am not satisfied; Steup explains, 'the same sentence that you passed yesterday' (which is very obscure); Gertz conjectured ἐσχάτῃ for αὐτῇ; perhaps ⟨ἅπαντας⟩ should be supplied after ζημίᾳ.

Note that the middle one of the three clauses is a generalization in form, οἱ διαφεύγοντες τῶν ἐπιβουλευσάντων, not ὑμεῖς ἐκείνων, like the other two; it is yet another example of variatio.

ἀναλγητότεροι: 'less sensitive', like δυσάλγητος in *O.T.* 12; but there it has a natural context, 'insensible to the ills of others'; here, on Kleon's lips, it means 'insensible to our own'. Cf. Melissos ap. Aristotle, *de Xenophane*, 974 a 10 ('insensitive to pain or danger'—L. and S.); *Eth. Nic.* i. 10. 12, 1100 b 32, iii. 7. 7, 1115 b 26; and *Rhet.* i. 9, 67 a 33 on the changeable meanings of words (see below, n. on τὸ δὲ σῶφρον, 82. 4), ληπτέον δὲ καὶ τὰ σύνεγγυς τοῖς ὑπάρχουσιν ὡς ταὐτὰ ὄντα καὶ πρὸς ἔπαινον καὶ πρὸς ψόγον, οἷον - - - τὸν ἠλίθιον χρηστὸν καὶ τὸν ἀνάλγητον πρᾷον.

6. μάλιστα δέ, κ.τ.λ.: explaining the last words only of the previous sentence. It is another γνώμη not particularly apt to the context. Certainly *Thucydides* was much given to this forming of *sententiae*; but so too were his contemporaries (cf. *The Clouds*), and examples were doubtless heard in the ekklesia. This particular one—'they would have taken precautions against a just resentment'—is well illustrated by the killing of Astyanax in *Troades*, a play inspired by the recent expedition against Melos, in which *the Athenians* so clearly προϋπῆρξαν ἀδικίας. Thucydides, Aristophanes, and Euripides all presuppose what we should call the normal sense of justice and proper conduct (cf. cc. 9–10 in the Mytilenean speech).

Note the inversion of the argument, which is: 'because ὁ μὴ ξὺν ἀνάγκῃ τι παθών is fiercer if he escape, therefore his enemies are thorough in their destruction, if possible; therefore, we who have escaped would be fiercer and our enemies the Mytileneans, who were the aggressors, would thoroughly destroy us if they could; therefore destroy them now first.' It is all very artificially expressed.

Stahl's διολλύναι for the MSS. διόλλυνται is not altogether satisfying; but no better correction has been suggested.

τοῦ ἀπὸ τῆς ἴσης ἐχθροῦ: an enemy fighting on the same grounds as yourself, as two imperialist powers fighting for the same territory, who have so often made a reasonable and lasting peace when one side has won.

7. ὅτι ἐγγύτατα τῇ γνώμῃ: see 38. 1 n.

πρὸ παντὸς ἂν ἐτιμήσασθε αὐτοὺς χειρώσασθαι: this surprises, in place of ἐτιμήσαντο ἐκεῖνοι ὑμᾶς χειρώσασθαι, as in § 5. Why 'you would have given much to conquer them', when in fact they had conquered them? We should bracket ἄν. Note ἀνταπόδοτε in the next sentence, which means 'give them what they would have given you'.

πρὸς τὸ παρὸν αὐτίκα: the redundancy is intended doubtless to emphasize the fleeting nature of the feeling of pity or delight in words or ἐπιείκεια. If τὸ παρόν means 'the present plight of the Mytileneans', αὐτίκα is less justified.

παράδειγμα: this is emphasized; see 39. 3 n.

τῶν πολεμίων ἀμελήσαντες: a vigorous ending. The idea is repeated from 39. 8, including the paradox μαχεῖσθε τοῖς ξυμμάχοις; for it is a paradox, even though Kleon is not at all sentimental about the 'allies'; cf. 10. 3.

41. Διόδοτος ὁ Εὐκράτους: it is singular that we know no more of the man who is given the notable speech which follows—notable, besides, because his cause won the day; no more than we know of Euphemos, the Athenian who is given the speech at Kamarina, vi. 81–88, but that speech is more conventional. Compare, too, Athenagoras and the somewhat different case of the two Plataians (iii. 52. 5); and contrast the *anonymi* at Sparta (i. 73) and at Melos. Diodotos' father may have been one of the well-known Eukratai, e.g. the tallow-chandler who is said to have preceded Kleon in demagogy (schol. Ar. *Equit.* 129); or the strategos of 432 B.C. (*I.G.* i.² 296; vol. i, p. 423); or he may have been related to Nikias, who had a brother Eukrates. But it is idle to guess. There is not much evidence of a moderate *party* at this time, consistently in favour of mildness towards the subject states, as was argued, for example, by West, *C.P.* xix, 1924, 132; see Ar. *Ach.* 641–2, cited above on 11. 7, and n. on 49. 4.

42. 1. τοὺς προθέντας - - - αὖθις: cf. 38. 1; elsewhere Diodotos refers to Kleon's words, cf. τάχος, below, with διατριβήν, ibid., ὀργήν with ὀργῇ, ibid., τούς τε λόγους, κ.τ.λ., with τῷ λέγειν πιστεύσας, 38. 2, etc. Sometimes there is special point in the reference: see nn. on εὖ εἰπεῖν, § 2; 44. 3–4; and de Romilly, p. 139, nn. 1 and 2.

τάχος τε καὶ ὀργήν: in this, as in the defence of debate in words below, Diodotos follows Perikles (ii. 40. 2–3); but Archidamos would also agree, as he would have agreed with much in Kleon (i. 84. 1–2, 85. 1). Cf. Antiphon, v. 71–73, 86, passages which contain γνῶμαι in the Thucydidean manner.

ὧν τὸ μέν, κ.τ.λ.: edd. in general take the first τό to be τάχος, the second ὀργή. I doubt this. To debate is to consider καθ' ἡσυχίαν, which takes time; and in the next sentence, the man who opposes debate is said to be ἀξύνετος (cf. 82. 4, which gives the other side: τὸ πρὸς ἅπαν ξυνετόν, ἐπὶ πᾶν ἀργόν). Ἀπαιδευσία, therefore, in this context, goes rather better with τάχος than with ὀργή. The latter accompanies ἄνοια (here almost the direct opposite of πρόνοια—cf. 38. 6 and as well 43. 4); τάχος goes with an illiterate and shallow (or trivial) mind.

2. τούς τε λόγους - - - μὴ διδασκάλους τῶν πραγμάτων γίγνεσθαι: Perikles' words in ii. 40. 2 are very close to this. μή is again primarily imperative—'he who fights for the doctrine, do not let words be our teachers'.

War was a different sort of διδάσκαλος: 82. 2.

ἢ ἀξύνετός ἐστιν ἢ ἰδίᾳ τι αὐτῷ διαφέρει: retorting to Kleon's ἢ τῷ

313

λέγειν πιστεύσας (in a ξυνέσεως ἀγών, 37. 5) - - - ἢ κέρδει ἐπαιρόμενος, 38. 2. Kleon could hardly object to being called ἀξύνετος.

εἰ ἄλλῳ τινὶ ἡγεῖται: as if there were other means than language for conveying our thoughts, or as if we should not think.

εὖ μὲν εἰπεῖν: he is again borrowing Kleon's words (38. 2, 4), but adapting them; for Diodotos means (I think) not 'to speak cleverly', but 'to speak well'; for he is defending words. Cf. ἄμεινον λέγοντα, § 5. Similarly εὖ διαβαλών recalls Kleon's τῶν λόγῳ καλῶς ἐπιτιμησάντων, though the purpose is different.

Finley, p. 172, well compares Eur. *Suppliants*, 409–16, though there the theme is the weaknesses of democratic government in general.

ἐκπλῆξαι: to browbeat, or bully, just like Kleon in *The Knights*. Compare, too, Euripides' complaint of Aeschylus in *The Frogs* (962); iv. 27. 5, 28. 1; and the passage from *Republic* quoted on ii. 65. 2.

3. χαλεπώτατοι δὲ καί, κ.τ.λ.: 'hardest to deal with (*or*, most to fear) are those who would prejudge the issue by accusations of bribery and oratorical display', to give an explanation rather than a translation, and reading προκατηγοροῦντες (C alone of the MSS.), not προσκατ. (cett.) with Stuart Jones. The accusation ἐπὶ χρήμασι can only be a special instance of εὖ διαβαλεῖν, hardly an additional charge; and προ- has a very apt meaning—not so much to make the charge before your opponent can speak, as to try to settle the issue before arguing on the merits of the case. Diodotos is not guiltless of the same trick in ἰδίᾳ τι αὐτῷ διαφέρει above.

In Aristophanes Kleon tries to browbeat with ready charges of 'oligarch', 'traitor', 'conspiring against the people's democracy' rather than of bribery.

4. ἥ τε πόλις οὐκ ὠφελεῖται: cf. Kleon again, 38. 3.

ἀδυνάτους λέγειν: presumably simply 'to be bad speakers'; but Diodotos comes near to questioning the value of free debate.

πεισθεῖεν: in the ordinary way a plural after ἡ πόλις would of course present no difficulty; but with τοὺς τοιούτους intervening, I prefer Classen's conjecture, πείσειαν.

5. μηδ' ἐλασσοῦν - - - μηδ' ἀτιμάζειν: I cannot see any distinction in meaning between the two instances of μηδέ; which means in each case 'not ... either'. In each case, too, the previous clause, μὴ προστιθέναι τιμήν and οὐχ ὅπως ζημιοῦν is concessive: 'do not, I agree, reward the good adviser with new honours, but do not take away what he has either; do not of course punish him for failure, but do not slight him either.' Not, 'do not even slight him'.

6. τῷ αὐτῷ χαριζόμενος: i.e. by the same means as the successful speaker. Classen takes ὁ κατορθῶν and ὁ μὴ ἐπιτυχών to mean the wise and the unwise adviser, not the orator who carries or fails to carry the majority with him, arguing from τὰ βέλτιστα λέγειν in 43. 1.

The carrying on of ἥκιστα ἄν through both clauses seems to me very difficult, a perverse piece of obscurity; it would have been more in Thucydides' manner, if he was not going to put ἥκιστα ἄν before ὅ τε κατορθῶν, to have written ἧσσον or οὐκ before ὀρέγοιτο. Cf. 43. 2, ὥστε δεῖν ὁμοίως, κ.τ.λ., for the normal order; and in fact it is easier to have a phrase like ἥκιστα ἄν apparently intended to qualify two clauses joined by τε - - - τε or τε - - - καί, but the second escaping its influence, as perhaps v. 22. 2.

The quarrel between Diodotos and Kleon is as much about how to conduct debate in the ekklesia as about the fate of Mytilene. And this is important; for, though Kleon was defeated in this case, he was still there, exercising his malign influence; and when he dies, there will be others like him, Hyperbolos, Kleophon, and more in the fourth century: a serious weakness of the democracy, especially in war-time.

43. 1. καὶ προσέτι ἦν τις καὶ ὑποπτεύηται, κ.τ.λ.: this is at first sight difficult, because the Greek for 'Yes, his advice is good, but he is getting some profit out of it' is βέλτιστα μὲν λέγει, κέρδους δὲ ἕνεκα πείθει (i.e. it is the μέν-clause which is concessive). But, as Classen has noticed, καί before ὑποπτεύηται belongs to βέλτιστα λέγειν, which in fact has the emphasis which one might expect to belong to κέρδους ἕνεκα, and ὑποπτεύηται is substituted for the more general δοκῇ or νομίζηται because κέρδους ἕνεκα intervenes. 'We do more; even if we think a man is giving the best possible advice—though, as we suspect, for private gain—resenting his apparent but uncertain profit we lose for the state the quite clear advantage of his advice.' L. and S. take the genitive τῆς δοκήσεως direct with φθονήσαντες; others suppose a genitive of origin. For δόκησις see ii. 35. 2 n. and below, 45. 2; and for the meaning, 10. 1, μετ' ἀρετῆς δοκούσης. Here the appearance is defined as οὐ βέβαιος.

2. καθέστηκε δέ: 'it is now the rule.'

τόν τε τὰ δεινότατα βουλόμενον πεῖσαι: cf. 42. 2, βουλόμενός τι αἰσχρὸν πεῖσαι, κ.τ.λ. And with ἀπάτῃ προσάγεσθαι Kleon's words, παράγειν πειράσεται, 38. 2.

ψευσάμενον πιστὸν γενέσθαι: an oxymoron, as Böhme noted, and only *variatio* for ἀπάτῃ προσάγεσθαι τὸ πλῆθος.

3. μόνην τε πόλιν, κ.τ.λ.: certainly, as Steup, sc. ἡμᾶς, 'we are the only city which, etc.', not, as many have taken it, 'the state, unlike individuals, is the only thing which'. Diodotos has no comparison with the private citizen in mind; and, if he had, he must have expressed it more clearly.

τὰς περινοίας: 'excessive cleverness', a word not found elsewhere in classical Greek (except Ps.-Plat. *Axioch.* 370 C); but cf. περινοεῖν ἅπαντα,

Ar. *Ran.* 958, and περιτέχνησις below, 82. 3. Superficially this is very like what Kleon condemned, 38. 5-7, and Archidamos; but Kleon had fine oratory and its audience in mind, Diodotos the ingenuities of suspicion, as Thucydides in 82. 5, and as Euripides prides himself in the passage in *The Frogs*, τεχνάζειν, κάχ' ὑποτοπεῖσθαι, περινοεῖν ἅπαντα. It is the opposite of τὸ εὔηθες in 83. 1.

ἀνθυποπτεύεται, κ.τ.λ.: 'get as his reward a suspicion that he will make some secret profit somewhere.'

4. καὶ ἐν τῷ τοιῷδε: 'even in these circumstances', as Haase and Steup, not 'and in such circumstances'. See below.

ἀξιοῦν τι ἡμᾶς: whether ἡμᾶς is the subject or the object of ἀξιοῦν (with ὑμᾶς understood) makes but little difference; the former is perhaps the more likely in view of the following participial clause. Take τι closely with the verb—'make some claim'.

περαιτέρω προνοοῦντας: by contrast with the ἄνοια which goes with ὀργή or τάχος (42. 1).

ὑπεύθυνον: not especially 'liable to the γραφὴ παρανόμων', the action of which is doubtful at this date; but, generally, 'held responsible for the advice we give'.

Is Diodotos, in ἀνεύθυνον τὴν ὑμετέραν ἀκρόασιν, in some degree defending the crowd's attitude to fine speeches which Kleon had condemned in c. 38? See also Ar. *Vesp.* 587.

5. εἰ γὰρ ὅ τε πείσας καὶ ὁ ἐπισπόμενος ὁμοίως ἐβλάπτοντο: contrast 42. 4, ἥ τε πόλις οὐκ ὠφελεῖται. But Diodotos is here thinking of the ekklesia not as the state, but as a collection of individuals; and βλάπτεσθαι here is nearly equivalent to 'suffer punishment', ζημιοῦσθαι below. The irresponsibility of the individual citizens was a constant worry to apologists of Greek democracy.

πρὸς ὀργὴν ἥντινα τύχητε: see L. and S., s.v. τυγχάνω, A. 4; 'according to your feelings at the moment', like τὸ τυχόν, ὡς ἔτυχε (ὅπως ἔτυχέ τῳ, v. 20. 2), ὁπόθεν τύχοιεν (iv. 26. 6), ὅ τι ἂν τύχωσι, τοῦτο πράξουσι (Plat. *Kriton*, 45 D). 'As it is, there are times when you fail and then you punish the single adviser according to your feelings at the moment' (of anger and sorrow, as after Sicily, of disappointment, or remorse, as in the condemnation of Kallixenos).

εἰ - - - ξυνεξήμαρτον: a not uncommon complaint against the Athenians; cf. ii. 61. 2, 64. 1, viii. 1.

It is not easy to see the logical connexion between §§ 4-5 and the earlier argument, nor indeed that between § 4 and § 5. Up to this point Diodotos has been complaining of the excessive 'punishment', in one form or another, of the politician; now he is emphasizing his proper responsibility.

44. 1. ἀντερῶν περὶ Μυτιληναίων: to contradict Kleon in the matter of Mytilene is to defend her.

316

οὐ γὰρ περὶ τῆς ἐκείνων ἀδικίας - - - εὐβουλίας; cf. Arist. *Rhet.* i. 3. 4, 1358 b, τέλος - - - τῷ μὲν συμβουλεύοντι τὸ συμφέρον καὶ βλαβερόν, - - - τοῖς δὲ δικαζομένοις τὸ δίκαιον καὶ τὸ ἄδικον. Not 'are *they* guilty?', a question to be put to a jury, but 'are *we* wise?' the question for debate in a parliament. See also i. 73. i.

2. ἦν τε γὰρ ἀποφήνω, κ.τ.λ.: in *C.Q.* xlii, 1948, 12–13, I have argued that we must assume a lacuna in the second half of the sentence, because a second negative is indispensable. Bergk, *Philol.* xxix, 1870, 320, saw this, and conjectured ἦν τε καὶ ἔχοντάς τι ⟨ξυγγνώμης, οὐ διὰ τοῦτο καὶ ἄξιοι ἂν⟩ εἶεν ξυγγνώμης. This may be on the right lines, except that I am sure that Thucydides did not repeat ξυγγνώμης in this way. There are two other difficulties, or peculiarities, one the use of ἔχειν τι ξυγγνώμης in a passive sense, like ἔχειν αἰτίαν, after its normal active use in 39. 2 (but Thucydides is free with this use of ἔχειν: cf. ἀποτροπήν τινα ἔχειν, 45. 7; τέκμαρσιν ἔχει, ii. 87. 1 n.; and for ξυγγνώμην ἔχειν we have Soph. *Trach.* 928; Eur. *Phoin.* 995); and the second that all our MSS. have ἔχοντες, ἔχοντας being Lindau's conjecture. Spratt ingeniously suggested εἶναι ἐν τῇ πόλει (cf. 39. 6), εἰ μὴ ἀγαθὸν φαίνοιτο. With this last in mind I have suggested ἦν τε καὶ ἔχοντές τι ξυγγνώμης φαίνωνται (or φανῶσιν), οὐδ' εἶναι ἐν τῇ πόλει, εἰ μὴ ἀγαθόν [φαίνοιτο]; not, however, with any conviction that the corruption is probable. Lindau's ἐᾶν (cf. Plat. *Euthyph.* 4 B) or Badham's ἀφεῖναι is possible, provided that we insert the negative—ἦν τε καὶ ἔχοντάς τι ξυγγνώμης, οὐδ' ἀφεῖναι, εἰ τῇ πόλει μὴ ἀ. φ.

Note as well the double protasis (ἤν - - - εἰ μή) in each half of the sentence, and the very unusual τε οὐ - - - τε οὐ in place of οὔτε - - - οὔτε.

3. καὶ τοῦτο ὃ μάλιστα Κλέων ἰσχυρίζεται, κ.τ.λ.: in the same article in *C.Q.* I maintained that ὅ (ABEFM) is right (ᾧ CG), and that τοῦτο is not only antecedent to it but the object of ἀντισχυριζόμενος. In both halves of the sentence the emphasis is on the future, ἐς τὸ λοιπὸν ξυμφέρον and περὶ τοῦ ἐς τὸ μέλλον καλῶς ἔχοντος, and resumes what has just been said, νομίζω δὲ περὶ τοῦ μέλλοντος, κ.τ.λ.; and the interpretation is: 'and this assertion in particular which Kleon makes, that we must have our eyes on the *future*, so as to reduce the number of revolts by, he argues, imposing the death penalty, I too make in my turn, that we must think of *future* advantage; but I come to the opposite conclusion.'

4. τῷ εὐπρεπεῖ τοῦ ἐκείνου λόγου: this is carrying the war into the enemy's camp; see 38. 2. Similarly ὅπως χρησίμως ἕξουσιν below is the answer to ξυμφόρως δεῖ κολάζεσθαι, 40. 4; and compare βουλευόμεθα περὶ αὐτῶν with the last words of c. 38.

Diodotos makes the complete, and very just, retort on Kleon. Kleon had imagined himself the hard realist; and Diodotos replies that on the contrary he concerned himself with right and wrong and what Mytilene deserved, and dealt in fine words, instead of confining himself to the facts and needs of the *situation*, as he, Diodotos, was doing. (See the scholiast on 42. 1.) Like so many realists, Kleon ignored most of the facts. 'All he can say is, "the Mytileneans deserve the worst—look how they have behaved to us. So decide at once, before your *feelings* are blunted". That is what his *Realpolitik* amounts to. Such an argument may appeal, in your present excited mood; but let us get back to the facts of the situation.' 'I am not appealing to your sense of pity or generosity, but to your own interests'; a natural argument in the circumstances, though a dangerous one. There was a close parallel in 1945: 'Food must be sent to Berlin, not from any pity for the conquered or generosity to Germans, but to prevent the spread of disease which would be dangerous to the Allies'. Grote, v. 174, aptly quotes a passage from Burke, on Conciliation with America (*Works*, iii. 69–74); but there remains, perhaps, a certain hardness characteristic of fifth-century Greece.

45. 1. ἐν οὖν ταῖς πόλεσι, κ.τ.λ.: the beginning of the 'realistic' argument against Kleon's theory, πρὸς τὸ ἧσσον ἀφίστασθαι θάνατον ζημίαν προθεῖσι (44. 3), is an elaborate statement of the case against all deterrent theories of punishment.

καὶ οὐδείς πω καταγνοὺς ἑαυτοῦ, κ.τ.λ.: 'no one has ever begun his dangerous task with the conviction that he will not survive it', the task of course being a crime, committed for gain, not an allotted duty. καταγνούς, 'after passing a verdict'. ἧλθεν ἐς τὸ δεινόν, a phrase taken from Kleon (39. 3).

2. πόλις τε ἀφισταμένη: 'so with a state, that would revolt.'

τίς πω ἧσσω τῇ δοκήσει, κ.τ.λ.: often enough, one would have said; and Diodotos says as much in § 6, below. τῇ δοκήσει here must be 'in their own opinion'.

3. πεφύκασί τε: note the emphatic position—'but it is in men's nature'. Steup, perhaps rightly, reads δέ for τε. ἁμαρτάνειν I understand to be here 'to make a mistake in judgement' (τῇ δοκήσει, above) not 'to break the law'.

οὐκ ἔστι νόμος ὅστις ἀπείρξει τούτου: cf. ii. 53. 4.

προστιθέντες: this is surely right here. προτιθέντες, which Krüger conjectured, 'promulgating', is colourless; they 'added' one punishment to another. So Bohme, Stahl, and Steup.

ὑπὸ τῶν κακούργων: a phrase suggesting a criminal *class*, which is far from being Diodotos' meaning.

καὶ εἰκὸς τὸ πάλαι, κ.τ.λ.: the opposite, liberal view that 'things are making for good on the whole' and punishments in consequence getting milder, is expressed by Lykourgos, c. Leocr. 65, ἐκεῖνοι (οἱ ἀρχαῖοι νομοθέται) - - - ὁμοίως ἐπὶ πᾶσι καὶ τοῖς ἐλαχίστοις παρανομήμασι θάνατον ὥρισαν εἶναι τὴν ζημίαν. Diodotos' more paradoxical opinion is perhaps supported by the history of the last twenty years. It will be found also in The Vicar of Wakefield, c. 27.

καὶ τοῦτο ὅμως παραβαίνεται: the sense is clear—'because of the repeated crimes most penalties were changed to the death penalty; but crime for all that continues', the passive of παραβαίνειν being used impersonally in both cases. But τοῦτο is a difficulty, and Krüger's κἂν τούτῳ, adopted by Steup (who notes that in i. 37. 4 there is just this divergence of reading in our MSS.), is attractive.

4. ἀλλ' ἡ μὲν πενία ἀνάγκῃ, κ.τ.λ.: Classen's analysis of this carefully composed sentence, which has little of Thucydides' usual variatio, is as follows. The external circumstances and internal passions, of individuals or states, are distinguished, and in the first two sentences particular circumstances and passions are mentioned, in the last both are generalized—πενία, ἐξουσία ('power' rather than 'wealth'; cf. i. 38. 5, 123. 1), and αἱ ἄλλαι ξυντυχίαι; τόλμα, πλεονεξία, and the general term ὀργή; and the 'assistants', so to speak, similarly—ἀνάγκῃ, ὕβρει καὶ φρονήματι, and ὑπ' ἀνηκέστου τινὸς κρείσσονος, which last is to be taken with κατέχεται. The only thing Classen finds disturbing is τῶν ἀνθρώπων, which, besides being unnecessary, leads one to expect ἕκαστός τις in the subordinate clause; and he alters to τὸν ἄνθρωπον. The objection to this is that ὀργῇ, both by its case and by its position, should correspond to ἀνάγκῃ and ὕβρει, not to τόλμαν; and τὸν ἄνθρωπον does away with no difficulties. Stahl emended to ὀργήν, sc. παρέχουσα (and bracketed τῶν ἀνθρώπων); but the order is against this. We must not press the antitheses too closely. As Classen saw, ἀνάγκῃ, which is external pressure and closely related to πενία, is not exactly analogous with ὕβρει καὶ φρονήματι, which are nearer to τόλμα. The last sentence, ὀργῇ - - - ἐξάγουσιν ἐς τοὺς κινδύνους, besides summing up the whole, is also in some sense parallel to ἀνάγκη τὴν τόλμαν παρέχουσα; and I would take ὑπ' ἀνηκέστου τ. κρ. as well as ὀργῇ, with ἐξάγουσιν. The only changes in the text which are improvements are Gertz's καὶ καταφρονήματι (φρόνημα has a complimentary meaning, ii. 43. 6, 62. 3, iv. 80. 3; cf. ii. 61. 3, i. 81. 6, vi. 18. 4; v. 43. 2 is nearest to meaning 'pride'; the scholiast here renders by μεγαλοφροσύνη), and Duker's ἑκάστῃ τις (cf. i. 17, and Hdt.'s use of κατέχεσθαι, i. 59. 1). 'Poverty by its pressure producing boldness, power through insolence and pride producing ambition (i.e. desire for more power), and other conditions of life lead men into undertaking risks, as they are held fast now by one now by another of these conditions, through some human passion, under the influence of an overmastering feeling.' 'Other conditions of life' include, in the case of states, subjection of one to another.

319

Many parallels could be quoted from Greek to this passage: e.g. Solon, 1. 33 ff., esp. 41–42,

$$\epsilon i \ \delta \acute{e} \ \tau \iota s \ \dot{a} \chi \rho \acute{\eta} \mu \omega \nu, \ \pi \epsilon \nu \acute{\iota} \eta s \ \delta \acute{e} \ \mu \iota \nu \ \acute{e} \rho \gamma a \ \beta \iota \hat{a} \tau a \iota,$$
$$\kappa \tau \acute{\eta} \sigma \epsilon \sigma \theta a \iota \ \pi \acute{a} \nu \tau \omega s \ \chi \rho \acute{\eta} \mu a \tau a \ \pi o \lambda \lambda \grave{a} \ \delta o \kappa \epsilon \hat{\iota}.$$

See Headlam ap. G. Thomson on Aesch. *Agam.* 228–31. With the whole chapter, cf. Antiphon Sophistes, fr. 15 Gernet (58 Diels: Stob. *Flor.* xx. 66); and contrast the different effect of Hdt. viii. 111 (Themistokles threatening Andros), though that is sophistic too. Contrast as well the grace of Themistokles' language with the harshness of Kleon's (esp. 39. 3), and the open cynicism of the Athenians at Melos.

5. ἥ τε ἐλπὶς καὶ ὁ ἔρως: a sentence which has led to much generalization about Thucydides' method of thought, especially by Cornford in *Thucydides Mythistoricus*. But this is not all that the historian said about $\dot{\epsilon} \lambda \pi \acute{\iota} s$: see ii. 62. 5 n., iv. 10. 1, 62. 4, v. 103. Diodotos here says, more picturesquely, much what Kleon had said, 39. 3. Adcock in his presidential address to the Classical Association in 1948 (*Proceedings*, xlv. 13) quoted Halifax on hope: "generally a wrong guide, though it is very good company by the way."

ἐκφροντίζων: 'thinking out a plan', 'carefully devising'. Edd. quote Ar. *Nub.* 695, $\dot{\epsilon} \kappa \phi \rho \acute{o} \nu \tau \iota \sigma \acute{o} \nu \ \tau \iota \ \tau \hat{\omega} \nu \ \sigma \epsilon a \upsilon \tau o \hat{\upsilon} \ \pi \rho a \gamma \mu \acute{a} \tau \omega \nu$ (Sokrates to Strepsiades); but the word, suitable to the $\phi \rho o \nu \tau \iota \sigma \tau \acute{\eta} \rho \iota o \nu$, seems wrong for $\acute{e} \rho \omega s$.

τὴν εὐπορίαν τῆς τύχης: 'the wealth of opportunity which fortune offers.'

ὄντα ἀφανῆ: because, not though, they are invisible. (It is rather the good things that hope and desire offer than hope and desire themselves, that are invisible.) Cf. ii. 61. 2, $\tau \grave{o} \ \mu \grave{e} \nu \ \lambda \upsilon \pi o \hat{\upsilon} \nu \ \acute{e} \chi \epsilon \iota \ \acute{\eta} \delta \eta \ \tau \grave{\eta} \nu$ $a \check{\iota} \sigma \theta \eta \sigma \iota \nu \ \dot{\epsilon} \kappa \acute{a} \sigma \tau \omega, \ \tau \hat{\eta} s \ \delta \grave{e} \ \dot{\omega} \phi \epsilon \lambda \acute{\iota} a s \ \acute{a} \pi \epsilon \sigma \tau \iota \nu \ \acute{e} \tau \iota \ \acute{\eta} \ \delta \acute{\eta} \lambda \omega \sigma \iota s \ \acute{a} \pi a \sigma \iota$, where the effect is different.

6. καὶ ἡ τύχη, κ.τ.λ.: 'and fortune does in fact play its part', $\dot{a} \delta o \kappa \acute{\eta}$-$\tau \omega s \ \acute{e} \sigma \tau \iota \nu \ \acute{o} \tau \epsilon \ \pi a \rho \iota \sigma \tau a \mu \acute{e} \nu \eta$; it is not altogether a mirage. A fragment of Euripides' *Peirithoos* (quoted by Adcock, above, on § 5, to illustrate Thucydides' judgement of Themistokles, i. 138. 3) has $\dot{\omega} s \ \tau o \hat{\iota} \sigma \iota \nu$ $\epsilon \hat{\upsilon} \ \phi \rho o \nu o \hat{\upsilon} \sigma \iota \ \sigma \upsilon \mu \mu a \chi \epsilon \hat{\iota} \ \tau \acute{\upsilon} \chi \eta$; which is very different from what we have here ('fortune sometimes aids us unexpectedly, even when we have been foolish'. Cf. iv. 18. 2 n.).

ἐκ τῶν ὑποδεεστέρων: resources not only insufficient, but known to be insufficient. See § 2 n.

ἐλευθερίας ἢ ἄλλων ἀρχῆς: obviously in a quarrel, e.g., between Mytilene and Athens, or Tegea and Sparta; but also, less obviously, in one between Athens and Sparta or Sparta and Argos. See ii. 63. 1 n. We expect $\langle \dot{o} \ \dot{a} \gamma \acute{\omega} \nu \rangle$. (We may translate *either* 'for one or other of the two alternatives, freedom or empire', *or* 'e.g. for freedom, or for empire'.)

καὶ μετὰ πάντων ἕκαστος - - - αὐτὸν ἐδόξασεν: the sense is clear— 'and, secondly, in assembly with his fellow citizens each man irrationally exaggerates his own capacity to overcome (or to play his part in overcoming) the danger' (cf. 43. 5); but, apart from the fact that all our good MSS. have αὐτῶν and only the *deteriores* αὐτόν, αὐτὸν δοξάζειν should have some adjectival phrase to explain it, as δοξάζειν ἑαυτοὺς βελτίους, Plat. *Phileb.* 48 E. L. and S. translate δοξάζειν here 'magnify, extol'; but the only other examples of this are from the Septuagint and Christian literature (though see Adam on Plat. *Rep.* vi. 511 A). Thucydides uses the word twice elsewhere, in the passive, vii. 75. 6, where it is a heightened form of ἐδόκει, and i. 120. 5, where it means contemplating a future action by contrast with the action itself, and so, in general sense, is not unlike its meaning here. I am not sure that we should not assume that a word is missing, ⟨ἰσχυρὸν⟩ αὐτόν or ἰσχυρότερον ἑαυτοῦ. ἐπὶ πλέον τι can then have its own natural meaning, 'over a wider field'. Classen objected to αὐτόν, that the *individual's* capacity is irrelevant here; but it is the total sum of individual capacities that is meant, and that is expressed in the Greek way. ii. 8. 4, ἐν τούτῳ τε κεκωλῦσθαι ἐδόκει ἑκάστῳ τὰ πράγματα ᾧ μή τις αὐτὸς παρέσται, is not very different in effect. For ἀλογίστως, cf. again Perikles, ii. 40. 2–3.

7. πολλῆς εὐηθείας: a nice hit at Kleon. (Steup's explanation of the grammatical construction may be right: 'and he who thinks it possible is a man of much simplicity.')

ἢ ἄλλῳ τῳ δεινῷ: 'or some other deterrent method.'

46. 1. οὔκουν χρή: we come to the conclusion to be derived from the elaborate argument of c. 45. Note how the words echo Kleon's conclusion, 40. 1.

2. καὶ ἀποστᾶσα: not 'even after revolting', but 'if they do revolt'; i.e. if they think their resources equal to it (cf. 45. 2) and later find they are not.

τὴν δαπάνην ἀποδοῦναι: as Samos, i. 117. 3, though Samos did not become a tribute-paying city in the strict sense (above, p. 17). Poteidaia had not been so treated; so that νῦν needs some qualification, though it might be said that she did resist to the end.

τίνα οἴεσθε ἥντινα οὐκ: as Kleon, 39. 7.

παρατενεῖσθαι ἐς τοὔσχατον: 'to extend themselves to the uttermost', to the point of exhaustion (note πόλιν ἐφθαρμένην below). Cf. παρατέταμαι λιπαρὰ κάπτων, Ar. fr. 506; γελῶντες - - - ὀλίγου παρετάθησαν, Plat. *Euthyd.* 303 B; see L. and S., s.v.

3. δαπανᾶν: as Kleon, 39. 8; and 31. 1, 33. 3. In πόλιν ἐφθαρμένην and

321

τῆς προσόδου - - - στέρεσθαι, he is more obviously answering Kleon's argument there, and making indeed the obvious answer.

ἰσχύομεν δέ: see 39. 8 n.

4. δικαστὰς - - - ἀκριβεῖς: 'strict judges', in the sense of adhering to the strict letter of the law.

καὶ τὴν φυλακήν, κ.τ.λ.: sound, but easy advice to give, and difficult to follow.

ἀπὸ τῶν νόμων τῆς δεινότητος: rather a reference to the generalizations of c. 45 than to any Athenian regulation relating to the punishment of seceding cities.

5. ἐλεύθερον καὶ βίᾳ ἀρχόμενον: 'independent states ruled by Athens in their own despite.' This would strictly apply to most other cities of the empire, not to Mytilene and Chios who enjoyed autonomy; but it is sound enough as a generalization and an answer to 39. 2. Cf. also 10. 5–11. 1, Mytilene's attitude.

εἰκότως: something between the two meanings of τὸ εἰκός in 40. 4–5— 'as was natural', and so to be expected, probable.

χαλεπῶς οἰόμεθα χρῆναι τιμωρεῖσθαι: in spite of Poteidaia, it is clear that severity was not yet the established practice. See 49. 4 n.

6. ἀφισταμένους: "(nicht ἀποστάντας) um den Moment zu bezeichnen, wo es zu spät ist: 'nicht erst wenn sie den Entschluss des Abfalls ausführen' "—Steup. But this would require an aorist. 'For revolting', 'as rebels', like οἱ προδιδόντες, 'the traitors', ii. 5. 7.

σφόδρα φυλάσσειν: τὰ τῶν ξυμμάχων διὰ χειρὸς ἔχειν, as Perikles put it (ii. 13. 2). Diodotos is still careful to avoid any appeal to pity or generosity.

47. 2. νῦν μὲν γὰρ ὑμῖν ὁ δῆμος ἐν πάσαις ταῖς πόλεσιν εὔνους ἐστί: this cannot be reconciled with Thucydides' very decisive opinion expressed in ii. 8. 4–5. We may allow something here for a pleader's exaggeration (whether Diodotos really so argued, or Thucydides made it up); but on the whole Thucydides' narrative, anyhow for the ten years' war, supports Diodotos' statement, especially the narrative of Brasidas' campaign; and the Mytilenean revolt certainly did not discover any enthusiasm for the 'cause of freedom' on the part of the masses there, or in other cities of the empire. Yet enthusiasm is just what Thucydides had stated in ii. 8. This is perhaps an indication that that chapter was written at a different time. See *J.H.S.* lxxi, 1951, 71–74.

It should also be clear from this statement, as from others (cf. iv. 88 n.), that *every* city in the empire did not have a 'democracy' imposed on it by Athens and an Athenian garrison to secure it.

πολέμιος εὐθύς: this, and οὔτε μετέσχε τῆς ἀποστάσεως below, would seem to be exaggerations, and Kleon's statement, 39. 6, rather nearer to the truth.

3. πρῶτον μὲν ἀδικήσετε τοὺς εὐεργέτας κτείνοντες: Diodotos cannot after all keep justice, the moral question, altogether out of the argument; so τοῖς ἀδικοῦσιν καὶ τοῖς μή below. But see § 5.

προδειξάντων: either 'having proclaimed for all to hear', as Steup, or 'having previously, by your treatment of Mytilene, made it clear'.

4. μὴ προσποιεῖσθαι: 'pretend that they have not.' Edd. compare Theophrastos, Char., περὶ εἰρωνείας, ἀκούσας τι μὴ προσποιεῖσθαι.

5. ἑκόντας ἡμᾶς ἀδικηθῆναι ἢ δικαίως οὓς μὴ δεῖ διαφθεῖραι: for all Diodotos' realism and his argument for Athenian interests above everything, this is a remarkable doctrine of empire; a doctrine which would lead in practice to wide toleration. ἀδικηθῆναι and δικαίως here refer to Kleon's argument for justice, not moral right and wrong as in § 3, above. μὴ δεῖ δ. is equivalent to μὴ ξυμφόρως ἂν διαφθείραιτε.

τὸ Κλέωνος τὸ αὐτὸ δίκαιον καὶ ξύμφορον: 'Kleon's identification of justice and interest', 40. 4. We must, of course, keep the MSS. ἐν αὐτῷ (i.e. ἐν τῷ αὐτοὺς διαφθεῖραι), rejecting Krüger's ἐν ταυτῷ, which would turn this sentence into a statement of universal application; which it clearly is not. Cf. 82. 8, οὐ μέχρι τοῦ δικαίου καὶ τῇ πόλει ξυμφόρου προτιθέντες. Steup's objection to ἐν αὐτῷ that it makes τῆς τιμωρίας superfluous is groundless, for τῆς τιμωρίας is 'the punishment, whatever it is, which we choose to inflict'; but his objection to ἅμα, since the 'identity of right and interest' is the subject of the verb, is sound. I should suppose, however, that the fault is Thucydides' own.

48. 1. γνόντες ἀμείνω τάδε εἶναι: Diodotos sums up, and at the same time restates his position—'it is quite different from what Kleon asserted (40. 2); I do not want you to yield to pity and generosity any more than he does'. προσάγεσθαι is easier if taken as passive of the middle verb (42. 6, 43. 2) than as middle with ἡμᾶς τοὺς λέγοντας as the implied subject; but Spratt's suggestion, παράγεσθαι, is attractive. With πείθεσθέ μοι, cf. Kleon's πειθόμενοι μὲν ἐμοί in his summing up (40. 4).

κρῖναι καθ' ἡσυχίαν: rejecting τάχος καὶ ὀργήν. (Perhaps the best parallel to καθ' ἡσυχίαν here is to be found in v. 26. 5.) μετὰ ἀνοίας too in 42. 1 is echoed in ἀνοίᾳ in the final sentence. But κρῖναι does not, I think, mean 'try by a regular court of justice' (δικαστὰς γενομένους, 46. 4); certainly 50. 1, Κλέωνος γνώμη διέφθειραν, suggests a decision at this meeting of the ekklesia, or at least at one very soon after. See Busolt, iii. 1030. 1, who thinks that Diodotos moved to send them for trial to the dicastery, but Kleon carried a motion to settle the matter there and then. He adds that this meant accepting without question Paches' judgement about οἱ αἰτιώτατοι; not necessarily—Kleon's motion may have been that 'death be the penalty for those found responsible'.

2. πρὸς τοὺς ἐναντίους: surely to be taken with εὖ βουλεύεται (as Classen and others), not as Steup, who prints a comma before πρός; εὖ βουλεύεται is much too commonplace by itself, and πρὸς τοὺς ἐναντίους ('with the enemy in mind') repeats τοῖς πολεμίοις above.

μετ' ἔργων ἰσχύος ἀνοίᾳ ἐπιών: 'attack with a combination of force and folly.' An effective close.

Finley, pp. 59–60, 172–4, has shown how well the rhetoric of these two speeches, both in style and composition and in the arguments used and the way they are used, is characteristic of exactly this period at Athens. In that sense these speeches are contemporary with the events narrated, whether they are freely invented by Thucydides or keep close to the general sense of what Kleon and Diodotos really said. Yet in one particular they appear somewhat remote from their context, inserted: Thucydides tells us that the second debate was held because the Athenians felt remorse for their first ruthless decision, and that the trireme sent to carry this order to Paches went slowly ἐπὶ πρᾶγμα ἀλλόκοτον—36. 4 and 49. 4, the two sentences which frame the debate; yet no speech is given which represents that feeling—Kleon opposes it, but no one expresses it. This might suggest that Diodotos' speech at least—but it would surely carry Kleon's with it—was composed later, and that the real debate had been simpler and less sophistical. Yet nothing in Diodotos' speech (except its literary style, for part of it) is at all unsuited to the occasion, a meeting of the ekklesia.

49. 1. ἦλθον μὲν ἐς ἀγῶνα ὅμως τῆς δόξης: various unlikely explanations of ὅμως have been attempted ('referring back' as far as 36. 4, 'in spite of the revulsion of feeling'; or, 'in spite of the full discussion') and equally unlikely emendations, such as Bredow's ὁμοίως (adopted by Hude). Of course an ἀγὼν τῆς δόξης is a probable, not an improbable result of the near-equality of the arguments on both sides. I do not doubt that Heilmann's forgotten suggestion to transfer ὅμως after ἐκράτησε δέ is correct. Cf. i. 105. 5–6, καὶ μάχης γενομένης ἰσορρόπου - - - ἐνόμισαν αὐτοὶ ἑκάτεροι οὐκ ἔλασσον ἔχειν ἐν τῷ ἔργῳ· καὶ οἱ μὲν Ἀθηναῖοι (ἐκράτησαν γὰρ ὅμως μᾶλλον), κ.τ.λ.; and vii. 34. 6.

2. φθασάσης τῆς προτέρας: all our good MSS. have δευτέρας, a notable agreement in obvious error. Valla translates as though he had προτέρας, but as likely as not by conjecture. I should prefer ἑτέρας (recc.), as a little more likely to give rise to the mistake.

3. οἴνῳ καὶ ἐλαίῳ: the ordinary μᾶζα was made of barley, oil, and water, not wine; but ἄλφιτα (cf. iv. 16. 1) is not necessarily barley, but may be 'groats': L. A. Moritz, C.Q. xliii, 1949, 113–17.

4. κατὰ τύχην δέ: Thucydides does seem now and then to

emphasize the part played by fortune, which is incalculable, in human affairs.

ἐπὶ πρᾶγμα ἀλλόκοτον: 'on so monstrous, inhuman an errand.' This is not only Thucydides' judgement, but what he says was the feeling of the Athenians, here, when the trireme went slowly, and in 36. 4. Why? Severity towards Poteidaia had, it would seem, been contemplated (ii. 70. 4 n.); Torone in 422 was not treated much better than had been threatened against Mytilene (v. 3. 4); and if Skione had caused especial anger at Athens (as Mytilene too had), the extreme sentence (which Kleon had urged) was carried out later when passion had had time to cool (iv. 122. 6, v. 32. 1); Melos fared no better in 416. In none of these cases do we hear of any difference of opinion or feeling in Athens, nor of any protest, whether on grounds of humanity or of self-interest—never any, for example, by Nikias. But so it is—what is at first felt to be an atrocity men become used to, and it becomes an established custom of war. Cf. Polybios, ii. 58. 9–10, the enslavement of men, women, and children (κατὰ τοὺς τοῦ πολέμου νόμους ὑπόκειται παθεῖν).

ἐπικατάγεται: 'arrived on the heels of the other', if one may use this metaphor of ships.

50. 1. Κλέωνος γνώμη: probably carried at the same ekklesia. See 48. 1 n.

ἦσαν δὲ ὀλίγῳ πλείους χιλίων: I am not sure that there is adequate reason for doubting this figure, though figures are easily corrupted and there are undoubtedly corrupt figures in the text of Thucydides. Those who think a much smaller number must have been meant (for example, Steup, ad loc., and Busolt, iii. 1031 n., who put the case best) stress the two superlatives, οἱ πράξαντες πρὸς τοὺς Λακεδαιμονίους μάλιστα τῶν M., 28. 2, and τοὺς αἰτιωτάτους here, and the facts related in 28. 2 (the taking refuge at the altars, the dispatch to Tenedos, and in 35. 1, εἴ τις ἄλλος, κ.τ.λ., which implies only a few more), and argue that this cannot mean more than 50–100 individuals, whereas 1,000 and more would mean the oligarchs in general, the governing class. Compare δέκα τοὺς αἰτιωτάτους of the oligarchs at Kerkyra, 75. 1; but also 75. 5—400 men take refuge in a precinct of Hera. (Others have said that 1,000 would be too large even for the governing class, out of a citizen population of 5,000; but the total citizen population of four cities of Lesbos is indeed quite unknown, but was almost certainly much larger than 5,000.) Besides this, Antiphon's client in *The Murder of Herodes* case, or rather his father, belonged apparently to the oligarch class—certainly he was well-to-do—and he had been spared (v. 76–79).[1] There is much in this

---

[1] Unless, of course, he got his wealth after the revolt, perhaps at the expense of the oligarchic families.

argument, except that οἱ αἰτιώτατοι might well mean the oligarchs as a party, by contrast with the whole citizen body who, certainly in the opinion of the Athenians, bore *some* responsibility for the war, whatever Diodotos might say (47. 3). If χιλίων is corrupt, it is idle to guess at the correct figure; the usual emendation, τριάκοντα ($\bar{\Lambda}$ for $\bar{A}$), palaeographically easy, gives, perhaps, too small a number. Nothing can be made of Diodoros (as so often when we are in a difficulty); in xii. 55 he gives, from Ephoros presumably, a brief account of the Mytilenean revolt, ending with the story of the ekklesia's first decision, and the change of heart at Athens, with nothing about the fate of the ringleaders; in xiii. 30. 4, where, probably from Timaios, in a speech given to Gylippos urging the execution of the Athenian prisoners at Syracuse,[1] he says that Athens had killed the men of Mytilene (τοὺς ἐν τῇ πόλει, certainly meaning τοὺς πολίτας, not, as some have supposed, 'those in Athens'), as they later killed the men of Skione and Melos. This second statement is simple error on the part of Diodoros or Timaios, or, if you will, a purposed exaggeration given by Timaios to Gylippos; cf. also Aelian, *V.H.* ii. 9, cited vol. i, p. 355, n. 1.

If, on the other hand, χιλίων is the correct reading, the number shocks; war often does.

τείχη καθεῖλον καὶ ναῦς παρέλαβον: as with Thasos (i. 101. 3) and Samos (i. 117. 3). The Chians, too, had to destroy their walls, the Athenians anticipating trouble in this case (iv. 51).

In the inventory of treasures in the Parthenon of 422–421 B.C., *I.G.* i.[2] 280 (Tod, 69), are some gold and silver objects from Lesbos (ἐγ Λέσβο: items 41–43), which may be dedications of public booty; but this is not certain. Immediately before them is listed a gold and ivory flute-case παρὰ Μεθυμναίον. All may have been sent to Athens a year or two later, when some harmony had been restored (below, p. 330).

2. φόρον μὲν οὐκ ἔταξαν: tribute had been imposed on Thasos, and payment of the cost of the war, by instalments, on Samos. See above, p. 33.

κλήρους δὲ ποιήσαντες τῆς γῆς - - - τρισχιλίους: the whole island of Lesbos is some 1,750 sq. km. in extent (or 1,614, according to Mantzouránes—see below), most of it, though there is some mountain land, very fertile; and, if we give to Methymna one-fifth of this, it will mean that each of these lots was of about 45 hectares: which would be large for a Greek holding, especially in a land which, like

---

[1] In answer to a speech by Nikolaos, an elderly Syracusan, in favour of mercy. It is a debate on a grand scale, fourteen chapters in Diodoros, and Nikolaos' speech is full of the most high-minded sentiments, very different from Diodotos': Timaios competing with and improving Thucydides. (Cf. Polyb. xii. 25–28 on Timaios' speeches: below, iv. 64. 5 n.)

Lesbos, produces mainly olives and vines. (It is probable that more corn was grown in antiquity than now, because it helped political independence. D. P. Mantzouránes, $To\ ἐτήσιο\ γεωργικὸ\ εἰσόδημα\ τῆς\ Λέσβου\ στὴν\ ἀρχαιότητα$ (Mytilene, 1950: see C.R., N.S. ii, 1952, 236), pp. 6–9, on the basis of Diocletian's census, I.G. xii.² 76–80, estimates that at that time, and probably in the fifth century B.C. as well, as much as 400,000 stremmata, out of a total of 750,000 under cultivation, were ploughed for wheat and barley (including the fallow), and not more than 45,000 were under olives and 35,000 under vines, whereas today, 300,000 stremmata are under corn, only 8,000 under vines, and 450,000 under olives. This is very speculative; but it may be on the right lines.) See below, n. on $δύο\ μνᾶς$.

$πλὴν\ τῆς\ Μηθυμναίων$: see vi. 85. 2, vii. 57. 5; also v. 84. 1, viii. 100.

$τριακοσίους\ μὲν\ τοῖς\ θεοῖς\ ἱερούς$: the usual tithe, as of war-booty; and as at Brea (below). The gods are presumably of Athens, Athena and the Other Gods, whose revenue, since the lands would be let at their full value, would be thus increased.

$σφῶν\ αὐτῶν\ κληρούχους\ τοὺς\ λαχόντας$: chosen by lot; probably from among the poorest citizens, zeugitai and thetes, as expressly stated in the inscription of the colony to Brea (I.G. i.² 45: Tod, 44).

$ἀπέπεμψαν$: they were certainly sent to Lesbos. See n. at the end of this chapter.

$δύο\ μνᾶς$: if, once more, we may take as a rough guide the money earned by workmen on the building of the Erechtheion in the last decade of the century (see ii. 13. 9 n., p. 45), 2 minae a year would be about 50 per cent. more than an unskilled labourer's income (at half a drachme a day for, say, 270 days), not enough for a hoplite, which an Athenian $κληροῦχος$ became (and an owner of 45 hectares, most of it good soil, in Attica would not be a poor man). It is also a small sum as rent for a holding of that size, and 100 tal. (2 minae × 3,000) small for the total annual value of four-fifths of the land of Lesbos; Aigina, for example, a much smaller and less fertile island (though it had had much trade), was able to pay 30 tal. a year as tribute to the Delian League. By this arrangement in fact the land could hardly be said to be confiscated, only somewhat heavily taxed. We are not told whether the property was actually conveyed to the $κληροῦχοι$, whether, for example, they were free to sell, or even to let it to whom they pleased; the words $αὐτοὶ\ εἰργάζοντο\ τὴν\ γῆν$ suggest that the Lesbian farmers had a right (subject to the 2 minae rental) to work the land of which the Athenian settlers could not deprive them. Nor, since the new $κλῆροι$ would be roughly equal in size or value, but the old properties presumably not, do we know how these rights of working the land were now distributed (Busolt, iii. 1033 n.). We must remember, at the same time, that some, perhaps nearly all, of the original land-owners had been executed, and, though we are not told so, their lands presumably confiscated. If in fact the old land-owning class had nearly all of it been destroyed, and if they had owned practically all the land, this measure would have amounted in general to a redistribution of land, at a low rental, among the demos of Mytilene, Eresos, Antissa, and Pyrrha. Cf. the possibly similar case of Chalkis, vol. i, p. 344. On the other hand, the statement in Antiphon, v. 77, ἐπεὶ δ' ὑμεῖς τοὺς αἰτίους τούτων ἐκολάσατε, τοῖς δ' ἄλλοις Μυτιληναίοις ἄδειαν ἐδώκατε οἰκεῖν τὴν σφετέραν αὐτῶν, which is but another way of putting Diodotos' proposal in 48. 1, is yet a more precise way, and, taken by itself, would be naturally interpreted as meaning that the majority of the population were left in possession of their land, as well as of their civil rights. It has, therefore, been suggested that not all the land of Lesbos (except Methymna's) was confiscated, but only what had belonged to the comparatively few oligarchs who had been executed, so that each lot was a good deal smaller than 45 hectares and 2 minae might be its full annual value. This is not what Thucydides' words imply (nor, for what it is worth, Diodoros, xii. 55. 10). In any case we must be careful about speculating; as Busolt says, we do not know anything precise about values of land or crops or anything else in Lesbos at this time. The doubts about the interpretation of *I.G.* i.² 60 (below, p. 329) also have a bearing on this problem.

3. τὰ ἐν τῇ ἠπείρῳ πολίσματα: cf. iv. 52. 2–3, 75. 1. They form a group, Ἀκταῖαι πόλεις, in the assessment lists of the Delian League of 425–424 and 421–420, within which the πολίσματα are assessed separately. See *A.T.L.* ii, A 9 and 10. As possessions of Mytilene they had not paid tribute before 427; now they were separated, and, unlike the Lesbian cities, did pay tribute: 14 in the first, 11 in the second assessment, headed by Antandros.

A last point. Almost immediately after the sentence quoted above, Antiphon has (79): ἠλλάξαντο μὲν πολλῆς εὐδαιμονίας πολλὴν κακοδαιμονίαν, ἐπεῖδον δὲ τὴν ἑαυτῶν πατρίδα ἀνάστατον γενομένην. Taken by itself this would indicate the total destruction of Mytilene, the execution of Kleon's decree; and so it would have been interpreted if we had only an account of a debate in Athens such as that of Diodoros and this sentence as a fragment of Antiphon. Which is a warning against too literal an interpretation of some words, especially orators' words.

The subsequent history of this cleruchy is as obscure as that of the cleruchy to Chalkis at the end of the sixth century (Hdt. v. 77. 2, vi. 100), or of the second to Chalkis in 447 or a little before (see vol. i, pp. 340, 344); and no satisfactory solution has been found, in spite of much discussion. That the cleruchs were settled at first in

Lesbos is clear from Thucydides and from *I.G.* i.² 60 (see below).¹
The natural supposition is that they formed a garrison, especially
perhaps to defend, in case of need, the Aktaia. Their pay as such, or,
much more probably, their earnings from work in their several
trades, supplemented by the 200 dr. a year from the κλῆροι, would
raise them to, or secure them in, the rank of hoplites, with the proper
rights and duties. But from vii. 57. 2 and 5 we can infer that none of
them (nor any Mytileneans) formed part of the Athenian forces in
Sicily, 415–413, though colonists were called from the other settlements. An exception might have been made if it had been thought
necessary to keep a garrison in a dangerous zone (though Thucydides might have said so in this detailed catalogue); but in 412 first
Mytilene, then Methymna revolted from Athens, and were quickly
recovered by an Athenian fleet (viii. 22–23), and there is no mention
of any action by Athenian settlers, then or later (viii. 100; Xen.
Hell. i. 6. 12–38, ii. 2. 5), still less by an Athenian garrison. They
were certainly not there.² Moreover, much earlier than that, in 424,
there was trouble in the Aktaia fomented by Mytilenean oligarchs
who had escaped three years before, and though Athens put it down,
it was not with any help from her citizens in Lesbos; at least not
as Thucydides tells it (iv. 52, 75. 1)—he may already have left Athens
never to return for twenty years, except perhaps to stand trial, but,
to judge by the rest of the narrative, that would not have prevented
him from learning the details of this campaign. Arnold says that
the klerouchoi "were sent out probably to ascertain the size and
situation of their respective shares, and to arrange matters with
their future tenants", and then returned; but Athens was not prodi-
gal of man-power, and only a small commission would be empowered
to settle such matters as these (cf. the arrangements at Brea). Busolt
and others say simply that the bulk of the settlers must soon have
returned to Athens, where the 200 dr. a year would have been a
useful supplement to their incomes in hard times; it would indeed—
and their envious fellow citizens sat by and watched them draw it?
Athens demanded more from her citizens than that.

The inscription, *I.G.* i.² 60, re-edited with an important rearrange-
ment of the fragments by P. H. Davis (*A.J.A.* xxx, 1926, 177–9; see

¹ For *I.G.* i.² 369, τὲς ἀποι[κίας] τὲς ἐς 'Ερ[- - - (vol. i, p. 344 n.), see now *A.T.L.*
iii, p. 284, with its distinction between ἄποικοι and κληροῦχοι. Clearly Eresos
cannot be restored here, and Erythrai is likely.

² In the discussion of ἀποικίαι and κληρουχίαι in *A.T.L.* iii. 284–94 (above,
p. 34, n. 1), the authors argue that in vii. 57. 2 the Lesbian klerouchoi are not
mentioned because they would be included under Ἀθηναῖοι, having remained
Athenian citizens, whereas the settlers in Hestiaia and Aigina were ἄποικοι and
formed new communities. The distinction may be valid; but I do not believe
that in vii. 57. 2, had klerouchoi from different parts of the empire been present
in the Athenian army, Thucydides would have said nothing about it.

Tod, 63), and as D 22 in *A.T.L.* ii, with photographs and new restorations, is an Athenian decree granting a treaty to Mytilene; it mentions the klerouchoi, and is therefore later than the summer of 427, though unfortunately it cannot be exactly dated. (*I.G.*, Tod, and *A.T.L.* give 427–426; but this is unwarranted; there is no certainty that it was a treaty in connexion with the first settlement.) In it Mytilene is promised autonomy by Athens and, perhaps, that Mytileneans are to have their own property: $\alpha\dot{v}\tau o[\nu\acute{o}]\mu os \ \delta o\kappa[\epsilon\hat{\imath} \ \acute{\epsilon}]\nu|[\alpha\iota \ \alpha\dot{v}\tau\grave{o}s \ \acute{\epsilon}\chi o\nu\tau\alpha s \ \ddot{\alpha}\pi\alpha\nu\tau\alpha] \ \tau[\grave{\alpha}] \ \sigma\phi[\acute{\epsilon}\tau\epsilon\rho\alpha] \ \alpha\dot{v}\tau\hat{o}[\nu$, according to Tod's most tempting emendation.[1] All difficulties, or all legal disputes between the parties, are to be settled, on a basis of mutual equality, $\kappa\alpha]\tau\grave{\alpha} \ \tau\grave{\alpha}s \ \chi\sigma v[\mu\beta o]\lambda\grave{\alpha}s \ \hat{\eta}\alpha\grave{\iota} \ \acute{\epsilon}\sigma\alpha\nu \ [\pi\rho\grave{o}s \ M\upsilon\tau\iota\lambda\epsilon\nu\alpha\acute{\iota}os]$, i.e. the agreements with Mytilene before 428.[2] Certain transactions between settlers and Mytileneans are regulated before the handing over of the land by the generals and army (if this restoration is adopted: see below). The Mytilenean delegates are invited to accept state hospitality. All is apparently decreed in a friendly atmosphere.[3] Then there is found, as a kind of rider, this mutilated beginning of a sentence: $\tau o\hat{\imath}s \ \delta\grave{\epsilon} \ \kappa\lambda[\epsilon\rho\acute{o}\chi o\iota s \ . . \ 17 \ . .] \ | \ \gamma\hat{\epsilon}s \ \dot{\alpha}\nu\tau\alpha\pi o\delta o \ . . \ 27 \ . . \ | \ . . \ \nu$, followed apparently by another decree. $\dot{\alpha}\nu\tau\alpha\pi o\delta\hat{o}\nu\alpha\iota$ (or $\dot{\alpha}\nu\tau\alpha\pi\acute{o}\delta o\sigma\iota\nu$) can surely only refer to a restoration of land to Mytileneans, in return for some payment to the klerouchoi (thus supporting Tod's restoration of ll. 11–12 given above). If this is correct, there occurred, some time after 427, a complete change of policy in Athens towards Mytilene, and the klerouchia was formally withdrawn—possibly the demos had given some help against the oligarchs in the Aktaia before 424; in that case the words of the decree which I translated above 'before the handing over of the land by the generals and the army', $\pi\rho\grave{\iota}\nu \ \dot{\alpha}[\pi o]\delta o\theta\hat{\epsilon}\nu\alpha\iota \ \alpha\dot{v}\tau o\hat{\imath}s \ [\tau\grave{\epsilon}\nu \ \gamma\grave{\epsilon}\nu \ \hat{\eta}\upsilon\pi\grave{o} \ \tau\hat{o}\nu \ | \ \sigma\tau]\rho\alpha\tau\epsilon\gamma\hat{o}\nu \ [\kappa\alpha\grave{\iota}] \ \tau\hat{o}\nu \ \sigma\tau\rho\alpha\tau\iota o\tau\hat{o}\nu$ (ll. 19–20), may refer not to the handing over of the land to the klerouchoi, but

---

[1] There is a small error in Tod: in accordance with his principles of transcription he prints $\epsilon\hat{\imath}\nu\alpha\iota$ for what on the stone would have been ΕΝΑΙ, but puts the end of the line after the iota instead of after the nu. With this corrected, his restoration of the next line is one letter short; so I have written $\ddot{\alpha}\pi\alpha\nu\tau\alpha$ for his $\pi\acute{\alpha}\nu\tau\alpha$, the absence of Η for the rough breathing being not uncommon in inscriptions of this period ($\hat{\upsilon}\pi\acute{o}$, *sic*, is restored by some scholars on l. 18 of this one).

This restoration, $\acute{\epsilon}\chi o\nu\tau\alpha s \ \ddot{\alpha}\pi\alpha\nu\tau\alpha$, is more convincing than that in *A.T.L.*, $o\dot{\iota}\kappa\hat{o}\nu\tau\alpha s \ \pi\acute{\alpha}\nu\tau\alpha$ (based on Antiphon, v. 77, above, p. 328; but $\pi\acute{\alpha}\nu\tau\alpha$ makes a lot of difference); and even if we accept $o\dot{\iota}\kappa\hat{o}\nu\tau\alpha s$, such a stipulation is hardly consistent with the land of these citizens being left in the possession of Athenians. The defendant in the Herodes case performed the usual duties of a rich citizen, $\chi o\rho\eta\gamma\acute{\iota}\alpha s \ \acute{\epsilon}\chi o\rho\acute{\eta}\gamma\epsilon\iota \ \kappa\alpha\grave{\iota} \ \tau\acute{\epsilon}\lambda\eta \ \kappa\alpha\tau\alpha\tau\acute{\iota}\theta\eta\sigma\iota\nu$, which also implies normal, free conditions in the state; and there is no reason to suppose that the $\tau\acute{\epsilon}\lambda\eta$ here mentioned must be the rent for the land paid to Athenian klerouchoi.

[2] For such $\xi\upsilon\mu\beta o\lambda\alpha\acute{\iota}$, see i. 77. 1 n., and R. J. Hopper, *J.H.S.* lxiii, 1943, 35–51.

[3] I might have mentioned this inscription in the argument about the Erythrai decree (vol. i, pp. 293–4); an apparent friendliness does not exclude the possibility of previous secession and even war.

to its restoration to the Mytileneans ($a\dot{v}\tau o\hat{\iota}s$ would admittedly more readily suggest the klerouchoi; but in a decree, such ambiguities are not unknown).[1] It seems then likely that this inscription gives the explanation for the absence of any mention of the Athenian klerouchoi in iv. 52, 75. 1, vii. 57, and viii. 22–23; and Antiphon's speech on the murder of Herodes, in which the Mytilenean defendant may have held land and which states that the Mytileneans in general were in possession of their property (above, p. 328), may well then date from c. 424, as Breuning maintained, C.Q. xxxi, 1937, 67–70.[2] Since the cities of the Aktaia were still separately assessed in 421 (above, p. 328), her old territory on the mainland was not restored to Mytilene.

For further discussion of the inscription see my article in *Robinson Studies*, ii. 334–9.

It is even possible, if this interpretation of *I.G.* i.[2] 60 is in general correct, and if it belongs to 425 or 424 B.C., that *Equit.* 830–5 may have a direct or indirect reference to it: the Sausage-monger to Kleon—

$$\tau \acute{\iota}\ \theta \alpha \lambda \alpha \tau \tau о к о \pi \epsilon \hat{\iota} s\ к \alpha \grave{\iota}\ \pi \lambda \alpha \tau \upsilon \gamma \acute{\iota} \zeta \epsilon \iota s,$$
$$\mu \iota \alpha \rho \acute{\omega} \tau \alpha \tau о s\ \ddot{\omega} \nu\ \pi \epsilon \rho \grave{\iota}\ \tau \grave{о} \nu\ \delta \hat{\eta} \mu о \nu$$

[1] The authors of *A.T.L.* restore this sentence quite differently, and have to omit $\tau \grave{\epsilon} \nu\ \gamma \hat{\epsilon} \nu$, which I think essential; and in other ways I find their interpretation unconvincing (see my article referred to above).

Meritt suggests that *I.G.* i.[2] 53, too, may be the record of a treaty between Athens and Mytilene (*A.J.P.* lxviii, 1947, 312–15; *S.E.G.* x. 46); it is the inscription which had been supposed to record a treaty with the Macedonian Philippos (see i. 57. 5 n., vol. i, p. 202: where, by the way, my footnote has been misunderstood in *S.E.G.*—I did not mean that $\mu \eta \delta \acute{\epsilon}$ was not on the stone, but that the restoration proposed required, grammatically, $\mu \acute{\eta} \tau \epsilon$ - - -$\mu \acute{\eta} \tau \epsilon$). It is very doubtful; and I am not sure that Philippos' name should not be restored again in l. 4: not indeed $\tau] \grave{\epsilon} \nu\ \gamma \hat{\epsilon} \nu\ \Phi \iota [\lambda \acute{\iota} \pi \pi о$, but $\tau] \grave{\epsilon} \nu\ \gamma \hat{\epsilon} \nu\cdot\ \Phi \iota [\lambda \acute{\iota} \pi \pi о \iota\ \delta \acute{\epsilon}$ - - -, or the like.

[2] Roussel, in *Mél. Glotz*, 1932, 817–22, shows that there is no proof that Herodes was an Athenian klerouchos, and the silence of the speaker about it, especially in 74–80, and the story about Herodes' relatives in 47, are against it. Nor need Lykinos have been Athenian either. (But Roussel's argument from $\lambda \upsilon \mu \alpha \acute{\iota} \nu \epsilon \sigma \theta \alpha \iota$ in 63, coll. Dem. xxiii. 28, is not, I think, sound; the word here only means 'roughly handled'.)

K. J. Dover (above, p. 278), arguing on points of style, says that the Herodes' speech is later than vi, which is 419–418 (Meritt, *Ath. Cal.* 121–2), and would put it c. 414 B.C. I am not altogether convinced: unless Antiphon was quite young in 420, and therefore still developing, I doubt whether there was a *noticeable* change between 419 and 414; the differences to be observed between the two speeches, that is, would not be due to development of the speaker's style.

It is not necessary to suppose that those bad Mytileneans, $\tau о \grave{\upsilon} s\ \epsilon \grave{\iota} s\ \tau \grave{\eta} \nu\ \mathring{\eta} \pi \epsilon \iota \rho о \nu$ $\mathring{\iota} \acute{о} \nu \tau \alpha s\ к \alpha \grave{\iota}\ о \grave{\iota} к о \hat{\upsilon} \nu \tau \alpha s\ \grave{\epsilon} \nu\ \tau о \hat{\iota} s\ \pi о \lambda \epsilon \mu \acute{\iota} о \iota s\ \tau о \hat{\iota} s\ \grave{\upsilon} \mu \epsilon \tau \acute{\epsilon} \rho о \iota s\ к \alpha \grave{\iota}\ \delta \acute{\iota} к \alpha s\ \grave{\alpha} \pi \grave{о}\ \xi \upsilon \mu \beta о \lambda \hat{\omega} \nu\ \grave{\upsilon} \mu \hat{\iota} \nu$ $\delta \iota к \alpha \zeta о \mu \acute{\epsilon} \nu о \upsilon s$, must be living in the Aktaian cities (Breuning, 69–70). They were more probably in the Persian Hellespont satrapy. The right $\delta \acute{\iota} к \alpha s\ \grave{\alpha} \pi \grave{о}\ \xi \upsilon \mu \beta о \lambda \hat{\omega} \nu$ $\grave{\upsilon} \mu \hat{\iota} \nu\ \delta \iota к \acute{\alpha} \zeta \epsilon \sigma \theta \alpha \iota$ they could have had by remaining in Mytilene, at least after the passing of the decree here discussed; the reference is here only an ironical or bitter one to some recent action and in general to the prosperous life of these enemies of the defendant and of Athens.

331

τὸν Ἀθηναίων; καί σ᾽ ἐπιδείξω,
νὴ τὴν Δήμητρ᾽, ἢ μὴ ζῴην,
δωροδοκήσαντ᾽ ἐκ Μυτιλήνης
πλεῖν ἢ μνᾶς τετταράκοντα.

It is the last charge to be expected against Kleon, the would-be butcher of Mytilene; but his enemy, by Demeter, ἢ μὴ ζῴη, will bring it. And it is not beyond Kleon to have made some proposal favourable to Mytilene in 425, which led directly or later to the decree which we have; or not beyond his opponents to say that he was prepared to do so, for a bribe, if such favourable proposals were being talked about. 'Forty minae' is an odd sum: it might be the rent of twenty κλῆροι about which there had been some scandal or rumour.

As a pendant to the unhappy story of the Mytilenean revolt as told by Thucydides, Paches' fate should be mentioned—ignored by the historian, as his manner was, for it was a personal matter only. Plutarch, Nik. 6. 1, tells us that, accused of some crime at his εὔθυνα, he killed himself in court—obviously therefore a crime which brought great disgrace. (He had, it seems, exercised considerable powers in settling matters himself in Lesbos, 35. 2; and he was thus exposed to attack, as Busolt points out, iii. 1034. 2; but not, ordinarily, to such as would lead to suicide.) A late epigram, by Agathias of the fifth century A.D., tells in execrable verse and in what would be Aeolic dialect, a story of Paches having violated two women of Mytilene, Hellanis and Lamaxis, whose husbands he had killed (against his express promise, 28. 1–2?); who appealed to the dicastery at Athens and thus sent him to his doom (Anth. Pal. vii. 614). This story is rejected by many, including Busolt and Adcock (C.A.H. v, p. 218. 3); but the very improbability of Paches' name surviving for nine centuries, unless in memory of some such incident, is some argument in favour of its truth. Agathias may have been prompted to write his poem by a tomb in Mytilene; but the tomb might record a fact. Certainly it is the kind of crime that might lead to suicide if discovered; and it is not inconsistent with human nature that the Athenians, who for a day were ready to sell all women of Mytilene for slaves, should later be ready to punish the violator of two of them. Busolt says that Plut. Aristeid. 26. 5, where Paches' fate is listed with that of many other Athenian strategoi who fell foul of an ungrateful demos, is inconsistent with Agathias' story. Why so? Paches' friends would have said that the charge was trumped up by political enemies, who would at least have supported it.

Financial record of the Mytilene campaign (below, iii. 116. 3 n.). We have no record for this, unless the very fragmentary *I.G.* i.²

294+299+308 (*S.E.G.* x. 226) belongs to the year 428–427. More probably, in my view, it belongs to 431–430. See above, ii. 47. 1 n.

51. *Athenian attack on Minoa*

51. 1. Νικίου τοῦ Νικηράτου: here mentioned for the first time by Thucydides, though according to Plutarch (*Nik.* 2. 2) he was already known as a good soldier; for he had been strategos in Perikles' lifetime, and had at once become prominent on Perikles' death, as both leader of the better sort, against Kleon, and as well personally popular with the masses. None of his earlier actions, however, are mentioned by Plutarch in his summary in c. 6: all the campaigns there referred to come from Thucydides.

Μινῴαν τὴν νῆσον: see n. on the topography at the end of this chapter. **πύργον ἐνοικοδομήσαντες**: see n. on δύο πύργω, § 3, below.

2. ἀπὸ τοῦ Βουδόρου καὶ τῆς Σαλαμῖνος: ii. 93. 4, 94. 3 nn. (Edd. cf. i. 116. 3, ii. 69. 1, for similar phrases; Steup supposes that after the incident of 429 B.C. other forts on Salamis, besides Boudoron, were used by the Athenians for watching Nisaia. Or it may be we should bracket καί.)

τούς τε Πελοποννησίους - - - μηδὲν ἐσπλεῖν: a truly remarkable sentence, to express a simple idea, deserving but not receiving the criticism of Dionysios. Hünnekes' πρός τε Π. (favoured by Steup) is an attractive emendation; τοῖς τε Πελοποννησίοις (*dativus incommodi*, parallel with τοῖς τε Μεγαρεῦσιν) might also serve. But probably the text should stand, with a construction somewhat like that of δεινόν γε τὸν κήρυκα - - - εἰ μηδέποτε νοστήσει πάλιν (Ar. *Av.* 1269–70), or, perhaps, 'on guard against the Peloponnesians - - -, and to prevent anything reaching Megara by sea'; but it is a notable instance of Thucydides' freedom from grammatical restrictions. (What is surely wrong is Stahl's τούς τε Π. ⟨σκοπῶν⟩, and his comment: "verbis autem τοῖς τε Μ. - - - ἐσπλεῖν scriptor ordinem antea institutum relinquit, cum haec non a σκοπῶν sed a τὴν φυλακὴν εἶναι pendeant (cf. adn. iv. 27. 4) pariter atque φυλάσσειν infinitivus sequitur." Thucydides did not say to himself, 'Now I may go back to the infinitive because I have used φυλακὴν εἶναι, and that is equivalent to φυλάσσειν, which may have an infinitive'. iv. 27. 4 is very much easier.)

ἔκπλους αὐτόθεν: there is a slight awkwardness that αὐτόθεν here, 'from Megara', has a different reference from αὐτόθεν just above, 'from Minoa', though the two places were very close together (Steup). **τὸ πρὶν γενόμενον**: ii. 93–94. For λῃστῶν cf. ii. 69. 1.

3. ἀπὸ τῆς Νισαίας - - - ἐκ θαλάσσης: as Steup rightly says, ἐκ θαλάσσης is not topographical in the sense of saying on which *side* of the island the attack was made, but means only 'from sea', i.e. from ships (not by the bridge mentioned below); and is not therefore

333

superfluous after ἀπὸ τῆς N. This last he interprets as 'on the side away from Nisaia'; but I doubt the possibility of this, that Thucydides, relying on his readers' memory that Nisaia has not yet been captured by the Athenians (i. 115. 1, ii. 31. 3, iv. 21. 3, 67–68), should use so ambiguous an expression. What else should ἑλὼν ἀπὸ τῆς N. mean but 'captured by attack from N.'? The words should either be transposed after ἔκπλους αὐτόθεν above, Nisaia being the harbour of Megara (C. F. Müller's suggestion), or be deleted as a marginal comment on that αὐτόθεν. (There is a late n. on each of the two αὐτόθεν: ἀπὸ τῆς Μινῴας.)

δύο πύργω: as Steup says, both towers must be on the island, and not apparently connected by a wall; so that perhaps πύργον in § 1 should be altered to πύργους.

μηχαναῖς: since the attack is from ships, in which no big 'engines' could be carried, these will be scaling ladders only.

ἐς τὸ μεταξὺ τῆς νήσου: i.e. according to most, 'into the space between the island and the main' (Krüger conjectured ⟨καὶ τῆς Νισαίας⟩), i.e. the harbour of Nisaia. Then why not ἐς τὸν λιμένα? Steup takes it to mean 'that part of the island between the two towers'; which gives some sense and is possible, though again ambiguous; and was there any special value in an entry to this point? Good landing ground, for example?

ἐλευθερώσας is used in a unique sense; Classen's κλειθρώσας would be a word uniquely used here, but his meaning for it is what is required (τοῖς Μεγαρεῦσιν μηδὲν ἐσπλεῖν).

καὶ τὸ ἐκ τῆς ἠπείρου: clearly different from the place where they landed ἐκ θαλάσσης, and from that occupied by the two towers (Steup), but facing Nisaia. They did not destroy the bridge over the marsh, for they might use it later themselves.

4. καὶ ἐν τῇ νήσῳ τεῖχος ἐγκαταλιπών, κ.τ.λ.: I agree with Steup that something must have been dropped from the text, though there is no need for his ὕστερον δὴ ⟨καὶ τὴν ἄλλην Μινῴαν ἑλών⟩ and τεῖχος ⟨ἐγκατοικοδομήσας ναῦς⟩ ἐγκαταλιπὼν καὶ φρουράν; only τεῖχος ⟨οἰκοδομήσας⟩ καὶ ἐγκαταλιπὼν φρουράν.

A chapter of great obscurity for a simple narrative.

Note on the Topography: Nisaia and Minoa

The relative positions of Nisaia and Minoa have been much discussed. I believe the only possible solution of the problem to be that of Bölte and Weicker in their article in Ath. Mitt. xxix, 1904, 79–100, namely that Nisaia is Paliókastro, the small hill on the coast southeast of the town of Megara, the harbour is the bay immediately to the east of it, and the island of Minoa the comparatively long and comparatively high range of hills to the east of that again, beginning with the hill of H. Geórgios on the west (where it is crowned by the chapel of St. George) and ending in the peninsula of Teichó to the east. Others (see, for example, Frazer on Pausanias, i. 44. 3; Casson, *B.S.A.* xix, 1913, 70–81) have maintained the opposite, that Palió-kastro is Minoa and H. Geórgios Nisaia; but the narrative of Athenian movements in iv. 66–67 makes it plain that Minoa was on the same side of the Long Walls between Megara and Nisaia as Eleusis, that is, to the east; for Demosthenes' force comes by land from Eleusis (cf. iv. 68. 5) and joins that of Hippokrates from Minoa at a gate in the Long Walls. It is also probable on *a priori* grounds that those walls should have been taken from Megara to the nearer suitable hill and place of defence on the coast rather than to the one farther away, and that the Athenians should attack first the fort nearer them; and the distance, 8 stades between Nisaia and the city-wall (iv. 66. 3), suits Paliókastro, not St. George;[1] and if the latter were Nisaia, its περιτείχισις (iv. 69) could not have been accomplished within two days. Further, there is archaeological evidence of prolonged habitation of Paliókastro, nothing but a wall on the hill of St. George.

But though I feel sure that this is the correct view, it is not without difficulties. Minoa is called an island, and was separated from the mainland by marshy ground crossed by a causeway. The chain of hills beginning with St. George is not now an island, and though there is extensive salt marsh to the east there is no marsh at the present time at the western end (north and west of the hill of St. George), which faces Megara itself and where the causeway must have been. There are streams flowing south and east of Megara (which join now south-east of the town) which bring down soil with them, and this may have led to the filling of the marsh and the joining of the 'island' to the mainland, and Strabo, ix. 1. 4, p. 391, calls Minoa ἄκρα, not νῆσος; but there are no signs of this on the spot today, and immediately below St. George to the west is an aerodrome, used during the 1939–45 war and still serviceable. Besides, when Hippokrates marched from Minoa to the Long Walls in 424 (iv. 67. 1), he must have crossed the marsh (presumably by the causeway); but no mention is made of it there. Strabo, describing the coast in the direction from Corinth to Attica, mentions Minoa first, as a headland forming the harbour of Nisaia; this would not suggest that Nisaia itself was a fortified hill which the traveller passed before reaching Minoa, and the explanation must be that Strabo kept inland and went only to Megara.[2]

---

[1] Strabo, however (see below), says 18 stadia, too far for either hill (the walls had been rebuilt: Plut. *Phok.* 15. 2). We must not rely too much on figures of distance.

[2] Pausanias, i. 44. 3, who had come in the opposite direction from Attica, mentions Nisaia before Minoa; but he clearly went to the city first, and then to the

335

The two towers on Minoa must have been on the south side, just above the shore. There is a small bay here formed by a low but rocky promontory just south of the hill on which is the chapel of St. George; the bay is still used for the export of products of the Megarid, must and wine, by steamers which come from abroad. This would be the natural place at which to attempt a landing, though its shore is rocky for triremes; but from it the capture of the St. George hill, and still more of the whole chain east to Teichó, would have been a difficult operation against defence of any vigour. Thucydides, I think, had no clear picture of Minoa in his mind.

There are small remains of a good Greek wall to the east of the chapel on the hill of St. George (described in some detail by Casson). Bolte and Weicker think it may be the fort built by Nikias. This is possible, but quite uncertain—it may be of the fourth century.

52. Fall of Plataia

52. 1. καὶ οἱ Πλαταιῆς: the narrative resumed from c. 24. καί presumably means, 'like Mytilene'.

Demosthenes, lix. 103, implies that some escaped at this last minute: οἱ δ' ὑπομείναντες - - - ἀπεσφάγησαν πάντες οἱ ἡβῶντες, παῖδες δὲ καὶ γυναῖκες ἐξηνδραποδίσθησαν, ὅσοι μὴ αἰσθόμενοι ἐπιόντας τοὺς Λακεδαιμονίους ὑπεξῆλθον Ἀθήναζε. This is inconsistent with Thucydides, and is partly (οἱ ἡβῶντες, κ.τ.λ.) just conventional.

οὐδὲ δυνάμενοι πολιορκεῖσθαι: 'not having the strength to endure the siege' (= πολιορκούμενοι ἀντέχειν, ii. 70. 1); a nice instance of a passive after δύνασθαι.

Those who are inclined at times to trust Diodoros should read xii. 56. 4, where he states that on the day following the escape of half the garrison the Spartans, incensed, attacked energetically and Plataia surrendered.

2. ὁ Λακεδαιμόνιος ἄρχων: unnamed. Because unknown? Yet Thucydides had been told the names of the chief Plataian speakers (§ 5); and often names Spartan and Corinthian commanders (iv. 42. 4, 57. 3, etc.). Cf. ii. 85. 5 n.

εἰ σπονδαὶ γίγνοιντο: as happened, v. 17. 2. With ὅσα πολέμῳ χωρία ἔχουσιν, cf. iv. 21. 3. Both Ἀθ. and Λακ. are to be understood as subject to ξυγχωροῖεν. We may note that Sparta concedes that she may not be able altogether to attain the object of the war—the liberation of Greece from the tyrant city; which is not surprising after her failure at Mytilene (Busolt, iii. 1035. 4).

λέγοντα, εἰ βούλονται, κ.τ.λ.: if, with Stuart Jones and others, we

harbour. He calls Minoa an island, either a literary reminiscence, or he mistakes one of the islets in the sea between the Megarid and Salamis for Minoa, which he knew from his reading as an island.

336

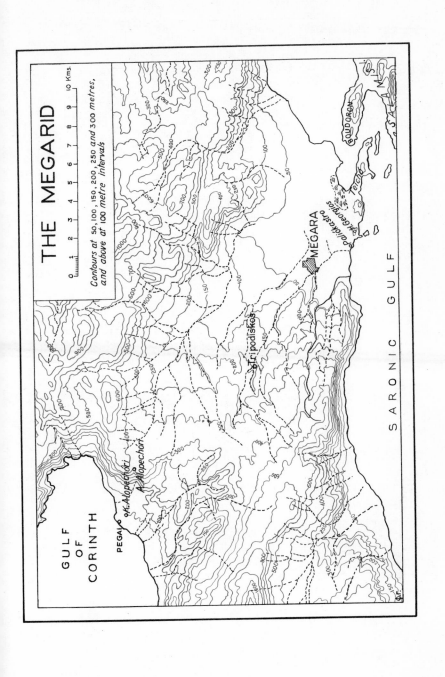

THE MEGARID

Contours at 50, 100, 150, 200, 250 and 300 metres, and above at 100 metre intervals

GULF OF CORINTH

SARONIC GULF

PEGAI

K. Alopechóri
Alopechóri

Tripodískos

MEGARA

Palaiókastro
Ag.Geórgios

Teichos
BUDORON
SALAMIS

take εἰ βούλονται - - - χρήσασθαι as protasis, and τούς τε ἀδίκους, κ.τ.λ., as apodosis, we must surely read κολάσειν for κολάζειν, as Krüger conjectured (from Valla), even though we should then like εἰ βούλοιντο. This interpretation makes it easy to understand τοὺς Λακ. or τοὺς δικαστάς as subject to κολάσειν. The sequence τε - - - δέ is not here expected (i. 11. 1, v. 9. 9, and viii. 16. 3 all seem to me easier); but to treat τε as connective ('asking whether they wished ... to have Sparta as judge, and for the punishment of the guilty'— Arnold, Spratt) makes a very harsh change of subject; and the same objection applies to punctuating with a comma after εἰ βούλονται: 'with the message, if they wished, to hand over the city to Sparta ..., and to have the guilty only punished.' These solutions, and a third which takes κολάζειν to be epexegetic (see Spratt), would besides require μηδένα for οὐδένα.

The sentence, τούς τε ἀδίκους κολάζειν, παρὰ δίκην δὲ οὐδένα, reminds one of the Athenians' μετάνοια, 36. 4, of Kleon, 40. 7, and of Diodotos, 48. 1. In the event the Spartans had it both ways.

3. οἱ ἐκ τῆς Λακεδαίμονος δικασταί: Aristomelidas, maternal grandfather of Agesilaos II, was one of them, Paus. iii. 9. 3.

4. εἴ τι Λακεδαιμονίους, κ.τ.λ.: Stahl compares the Roman question to Capua in the second Punic war, 'ecquis Campanorum bene meritus de republica Romana esset' (Livy, xxxvi. 33).

5. Ἀστύμαχόν τε - - - καὶ Λάκωνα: names that are only names to us, but notables of Plataia. Nothing, as far as we can see, is *added* to the narrative by the mention of the names of the speakers any more than by Diodotos' name (41 n.) or Euphemos'. Here especially they are merged in their state; and at c. 60 we have τοιαῦτα μὲν οἱ Πλαταιῆς εἶπον. In any case we have two names and one speech: cf. vii. 65. Asopolaos is a local name, from the river Asopos (the boundary between Plataia and Thebes); for a personal name of the type Lakon, cf. Kimon's son Lakedaimonios, i. 45. 2, Athenaios the Lacedaemonian, iv. 119. 2 n., and Boiotos the Athenian (Dem. xxxix, xl).

53–68. *The Trial*

53–59. *Speech of the Plataians*

Poppo analyses the rhetorical parts of this speech, so much admired in antiquity and in modern times, as follows: "post exordium (cc. 53–54. 1) legitur A) τὸ διδακτικὸν μέρος (cc. 54–57), in quo 1) de iusto (cc. 54–56) sic, ut a) defensio Plataeensium (cc. 54, 55), b) accusatio Thebanorum (c. 56) eo loco contineatur, tum 2) de utili (c. 57) explicatur. Sequitur B) τὸ παραινετικὸν καὶ ἐντρεπτικὸν μέρος (58. 1–59. 2) cum peroratione (59. 3–4)." It is, however, not quite so rigid as this: see esp. c. 56.

337

53. 1. ἐν δικασταῖς οὐκ ἂν ἄλλοις δεξάμενοι: if we accept Dobree's ἄν for the second ἐν, with Hude and Stuart Jones, the participles οἰόμενοι and ἂν δεξάμενοι are co-ordinate, and ἡγούμενοι is causal, dependent on the latter. If we keep the double ἐν of the MSS. (as Stahl, Classen, and Steup), with vi. 82. 4 (from Euphemos' speech), ἐπὶ τὴν μητρόπολιν, ἐφ' ἡμᾶς, to defend it, οἰόμενοι and ἡγούμενοι are co-ordinate and δεξάμενοι equals εἰ δεξαίμεθα, protasis to ἂν φέρεσθαι. The former is more idiomatic, and the highly rhetorical ἐπὶ τὴν μητρόπολιν, ἐφ' ἡμᾶς is not a true parallel.

Hude and Stuart Jones–Powell bracket ἢ ὑμῖν on the ground that the scholiast did not read the words, but gives them as an explanation. This may be right; but I am inclined to insert ἐν ὑμῖν (or παρ' ὑμῖν) before ἂν φέρεσθαι. 'We surrendered because we expected that a different matter (not life and death) would be in issue, and because we would not accept other judges, supposing that we should find in Sparta impartial ones.'

For δεξάμενοι - - - γενέσθαι, cf. i. 143. 2.

2. τεκμαιρόμενοι προκατηγορίας τε - - - τό τε ἐπερώτημα, κ.τ.λ.: 'inferring this from two facts, that (1)', etc., a peculiarly perverse instance of *variatio*. Spratt's argument, "Thucydides' free coordination allows of the collocation of gen. absol. with accus. absolute. Cf. viii. 96. 2, αὐτῶν τε στασιαζόντων καὶ ἄδηλον ὂν ὁπότε σφίσιν αὐτοῖς ξυρράξουσι", is very weak. Classen's, that, after the parenthesis, the construction continues as if λογιζόμενοι or σκοποῦντες had preceded, is better; but it hardly helps. Mervyn Jones suggests that τεκμαίρεσθαι is used in two senses, 'concluding' with the genitive absolute, and 'noting, as evidence for our conclusion, the brevity of the question put to us'. Yet Dionysios in his praise of the speech, as the best in Thucydides, says, τὸ μὴ βεβασανίσθαι μηδὲ κατεπιτηδεῦσθαι, ἀληθεῖ δέ τινι καὶ φυσικῷ κεκοσμῆσθαι χρώματι. τά τε γὰρ ἐνθυμήματα πάθους ἐστὶ μεστά, καὶ ἡ λέξις οὐκ ἀποστρέφουσα τὰς ἀκοάς· ἥ τε γὰρ σύνθεσις εὐεπής, καὶ τὰ σχήματα τῶν πραγμάτων ἴδια (de Thuc. 42, pp. 921–2). Cf. 56. 3, 7, which are not easier; 57. 1, 58. 1, 59. 1, 2.

ᾧ τὰ μὲν ἀληθῆ, κ.τ.λ.: with Poppo, Böhme, and Steup, τὰ ἀληθῆ, like τὰ ψευδῆ, is to be taken as the object of ἀποκρίνασθαι, and the infinitive is the subject of ἐναντία γίγνεται and of ἔλεγχον ἔχει; the plural ἐναντία is like ἀδύνατα, i. 59. 2, al., and it means 'inimical to' or 'presenting obstacles to' the defendant, τῷ ἀποκρινομένῳ. But it would certainly be easier if we had ἐναντίον, or ἐναντίως.

3. πανταχόθεν δὲ ἄποροι καθεστῶτες: as in ii. 59. 2, but that *there* τῇ γνώμῃ qualifies, and 61. 2 gives the answer; here there is no escape.

4. ἡ πειθώ: 'the chance of persuading you', the word, often found with ἐλπίς and ἔρως in other writers, only found here in Thucydides. οὐχί: an emphatic negative, found in five other places in Thucydides,

338

all in speeches (except vii. 56. 3, where the confident hopes of the Syracusans are expressed as in a speech).

ἄλλοις χάριν φέροντες - - - καθιστώμεθα: not a 'confusion' of construction, for ἡμᾶς καθίστητε, but said in bitter irony: 'we are here, facing a predetermined verdict in order to gratify others', i.e. a third party.

The distinction between the two halves of the sentence, between προκαταγνόντες and διεγνωσμένην, primarily of course rhetorical, might be rendered 'not that you are prejudiced against us (so that you *may* bring in a verdict of guilty), but that the verdict has already been decided'.

54. 3. μόνοι Βοιωτῶν: a notable falsehood, for Thespiai played a gallant part at Thermopylai. Cf. Hdt. vii. 132. 1, 202, viii. 50. 2. According to Pausanias, ix. 32. 4, Haliartos also took the national side, and the city was burnt. But claims to have stood alone tend to be exaggerated: cf. i. 73. 4.

4. ἠπειρῶται - - - ἐπ' Ἀρτεμισίῳ: ὑπὸ δὲ ἀρετῆς καὶ προθυμίης Πλαταιέες, ἄπειροι τῆς ναυτικῆς ἐόντες, συνεπλήρουν τοῖσι Ἀθηναίοισι τὰς νέας: Hdt. viii. 1. 1. The Plataians were not at Salamis, ibid. 44. 1 (with a very poor reason given for their absence). (J. E. Powell, in his note on Herodotos, observes that the Plataian speech of Thucydides owes much to Herodotos.)

μάχῃ τε τῇ ἐν τῇ ἡμετέρᾳ γῇ γενομένῃ: Hdt. ix. 28. 6.

εἴ τέ τι ἄλλο, κ.τ.λ.: presumably a reference to Marathon, a delicate one for Spartan ears, unlike the manner of the Athenians (i. 73). Cf. 56. 6 n. (My n. on i. 73. 4 should be modified.) Dem. lix. 95 says they were present at Salamis and Thermopylai; but this is clearly wrong.

5. ὅτεπερ δή: 'just then when', in the hour of your greatest danger. See i. 102. 1 n.

55. 1. ἠξιώσαμεν εἶναι: "wir haben unsre Ehre darein gesetzt"; cf. i. 22. 2—Classen. 'It was our aim', or 'our ambition'.

δεομένων γὰρ ξυμμαχίας, κ.τ.λ.: Hdt. vi. 108, whom Thucydides follows. For the date, see 68. 5 n. The Theban point of view is given in 61. 2. Note that, though this is to be by contrast with τὰ μὲν παλαιά, Thucydides begins by going back to an even earlier event.

2. ἐκπρεπέστερον: 'irregular', 'abnormal', as i. 38. 4.

3. ὑμῶν κελευσάντων: see 68. 1 (the Spartan view), ii. 72.

οὐκέτι ἦν καλόν: i.e. after Athens had given help to us. This is generally referred to the Theban attack in 431 B.C., as ἐν τῷ πολέμῳ above suggests; but ὅτε ὑμεῖς ἀπωκνεῖτε appears to refer back to the original alliance—at least there is no suggestion of an appeal to Sparta in ii. 2–6; and 56. 1 gives the required reference to the event of 431.

πολιτείας μετέλαβεν: cf. 63. 2, Ἀθηναίων ξύμμαχοι καὶ πολῖται; Dem.

lix. 104–6; Isokr. xii. 94; Lys. xxiii. 2. The right of $\dot{\iota}\sigma\sigma\pi\sigma\lambda\iota\tau\epsilon\dot{\iota}a$ did not mean the merging of two states in one, but the grant of honorary citizenship to all citizens of the favoured state and of all (or most) of the rights of citizenship to such of those citizens as settled in the granting state. Cf. the case of Samos in 405, *I.G.* ii. 1. 1 (Tod, 96). When a large number from the favoured state migrated as a body, like the Plataians to Athens, they might continue to form a group in their new state and keep their old name (cf. Ar. *Ran.* 693–4; Hellanikos, F. 171), and might serve as a separate unit in the army (below, iv. 67). This was doubtless because their ultimate fate was undecided, and the Plataians would themselves have hoped, in 427, that they would be restored to their own city at the end of the war—honorary citizens of Athens still, like the Samians in 405, but forming their own $\pi\acute{o}\lambda\iota s$. When they were settled in the territory of conquered Skione in 420 (v. 32), they became a new $\pi\acute{o}\lambda\iota s$.

It is this possibility of double citizenship which makes me doubt the argument that Thucydides makes a mistake here about the date of the grant of Athenian citizenship to the Plataians (Isokrates implies that it was given after this trial): see Busolt, iii. 1059 n., who argues that, by the use of $\xi\acute{v}\mu\mu\alpha\chi\sigma\iota$ in ii. 2. 1 and 73. 3, Thucydides must mean that citizenship had not then been granted, whereas our present passage implies that it had. For, so long as Plataia existed as a separate state, their alliance with Athens was more important than their honorary citizenship; they would behave as allies, sending ambassadors to one another and consulting together, just as is proposed in the decree for Samos. It would be important if Thucydides were inconsistent and here in error; for it would show that these two speeches were composed not only some time later than the events, but later also than his narrative of the events: but that is not proved. Cf. 56. 2 n.

$\dot{\iota}\acute{\epsilon}\nu\alpha\iota\ \delta\acute{\epsilon}$ - - - $\epsilon\dot{\iota}\kappa\grave{o}s\ \mathring{\eta}\nu$: we could do without $\epsilon\dot{\iota}\kappa\grave{o}s\ \mathring{\eta}\nu$, for the order of words suggests that $\dot{\iota}\acute{\epsilon}\nu\alpha\iota$ is governed by $\kappa\alpha\lambda\acute{o}\nu$ above.

4. $o\dot{v}\chi\ o\dot{\iota}\ \dot{\epsilon}\pi\acute{o}\mu\epsilon\nu\sigma\iota$, $\kappa.\tau.\lambda.$: words repeated, with a twisted meaning, by the Thebans, 65. 2.

56. 2. $\dot{\epsilon}\nu\ \sigma\pi\sigma\nu\delta\alpha\hat{\iota}s$: ii. 2. 3, 5. 5.

$\dot{\iota}\epsilon\rho\sigma\mu\eta\nu\acute{\iota}\alpha$: repeated, 65. 1. This particular is not to be found in the narrative, ii. 2–6; but it may very well mean 'the first of the month festival', the first of every month being regarded as a $\dot{\iota}\epsilon\rho\sigma\mu\eta\nu\acute{\iota}a$. It should be noted that Thucydides does not say that the Thebans attacked on the day of the new moon (which would begin at sunset) but on a day, or perhaps two days, before it ($\tau\epsilon\lambda\epsilon\upsilon\tau\hat{\omega}\nu\tau\sigma s\ \tau\sigma\hat{v}\ \mu\eta\nu\acute{o}s$, ii. 4. 2: see above, pp. 70–71); and this may be, to that extent, a false statement, though if it were so intended, its repetition by the Thebans in their answer is unexpected. Perhaps we should there bracket $\kappa\alpha\grave{\iota}$

340

ἱερομηνίᾳ (it is in any case far from wanted), as an adscript borrowed from this passage. If not, then Thucydides is in error; for if the day before that new moon in 431, or the day before that, was in fact a festival in Plataia, he should certainly have mentioned it in the narrative. Cf. above, n. on πολιτείας μετέλαβεν, 55. 3.

ὀρθῶς τε ἐτιμωρησάμεθα: 'we were right to take our revenge', or 'to punish them'. We should, with ABEFM and the earlier edd., omit τε, and put a colon after ἀμύνεσθαι; a new point begins with καὶ νῦν.

τιμωρεῖσθαι is not the same as ἀμύνεσθαι, and that is one point at issue—the execution of the Theban prisoners (ii. 5. 5–7); a matter over which the Plataian speakers hurry, the Thebans dwell (66), as Classen points out.

3. εἰ γὰρ τῷ αὐτίκα χρησίμῳ, κ.τ.λ.: 'if you measure justice by what is at the same time your immediate advantage and Theban hostility.' So Classen and Stahl, who compare Dem. xviii. 31, τὸ - - - ἐν τῇ πρεσβείᾳ πρῶτον κλέμμα μὲν Φιλίππου, δωροδόκημα δὲ τῶν ἀδίκων τούτων ἀνθρώπων. But note first that in Demosthenes the order is normal, for τὸ ἐν τῇ πρεσβείᾳ πρῶτον belongs to both the μέν and the δέ-clause, and he does not write κλέμμα Φιλίππου μέν, τῶν δὲ ἀδίκων τούτων δωροδόκημα; and that there is no such ambiguity as arises in this sentence from the juxtaposition of ὑμῶν τε καὶ ἐκείνων. Secondly, Demosthenes is referring to one thing which was at once Philip's 'theft' or ruse, and the defendants' bribe (for a similar expression in Thucydides, cf. above, 47. 5); but no one thing can be both Spartan advantage and the Thebans' hostile attitude, and the translation I have given above is in fact nonsense; and neither Stahl nor Classen translate the sentence as they explain its grammar. (The two genitives are different, ὑμῶν being objective, ἐκείνων subjective.) Spratt does his best with "if you intend to fix your estimate of justice by that vindictiveness of theirs which tallies for the moment with your own interests"; but that is some way from the Greek. The transposition of τε, therefore, not of course unexampled, is here very awkward, for since there are two different measures of justice it should strictly come after τῷ; and its result is an artificial obscurity. Cf. 53. 2 n. It should be noticed that C ⟨G⟩ omit τε; but that does not in itself make the sentence easier. Classen objects to Krüger's πολεμίως (which is otherwise too not convincing) that in the context there is no mention of the advantage to the Thebans of Spartan action; the same objection, and others, apply to Hude's bracketing of πολεμίῳ.

4. καίτοι εἰ νῦν, κ.τ.λ.: Gertz's ⟨οἶδε⟩ after ὠφέλιμοι would be an improvement, except that we have it again in the next sentence.

ἦτε: a compliment to Sparta, that the danger is said to have been hers.

5. σπάνιον ἦν τῶν Ἑλλήνων: τῶν Βοιωτῶν would have been more accurate, and better pointed at Thebes; but τῶν Ἑλλήνων is more flattering to Sparta ('you saved Greece') as well as to themselves.

ἐπῃνοῦντό τε μᾶλλον: 'more than now, when their deeds are forgotten', according to Classen; but this is very obscure. It is rather, 'those were praised, not blamed, who', etc.

6. τιμηθέντες ἐς τὰ πρῶτα: see ii. 71. 2; Plut. Arist. 20. 2-3.

ἐπὶ τοῖς αὐτοῖς: as this is explained by Ἀθηναίους ἑλόμενοι, with δικαίως emphasized ('we did then what we have done now, rightly choose the Athenian side'; which cannot mean the war of 480-479), we have another oblique reference to Marathon, for which they also received praise at the time. Cf. 54. 4 n. If not, we must expand the meaning to, 'because, in choosing the Athenian side rather than yours, we are again preferring justice to selfish advantage'.

7. ταὐτὰ περὶ τῶν αὐτῶν - - - γιγνώσκοντας: a doctrine Sparta is forgetting if she judges Plataia now otherwise than she did in 490 and 479; a somewhat specious argument. Cf. Isokr. ii. 18.

ὅταν αἰεὶ βέβαιον, κ.τ.λ.: it is essential that in this sentence καὶ τὸ παραυτίκα που ὑμῖν ὠφέλιμον καθιστῆται take a subordinate place, and that all the emphasis should be on the first half (note που, your supposed immediate interests); otherwise we get a sentence which gives a sense the opposite of what we require, just as we have in ii. 42. 4, τῶν δὲ ἐφίεσθαι, if the MSS. reading there is kept. To secure this we should adopt Heilmann's admirable ἔχουσι (the participle), which, by making one finite sentence out of two, puts the emphasis, by the order of words, on the participial clause. It has the further advantage, as Stahl points out, that the direct relation of the whole sentence to Sparta is preserved, whereas ἔχωσι must equal ἔχῃ τις, and the first half is generalized, the second (with ὑμῖν) particular. 'True advantage is only secured when your presumed immediate interest too is established by keeping constant your gratitude to those of your allies who have deserved it by their valour.' If we do not accept ἔχουσι, we must, I think, read with Dobree κἂν μή for καί; which is simpler but less elegant, and is open to Stahl's objection to the MSS. reading. Cf. v. 105. 4, for the application of this doctrine to Sparta.

57. 1. παράδειγμα - - - ἀνδραγαθίας: 'the example to all of upright conduct.' Cf. ii. 42. 3 (where it is qualified, ἐς τοὺς πολεμίους), 63. 2 n.

ἐπαινούμενοι: 'as men of fame and reputation'; yet a bold use (for ἐλλόγιμοι or the like), for after τὴν δίκην τήνδε, it could so naturally mean 'applauded for this conduct', 'conduct to which men will assent', and περὶ οὐδ' ἡμῶν μεμπτῶν seems to support this.

Cf. Sallust's imitation, Cat. 51, and Gorgias, Palamedes, 8.

ἐπιγνῶναι: I find it difficult to recognize the proper meaning of this compound here (ii. 65. 11, i. 70. 2; cf. i. 132. 5); and there is much to be said for Hude's γνῶναι, with a mistake due to dittography; a conjecture, however, which he gave up in his 1913 edition.

2. πανοικεσίᾳ διὰ Θηβαίους ἐξαλεῖψαι: 'obliterate the whole city, buildings and all, for the sake of Thebes.' The separate *state* of Plataia would disappear (though all but a small minority of its citizens would live on as citizens of Athens); χώραν τὴν Πλαταιίδα Θηβαῖδα ποιήσετε (58. 5, like ἐν τῇ Μεσσηνίᾳ ποτὲ οὔσῃ γῇ, iv. 3. 2). ἐξαλεῖψαι is the proper word for erasing a name or a sentence from a public record: e.g. if a man has been posted as a public debtor and later pays his debt; or as a benefactor and is later found to be a traitor. The name of Plataia was recorded in the finest monument of all, at Delphi.

3. ἀπωλλύμεθα: the city was destroyed by the Persians, also at the behest of the Thebans, after their victory at Thermopylai (Hdt. viii. 44. 1 and 50. 2); and would have remained for ever extinct, had Persia won the war.

Θηβαίων ἡσσώμεθα: 'we take second place to Thebes', or 'we lose our case against Thebes in this *Spartan* court of justice'.

τότε μέν, τὴν πόλιν εἰ μὴ παρέδομεν: referred by most edd. to the surrender a few days back, 52. 1, 59. 3; and every word but τότε, especially λιμῷ, supports such a view. But how, in this context, can τότε refer to anything but 480–479 B.C., especially with τῶν τότε ξυμμάχων to follow so soon? And what is the point of any comparison with yesterday's surrender? It is not that a surrender by the Plataians under threat of starvation in 480 is incompatible with Herodotos' brief (surprisingly brief) narrative; there may well have been a story, even a true story, of a siege and much suffering. What is wrong is that λιμῷ *seems* so clearly to point to 52. 1. We expect ἅπαντας or βίᾳ διαφθαρῆναι. I cannot but suspect something wrong with the text.

4. παρὰ δύναμιν: as in 54. 4.

τῶν τότε ξυμμάχων - - - οὐδείς: not Sparta; but also, not even Athens. καί at the beginning of the sentence has perhaps more feeling than a more conventional γάρ.

ἡ μόνη ἐλπίς: for was not Sparta the liberator of Greece, and her foremost defender? cf. the Melians, v. 104, and the Athenian answer. Compare also other uses of ἐλπίς in Thucydides, as ii. 62. 5 and iii. 45. 5. μὴ οὐ βέβαιοι ἦτε: βέβαιος as in 56. 7. The Spartans do not stand firm; they are swayed by Thebes—διὰ Θηβαίους, Θηβαίων ἡσσώμεθα, above. See n. on καμφθῆναι, 58. 1.

58. 1. τῶν ξυμμαχικῶν ποτὲ γενομένων: Valla translates τότε, which may be by mistake, or conjecture; but it seems the better reading (cf. τῶν τότε ξ., 57. 4). Contrast ὁμαίχμοις ποτὲ γενομένοις, § 4, where ποτέ is obviously right.

343

καμφθῆναι ὑμᾶς: in the last chapter the fear was that Sparta was not firm enough; here that she will obstinately abide by a promise given to Thebes.

ἀνταπαιτῆσαι αὐτούς: 'ask for the gift back', 'you gave Thebes as a gift the promise to kill us; ask for this gift back, not to kill us', a somewhat frigid conceit in this context.

2. οὐκ ἐχθρούς, κ.τ.λ.: as before (56. 2), the Plataians (naturally enough) ignore what was the main argument, if not the chief motive, of their enemies; which is not that they were hostile, but that they had killed their Theban prisoners, and after a promise to spare them. It was not the ordinary Greek view that prisoners of war were to be killed, frequent as such cruelty was; the next sentence indeed suggests that it was among the worst of crimes.

3. προνοοῦντες: "die Erklärung 'vorher erwägen' ergiebt hier ebensowenig einen passenden Sinn wie c. 57. 1 für die überlieferte Lesart προσκέψασθε"—Steup (who adopts Meineke's προσσκέψασθε there); but προνοοῦντες refers to ἐπίπονον τὴν δύσκλειαν ἀφανίσαι, and 'foreseeing' or 'taking precaution' is the meaning. See Steup's n. for a certain logical confusion here, in the junction καὶ ποιοῦντες and καὶ προνοοῦντες (which, I think, is not removed by his καὶ τῶν⟨δε ἕνεκα τῶν⟩ σωμάτων); but the Greek is rhetorically sound.

4. ἐς πατέρων - - - θήκας: Hdt. ix. 85; Paus. ix. 2. 5.

ἐτιμῶμεν κατὰ ἔτος ἕκαστον: Plut. Arist. 21. See the discussion of the terms of this covenant in A.T.L. iii. 101–3. There was also a four-yearly festival, the Eleutheria, which was still celebrated in Pausanias' day, two generations or so after Plutarch.

ἐσθήμασι: a word used mainly in poetry, proper in this highly poetical passage (cf. ὁμαίχμοις, αὐθένταις, ἐσσαμένων, etc.); and explained either by offerings of clothes to the dead, which can be paralleled (Steup), or by the special clothes worn by the Plataian archon at this festival as narrated by Plutarch (Classen, Stahl). The former goes better with ὅσα τε ἡ γῆ, κ.τ.λ.; but this is not compelling.

εὖνοι μὲν ἐκ φιλίας χώρας, κ.τ.λ.: in Gorgias' manner, but sincere. φιλίας: they were, as they have already said, not ἐχθροί to Sparta. ξύμμαχοι δέ, κ.τ.λ.: 'allies of our one-time comrades-in-arms.' The solemn rhythm of this whole passage reminds one of the closing chapter of Agricola.

5. ἔθαπτεν: imperfect, not 'gave them burial', but 'found them a burial place', or the like.

Θηβαΐδα: Βοιωτίαν, the Thebans would have said (ii. 2. 4); but Theban it became (68. 3).

οἷς εὐξάμενοι Μήδων ἐκράτησαν: as Archidamos, ii. 74. 2.

ἐρημοῦτε: unless this can stand as a future form, which is very improbable, the text is surely corrupt. The simple change to ἐρημώσετε

344

(Herwerden) is just possible. Stahl's ἐρημοῦντες, provided that we bracket as well the following καί, and interpret τῶν ἐσσαμένων καὶ κτισάντων (a purely rhetorical doublet) as the founders of both temples and temple-services, i.e. the Plataian people, may be right; but it loses much of the rhetorical effect, and gets the balance wrong. It should be recorded that $Π^{10}$ has ἐρημοῦτε.

59. 1. ἐπικλασθῆναι τῇ γνώμῃ: cf. 67. 2, and καμφθῆναι, 58. 1 n.; and for the phrase in a very different context, iv. 57. 1.

οἴκτῳ σώφρονι: the Plataians may appeal to that feeling which Kleon spurned in the Mytilenean case and Diodotos would not make use of; their fate, however, was worse than Mytilene's. σώφρονι, as in σώφρονα χάριν, 58. 1, because this is an appeal to Spartans, who claimed σωφροσύνη as their own virtue: they would not be influenced by merely emotional pleading; see i. 84. 2, and below, iii. 62. 3.

ἀστάθμητον τὸ τῆς ξυμφορᾶς, κ.τ.λ.: a construction in Thucydides' more obscure manner (53. 1 n.)—"quam sit incertum, cuinam calamitas vel immerenti sit eventura" (Portus, ap. Stahl; though I think ξυμφορά is perhaps more general—'events are uncertain and may hit those who do not deserve misfortune').

2. θεοὺς τοὺς ὁμοβωμίους: normally this means gods who share an altar, as the Boeotian ὁμωχέτας, iv. 97. 4; but here, as Classen says, gods worshipped by us and you and all Greece (not the specifically ἐγχώριοι θεοί, ii. 71. 4).

πεῖσαι τάδε: with Stuart Jones's punctuation the meaning is, 'in calling on our common gods to persuade you of this, namely, that in bringing your fathers' oaths to our defence we are suppliants and that we call in aid the dead', etc. Not only does this make αἰτούμεθα of little meaning and separate unnaturally the calling on the gods from the bringing of the oaths to witness, as Classen shows, but ἐπικαλούμεθα τοὺς κεκμηκότας is not in itself something of which the judges need to be persuaded (but μὴ γενέσθαι ὑπὸ Θηβαίοις: even with the emphasis on the participial clause, it is difficult), still less ἡμέρας τε ἀναμιμνῄσκομεν, though, as a third member, it might be divorced from the common source, πεῖσαι τάδε, as it is by Stuart Jones's stop after παραδοθῆναι. It is better, therefore, to give τάδε a backward reference, and insert καί before προφερόμενοι. (Stahl's προφερόμενοί τε with τε as the connective will hardly do.)

τοῖς ἐχθίστοις φίλτατοι ὄντες: τοῖς κεκμηκόσιν is to be understood with both these adjectives—we their best friends, the Thebans their bitterest enemies.

ἐκείνης ᾗ: with strict reference to the participle only of the relative clause; which I find uncommonly harsh. ἀναμιμνῃσκόμενοι - - - ἐπράξαμεν would have been much easier.

3. τῷ αἰσχίστῳ ὀλέθρῳ λιμῷ: the scholiast notes Od. xii. 342; and

345

Stahl the imitations of Sallust, fr. 3. 11, and Livy, xxi. 41. 11, xxvii. 44. 8 ('fame ac frigore, quae miserrima mortis genera sint').

In the copy of the oath said to have been taken before the battle of Plataia of 479 B.C. (above, ii. 71. 4 n.) occurs the clause: οὐδὲ λιμῷ περιόψομαι ἐργομένους οὐδὲ ὑδάτων ναματιαίων εἴρξω οὔτε φίλους ὄντας οὔτε πολεμίους (this follows οὐκ ἀναστήσω Ἀθήνας οὐδὲ Σπάρτην οὐδὲ Πλαταιάς, nor any other of the allied states). This is a formula taken from the Amphiktyonic 'rules of war' (Aischines, ii. 115–16, iii. 110; see Tod, ii, p. 307); if the oath is genuine, the Plataians might have made a special appeal to it (52. 1), especially to the words οὔτε πολεμίους.

4. τοῖς ἡμῖν ἐχθίστοις: perhaps τοῖς ἡμῖν ⟨τε καὶ ὑμῖν⟩ ἐχθίστοις, sc. γενομένοις.

From what source did Thucydides hear anything of the Plataian speech? Was there some honest Spartan or Theban (or Thespian?) present who gave him the drift of it? In no other case, not even the Theban speech which follows, must Thucydides' sources have been so doubtfully accurate as in this. Yet he knew something of what happened in Plataia after the escape of half the garrison (24. 3 n.); and he gives the names of the speakers here: or did he make that up too, knowing only that two of those who had remained behind at Plataia and so, presumably, had been caught in the final disaster, were Astymachos and Lakon? If he did not (and I find it nearly as difficult to believe that he did as that Perikles delivered *no* funeral speech in 431), someone was interested enough to remember the speakers' names and tell them to the historian. He may have told him also that the speeches were particularly affecting and in a better world would have been effective; if Thucydides asked, what did they say? the answer may have been, 'only the usual things—the Persian wars, the gods and the oaths, the special sanctity of Plataia, the honour of Sparta; but it was very honestly done'; and in that event he clothed it in the language that we have, and made it of such and such a length, because he wanted it for his purpose. As to that purpose, see below, p. 354.

60–67. *Speech of the Thebans*

60. παρελθόντες: normally used of 'coming forward' on to the platform, or what not, after the speaker has been called on. Hence Ullrich's προσελθόντες here, 'approached the judges', accepted by Hude.

61.1. τοὺς μὲν λόγους, κ.τ.λ.: the exordium reads very convincingly, as if this was what the Thebans did say.

Hude's οὗτοι for αὐτοί is surely right.

346

ἡ ἡμετέρα - - - κακία: 'our bad name.' Cf. the use of the verb κακίζω, i. 105. 6, ii. 21. 3; and ἀρετή meaning 'reputation for virtue', i. 33. 2.

2. ὕστερον τῆς ἄλλης Βοιωτίας: for the Boiotoi in Boeotia see i. 12. 3 n.

ξυμμείκτους ἀνθρώπους: cf. Ephoros F. 21; Strabo, ix. 2. 3, p. 401.

ἡγεμονεύεσθαι: Thebes was head of a federation, of all the Boeotian states except Plataia. Cf. iv. 91–92.

τὰ πάτρια: ii. 2. 4, and below, 65. 2.

62. 2. μηδίσαι μὲν - - - τῇ μέντοι, κ.τ.λ.: as often in μέν - - - δέ and normally in μέν - - - μέντοι sentences, the first clause is concessive, 'we agree that Plataia did not medize'; but its subordinate clause, διότι οὐδ' Ἀθηναίους, is not concessive, but in effect an independent assertion, 'but it was because Athens did not either'; and with that the logical connexion would be, 'so, similarly, they were the only Boeotians to Atticize'. The argument is repeated in 64. 1. It is the same attitude as that which Herodotos asserts of the Phokians in 480, viii. 30; for which Plutarch, Mor. 868 B (de Her. mal. 35), takes him to task.

(Classen says we should accent οὖ φαμέν, in order that οὖ, which belongs closely to αὐτούς, may be kept separate from φαμέν. But this would be ἡμεῖς δέ φαμεν μηδίσαι μὲν αὐτοὺς οὖ, as φασὶ μόνοι just above?)

2–3. τῇ - - - αὐτῇ ἰδέᾳ - - - ἐν οἵῳ εἴδει: "i.e. τῷ αὐτῷ τρόπῳ. Iungenda igitur haec sunt cum ἰόντων verbo ... i.e. τρόπῳ πολιτείας, in quo statu" —Stahl. " 'Nach derselben Handlungsweise, demselben Grundsatz' (ebenso vi. 76. 3), mit μόνους ἀττικίσαι zu verbinden ... Hier stehen daher ἰδέα u. εἶδος als Bezeichnung des innern u. äussern Verhaltens sich gegenüber: doch lässt die gemeinsame Bedeutung beider Worte, 'die Gestalt, das Aussehen', einen Wechsel des Gebrauches zu: vgl. i. 109. 1, wo ἰδέα die äussere Erscheinung, u. vi. 77. 2, viii. 56. 2, wo εἶδος die Handlungsweise bezeichnet"—Classen. I believe both words mean, essentially, the same here, 'external form', 'the form which all can see'; it is another case of variatio, like vi. 76. 3 and 77. 2 (both from Hermokrates' speech). τῇ αὐτῇ ἰδέᾳ is to be taken with ἀττικίσαι, as Classen, and does not refer to the constitution. The Athenians did, according to the Theban view, act in the same way as the Mede; but that is shown by the words ἦλθεν ἐπὶ τὴν Ἑλλάδα above and ἰόντων ἐπὶ τοὺς Ἕλληνας here.

3. κατ' ὀλιγαρχίαν ἰσόνομον: i.e. a constitutional, law-abiding government, in which all citizens have equal civil rights, though not equal political power (cf. ii. 37. 1 and iii. 82. 8 for democratic ἰσονομία); in a δυναστεία, as in a tyranny, the rulers, a narrow clique, govern according to their own wishes—Arist. Pol. iv. 5. 1, 1292 b. Cf. iv. 126. 2 n. Such passages as this and iv. 78. 3 show that it is wrong simply to treat ἰσονομία as a democratic catchword and εὐνομία as oligarchic.

347

τῷ σωφρονεστάτῳ ἐναντιώτατον: 'the opposite extreme of the ideal of orderly government', if the first superlative may stand. (Herwerden ingeniously conjectured τῷ σώφρονι πάντων ἐναντιώτατον.) It is again, with νόμοις, a compliment to Sparta; cf. 58. 1, 59. 1, and for ἀριστοκρατία σώφρων, 82. 8.

ἐγγυτάτω δὲ τυράννου: Poppo quotes Tacitus, *Ann.* vi. 42, 'paucorum dominatio regiae libidini proprior est'.

ὀλίγων ἀνδρῶν: Herodotos mentions Attaginos and Timagenidas as the most prominent leaders of the Median faction at Thebes (ix. 86. 1; cf. 15. 4). Leontiadas, father of the Eurymachos who had led the Theban attack on Plataia in 431, had commanded the Theban contingent at Thermopylai (but see n. on ii. 2. 3); Herodotos' account of the Thebans there is certainly heavily biased against them, and Leontiadas may have been no medizer; but he was clearly a prominent man; and this simple picture of Thebes governed autocratically by a small group of medizing politicians must be far from the truth. Cf. Plut. *Aristeid.* 18. 7.

Thebes made a similar excuse to Athens in 395 for its conduct in 404 B.C., according to Xen. *Hell.* iii. 5. 8.

4. ἰδίας δυνάμεις: the fatal weakness of Greek politicians; see 82. 8.

σχήσειν: not 'retain', as Stahl, but 'obtain' (see Neil on Ar. *Equit.* 130, though his statement is too absolute: cf. vi. 11. 1).

καὶ ἡ ξύμπασα πόλις, κ.τ.λ.: just the argument that had been used on Mytilene's behalf, but not by her Theban allies. The order here is awkward: we expect either οὐχ ἡ ξ. πόλις αὐτ. οὖσα (as Cobet suggested), or οὐ τοῦτ' ἔπραξεν; or we might accept Steup's οὔτε - - - οὔτε for οὐκ - - - οὐδέ. Classen put a comma after ἐπηγάγοντο αὐτόν and a colon after ἔπραξεν.

5. κατὰ στάσιν ἤδη ἐχόντων αὐτῆς τὰ πολλά: i. 108. 2–3. See my n. there, with the reference to Ps.-Xen. 3. 10–11, and *Athenian Studies*, p. 230, n. 1.

ἐν Κορωνείᾳ: i. 113. 2.

ἵππους τε παρέχοντες: we certainly expect ἱππέας or ἵππον (Cobet; ii. 100. 2, to which Classen refers, is not exactly parallel); and, as well ⟨καὶ ὁπλίτας⟩. Even though it was Boeotian cavalry who were more useful in Attica (ii. 12. 5, 22. 2), their hoplites were not absent; and at Plataia they must have been prominent, and later, at Delion and at Syracuse, they played a decisive part.

63. 1. ἀξιώτεροί ἐστε πάσης ζημίας: Arnold points out that the memory of Theban conduct in 480, and of the sentence passed against them and all medizers (Hdt. vii. 132), was kept alive into the fourth century by interested parties (Xen. *Hell.* vi. 3. 20, 5. 35).

2. ἐπὶ τῇ ἡμετέρᾳ τιμωρίᾳ: 'for vengeance' rather than 'for defence,

348

against us'—so L. and S.—unless ἡμᾶς ὑμῶν ἀποτρέπειν repeats the meaning.

καὶ πολῖται: 55. 3 n.

ὑπάρχον γε: no one could complain of undue simplicity of construction, when we have to supply mentally μὴ ξυνεπιέναι and to see at once that τῆς - - - ξυμμαχίας γεγενημένης is a causal participial clause dependent on ὑπάρχον—'as you might have done, for there was the alliance with our friends the Spartans at your command'. Besides which, ἱκανή γε ἦν, following closely on ὑπάρχον γε (not to mention πολὺ δέ γε soon afterwards) is inelegant; and of the two, ἱκανή γε ἦν, besides being the better attested by the MSS., is the more idiomatic (Neil, ed. *Knights*, p. 188; perhaps ironic, Denniston, pp. 129–30). I have thought of ὑπάρχον τε (the reading of ABCFG) - - - ⟨καὶ⟩ τῆς τῶν Λ., κ.τ.λ., even though the genitive absolute is causal in sense.

εἴ τι καὶ ἄκοντες: cf. again the Mytilenean argument, 11. 4.

ἦν - - - προβάλλεσθε: 'which you put up as a defence, or screen', 'behind which you shelter'. Cf. i. 37. 4; also i. 73. 2.

ἱκανή γε ἦν ἡμᾶς τε ὑμῶν ἀποτρέπειν, κ.τ.λ.: just what it would not be according to Herodotos' statement of the argument of Kleomenes at the time (vi. 108. 2; and n. on 55. 1, above); and certainly would not be in the stress of a world war.

3. τοὺς δὲ ἐλευθεροῦντας: doubtless the whole Peloponnesian League is meant (cf. i. 124. 3), as Classen notes; but grammatically this agrees with τοὺς πάντας Ἕλληνας, which is illogical.

4. οὐδὲ αἰσχύνης ἀπηλλαγμένην: cf. i. 122. 4, and ii. 42. 4, ad fin., with n.

καίτοι τὰς ὁμοίας χάριτας, κ.τ.λ.: one expects ὁμοίας τὰς χάριτας, 'make your return of services similar'. For the meaning of the whole, Arnold compares Cicero, *de Off.* i. 15: 'non reddere beneficium (μὴ ἀντιδιδόναι χάριν) viro bono non licet (αἰσχρόν), modo id facere possit sine iniuria (τὰς ὁμοίας χάριτας).' "But if it can only be returned *cum iniuria* (ἐς ἀδικίαν ἀποδιδομένας), then the not returning it is allowable in a good man (οὐκ αἰσχρόν)." Cf. also Arist. *Eth. Nic.* viii. 13. 9; Plat. *Rep.* i. 331 c.

But it is all frigidly and obscurely expressed. A negative in each sentence (⟨οὐκ⟩ ἀδικούμενοι and, as Campe suggested from the scholia, ⟨οὐ τὸ⟩ τὰς ὁμοίας χάριτας) would make for easier reading; but for that reason is perhaps not to be accepted. μετὰ δικαιοσύνης ὀφειληθείσας—because Athens went to the aid of Plataia when the latter (as she asserted) was being wronged; either on the occasion of the first alliance, or in 431.

64. 1. ὑμεῖς δέ, κ.τ.λ.: 'and *you* did not medize only because you identified yourselves with the ambitions of Athens, and were the enemies of Greece'—unlike the Spartans, it is implied, who were the

349

true defenders of Greece. As Stahl says, it is absurd to say that Plataia in 480 τοῖς Ἕλλησι τἀναντία ἐβούλοντο, which is what must be meant; but it is not, therefore, absurd to attribute the words to the Theban speakers: cf. πᾶσι τοῖς Ἕλλησι μισοῖντο, § 4; εἴ τις ἄρα καὶ ἐγένετο, 67. 2. Stahl, followed by Classen and Steup, read ἡμεῖς δέ with ABEFM, with a comma after it, 'because the Athenians did not either, and we did', mainly to explain away (unnecessarily) the presence of ὑμεῖς δέ ("utrumque vocabulum, cum oppositum desit, adeo omni pondere carere, ut abesse non solum possint, sed etiam debeant"), but partly so that the second τοῖς can mean the Thebans. (I should prefer, if we adopt this reading, to interpret the last clause, 'joining some, opposing others', out of a spirit of contrariness, 'not from any loyalty to Greece'; I doubt whether τοῖς could mean the speakers' own city.)

2. τούτοις ξυναγωνίζεσθε: 'continue in their camp, do not talk about being friends and allies with Sparta, or neutrals.' An apparently good argument, but only for the destruction of Plataian independence, not for the trial and execution, unless it was a rule that all prisoners of war (here Athenians as well as Plataians) were to be executed; but this is passed over. The only good ground for punishing the Plataians (or their leaders only?) was their execution of the Theban prisoners in 431; but the Thebans did not feel that this argument was in itself strong enough (c. 65).

3. ξυγκατεδουλοῦσθε μᾶλλον: Archidamos, ii. 72. 1, had asked them, τοὺς ἄλλους ξυνελευθεροῦτε.

καὶ ἄλλους τινάς: there is no need to ask who these were, as Stahl elaborately does. For τῶν ξυνομοσάντων, see ii. 71. 4 n.

ἔχοντές τε τοὺς νόμους: 'under your own constitutional government.' Neither Plataia nor Thebes suggests that Athens actually forced a decision on Plataia in 431.

πρόκλησιν ἐς ἡσυχίαν ἡμῶν: ii. 72. 1, and below, 68. 1. There is, I think, a slight preference for ὑμῶν (AEM1).

4. ἀνδραγαθίαν προύθεσθε: 57. 1 n.

ἐπεδείξατε: if this is right (ἀπεδ. coni. Classen), it must mean not 'showed as an afterthought', as suggested in L. and S., but 'exhibited', 'gave specimens of', as λόγον, σοφίαν ἐπιδεῖξαι (δύναμιν ἐπιδεῖξαι, vi. 47), and in middle, μουσικὰν ὀρθάν (Pind., fr. 32 Schr. = 13 Bowra), τὴν αὐτοῦ δύναμιν ([Andok.] iv. 14); or as Equit. 932; with an ironical colouring: 'you gave an example of your virtues and thereby showed they were not your own', or 'not genuine'. οὐ προσήκοντα as τῆς μὴ προσηκούσης, ii. 61. 4; cf. ii. 65. 8, and below, 67. 2, where the meaning is slightly different.

μετὰ γὰρ Ἀθηναίων ἄδικον ὁδόν ἰόντων ἐχωρήσατε: we seem to have the Greek for 'fellow-travellers' here. χωρεῖν, here and 66. 2, as in Ar. Equit. 511 (Neil, ad loc.).

350

65. 1. καὶ ἱερομηνίᾳ: perhaps to be bracketed; see 56. 2 n.

2. ἄνδρες ὑμῶν οἱ πρῶτοι: see ii. 2. 2.

τὰ κοινὰ - - - πάτρια: see 61. 2.

οἱ γὰρ ἄγοντες: a parody, and only a verbal parody, of 55. 4.

3. πλείω παραβαλλόμενοι: throughout this chapter the Thebans take a frankly oligarchic view, which is inconsistent, strictly, with their argument in 64. 3, ἔχοντες τοὺς νόμους. Cf. also 66. 2, εἰ - - - ἀνεπιεικέστερον - - - οὐ μετὰ τοῦ πλήθους ὑμῶν ἐσελθόντες.

φιλίως, οὐ πολεμίως: 'amico, non hostili (in civitatem) animo' (Stahl). If this is correct, it points forward to the explanation, ἐβούλοντο, κ.τ.λ., 'in a friendly spirit (towards you) they wished to reform you'. Yet πολεμίως surely refers back to the Plataian conspirators' relation to the Thebans—they admitted us in a friendly, not a hostile spirit; i.e. as friends and allies, not as citizens of a country at war with you; hence Steup's φιλίους, οὐ πολεμίους is to be preferred. Cf. below, ἐχθροὺς οὐδενὶ καθιστάντες, ἅπασι δὲ ὁμοίως ἐνσπόνδους, and πολεμίως, 66. 1.

τούς τε ὑμῶν χείρους μηκέτι μᾶλλον γενέσθαι: χείρους understood with γενέσθαι. "μᾶλλον igitur cum comparativo iunctum est. In quo hic eo minus offendimus, quia, cum ipse comparativus non sit iteratus, ex eo positivus repeti potest. Certe aut adiectivum iterandum aut μᾶλλον addi necesse fuit"—Stahl. Classen renders μηκέτι μᾶλλον "nicht noch mehr". But, apart from these singularities, and the rare order of words, τοὺς ὑμῶν χείρους, is 'in the desire that the worse among you should not deteriorate yet further' (or, 'should no longer deteriorate') the meaning required? Hude condemned γενέσθαι; and some word like ὑβρίζειν (note σωφρονισταὶ τῆς γνώμης, below) seems required, and μᾶλλον to go with ἐβούλοντο; or μηκέτι ⟨κρείσσους⟩. Spratt suggested μεγαλύνεσθαι, comparing v. 98, which seems not quite to fit ('no longer to be increased in power'? or 'to boast', or 'to be lauded'?); σεμνύνεσθαι would be better. Simpler than any of these suggestions would be τούς τε ⟨πολλοὺς⟩ ὑμῶν, with χείρους γενέσθαι as in i. 95. 7 (which in practice means ὑβρίζειν) and μᾶλλον taken with ἐβούλοντο.

σωφρονισταὶ ὄντες τῆς γνώμης: cf. vi. 87. 3 (Sicilian cities as σωφρονισταί of Athens) and viii. 48. 6 (where the demos is σωφρονιστής of powerful individuals). Spratt compares (for the statement of 'moderate' policy which follows) Plat. *Rep.* v. 471 A, εὐμενῶς δὴ σωφρονιοῦσιν, οὐκ ἐπὶ δουλείᾳ κολάζοντες οὐδ᾽ ἐπ᾽ ὀλέθρῳ, σωφρονισταὶ ὄντες, οὐ πολέμιοι. For τῶν σωμάτων τὴν πόλιν, where we might expect τὰ σώματα τῆς πόλεως, edd. compare i. 40. 2; but ἀλλοτριοῦντες simply in the sense of ἀποστεροῦντες is difficult; cf. i. 34. 1, 35. 5 (with my n.), viii. 73. 4, where the word means 'make hostile', 'estrange from'. There is much in favour of Weil's suggestion, σ. ὅ. τ. γν. ⟨καὶ οὐ⟩ τῶν σωμάτων, τήν ⟨τε⟩ πόλιν οὐκ ἀ., κ.τ.λ. (The scholiast takes τῶν σωμάτων with σωφρονισταί, but the negative is much better, giving the meaning, 'we are not going to punish by exile or death'.)

ἐχθροὺς οὐδενί, κ.τ.λ.: οὐδενί and ἅπασι are not to be confined to Boeotia, but comprise all Greek states. Cf. 64. 1 n. The Thebans can be smooth speakers.

66. 1. προείπομεν: ii. 2. 4.

2. ἄσμενοι: a nice exaggeration.

ἀνεπιεικέστερον: they do not say ἀδικώτερον; they will not admit to a *crime*, only something not quite justifiable, not altogether well-mannered.

οὐ μετὰ τοῦ πλήθους ὑμῶν: see 65. 3, n. on πλείω παραβαλλόμενοι.

πείθειν: all edd. accept this emendation (Classen's) of the MSS. πείσειν; but πεῖσαι would be as good Greek, though πείθειν is one of those verbs which tend to be used in the present and imperfect; and confusion of aorist and future infinitive is very common in our MSS.

κατὰ νόμον γὰρ δή τινα ἔπασχον: the ordinary laws of war; cf. 54. 2 and 68. 1 n.; the only thing here that the Thebans can urge is the breaking of the first truce (ii. 3. 1-2).

χεῖρας προϊσχομένους: as prisoners of war; the words again taken from the Plataians' speech and describing their situation, 58. 3.

ὑποσχόμενοι: cf. τὴν ὑπόσχεσιν, below. It is perhaps of some significance that the Thebans do not here say that the Plataians confirmed their promise with an oath, as ii. 5. 5-6.

ὕστερον μὴ κτενεῖν: ὕστερον with ὑποσχόμενοι; but Hude's transposition, μὴ κτενεῖν ὕστερον - - - διεφθείρατε, is attractive.

3. τὸν ὕστερον θάνατον καὶ τὴν - - - ψευσθεῖσαν ὑπόσχεσιν: two separate crimes, the killing of 'suppliants' in any case, and the breaking of a solemn promise.

This is really the only ground for any punishment of the Plataian prisoners—as war criminals; but, though the Thebans go into the matter at greater length than the Plataians had done (56. 2, 58. 2 nn.), naturally enough, it still does not take up much of their argument—for it would not appeal to the Spartans.

67. 1. ἡμεῖς δέ, κ.τ.λ.: 'while we may know that we are yet more righteously avenged.' Classen and others have found unnecessary difficulty here: 'grammatically εἰδῶμεν, but logically an intransitive or passive verb, e.g. φαινώμεθα, must be in the speaker's mind'; and various emendations have been made. But ἡμεῖς δὲ (εἰδῶμεν) is the proper consequence of ἐπεξήλθομεν καὶ ὑπὲρ ὑμῶν καὶ ἡμῶν. τετιμωρημένοι anticipates the verdict, which is only to be based on the answer to the 'short question'.

2. παλαιὰς ἀρετάς: in the Plataian speech, 56. 5; also 56. 7, 57. 2, 58. 1.

ἐπικλασθῆτε: cf. 59. 1.

διπλασίας ζημίας: 'should entail double punishment.' For the thought, cf. Sthenelaḯdas' speech, i. 86. 1.

οὐκ ἐκ προσηκόντων: cf. 64. 4 n.

μηδὲ ὀλοφυρμῷ καὶ οἴκτῳ: again, as in the Mytilene debate.

πατέρων τε τάφους - - - ἐρημίαν: 59. 2, 57. 4, and § 5, below. And for ἐρημία in this political sense ('isolation'), i. 71. 5, 32. 4.

3. πρὸς ὑμᾶς τὴν Βοιωτίαν ἄγοντες: a flattering way to put it.

καὶ οἰκίαι ἐρῆμοι: I agree with Stuart Jones that this should stand, against Stahl's κατ' οἰκίας (better καὶ ⟨κατ'⟩ οἰκίας?); but Krüger's καὶ ⟨αἱ⟩ οἰκίαι ('and their empty houses') is attractive.

4. ἐπίχαρτοι εἶναι: ἐπιχαίρειν is the vox propria for rejoicing over another's misfortune—Soph. Ajax, 961; Ar. Pax, 1015; Dem. ix. 61; ταῖς ἀτυχίαισι μὴ 'πίχαιρε τῶν πέλας, Menander, fr. 673. Cf. Arist. Eth. Nic. vi. 1107 a 10. The Thebans do not quite mean this, but that good men rejoice at the punishment of the wicked (Stahl quotes here from the Septuagint, Proverbs, xi. 3, ἀσεβῶν ἀπώλεια ἐπίχαρτος); but in the course of this very well conceived speech, especially in this last chapter, the Thebans become more and more envious (εἴ τις ἄρα καὶ ἐγένετο), malevolent (τὴν σφετέραν ἐρημίαν), and hateful, ending with this ἐπίχαρτοι; and their own appeal, ὧν πατέρες οἱ μέν, κ.τ.λ., must have fallen on very deaf ears. Yet they had a case, in the execution of prisoners in 431, and a political argument, which they put effectively enough in the next sentence; but when they go on with οὐ προπαθόντες ὑφ' ἡμῶν, the hypocritical μίσει πλέον ἢ δίκῃ κρίναντες, and the sophistic οὐχὶ ἐκ μάχης, κ.τ.λ., they do not exactly win our sympathy. There is no palliation in Thucydides.

5. τοὺς - - - ξυμμάχους - - - ἀπεώσαντο: the retort to 57. 4, περιεώσμεθα ἐκ πάντων.

ἀνταποδόντες: Poppo defended the aorist as an anticipation of the verdict, or as description of the Plataians' hopeless state in being tried on the particular charge in the 'short question', comparing τετιμωρημένοι in § 1. But Dobree's ⟨ἄν⟩ ἀνταποδόντες, or Poppo's own ἀνταποδώσοντες, is surely right, for the other aorist κρίναντες so clearly refers to a past action. We might have expected οὐδὲ νῦν for οὐ - - - νῦν; and Widmann in Bursian, cxxv, 1905, 174, records an elegant conjecture by Beintker, ἀνταποδόντες ⟨ἐς⟩ νῦν, coll. Plat. Tim. 20 c; which is perhaps to be preferred. With τὴν ἴσην τιμωρίαν ἀνταποδόντες and the argument here, cf. τὰς ὁμοίας χάριτας ἀντιδιδόναι, 63. 4, and the argument there. How much in Thucydides is payment for something, for past benefits or past folly (lack of πρόνοια), or, in the words of a Kleon or these Thebans, for past wickedness.

οὐχί: see 53. 4 n. Here it is direct contradiction.

ὥσπερ φασίν: 58. 3. But not only 'as they assert', but 'as our soldiers suffered whom they executed', 66. 2; and it is a little curious that

353

this is not expressed here, for it is this difference that makes the Plataian punishment οὐκ ἴση.

The argument, though hateful and sophistic, is not entirely empty: it was wrong to kill an enemy in battle who offered to surrender; but if he surrendered unconditionally, he could, legally, be executed—like the Mytileneans, as well as the Plataians.

6. τῷ τῶν Ἑλλήνων νόμῳ: see 58. 3, and 59. 1 for the Plataian view, 66. 2 for the Theban.

ἀνταπόδοτε χάριν δικαίαν: see 58. 1, δωρεὰν ἀνταπαιτῆσαι - - - σώφρονα ἀντὶ αἰσχρᾶς κομίσασθαι χάριν. There is also an echo of the Plataians' words (59. 4) in ὧν πρόθυμοι γεγενήμεθα, and a tasteless one; and again in περιωσθῶμεν (57. 4).

τοῖς Ἕλλησι παράδειγμα: for the Plataians, too, the Spartan decision was to be one for the whole Greek world to understand (57. 1). So did Kleon argue that the Athenian decision on Mytilene was to be meant for all her subjects (40. 7).

οὐ λόγων τοὺς ἀγῶνας προθήσοντες: another point of agreement between oligarch or Peloponnesian and Kleon (37. 5, 38).

ἁμαρτανομένων: passive, as in ii. 65. 11, but here crimes, not blunders (as also 54. 2); cf. παραβαινομένων, 45. 3.

For λόγοι ἔπεσι κοσμηθέντες, cf. Jebb on Soph. *Ajax*, 1096; and, in a different context, i. 21. 1.

7. κεφαλαιώσαντες: the emphasis falls on this word, and on οἱ ἡγεμόνες: 'if only leaders will sum up before (*or* in) making their decisions, for all to hear'; and this is supposed to mean, in this case, 'if only you will repeat your brief question, and nothing else, others will be less eager to clothe foul deeds in fair words'. This is indeed what it must mean; but it is a lot to get out of κεφαλαιώσαντες.

Thucydides might have had more information about the Theban speech than about the Plataian, for the latter depended on enemies. But the chief point of interest is the length of the speeches, the great emphasis Thucydides wished to put on the whole episode of the fall of Plataia. He was, as a military historian, much interested in the details of circumvallation and in the manner of escape by half the garrison; but he was still more interested in the political and moral issues raised by Plataia's alliance with Athens, her obliteration, and the cold-blooded execution of the survivors. The *fall* of Plataia was of little military importance, and had not much effect on the issue of the war (below, iv. 76.5, n.); but all its circumstances illustrated the *mores* of men at war in a most vivid way; and for that reason Thucydides treats it at such length and in so impressive a manner. Immediately before, we had the debate on Mytilene; now that on Plataia: 'that is what Athens was like; this was Sparta, the liberator.' But he does not make the comment explicitly; it is for the reader to understand. So Melos precedes Syracuse: not the events—that is merely what happened, ἃ ἐγένετο, as Aristotle would say; but Thucydides' method of narrating them puts the whole story, a historically true story, into the category of τὰ καθόλου, οἷα ἂν γένοιτο.

Mme de Romilly, p. 148, notes a different antithesis—Mytilene the rebellious, Plataia the faithful ally—but I do not think that this is of great significance for Thucydides. Her analysis, however (pp. 146-9), of the close connexion between the two debates and the events which gave rise to them, is sound, especially of the Mytilene debate which is concerned only with the point at issue, the punishment of a rebellious city, just that and not with Athenian imperialism seen from the point of view of 404 B.C.

68.1. διότι τόν τε ἄλλον χρόνον, κ.τ.λ.: if we take the sentence-construction at its simplest, i.e. assume no displacement of τε, so that τὸν ἄλλον χρόνον will be joined with another temporal clause, and if further we keep ὡς οὐκ ἐδέξαντο as a typical parenthetical clause (cf. e.g. in another long sentence, ὡς ἀπῇσαν ἐπ' οἴκου, v. 36. 1), we will not delete ὅτε nor alter it to ὅτι, nor delete ὡς, nor both of them, nor even, with C. F. Smith, A.J.P. x, 1889, 210, read οὐδ' ὣς for ὡς οὐκ (an ingenious suggestion); but we will bracket ἅ, as Heilmann suggested, or, perhaps better, adopt Gertz's emendation αὖ. This gives a proper meaning; and though other changes are possible enough, and simplicity of construction is not always to be predicated of Thucydides, we may be content with it. I do not understand how Stuart Jones took the passage with no change. There is no indication of difficulty or peculiarity in the scholia or in Dionysios.

τόν τε ἄλλον χρόνον ἠξίουν δῆθεν: we know nothing of this but for Archidamos' statement, ii. 72. 1, ἅπερ καὶ πρότερον ἤδη προυκαλεσάμεθα; and it is clear that Thucydides thought little of its sincerity or relevance. (I cannot agree with the interpretation of δῆθεν in A.T.L. iii. 103. 35.) καὶ ὅτε ὕστερον, κ.τ.λ., refers of course to the offer in ii. 72. 1 (see iii. 64. 3).

κατὰ τὰς παλαιὰς - - - σπονδάς: στρατεῦσαι μηδένα ποτὲ ἀδίκως ἐπ' αὐτούς, ii. 71. 2 (Πλαταιεῖς ἀσύλους καὶ ἱεροὺς ἀφεῖσθαι, Plut. Aristeid. 21. 2); and n. on ii. 71. 4.

ὡς οὐκ ἐδέξαντο, ἡγούμενοι: added by way of explanation of νομίζοντες - - - διότι, κ.τ.λ., above (Steup).

τῇ ἑαυτῶν δικαίᾳ βουλήσει ἔκσπονδοι ἤδη: this is supposed to mean 'by the rejection of their own just desires they were now free from the former treaty obligations towards Plataia'. Stahl ingeniously conjectured δικαιώσει 'just claims', for δικ. β. (supporting this by a scholion on τῇ δικαιώσει, 82. 4, ἀντὶ τοῦ τῇ ἑαυτῶν δικαίᾳ κρίσει—but see Hude's edition of the scholia—and by the dubious note on

355

v. 17. 2). This is an improvement; but to understand 'the Plataian rejection of' the claims is too much. Rauchenstein's $\tau\hat{\eta}$ $a\dot{v}\tau\hat{\omega}\nu$ $\delta\iota\kappa\alpha\iota\dot{\omega}\sigma\epsilon\iota$ (*Philol.* xxxv, 1876, 539) is to that extent better: they had been injured by the Plataians' claim—a claim, as the Peloponnesians saw it, to be at once neutral and an ally of Athens. But the phrase is barely intelligible, and the corruption may lie deeper. We could do well, too, with $\ddot{\epsilon}\kappa\sigma\pi\sigma\nu\delta\sigma\iota$ $\ddot{\eta}\delta\eta$ $\langle\gamma\epsilon\nu\dot{\sigma}\mu\epsilon\nu\sigma\iota\rangle$ or $\langle\ddot{\sigma}\nu\tau\epsilon\varsigma\rangle$.

Nor is $\ddot{\epsilon}\kappa\sigma\pi\sigma\nu\delta\sigma\iota$ to be interpreted simply, in Arnold's words, "being $\ddot{\epsilon}\kappa\sigma\pi\sigma\nu\delta\sigma\iota$, according to Greek notions, they were placed in a mere state of nature with regard to them, and nothing hindered them from putting them to death, just as they would barbarians if taken in war, or as they were in the habit of treating their Greek enemies, as appears from ii. 67. 4, iii. 32. 1". For the Plataians say, 54. 2, $\epsilon\dot{\iota}$ $\mu\dot{\epsilon}\nu$ $\dot{\omega}\varsigma$ $\pi\sigma\lambda\epsilon\mu\dot{\iota}\sigma\upsilon\varsigma$ $\dot{\epsilon}\rho\omega\tau\hat{a}\tau\epsilon$, $\sigma\dot{\upsilon}\kappa$ $\dot{a}\delta\iota\kappa\epsilon\hat{\iota}\sigma\theta\alpha\iota$ $\dot{\upsilon}\mu\hat{a}\varsigma$ $\mu\dot{\eta}$ $\epsilon\dot{\upsilon}$ $\pi\alpha\theta\dot{\sigma}\nu\tau\alpha\varsigma$ (and 58. 3, 59. 1); and the Thebans accept this, 66. 2–3: it is, they say, the Greek notion (67. 6). $\ddot{\epsilon}\nu\sigma\pi\sigma\nu\delta\sigma\iota$ $\ddot{\epsilon}\tau\iota$ $\kappa\alpha\kappa\hat{\omega}\varsigma$ $\pi\alpha\theta\epsilon\hat{\iota}\nu$ would, in fact, have been a stronger argument for demanding retribution—it is almost the Theban claim (66. 2). Yet the meaning must be that the Spartans now felt themselves free from the special claims contained in the Regent Pausanias' promise to Plataia, and, as sufferers by Plataian action, that they could now be as ruthless and as unscrupulous as they wished. They are ignoring the Theban claim, thinking only of their own rights and interests; but even so, even if they had persuaded themselves that they might without doing wrong act as judges and executioners of the Plataians, what was their claim against the twenty-five Athenian prisoners who had surrendered at the same time? In ruthlessness Kleon had been their equal, but not in deceit and dishonesty. They had actually secured the 'surrender' of Plataia, instead of its capture, so that they might claim, if necessary, that the city was 'non-returnable' because it had 'willingly joined them'; and then executed these new allies, to please Thebes. No wonder that the unscrupulous *dishonesty* of Sparta aroused especial indignation in her enemies; and no doubt this is reflected in some of Euripides' plays: *Andromache*, for example, may belong to this time (but see D. S. Robertson, *C.R.* xxxvii, 1923, 58–60; and for the orthodox view, P. Treves, *J.H.S.* lxiv, 1944, 104, n. 8); perhaps also *The Suppliants* with its unsympathetic picture of Thebes: only dislike of Thebes in Athens could be aroused at any time. And the indignation of the Acharnians is understandable enough, however much it was laughed at—

$\pi\hat{\omega}\varsigma$ $\delta\dot{\epsilon}$ γ' $\ddot{a}\nu$ $\kappa\alpha\lambda\hat{\omega}\varsigma$ $\lambda\dot{\epsilon}\gamma\sigma\iota\varsigma$ $\ddot{a}\nu$, $\epsilon\ddot{\iota}\pi\epsilon\rho$ $\dot{\epsilon}\sigma\pi\epsilon\dot{\iota}\sigma\omega$ γ' $\ddot{a}\pi\alpha\xi$
$\sigma\hat{\iota}\sigma\iota\nu$ $\sigma\ddot{\upsilon}\tau\epsilon$ $\beta\omega\mu\dot{\sigma}\varsigma$ $\sigma\ddot{\upsilon}\tau\epsilon$ $\pi\dot{\iota}\sigma\tau\iota\varsigma$ $\sigma\ddot{\upsilon}\theta'$ $\ddot{\sigma}\rho\kappa\sigma\varsigma$ $\mu\dot{\epsilon}\nu\epsilon\iota$; $\kappa.\tau.\lambda.$

(*Ach.* 307 ff.)

2. δıακοσίων - - - πέντε καὶ εἴκοσιν: there were about 480 defenders

356

originally, ii. 78. 3; 212 escaped, iii. 24. 2; about 225 were now made prisoners and executed. So there had only been some forty deaths in the first attacks and the long siege; and οἱ μὲν ἡμιοεῖς, iii. 20. 2, implies that these had occurred at the beginning: in itself a comment on Greek siege warfare.

ἠνδραπόδισαν: this ought to mean that the women were free, i.e. citizens of Plataia (cf. e.g. v. 32. 1); but most assume it to mean 'sold' simply in contrast to ἀπέκτειναν, and that the women were slaves. See e.g. Velsen ap. Stahl on ii. 78. 3–4, and Classen–Steup here. It is possible that some were free and some slaves. Compare, perhaps by contrast, i. 55. 1, καὶ τῶν Κερκυραίων ὀκτακοσίους μὲν οἳ ἦσαν δοῦλοι ἀπέδοντο, and iv. 48. 4, τὰς γυναῖκας - - - ἠνδραποδίσαντο, who were surely free women (not slaves, as B. Schmidt, *Kork. Stud.*, n. 61, p. 84), and the many other places where ἀνδραποδίσαι has free persons as object. On the other hand, ἀπέδοντο is used of free men in i. 29. 5 and vii. 84. 3. The σιτοποιοί in the armada for Sicily seem to have been free men, vi. 22.

3. [Θηβαῖοι]: perhaps Classen was right to bracket this. It is natural to assume that οἱ Πελοποννήσιοι (the enemies of Plataia in general) is the continuing subject; § 4 seems to imply it; and marginal adscripts of the type οἱ Θηβαῖοι δηλονότι, often wrong, are so common that the deletion has little against it. But all of Classen's reasons are not sound: τὰ σφέτερα φρονοῦντες might more easily refer to Thebes (cf. also v. 17. 2); Plataian territory was practically incorporated in Thebes (58. 5, above, and v. 17. 2) and it was surely Thebans, by agreement with Sparta, but not Spartans, nor Peloponnesians generally, who pulled down all the buildings in Plataia, and built the temple to Hera; nor would the repetition of Θηβαῖοι at the end, καὶ ἐνέμοντο Θηβαῖοι, in place of αὐτοί, offend or surprise, after so long an interval. See Busolt, iii. 1037. 3. It looks as though the narrative is somewhat confused; § 4 implies at least that for a year (§ 3, init.) Sparta kept control, Plataia having been surrendered to her. Perhaps she did attempt this compromise, but surrendered to Theban intransigence after a year.

πρὸς τῷ Ἡραίῳ: Hdt. ix. 52, 53; Paus. ix. 2. 7 (θέας ἄξιος μεγέθει τε καὶ ἐς τῶν ἀγαλμάτων τὸν κόσμον: some of the statues at least were later); Plut. *Aristeid.* 18. 1.

Was there a temple here, within the precinct, in 480, destroyed by the Persians? Some building there surely was that could be called νεώς; but did the Persians destroy any temples outside Attica? The question raises others: in the Congress decree (Plutarch, *Per.* 17; see *A.T.L.* ii, D 12; iii. 279–81) one proposal was the restoration of the temples destroyed by the enemy; a temple at Plataia would certainly have been included. Was it said, after the failure of the congress to meet, that Athens ought to have shared with Plataia the Hellenic money which was spent on rebuilding the temples of Athens? And did Sparta and Thebes now say that they were doing what Athens had neglected?

καταγώγιον: necessary, because the festivals, not only the Eleutheria but others, were to be continued, of set policy, κατὰ τὰ τῶν πάντων Βοιωτῶν πάτρια; and the town, which before would have housed the visitors, was destroyed.

ἐν τῷ τείχει: 'within the walls', i.e. in the town; as ἐς τὸ τεῖχος κατέφυγον, i. 62. 6, al.

4. ἄρτι τότε καθιστάμενον: see 3. 1 n., for the meaning. The words were clearly not written till a good many years after, probably later than the Peace of Nikias at least.

5. ἔτει τρίτῳ καὶ ἐνενηκοστῷ: this would be 519 B.C. The figure is often emended, to ὀγδοηκοστῷ or to ἑβδομηκοστῷ (for the latter see Mahaffy, Essays presented to Wm. Ridgeway, 1913, p. 196, who argues that $\overline{OΓ}$ was mistaken for $\overline{ϘΓ}$); but it is wrong to change Thucydides' text, for there is no good evidence against 519 B.C. and nothing particularly in favour of either 509 or 499 (see e.g. Wells, J.H.S. xxv, 1905, 193–203; accepted by Lenschau, in Bursian, cxxxv, 1907, 90).

69–85. Campaign in Kerkyra. The great στάσις

69. 1. αἱ δὲ τεσσαράκοντα νῆες: 29. 1; and 26. 1 n.

ὡς τότε φεύγουσαι - - - ἐπιδιωχθεῖσαι: 33. 1, 3.

καὶ ἀπ' αὐτῆς σποράδες: Thucydides could easily write χειμασθεῖσαι καὶ σποράδες; but here, I feel sure, Classen was right to bracket καί.

ἐν τῇ Κυλλήνῃ: i. 30. 2 n., ii. 84. 5.

Βρασίδαν - - - ξύμβουλον: this was the nearest the Spartans would go to recalling an incompetent and unsuccessful commander (though they often prosecuted kings, when a campaign was over). See ii. 85. 1. The nearest also that they would go, apparently, to entrusting Brasidas with a command, up to the present time. Thucydides hints, but hardly does more than hint, at personal and political rivalries among the χρηστοί of Sparta as envious as any in democratic Athens; see iv. 81. 1 n., 108. 7; but Sparta did not wash her linen in public.

2. δώδεκα μὲν ναυσί, κ.τ.λ.: in the previous year Asopios also had twelve ships (7. 3). The Peloponnesians, though baffled by Phormion, hoped again from the small numbers of the Athenians at Naupaktos; but Nikostratos was to prove himself as good as Phormion.

The μέν - - - δέ-clauses are, as Classen says, only two sides of the same thing; but "durch diese parataktische Anordnung begleitet der Ausdruck den Fortschritt der Reflexion". 'Let us make for Kerkyra; there are only a dozen ships at Naupaktos. And let us go at once, before they are reinforced.'

358

We could do without ναυτικόν after ἐκ τῶν Ἀθηνῶν; we have just had τὸ ναυτικόν above, and there was no doubt about the nature of Athenian reinforcement.

70. 1. οἱ αἰχμάλωτοι: some 250 in number, the majority of them among the foremost men in Kerkyra (i. 54, 55).

περὶ Ἐπίδαμνον: the battle of Sybota was fought a long way from Epidamnos; and Classen suggested Ἐπιδάμνου.

ὑπὸ Κορινθίων ἀφεθέντες: clearly not long before the sedition broke out in Kerkyra in the spring of 427, when Mytilene was under blockade, but it was hoped that it would be relieved, and that other cities would revolt and Athens' whole attention be thus occupied in that quarter (Grote, v, p. 185); that is, before Alkidas set sail for Ionia. Some have thought that this argues too long a time taken in the persuasion of the prisoners, whom the Corinthians had cherished from the beginning (i. 55. 1); but perhaps the majority of them were moderately honest and patriotic men. In 435 they at the least had not opposed the war with Corinth and Epidamnos, and had perhaps favoured it; for Kerkyra supported the oligarchs against the democrats of Epidamnos (i. 24, 26. 3; see Busolt, iii. 766. 2). There had not always been friendship between Corinth and the 'first families' in Kerkyra, either under a tyrant's or oligarchic government in Corinth: Hdt. iii. 48–49.

ὀκτακοσίων ταλάντων: although this was only a story, it had to be a credible one, or it would have served no purpose. But 800 tal. seems impossibly large, twice the annual revenue of the Delian League, and over 3 tal. each. Herodotos, vi. 79. 1, gives 2 minae as the normal ransom for a Peloponnesian hoplite; and though the majority of these Kerkyraians were wealthy men, that would not mean increasing their value nearly a hundredfold. True, Nikias in 413 suggested that Athens pay as indemnity to Syracuse all the costs of the war and give hostages at the rate of one man per talent till it was paid (vii. 83. 2); but he must put the figure as high as possible, or all Athenian manhood would have been engaged. True also, a century later (when most prices, and some salaries at least, had doubled), 9 tal. is mentioned for a ransom, but as an exorbitant sum illegally exacted ([Dem.] xii. 3); it justifies nothing in 3 tal. each for so large a number. Besides, how many were the proxenoi who were said to have stood surety for this immense sum? Eighty talents, instead of 800, would mean 20 minae per man, and must be near the maximum likely sum; 800 minae is possible. Diodoros, xii. 57. 2, has ἱκανῶν τινῶν ταλάντων only, which might mean that Ephoros had a much lower figure than 800; but his account of these events at Kerkyra is so perverse (there was no terror, and the democrats,

359

διὰ τὴν πρὸς θεοὺς εὐσέβειαν, spared the lives of all the suppliants and sent them out of the country) that we cannot rely on anything in it.

2. κατὰ τὰ ξυγκείμενα: it was a defensive alliance only, i. 44. 1; and Kerkyra had given help to Athens once only during the war, in 431, ii. 25. 1. Cf. iii. 95. 2. But she was of the greatest importance to Athens as an ally because of her position on the way to the west (already noted, i. 36. 2, 44. 3).

Πελοποννησίοις δὲ φίλοι: the Greeks could equal us in make-believe and self-deluding diplomacy. Yet the pro-Peloponnesian party had won something—the reassertion of old friendship and of the terms of the alliance with Athens, with which the action in 431 might strictly be said to have conflicted. They had won a moral victory, and they go on to attack Peithias for wanting to go farther than the resolution allowed in the alliance with Athens, and were prepared to call his policy 'trying to enslave the city to Athens'. See Steup's n. here.

Cf. Hermippos, fr. 63 (below, p. 362).

3. ἐθελοπρόξενος: a word only found here; but presumably a πρόξενος not recognized officially by the state (here Athens) for whom he worked: self-appointed; or perhaps, as the scholiast says, not confirmed by his own city. Cf. vi. 89. 2.

4. τέμνειν χάρακας: the present tense, as edd. say, means that they were accused of doing it regularly, as of right or custom. See Arnold's n. This explains too the size of the fine: they had been doing it for years (see below on στατήρ). But how taking the props which supported the vines (see L. and S.) could be so serious a crime it is more difficult to see. Presumably these men, as lessees, had been cultivating fields owned by the temples of Zeus and Alkinoos, and had treated the stakes as their own property; but for what purpose? Not surely to use in their own vineyards, a simple case of theft and sacrilege? Or had they cut timber from the precincts to use as stakes for their vines? (At one time I thought that the charge might be of taking cuttings from the sacred olive-trees for their own use, for L. and S. give this as one of the meanings of χάραξ; but in Theophrastos, Hist. Plant. ii. 1. 2 and 4, at least, it clearly means stake or post, and it may mean this at Caus. Plant. i. 12. 9 and v. 1. 4.) χάρακες in very large numbers (over 10,000 in either case; in one designated as ὑπὸ ταῖς ἀμπέλοις) are twice listed in the property of the profaners of the Mysteries in 415, on the poletai inscriptions, now adequately published by Pritchett, Hesperia, xxii, 1953, 255–99.

τοῦ Ἀλκίνου: for the tradition of Phaiakians in Kerkyra, see i. 25. 4. The site of the sanctuary is unknown. One of the harbours may have been known as that of Alkinoos: below, p. 372.

στατήρ: the Corinthian stater of 3 dr., the near equivalent of 2 Attic dr. Busolt, iii. 1043. 1, points out that, in order that the fine should amount to a sum large enough to be oppressive to these five very rich men, they must have been accused of cutting thousands of χάρακες, over a number of years, almost of laying waste the τέμενος; and this is so unlikely that he thinks that στατήρ is corrupt. He compares *I.G.* i.² 76, ll. 54–59, where the fine for cutting stone in the Pelargikon at Athens (ii. 17. 1 n.), or taking earth and stone from it, is as high as 500 dr.; and ii.² 1362 (end of 4th century B.C.) in which it is forbidden to cut wood in a sanctuary of Apollo or to carry away from it timber or loppings (κοῦρος: branches or twigs cut in pruning?) or brushwood or fallen leaves, under a penalty of 50 dr. for a free man and fifty lashes for a slave—but the penalty is for each offence, not for each twig or leaf. Cf. also *I.G.* ii.² 1177 (mid-4th century); Prott–Ziehen, ii. 1, nn. 33, 34, p. 104, who cite Paus. ii. 28. 7 for another case where the carrying away of broken branches (τὰ θρανόμενα) of olives and other trees, in a sanctuary of Hyrnetho, was forbidden. (It reads, however, as though such an order was exceptional.)

5. ὅπως ταξάμενοι ἀποδῶσιν: this probably means 'so that they might pay the debt by means of assessed instalments'. Cf. i. 117. 3, where κατὰ χρόνους is added. Others take it to mean 'by agreement as to the sum to be paid', by a compromise and reduction of the total due; which seems less likely.

ἐτύγχανε γὰρ καὶ βουλῆς ὤν: either the boule had executive powers in such matters—the duty of seeing that punishments awarded by the courts were carried out—or it had been expressly given powers in this case.

6. οἱ δέ: they must be not these five rich men only, but the oligarchical faction generally; for five men, unless accompanied by faithful servants, could hardly have overpowered the boule.

τοὺς αὐτοὺς Ἀθηναίοις φίλους, κ.τ.λ.: see § 2 n.

71. 1. ἡσυχάζοντας: to judge from ii. 7. 2, this agrees with the implied subject of δέχεσθαι (Κερκυραίους), not with the object. See also vi. 52. 1.

2. διδάξοντας ὡς ξυνέφερε: "qui et res gestas nuntiarent, ut ipsis commodum erat. Nam minus apta videtur haec sententia: qui et res gestas utiles (Atheniensibus) fuisse demonstrarent"—Stahl. I prefer the latter, though with a more general meaning: 'that their action was for the best.'

τοὺς ἐκεῖ καταπεφευγότας: one must suppose, from the tense, that the Attic trireme (70. 6), with the delegates and the refugees on board, had left for Athens immediately after the *coup d'état* (sending a warning to Nikostratos at Naupaktos on the way?—75. 1) and so

361

arrived before the representatives of the new government at Ker-kyra. But it could not have been long before, and the perfect parti-ciple instead of the aorist (for 'had taken refuge') is unexpected. See below, 80. 2 n., for the time-table of events at Kerkyra.

μή τις ἐπιστροφὴ γένηται: 'lest some counter-action be taken' by Athens (Arnold, who compares the military use of ἐπιστροφή, of a force changing direction in a counter-manœuvre: cf. ii. 90. 5; so L. and S.); or 'lest attention be drawn to their actions'. The former is preferable; for their very presence must draw attention to what had happened.

Hermippos, fr. 63 (the passage on the imports into Athens cited in vol. i, p. 201), 10-11,

$$\kappa a i \ K \epsilon \rho \kappa \upsilon \rho a i o \upsilon s \ \dot{o} \ \Pi o \sigma \epsilon \iota \delta \hat{\omega} \nu \ \dot{\epsilon} \xi o \lambda \dot{\epsilon} \sigma \epsilon \iota \epsilon \nu$$
$$\nu a \upsilon \sigma i \nu \ \dot{\epsilon} \pi i \ \gamma \lambda a \phi \upsilon \rho a \hat{\iota} s, \ \dot{o} \tau i \dot{\eta} \ \delta i \chi a \ \theta \upsilon \mu \dot{o} \nu \ \ddot{\epsilon} \chi o \upsilon \sigma \iota \nu,$$

may have been written with direct reference to these events (Wilamo-witz, Obs. crit. 35. 6); and the 'hollow ships' may be those in which the Kerkyraioi fought so ingloriously (76-78), especially if γλαφυρός was coming into use to mean elegant, neat, skilful (Ar. Av. 1272; see L. and S.). (If this is so, the play, the Phormophoroi, was pro-duced in 426 or soon after, not 427, as I wrote, vol. i, p. 201.) Cf. also above, p. 215.

Adcock, J.H.S. lxxi, 1951, 5, notes that the argument, 'Kerkyra will prove an untrustworthy and wavering ally', 'ever in two minds', was not used by the Corinthians in their speech at Athens in 433, and that this is an indication that the speech was composed before 427.

72. 1. τούς τε πρέσβεις - - - ξυλλαβόντες: an action against the ac-cepted standard of international morals? It may be that Athens held them on behalf of the rightful government in Kerkyra. The subsequent fortunes of these men are unknown.

2. τριήρους Κορινθίας: the other (70. 2) had presumably left after the first debate, even before the Athenian; but one expects ἄλλης or ἑτέρας τρ. K. In 74. 3 only one is in mind.

3. ἐς τὴν ἀκρόπολιν: for the topography of the city of Kerkyra, see below, 75. 5 n.

οὗπερ οἱ πολλοὶ ᾤκουν αὐτῶν: doubtless absentee landlords of wide agricultural domains, most of them; some of them merchants. It was a characteristic of the older and richer families to live in or near the political centre; see my Population of Athens, pp. 37-39.

73. ἐς τοὺς ἀγροὺς - - - τοὺς δούλους: Kerkyra and Chios seem to have been among the few states of the Greek world in which agricul-ture was regularly carried on by slaves. In most the land was held by small peasant proprietors, who were αὐτουργοί, like Dikaiopolis and Trygaios, and most Peloponnesians (i. 141. 3) ; while Sparta, the states of Thessaly, and, intermittently, Argos, had serfs. Kerkyra was a large island for a single state, and exceptionally fertile. One wonders what the Spartan ambassadors, doubtless preaching σωφρο-σύνη (the pride of the Dorians), thought of this action by the Dorian aristocrats of Kerkyra.

Similarly, unlike Athens, Kerkyra employed slaves to row in triremes, in large numbers, if not exclusively (i. 55. 1 ; and 75. 2, below).

74. 1. διαλιπούσης δ' ἡμέρας: according to Classen this is the day occupied by the skirmishes and appeals of c. 73. This is improbable. We should allow some time for the slaves and the foreign mercenaries to arrive, even if we may suppose that the appeals for help were sent out before the skirmishing began.

2. τοῦ τε νεωρίου: "dass Th. über die Lage des hier erwähnten νεώριον gar nichts bemerkt, scheint zu beweisen, dass er ein νεώριον als zu jedem Hafen gehörig ansah"—Steup. There may have been another νεώριον in the Hyllaic harbour; but Steup's reason is, unfortunately, insufficient; and one would suppose a special fear on the part of the oligarchs, not that their enemy might master the agora harbour and therewith its arsenal, but that they might seize the arsenal. See 81. 2 n.

τὰς ξυνοικίας: houses let to several families. Ps.-Xen. i. 17 ; Aischines, i. 124.

ὅπως μὴ ᾖ ἔφοδος: through narrow streets which the demos would know well? Ordinarily one would suppose that such streets could be easily defended, and that their destruction by fire, except while it was actually raging, would make the agora more accessible to the enemy. Perhaps the houses were fired only to keep off the immediate attack.

75. 1. τῇ δὲ ἐπιγιγνομένῃ ἡμέρᾳ: see 80. 2 n.

Νικόστρατος ὁ Διειτρέφους: we know nothing of this distinguished man except from Thucydides. He may be the Nikostratos of Vesp. 81-84; but that tells us little (a hit at him for being the friend of such a man as Philoxenos?).

ἐκ Ναυπάκτου δώδεκα ναυσί: see 69. 2. Nikostratos must have left Naupaktos three or four days before the Peloponnesians left Kyllene (76) ; but it did not apparently occur to Alkidas and Brasidas to make an attack on Naupaktos in the absence of the Athenian squadron and of 500 of the land garrison. It would not have been easy—it has always been difficult to storm a fortified port from the sea; but at least as easy as the attempt in 429 (ii. 90), and much easier than that on Peiraeus (ii. 93). A surprise attack might have succeeded. See also 77. 3 n.

πείθει ὥστε ξυγχωρῆσαι ἀλλήλοις: πείθει ὥστε is good Greek; but I suspect that Thucydides wrote πείθει ξυγχ. ἀ. ὥστε.

οἳ οὐκέτι ἔμειναν: 'who had not stayed for the outcome of the negotiations, and were already clear.' A most humane compromise. The only security measure that Nikostratos asks is the strengthening of the alliance with Athens (cf. 70. 2, 6).

καὶ πρὸς Ἀθηναίους, ὥστε, κ.τ.λ.: F. Hampl, Philol. xci, 1936, 153–60, in a study of the term σπονδαί, would insert ⟨ξυμμαχίαν⟩ after Ἀθηναίους, on the ground that σπονδαί does not have the generic sense, 'pact'. See v. 24. 2 n.

2. τοὺς ἐχθροὺς κατέλεγον: the majority at least of rowers in Kerkyraian triremes had been slaves (i. 55. 1); and in the old-fashioned fighting at Sybota in 433 there had been many hoplites on board (i. 49. 3). We have no reason to suppose that either ships or training had been brought up to date; and these drafted men were probably all ἐπιβάται—200 of them, if there were 40 per ship, as at Salamis. Apart from their political waywardness, these five ships would not be an asset to Nikostratos' small squadron; and he was bold enough to divide that.

This was an old trick, to draft your political enemies for service abroad: Polykrates of Samos had tried it, Hdt. iii. 44.

4. ὁπλισθείς: Cobet conjectured ὀργισθείς, unnecessarily. We are not to suppose that the demos of Kerkyra, like that of Mytilene (27. 2–3), had no ὅπλα of their own, and so could not arm themselves till they had got their enemies' weapons from their houses.

ἐπὶ τῇ προφάσει ταύτῃ: see 13. 1 n.

5. οἱ ἄλλοι: 'the rest of the oligarchs', that is, those who had not taken refuge at the Dioskoroi, as well as those who had not been called for service in the five ships. But the figure of 400 which is now given seems to describe all the oligarchs who were nervous of democratic promises, which means most oligarchs (82. 7). Yet there is nothing whatever to indicate that the suppliants of the Dioskoroi had left for the safer protection of Hera, as Stahl, following Bloomfield, maintains. There were, naturally, yet other 'oligarchs' who were not revolutionaries (τοῖς ἄλλοις of 80. 1).

ἐς τὸ Ἡραιον: the shrine at which the Epidamnian exiles had taken refuge in 436–435, i. 24. 7. For its position, see below, p. 370.

ἐς τὴν πρὸ τοῦ Ἡραίου νῆσον: see p. 371.

76. ἔφορμοι οὖσαι: not only is ἔφορμος not known elsewhere in classical Greek as an adjective, but, if it were admissible as one, it should mean 'on the watch', 'at anchor over against a place', the regular meaning of ἐφορμεῖν. Cf. also ἐφορμίσασθαι, iv. 8. 5. The

364

emendation ἐφορμοῦσαι is to be rejected for this same reason; for the Peloponnesian fleet was only preparing and waiting, in a distant home harbour. (Steup instances λιμένα καὶ ἐφόρμησιν, vi. 48, to show that ἐφορμεῖν need not necessarily mean 'to blockade'; but it certainly means there to *watch the enemy*, for the simple meaning 'anchorage' has already been expressed by λιμένα.) Stahl's ἐφ' ὅρμῳ οὖσαι, ingenious enough, also suffers from the fact that it is not found elsewhere for 'being at anchor'. ἐκεῖ ὁρμοῦσαι is what we need; or, indeed, ἐπισκευασθεῖσαι.

τρεῖς καὶ πεντήκοντα: 69. 1.

ἐπέπλει: note ἐπέπλεον immediately following, with a very different meaning.

Σύβοτα λιμένα τῆς ἠπείρου: see the map in vol. i, facing p. 196; but my nn. on i. 46. 4, 47. 1, and 50. 3, on the topography of the Epeiros coast opposite the southern end of Kerkyra Is., must be modified in the light of N. G. L. Hammond's article, on the topography and on the campaigns of 435 and 433 B.C., in *J.H.S.* lxv, 1945, 26–37. He places 'mainland Sybota' not at Mourteméno Bay, but at Moúrtzo to the north of it, in the narrow channel between Sybota Is. and the mainland.

He also makes it probable that Cheimerion harbour (i. 30. 3, 46. 3–4), the main Corinthian base from 435 to 433, was at Vemókastro, a bay south of Aríla and north of C. Varlaám (not marked on my map, and I have not seen it). I have some doubt whether it is large enough for the Corinthian fleet, and whether it is not too far north to have served the Corinthians in 435–434; but this site would make the actions of the twenty ships of the Kerkyraian left wing at Sybota much easier to understand (vol. i, p. 195). There would remain, however, one error in Thucydides' topography (shared by Strabo) which Hammond does not explain: namely, the belief that Cheimerion was near the mouth of the Acheron (i. 46. 4); for that, at Phanári Bay, is 14 or 15 miles from Vemókastro.

77. 1. παρεσκευάζοντό τε ἅμα: I suspect that we should read ὅμως for ἅμα (cf. 80. 1); ἅμα occurs just below in a proper context. 'They were preparing and sending out one by one' hardly needs 'at the same time' to help the meaning.

2. οὐδεὶς κόσμος: contrast Sparta, ii. 11. 9; and Athens, ii. 89. 9.

3. Σαλαμινία καὶ Πάραλος: these two vessels had been (like Alkidas and his fleet) in the Aegean not long before (33. 1). Steup suggests that, as they were not part of the normal garrison at Naupaktos, the twelve vessels there (69. 2) did not include them; Nikostratos may well have left at least two triremes to help guard the harbour (see n. on 75. 1; and Thucydides does not there say ταῖς δώδεκα ναυσί), in which case the Salaminia and Paralos will have joined him as he was *en route* for Kerkyra. Or, if he had to wait for orders from Athens before he left Naupaktos, they were sent to him there with those orders as soon as Athens heard of the oligarchic movement in Kerkyra (so Busolt, iii. 1044. 3). In spite of a long voyage round the Peloponnese, during which they should have been observed, they escaped all attention from the enemy at Kyllene. See below, 80. 2 n., for the chronology.

78. 1. ἀθρόαις μὲν οὐ προσέπιπτον: although κατὰ κέρας below ('on one wing of the enemy') is opposed to κατὰ μέσον rather than to ἀθρόαις, edd. are probably right in taking ἀ. with ταῖς - - - τεταγμέναις, rather than as 'with all their ships at once' (as 77. 1, πάσαις - - - ἐπιγενέσθαι).

2. ὅπερ ἐν Ναυπάκτῳ: ii. 84.

3. πρύμναν κρουόμενοι: see i. 50. 5 n. We must remember that the rowers had their backs to the enemy, as they had when attacking. (The scholiast on i. 50. 5 did not notice this.) This shows rare courage, discipline and confidence in their officers.

ἑαυτῶν σχολῇ τε, κ.τ.λ.: a nice case of genitive absolute, where the subject of the main verb is formally the same (cf. 55. 1, a simpler instance), with the implication 'forget about us; we will get back in good time and the enemy will attend only to us. You get away as best you can'. Note, too, the order ἑαυτῶν σχολῇ τε - - - καὶ πρὸς σφᾶς, the emphasis on the two pronouns and the position of τε. ἑαυτῶν followed by σφᾶς is not just a case of *variatio*: in direct speech and with a co-ordinate clause, it would be αὐτοί τε γὰρ σχολῇ ὑποχωρήσομεν καὶ πρὸς ἡμᾶς τετάξονται οἱ ἐναντίοι. It is as good a case as one could wish both of the elegance and the precision of Greek speech.

4. τοιαύτη γενομένη: this brilliant little engagement, for skill, daring, and coolness in judgement and action, is the equal of Phormion's best battles; and the political intelligence and humanity shown by Nikostratos was of a kind nowhere claimed for Phormion, nor indeed for any other Athenian, though doubtless if we had more details of Perikles' career we should find it in him; for it springs from a certain μεγαλοφροσύνη which very much belonged to him (μόνοι οὐ τοῦ ξυμφέροντος μᾶλλον λογισμῷ ἢ τῆς ἐλευθερίας τῷ πιστῷ ἀδεῶς τινὰ ὠφελοῦμεν, ii. 40. 5). It is possible enough that Nikostratos was not *bon camarade* with his sailors as Phormion was, and did not so conspicuously share their hardships and rough living; was more reserved; could be more easily attacked for his virtues, as an appeaser; and hence had not that same wide popularity; but if there had been but a few more like him in Athens—had Alkibiades, for example, really possessed the aristocratic virtues which he claimed—it could with more truth have been said of her, οὔτε τῷ πολεμίῳ ἐπελθόντι ἀγανάκτησιν ἔχει ὑφ' οἵων κακοπαθεῖ οὔτε τῷ ὑπηκόῳ κατάμεμψιν ὡς οὐχ ὑπ' ἀξίων ἄρχεται.

366

From the way certain events in the story of Kerkyra are told, without explanation, e.g. the arrival of ambassadors (70. 2, 72. 2), of Nikostratos (75. 1), and of the Paralos and Salaminia (77. 3), Busolt, iii, 1041. 2, concluded that Thucydides had Kerkyraian informants, who could tell him the simple facts but not explain how they happened. This seems plausible; but what are we to think of cc. 77–78, and the story after the arrival of Eurymedon? It must have been a very impartial man who related them to the historian if he was a Kerkyraian.

79. 1. ἐς τὸ Ἥραιον: see n. on the topography, below, p. 370.

3. οὐδὲν μᾶλλον ἐπέπλεον: they had rowed the previous evening 40 or 45 miles from their base, Sybota on the mainland, and back (76) besides fighting in the battle; and it should already have been clear that they would not (in all probability) row back again next day. Leukimme was much closer to Sybota, not more than 8 or 9 miles (see i. 47. 2 n., and map, vol. i, opp. p. 196). It may be that Thucydides had an incorrect idea of the distances.

ὡς λέγεται: it was the inevitable surmise, but, as Thucydides clearly thought, perhaps true.

80. 1. καί τινας αὐτῶν ἔπεισαν: from the narrative here (cf. 75. 2, 81. 2) and from i. 55. 1 it would appear that it was the richer classes in the main who served, as epibatai, on board ship; for it does not appear that the whole hoplite force of Kerkyra was drawn from the Few (75. 4 n.).

2. ἐφρυκτωρήθησαν ἐξήκοντα νῆες, κ.τ.λ.: was the signal (a fire signal of some kind) simply 'enemy in sight', with Thucydides adding, 'namely 60 Athenian vessels approaching from Leukas', or was it '60 enemy ships sighted approaching from Leukas'? See 22. 7–8 nn. ἀπὸ Λευκάδος is naturally taken with προσπλέουσαι; but this makes little difference, for a 'signal from Leukas' would inevitably announce ships seen from Leukas and so approaching Kerkyra from Leukas. See 81. 1 n. The distance between the southern part of Kerkyra, or Sybota, and Leukas is about 80 km., and there may have been a chain of signals.

πυνθανόμενοι τὴν στάσιν: from their trireme which had brought democratic refugees to Athens and from the Kerkyraian delegates (71. 2). The story is very like that of i. 50. 5; and so is Thucydides' method of telling it—no mention in 72. 1 of the Athenian intention to send reinforcements.

Εὐρυμέδοντα τὸν Θουκλέους: the first mention of this prominent and commonplace Athenian strategos.

　Busolt, iii. 1044. 3, has a note on the times of the events at Kerkyra. The first Athenian trireme must have sailed as quickly as possible to Athens, with the Kerkyraian refugees on board; there they were found by the Kerkyraian oligarchic leaders who were sent to Athens not long after (71. 2 n.). The Athenians then, presumably, sent the Paralos and Salaminia to Naupaktos with instructions to Nikostratos to intervene at Kerkyra. It is some 750 km. from Athens to Kerkyra, 600 from Athens to Naupaktos, and from Naupaktos to Kerkyra, 270. Accordingly we should have a time-table somewhat as follows: 5 days for the first Attic trireme from Kerkyra to Athens; 3–4 days for the decision to send to Nikostratos and get the two triremes ready; 4 days to Naupaktos; perhaps 5 days for Nikostratos' preparations and voyage to Kerkyra: that is, he would arrive in Kerkyra 18–20 days after the murder of Peithias (assuming that he must wait for orders from Athens before leaving Naupaktos: this seems probable; or at least he must otherwise have waited till he knew that Alkidas' fleet had left Kyllene).

81. 1. ὑπερενεγκόντες τὸν Λευκαδίων ἰσθμὸν τὰς ναῦς: so again in 425, iv. 8. 2, but then because it was quicker than sailing round the island. Steup thinks that this was the reason now, and suspects ὅπως μὴ ὀφθῶσιν as a marginal and mistaken explanation; for if the Athenian fleet was 'approaching from Leukas' when the Peloponnesians were in Sybota, it would have been long past Leukas, almost in Kerkyraian waters, by the time the Peloponnesians reached the isthmus, and there would have been no danger of their being seen. This is over fine. The distance from Sybota to Leukas was more than they could cover in the hours of darkness (see vol. i, p. 20, and ii. 97. 1 n.), for the signal was not given till after dark, and some time must have been taken in preparing for departure; and, in the ordinary way, ships intending to round Leukas would not hug the Epeirote shore, and the Peloponnesians would have been near the path of the Athenians coming in the opposite direction by dawn. We have only to suppose that ἀπὸ Λευκάδος in 80. 2 means 'we have seen them from Leukas' (whether such a message could be included in the signal, or is simply implied by the signalling station being situated on Leukas), to make Alkidas' fears quite natural, his hugging the shore and crossing the isthmus.

For the low neck of land, mostly silted sand, which connects Leukas with the mainland, see Leake, i. 172, iii. 10; Oberhummer, *Akarnanien*, 7–14; Partsch, *Petermanns Mitt.*, Ergänzungsheft 95, 2 ff. For the canal, cf. Strabo, x. 2. 8, p. 452.

2. λαβόντες τούς τε Μεσσηνίους: the Ambrosianus of Dionysios, *de Thuc. iud.* 28 (p. 883. 14), in his quotation of this paragraph, omits τε (ed. Usener and Radermacher); which certainly makes an unnecessary λαβόντες much easier. Hude's λαθόντες seems condemned by the transposed τε; and what need was there for secrecy? Classen would bracket the word as having arisen from εἴ τινα λάβοιεν below. For the Messenians, see 75. 1.

ἐς τὸν Ὑλλαϊκὸν λιμένα: see below, p. 370. They had been at the other harbour near the agora, where was the νεώριον (but see 74. 2 n.); and were now sent to the quarter where the democrats were more clearly masters, and to separate the oligarchs among the crews from their friends.

4. ὁ Εὐρυμέδων - - - παρέμεινε: the implication is that Eurymedon was, to this extent, responsible for the massacre, that with sixty ships he could have done what Nikostratos did with twelve, but took no trouble to interfere; and that Nikostratos either left soon after Eurymedon's arrival (cf. 75. 2, ἔμελλεν ἀποπλεύσεσθαι, and there was need probably to defend Naupaktos after the Peloponnesian fleet left Kerkyra; though once more the Peloponnesians do not take their chance), or was expressly subordinate in the command. If he had left, he had not taken his Messenians with him. At the same time, as Steup observed, we must not suppose that Thucydides saddles the Messenians with responsibility for the terror, or even with taking any part in it.

τὴν μὲν αἰτίαν ἐπιφέροντες, κ.τ.λ.: i.e. bringing the charge (of conspiracy against the state, before the courts) against the revolutionaries; but, besides that, many were killed from private enmity, etc. with no sort of charge brought against them, still less any trial or pretence of trial, but killed in the streets or in their houses, under cover of the general terror—men, in Arnold's words, "whom in fact the victorious party had no intention of molesting, as they were not politically obnoxious"). This would be all right if instead of τὴν αἰτίαν ἐπιφέροντες we had ἐς δίκην ἄγοντες or the like; for what is *the* charge, except that of attempting to overthrow the demos? That is, we need an explanation of '*the* charge'. Or if that can be assumed, we should have at least τοῖς ⟨ἔργῳ⟩ τὸν δῆμον καταλύουσι; cf. 46. 4, where the meaning of τὴν αἰτίαν is clear and the object of τὴν αἰτίαν ἐπιφέρειν is defined. But does Thucydides mean that the victorious democrats were scrupulous to bring a legal indictment only against the real offenders? For all these reasons, I feel that Duker's αὐτοῖς ὡς for τοῖς is to be adopted: the charge of revolutionary conspiracy was brought against all enemies. Debtors would certainly call their creditors conspirators and oligarchs and agents of a foreign power; and all or most of those in the second group will have been put on trial as conspirators, like those in the first. The MSS. of Dionysios (*de Thuc.* 884) agree with those of Thucydides; but Dionysios has no complaint to make of the style here (883).

ὑπὸ τῶν λαβόντων: either 'by their captors', with ὀφειλομένων ('others, to whom money was owed by their captors'), or 'by their debtors', those who had received the money, with ἀπέθανον ('others, to whom money was owed, by their debtors'). The former has more point, and, in the context, gives the readier meaning to οἱ λαβόντες; cf. τῶν ἐχθρῶν εἴ τινα λάβοιεν, § 2. They are perhaps contrasted with those in the second group (those killed ἰδίας ἔχθρας ἕνεκα), who were at least put on trial. Dionysios does not note any dubiety of meaning.

5. οὐδὲν ὅτι οὐ ξυνέβη καὶ ἔτι περαιτέρω: a turn of speech that would inevitably be imitated by Sallust (and doubtless by others), Jug. 44. 5, 'postremo quaecunque dici aut fingi queunt ignaviae luxuriae-que probra in illo exercitu cuncta fuere et alia amplius'; and, in Sallust, it marks an artificial excitement of the emotions.

ἐν τοῦ Διονύσου τῷ ἱερῷ: the site is unknown. The men immured in the precinct were presumably starved to death; cf. the case of Pausanias the Regent, i. 134. 1–3.

The Topography of the City of Kerkyra

Since the publication of B. Schmidt's Korkyräische Studien in 1890, his general view of the topography of the town has been accepted: namely, that the ancient akropolis was on the slight eminence formed by the peninsula now called Palaiópolis; the Hyllaic harbour (72. 3, 81. 2) was the shallow bay called Chalikiópoulo west of Palaiópolis, and the harbour by the agora and opposite the mainland (72. 3) was the Bay of Kastrádes, with the νεώριον (74. 2) at its southern end, and the agora near by, below the north end of Palaiópolis; the Heraion was near the agora, on the north slopes of the 'akropolis', and the island opposite it (75. 5) in consequence was the Fortezza Vecchia, which juts out eastwards into the sea at the north-east corner of the modern town; and that the islet of Vido, opposite the modern harbour, is Ptychia (iv. 46. 3). Fort Abraham (Fortezza Nuova) to the west of the town Schmidt identified with the height occupied by Mnasippos in 374 B.C. (Xen. Hell. vi. 2. 2–38).

Unfortunately, no known building, e.g. Dioskoreion (75. 3), sanctuary of Dionysos (81. 5), Heraion, or arsenal (74. 2), has been identified. For several reasons I find it impossible to accept Schmidt's view. First, it is difficult to believe that the Greek settlers did not at once occupy the prominent heights of the two forts, either of which would make a typical akropolis, in preference to the low hill to the south with its gentle slopes; according to Schmidt the Kerkyraioi did not even occupy Fort Abraham as a καρτερὸς λόφος outside the town (cf. iv. 129. 3, Mende, and 131. 1, Skione). Schmidt himself likens the Old Fort to the 'island' of Syracuse, without noting that at Syracuse the island did form the akropolis. Secondly, I do not believe that Fortezza Vecchia would ever have been described as 'the island in front of the Heraion'. It is now an island in the sense that it is and has been at least since the early Byzantine age cut off from the main part of the town by an artificial canal; and

370

there may have been a canal cut in classical times. It may even, though there seems to be no evidence for this, at one time have been a natural island; but never, surely, called the island in front of the Heraion, with that sanctuary on the northern slopes of Palaiópolis. Besides, in 79. 1, the democrats of Kerkyra, after the sea-fight, remove the prisoners from the island back to the Heraion, because the enemy, now superior at sea, might rescue them; if the Fortezza Vecchia were the island, no superiority at sea alone would put it into the hands of an enemy. The island must be Vido, as earlier scholars had maintained, and the Heraion in consequence near the shore north or east of the fort, perhaps near H. Nikólaos (rather than on the slopes of Fortezza Nuova, where Partsch placed it: *Die Insel Corfu, Petermanns Mitt.* Suppl. Bd. 1887).

The democrats, at the beginning of the fighting in the town, held the akropolis and τὰ μετέωρα τῆς πόλεως, and the Hyllaic harbour (72. 3). The 'high parts' are naturally to be taken as the Fortezza Nuova (Fort Abraham), if the Vecchia is the akropolis, and the present-day harbour, or the smaller bay just north of the Vecchia, will be that called Hyllaic. It is again reasonable to suppose that the citizens of the ancient town would use the best harbour in the place. The other harbour, opposite the mainland, with the νεώριον, will have been in the bay of Kastrádes, as has been generally agreed, but probably towards its northern end, with the agora near by (72. 3, 74. 2, and 77). An objection to supposing that the Hyllaic harbour was Chalikiópoulo is that it is much too shallow, practically marsh, and there is no evidence that it was deeper in ancient times; and if this harbour must be put elsewhere, the only argument for the ancient akropolis being on Palaiópolis disappears. Such classical remains as have been found on that hill, including a temple, a cemetery, and the tomb of Menekrates, are of course consistent with its having been outside the city. Finally, Ptychia island, iv. 46. 3 (which, as Schmidt says, should be different from the island in front of the Heraion), is probably Latsaréto to the west of Vido, which is quite consistent with what Ptolemy tells us.

A few words should be added about the other evidence. Xenophon's account of Mnasippos' siege of Kerkyra, by sea and land, is consistent with the topography suggested above, and not always easily to be understood if Palaiopolis were the akropolis (esp. §§17–20); the hill occupied by Mnasippos (§ 7) will be one to the west of Fort Abraham; his fleet he sent into Kastrádes Bay, εἰς τἀπὶ θάτερα τῆς πόλεως, whence it could watch for the approach of an Athenian fleet from the south (ibid.; cf. § 25). Diodoros, xiii. 48, the story of renewed civil war in the city in 410, does not help; and much of it seems to be taken from Thucydides' account of the stasis in 427, and is a conventional picture (Diodoros' account of the earlier stasis,

371

xiii. 57, having no such detail). Ps.-Skylax, 29, mentions three harbours: these will correspond to the present harbour, that to the east of it north of Fortezza Vecchia, and that in the bay of Kastrádes. Dionysios Periegetes, 492, c. schol., mentions a 'harbour of Alkinoos', 'between the peaks'; this also best suits the modern harbour between the Old Fort and Fort Abraham, or perhaps the small harbour to the north of the Old Fort, between its two high points.

82. 1. ἐν τοῖς πρώτη ἐγένετο: clearly here 'it was the first of all' (or, the first in this war: cf. ii. 85. 2 n.), not 'it was among the first'. See 17. 1 n.; and for the effect of a first example, compare iv. 81. 3 and my n. there. It is part of the irony of history that Kerkyra, which had enjoyed a Phaeacian peace before 434 and had been pleased with its ἡσυχία and ἀπραγμοσύνη, should have been the scene of this violent *stasis*, and have shown the way to the rest (Ullrich, p. 100, n. 117). καὶ ἔδοξε μᾶλλον, because afterwards people got used to them, accepting them as a natural thing, at least in war-time.

ὕστερόν γε - - - ἐκινήθη: this means, surely, that this famous passage, cc. 82–83, was written after 413 B.C. Cf. i. 1. 1–2, and my article in *J.H.S.* lxxi, 1951, 70–80. It does not follow that much of it was not thought out and written down some time earlier. Note that formally at least, as shown by the next clause, Athens is not included among the sufferers from στάσις; contrast ii. 65. 11–12.

ἐκινήθη: cf. i. 1. 2, κίνησις γὰρ αὕτη μεγίστη, though there the word has a more comprehensive meaning. Elsewhere it may mean 'movement' simply, with no disturbance (v. 8. 1; and n. on v. 9. 5).

καὶ ἐν μὲν εἰρήνῃ, κ.τ.λ.: I believe that those edd. are right who think that this sentence, with its remarkable anacoluthon (no main verb in the μέν-clause), cannot stand in its present form as what Thucydides wrote. The examples quoted as parallels, as 81. 4, ii. 47. 3, iv. 6. 1, vi. 69. 1, are, as Steup says, quite different. On the other hand, the conjecture ἐτόλμων for ἑτοίμων (variously attributed to C. F. Müller, Vollgraff, and Classen), ingenious enough, and getting rid at the same time of the difficulty caused by the absence of ὄντων with ἑτοίμων, will not do, for the subject of this verb and of the participle, ἐχόντων, is clearly the same, the faction leaders; οὐκ ἂν ἐχόντων πρόφασιν does not mean, as Steup wishes, 'Athens and Sparta not having occasion to intervene'. We should also have to change οὐδέ to οὐκ. What we need is some such phrase as ⟨ἡσύχαζον μᾶλλον αἱ πόλεις⟩ after παρακαλεῖν αὐτούς, which would give a proper distinction between the general body of citizens in each state and the party leaders (again as in ii. 65. 11). Marchant's suggestion, to put a comma after τοὺς Λακεδαιμονίους, making one sentence from ἐπεὶ ὕστερόν γε to ἐπορίζοντο, so that ἐν μὲν εἰρήνῃ οὐκ ἂν ἐχόντων, κ.τ.λ., is a second genitive absolute parallel with διαφορῶν οὐσῶν, does

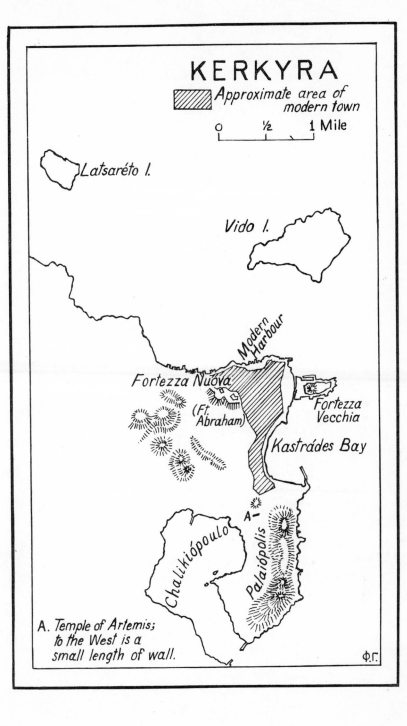

KERKYRA

Approximate area of modern town

0   ½   1 Mile

Latsaréto I.

Vido I.

Modern Harbour

Fortezza Nuóva

(Fr. Abraham)

Fortezza Vecchia

Kastrádes Bay

Chalikiópoulo

Palaiópolis

A

A. Temple of Artemis; to the West is a small length of wall.

Φ.Γ.

produce a grammatical structure like that of 81. 4, 87. 1, or ii. 47. 3. But the break in the sequence of thought at καὶ ἐν μὲν εἰρήνῃ makes this impossible. It is to be noted that none of the longish scholia on this section (except those of the Bâle MS.) have any mention of the anacoluthon; and that Dionysios does not include it to illustrate the σκολιὰ καὶ δυσπαρακολούθητα, κ.τ.λ., of the rest of this chapter (29. 885).

πολεμουμένων δέ, κ.τ.λ.: the run of the sentence requires, I think, that καὶ ξυμμαχίας be taken as another genitive absolute, so that πολεμουμένων ('in war-time', or 'when they, i.e. the Greek cities generally, were at war') answers exactly to ἐν εἰρήνῃ and ξυμμαχίας - - - προσποιήσει το οὐκ ἂν ἐχόντων - - - παρακαλεῖν αὐτούς, even though this leaves ξυμμαχίας without its participle, ὑπαρχούσης or διδομένης (or perhaps δεομένοις, which is found in the Bâle scholia: Powell, C.Q. xxx, 1936, 85), like ἑτοίμων in the previous clause. Stahl, followed by Steup, takes ξυμμαχίας as objective genitive with αἱ ἐπαγωγαί, and Steup further supposes that ἑκατέροις (for ὑφ' ἑκατέρων) and σφίσιν αὐτοῖς, and the subject of πολεμουμένων, are Athens and Sparta; which seems forced. 'But in war and when help from outside was available to either party to get the better of their opponents and acquire strength for themselves, occasions to call in Athens or Sparta were readily at hand for the party prepared for revolution.' κακώσει and προσποιήσει are datives of motive, and the latter has the meaning of the verb in the middle voice.

For the general sense cf. Plat. Rep. viii. 556 E, where also there is a similar use of πρόφασις (cf. 13. 1 n.).

2. γιγνόμενα μὲν καὶ αἰεὶ ἐσόμενα, κ.τ.λ.: 'they happened and will continue to happen so long as human nature remains the same, with greater or less violence and varying in form, according as changes of circumstances impose themselves in individual cases.' For the general conviction, cf. i. 22. 4; but, again, it does not imply a 'cyclical' view of history.

Krüger proposed ἑκάστοις, Hude ἑκάσταις, for ἕκασται or ἕκαστα of the MSS., with some reason.

τοῦ καθ' ἡμέραν: Krüger's suggestion ⟨βίου⟩ has much to be said for it, though edd. have not accepted it.

βίαιος διδάσκαλος: 'a teacher of violence', so that violence within a state is a natural consequence of war between states. I have always regarded this as one of the strongest and deepest of Thucydides' personal convictions, and clearly expressed; cf. my Essays, c. vi; but I have not found many to agree with me. He appears here to be expressly dissociating himself from the cynical doctrine of force which he puts so often in the mouths of others; and we will not forget that he has called Kleon βιαιότατος τῶν πολιτῶν.

τὰς ὀργάς: 'their tempers, emotions', rather than simply their 'dispositions', as the schol. ($\nu\tilde{\upsilon}\nu$ $\gamma\grave{\alpha}\rho$ $\dot{\delta}\rho\gamma\grave{\alpha}s$ $\tau\grave{\alpha}s$ $\gamma\nu\acute{\omega}\mu\alpha s$ $\kappa\alpha\grave{\iota}$ $\tau\upsilon\grave{\upsilon}s$ $\tau\rho\acute{\delta}\pi\upsilon\upsilon s$ $\dot{\epsilon}\kappa\acute{\alpha}\lambda\epsilon\sigma\epsilon\nu$). For Thucydides here uses $\tau\grave{\alpha}s$ $\dot{\delta}\rho\gamma\acute{\alpha}s$ of set purpose by way of contrast with $\tau\grave{\alpha}s$ $\gamma\nu\acute{\omega}\mu\alpha s$ above: men's passions in war and in time of stress not only deteriorate, but tend to dominate their minds. This is what Kleon and men like him wanted: 38. 1, 40. 7. Cf. the lines on $\sigma\tau\acute{\alpha}\sigma\iota s$ in *Eumenides*, 976–87 ($\delta\iota$' $\dot{\delta}\rho\gamma\acute{\alpha}\nu$, 981). If, on the other hand, $\alpha\acute{\iota}$ $\dot{\delta}\rho\gamma\alpha\acute{\iota}$ here is equivalent to $\upsilon\acute{\iota}$ $\tau\rho\acute{\delta}\pi\upsilon\upsilon$, cf. *Ajax*, 638–40,

$$o\dot{\upsilon}\kappa\acute{\epsilon}\tau\iota \ \sigma\upsilon\nu\tau\rho\acute{\delta}\phi\upsilon\iota s$$
$$\dot{\delta}\rho\gamma\alpha\tilde{\iota}s \ \acute{\epsilon}\mu\pi\epsilon\delta\upsilon s, \ \dot{\alpha}\lambda\lambda' \ \dot{\epsilon}\kappa\tau\grave{\delta}s \ \dot{\delta}\mu\iota\lambda\epsilon\tilde{\iota}.$$

τῶν πολλῶν: 'of the majority of men' (not 'of the masses' in a political sense, as it has sometimes been translated).

3. ἐστασίαζέ τε οὖν: note the order of thought in this chapter: from *stasis* in Kerkyra to *stasis* in the Greek world generally and one of its causes (the war between democratic Athens and oligarchic Sparta); to universal conditions of *stasis* and war as its stimulus; then back to *stasis* in Greece, and its particular characteristics. I am not sure that it was all written at one time; note, for example, $\kappa\alpha\grave{\iota}$ $\dot{\epsilon}\nu$ $\mu\grave{\epsilon}\nu$ $\epsilon\dot{\iota}\rho\acute{\eta}\nu\eta$ followed soon by $\dot{\epsilon}\nu$ $\mu\grave{\epsilon}\nu$ $\gamma\grave{\alpha}\rho$ $\epsilon\dot{\iota}\rho\acute{\eta}\nu\eta$.

πολὺ ἐπέφερε: I prefer Reiske's $\pi\upsilon\lambda\lambda\acute{\eta}\nu$, from one MS. of Dionysios.

περιτεχνήσει: a word not found again before Dio Cassius, nor are any of its cognates ($\pi\epsilon\rho\iota\tau\epsilon\chi\nu\tilde{\alpha}\sigma\theta\alpha\iota$, etc.) preserved from classical Greek: 'excessive ingenuity'; cf. n. on $\tau\grave{\alpha}s$ $\pi\epsilon\rho\iota\nu\upsilon\acute{\iota}\alpha s$, 43. 3. $\dot{\alpha}\tau\upsilon\pi\acute{\iota}\alpha$ is 'enormity', and $\tau\iota\mu\omega\rho\acute{\iota}\alpha\iota$ 'reprisals'.

4. τῇ δικαιώσει: as Dionysios paraphrases, $\dot{\alpha}\lambda\lambda\omega s$ $\dot{\eta}\xi\acute{\iota}\upsilon\upsilon\nu$ $\alpha\dot{\upsilon}\tau\grave{\alpha}$ $\kappa\alpha\lambda\epsilon\tilde{\iota}\nu$; they 'claimed the right' to impose new interpretations on old words. $\dot{\epsilon}s$ $\tau\grave{\alpha}$ $\acute{\epsilon}\rho\gamma\alpha$ goes surely with $\dot{\alpha}\nu\tau\acute{\eta}\lambda\lambda\alpha\xi\alpha\nu$ 'with a view to their actions', not with $\tau\grave{\eta}\nu$ $\dot{\alpha}\xi\acute{\iota}\omega\sigma\iota\nu$.

Finley, pp. 229–32, points out how Alkibiades' speech at Sparta illustrates this distortion of meanings: e.g. $\phi\iota\lambda\acute{\delta}\pi\upsilon\lambda\iota s$, vi. 92. 2, coll. ii. 60. 5.

τόλμα - - - ἀλόγιστος: the words used to describe Harmodios' and Aristogeiton's murder of Hipparchos, which was caused by $\tau\upsilon\tilde{\upsilon}$ $\pi\alpha\rho\alpha$-$\chi\rho\tilde{\eta}\mu\alpha$ $\pi\epsilon\rho\iota\delta\epsilon\upsilon\tilde{\upsilon}s$, vi. 59. 1.

φιλέταιρος: $\pi\alpha\rho\epsilon\lambda\kappa\acute{\delta}\nu\tau\omega s$ $\kappa\epsilon\tilde{\iota}\tau\alpha\iota$· $\kappa\acute{\epsilon}\chi\rho\eta\tau\alpha\iota$ $\delta\grave{\epsilon}$ $\alpha\dot{\upsilon}\tau\tilde{\omega}$ $\delta\iota\grave{\alpha}$ $\tau\grave{\delta}$ $\pi\rho\upsilon\theta\epsilon\tilde{\iota}\nu\alpha\iota$ $\tau\acute{\delta}\lambda\mu\alpha\nu$ $\dot{\alpha}\lambda\acute{\delta}\gamma\iota\sigma\tau\upsilon\nu$, $\acute{\iota}\nu\alpha$ $\pi\alpha\rho\acute{\iota}\sigma\omega\sigma\iota s$ $\gamma\acute{\epsilon}\nu\eta\tau\alpha\iota$—schol. This is the sort of thing Gorgias did, and that Dionysios expected to find in Thucydides; the latter, p. 887, says that *all* the epithets in this sentence are nothing but ornament. This is the reverse of the truth; and $\phi\iota\lambda\acute{\epsilon}\tau\alpha\iota\rho\upsilon s$ is a key-word, 'in the interests of the party'.

Ros, p. 103, strangely takes $\tau\acute{\delta}\lambda\mu\alpha$ and $\dot{\alpha}\nu\delta\rho\epsilon\acute{\iota}\alpha$ as an instance of ordinary *variatio*, as though Thucydides was *not* illustrating changes in the meaning of words; on p. 104 he takes $\tau\grave{\delta}$ $\sigma\tilde{\omega}\phi\rho\upsilon\nu$ and $\tau\grave{\delta}$ $\xi\upsilon\nu\epsilon\tau\acute{\delta}\nu$ similarly, which is also clearly wrong.

μέλλησις δὲ προμηθής: the exact antithesis of $\tau\acute{\delta}\lambda\mu\alpha$ $\dot{\alpha}\lambda\acute{\delta}\gamma\iota\sigma\tau\upsilon s$—a hesitation based on foresight. τὸ σῶφρον and τὸ - - - ξυνετόν form together another contrary to τόλμα ἀλόγιστος.

τὸ δὲ σῶφρον τοῦ ἀνάνδρου πρόσχημα: cf. Plat. *Rep.* viii. 560 D, σωφροσύνην δὲ ἀνανδρίαν καλοῦντές τε καὶ προπηλακίζοντες ἐκβάλλουσι; but in this part of the *Republic*, in which στάσις first in the oligarchic and then in the democratic state is described, the differences from Thucydides are as important as the resemblances. See also Aristotle's note on the changeable meanings of words, so valuable to the *rhetor*, *Rhet.* i. 9. 67 a 33, esp. οἷον τὸν εὐλαβῆ ψυχρὸν καὶ ἐπίβουλον καὶ τὸν ἠλίθιον χρηστόν, κ.τ.λ. (above, n. on ἀναλγητότεροι, 40. 5).

τὸ πρὸς ἅπαν ξυνετόν, κ.τ.λ.: 'an intelligence which can grasp the whole amounted to inactivity in everything.'

τὸ δ' ἐμπλήκτως ὀξύ, κ.τ.λ.: Stahl's general analysis of this passage is sound—"non solum vera cuiusque nominis notio falsae quam brevissime opponitur, sed etiam vitio in virtutem mutato contraria virtus in vitium versa respondet. Sequitur ut hoc quoque loco eadem verae et falsae notionis brevissima sit oppositio neque quidquam explicationis causa addatur, deinde ut vesanae temeritati pro animo virili acceptae contraria virtus ignaviae loco habita ex adverso sit". ἀνδρὸς μοίρᾳ comprises a virtue, and ἀποτροπῆς πρόφασις εὔλογος is its contrary weakness; in consequence τὸ ἐμπλήκτως ὀξύ and τὸ ἐπιβουλεύσασθαι must be opposing vice and virtue respectively which may be labelled in the heat of party strife 'belonging to a true man' and 'a specious excuse for evasion'. ἀσφαλείᾳ τὸ ἐπιβουλεύσασθαι in consequence means, as the scholiast says, τὸ ἐπὶ πολὺ βουλεύσασθαι δι' ἀσφάλειαν, 'prolonged thought in order to avoid pitfalls' (for ἀσφαλείᾳ, cf. 56. 5, and Soph. *O.T.* 51, with Jebb's n.), not "zur eignen Sicherung wurde tückische Arglist gerechnet" (Classen), but rather "zum Zwecke der Sicherheit eines Unternehmens überlegen" (Steup; for ἐπιβουλεύειν in the simple sense of 'to plan', compare 20. 1, 109. 3). Further, 'careful thought' stresses the intellectual rather than the moral aspect; τὸ ἐμπλήκτως ὀξύ, therefore, should be more an intellectual than a moral vice; not *vesanus animi impetus* (*ardor*) or *vesana temeritas* (Stahl), nor "ein wahnsinniges Drauflosgehen" (Classen, Steup), but τὸ ὀξύ will here mean 'sharpness', 'quickness'. Such a quality may be praised (i. 70. 2, viii. 96. 5, of the Athenians by contrast with Spartans; or ii. 11. 9); cf. vi. 11. 7, ὅπως πόλιν δι' ὀλιγαρχίας ἐπιβουλεύουσαν ὀξέως φυλαξόμεθα ('keep a sharp look-out'); or it may be deprecated as 'hastiness' (in the same speech of Nikias, τὸ πρᾶγμα μέγα εἶναι καὶ μὴ οἷον νεωτέρῳ βουλεύσασθαί τε καὶ ὀξέως μεταχειρίσαι, vi. 12. 2—note βουλεύσασθαι in this context); or it may be that particular quality of sharpness and cunning characteristic of certain kinds of men, including, as is relevant here, ambitious politicians: *Rep.* vii. 519 A, ἢ οὔπω ἐννενόηκας τῶν λεγομένων πονηρῶν μέν, σοφῶν δέ, ὡς δριμὺ μὲν βλέπει τὸ ψυχάριον καὶ ὀξέως διορᾷ ταῦτα

375

ἐφ' ἃ τέτραπται, ὡς οὐ φαύλην ἔχον τὴν ὄψιν, κακίᾳ δ' ἠναγκασμένον ὑπηρετεῖν, ὥστε ὅσῳ ἂν ὀξύτερον βλέπῃ τοσούτῳ πλείω κακὰ ἐργαζόμενον; cf. ii. 368 C, iii. 401 E, and also vii. 503 C; viii. 567 B, of the tyrant, ὀξέως ἄρα δεῖ ὁρᾶν αὐτόν, τίς ἀνδρεῖος, τίς μεγαλόφρων, κ.τ.λ. Doubtless, ὀξίνης 'Υπέρβολος, Ar. Eq. 1304, includes a similar idea. I take τὸ ὀξύ, therefore, to be the small sharpness of a little soul, and ἐμπλήκτως to be 'capricious', as Aischin. ii. 164, πολιτείας ἐμπληξία, Soph. Aj. 1358, and Eur. Tro. 1205,

αἱ τύχαι,
ἔμπληκτος ὡς ἄνθρωπος, ἄλλοτ' ἄλλοσε
πηδῶσι.

προσετέθη is to be understood literally, 'was *added* to the other qualities of a true man', 'to a man's portion', for τόλμα ἀλόγιστος has already been mentioned as one of those qualities, and a very important one. That, and μέλλησις προμηθής, were rather moral qualities, rashness and prudence; here we have the intellectual side. For the use of βουλεύεσθαι where 'deliberation' might be an excuse for avoiding action, cf. Plut. Nik. 14. 4, οὐκ ἐπαύσατο καθήμενος ἢ περιπλέων ἢ βουλευόμενος πρὶν ἐγγηρᾶσαι μὲν αὐτῶν τὴν ἀκμὴν τῆς ἐλπίδος, κ.τ.λ. It is used scornfully by Sthenelaïdas, i. 86. 4, to indicate how a man should *think* when meditating a crime. The meaning of ἀποτροπή is taken from the middle voice of the verb, 'shrinking from', or, according to L. and S., 'deserting the party, ratting'. If any emendation is required, we might have ἀποστροφῆς from ἀποστρέφεσθαι, 'to turn away from, to abandon'.

The difficulties in the way of this interpretation are two. The first is slight, the position of ἀσφαλείᾳ, outside the phrase, τὸ ἐπιβουλεύσασθαι, to which it belongs; as such this is not difficult, it is a matter of emphasis (cf. i. 42. 4), but here it has some awkwardness, for at first sight a dative would appear to correspond to ἀνδρὸς μοίρᾳ; and there is some case for the reading ἀσφάλεια δὲ τοῦ ἐπιβουλεύσασθαι, adopted by Hude. Since, however, ἀσφάλεια cannot by itself be either a virtue or a vice, the construction, though obscure, is not doubtful. The other difficulty is more serious, the use of ἐπιβουλεύσασθαι to mean 'intent deliberation'. Stahl compared ἐπινοῆσαι, ἐπιγνῶναι, i. 70. 2, as similar compounds; but Classen was surely right to reject this. The middle of this verb is anyhow rare; and I believe that we must emend, and that the scholiast's words quoted above give the text of Thucydides himself, τὸ ἐπὶ πολὺ βουλεύσασθαι (cf. 89. 2, n. on ἐπανελθοῦσα). The aorist is used as in Aischines' σιγῶ καὶ λέγω βουλευσάμενος, iii. 218. (Lupus conjectured ἔτι βουλεύσασθαι, which showed a true sense of the difficulty; but ἔτι has been rightly condemned. L. and S. make no mention of this passage, s.v. ἐπιβουλεύω; for the reference "Th. iii. 82" is evidently to ἐπιβουλεύσας below.)

376

εὔλογος might be either 'well-thought', 'reasonable', or perhaps in this context 'well-phrased', as εὖ λέγειν.

5. ἐπιβουλεύσας δέ τις, κ.τ.λ.: 'in a plot a man who was successful was thought intelligent, one who suspected a plot even cleverer.' Dionysios' MSS. read τυχών τε (twice: de Thuc. 889 and de Dem. 954); this is preferable, 'one who plotted and was successful'. There is, I feel sure, a double edge to Thucydides' language here: not only was suspicion (which ὀξέως βλέπει) regarded more highly even than success, but it was thought better to be clever than intelligent. 'A is an intelligent man'; 'yes, but B is even cleverer'. δεινός is by no means always a complimentary term, as ξυνετός is. Cf. also Plato's description of ὁ δεινὸς ἐκεῖνος καὶ καχύποπτος, Rep. iii. 409 C.

προβουλεύσας δέ: "von einem dritten, der sich möglichst von den Parteiumtrieben fern hielt"—Classen. It goes deeper than this: it refers to one who may be taking a leading part in affairs, but (in face, perhaps, of external danger) proposes some approach to the other party—to prevent both plot and counterplot, and endless suspicion—or open and constitutional (μετὰ τῶν κειμένων νόμων, below) rather than secret and violent methods to gain the desired end.

ὁ ἐπικελεύσας τὸν μὴ διανοούμενον: again we seem to be going from bad to worse. ὁ φθάσας was at least a man of some energy, one who took a risk; ὁ ἐπικελεύσας only cheered on a man who would otherwise have taken no part in the conspiracy. Classen took τὸν μέλλοντα, like τὸν μὴ διανοούμενον, to be a member of the same party, not an enemy; but I doubt this. (L. and S. say that παρακελεύεσθαι properly means 'cheer one on to an act not begun, ἐπικ. to one already begun'. Not apparently here.)

6. καὶ μὴν καὶ τὸ ξυγγενές, κ.τ.λ.: "to be kin to another was not so near as to be of his society"—Hobbes.

ἑτοιμότερον εἶναι, κ.τ.λ.: 'they were more ready to undertake any action without demur (on behalf of the party)'; or perhaps, 'without cause', ἀπ' οὐδεμιᾶς προφάσεως.

οὐ γὰρ μετὰ τῶν κειμένων νόμων: there were such ἑταιρεῖαι, in Athens and elsewhere, which confined themselves to aiding their members by making use of established laws. In Athens they did not attempt unconstitutional methods till 411 B.C.; and in Kerkyra men had begun by actions in the law-courts, even if only for party ends.

We must surely, with most edd., adopt Poppo's emendation ὠφελίᾳ; it is a trifling change, the run of the sentence demands it, and it is implied by Dionysios' paraphrase: οὐ γὰρ ἐπὶ ταῖς κατὰ νόμον ὠφελείαις - - -, ἀλλ' ἐπὶ τῷ παρὰ τοὺς νόμους τι πλεονεκτεῖν.

αἱ τοιαῦται ξύνοδοι: cf. Equit. 475-7 (Kleon speaking):

ἐγὼ μὲν οὖν αὐτίκα μάλ' εἰς βουλὴν ἰών
ὑμῶν ἁπάντων τὰς ξυνωμοσίας ἐρῶ,
καὶ τὰς ξυνόδους τὰς νυκτερινὰς ἐπὶ τῇ πόλει,

with Neil's n.

377

7. τά τε ἀπὸ τῶν ἐναντίων, κ.τ.λ.: 'fair proposals coming from the other side were accepted (when accepted at all) by the stronger party only with precautionary action, not in a spirit of generosity.' Peace proposals *were* accepted sometimes, but only if the party approached was (or thought itself to be) the stronger, and only when the acceptance was accompanied by further steps in self-defence. The subject of προύχοιεν is more probably οἱ ἐνδεχόμενοι than οἱ ἐναντίοι, for, as Herbst saw, it is the stronger side that might show generosity—and perhaps only the weaker would make proposals for peace (Arnold compares i. 29. 1); and ἔργων is better taken as a genitive of definition than objective (precautionary *action*, not 'precaution against action by the others'), in order to keep a better contrast between τὰ λεγόμενα and ἔργων: the words of one side were met by deeds on the other. See below, 83. 2.

διδόμενοι: 'offered', as in the phrase ὅρκους διδόναι καὶ λαμβάνειν. 'When binding agreements under oath *were* made, because the offer of an oath was only made, on either side, to get out of an *impasse*, they were observed only for the moment, while (*or* because) one side or the other could get no support from elsewhere.' ἄλλοθεν δύναμιν, if it has a particular reference, means the support of other states (§ 1).

ἐν δὲ τῷ παρατυχόντι: 'as occasion offered', as i. 122. 1. The rare infinitive after φθάσας must be for euphony; but it is natural variation.

ξυνέσεως ἀγώνισμα προσελάμβανεν: 'won the laurels for intelligence.' Cf. Kleon's words in 37. 5, 38. 4.

ῥᾷον δ' οἱ πολλοί, κ.τ.λ.: I have discussed this passage in *C.Q.* xlii, 1948, 14. The difficulty in the usual interpretation (as the scholiast's, Arnold's or Stahl's) is that ἀμαθεῖς is translated as though it were εὐηθεῖς, whereas it means 'ignorant' or 'stupid' (cf. i. 84. 3 n., iii. 37. 3, ἀμαθία μετὰ σωφροσύνης); 'most men are more readily called clever when knaves than fools when honest'. Why 'fools when honest'? To understand ὄντες with ἀμαθεῖς rather than with ἀγαθοί is not only, I think, wrong, but does not help: e.g. Forster Smith's "it is easier for rogues to get themselves called clever than for the stupid to be reputed good". Why should the stupid be thought good? Contrast Eur. *Ion*, 834–5,

> φαῦλον χρηστὸν ἂν λαβεῖν φίλον
> θέλοιμι μᾶλλον ἢ κακὸν σοφώτερον.

For once Dionysios' objections to the obscurity of this chapter (p. 893) seem justified. Krüger, followed by Steup, translates: "die meisten lassen sich aber lieber gewandte Schelme als ungebildete Biedermänner nennen"; but this requires the bracketing of ὄντες; and even so the alternative is forced: why must one choose between

378

being a clever rogue and an uneducated *Biedermann*? I propose, therefore, to insert $\H{\eta}$ after οἱ πολλοί: 'the majority of men are readily (*perhaps*, more readily than in normal times) called either clever if they are knaves or fools if they are honest.' But it must be admitted that the puzzlement of Dionysios and the imitation of Prokopios, quoted by Poppo (p. 293, 36: ῥᾷον γὰρ οἱ θρασεῖς εὔτολμοι κέκληνται ἢ οἱ προμηθεῖς ἀσφαλεῖς, borrowed as much from § 4 as from here), show that they had our MSS. text in front of them; and if, of course, we could translate οἱ πολλοὶ ῥᾷον κέκληνται, 'most men *would rather be* called' clever if rascals than stupid (as they would be called) if honest, there would be no need for emendation.[1]

The similarity with the views of Kallikles in *Gorgias* is to be noted; and compare *Republic*, iii. 409 A, quoted below on 113. 4, καὶ μὲν δή, κ.τ.λ., and Arist. *Rhet.* i. 9, quoted above on § 4.

8. πάντων δ' αὐτῶν αἴτιον ἀρχὴ ἡ διὰ πλεονεξίαν: there is no good ground for Madvig's bracketing of αἴτιον which Hude adopts, nor for Hude's own bracketing of ἡ, and some loss follows. 'The cause of it all was power pursued for the sake of greed and personal ambition'; not all ἀρχή, obviously, brings such bad results, only ἡ διὰ πλεονεξίαν, κ.τ.λ. And arising from that is the 'keenness in faction' shown when once party strife begins. τὸ πρόθυμον is illustrated particularly by the sentence παντὶ δὲ τρόπῳ - - - ἐτόλμησαν, below. For Plato, too, πλεονεξία was a chief cause of evil in public affairs: see R. G. Bury, *C.Q.*, N.S. i, 1951, 88.

ἰσονομίας - - - ἀριστοκρατίας: this is not an instance of polite terms used in place of offensive ones (here δημοκρατία and ὀλιγαρχία), as Classen and others (δημοκρατία at least was not an offensive word, any more than 'democracy' is now); rather do they describe certain conditions which ideally should accompany the two forms of government. In a democracy we ought always to see equality before the law, such as befits free citizens (πολιτικῆς), for *all* (πλήθους), and (it is implied) we must have the rule of law; in an oligarchy, the rule of the best citizens, whose guiding principle will be σωφροσύνη. We must remember that τὸ ἰσόνομον can be used of an oligarchy, provided that it is law-abiding and constitutional, and is not government by a small clique (62. 3, above, iv. 78. 3); and that ἀριστοκρατία does not describe a form of constitution, but a condition of any of the three forms, monarchy, oligarchy, or democracy, at its best (above, p. 109). Naturally democrats asserted that only in a democracy was true ἰσονομία in fact to be found, and oligarchs that only an oligarchy could ensure rule by the best. πλήθους is added because ἰσονομία might be used of an oligarchy; σώφρονος because σωφροσύνη

---

[1] Hude reports ABF as reading ῥάδιον for ῥᾷον, which, emended to ῥᾳδίως, would support my conjecture; but Stuart Jones and Powell have no mention of this.

was, so they claimed, the special oligarchic virtue—democracies, owing to the passion for equality, tending always to lawlessness (so Plato, *Rep*. viii. 557 B–563 E).

ἆθλα ἐποιοῦντο: cf. 38. 3; ii. 65. 7. The idea is continued in ἀγωνιζόμενοι.

προτιθέντες: between this, the MSS. reading, and προστιθέντες, the reading of Dionysios and of a scholiast, it is difficult to determine, and edd. are divided. For the former, cf. 40. 1, but we lack an object to the verb; for the latter, cf. 39. 7, 45. 3, viii. 17. 2, and we may take τὰς τιμωρίας as its object.

τὸ - - - ἡδονὴν ἔχον: cf. n. on ii. 53. 1.

κτώμενοι τὸ κρατεῖν: 'in their efforts to gain power.' We might take these words either with both alternatives ('grasping at power either by ... or by ...'), or with χειρί only ('either by ..., or by using violence to obtain power'); Classen–Steup argue that the latter must be correct (which would provide a case of *variatio* of prepositional phrase, μετὰ - - - καταγνώσεως, with participial: so also Ros, p. 192), because of the great inequality in length of the two clauses, ἢ - - - καταγνώσεως and ἢ χειρί, if we take κτώμενοι τὸ κρατεῖν with both. But Thucydides is not so rigid; indeed one form of *variatio* may lie in the different length of antithetical clauses (cf. vi. 17. 3, ἐκ τοῦ λέγων πείθειν ἢ στασιάζων); and we must not weaken the stress either on χειρί or on κτώμενοι τὸ κρατεῖν. ἑτοῖμοι ἦσαν, 'they were equally ready' for either method. ψήφου ἀδίκου can imply either a packed jury or a verdict clearly against the weight of the evidence, given for political reasons.

εὐσεβείᾳ: a scrupulous integrity, regard for truth, for those standards of morality which are binding (whether ordained by the gods or not, Thucydides might have said). Cf. Soph. *Phil*. 1050–2.

εὐπρεπείᾳ δὲ λόγου, κ.τ.λ.: all alike were unscrupulous, but 'those who succeeded in doing something in an odious way under cover of some fine phrase were thought of more highly'.

τὰ δὲ μέσα τῶν πολιτῶν: neutrals, who refused to take sides, not the middle classes; though, as Arnold observed, they might in fact mostly belong to the middle classes if the two opposing factions were the rich and the poor. I doubt, however, whether in most cases they could be accurately so described.

We should make the inevitable comparison with Solon's νόμος ἴδιος καὶ παράδοξος (Plut. *Sol*. 20. 1; Ἀθπ. 8. 5: see ii. 40. 2); for which see Lavagnini, *Accad. Palermo*, vi, 1945–6, pt. 2.

83. 1. κακοτροπίας: from τρόποι as the word is used in the Epitaphios, ii. 36. 4, 39. 4, 41. 2 (Classen). 'Ill manners' in the very widest sense.

τὸ εὔηθες, κ.τ.λ.: 'that simplicity in which a sense of honour has so large a part'; a definition of τὸ εὔηθες of course, not of τὸ γενναῖον.

The word is very like our 'simple' in its double sense: contrast 45. 7, and see Plat. *Rep.* iii. 400 E ((1) a polite term for ἄνοια; (2) its true and original sense, ἡ ὡς ἀληθῶς εὖ τε καὶ καλῶς τὸ ἦθος κατεσκευασμένη διάνοια), and 409 A–B (quoted below, n. on 113. 4, καὶ μὲν δή). Later in *Republic*, viii. 560 D (see n. on 82. 4, τὸ δὲ σῶφρον), Plato has καὶ τὴν μὲν αἰδῶ ἠλιθιότητα ὀνομάζοντες ὠθοῦσιν ἔξω ἀτίμως φυγάδα. With ἠφανίσθη cf. *Agamemnon*, 383–4, λακτίσαντι μέγαν Δίκας βωμὸν εἰς ἀφάνειαν.

τὸ δὲ ἀντιτετάχθαι, κ.τ.λ.: 'being in opposite ideological camps', ugly as our modern phrase is, gives a very near meaning; it is a military metaphor. τῇ γνώμῃ of course belongs with this infinitive; but I doubt whether the run of the words in Greek will allow that ἀπίστως does too, as most edd. assume. I prefer to take it with διήνεγκεν, 'so as to produce distrust everywhere'. The next sentence explains this.

2. κρείσσους δὲ ὄντες, κ.τ.λ.: there can be little doubt that Steup's interpretation is right (against Stahl and Classen): 'everybody, when they found themselves stronger than their enemies, calculating that security was not to be hoped for (from promise or oath), took precautions against injury, and were incapable of trusting anyone.' The meaning comes near to that of 82. 7, τά τε ἀπὸ τῶν ἐναντίων, κ.τ.λ.; but in that passage to get in a counterblow was more important than to have suffered no blow oneself first. Here join λογισμῷ (emphatic by position) with προυσκόπουν: they acted on the calculation that, etc., instead of relying on oath or promise. For ἐδύναντο, cf. i. 130. 1. Hobbes translates "being, the more they considered, the more desperate of assurance"; which perhaps renders the paradox of λογισμός unaccompanied by τὸ βέβαιον. Steup thinks that the similarity between this and 82. 7, and the sudden changes of thought to be found in these two chapters, are an indication that they consist of pieces written at different times.

3. τοῦ πολυτρόπου: the characteristic of Odysseus, who in fifth-century literature turned his ability as often to base ends, so that it was indistinguishable from a low cunning, as to the overcoming of varied difficulties.

For the meaning of οἱ φαυλότεροι γνώμην, see Eur. *Ion*, 834–5, quoted above on 82. 7; for their success, cf. iii. 37. 3, though it is there of a different kind, and Plat. *Apol.* 22 A; and for another use of τὸ φαῦλον in a political context, vi. 18. 6; and οἱ φαυλότατοι, 'the humblest among you', vii. 77. 2.

φθάσωσι προεπιβουλευόμενοι: Thucydides was fond of this double; cf. 112. 1, ii. 91. 1, vii. 25. 9. It was doubtless a stage on the road by which φθάνειν from meaning 'arrive first' came to its modern meaning 'arrive'.

4. καταφρονοῦντες κἂν προαισθέσθαι: for this use of καταφρονεῖν

381

edd. compare Hdt. i. 66. 1. It is not unlike that of other compounds of κατά in Thucydides, as ii. 41. 3, iii. 16. 1. For a commoner instance of the stronger despising the weaker, with disastrous results, see ii. 11. 4.

Have we in the last two sentences the conflict between two sets of rascals, the brutish and the cunning, both, that is, aiming at power διὰ πλεονεξίαν καὶ φιλοτιμίαν, or an explanation how, in a *stasis* of this kind, men of second-rate minds get the better of the intelligent, who, as intelligent men, wish to end the strife in a sensible manner (82. 5)? τὸ τῶν ἐναντίων ξυνετόν would suggest the latter, if it were not that the whole sentence from τῷ δεδιέναι explains what is passing in the mind of the φαυλότεροι; while the words ἔργῳ οὐδὲν σφᾶς δεῖν λαμβάνειν ἃ γνώμῃ ἔξεστιν certainly seem in themselves to imply that the more intelligent are equally in the game of striving for power.

In either case, but especially in the latter, though subtly observed, §§ 3–4 of this chapter form a somewhat lame conclusion to the whole of 82–83. The observations on στάσις are not rounded off; it is possible that Thucydides did not complete what he had intended to write, and certainly easy to believe that another could *think* it incomplete, and compose c. 84 as an example of what Thucydides might have and perhaps ought to have written.

84. That c. 84 is not genuine has been agreed by most. According to one scholion, it was not accepted by ancient commentators (ἐξήγηται)—this should be an early note, or the abridgement of one, for such ἐξήγησις is all early; and, negatively, it has been noted that there are no old scholia in our MSS. to interpret it; and that Dionysios, who quotes most of cc. 82 and 83 (as Thucydides' reflections on the *stasis*) in order to criticize, has no reference to 84, which, besides being part of the whole if genuine, offers many more targets for his attack. After quoting most of c. 82 and criticizing it sentence by sentence, he goes on θήσω δὲ καὶ τὰ ἑξῆς οὐδεμίαν ἔτι λέξιν ἐμαυτοῦ προστιθείς, and quotes from 82. 8, πάντων δὲ αἴτιον, to the end of 83. I do not myself doubt that it is spurious. It apparently returns to the special case of Kerkyra, only to generalize again after the first clause; and we return again to Kerkyra in 85. 1 (προυτολμήθη, 84. 1, and ὀργαῖς ταῖς πρώταις, 85. 1). Various phrases show a later date: διὰ πάθους, 'passionately' (and, as Classen says, why is this πάθος confined to the envious poor?), τῶν νόμων κρατήσασα ἡ ἀνθρωπεία φύσις (cf. 45. 7), βλάπτουσαν ἰσχύν ('injurious strength'); ἀπὸ ἴσου - - - ἐπιόντες suggests a careless copying of a Thucydidean phrase, for in Thucydides it would mean 'attacking with equal resources', but here 'not from greed, for they were as rich as their enemies'; ἀπαιδευσία ὀργῆς is from 42. 1; ἀκρατὴς μὲν ὀργῆς οὖσα, κρείσσων δὲ

382

τοῦ δικαίου is a good imitation, or a clever parody, but Thucydides wrote χρημάτων κρείσσων (ii. 60. 5); I doubt whether he would have written the other, nor ἀκρατὴς ὀργῆς; and ἀρχόμενοι - - - ὑπὸ τῶν τὴν τιμωρίαν παρασχόντων (Göller demanded παρεχόντων) seems rather an imitation of ἀπέθανον ὑπὸ τῶν λαβόντων, 81. 4, than a similar phrase by the same writer. Further, since καὶ ὁπόσα means 'and all those deeds which', with προυτολμήθη understood after καί, the deeds should be those done in Kerkyra, and we expect ἔδρασαν, ἔγνωσαν, ἐπῆλθον.

It is, however, moderately good imitation of Thucydides—not, I think, written in parody, and perhaps not with intent to deceive— and it was perhaps in its turn imitated by Josephus (ὀργῆς μὲν ἥσσων, κρείσσων δὲ τοῦ δικαίου, Ant. Iud. xvii. 8. 1), though it is by no means certain that what he imitated he found in his text of Thucydides. The supposed imitations of Dio Cassius (lii. 34. 6–8) seem to me to be commonplaces that Dio could have got from any one of a dozen writers or have thought of for himself, and to have nothing to do with this chapter; if Dio was influenced by anything in Thucydides, it was by iii. 45.

Among modern scholars who have accepted c. 84 as written by Thucydides are Schwartz, Geschichtswerk, 282–5, and Adcock (above, c. 17 n.); who take it to be a first draft, or rather the beginning of one, of which cc. 82 and 83 were a later elaboration by the historian, intended by him to take the place of 84, but the editor put in everything of Thucydides he could find. But I am not convinced. It may be a simple case of prejudging, but, quite apart from its language, when I read cc. 82–85 init. in translation without reference to the Greek, Hobbes's or Forster Smith's or Heilmann's, c. 84 seems a spurious addition simply from its contents and arrangement.

The importance of cc. 82 and 83 is so great, and Thucydides' language, clearly chosen with much care, is yet so difficult, that I have attempted a translation.

'So the savage strife proceeded, and, because this was the first example of it, it seemed even worse than it was; later, practically the whole of the Greek world was in commotion, because in every state quarrels gave occasion to the democratic leaders to ask for aid from Athens, to the oligarchs to ask Sparta. In peace time, without the excuse and indeed without the readiness to summon them ⟨they would settle their differences without fighting⟩; but in war and with an alliance at hand for either side, to injure their enemies and get more strength for themselves, requests for intervention were easily made by those ready for revolution. Many were the calamities which befell the Greek states through this civil strife: they happened then and will happen again so long as human nature remains the same, with greater or less violence and varying only according to the changing conditions in each state. In peace and in prosperous times, both states and individuals are better disposed because they are not oppressed by inescapable wants; but war, destroying the ease of everyday life, is a violent taskmaster; and assimilates most men's tempers to the conditions around them.

'So, as strife followed strife from city to city, the later outbreaks, by knowledge of what had gone before, were marked by ever increasing novelty of plan, shown both in the ingenuity of attack and in the enormity of revenge. The customary meanings of words were changed as men claimed the right to use them as they would to suit their actions: an unreasoning daring was called courage and loyalty to party, a prudent delay specious cowardice; moderation and self-control came to be reckoned but the cloak of timidity, to have an understanding of the whole to be everywhere unwilling to act. A capricious cunning was added to the brave man's portion; to deliberate for long so as to avoid mistakes was supposed a well-thought excuse for avoiding action. So the man who quarrelled was always believed, his opponent always suspect. If a man plotted and succeeded, he was intelligent; if he suspected a plot he was even cleverer; and one who took care so that neither plot nor suspicion be needed was a subverter of his party and intimidated by the other side. Applause, in a word, went to one who got in first with some evil act, and to him who cheered on another to attempt some crime that he was not thinking of. Kinship became more foreign than party, for party friends were readier for action without demur; for such associations were formed not for the sake of mutual aid under the existing laws, but for gain by illegal means. Good faith between the members of a party was secured not by the sanction of divine law so much as by partnership in crime; and as for fair offers from opponents, they were received only with precautionary *action* by the stronger party, not with candour and generosity. A man thought more of avenging an injury than of having no injury to avenge. When sworn treaties *were* agreed to, the oaths taken stood for a brief time while each party was in difficulties and had no help from outside; but in a moment, the man who plucked up courage first when he saw his enemy off his guard, was more delighted with his revenge because of the good faith broken than he would have been with an open fight—the safety of the deed was considered and, because he had won by a trick, he got the laurels for intelligence. At such times most men are readily called either, if they are knaves, clever, or fools if they are honest, and they are ashamed of the latter and glory in the former.

'The cause of it all was love of power to gratify greed and personal ambition; from that came the eagerness to quarrel which appeared once strife had begun. The leading men of either side in the cities armed themselves with fine-sounding names, equality for all free citizens or prudent government by the best, but all alike made a prize of the public interest which they pretended to be serving; and using every means in the fight to get the better of each other they boldly committed villainous outrages and took even more villainous revenge, not stopping where justice or the city's interest demanded, but limiting their actions only by their appetites; seizing power either by misuse of process of law, or by violence, all were equally ready to satisfy their immediate rivalries. Neither side made any use of honour, but if a man succeeded in accomplishing some odious deed under the cloak of a fine phrase he was the more applauded. Those citizens who were neutral were destroyed by both factions, either just because they would not take sides, or from envy because they might survive.

'Thus did every sort of evil take root in Greece, fed by these civil wars. That simplicity of which a sense of honour is so large a part was laughed out of court and disappeared; division into two hostile camps prevailed over a wide area and destroyed all trust, for no promise was strong enough, no oath awful enough, to reconcile them; all alike, when they got the upper hand, calculating that security was not to be hoped for, took precautions against danger and were incapable of trusting anyone. Men of more common mind were on the whole the survivors; for fearing their own defects and their adversaries' intelligence, afraid of getting the worse of argument and lest the others by their abundant cleverness might deal some cunning blow first, they boldly went to work with deeds. The others, contemptuously sure that they would foresee an attack and not thinking it necessary to get by force what they might secure by wit, were often caught off their guard and destroyed.'

Thucydides was deeply moved when he wrote this analysis of civil war in Greek cities, even more deeply than in the writing of the speech of the Plataians; but here, too, he will not expressly attach blame to anyone, not to one party or state rather than another, nor to any individual—not, for example, to Eurymedon by contrast with Nikostratos. It was something which happened, and which, given war and certain political conditions, we must expect to happen. The *stasis* at Kerkyra, too, like the fall of Plataia, was not an event which was decisive or even important for the outcome of the war— whether the issue was just victory for either side, or the maintenance of the Athenian empire or the liberation of Greece or the substitution of Spartan for Athenian rule; but it was important for showing what the war was like, or one aspect of it at least—how human beings behaved in such a κίνησις as the Peloponnesian war. For the history of the Archidamian war cc. 1–83 of the third book are central: of

385

this impressive section the greater part is not a tale of fighting, but of imperial politics and civil strife, told in speech and commentary; all of it concerned with morals, and in 82–83 Thucydides makes it clear where he stands. Yet some have thought that he stood, intellectually, with the outright imperialists and with those sophists among his contemporaries who denied the validity of any principle of morality but a short-sighted self-interest.

85. 1. οἱ μὲν οὖν κατὰ τὴν πόλιν Κερκυραῖοι: the phrase should distinguish them from some Kerkyraians not in the city. These should not be οἱ φεύγοντες of § 2, for that group was not yet formed, and the individuals in it had been very much involved in the strife κατὰ τὴν πόλιν. Steup would delete κατὰ τὴν πόλιν; we might perhaps transpose to after ταῖς πρώταις.

ταῖς πρώταις: 'the first in Kerkyra', by contrast with those related in iv. 46–48, or with ὕστερον δέ in § 2, below (Stahl), or 'in Kerkyra, first of any state in Greece', as ἐν τοῖς πρώτη, 82. 1 (Classen, Steup)? The last surely; ὕστερον refers to the departure of Eurymedon, and the establishment of the 500 on the opposite coast is not included amongst the manifestations of passion.

2. τῆς πέραν οἰκείας γῆς: like Mytilene, Samos, and other islands (see iv. 52, iii. 32. 2 n.), Kerkyra possessed territory on the opposite mainland, which is at no great distance—within 10 miles opposite the city, and considerably less farther north. This helps to explain the hostility of most of the Epeirote tribes to Kerkyra and their friendliness to Corinth (see Beaumont in *J.H.S.* lxxii, 1952, 63–64).

3. κρατεῖν τῆς γῆς: 'to be masters of the open country', not of the island as such, would be the natural meaning, as below; cf. 6. 2, 18. 3–5, *al.*; and Krüger was probably right to bracket τῆς γῆς.

τὴν Ἰστώνην: this mountain has not been identified, for, as B. Schmidt has argued, *Korkyräische Studien*, 61, it need not be very close to the city itself; as Thucydides mentions it, perhaps, as well-known, it may be Pantokrátor, the highest in the island, to the north of the city. (Schmidt thinks that Istone was the name of the district in the north to north-west, and would read τῆς Ἰστώνης here, as our MSS. do in iv. 46. 1.) What perhaps surprises is that the insurgents should apparently have had only one, fixed, base, though this is like the Messenians at Ithome in 464–459 (vol. i, pp. 301–2).

ἔφθειρον - - - ἐκράτουν: imperfects. The destruction and the conquest were as yet incomplete, and these actions continue till the events related in iv. 46.

86. *First Athenian Expedition to Sicily*

86. 1. τοῦ δ' αὐτοῦ θέρους τελευτῶντος: this might be the end of summer, shortly before autumn, *c.* end of August, or, as can be seen from the contrast with χειμῶνος, c. 87. 1, shortly before winter, towards the end of October. The earlier date is perhaps the more likely for an expedition to Sicily.

Λάχητα τὸν Μελανώπου: of the deme Aixone, the man well known also from Aristophanes and Plato. He was older than Sokrates, who was born in 469 (Lach. 181 D), so approaching 50 at least in 427. He was killed as a veteran at Mantineia in 418.

Χαροιάδην τὸν Εὐφιλήτου: Thucydides tells us all that we know of him, except the detail we learn from the papyrus-fragment in Florence (below, 88. 4 n.), and perhaps a mention in I.G. i.² 300₉ (Wade-Gery, J.H.S. liii, 1933, 136; S.E.G. x. 226, init.). See 90. 2.

2. οἱ γὰρ Συρακόσιοι, κ.τ.λ.: we do not know when this war had broken out.

πλὴν Καμαριναίων αἱ ἄλλαι Δωρίδες: the ancient divisions of the Greek people were still of some force; cf. vii. 57–58; but the separation from eastern Greece was becoming more important (οὐ μέντοι ξυνεπολέμησάν γε). For the exceptional Kamarina, see vi. 5. 3; and for the alliance with Sparta at the beginning of the war, ii. 7. 2 n.

κατὰ τὸ ξυγγενές: the kinship was closer than between the Dorian states, for Naxos, Leontinoi, and Rhegion had all been founded from Chalkis.

3. οἱ τῶν Λεοντίνων ξύμμαχοι: not excluding Leontinoi herself, but 'the Leontine alliance', as one body. This was the embassy on which Gorgias of Leontinoi served and made so great an impression on Athens: Plat. Hipp. mai. 282 B. Thucydides' silence is as characteristic as the enthusiasm of Timaios (if Diodoros, xii. 53–54 comes, as is probable, from him); Timaios, however, did not add anything of value to Thucydides' narrative.

κατά τε παλαιὰν ξυμμαχίαν: for the inscriptions recording the alliances with Leontinoi and Rhegion, c. 446, renewed in 433–432 (I.G. i.² 51–52, Tod, 58, 57), see vol. i, p. 198, and, more recently, the Addenda in Tod's second edition, Raubitschek, T.A.P.A. lxxv, 1944, 10. 2, and Meritt, in C.Q. xl, 1946, 85–91 (S.E.G. x, 1949, No. 48). Meritt gives important new readings, and shows that the original alliances had been 'for all time', yet were renewed in 433. See also iv. 63. 1 n. Accame, Riv. d. Filol. xxx, 1952, 127–36, puts the original treaty with Rhegion c. 460 (largely because Athens would surely not make a treaty with Egesta in western Sicily without an allied base in the straits, and the alliance with Egesta was probably made in 458–457: S.E.G. x. 7); and has other suggestions to make about the two inscriptions, I.G. i.² 51 and 52.

4. πρόπειράν τε ποιούμενοι: apparently written after the great campaign of 415–413, as most scholars suppose. Yet it is to be observed that the sparse details of the campaign given in cc. 88, 90, 99, 103 are

clearly, I think, related as Thucydides heard of them at the time (see 90. 1 n.)—they at least are not retold in the light of later events. I am not sure that πρόπειρα does not point only to the greater expedition of Eurymedon and Sophokles in 425–424.

5. τὸν πόλεμον ἐποιοῦντο: the story is renewed in c. 88.

87. Return of the Pestilence to Athens

87. 2. ἐπίεσε καὶ ἐκάκωσε τὴν δύναμιν: 'oppressed them and weakened their military strength', i.e. demoralized them and caused great loss in man-power. For the MSS. support of the reading ἐπίεσε καί, see Powell's crit. n.; it should, however, be observed that the following sentence refers strictly only to the loss in man-power. See also J. v. Straub, Philol. lxx, 1911, pp. 565–9.

Ullrich, Beiträge, 90–92, argued that δύναμις here must include other forms of military strength (finance, ships, allies) even though the pestilence did not directly affect them, and that, since the Sicilian expedition caused greater loss on the whole (vii. 87. 4–6, viii. 1. 2; cf. vi. 26. 2), this chapter must have been written before 415; Classen–Steup agree. I do not find this argument convincing: no single disaster in fact caused such weakening of spirit (Ullrich and Classen–Steup did not read ἐπίεσε καί in their texts) and such loss in man-power, not even the Sicilian expedition; but this does not prove that Ullrich's conclusion is not right.

3. ἐκ τῶν τάξεων: this should, and doubtless does, mean, 'from the hoplite ranks', i.e. 4,400 out of about 13,000 men (ii. 13. 6 n.), a loss of one in three, slightly higher than that of the cavalry, 300 out of 1,000. Most take ἐκ τῶν τάξεων, arbitrarily, to mean ἐκ τοῦ καταλόγου, i.e. from all liable to serve, and those liable to serve at home as reserve, as well as in the field, i.e. a loss of 4,400 out of c. 18,000. See ii. 13. 7, iv. 94. 1 nn.; and Pop. of Athens, p. 6.

τοῦ δὲ ἄλλου ὄχλου ἀνεξεύρετος ἀριθμός: metics, foreigners, women and children, slaves (both men and women); the number never ascertained because there was no muster of them all, and so no countable gaps in their ranks, strange as this appears in a case which so greatly affected the number available for the navy, and in general that of all citizens; cf. J.H.S. lxvi, 1946, 129. One might suppose that the losses among the poorer citizens and foreigners and the slaves were even heavier, because their living conditions, especially at this time, would be worse; and the same may be true of the women, less well fed, and the younger children, naturally weaker (but see above, p. 153). The mortality must have been very high; and the loss among citizen women and children will have affected the size of the citizen body for a generation at least to come.

It is characteristic of the loose conventional use of figures by later writers, and especially of μύριοι (cf. p. 128 of my n. in *J.H.S.*, above), that Diodoros, xii. 58. 2, presumably from Ephoros (cf. ii. 13. 6 n., above, p. 38), has 'over 4,000 hoplites, 400 cavalry, and of the rest, free and slave, ὑπὲρ τοὺς μυρίους'. He is, if anything, exaggerating; but the losses of the last group must have amounted to near 70,000 or 80,000.

4. οἱ πολλοὶ σεισμοὶ τότε τῆς γῆς: this winter was *known* for the number of its earthquakes. "So one might say, when relating the events of the year 1746, 'this was the period of *the famous* great frost' " (Arnold); or 'this was the Olympic meeting at which Dorieus of Rhodes won his second victory' (8. 1).

Does Thucydides imply any connexion between the frequency of these earthquakes and the war? See i. 23. 3 n. The brevity with which they are referred to suggests perhaps that he is dismissing a popular view; but I feel that the detailed description and explanation of the great tidal wave immediately below, c. 89, was not written at the same time as this note. See 89. 1 n.

88. *Athenians in Sicily attack the Lipara Is. without success*

F. Gr. Hist. iii B, 577 (Philistos?)

88. 1. τριάκοντα ναυσί: see 86. 1, Rhegion presumably contributing ten. See n. on § 3, below.

τὰς Αἰόλου νήσους: see Strabo, vi. 2. 10, p. 275.

δι' ἀνυδρίαν: this illustrates, briefly but clearly, one of the chief purposes of the chronological system of summers and winters: it shows the military conditions. See Ziegler in *R.E.* xiii. 1 (1926), 720.

2. οὐ μεγάλη: but the biggest of them.

3. ἐν τῇ Ἱερᾷ: the island now called Volcano. Today, of course, the visible fire is from Stromboli (Strongyle), not from Volcano.

Σικελῶν καὶ Μεσσηνίων: i.e. the north coast.

4. ἀπέπλευσαν: a singularly unimpressive end to an unimportant expedition.

The similarity between much of this chapter and Pausanias, x. 11. 3-4, and the fact that Pausanias gives Antiochos of Syracuse (F 1) as the source for one detail at least, have led K. J. Dover, *Maia*, vi, 1953, 8-9, to conjecture that Antiochos was Thucydides' source not only for the geographical and demographic details here given, but for his account of the Athenian campaign in Sicily. But it is not at once apparent that Thucydides here, contrary to his practice everywhere else when narrating contemporary events, was using a written source. See also 90. 1 n.

The interesting papyrus-fragment of a history published first by Coppola, and more fully by Bartoletti, *P.D.S.I.* xii, 1950, No. 1283 (see *F. Gr. Hist.*, No. 577, F 2), gives the story of this expedition with more detail about its circumstances than we find in Thucydides. Laches and Charoiades had apparently been campaigning separately, Laches off Kamarina (by arrangement, with a naval command), Charoiades off Megara on the east coast of Sicily. The latter was mortally wounded in an engagement with the Syracusans, in which apparently the Athenians had some losses in ships. Laches then rejoined this squadron, and the whole force, together with ten ships from Rhegion (above, § 1 n.), attacked Lipara. Soon after their failure there, Laches invaded and ravaged part of the territory of Lokroi, and apparently, on withdrawing, met a small Lokrian squadron and inflicted on it some loss. This last incident is not mentioned by Thucydides; it may be the one narrated by Diodoros, xii. 54. 4, though his narrative is (as usual) confused. The skirmishes at the Kaïkinos and the Alex rivers (Thuc. 103. 3 and 99) are told in the reverse order.

The author of this small fragment has been confidently said to be Philistos; and this is possible enough, though there is nothing in it characteristic of an imitator of Thucydides. Jacoby is doubtful; and we should remember how many histories were written of which we have no record. This one clearly gave the story of this campaign in greater detail than Thucydides; but even so we cannot be quite sure that the fragment even comes from a Σικελιῶτις ἱστορία. If the writer is accurate, Thucydides has made some small blunders, and has not consistently fulfilled his promise (90. 1).

YEAR 6: 426–425 B.C. (CC. 89–116)

89. *Abortive Peloponnesian Invasion of Attica. Tidal Wave at Orobiai*

89. 1. τοῦ δ' ἐπιγιγνομένου θέρους: presumably at the usual time for such invasions, mid-May or a little earlier (ii. 19. 1 n.). Nothing of note had happened earlier this year.

Ἄγιδος τοῦ Ἀρχιδάμου: see 26. 2 n.

σεισμῶν δὲ γενομένων πολλῶν: clearly the same *series* as that mentioned above, 87. 4; but the two passages are but indifferently combined. The final revision is lacking.

καὶ οὐκ ἐγένετο ἐσβολή: this seems almost like an omen of Agis' unsuccessful career. Another Spartan, Melanchridas the nauarchos, was even more unfortunate, for he was given no further chance of fulfilling his ambitions, but disappeared from history as soon as he first appeared: viii. 6. 5. Cf. also vi. 95. 1.

We must not attribute *all* these failures to superstition, still less the postponement of a meeting of the ekklesia because of earthquake (v. 45. 4); earthquakes can be destructive. On the other hand, it would not seem, from Thucydides' careful description of tidal action of the sea on this occasion, that there was any great destruction, nor that within his lifetime any very disastrous earthquake occurred, in spite of what he says in i. 23. 3.

The well-known lines in *The Acharnians*, 652–4,

διὰ ταῦθ' ὑμᾶς Λακεδαιμόνιοι τὴν εἰρήνην προκαλοῦνται
καὶ τὴν Αἴγιναν ἀπαιτοῦσιν· καὶ τῆς νήσου μὲν ἐκείνης
οὐ φροντίζουσ', ἀλλ' ἵνα τοῦτον τὸν ποιητὴν ἀφέλωνται,

have been considered by many to refer to a specific offer of peace made by Sparta about this time (nine months or so before the production of the play) or later this summer. "The ephors", says Adcock (after Beloch), "took advantage of an earthquake ... to open negotiations for peace"; and the proposals may have taken the form of a return to the Thirty Years' Peace. This, of course, would have conceded the victory to Athens—it was what Perikles had wanted to fight for; but it would, incidentally as it were, have involved the restitution of Aigina to the Aiginetans (*C.A.H.* v. 226–7). Busolt, iii. 1079. 5, would put the offer in the autumn after the Peloponnesian defeat in Amphilochia; and he notes that Dikaiopolis likes the idea of a thirty years' peace (ll. 194–7). Some such proposals may have been made at some time not long before the end of 426; but I would not agree with Adcock that "the sanguine and violent popular leaders found it easy to arouse the spirit of the demos, and the Lacedaemonians were dismissed with contumely. It is significant that Thucydides does not think it worth while even to mention these proposals which were rejected as soon as they were made." It is easier to suppose that, with the return of Pleistoanax (v. 16. 3 n.), there was some unofficial 'kite-flying', much hinting of peace in Sparta and Corinth, with 'back to the Thirty Years' Peace' as a general basis, rather than an embassy with specific proposals; and it would be Athenians, not Peloponnesians, who would point out that 'back to 445' involved the withdrawal of the Athenian settlers in Aigina. Either that, or in answer to unofficial peace-feelers from Athens, the Peloponnesians were saying, 'we cannot make peace unless Aigina is restored to its rightful citizens'; or were reported in Athens to be saying this. It is even possible that the reference is to the abortive negotiations of 430 (ii. 59. 2), when Athens asked for peace, and the Peloponnesians perhaps replied, 'Yes, if you will give up Aigina altogether, end the blockade of Megara, etc., etc.'.

I agree with Rennie (n. ad loc.) that v. 654 "must be the merest *jeu d'esprit*. The poet ... must have had some connexion with Aegina ... it would be a fair assumption, in Comedy, that he would go with the island" (only the poet was Aristophanes, not Kallistratos).

2. τῆς Εὐβοίας ἐν 'Οροβίαις: this small place, which was not a πόλις but in the territory of Histiaia, has kept to this day its ancient name

(in the form 'Ροβιές). It was on the coast of the Atalante channel, opposite Atalante island. Athena, goddess of Athens, had a precinct there in the days of the empire: $I.G.$ i.[2] 376 (see Raubitschek, $Hesp.$ xii, 1943, No. 6).

ἐπανελθοῦσα: a correction, and a proper one, of the MSS. ἐπελθοῦσα, based on the scholion, ἐπανελθοῦσα ἡ θάλασσα μέρος ἀπὸ τῆς τότε οὔσης γῆς ἐπῆλθε καὶ κατέλαβε, and adopted by all edd., including those who in other places, e.g. ii. 96. 1, use scholia of this kind as evidence that words in them were not in the original text.

τὸ δ' ὑπενόστησε: the use of τό - - - τό certainly makes it probable that ἡ θάλασσα is the subject of both verbs, 'flooded in one direction, and withdrew in another' (as ὑπονοστήσαντος τοῦ ποταμοῦ, Hdt. i. 191. 3); but the consequence, 'there is now sea where there was once land', suggests that the second clause means 'there was a subsidence of the land' (as a stack of wood 'settles' ὑπὸ τῶν χειμώνων, Hdt. iv. 62. 2).

3. Ἀταλάντην: for this islet (which has also kept its name) and the Athenian fort on it, see ii. 32.

4. ἐν Πεπαρήθῳ: one of the group of islands north-east of Euboea, the modern Skopelos: $A.T.L.$ i, Gazetteer.

5. ἐπισπωμένην: I believe Stuart Jones is right in keeping the MSS. reading here, with ἀποστέλλειν intransitive (if this is not only a colloquial use: cf. Dem. xxxii. 5) and τὴν θάλασσαν subject of both infinitives, instead of ἐπισπώμενον, from the scholiast (Madvig, Hude) or ἐπισπωμένης (coni. Meineke; Stahl, Classen), with τὸν σεισμόν as the subject. Herwerden's objection that with τὴν θάλασσαν as subject we must have τὴν ἐπίκλυσιν ποιεῖσθαι is not conclusive; apart from cases of the active of ποιεῖν such as ii. 15. 2 ad fin., it is correct that the sea 'causes the flood' (ἐ. ποιεῖν); ἐ. ποιεῖσθαι is 'to be in flood', and would more naturally be used of a river than of the sea.

ἄνευ δὲ σεισμοῦ: the tidal waves are natural phenomena, not sent specially by a god called Poseidon.

For another, apparently even more serious earthquake, accompanied by flooding from the sea, in this same region, see Demetrios Kallatianos, $F. Gr. Hist.$ 85 F 6 (ap. Strabo, i. 3. 20, p. 60); Capelle in $R.E.$, s.v. 'Erdbebenforschung', suppl. vol. iv. 348. 25.

90. Further Fighting in Sicily

90. 1. ἐπολέμουν μὲν καὶ ἄλλοι: I would adopt Poppo's ἄλλα for ἄλλοι (Böhme, Stahl, Classen); for there is no one to whom ἄλλοι can refer. Steup's objections seem insufficient, and i. 65. 2 a sufficient parallel.

αὐτοὶ οἱ Σικελιῶται, κ.τ.λ.: as later, iv. 25. 12.

ἃ δὲ λόγου μάλιστα ἄξια: Dover (above, 88. 4 n.) thinks that this implies that a more copious history was already written (Antiochos' Σικελιῶτις συγγραφή); but I doubt it. See above, 86. 4 n.

2. Χαροιάδου γὰρ ἤδη - - - τεθνηκότος - - - πολέμῳ: when we note what events in this Sicilian fighting Thucydides did choose to relate as among 'the most important', it is surprising that the skirmish in which Charoiades fell is not one of them. See above, 88. 4 n.

Μυλάς: on the site of Milazzo, on the north coast.

δύο φυλαί: as was frequent in Greek cities, the military organization was based on the civil, and members of one *phyle* formed a regiment. Cf. for Athens and Syracuse, vi. 98. 4, 100. 1. We do not, however, know the number of *phylai* at Messene.

The story of this campaign is resumed in c. 99. For a reference to it in the newly discovered papyrus-fragment perhaps to be attributed to Philistos, see Bartoletti, *Pap. Soc. Ital.* xii, 1950, fasc. 2; *F. Gr. Hist.*, No. 577. See also 103. 3 n.

91. *Athenian Expeditions round Peloponnese, against Melos, and to Tanagra*

91. 1. Δημοσθένης: the first mention of this famous man.

Προκλῆς: killed later in the year, 98. 4. Nothing more is known of him.

The story of this expedition begins in c. 94. It presumably set sail just before that of Nikias to Melos.

ἐς Μῆλον: see ii. 8. 4 n. This was a considerable force, and Nikias does little with it (R. Cohen, in *Mél. Glotz*, 1932, 227–39). We may note, too, Nikias' connexion with the 'expansionist' policy at sea in this campaign (ii. 65. 7 n., and my article in *J.H.S.* lxxi, 1951, 75–80).

Νικίας: he had been strategos the year before too, c. 51.

2. ὄντας νησιώτας: Athenian claims on all islands are put at greater length in the Melian dialogue, v. 97, 99. Cf. also iv. 121. 2 n. (In Stuart Jones's text ἐς τὸ αὐτῶν ξυμμαχικόν should be read, with Krüger's αὐτῶν an emendation—an unnecessary one—as quoted in crit. n.)

3. τῆς Γραϊκῆς: see ii. 23. 3 n. The schol. here implies this reading by the note, ταύτην τὴν Τάναγραν Ὅμηρος (*Il.* ii. 498) Γραῖαν καλεῖ.

4. Ἱππονίκου τοῦ Καλλίου: the well-known, very rich Hipponikos, whose father had been ambassador to Sparta in 446–445 (i. 115. 1 n.); only here mentioned in Thucydides. According to Ps.-Andokides, iv. 13 (a very unimpressive authority), he was killed as a strategos at Delion. This presumably is only a confusion with Hippokrates (iv. 101. 2); certainly Athenaios, v. 218 b, knew nothing of it, who says only that from Eupolis' *Kolakes* (fr. 154) it was clear that Hipponikos had died shortly before 422.

If his wife, the mother of the younger Kallias (Plat. *Protag.* 314 E; *Apol.* 20 A), was married to him before she married Perikles and became the mother of Xanthippos and Paralos (Plut. *Per.* 24. 8),

Hipponikos himself must have been well over 50 in 426, for Xanthippos was already married when he died in the pestilence in 430-429 (Plut. *Per.* 36. 2)—Kallias therefore at least 26 or 27, and Hipponikos at least 55, in 430. (A man over 50 was not called for military service abroad unless he was strategos.)

Alkibiades married Hipponikos' daughter, Hipparete, Plut. *Alkib.* 8. 3; but that did not prevent him from spending more than his income.

5. ἐν τῇ Τανάγρᾳ: Tanagra was not more than 18 km. west of Oropos, by an easy road; and the Athenians will not have gone so far, but into the territory of Tanagra only, not far from the scene of the later battle of Delion. Indeed this whole episode seems to anticipate the campaign of 424, except in its outcome; with more modest aims, the co-operation of Nikias with Hipponikos and Eurymedon was more successful than Demosthenes and Hippokrates were. Not much indeed was gained; but this whole chapter, though not a chronicle of victory, relates a sensible use of sea-power, directed both against Sparta (who could not intervene to help Melos) and more particularly Sparta's allies.

6. τῆς Λοκρίδος τὰ ἐπιθαλάσσια: cf. ii. 26, 32.

92-93. *Lacedaemonian Colony in Trachinia*

92. 1. ὑπὸ δὲ τὸν χρόνον τοῦτον: this event interrupts the account of Athenian naval measures, 91 and 94, clearly for chronological reasons; it followed immediately Nikias' raid in Lokris (Classen). But does this mean Spartan resolve or Spartan action? It would take some time to collect settlers and arrange all matters for the colony; probably the resolution had already been taken and a beginning with the new colony was made soon after the departure of Demosthenes and of Nikias from Athens (91. 1).

2. Μηλιῆς: the inhabitants of the lower valley of the Spercheios and of some heights to the south of it; but their boundaries are unknown—cf. 93, 2, n. on ὧν ἐπὶ τῇ γῇ ἐκτίζετο. See Béquignon, *La Vallée du Spercheios,* pp. 158-67; Grundy, *Great Persian War,* c. vii. The area of the valley here has been much altered by the great advance of the coastline eastwards since the fifth century B.C., and the change in the course of the Spercheios river.

Ἰριῆς: their exact location is unknown. They owe this spelling not to the MSS. of Thucydides but to those of Steph. Byz. (see Bursian, *Geographie,* i. 95); on which see 101. 2 n.

ὑπὸ Οἰταίων: indicated as living in the mountains to the south of the Trachinioi by Herodotos, vii. 217. 1 (unless Herodotos here means that the famous path in its course up the Asopos gorge divided the mountains belonging to the Oitaioi to the west from those belonging to the Trachinioi to the east, because Melian territory extended east-wards as far as Alpenos of the Lokrians, 216; it looks like it, but would be confusing, for the old, like the new city, of the Trachinioi was to the west of the Asopos, and above it were the Trachinian cliffs: see below, on § 6).

For a further account of the Trachinian mountains, see A. R. Burn in *Studies Presented to D. M. Robinson*, i. 480–9.

δείσαντες δὲ μὴ οὐ σφίσι πιστοὶ ὦσι: like so many who distrusted Athens, they found Sparta a worse master in the end.

Τεισαμενόν: another case of a name in Thucydides, without further significance.

3. Δωριῆς: to the south of the Oitaioi, at the head-waters of the Boeotian Kephissos. Cf. i. 107. 2 n.

4. ἐπί τε γὰρ τῇ Εὐβοίᾳ ναυτικόν, κ.τ.λ.: quite suddenly Sparta shows initiative. Clearly she was beginning to understand that her annual invasions of Attica would not end the war—just then she would understand it particularly well, because doubtless one reason for giving up the invasion this year after the earthquake (89. 1) was a lack of all enthusiasm for it even in good weather; but instead of looking round for some means of making peace, she thinks of attack by sea and of a distant expedition by land. Clearly we can see the mind of Brasidas behind this; but Thucydides does not here say so, even with λέγεται, as in 79. 3, nor mark the occasion as at all ex-ceptional.

The new colony did in fact serve as Brasidas' starting-point (iv. 78. 1; cf. v. 12. 1); and it may be noted that Doris too is on the route to Thessaly from the Corinthian gulf via Amphissa.

5. Ἀχαιῶν: presumably because of their ambiguous attitude at the beginning of the war, ii. 9. 2. They seem to have been admitted later, but unwisely, if the Achaioi who betrayed the colony in 408–407 (Xen. *Hell.* i. 2. 18) are from the Peloponnese.

ἔστιν ὧν ἄλλων ἐθνῶν: for example the Akarnanians (except Oiniadai). Ἀλκίδας: doubtless the discredited nauarchos of the Ionian and Kerkyra expeditions, rewarded with an easy post in the aristocratic manner: perhaps as a compromise between Brasidas and his political enemies. The choice was not likely to make the new colony popular; but any Spartiate, it was supposed, would do. Cf. iv. 132. 3, n. on τοῖς ἐντυχοῦσιν.

6. ἐκ καινῆς, ἣ νῦν Ἡράκλεια καλεῖται: in itself this would not neces-sarily mean that the site of the new city was different from the old, only that the fortifications were renewed, and perhaps enlarged, and the name changed; but the careful geographical details that follow suggest a new site. Cf. Hermippos, fr. 70, εἶδον οὖν τὴν Ἡράκλειαν καὶ μάλ' ὡραίαν πόλιν (ap. Athen. xi. 461 E, who points out that this Herakleia is meant).

395

ἀπέχουσα Θερμοπυλῶν, κ.τ.λ.: unfortunately we do not know what part of the pass Thucydides means, and since the pass itself is about 35 stades long, this is important in a matter of 40 stades. If, as seems likely, Thermopylai, when used precisely, meant the hot springs (cf. Hdt. vii. 176. 2), a point 40 stades to the west, or better, west by south, on the foothills below the Trachinian cliffs, is still just east of the Asopos river; 40 stades from the narrow part of the pass, west of the springs, where the Phocian wall had been, is just west of the Asopos. See next n.

τῆς δὲ θαλάσσης εἴκοσι: Strabo, ix. 4. 17, p. 429, is quoted as saying 40 stades; but he is speaking of a different harbour, by Thermopylai itself, with a sanctuary of Demeter where the Amphiktyons met. Thucydides clearly means to show the distance between Herakleia's city-wall and her own νεώρια. Now, as is well known, the sea is a long way, as much as 70 stades, from the site of Herakleia, and 35 to 40 stades from Thermopylai itself. (Stählin, in R.E., s.v. 'Thermopylai', 2409, says that Thucydides' figure is too low, the sea being at least 4.8 km. from Herakleia (20 stades being a little less than 4 km.); but we are not sure where the coastline was in the fifth century, nor of the extent of the city-walls.)

The most careful description of the country around Trachis, and of the possible sites of old Trachis and of Herakleia, are to be found in Grundy's Great Persian War and Béquignon (above, § 2), 244–62; but though traces of walls and pottery have been found the sites are not precisely known; and, unfortunately, it is difficult to follow the latter's argument, for his maps are almost illegible. Below the precipitous Trachinian cliffs there are low, gently sloping, cultivated foothills to the west (below the railway station called Arpenoi), about 150 feet above the Spercheios level, with a lower shelf to the north about 50 feet above the valley, and descending gradually as you go east, towards Thermopylai, across the Dyras, Melas, and Asopos rivers near where they issue from deep gorges in the cliffs. Trachis, according to Herodotos, vii. 198–9, was situated between the two last-named rivers; and Mycenaean pottery of the thirteenth century has been found recently in that area (it will be remembered that Trachis is mentioned in the Catalogue), though at Vardátes, a village nearer the Melas river (the modern Xeriás) than to the Asopos, and thus a good deal farther from Thermopylai. Béquignon thinks that the site of old Trachis, on this hilly ground, was used as the akropolis of the new city, and that the lower town spread northwards or north-eastwards into the plain where traces of walls have been found and pottery of the fifth and fourth centuries. The question cannot be finally settled till further excavations can be made— we need, for example, the confirmation of classical remains too on the site of old Trachis.

εἶρξαν τὸ κατὰ Θερμοπύλας: all edd. since Classen have accepted this reading (from E) against ἤρξαντο κατὰ Θ. (cett.), which by itself is clearly impossible; but the result is not satisfactory. Classen himself says that with E's text we get "die Erwähnung eines Umstandes, der in dem Zusammenhang der Sache aufs beste begründet ist. Gerade gegen die feindlichen Thessaler welche die Ansiedlung ungern sahen, musste Vorkehr getroffen werden, und diese konnte in nichts anderm bestehen, als in dem, was in alten Zeiten die Phokier, als sie noch im Besitz dieser Landschaft waren, gethan hatten: ἔδειμαν τὸ τεῖχος δείσαντες, ἐπεὶ Θεσσαλοὶ ἦλθον ἐκ Θεσπρωτῶν οἰκήσοντες γῆν τὴν Αἰολίδα τήν περ νῦν ἐκτέαται. ἅτε δὴ πειρωμένων τῶν Θεσσαλῶν καταστρέφεσθαί σφεας, τοῦτο προεφυλάξαντο οἱ Φωκέες, Hdt. vii. 176. 4".

True; but of course the Phokians εἶρξαν τὸ κατὰ Θερμοπύλας from the other side, the east, against the Thessalian threat from the west end of the pass, just as the Greeks did against Xerxes; and Herakleia is to the west and can only have "blocked the pass" against the friendly Lokroi, not against the hostile Thessalians. What Sparta had done by the new walls (or rather, hoped to do) was to secure Thermopylai, that is, the easiest passage from central to northern Greece and Macedonia, for herself, and at the same time remove any threat from Thessaly against her allies, Lokrians, Phokians, and Boeotians (cf. ii. 22. 2 n.); this would increase the hostility of the Thessalians, but the barrier against them would be not at Thermopylai, but to the north of Herakleia, say at the Spercheios, the crossing of which considerable river might have been barred. Should we read ἤρξαντο ⟨τὸ⟩ κατὰ Θ. ⟨ἀποικοδομεῖν⟩?

By what route Brasidas reached Herakleia (iv. 78. 1) we are not told—probably by land all the way, since he had concentrated his forces at Corinth and Megara was now safe, by Megara, Thebes, Elateia, and Thermopylai. Even if he crossed the gulf from Corinth to Krisa, and went thence by Amphissa into Doris (§ 3, above), he may still have made the detour by Elateia and Thermopylai rather than have gone by the difficult pass due north from Doris and just east of the Asopos gorge.

It was surely this pass, by the way (which covered the Anopaia path as well against an enemy from the north), which the Phokians were intended to guard in 480, not the Anopaia alone. Munro, in C.A.H. iv. 293, chooses, like most historians, the latter alternative, and puts the Lokrians in Trachis to control the pass up the Asopos valley. Apart from the fact that Herodotos, vii. 201–3, leaves it doubtful whether the Persians or the Greeks actually occupied Trachis at the beginning of the fighting at Thermopylai, a force within the walls of Trachis could not 'control' the pass east of the Asopos, especially against a force as large as that of Xerxes. The Persians needed only to send one force to contain Trachis, and another, equally small, to contain the Phokians on the Anopaia, and could have marched without opposition up the gorge southward to the upper Kephissos valley in Doris. What the Phokians did when Hydarnes apparently threatened to do just this was to retreat to the most defensible part of the pass, and thereby open the little-used and forgotten path by Anopaia.

93. 1. ἐπὶ τῇ Εὐβοίᾳ μάλιστα: it took the Athenians a long time to appreciate the threat to their positions in Thrace. See nn. on iv. 7, 78. 1.

Kenaion is the extreme north-western peninsula of Euboea: Strabo, x. 1. 2, p. 444; '70 stades from Thermopylai', ix. 4. 17, p. 429, 5. 13, p. 435 (considerably less than the true distance). There was a temple of Zeus there, known to Athenians, Soph. *Trach.* 237–8. **οὐ γὰρ ἐγένετο ἀπ' αὐτῆς δεινὸν οὐδέν:** i.e. against Euboea, and against the land neighbours of Herakleia. Here Thucydides himself seems to be forgetting the πάροδος to Thrace.

2. αἴτιον δὲ ἦν, κ.τ.λ.: many edd., Stahl, Böhme, Classen, Steup, by punctuating with a colon after ἦν and no comma after χωρίων, make οἵ τε Θεσσαλοί, κ.τ.λ. an independent clause, and οἱ Θ. the subject of the whole sentence down to πάνυ πολλούς; ὧν dependent, like χωρίων, on ἐν δυνάμει ὄντες; and τε in οἵ τε Θ. answered by μέντοι of the next sentence—'for Thucydides must have had in mind at the beginning the two main causes of the failure, Thessalian hostility and the incompetence of the Spartan commanders'. I am sure that, if this is in general the right construction, Cobet was correct in bracketing ἦν (though there was no need for him to insist on a following γάρ, οἱ γὰρ Θ., in place of the unoffending τε): cf. τεκμήριον δέ, ii. 15. 4, ii. 50. 2; αἴτιον δὲ τούτων, Dem. viii. 32; τὸ δ' αἴτιον τούτου τόδε, Plat. *Theait.* 150 C; I am even surer that Stuart Jones was right to take ὧν ἐπὶ τῇ γῇ ἐκτίζετο, with the scholiast, as ἐκεῖνοι ὧν, κ.τ.λ., parallel with οἱ Θεσσαλοί; for, with both genitives dependent on ἐν δυνάμει ὄντες (as Stahl and others), what is the distinction between τὰ ταύτῃ χωρία and ὧν ἐπὶ τῇ γῇ ἐ.? Clearly Thucydides says that both the dominant Thessalians and the tribes in whose immediate neighbourhood the new colony was planted kept up an unremitting hostility (as v. 51. 1). τε may, however, still connect with μέντοι, not with this καί.

It is not clear, however, how Stuart Jones understood the construction of the whole sentence in putting no stop after ἦν and a comma after χωρίων: presumably the first clause is to be taken like iv. 26. 5, αἴτιον ἦν followed by noun and participle, and the second, though connected with the first by τε - - - καί, continues, by a harsh anacoluthon with principal verbs instead of participles (so Matthiae, quoted by Spratt); the anacoluthon is harsh, because it makes (ἐκεῖνοι) ὧν ἐπὶ τῇ γῇ ἐκτίζετο alone the subject of ἔφθειρον, ἐπολέμουν, and ἐξετρύχωσαν, to the exclusion of οἱ Θ., which, in point of sense, is clearly not meant; moreover, 'the cause' was not the Thessalian influence in these parts, but their active hostility. There is, therefore, much in favour of Spratt's suggestion, αἴτιον δὲ ἦν ὅτι Θ. (omitting οἵ τε); only I would prefer ὅτι Θ. οἵ τε—not all Thessalians by any means, but the southern states (cf. v. 51. 1, ii. 101. 2). By this the connexion between τε and μέντοι, in itself desirable, is lost; and perhaps Cobet's suggestion (but with οἵ τε Θ. ⟨οἱ⟩) is best.

ὧν ἐπὶ τῇ γῇ ἐκτίζετο: i.e. Ainianes, Dolopes, and Melieis; see v. 51. 1–2. But, of the Melieis, presumably the Trachinioi (93. 2) are not here included, though they may already have been hostile in 420. We should note that this Thessalian hostility to the Spartan colony did not prevent an important faction from supporting Brasidas in 424. See iv. 78. 3 n.

γενομένους τὸ πρῶτον καὶ πάνυ πολλούς: Ps.-Skymnos, 597, and Diodoros, xii. 59. 3–5, both probably from Ephoros, say they were 10,000 in number, Diodoros with the refinement that 4,000 of them were Peloponnesians and 6,000 from the rest of Greece; but Ephoros is not to be trusted in these matters, and the figure is almost certainly much too high—it would mean that Herakleia was one of the largest states in Greece. See Béquignon, 253.

Λακεδαιμονίων οἰκιζόντων: the old confidence in Sparta took a long time to die, and was only succeeded, before and after 404, by fear.

τὰ πράγματά τε ἔφθειρον: I would suggest ἔφθειραν here, as κατέστησαν, and by contrast with the very clear imperfect ἔφθειρον above. But see Ros, pp. 320, 324.

χαλεπῶς τε: I incline to think that χαλεπῶς should be taken with ἐκφοβήσαντες, with post-position of τε, and ἐξηγούμενοι, more narrowly, of military leadership—'by terrorizing the majority (of the citizens) with their harsh treatment and by some failures in command'.

In any case οὐ καλῶς probably means 'unsuccessfully', rather than 'dishonourably'.

This is one of the occasions on which Thucydides carries the story beyond the chronological order, certainly to 420 (v. 51–52. 1), perhaps to 413 (viii. 3. 1). The date of composition is of some importance, for the note about the later history of Herakleia does not look especially like an addition to the rest.

94–98. *Demosthenes in Leukas and in Aitolia, where he is defeated*

94. 1. ἐν Ἑλλομενῷ τῆς Λευκαδίας: Λευκαδίας is the reading of E, the rest have Ἀρκαδίας, which is clearly impossible. But I am not confident that Λευκαδίας is right: περὶ Πελοπόννησον ὄντες may be

399

a temporal participle, and therefore Ellomenos in the Peloponnese (we have no evidence for it anywhere), and ἐπὶ Λευκάδα is to me suspicious after Λευκαδίας: had Thucydides meant that after a raid on one part of the island the Athenians made a major attempt to capture the capital, he would have written ἐπὶ τὴν πόλιν and probably have added αὐτήν; he would also, I believe, have written 'E. τῆς Λευκάδος on his first mention of the island. K. J. Dover, in an article on the Palatine MS., C.Q. iv, 1954, 76–83, defends Λευκαδίας, as well as other independent readings of E. If this is right, Leukadia is probably the peraia of Leukas (above, ii. 30. 1 n.). Cf. iv. 42. 3 crit. n.

The last attack on Leukas was the unsuccessful one by Phormion's son, 7. 4–5. There had been an attempt on Oiniadai at the same time.

Κερκυραίων πέντε καὶ δέκα ναυσίν: probably as many as they could successfully man and afford to send abroad after the recent fighting and in the existing conditions (85).

2. ἐν ᾗ καὶ ἡ Λευκάς ἐστι: for a description of the isthmus joining the 'island' to the mainland, see Leake, iii. 10-23, and the map in Arnold's edition; and Strabo, x. 2. 8, pp. 451–2.

ἀποτειχίζειν: to cut off by a wall; but in this case by a complete circumvallation (95. 2).

ῥᾳδίως γ' ἂν - - - καὶ πόλεως: this adoption of the reading of C ⟨G⟩ by Hude and Stuart Jones, in place of ῥᾳδίως τ' ἂν - - - πόλεως τε, seems to me a mistake. γε has no place here; and the change from καί to the second τε is unexplained, whereas the reverse change is easily understood once the first τε had been misread as γε. 'It would both be an *easy* matter to conquer the place, and success would get rid of an inveterate enemy.'

3. στρατιᾶς τοσαύτης ξυνειλεγμένης: without the Akarnanians it was by no means a large force, and not particularly select; and clearly the Messenians ought from the first to have reckoned with a refusal by the Akarnanians. Even the addition of the Lokrians (95. 3) would not make it exceptionally big. Cf. 98. 4, n. on βέλτιστοι δὴ ἄνδρες. See also 102. 6 n.

Ἠπειρωτικὸν τὸ ταύτῃ: I agree with all those who would spell ἠπειρωτικόν with a small initial; τὸ ταύτῃ is sufficient to show that it is not a proper name here. (It may be only a misprint in Stuart Jones; cf. 102. 6). It is difficult to see what part of the mainland is meant: for Aitolia was *ex hypothesi* conquered and the Akarnanians and Lokroi Ozoloi already friendly. See n. on τούτων γὰρ ληφθέντων, § 5, and ἠπειρώταις, 95. 1.

4. σκευῇ ψιλῇ χρώμενον: this was to prove their strength, not their weakness.

5. Ἀποδωτοῖς, κ.τ.λ.: for a general description of Aitolian geography and topography, Woodhouse's book is still our best authority (see particularly pp. 3–8, 40–49), though many of his identifications of

ancient sites are quite uncertain and much of his argument is weak. The boundaries of these three divisions of the Aitolian peoples are unknown; only those of the Apodotoi, however, both with Ozolian Lokris on the south and with the Ophioneis to the north, concern us here (see 96. 2 and 97. 2 n.). Woodhouse, pp. 57–59, thinks that the mountain range which stretches between the east–west course of the Mórnos river (for which see below, n. on 95. 1) and the coastal area was the northern boundary of Lokris, which is thus left with but a narrow strip of territory between mountain and sea, and that the Mórnos was the boundary between the Apodotoi and the Ophioneis. This may in general be right, for it fits the only figure of distance which Thucydides gives us (97. 2, with n.); but we have to allow a much greater extension of Lokris northwards in its eastern half than Woodhouse supposed (see 101. 2 nn.).

He noted (pp. 55–56) the very great contrast between Homeric Aitolia, confined to the coastal plains and hills west of the narrows (Rion and Antirrion) and so famous in legend—the region crossed by the Peloponnesians later in this year (102. 5)—and the extensive, wild, and almost unknown mountain country of the interior which was regarded as the home of the Aitolians in the fifth century and which is Thucydides' concern here. Some scholars, as Wilamowitz, *Sitzb. Berlin*, 1921, 729–30, have assumed a difference of race between Homer's Αἰτωλοί and those of later ages, who had only the name in common. In the seventh and sixth centuries, too, 'Homeric' Aitolia (i.e. the country between the Mesolónghi lagoons and the Euenos valley), was highly civilized, and not at all provincial; so was Thermon farther north in the hills to the east of Lake Trichonis (E. Dyggve, *Das Laphrion*, Copenhagen, 1948: see Dunbabin, *J.H.S.* xlix, 1949, 100).

ὠμοφάγοι εἰσίν, ὡς λέγονται: Thucydides will not vouch for this; which is in itself improbable, for the greater part of Aitolia was and is well wooded, and cold in winter and cool at nights in summer: that is, fires must have been common and cooking therefore natural. Their language was difficult to understand; but this means not that it was not as pure Greek as any other dialect (it was perhaps purer), but that it was pronounced in a difficult and provincial manner. Polybios' Αἰτωλῶν οὔκ εἰσιν Ἕλληνες οἱ πλείους (xviii. 5. 7), gravely quoted by some edd. here, is from the speech of Philip V at the conference of Nikaia in 198 B.C.; and the whole passage runs, ποίας δὲ κελεύετέ με ἐκχωρεῖν Ἑλλάδος καὶ πῶς ἀφορίζετε ταύτην; αὐτῶν γὰρ Αἰτωλῶν οὔκ εἰσιν Ἕλληνες οἱ πλείους· τὸ γὰρ τῶν Ἀγραίων ἔθνος καὶ τὸ τῶν Ἀποδωτῶν, ἔτι δὲ τῶν Ἀμφιλόχων, οὔκ ἐστιν Ἑλλάς. (For the Amphilochoi, cf. above, ii. 68. 5; the Agraioi, below, iii. 106. 2: neither was Aitolian in the fifth century.) It would serve better to quote Euripides' μειξοβάρβαρος (see below, 97. 2 n.).

τούτων γὰρ ληφθέντων ῥᾳδίως καὶ τἄλλα προσχωρήσειν: τούτων are clearly the Eurytanes, and τἄλλα would naturally be the rest of the Aitolians; but that they cannot be, for the Eurytanes are to be attacked only after the conquest of the others. τἄλλα must therefore be τὸ ἄλλο ἠπειρωτικὸν τὸ ταύτῃ, § 3.

95. 1. τοῖς ἠπειρώταις: clearly the same as τὸ ἠπειρωτικὸν τὸ ταύτῃ, 94. 3, and as ambiguously expressed, though here it might have meant the Akarnanians and Lokrians.

κατὰ γῆν ἐλθεῖν ἐπὶ Βοιωτούς: the ultimate objective placed first (Classen). There were two major differences between Demosthenes' first plan for the overthrow of Boeotia and his second two years later: the former was to be carried out ἄνευ τῆς τῶν Ἀθηναίων δυνά-μεως, and it was to be κατὰ γῆν from the west. The detail of his proposed route of invasion is not clear, and it is not certain that Thucydides was himself aware of the chief geographical features (cf. 102. 1–2 n.). Ozolian Lokrian territory extended from the lower Mornos valley eastwards to the plain of Krisa below Delphi, and northwards but a short distance from the sea to the mountains of Aitolia. Except for the lower Mórnos valley the territory is itself mountainous, but not very difficult to cross, the valleys being open and the mountains not high or steep (see c. 101, below). From it run two main routes northward, the more westerly up the little-known Mórnos valley,[1] the eastern by the pass from Krisa through Amphissa to the upper Kephissos valley, so well known both in ancient and modern times to visitors to Delphi, and to armies moving north and south (cf. i. 107. 2–3, iii. 92. 6 n.); and as well to all Amphiktyonic delegates. Delphi was at this time under Pelopon-nesian control (cf. 92. 5, 101. 1, as well as i. 118. 3); and Amphissa, though Lokrian, was at least prepared to welcome Peloponnesians, if only through fear of the Phokians who were kept hostile to Athens (ii. 9. 2) only by their isolation and their exposure to Boeotian and Peloponnesian pressure (below, 101. 2). Demosthenes, therefore, can hardly have had this route in mind; besides, it does not go through Aitolia; and his Lokrian friends must have told him of the Mórnos valley route. This river flows nearly due south for some distance from western Doris (near the modern villages of Mavrolithari and Mousounítsa) in a narrow but not otherwise difficult valley, before it turns west-south-west to run through southern Aitolia and then finally south for a short distance to the sea, east of Naupaktos and perhaps there marking the boundary between Naupaktos and Lok-rian Oineon (§ 3). It is a considerable river, fast flowing and difficult to cross, till it reaches the plain only three miles or so from its mouth;

[1] The Mórnos is shown, though not named, on my map of Greece, flowing from west of Doris to enter the sea just east of Naupaktos.

in this part it spreads out into a wide, stony bed. In its north-south course it is bounded on the east by the very steep slopes of Mt. Ghióna ($\Gamma\kappa\iota\acute{o}\nu\alpha$), which separates this pass from the neighbouring pass by Amphissa, and which though not so impressive as Parnassos and not visible from so many directions and at such great distances, is yet a higher mountain, indeed the highest in Greece south of Olympos; on the west of the valley is Mt. Vardousi, nearly as steep and nearly as high. So little was it visited in ancient times that we do not know for certain the classical names of these two mountains (each over 8,000 ft.); one of them was Korax (Strabo, vii, fr. 6; ix. 3. 1, p. 417; x. 2. 4, p. 450); nor that of the Mórnos river (probably the Daphnos: Plut. *Mor.* 162 D). Going to Doris by this route (which he could only use with the Aitolians cowed or friendly) Demosthenes would go through Lokrian territory, $\delta\iota\grave{a}$ $\Lambda o\kappa\rho\hat{\omega}\nu$ $\tau\hat{\omega}\nu$ '$O\zeta o\lambda\hat{\omega}\nu$, as far as the bend of the valley northwards (see n. on Aigition, 97. 2), and thereafter would have Mt. Ghiona, not Parnassos, on his right, until he turned eastwards and, crossing the saddle to the Kephissos valley, 'descended to the Phokians'.[1] Classen thinks that by $\acute{e}\nu$ $\delta\epsilon\xi\iota\hat{q}$ $\acute{e}\chi\omega\nu$ $\tau\grave{o}\nu$ $\Pi\alpha\rho\nu\alpha\sigma\sigma\acute{o}\nu$ Thucydides does mean the north side of Parnassos which would be on the right to one descending through Doris and Phokis, not the western which is to the right of the pass by Amphissa to one going north; but the position of the words in the sentence hardly suggests this, and I believe that Thucydides, and probably Demosthenes too, had but vague information about the routes north from Ozolian Lokris, and meant simply 'with Parnassos to the east'.

In the 'Congress Decree' of perhaps 449 B.C. (Plut. *Per.* 17; *A.T.L.* ii, D 12; see my vol. i, pp. 366–7), one group of delegates was to go $\epsilon\grave{\iota}s$ $Bo\iota\omega\tau\acute{\iota}\alpha\nu$ $\kappa\alpha\grave{\iota}$ $\Phi\omega\kappa\acute{\iota}\delta\alpha$ $\kappa\alpha\grave{\iota}$ $\Pi\epsilon\lambda o\pi\acute{o}\nu\nu\eta\sigma o\nu$, $\acute{\epsilon}\kappa$ $\delta\grave{\epsilon}$ $\tau\alpha\acute{\upsilon}\tau\eta s$ $\delta\iota\grave{a}$ $\Lambda o\kappa\rho\hat{\omega}\nu$ - - - $\acute{\epsilon}\omega s$ $A\kappa\alpha\rho\nu\alpha\nu\acute{\iota}\alpha s$ $\kappa\alpha\grave{\iota}$ $A\mu\beta\rho\alpha\kappa\acute{\iota}\alpha s$. They will have travelled by the Amphissa route from Phokis to Lokris. (The Peloponnese is out of place, and strangely unimportant-seeming; why should delegates go there from Athens by this way round? And if they did, why did they return to Krisa in order to reach Lokris and Akarnania?)

$\delta\iota\grave{a}$ $\Lambda o\kappa\rho\hat{\omega}\nu$ $\tau\hat{\omega}\nu$ '$O\zeta o\lambda\hat{\omega}\nu$: now allied with Athens (§ 3, below), though not at the beginning of the war (ii. 9. 4), and not very staunch, some of them, now (101–2, below). The other Lokrians, of Opous and in Italy, were hostile (91. 6, 86. 2). For the country, see below, 101. 2 n.

$\acute{\epsilon}s$ $K\upsilon\tau\acute{\iota}\nu\iota o\nu$ $\tau\grave{o}$ $\Delta\omega\rho\iota\kappa\acute{o}\nu$: generally assumed to have been near Graviá, which is in the Kephissos valley at the opening of the Amphissa Pass from Krisa. If this is correct, then Thucydides had no very clear

---

[1] It was probably by this route, the Mórnos valley, that M. Acilius Glabrio marched in 191 B.C., in the opposite direction, from Thermopylai to Naupaktos, the Aitolians having failed to guard the pass (Livy, xxxvi. 30; the easier pass, by Amphissa, was used by the Romans in 190, xxxvii. 45). Livy too mentions Mt. Korax.

idea of the Mórnos valley route, which was probably the one indicated to Demosthenes.

κατὰ τὴν Ἀθηναίων αἰεί ποτε φιλίαν: cf. i. 107. 2, 111. 1, 112. 5; ii. 9. 2 n. καὶ Φωκεῦσιν ἤδη, κ.τ.λ.: i.e. if he got thus far, he would *already* have reached his goal (Classen).

Σόλλιον: ii. 30. 1 n.

2. τοῖς ἐπιβάταις: ten to each vessel in accordance with contemporary Athenian practice (i. 13. 2 n.). These men, recruited, like the rowers, from the thetic class, were armed with hoplite armour by the state and were part of the ship's complement, who must defend the unarmed rowers: how much training had they had in fighting on land? And were their ships, left at Naupaktos, regarded as in commission in their absence? Demosthenes was taking more than one risk in invading Aitolia.

αἱ γὰρ πέντε καὶ δέκα, κ.τ.λ.: the Kerkyraioi certainly live up to their reputation. Cf. 70. 2 n.

3. ἐξ Οἰνεῶνος τῆς Λοκρίδος: its position is not further defined by Thucydides, but it was the first city in Lokris, suitable as a base, reached by one travelling from Naupaktos eastward. See below, 101. 2 n. Thucydides takes no notice of the river Mórnos, the boundary of Lokris (cf. 102. 1–2 n.); but Demosthenes will have gone by sea as far as Oineon.

96. 1. αὐλισάμενος: i.e. at the end of the first day's march out from Oineon, according to edd. Not necessarily; the precinct of Nemean Zeus may have been quite close to the town, for ὡρμᾶτο in 95. 3 does not mean 'he set out', but 'he was going to use as a base', as Bloomfield and Crawley saw; 'he established his base at Oineon'. Soteriádhes thought he had found the foundations of the temple, *Ath. Mitt.* xxxi, 1906, 394–5; but it is uncertain still.

Ἡσίοδος ὁ ποιητής: see Plutarch, *Sept. Sap. Conv.* 19 (*Mor.* 162 D–F); Paus. ix. 31. 6. We can observe the irony in χρησθὲν αὐτῷ ἐν Νεμέᾳ τοῦτο παθεῖν; it was a very typical oracle.

2. Ποτιδανίαν - - - Κροκύλειον - - - Τείχιον: the positions of these small places are quite uncertain. Woodhouse, pp. 340–62, identifies them with ruins of walls (of uncertain date, though classical) in the mountains south of the Mórnos, Teichion just above the south (left) bank of the river. This may be correct; but we must remember that in Thucydides' day they were unwalled, or so reported, and the ease with which the Athenians took them shows that the report was true; see n. on Aigition, 97. 2. Teichion would be about 12 km. from Oineon, as the crow flies; a good deal farther for Demosthenes' troops; see ὀγδοήκοντα σταδίους, 97. 2.

For Eupalion in Lokris, see 102. 1 n.

τὴν γὰρ γνώμην, κ.τ.λ.: not very elegantly expressed—'his plan was

404

only after conquering the rest to march later against the Ophioneis, if they would not come to terms, after a return to Naupaktos'. This plan would be contrary to the advice already given him by the Messenians (οὐ χαλεπὸν ἀπέφαινον, πρὶν ξυμβοηθῆσαι, καταστραφῆναι, 94. 4), and given him again (97. 1); but 96. 2 and 97. 1 do not seem to be properly co-ordinated, and 96. 3 has been awkwardly inserted between them; perhaps Thucydides inserted it only when he came to 97. 3, βεβοηθηκότες γὰρ ἤδη ἦσαν ἐπὶ τὸ Αἰγίτιον. Classen says that Demosthenes' first idea was to return to Naupaktos for fresh forces; doubtless, and these forces were probably the Lokrians (97. 2); but Thucydides might have said so in 96. 2.

The Ophioneis, as we learn from § 3, were away to the north and north-east, their last tribes being to the south of the Melieis in the Spercheios valley (cf. Strabo, x. 2. 5, p. 451; Paus. x. 22. 3); that is, they were the group through whose territory he must pass to get to Doris. Kallipolis (Livy, xxxvi. 30) may have been the (later) capital of the Kallieis, and its site north-west of Mavrolithári, where there are remains of walls (Woodhouse, p. 371).

97. 1. τῷ δὲ Δημοσθένει, κ.τ.λ.: that is, the Messenians repeated the advice they gave before, not to give the Aitolians time to bring all their forces into action together. The older edd. used to punctuate this sentence at τὸ πρῶτον (and so Hude); Classen changed this and put the stop after ἡ αἵρεσις; Stuart Jones puts it after παρῄνουν. I think Classen right in principle, though I would keep the comma after ἡ αἵρεσις and bracket ἐκέλευον; but he is surely wrong in saying that ἀναδιδάσκοντες means simply 'advise' ('as in i. 32. 1, viii. 86. 1': so L. and S.), not 'give better, or different advice', because 'Thucydides does not mean that Demosthenes had been of a different opinion about attacking Aitolia'; on the contrary, I agree with Stahl that here, as also at i. 32. 1 and at viii. 86. 1, ἀναδιδάσκειν has its proper meaning, and refers to Demosthenes' own plan, 96. 2.

2. ψιλῶν γὰρ ἀκοντιστῶν ἐνδεὴς ἦν μάλιστα: cf. Euripides, *Phoin.* 133–40:

Παιδαγωγός.   παῖς μὲν Οἰνέως ἔφυ
               Τυδεύς, Ἄρη δ' Αἰτωλὸν ἐν στέρνοις ἔχει.

Ἀντιγόνη.   ὡς ἀλλόχρως ὅπλοισι, μειξοβάρβαρος.
Παιδ.   σακεσφόροι γὰρ πάντες Αἰτωλοί, τέκνον,
               λόγχαις δ' ἀκοντιστῆρες εὐστοχώτατοι.

And 1165 ff.

ἐπὶ Αἰγιτίου: Woodhouse, pp. 363–76, says that this must be in the territory of the Ophioneis, and so north of the Mórnos, and identifies it with the site of some considerable ruins, with a finely built wall, just north of the Stenó, near where the river makes its bend from south to west-south-west direction, and to its junction with the Kókkinos: the Kástro of Veloúchovo, "the strongest site" in Aitolia and "the only first-class fortress in Ophioneia". Later he suggests, as an alternative site, Paliokátouno, west of Veloúchovo and north-west of Teichion, in the wild mountain country north of the river. But (1) it is by no means certain from Thucydides' narrative (our only evidence) that Aigition was not still in the Apodotoi country; (2) Veloúchovo is $c.$ 20 km., Paliokátouno $c.$ 18 km. (100 stades and 90 stades) in a direct line from the nearest point on the coast; but Thucydides, when he says below ἀπέχουσα τῆς θαλάσσης ὀγδοήκοντα σταδίους, is surely thinking of Demosthenes' base at Oineon as the starting-point, and mountain paths by which the troops must re-treat, not direct lines, for distance. Reckoned this way, Velouchovo is more than 35 km. from the sea, and Paliokátouno at least 30; (3) again, we must not think in terms of first-class fortresses, but of unwalled villages; and (4) Thucydides would have been guilty of a bad blunder in omitting to mention the crossing of the Mórnos either in the advance or the retreat. True, he does not mention its crossing by Eurylochos later this summer (102. 1–2); but that was a very different matter. In the plain before Naupaktos the river is sprawling, with a wide shingly bed, but easily fordable;[1] and Eury-lochos was unopposed; the Athenians would have had to cross a deep and fast river running between steep mountain sides. It does not help to say that Thucydides' descriptions of country are "graphic, rather than accurate", as Jowett put it, and consist only of generali-ties (Woodhouse, p. 340); for a mention of getting across such a river, on the retreat especially, would have been not the least graphic part of the narrative; the survivors who were Thucydides' infor-mants must have mentioned it, just as they would have exaggerated rather than minimized the distance they had covered. The only argument in favour of Veloúchovo as the site of Aigition is that it would be a very suitable place for Aitolians from distant parts (especially from the north) to concentrate (§ 3); but even so they could easily have met there and moved thence towards Aigition. Woodhouse, with his fortress and his place of concentration, was really thinking of Aitolia in the third and second centuries. Aigition should be placed somewhere on the northern slopes of the mountains south of the Mórnos; they are rugged and intractable enough to fit the narrative, and perhaps, since Aigition is not known from later history, no ancient fortified site should be looked for.

(A subsequent view is that the Kástro of Veloúchovo is Kallipolis,

---

[1] In 1938 when the road from Amphissa to Naupaktos, which goes via Stenó down the Mórnos valley, was being made and the bridge over this section of the river was under construction, lorries crossed the river, in June, without much difficulty.

the (later) chief city of the Kallieis; it is supported by the discovery of an inscription of the Kallipolitai ([Καλλιπολ]ῖται, restored, with some probability, by Dittenberger, *S.I.G.*³ 369) in honour of Pyrrhos of Epeiros, perhaps of 289 B.C.: Soteriádhes, *B.C.H.* xxxi, 1907, 310; v. Geisau, in *R.E.*, s.v. 'Kallipolis', 1919; Klaffenbach in *I.G.* ix.² 1. 154 accepts it. This is much more reasonable than Woodhouse's suggestion; but it does not suit Livy, xxxvi. 30. 4 (above, p. 405), 'ad Coracem (mons est altissimus inter Callipolin et Naupactum)', if Korax is, as seems certain, Vardhoúsi or Ghióna.)

ὑπέφευγον γάρ: we must surely accept Herwerden's correction, ὑπέφυγον, with Steup and Hude. As Steup says, καὶ ἐκάθηντο implies a completed action before it. Stahl's n. is "de imperfecto, cf. adn. 68. 2", which presumably refers to οἱ ξυνεπολιορκοῦντο; which, however, is different, and means 'who were their fellow-besieged', like οἱ προδιδόντες, 'the betrayers', φεύγοντες, 'in exile'.

ἦν γὰρ ἐφ' ὑψηλῶν χωρίων, κ.τ.λ.: see n. on ἐπὶ Αἰγιτίου, above.

3. ὅτε μὲν ἐπίοι, κ.τ.λ.: the usual tactics of light-armed against hoplites, as ii. 79. 6, iv. 33. 2, and generally successful if properly conducted in the right conditions.

98. 1. οἱ δὲ ἀντεῖχον: the whole force, Athenians and their allies, with reference to αὐτοῖς above, not οἱ τοξόται.

ἔς τε χαράδρας, κ.τ.λ.: see n. on ἐπὶ Αἰγιτίου, 97. 2.

Χρόμων ὁ Μεσσήνιος: Thucydides did not record the name of the other Messenian, who distinguished himself on Sphakteria, iv. 36. 1 n.

2. ποδώκεις καὶ ψιλοί: the repetition after ἄνθρωποι ψιλοί in § 1 is notable; but there the disadvantage of being ψιλοί was in point (unlike the hoplites they had no effective defence-armour), here the advantage; while ποδώκεις means a natural gift.

4. τοσοῦτοι μὲν τὸ πλῆθος καὶ ἡλικία ἡ αὐτή: 'So many in number and all of the same age'; that is, 120, which would not be so large a loss from the hoplite force in general, was large in relation to the force then engaged (300: 95. 2), and the loss was particularly felt because they were all taken from the same age-group. As Stahl says, ἡλικία ἡ αὐτή = ὁμήλικες (though perhaps we must not interpret too narrowly: two, or even three, contiguous age-groups might be said to consist of ὁμήλικες). I see no justification for Hude's ἡ πρώτη, which he would render, *aetatis praestantissimae*, cf. iv. 95. 3 (*Comm. crit.* 116).

βέλτιστοι δὴ ἄνδρες: nothing whatever is said in 91. 1, or 94. 1, or 95. 2, to suggest that the 300 Athenian hoplites, all ἐπιβάται, were specially selected troops; and ἄνευ τῆς τῶν Ἀθ. δυνάμεως, 95. 1, implies that on this occasion, too, the main hoplite force was not engaged. Normally *epibatai* were recruited from the thetic class (vi. 43), and we need suppose no exception on this occasion; and even when hoplites were drafted as epibatai to meet particular dangers (iii. 16. 1,

viii. 24. 2), they were not a chosen body like, for example, the 1,000 of Argos in 418 (v. 67. 2). Arnold supposes that "some young men of higher families" had been induced to serve partly by the popular character of Demosthenes and partly by the hopes of plunder; but, aside from Thucydides' silence, we do not know whether Demosthenes was yet popular (this is his first known command), and this expedition in Akarnania or against the rude Aitolians offered rather less opportunity for loot than most others. Either Thucydides means, very succinctly, almost silently, that these 300 had proved themselves a specially gallant body of men (should we read $\langle\gamma\epsilon\nu\acute{o}\mu\epsilon\nu\sigma\iota\rangle$?); or there is something missing from his narrative. I have suggested above that $\sigma\tau\rho\alpha\tau\iota\hat{\alpha}s$ $\tau\sigma\sigma\alpha\acute{\nu}\tau\eta s$, 94. 3, is not properly explained either. Diodoros, xii. 60. 1, in a very summary account of the campaign (and wrongly dated), has $\mu\epsilon\tau\grave{\alpha}$ $\nu\epsilon\hat{\omega}\nu$ $\tau\rho\iota\acute{\alpha}\kappa\sigma\nu\tau\alpha$ $\kappa\alpha\grave{\iota}$ $\sigma\tau\rho\alpha\tau\iota\omega\tau\hat{\omega}\nu$ $\acute{\iota}\kappa\alpha\nu\hat{\omega}\nu$; which *may* be significant.

$\acute{\epsilon}\nu$ $\tau\hat{\omega}$ $\pi\sigma\lambda\acute{\epsilon}\mu\omega$ $\tau\hat{\omega}\delta\epsilon$: here I feel assured that only the ten years' war can be meant. Even so, the emphasis on the loss of the 120 is remarkable when Delion and the second battle of Amphipolis were to come.

5. $\mathbf{\Delta\eta\mu\sigma\sigma\theta\acute{\epsilon}\nu\eta s}$ $\delta\grave{\epsilon}$ - - - $\acute{\upsilon}\pi\epsilon\lambda\epsilon\acute{\iota}\phi\theta\eta$: whether he was deprived of his command we are not told; we might expect it, since he was almost self-condemned, and he is expressly called $\acute{\iota}\delta\iota\acute{\omega}\tau\eta s$ in the spring of next year, iv. 2. 4; but see 105. 3 n.

The fleet returned later, that is, perhaps later than the events of cc. 100–2. We are still in the summer of 426, though near autumn (100. 1, 2), i.e. probably already in the archon-year 426–425.

99. *The Fighting in Sicily continued*

99. $\pi\epsilon\rho\iota\pi\acute{o}\lambda\iota\sigma\nu$: "a guard fort or station of the $\pi\epsilon\rho\acute{\iota}\pi\sigma\lambda\sigma\iota$. Cf. iv. 67. 2, vi. 45, vii. 48" (Arnold). It is called a $\phi\rho\sigma\acute{\upsilon}\rho\iota\sigma\nu$ below, 115. 6.

$\tau\hat{\omega}$ $\mathbf{'A\lambda\eta\kappa\iota}$ $\pi\sigma\tau\alpha\mu\hat{\omega}$: the river that divided the territories of Lokroi and Rhegion, Strabo, vi. 1. 9, p. 260.

100–2. *Peloponnesian Invasion of Lokris Ozolia*

100. 1. $\pi\rho\sigma\pi\acute{\epsilon}\mu\psi\alpha\nu\tau\epsilon s$ $\pi\rho\acute{o}\tau\epsilon\rho\sigma\nu$: usually explained as being before the Athenian invasion of Aitolia, owing to the old hostility between Naupaktos and the Aitolians (94. 3), or as soon as the Aitolians had got wind of the Messenians' plan (96. 3); but, as Steup says, this is vague, and it does not seem consistent with $\delta\iota\grave{\alpha}$ $\tau\grave{\eta}\nu$ $\tau\hat{\omega}\nu$ $A\theta\eta\nu\alpha\acute{\iota}\omega\nu$ $\acute{\epsilon}\pi\alpha\gamma\omega\gamma\acute{\eta}\nu$. Steup also points out that nothing seems to have come of the embassy to Corinth; but this might easily mean simply that Corinth took up their cause and accompanied them to Sparta, promising their share in whatever was given.

$\mathbf{T\acute{o}\lambda\sigma\phi\acute{o}\nu}$ $\tau\epsilon$ $\tau\grave{o}\nu$ $\mathbf{'O\phi\iota\sigma\nu\acute{\epsilon}\alpha}$, $\kappa.\tau.\lambda.$: one from each of the main divisions of the Aitolians (94. 5). As so often, the names remain but names to us.

2. περὶ τὸ φθινόπωρον: about the end of September or early October. See Appendix.

ὁπλίτας τῶν ξυμμάχων: see 109. 2 n.

ἐξ Ἡρακλείας: mentioned because it was a notable action by a new state; but the 500 play no noteworthy part in the campaign. Herakleia was near the outer tribes of the Ophioneis (96. 3).

οἱ Σπαρτιᾶται: the article is explained by Arnold to mean that Makarios and Menedaïos made up the usual complement of three (one leader and two to take his place, successively, if he is killed: see iv. 38. 1 n.); just as τὸν Ὀφιονέα, etc., above, indicate that each division must have its representative. This is perhaps right; but in spite of instances such as Σάλαιθος ὁ Λακεδαιμόνιος, 25. 1, I feel that the expression is barely possible here after Σπαρτιάτης δ᾽ ἦρχεν Εὐρύλοχος, and suggest καὶ αὐτοί for οἱ (or better, Σπ. καὶ αὐτοί).

101. 1. διὰ τούτων γὰρ ἡ ὁδὸς ἦν ἐς Ναύπακτον: see above, 95. 1 n. on κατὰ γῆν ἐλθεῖν, and below, n. on § 2.

2. τῶν Λοκρῶν: according to Steup this genitive is to be taken not with μάλιστα but with Ἀμφισσῆς, as Παλῆς Κεφαλλήνων, i. 27. 2, and Ἀρκάδων Ἡραιεῖς v. 67. 1; and he would even change αὐτῷ to αὐτῶν, to bring out the fact of Amphissa belonging to Lokris. This is mistaken; Λοκροῖς τοῖς Ὀζόλαις above shows the relationship clearly.

Μυονέας: cf. Paus. vi. 19. 4–5, x. 38. 8; who says it was only 30 stades from Amphissa, on a height above it and πρὸς ἤπειρον (i.e. not towards the gulf of Krisa). See below. The road from Amphissa to Naupaktos rises rapidly over a pass to the west, and 'here is the most difficult part of the road into Lokris' (not, as it might seem at first sight, 'the most difficult of all the passes into Lokris'). Amphissa, in the valley above Krisa, though Lokrian, was geographically separated from the rest of the Lokrian territory.

For the country and the sites, where known or conjectured, of the townships mentioned by Thucydides (clearly again from notes made at the time, and suggesting that the country was little known in the rest of Greece: cf. Woodhouse, p. 339), see, besides Leake and Bursian, an old and a recent account: Gell, *Itinerary of Greece*, p. 197, and two important articles in *B.C.H.*, L. Lerat, 'La Liste des peuples locriens dans Thuc. iii. 101' (lxx, 1946, 329–36; see also a summary of some of Lerat's conclusions on problems of identification in *R.E.G.* lvi, 1943, pp. xiii–xv); and Lerat and F. Chamoux, 'Voyage en Locride occidentale' (lxxi–lxxii, 1947–8, 47–80). See also ibid. lxxv, 238–9, 141–2. The latter describes in detail the various walled sites and towers, the building being generally of good quality from the second half of the fourth century; the former gives the inscriptional evidence and suggests identifications with the towns mentioned by Thucydides; from which he argues convincingly that, contrary to received opinion, Thucydides' list is in geographical order, for one invading Lokris from the east. The only certainties or near-certainties are the two extremes, Amphissa and Naupaktos, and Myoneis (H. Efthymía: see Pappadákes, $Ἀρχ. Δελτ.$ vi, 1920–1, 148–9) near the one, and Oineon (Klíma, near C. Marathiás, $c.$ 10 km. east of the Mórnos crossing) and Eupalion (Soúles, immediately east of the river, and north of the ford near its issue from the mountains: Klaffenbach, $Sitzb. Berlin$, 1935, 695–6: so Woodhouse already, pp. 340–62) near the other; but others can be inferred with probability from inscriptions, as that Polis of the Hyaioi was at Glýpha, and Alpaioi to the west of it, and that Hypneis and Myoneis, Triteeis and Chaleieis were neighbours. Further it is probable that Chaleion was at Galaxeídi (not at Itéa), Tolophon at Vídavi to the west along the coast, and Oiantheis (cf. Polyb. iv. 57. 2; Paus. x. 38. 5) not at Galaxeídi, where it has been generally placed, but farther west at Vitrinítsa. (Triteeis cannot be the same as $Τριτέες$ of Hdt. viii. 33, which was in the Kephissos valley, in Phokis; but W. A. Oldfather, in $R.E.$, s.v. (1948), conjectures that the inhabitants of the Phokian city did not return to it after the retreat of the Persians, but settled in Ozolian Lokris; and that Lokrian Triteeis must be looked for near the Phokian border, and probably at H. Efthymía. This does not agree with Thucydides' order of mention, according to which it should be west or north-west of Galaxeídi.)

Since the critical apparatus of modern editions, including O.C.T., is defective in its reference to the evidence for the spelling of some of these names, it will be as well to give Lerat's conclusions in this matter too. The inscriptions are most of them from Delphi. $Μυανέας$ is the Doric form of $Μυωνέας$, which in the fifth century would be written $Μυονέας$ and was perhaps so written by Thucydides; to be consistent we should print $Μυωνέας$. $Ἰπνέας$ should be $Ὑπνέας$, and so printed, $Τριταιέας$ $Τριτέας$ (the former being only due to confusion with Tritaieis in Achaia); $Χαλαίους$ is an impossible form, the town being $Χάλειον$ and the ethnic appearing on inscriptions as $Χαλειεύς$, $-ηεύς$ or $-εύς$. $Τολοφώνιοι$ is generally $Τολφώνιοι$, but the longer form is found. $Ἡσσίους$ should be $Ἰσίους$ and should be so printed in Thucydides (the form is found in Polybios, xviii. 3. 1). $Ὀλπαῖοι$ is $Ἀλπαῖοι$ on the inscriptions, and the traditional spelling is only due to confusion with Olpai in Amphilochian Argeia (105. 1); Strabo's Alope, ix. 4. 9, p. 427, is a lengthened form, like Tolophon for Tolphon. Lerat believes that the spelling of Stephanos of Byzantion is not to be trusted, for he compiled only from books and may repeat their errors. Cf. p. 672 n.

102. 1. Οἰνεῶνα - - - καὶ Εὐπάλιον: see above, p. 410.

2. γενόμενοι δ' ἐν τῇ Ναυπακτίᾳ: to do this the army must cross the Mórnos river, a considerable stream, though fordable in late summer, in a wide, shingle-covered bed: see above, p. 406. It is notable that Thucydides takes no notice of this, nor of the Euenos and the intervening mountain country, in § 5 below.

Μολύκρειον: ii. 84. 4 n. For Κορινθίων μὲν ἀποικίαν see below, n. on iv. 104. 4. The colony may have been settled in the late seventh century, under Kypselos; we know that Corinthian influence was strong then in southern Aitolia. Molykreion does not reappear in history after its capture by Eurylochos; who may have destroyed it (so Oldfather).

3. Δημοσθένης δ' ὁ Ἀθηναῖος: edd. have thought it necessary to defend (or even alter) ὁ Ἀθηναῖος. We forget that Demosthenes was not then as eminent as he is now, and that Thucydides was not writing for an Athenian audience only.

4. ἐπὶ τῶν νεῶν: these, says Classen (followed by Stahl and Steup), must be the Akarnanian fleet, for the thirty Athenian ships had sailed home (98. 5) and the new squadron of twenty (105. 3) had not yet arrived; true, no other mention is made of an Akarnanian fleet, but they had a coast and must have had one. Some would insert σφετέρων; Steup would prefer τινῶν for τῶν. More probably the ships are the thirty Athenian, which are not said to have already returned: all that we are told in 98. 5 is that they returned later. What Thucydides has failed to mention is the dispersal of Demosthenes' army after his defeat, a failure the more notable in that it was described as a large army (στρατιᾶς τοσαύτης, 94. 3, where see n.), and now they were too few to defend Naupaktos. Those Athenian hoplites who got back safely from Aitolia were probably all back on their ships, as ἐπιβάται. If these ships are Athenian, note that Demosthenes appears to be still in command of them (see 105. 3 n.).

μεγάλου ὄντος τοῦ τείχους: so Livy, xxxvi. 30. 6, 34. 2 (of the siege by Acilius in 191 B.C.). The line of the walls is almost fixed by the nature of the site, which slopes steeply down to the very small harbour; moreover, traces of the Hellenic wall (perhaps, however, of the fourth or third century) can be seen at the base of the still standing medieval: see Oldfather, *R.E.*, s.v. 'Naupaktos' (1935). I have not seen figures for the length of the walls; but to my recollection of them, the statement that it was a large fortress is surprising.

5. οὐκ ἐπὶ Πελοποννήσου: again unwonted enterprise by a Spartan commander, even though at the expense of allied, not of Spartan, troops (100. 2).

ἐς τὴν Αἰολίδα, κ.τ.λ.: I agree with those who would write here ἐς τὴν Αἰολίδα νῦν καλουμένην, Κ. καὶ Πλ. καὶ τὰ ταύτῃ χωρία; see Steup, p. 278. For the name Aiolis, cf. Strabo, x. 3. 4, p. 464; and for traces of Aeolic speech there, see Buck, *Greek Dialects²*, 4; L. A. Mackay, *Wrath of Homer* (Toronto, 1948), 13–14. Since Aiolis is presumably the older name, or so supposed, we should perhaps read ἔτι νῦν for τὴν νῦν.

As noted above, §§ 1–2, Thucydides says nothing of the difficult country between Naupaktos and Pleuron, nor of the river Euenos, which is nearly as big as the Mórnos, though he knew of its existence (ii. 83. 3; see Strabo, x. 2. 3–5, pp. 450–1; 21, pp. 459–60). The river would be easily fordable in early autumn, with but 2 feet of water, at the ford near where the railway from Kryonéri to Agrinion crosses it. It seems likely that Eurylochos marched inland of the two formidable mountains that lie between Naupaktos and the Euenos, Taphiassos (Klókova), and Chalkis (Varássova), by the path that reaches the river near the ford. There is a path on the south slopes of Klókova, well above the coastline (Kaké Skala, clearly visible from steamers entering the Gulf of Corinth), but there was no reason why Eurylochos should take it; and there seems to be none round the south side of Varássova. Both mountains slope very steeply to the sea, and have only a narrow valley between them. See Woodhouse, pp. 322–31. Up this valley was the Aitolian Chalkis (ii. 83. 3).

Kalydon was the Kástro of Kourtagá, about ½ hour from the west bank of the Euenos, just north of the ford and the railway bridge. Its exterior remains have been excavated and described by Poulsen and Rhomaios, *Erster vorläufiger Bericht über ... Kalydon* (Copenhagen, 1927), Dyggve, Poulsen, and Rhomaios, *Das Heroon v. Kalydon* (1934), and Dyggve, *Das Laphrion* (1948). The site of Pleuron is also well known, the Kástro of Kyrá-Eiréne about 4 km. north of Mesolónghi on the west foothills of Mt. Arakynthos (Zygós), on the right-hand side of the railway to Agrinion, here going north-west along the shore of the lagoon; its walls descend as far as the shore. See besides the work of Dyggve, Poulsen and Rhomaios, E. Kirsten in *R.E.*, s.v. 'Pleuron' (1951).

The site of Proschion, however, is quite uncertain. Two roads come south from the plain of Agrinion to Mesolónghi: one almost due south from Agrinion by a causeway across the marshland between the two lakes (Trichonis and Anghelókastro) and then through the remarkable gorge (the Kleisoúra) to the north end of the lagoons; the other goes south-west of Agrinion, rounds the lake of Angelókastro, and goes thence south-east to join the first just south of the Kleisoúra. Proschion may have been near the junction of these two roads, perhaps at the ancient site near Sideroporta (Woodhouse, pp. 142–3). Woodhouse himself put it farther south, nearer to Pleuron; for my part, since Thucydides says expressly that it is in Aitolia, i.e. not in what is called Aiolis, I should put it farther north, near the western end of the lakes and the crossing of the Acheloos (106. 1). Pleuron by itself was strategically well placed to guard the road between the upper and the lower plains.

6. οἱ γὰρ Ἀμπρακιῶται, κ.τ.λ.: they revive their ambitious plans of 429 B.C., ii. 80.

Ἀκαρνανίᾳ ἅμα: Stuart Jones followed Bekker, Poppo (but not Stahl), and Classen in putting the comma after ἅμα, not before it. Of course Thucydides often has the sequence τε and καὶ - - - ἅμα, but not with ἅμα at the end of the clause. ἅμα λέγοντες makes good sense: 'explaining at the same time the prospects of great advantage accruing.'

πᾶν τὸ ἠπειρωτικόν: a similar promise, almost in the same words, had been made to Demosthenes by the Messenians of Naupaktos; and, like the Athenian, Eurylochos is persuaded, and leaves one set of allies in the lurch in order to get the assistance of others (94. 3–95. 1). Further, though this is not expressed for Eurylochos, each commander hoped that his city would make a big conquest ἄνευ τῆς ἑαυτῶν δυνάμεως. The only difference between them is that the Athenian did not wait for his allies, while the Spartan did. The result of similar promises and hopes and different strategy was equally bad in the end. Compare also the promises made to Knemos in 429, ii. 80. 1.

Sparta is not accused of rashness, of attempting things ἔξω τοῦ πολέμου δοκοῦντα εἶναι, nor of τοῦ πλέονος ὀρέγεσθαι.

7. τοὺς Αἰτωλοὺς ἀφείς: also the Lokrians, as Classen notes, who might suffer more in consequence.

103. *The Fighting in Sicily continued*

The interruption of the narrative for the sake of the chronological order is carried to an extreme in the account of this campaign (86, 90, 99, 103, iv. 1), and, since the campaign is not of the first importance and not very interesting, might, if taken by itself, justify Dionysios' and others' criticism of Thucydides' 'unfortunate chronological method'. Cf., however, n. on iv. 78. 1, p. 540.

103. 1. ἐπ' Ἴνησσαν: about 80 stades inland from Katane and near Kentoripa, Strabo, vi. 2. 3, p. 268, 2. 8, p. 273; cf. Thuc. vi. 94. 3; later called Aetna, as by Cicero *in Verrem*.

οὗ τὴν ἀκρόπολιν Συρακόσιοι εἶχον: Arnold compares vi. 88. 5.

προσέβαλον: according to edd., except Stuart Jones–Powell, all our good MSS. except M read προσέβαλλον, and in M προσέβαλον is corrected. The aorist is far preferable, as Steup and Stuart Jones.

3. ὁ Λάχης: mentioned here in a way that implies that he had not been in command against Inessa.

413

κατὰ τὸν Καϊκῖνον ποταμόν: clearly a different river from the Alex (99), though Pausanias, vi. 6. 4, gives it the same function of marking the boundary between Rhegine and Lokrian territory; the boundaries may have changed with the years (Steup), or Pausanias may have made a mistake. The river has not been identified; there are many mountain streams in the area.

μετὰ Προξένου τοῦ Καπάτωνος: an extreme case of the unimportant note made at the time and now preserved in the narrative. (B. Keil, Hermes, l, 1915, 635, reads Καπάρωνος, a spelling obtained from an inscription.)

104. Purification of Delos

104. 1. Δῆλον ἐκάθηραν Ἀθηναῖοι: the immediate occasion being presumably thanksgiving for the cessation of the pestilence (87) or a prayer that it might cease, as asserted by Ephoros (Diod. xii. 58. 6–7); and the opportunity was taken to assert Athenian interest in Apollo, who at Delphi seemed now almost exclusively Peloponnesian and Dorian, and to start another international festival, the other four being, as it happened, in Peloponnesian hands.

This purification was mentioned in i. 8. 1.

κατὰ χρησμὸν δή τινα: Classen compares i. 24. 2 and denies the possibility of irony here. I can compare the two passages and see irony in this one. Cf. iv. 117. 2 n.

Πεισίστρατος: Thucydides' interest in past history, and in Homer (which he shared with all men), leads him to a digression here; but the digression explains also the Athenian purpose. There is no reason to suppose that he is again correcting common error. He certainly agrees with Herodotos, i. 64. 2, about Peisistratos' part.

2. ἀπέχει δὲ ἡ Ῥήνεια, κ.τ.λ.: 4 stades only, according to Strabo, x. 55, p. 486; in fact c. 700 metres at the narrowest part of the strait, and with an islet in the middle. Cf. Plut. Nik. 3. 5.

The sanctuary on Delos, at least in the fourth century and later, owned much land on Rheneia, and we possess inscriptions recording the letting of it: see the valuable article by J. H. Kent, Hesperia, xvii, 1948, 243–338.

Πολυκράτης: see i. 13. 6. See Parke in C.Q. xl, 1946, 105–8, who dates this shortly before Polykrates' death, c. 523 B.C.

τὰ Δήλια: "Byzantinis utile additamentum, Graecis non item", Herwerden. This would be in any case insufficient reason for bracketing the words; but the reverse is true; for τὰ Δήλια would be but words to the Byzantines, but would have meant something to Thucydides' contemporaries.

3. ἦν δέ ποτε καὶ τὸ πάλαι, κ.τ.λ.: Athens was reviving an old Ionian festival, celebrated by Homer, and making it more splendid—in accordance with her general policy (see vol. i, p. 388), and this time

414

with a special appeal to the Ionians. For the festival in relation to the Delian League, see Highby, *Klio*, Beiheft 36, 1936, pp. 11–13.

τῶν Ἰώνων τε: Classen would insert here ⟨καὶ Ἀθηναίων⟩ on the ground that the 'Ionians' here can be only those of Asia Minor. Unnecessarily: Thucydides might be using an old title (cf. the poetic περικτιόνων) in which 'Ionians' would include Athenians, even though 'Ionians and neighbour islanders' is not itself completely logical.

τὰ Ἐφέσια: little is known of this festival of the Ionians. For what is known, see Nilsson, *Gr. Feste*, 243.

4. Ὅμηρος: in later times at least, and perhaps already in Thucydides' day, the Hymn to Apollo was said not to be Homer's, and some said it was by Kynaithos of Chios (see schol. Pind. *Nem*. ii. 1; *F. Gr. Hist.*, 568 F 5). The six other cities who each claimed Homer for a citizen naturally rejected the testimony of this hymn.

ἐκ προοιμίου Ἀπόλλωνος: ὕμνου Ἀπόλλωνος· τοὺς γὰρ ὕμνους προοίμια ἐκάλουν—schol.; and this is likely to be a true explanation—i.e. the μουσικὸς ἀγών (whatever form the earliest musical festivals took) began with a hymn to a god, which was thus a προοίμιον to the whole. The quotations are from vv. 146–50 and 165–72 of our texts. There are many differences between the readings in the two sets of MSS.; e.g. in verse 146, ἀλλὰ σύ for ἀλλ' ὅτε; the latter is difficult to construe, so that it hardly helps to say that Thucydides is quoting from memory.

6. τοὺς μὲν χορούς: all that was left of the old festival. Bohme rightly interpreted καὶ τὰ πλεῖστα 'and the greater part of it altogether'. 'Not only had the agones ceased, but the Ionians were no longer there, and the women and children did not go' (Steup). The absence of the Ionians of Asia Minor (implied by οἱ νησιῶται καὶ οἱ Ἀθηναῖοι) was presumably due to the Lydian and Persian conquests, at least indirectly; hence Peisistratos had not been able to get them back. The Athenians now restored everything, and enlarged the festival with chariot-racing. Plutarch, *Nik*. 3. 5–7, tells us of the carelessness and disorder which used to attend the sending of the χοροί from the cities, and how Nikias restored both order and magnificence; but he does not connect this with the purification of Delos, of which he says nothing. We would naturally suppose that Nikias had some say in it.

105–14. *The Peloponnesian Defeat in Akarnania*

105. 1. Ἄργος τὸ Ἀμφιλοχικόν: see ii. 68. 3–5, and vol. i, pp. 96–97. For the sites of Argos and Olpai, and for the geography of this region, see Hammond in *B.S.A.* xxxvii, 1936–7, 128–40, and the discussion below, pp. 426–8.

τρισχιλίοις ὁπλίταις: see n. on πανδημεί, § 4.

ὅ ποτε Ἀκαρνᾶνες τειχισάμενοι κοινῷ δικαστηρίῳ ἐχρῶντο : the reader of ii. 68. 5–7 would assume that whatever the date of the introduction of Amprakiot settlers in Argos ('many generations after' Amphilochos its founder, but sufficiently long before the Peloponnesian war for the Amphilochoi to become Greek speakers), the expulsion of the original Argeioi by these Amprakiots did not take place long before the union of the Argeioi with the Akarnanians and the joint summons to Athens for help, and the consequent expedition of Phormion and recovery of Argos. This last is generally put c. 437, e.g. Busolt, iii. 736. 6, $P.A.$, and Adcock in $C.A.H.$ v. 474–5 (cf. my vol. i, p. 367), but only on the ground that it cannot be much later, or it would have directly affected τὰ Κερκυραϊκά of 435–432, nor earlier than the Samian war of 440–439, for in that case Corinth would not have been friendly to Athens (i. 40. 5), and Thucydides would have mentioned it in its place in the *Pentekontaetia*. See also Wade-Gery, *J.H.S.* lii, 1932, 216, who is followed by Beaumont (*J.H.S.* lxxii, 1952, 62–73). On the other hand, ποτέ here would naturally mean a much earlier date than a dozen years before; and, since the Akarnanians did not hold the place before Phormion's expedition, I now incline to put this a good deal earlier, perhaps in the 50's, at least as early as the Athenian campaign at Delphi in c. 448 (vol. i, p. 409). Cf. Beloch, ii. 2. 299, n. 2. There are other events of the fifty years which Thucydides has omitted; and this may have been only one incident in a *periplous* of the Peloponnese, e.g. that of i. 111. 4 (in 453 B.C. perhaps), though more probably in a *periplous* not mentioned at all. There is some reason to suppose that Phormion was an oldish man in 427 (above, 7. 1 n.) and so could have been in command twenty-five or even thirty years earlier. Or a date in the late 40's is possible. Corinth's 'friendly attitude' towards Athens in 440 can be explained in many ways.

Some, e.g. Steup, followed by Busolt, iii. 763. 1, have thought that ποτέ must go with ἐχρῶντο ('they once used the place as a κοινὸν δικαστήριον, but do so no longer') since it is otiose with τειχισάμενοι; and most have argued that the 'common place of judgement' means common to all the states of Akarnania, not common to Akarnanians and Amphilochoi. But, apart from the improbability, amounting almost to impossibility, of the Akarnanians choosing a border town, outside their own territory, and recently conquered, as a common centre, for a short period (for they had a common centre again later, but at Stratos, e.g. Xen. *Hell.* iv. 6. 4), the words in ii. 68. 7, κοινῇ τε ᾤκισαν αὐτὸ Ἀμφίλοχοι καὶ Ἀκαρνᾶνες, themselves suggest that the κοινὸν δικαστήριον belonged to these two peoples, who, as Stahl noted, are still mentioned as separate states below in 114. 2. Steup's view that the Akarnanians fortified Olpai at the time of the ξυμφοραί of Argos (ii. 68. 5), and then used it as their common centre, and may

416

have handed it back to the Argives at the time of the close alliance between the two, seems quite inconsistent with ii. 68. I see no reason why ποτέ should not be taken with τειχισάμενοι only ('which they had earlier fortified and were using as a common centre'); and if it is necessary, in order to make this meaning of κοινόν clear, that the Amphilochoi be mentioned, we should adopt Niese's Ἀκαρνᾶνες ⟨καὶ Ἀμφίλοχοι⟩, or κ. δικ. ⟨μετ' Ἀμφιλόχων⟩ (which Steph. Byz. may have read in his text of Thucydides: Ὄλπαι φρούριον, κοινὸν Ἀκαρνάνων καὶ Ἀμφιλόχων δικαστήριον. Θουκυδίδης τρίτῃ). Hammond, p. 133, agrees with this interpretation.

2. Κρῆναι: see below, pp. 426–8.

3. ἐπὶ Δημοσθένη τὸν ἐς τὴν Αἰτωλίαν Ἀθηναίων στρατηγήσαντα: this is a more remarkable explanatory note than that in 102. 3 (see n. there), especially in coming so soon after 102. 3; written, I think, at a different time (not necessarily long after, or before), and not finally revised.

I agree with Steup that στρατηγήσαντα here does not necessarily imply that he was no longer strategos, deprived of his command in consequence of his defeat in Aitolia, and, further, that probably he would not have been able to answer the Akarnanians' appeal with Messenians and Athenian archers (107. 1) unless he was still in office. Compare the action of Simonides, strategos in Chalkidike next year, ξυλλέξας Ἀθηναίους τε ὀλίγους ἐκ τῶν φρουρίων καὶ τῶν ἐκείνῃ ξυμμάχων πλῆθος (iv. 7).[1] This suits the description, ὄντι ἰδιώτῃ μετὰ τὴν ἀναχώρησιν τὴν ἐξ Ἀκαρνανίας, iv. 2. 4: which could well mean that he was not dismissed from office, but was not re-elected in the spring of 425. See, however, n. on ἀδεεστέρα ἡ κάθοδος, 114. 1; also on τὰ μὲν τῶν Ἀθηναίων, ibid. as well as, for a different view, Busolt, iii. 1059. 1; and it is to be admitted that we would have expected simply τὸν Ἀθηναίων στρατηγόν here, as in 94. 2 (cf. 102. 3). He had clearly won back his old ascendancy among the Akarnanians, for they wanted him as their leader.

αἳ ἔτυχον περὶ Πελοπόννησον οὖσαι: 'which were at that time off the Peloponnese.' They formed a new squadron sent out from Athens when news came of Eurylochos' expedition.

Ἀριστοτέλης τε, κ.τ.λ.: nothing more is known for certain of either of these strategoi nor of their fathers—though an Aristoteles was hellenotamias in 421–420 (A.T.L. List 34 = Tod, 71) and the name

---

[1] Similarly, if the fleet mentioned in 102. 4 was Athenian (see n. there), Demosthenes could not have ordered its movement except as strategos. Adcock must surely be wrong in saying (C.A.H. v. 229), the Akarnanians invited "Demosthenes to lead them. Calling up a squadron of 20 Athenian triremes that had appeared off the north-west of the Peloponnese with two generals, who were no doubt sent to supersede him, he brought his Messenians and 60 Athenian archers and took command" (107. 2). What had Aristoteles and Hierophon to say to this?

may be rightly restored in *I.G.* i.[2] 299 ($[Ἀριστοτ]έλει\ Θορα[ιεῖ]$), as strategos. The date of this very small fragment of a financial document is disputed, but is probably 431–430: see Wade-Gery, *J.H.S.* l, 1930, 288–93; liii, 136; West, *T.A.P.A.* lxi, 1930, 217–39; Meritt, *A.F.D.* 65–68, 82–86; *S.E.G.* x. 176, 226. All these references are probably to the same man.

4. πανδημεί: they had already set out with a large force, 3,000 hoplites (§ 1), yet this was by no means their whole army. Some, e.g. Beloch, *Bevölkerung*, pp. 193–4, have thought the number too high, and have used Diodoros' statement (xii. 60. 4) that there were 1,000 to correct Thucydides' text, though Diodoros' narrative here is very confused. We are hardly in a position to question our text on grounds of general probability; and Amprakia was at least large enough to hold its own, generally, against the whole body of Akarnanians; but the account of the battle in 107–8 is also more difficult to follow, if so large a force of Amprakiots was present (see e.g. 108. 2, 113. 6 nn.). Beaumont (above, ii. 30. 1 n.) keeps the figures of Thucydides, the 3,000 *plus* (at least 5,000 in all); it is as large as the force of Corinth at Plataia in 479 according to Herodotos, and much larger (5 : 3) than that of Sikyon. Amprakia, if this is correct, was one of the larger Greek cities, and much the largest in these parts.

106. 1. ἐκ τοῦ Προσχίου: 102. 5 n.

διαβάντες τὸν Ἀχελῷον: there is a ford a mile or so below the present bridge over which goes the road from Agrinion to Arta (Amprakia) and Yánnina. The river is a large one, for Greece, and in November might have been difficult to cross; however, it would not be in spate, unless exceptionally, till the melting of the snow in spring. It was here the boundary between the Aitolian territory and the Akarnanian (Strabo, x. 2. 1, pp. 449–50). Cf. ii. 102. 2. No reason is given why Eurylochos should march by this route, through enemy territory, when he might have continued in Aitolia till he had reached the Agraioi. Presumably it was the difficulty of the country which deterred him (114. 4), and perhaps the Aitolians were not too friendly.

οὔσης ἐρήμου: a very good instance of this use of ἐρῆμος, for it ignores even the garrison of Stratos, and perhaps of other cities, which may have consisted of the 'oldest and youngest' only (ii. 13. 7). It is remarkable that even in winter the Akarnanians should leave their land undefended on the south, open to one enemy, trying to prevent his joining the other by mustering at Krenai instead of at the crossing of the Acheloos near Stratos.

τὴν Στρατίων πόλιν: see ii. 80. 8 n. Eurylochos is marching by the same road, in the opposite direction, as Knemos in 429.

ἐν ἀριστερᾷ δέ: this contrast suggests that above Stratos, whose territory reached the right bank of the river, the 'rest of Akarnania' did not extend as far as the river (which is here flowing from the north-east), but only to the hills which separate its valley from the two lakes (ii. 80. 8 n.) ; and that it was only from Stratos to its mouth by Oiniadai that the river was the boundary. Note also παρ' ἔσχατα, below.

2. διὰ τῆς Φυτίας καὶ αὖθις Μεδεῶνος: see Oberhummer, *Akarnanien*, 37, 38, who follows Leake, iii. 575, in placing Phytia (Φοιτία, Polyb. iv. 63. 7) at the ruins near Pórta, some 15 km. west of Stratos, and Medeon north-east of the southern of the two lakes mentioned below, p. 427, near Katoúna, with territory stretching north to the gulf at Loutráki Bay. Pórta seems to be too far west for Thucydides' account of Eurylochos' march.

τῆς Ἀγραίων: on the extent of Agraian territory and the identification of Mt. Thyamos, see below, p. 427.

3. μεταξὺ τῆς τε Ἀργείων πόλεως καὶ τῆς ἐπὶ Κρήναις - - - φυλακῆς: it is clear that Argos, by the sea (105. 1), was on the regular road from Akarnania northwards along the east end of the gulf, and that Krenai was inland and off the main route, on a more mountainous path by which the Peloponnesians could be expected since Argos was occupied by their enemy. That is, on their march north from Stratos, some time before they reach the coast at the south-east corner of the gulf, they diverged from the main road, eastwards and northwards into Agraian territory, and then turned north-westwards, before getting as far as Krenai. Below, pp. 426–8.

107. 1. ἐπὶ τὴν Μητρόπολιν καλουμένην: except that we can infer that it was not far from Olpai and near and north of the wide χαράδρα of § 3, we have no means of identifying Metropolis, nor of knowing what sort of place it was.

καὶ Δημοσθένης: how did his force reach Amphilochia? By land, on the heels of the Peloponnesians, or by sea? And if the latter, on what ships? Possibly they were embarked by the squadron of twenty; if the ships of 102. 4 were Akarnanian, they could have used them, but see n. there; or there may always have been some transports at Naupaktos. More probably, however, they marched by land (so Hammond, op. cit.).

The force of sixty Athenian archers may have been part of the permanent garrison of Naupaktos (Steup, Busolt, iii. 1073. 3). As noted in 105. 3, it seems probable that Demosthenes was still in office as strategos. This is one of the very few occasions on which the citizen bowmen of Athens are mentioned, and a very small force is used. See ii. 13. 8 n.

2. περὶ τὰς Ὄλπας τὸν λόφον: there is so little need for τὸν λόφον (secl. Herwerden) that it is strange that, if it is not original, it should

419

ever have been inserted. The Athenian watch at sea could not have been in any way decisive, for, until their defeat on land, the Amprakiots and Peloponnesians could get whatever they needed from Amprakia.

οἱ γὰρ πλείους - - - βίᾳ κατείχοντο: Classen refers to 114. 3 to explain this.

3. μεῖζον γὰρ ἐγένετο, κ.τ.λ.: 'it proved to be larger and outflanked the enemy', when the troops were drawn up in line of battle.

4. ἦσαν ἐς χεῖρας: Thucydides does not tell us which side took the initiative in forcing an action, nor, what is at least as important, which attempted to cross the wide charadra that separated the two armies. Cf. Arist. Pol. v. 2. 12, 1303 b 12, quoted in vol. i, p. 10.

Ἀθηναίων ὀλίγων: Steup, observing that ὀλίγων is otiose after ἑξήκοντα τοξότας Ἀθηναίων, § 1, supposes a lacuna, e.g. Ἀθ. ⟨καὶ Ἀμφιλόχων ὁπλιτῶν⟩ ὀλίγων, or ⟨κ. Ἀ. σφενδονητῶν⟩ (by contrast with the ἀκοντισταί mentioned below). But he should have seen that only hoplites are in question here, in the regular line of battle, and that the few Athenians must be hoplites, not archers, and very likely the epibatai from the twenty ships. The Amphilochian ἀκοντισταί wili have been on the flank of the left wing; and the Athenian archers probably with the 400 in the sunken road. Hammond's belief that Demosthenes' force consisted mainly of light-armed is surely wrong; had it been, the battle would have taken a very different form or (almost certainly) have had a different result. It is often assumed that the Akarnanians had only light-armed troops, an assumption based on statements of their skill with the sling and the javelin (ii. 81. 8) and the use of some of them as light-armed with Demosthenes' forces in Sicily (vii. 31. 5, 67. 2); but they had recently sent 1,000 hoplites to Naupaktos (102. 4) and Ἀμφιλόχων οἱ παρόντες ἀκοντισταί below itself implies that here at Olpai the main Akarnanian force consisted of hoplites.

ἀναμὶξ τεταγμένοι: the words πλὴν Μαντινέων and οὗτοι - - - ἀθρόοι ἦσαν show that the other Peloponnesian contingents were not brigaded as units; which is strange at first sight, unless no one city except Mantineia (and Herakleia Trachinia, 100. 2, which is here neglected) had sent more than small numbers, and those all volunteers for an 'international force'. The Mantineans kept their usual position in the line, and the rest of the Peloponnesians were posted with the Amprakiots, presumably to stiffen their ranks; yet even this is not easy, in view of 108. 2, unless the fact that the Amprakiots were the best fighting troops of those parts—better than the Akarnanians, amongst others—is not meant as a very high compliment. Compare the description of the Chaones in the earlier campaign, ii. 81. 4. See, further, n. on τὸν μισθοφόρον ὄχλον, 109. 2.

ἐν τῷ εὐωνύμῳ μᾶλλον, κ.τ.λ.: i.e. 'they were posted on the left wing, though not on the extreme left where were Eurylochos and his company, opposite Demosthenes and his Messenians'.

καὶ οἱ μετ' αὐτοῦ: who were they? Some selected corps, but one expects further elucidation. They were not, it would seem, identical with τὸ κατ' Εὐρύλοχον καὶ ὃ κράτιστον ἦν of 108. 1, for these should include the Mantineans.

108. 1. ὥστε μήτε ἐς ἀλκὴν ὑπομεῖναι, κ.τ.λ.: the very simple device of Demosthenes has a remarkably decisive effect. The traditional Peloponnesian hoplite methods were no match for novel tactics (i. 71. 2–3); yet compare Brasidas' description of his plan at Amphipolis, v. 9. 4–5, 8.

2. οἱ δὲ Ἀμπρακιῶται καὶ οἱ κατὰ τὸ δεξιὸν κέρας: i.e. the mixed Amprakiot and Peloponnesian force; and again the sentence is not very easy, for the next καὶ γὰρ μαχιμώτατοι, κ.τ.λ., refers to the Amprakiots only. I would suggest inserting οὗτοι after μαχιμώτατοι. Moreover, the Amprakiots were 3,000 strong (105. 1). Who then formed τὸ πλέον νενικημένον just below, seeing that there were only 3,000 Peloponnesians in all (100. 2)? It may be we should understand that Eurylochos had Lokrians with him, and perhaps some Aitolians too, in spite of 102. 7. An alternative remedy would be to bracket καί before οἱ κατὰ τὸ δεξιὸν κέρας—not all the 3,000 Amprakiots formed the right wing. Or were the majority of them still pressing the siege of Argos (107. 2)?

ἐνίκων - - - καὶ - - - ἀπεδίωξαν: 'were victorious and had driven off the field.'

3. ἀτάκτως - - - προσπίπτοντες πλὴν Μαντινέων:.there are two more difficulties here—προσπίπτοντες in the sense of 'hurrying on to', which is difficult in the context, especially after the use of the verb in § 1 in its ordinary sense (vi. 97. 4 seems to me no sort of parallel, and viii. 84. 2 not similar); and πλὴν Μαντινέων, when we have thought up to this point that only the Amprakiots and Peloponnesians on the right wing were concerned. In effect the subject of διεσώζοντο is the whole army (as Jowett translated); and it is difficult to see how this can be made clear without supposing the loss of a sentence.

It will be noticed what a number of small difficulties there are within a short space in an otherwise simple and vivid narrative.

109. 1. ἐκ θαλάσσης ταῖς Ἀττικαῖς ναυσὶν ἀποκεκλημένος: nothing is said of any attempt by Amprakia to use her own fleet to break the blockade or at least harass the Athenians. They had twenty-seven ships at Sybota in 433; but they had heavy losses there (i. 46. 1, 48. 4, 49. 5; see vol. i, pp. 191–3) at the hand of twenty Kerkyraian vessels, and they were doubtless in no mood to face twenty Athenian now.

Δημοσθένει καὶ τοῖς Ἀκαρνάνων στρατηγοῖς: Demosthenes was in command (107. 2), but on a *political* question of this nature the Akarnanian leaders would certainly want to be consulted.

2. σπένδονται: this is a remarkable plural, and it is perhaps worth noting that for παρεσκευάζετο, 110. 2, the writer of C, according to Hude, first wrote παρεσκευάζοντο.

τὸν μισθοφόρον ὄχλον: Steup argues, from § 3, οἷς ἐδέδοτο, from 111. 1, 113. 1, and, perhaps, 114. 2, that not all the Peloponnesians who had been engaged to serve with Eurylochos were granted an armistice and freedom to leave Akarnania; and that therefore the mercenaries mentioned here must include some of the Peloponnesians at least, and were not only Epeirots and others of this part of Greece. If this is correct, we must suppose that the Mantineans were in a separate category, and that there were some others, or their officers, who were not called mercenaries; but perhaps all the rest were, like those who went with Brasidas to Thrace (iv. 80. 5). See Busolt, iii. 1070. 1. It is surprising, however, that we were not told this in 100. 2, where ὁπλίτας τῶν ξυμμάχων does not suggest a paid volunteer force; and the use of Πελοποννήσιος in 111. 3–4 would naturally imply a single body. Steup regards it as a sign that the *History* is unfinished; but this would not explain the omission, and I incline to the view that all the Peloponnesians were granted permission to leave. It was a secret business, and all may not have got away.

Classen defended τὸν ξενικόν on the ground that Thucydides wanted to define more closely the two elements which went with the mercenary status—service for pay and with foreign states. But since all these men were recruited from among Sparta's allies (100. 2), this argument will not serve here.

Ἕλληνας ὡς καταπροδόντες: Steup puts a comma before Ἕλληνας to mark it as object of the participle and not belonging to ἐς τοὺς ἐκείνῃ. Stahl's objection that the Spartan leaders were betraying not Greece but only Amprakia is singularly weak; Sparta had proclaimed her mission to be to free Greece, both from tyranny and from the threat of tyranny. But while I feel that we want an object to καταπροδόντες, the sentence as it stands demands the construction ἐς τοὺς ἐκείνῃ Ἕ.; and while Ἕλληνας has, naturally, some emphasis, the emphasis is not of the kind indicated by the order Ἕ. ὡς καταπρ. ('it was Greece they had betrayed'). I incline, therefore, to get what Steup wished by altering the order to ὡς Ἕλληνας καταπροδόντες (or ⟨τοὺς⟩ Ἕ.: cf. 10. 3, iv. 87. 3, 6): 'that this preference for their own interests was a betrayal of Greece'; otherwise we must translate 'to discredit Sparta and the Peloponnese with the Greeks there, showing that in betraying them they were simply regarding their own interests'. See Nachmansson, *Eranos*, xii, 1912, 181–8.

422

110. 2. τὰς ὁδοὺς προλοχιοῦντας: Thucydides does not say why this would be especially effective. In fact the country to the north and to the east of the Amphilochian plain is exceptionally rugged and difficult; see below, pp. 426-8.

111. 1. ἐπὶ λαχανισμόν: edible herbs are common, growing wild, in most parts of Greece, and make very good dishes.

ὑπαπῇσαν κατ᾽ ὀλίγους: an inglorious action for Peloponnesians and liberators.

2. ὅσοι μέν, κ.τ.λ.: there is no scholion on this sentence, which at least suggests that no difficulty was felt and that our MSS. text is therefore corrupt. Corrections have been made along two lines, as Classen's ὅσοι μονούμενοι ἐτύγχανον οὕτως, ἀθρόοι ξυνελθόντες, ὡς ἔγνωσαν, κ.τ.λ.: where the position of οὕτως is clearly suspect; and Hude's ὅσοι μὴ ἐτύγχανον τούτοις ἀθρόοι ξυνεξελθόντες (see crit. n. for the v.l. in our MSS.), where ἀθρόοι has no good meaning (as Hude himself felt when he once conjectured ἄθροοι). I incline to the view that, as often, there is a lacuna, and that ὅσοι μέν is genuine, the general subject, οἱ δ᾽ Ἀ. καὶ οἱ ἄλλοι, being broken up into two parts: perhaps ὅσοι μὲν ἐτύγχανον ξυνεξελθόντες προυχώρουν μετὰ τούτων, οἱ δὲ ἐν τῷ τείχει ἔτι, ὡς ἔγνωσαν ἀπιόντας, ἀθρόοι ὥρμησαν καὶ αὐτοί gives the right sense. As Steup noted, the need for food and fuel was genuine, and we cannot believe that the collection of this was to be left entirely to the Mantineans and the officers and distinguished persons among the Peloponnesians. It is clear from § 3 ad fin. that while there was some confusion between Amprakiots and those who were getting away under the truce, the main body of the Amprakiots could be distinguished. See also n. on 113. 1.

3. οἱ δὲ Ἀκαρνᾶνες - - - ἐπεδίωκον: this will mean that the main body of the Akarnanians, knowing nothing of the truce, thought that *all* alike were getting away, without any truce, and began pursuing the Peloponnesians. But why this emphasis on πάντας ὁμοίως if to the Akarnanians in general it would have been wrong to let any of the enemy retreat unmolested? I suspect that we should read νομίσαντες for ἐνόμισαν: 'the Akarnanians [who had been let into the secret (κρύφα σπένδονται, 109. 2: i.e. not specifically here the Akarnanian soldiers as opposed to their generals)], seeing the Amprakiots and the rest join in the retreat, thought that *all* were getting away, like the Peloponnesians, contrary to the truce, and so pursued them.' They attacked all, Peloponnesian and Amprakiot alike, because they thought that the former were breaking the truce by allowing the Amprakiots to get away with them under its cover. The commanding officers told them about the truce in the belief that those attacking knew nothing of it.

τοὺς Πελοποννησίους ἀφίεσαν: not consistent with the view that

423

only a minority of the Peloponnesian force got away under the truce (see 109. 2, n. on τὸν μισθοφόρον ὄχλον).

4. ἐς διακοσίους μέν τινας αὐτῶν: i.e. of both Peloponnesians and Amprakiots. Some of the latter got away safely into the Agraïs (113. 1).

112. 1. ἐπ' Ἰδομενήν: for the site, see below, pp. 426–8.

2. δειπνήσας: a mark of time, 'late in the day', rather than a purposeful reference to army supplies.

4. Δωρίδα τε γλῶσσαν ἱέντας: cf. iv. 3. 3, 41. 2. The Amprakiots were Dorian as colonists of Corinth. It would seem that there had been little change in idiom and pronunciation since very early times, if the Amprakiots could be so easily deceived; yet this is contrary to what we know of the Dorian, as of other Greek dialects.

6. ψιλῶν πρὸς ὁπλίτας: in circumstances in which it was a disadvantage to be a hoplite.

7. ὑπὸ τῶν βαρβάρων καὶ ἐχθίστων Ἀμφιλόχων: not just a statement of fact as in ii. 68. 5, but a reflection of the feelings of the Amprakiots, who "affected to regard the Amphilochians as barbarians, because they were in reality a mixed race" (Arnold); or indeed because they were neighbours and enemies.

113. 1. ξυνεξῆσαν: 'made the attempt to get away with the Mantineans.' As Steup says, there is no reason why ξυνεξελθόντες in 111. 2 must refer to the same action; the latter may well mean only 'went out of Olpai with the others to collect food'. The dead of the first battle itself had been handed back earlier (109. 2).

3. καί τις αὐτὸν ἤρετο: the sites of the two battles must have been close to one another and the collection of the armour from the dead quickly done, for it had taken little more than a day to get all to a place where the herald from the troops in the Agraïs might expect to find them.

διακοσίους μάλιστα: here is a case where μάλιστα may well have the meaning 'at most'; 'not more than two hundred'.

4. οὔκουν τὰ ὅπλα ταυτὶ φαίνεται: λείπει τὸ διακοσίων εἶναι μόνων, schol.; and Krüger, followed by many, inserted διακοσίων (σ̄) after ταυτί. Certainly a predicate is required; Spratt suggested ἐκείνων after οὔκουν, but this anticipates the herald's answer, οὐκ ἄρα τῶν, κ.τ.λ. (see below), and does not correspond with ἀλλὰ πλέον ἢ χιλίων. Denniston, C.Q. xliv, 1930, 213–14, conjectured ταυτὶ ⟨τοσαῦτα⟩, which may be right; but we must note that the word had dropped out, if it had dropped out, before the date of the scholiast's note. Denniston also thought that we should read τά ⟨γ'⟩ ὅπλα, on the ground that emphatic οὔκουν always requires γε (as Aesch. P.V. 324, 518; cf. μὴ οὖν - - - γε, viii. 91. 3, etc.), but his translation "anyhow

424

these arms don't look like the arms of 200" is not the meaning we want, but 'these are not the arms of 200' ($\phi\alpha\acute{\iota}\nu\epsilon\tau\alpha\iota$ ὄντα, not ϕ. εἶναι). οὐκ ἄρα - - - ἐστίν: I agree with Marchant that this should be a question; this makes the answer clearer, εἴπερ γε, κ.τ.λ., 'yes, if'. Otherwise we must understand ἔστι μέντοι before εἴπερ γε, as Classen. καὶ μὲν δή, κ.τ.λ.: 'and we did fight with them, yesterday, when they arrived from the city.' καὶ μὲν δή is not here at vero (Stahl and others), but used in what Denniston, pp. 395–7, calls its 'progressive' sense. It is an unsympathetic, harsh answer to the herald of the beaten side. Plato, Rep. 409 A, εὐήθεις νέοι ὄντες οἱ ἐπιεικεῖς φαίνονται καὶ εὐεξαπάτητοι ὑπὸ τῶν ἀδίκων - - - Καὶ μὲν δή, ἔφη, σφόδρα γε αὐτὸ πάσχουσι, called by Denniston 'assentient', is very near in meaning ('and they are badly deceived'); it is the appearance of agreeing which makes the Akarnanian's answer so harsh.

6. μέγιστον δὴ τῶν κατὰ τὸν πόλεμον τόνδε: it seems most likely that Thucydides wrote this about 420 B.C. and was referring, therefore, to the Archidamian war (certainly not that he wrote it later and specifically meant the Archidamian war by the phrase ὁ πόλεμος ὅδε). Cf. vii. 29. 5, 30. 3, the description of the disaster to Mykalessos; which was of course a much smaller city than Amprakia, but that should not affect this particular statement.

If Euripides wrote his Suppliants shortly after this time, it may be that it was the story of the slaughter of the Amprakiots, as well as the end of Plataia, the threat to the Mytileneans and the civil war in Kerkyra, that stirred him to write vv. 476–93:

εἰ δ' ἦν παρ' ὄμμα θάνατος ἐν ψήφου φορᾷ,
οὐκ ἄν ποθ' Ἑλλὰς δοριμανὴς ἀπώλλυτο.

Cf. G. Murray, J.H.S. lxiv, 1944, 1. The anti-Spartan tone of Andromache (above, n. on 68. 1) may have been caused in part by this campaign as well as by Plataia, especially if it was produced in Molossia (D. S. Robertson, C.R. xxxvii, 1923, 58–60); see also below, p. 674.

ἀριθμὸν οὐκ ἔγραψα: more than a thousand (§ 4, above); and a good many more, for many of the arms of men killed in scattered fighting had perhaps not yet been collected (perhaps never were all collected —Grote, v, p. 223), and the Amprakiots at Olpai had had considerable losses too (108. 3). We must certainly suppose many more if the figure of 3,000 for the first Amprakiot hoplite force is correct (105. 4 n.); and the 300 panoplies allotted to Demosthenes personally (114. 1) indicate a much larger number than 1,000.

ἄπιστον τὸ πλῆθος λέγεται ἀπολέσθαι: it was, then, not soon confirmed by a subsequent muster of the survivors, or a counting of the dead when the bodies were picked up? or were they not picked up even later (οὐκέτι ἀπῄτει τοὺς νεκρούς)? Or is it simply that the

425

report brought to Thucydides in Athens, by reputable persons (by Demosthenes? cf. below, p. 485), seemed incredible to him? The detail of the conversation between the herald and the Akarnanian, an episode so foreign to Thucydides' normal manner of writing, and as well the confident statement, οἶδα ὅτι Amprakia would for certain have fallen to a quick attack, suggest that he may have been himself present on this campaign; the conversation has point mainly from its immediacy. Köhler, however, thought Thucydides got his certainty about Amprakia's weakness from inquiry, presumably later, in Amprakia itself (Hermes, xxvi, 1891, 47); and Hammond, p. 139, thinks that the vagueness of some of the geographical detail, e.g. of the site of Idomene, shows that Thucydides was never in Amphilochia. I doubt this last argument; he is as precise, or nearly so, about this country as about Amphipolis; and he may not have been able to cover all the ground by any means. But see nn. on 107. 4 and 108. 3. χαλεπώτεροι σφίσι πάροικοι: see iv. 92. 5 n.

Topography of the Amphilochian Campaign (Map, opp. p. 428)

Much the most important account of the topography of Amphilochia is that of Hammond in his article referred to in 105. 1 n.; he made a proper study of the whole region, particularly of the mountain country which separates the plain of Arta (Amprakia) to the north and that of Karvassará or Loutró (Amphilochia) to the south of the eastern end of the Amprakiot Gulf. There are, however, certain difficulties in his interpretation of Thucydides' account, which must be discussed; though I do so with considerable hesitation, since all that I have seen of the district is the arid mountain area west of Karvassará, on a journey from Karpenési, and the ordinary road along the coast between Karvassará and Arta, including the narrow Makrinóros pass between mountains and the sea, which is 7–8 km. long.

Hammond places Argos Amphilochikon itself, without discussion, on the site "with extensive ruins" just north of the H. Ioánnes branch of the Bótoko river, before the junction of the two beds, in a commanding position overlooking the plain; Olpai on the hill Agrilovoúni, south of the Loutró river mouth (near Arápes), where Leake and others put it; Krenai (105. 2, 106. 3) also near the coast at the foot of another hill, Palio-Avlí, west-south-west of Argos; Metropolis (107. 1) somewhere east of Agrilovoúni, c. 4 km. distant, where the Loutró river reaches the plain; and Idomene (112. 1) well away to the north in the mountain country on the saddle near Tsanochóri between two ridges running north-north-west to south-south-east, Makrinóros and Liapochóri, the two hills of Idomene being peaks of the two ranges, or the two ranges themselves (Hammond is not quite clear: pp. 137–8) north of the Tsanochóri saddle and some 3 to 4 km. distant from each other, with steep gullies between them. The whole of this mountain country between Arta and the plain of Loutró he includes in Amphilochia, and names the whole of the plain of Loutró Argeia. He maintains too that, before the cutting of the carriage road along the coast where Makrinoros falls steeply to the sea, the natural way from Amprakia to Argos lay, not by the coast, but on one or other of the parallel ridges to the east of the coastline, the best of these being up the second ridge to Langada and either along it to the descent at Loutro or across the saddle at Tsanochori and the southern part of Makrinóros (or down the valley between them). Agrais is the mountain land east of Karvassará and the plain, and Mt. Thyamos (106. 3) one of the heights at the southern end of the Seriakısı ridge; but the extent of Agraiïs, whether eastwards towards Eurytania in Aitolia (94. 5) or north and south, is unknown.

Limnaia (106. 2), which was in Akarnania, near or at the northern border, Hammond puts at Karvassará, also without discussion. Further he distinguishes Olpai (105. 1, 4, 106. 1, 3, 107. 1, 108. 3, 110. 1) from Olpe (107. 3, 111. 1, 113. 1), and makes the latter the scene of the battle, just below a hill south of the Loutró river, south or south-east of Metropolis.

The difficulties in the way of this last suggestion are obvious: Thucydides gives some geographical description of Olpai, and he must have given some indication of the site of Olpe had it been 4 km. away inland. In these same chapters he uses both Idomenai and Idomene (113. 3 and 4), and the variation between Plataia and Plataiai is well known. Nor can I believe that the twin hills of Idomene were on two widely separated ridges, but rather like those of Megara or Syra; nor that the battle of Idomene took place so far from Olpai as Hammond puts it (113. 3 n.).[1] And for Krenai: "the name Krenae, 'the wells'," he says, "is appropriate to the plain just N.E. of Paleo-avle, where the Botoko stream runs dry in the summer but water is obtained by digging wells" (p. 133). But $\kappa\rho\hat{\eta}\nu\alpha\iota$ means springs, not wells, and the place must be sought, as most travellers have observed, somewhere at the foot of the hills to the east of the plain.

Argos is called $\epsilon\pi\iota\theta\alpha\lambda\alpha\sigma\sigma\iota\alpha$ by Thucydides, 105. 1, and should not be 4 km. inland by contrast with Olpai. Limnaia, from its name, might well have been near the northernmost of the two lakes by which the road from Stratos passes (above, p. 215) or the 'district of the

---

[1] One would guess a misprint on p. 138 of Hammond's article, where he gives the time taken from Langáda to Krikélo (between Loutró and Agrilovoúni, at the southern foot of Makrinóros) as 2 hours; the distance is 14 km. as the crow flies, and it is rough country; for he gives 2 hours to his walk from Argos to Karavassara, which is about 9 km. and easier going.

lakes' here; and if so, Argos could be placed at Karvassará and Olpai at Palio-avlí, 5–6 km. away, a little more than Thucydides' 25 stades. In favour of this is the short distance to the east of the Bótoko valley, which may be the wide ravine of 107. 3, and within it may be found the 'sunken path covered with bushes'; or else these are to be found farther east (as Hammond says, the distances are not great). In this case the Amprakiot reinforcements will have advanced by the ridge of Liapochóri to Loutró, and have been caught probably in the hills to the south of Loutró, east or north-east of Palio-avlí. Or, if Argos cannot be Karvassará, it should be placed at Palio-avlí, with Olpai at Agrilovoúni, about 4½ km. away; and the battle must have taken place near where Hammond puts it; for there is no sunken path near Agrilovoúni. If so, the reinforcements could have come either by the coast road or by one of the two nearer inland routes, and have been caught in the hills north of the Loutró river. ἡ ἐσβολή, 112. 2, can easily be the entrance to a pass either here, or to the east of Palio-avlí. The Akarnanians will have posted their forces at Krenai knowing that Eurylochos would not march too near to Argos, which they held, and would prefer the mountain road; they had not expected him to slip between Krenai and Argos during the night. It would suit better, since he marched διὰ Λιμναίας (106. 2), if Limnaia were the region of the two lakes, or of the north lake, rather than a town on the coast.

114. 1. τρίτον μέρος - - - τοῖς Ἀθηναίοις: their official allotment (as distinct from that of Demosthenes—see below), due to their fleet and their few land troops and perhaps to the Messenians; i.e. τὰ ἄλλα κατὰ τὰς πόλεις would not include anything to Naupaktos.

πλέοντα ἑάλω: we are not told how, or when. The Athenian fleet returned to Naupaktos (§ 2); so this booty may have been carried in a single vessel unescorted. So may Demosthenes'.

In spite of the loss the Athenians set up a statue of Athena Nike from the spoils of Amprakia, of Anaktorion (§ 3, below), and of the oligarchs in Kerkyra, a statue which had to be repaired a century later (*I.G.* ii.² 403; *S.E.G.* iii. 85). The Messenians of Naupaktos put up a monument in the Athenian portico at Delphi (Tod, p. 147).

Δημοσθένει ἐξῃρέθησαν: a personal gift to Demosthenes by the Akarnanians and Amphilochians because he was their leader and, clearly, popular as well as successful. And it was he who dedicated them on his return in Attic temples—he tactfully kept none for himself. Grote, v. 227–8, was therefore not only rash in assuming a ratio (of 6 to 1) between the Athenian state's allotment and that of Demosthenes, and calculating therefrom round figures for the Amprakiot losses, but wrong in principle; for Demosthenes did not receive this booty as Athenian strategos.

428

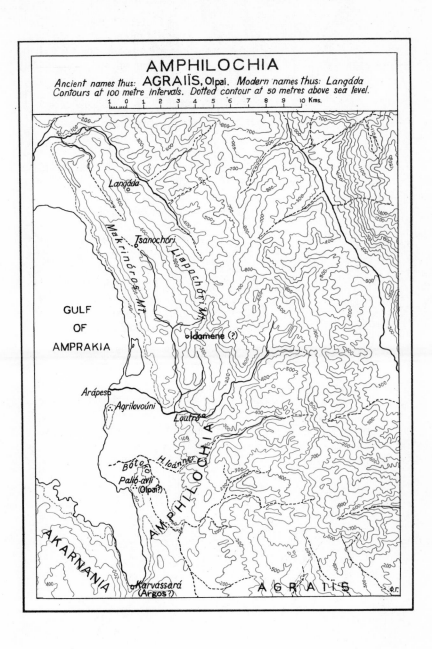

AMPHILOCHIA

Ancient names thus: AGRAIÏS, Olpai. Modern names thus: Langáda
Contours at 100 metre intervals. Dotted contour at 50 metres above sea level.

Langáda

Tsanochóri

Makrinóros Mt.

Liapachóri Mt.

GULF
OF
AMPRAKIA

Idomene (?)

Arápeso

Agrilovoúni

Loutró

AMPHILOCHIA

Bóto

H.Ioánner

Palió-avli
(Olpai?)

AKARNANIA

Karvassará
(Argos?)

AGRAIÏS

ἀδεεστέρα ἡ κάθοδος: cf. 98. 5. "Ut alibi de exulum, ita hic de Demosthenis sua sponte exulantis reditu in patriam legitur"—Stahl. As stated above, 105. 3 n., there is no actual evidence that Demosthenes had been deprived of his command, only that he was not re-elected in the ensuing spring; if his fears were justified, however, it would be surprising—the Athenians being what they were—if he had not been deposed.

2. ἀναχώρησιν ἐσπείσαντο ἐξ Οἰνιαδῶν: they had no ships, and so could not get across to the Peloponnese without a truce; so edd. explain this, with μετανέστησαν in the pluperfect sense so common in relative and other subordinate clauses. But how did they get to Oiniadai? Through Aitolia perhaps; but why did the Amprakiots among them trouble to move so far away from their own country? And the truce must come almost exclusively from the Athenians at Naupaktos if it was only a question of a sea-voyage. I think, therefore, that Oberhummer, *Akarnanien*, 112, was right in thinking that the truce was for the journey to Oiniadai as well as (as far as this concerned the Akarnanians) for unhindered departure from there; but there is no need to alter the text to ἐπ' Οἰνιαδῶν—the truce was for a 'departure from Oiniadai', and for that purpose they get a safe passage to Oiniadai. οἷπερ καὶ μετανέστησαν παρὰ Σ. will then have the meaning, 'whither they then departed from Salynthios' kingdom'; οἷπερ καί suits this interpretation. We must bear in mind that Menedaïos and the Mantineans had had transports to take them across the gulf. Knemos in 429 had been able to cross from Oiniadai with Phormion at Naupaktos (ii. 82).

3. ξυμμαχίαν - - - ἐπὶ τοῖσδε: really an ἐπιμαχία, with similar terms to that between Kerkyra and Athens in 433, i. 44. 1; but apparently less stable, for while Akarnania is excused from participation in war against Athens and Amprakia from war against Peloponnesians, they are to give each other mutual help against aggression; and who so likely to attack Akarnania as the Peloponnesians, or Amprakia as the Athenians (especially with a Corinthian garrison inside it, § 4, below)? They are, in reality, only promising to help each other against neighbours, Aitolians and Agraioi and other mountain tribes. See Busolt, iii. 1078. 1. Akarnania, it would seem from v. 30. 2 (Sollion and Anaktorion not given back to Corinth after the peace of 421), remained an ally of Athens.

Amprakia gets off very lightly after her defeat, and Athens got little by the victory of Demosthenes. Her forces had been small, especially on land, and hence the Akarnanians were able to refuse the request to attack and capture Amprakia.

Ἀνακτόριον - - - πολέμιον ὂν Ἀκαρνᾶσιν: see ii. 80. 5, and n. on πλέοντα ἑάλω, § 1, above; Anaktorion fell to the Akarnanians next year, iv. 49.

4. Κορίνθιοι: Amprakia had been a Corinthian colony, ii. 80. 3.

τριακοσίους ὁπλίτας: as a garrison, for purely defensive purposes behind a wall, or to repulse raiding in the fields this was a useful force; but its numbers show, nevertheless, to what straits Amprakia had been reduced.

Ξενοκλείδαν: he had been in command against Kerkyra in 433 (i. 46. 2).

χαλεπῶς διὰ τῆς ἠπείρου: through Aitolia, a difficult journey whether from Delphi and across country more or less direct, or by Trachis, up the valley of the Spercheios, and through Eurytania. In peacetime Greeks would always have made the journey by sea.

For Peloponnesian proposals of peace, perhaps consequent on this defeat, see 89. 1 n.

115. The Campaign in Sicily

115. 1. οἱ δ' ἐν τῇ Σικελίᾳ Ἀθηναῖοι: the narrative of this campaign resumed from 103. 3.

τὴν Ἱμεραίαν: see vi. 5. 1, 62. 2. The fact that some information about its geographical position is given in vi. 62. 2 might suggest that that passage was written before this; but Thucydides is not so systematic. Σικελῶν τῶν ἄνωθεν: this convincing emendation by Dobree (cf. vii. 57. 11, where a similar correction is certain, though a papyrus of the second century A.D. supports the MSS.), or Bloomfield's Σικελῶν without the following article, which is not so good, has been accepted by most edd., except Classen and Steup; the latter objects that ἀπόβασιν ἐποιήσαντο --- μετά must imply that the allies of the Athenians made the landing with them, which the inland Sikels could not have done, and therefore suggests a lacuna (e.g. Σικελιωτῶν ⟨ξυμμάχων καὶ τῶν Σικελῶν⟩ ἄνωθεν). But the objection is unfounded.

For τῶν ἄνωθεν, cf. vi. 88. 4.

τὰς Αἰόλου νήσους: see 88. 1.

2. Πυθόδωρον τὸν Ἰσολόχου: he was banished for corruption on this campaign, iv. 65. 3, and so was not the Pythodoros who took the oath at the peace treaty of 421 (v. 19. 2, 24. 1); but he may have been recalled then and so may be the Pythodoros who led a foray into Epidaurian territory in 414, vi. 105. 2. Or he may have been the archon of 432–431, ii. 2. 1, and an ἔργων ἐπιστάτης, c. 445 (I.G. i.² 335. 51); but the name was not uncommon in Athens. See P.A. 12399, 12402, 12410. See also Plat. Alkib. I, 119 A; Parmen. 126 B, 127 B–C: he had been a pupil of the older sophists, some years before the war.

See also below, p. 679.

ὁ Λάχης: see 86. 1. It is generally assumed from Ar. Vesp. 240–2 and 836 ff., and the schol. on 240 and 895, that Laches was prosecuted by Kleon for misconduct on this expedition (κλοπῆς, malversation of public funds, at his εὐθύναι), but was acquitted; see, e.g., Busolt,

430

iii. 1083—"eine empfindliche Niederlage Kleons". *The Wasps*, however, was not produced till 422 B.C.; and, meanwhile, Laches had played a prominent part in obtaining the year's truce of 423 (iv. 118. 11). I prefer to think, especially from *Vesp.* 240, that Kleon and others were frequently abusing Laches, asserting his dishonesty, and threatening trial, but did not prosecute. The scholiast here, who quotes Philochoros (F 127), only quotes him (characteristically) for what came from Thucydides, not for the prosecution; which is only an inference from Aristophanes.

Busolt speaks, too, of a revival of the "peace party" in Athens at the elections to the *strategia* in the following spring, because Nikias, Nikostratos, and Autokles were all successful; indicated too by Nikias' personal success at the first celebration of the Delia (above, 104. 6 n.), and by the first prize awarded to Aristophanes' *Acharnians* produced at the Lenaia in 425 (just before the end of the winter). None of these events seems to me to have the significance which Busolt and others have given them.

3. τῆς δὲ θαλάσσης - - - εἰργόμενοι: compare their position earlier, 86. 3.

4. μελέτην τοῦ ναυτικοῦ ποιεῖσθαι: "it has been pointed out that this is probably intentional irony on the part of Thucydides, who repeats the statements of the war-party of the day. There was an unlimited field for Athenian naval activity round the coasts of Peloponnese without sending fleets to Sicily"—Marchant. There may be something in this; but Athenian vessels sailing round the Peloponnese no longer met with an enemy *fleet*.

5. Σοφοκλέα: banished with Pythodoros in 424 (iv. 65. 3); he may have been the Sophokles who was one of the Thirty, Xen. *Hell.* ii. 3. 2 (*P.A.* 12827).

ἀποπέμψειν ἔμελλον: see iv. 2. 2.

6. τὸ Λοκρῶν φρούριον: see 99. The Lokrians had presumably recaptured it in the interval.

116. *Eruption of Mt. Etna*

116. 1. περὶ αὐτὸ τὸ ἔαρ τοῦτο: just at the turn of winter and spring; cf. τελευτῶντος τοῦ χειμῶνος just above and κατὰ τὸν χειμῶνα τοῦτον below; and Appendix.

ὁ ῥύαξ τοῦ πυρός: a well-known phenomenon, and peculiar, within the knowledge of the Greeks, to Etna. Pindar, *Pyth.* i. 21–28, had brilliantly described the earlier eruption; and doubtless others had attempted to do it as well.

ὑπὸ τῇ Αἴτνῃ τῷ ὄρει: τῷ ὄρει added to distinguish it from the city of this name founded by Hieron. But why was this necessary immediately after the mention of ἡ Αἴτνη, which must be the mountain?

431

And why is ὅπερ μέγιστόν ἐστιν ὄρος ἐν τῇ Σικελίᾳ added here and not just above, if at all? I suspect *additamenta*; but see Steup's n.

2. πεντηκοστῷ ἔτει: not, I think, intended as a round number, but for the year which we call 474 B.C. *Marmor Parium* (*F.Gr. Hist.* 239), 52, dates it in 479; Schol. ad Aesch. *Prom.* 384, κατὰ τοὺς 'Ιέρωνος χρόνους. The date of the first *Pythian* is not certain, but it is later than the foundation of Aitne, which is put in 475 (Hackforth in *C.A.H.* v. 147). Thucydides is not vouching for the accuracy of his date.

τρὶς γεγενῆσθαι: all agree that the third eruption must have been, not that of 396 B.C. recorded by Diodoros, xiv. 59. 3, but one earlier than that celebrated by Pindar; and this is proved by the construction after λέγεται being continued. Two things were told to Thucydides: (1) that the eruption next before this of 425 occurred forty-nine years before (this earlier eruption being well known: it is here being dated), and (2) that there had been three altogether. This could not have been so written had the eruption of 396 been in Thucydides' mind.

This sentence was clearly written before 396, and most assume that it is proof that Thucydides died before then. It is not, by any means; but the opinion that he did is so probable on other grounds that we need not discuss it.

3. The scholia tell us that in the thirteen-book edition of the *History*, book v ended here.

Note on Athenian Finance (I.G. i.² 324)

Thucydides only once tells us the cost of an Athenian military operation, the 2,000 tal. for the campaign and long siege of Poteidaia (ii. 70. 2); elsewhere we have only general statements, as of the great expense of the Syracusan expedition (vi. 31), the financial strain felt in Athens in the fourth year of the war (iii. 13. 3, in the Mytilenean speech at Olympia, where the strain is exaggerated), and the partial recovery after 421 (minimized by Nikias, vi. 12. 1), and occasional statements of sums expended, as the 120 tal. taken by Eurymedon to support the forces in Sicily (vii. 16. 2). Nor does he tell us in v. 20–24 (see v. 20. 3 n.) how much of the reserve fund of 5,000 tal. (ii. 13. 3 and 24. 1) had been spent by the end of the ten years' war— we only know that the special reserve of 1,000 tal. had not been touched; with the result that, as pointed out above (pp. 43–44), his figures for the reserve existing in 431 and for the yearly income of the Delian League lack their proper significance. Doubtless the main reason for the omission is that he had not made notes of public expenditure before he left Athens for the last time, and had no access to them afterwards; the wording especially of vi. 31. 5, εἰ γάρ

432

τις ἐλογίσατο - - -, πολλὰ ἂν τάλαντα ηὑρέθη ἐκ τῆς πόλεως τὰ πάντα ἐξαγόμενα, indicates that he would have given us figures had he known them.

The records of the *logistai*, who had examined the accounts of the *tamiai* of Athena (and Athena Nike), and of the Other Gods for the Panathenaic period of four years from 426–425 to 423–422, and give as well the totals for the previous seven years, help us in some measure to fill this gap. These are found on *I.G.* i.² 324 (Tod, 64; *S.E.G.* x. 227: in the latter and in Tod's second edition the most recent bibliography is given. The main work of reconstruction and restoration of the inscription in recent years has been by Meritt in *The Athenian Calendar* and *Athenian Financial Documents*; for some important criticism see Pritchett-Neugebauer, 94–108). Unfortunately, unlike the records of the *tamiai* themselves (*I.G.* i.² 293–309), the *logistai* seldom record the purpose of the individual payments; and to that extent we have to use surmise more than we should like in relating their information to what we get from Thucydides. Secondly, we do not know how the yearly income from the tribute, which after 425 amounted to something like 1,000 tal. a year (below, p. 503)—a very large sum, when we compare it with the payments listed in *I.G.* i.² 324—was administered: how much of it, that is to say, reached the treasury of Athena, how much was handed direct by the hellenotamiai to strategoi for an expedition, and how much might be expended by strategoi themselves without having been through the hands even of the hellenotamiai. It has been noticed by Wade-Gery (*C.Q.* xxiv, 1930, 38: cf. Tod, p. 145) that some payments from Athena, loans from her treasury, were made immediately after the Dionysia, when the tribute was brought to Athens and it might be supposed that the hellenotamiai's own treasury was full; note especially on Table A below, the payment of 100 tal. in April 422 (archonship of Ameinias), which fell in the period following the year's armistice, during which we know that no major fighting took place (v. 1) and the siege of Skione was the only important operation: we should certainly expect that the expense for that and for routine inspection in the empire could have been met from the tribute of the year. It may be that every year, after a certain sum (which would be a large one) had been put aside for maintenance of ships and arsenals, training of crews, and routine exercises, and perhaps for building new ships,[1] the rest was automatically handed over to the tamiai of Athena to be placed in her treasury—that is, that it was not just the true surplus, if any, of income over expenditure as certified at the end of a financial year that was put to reserve, but, after the Dionysia each year, the difference between the total of the

[1] On the tamiai accounts of, probably, 431–430 B.C. (see ii. 47. 1 n.), there is mention of a sum from Athena for new triremes; but none on i.² 324.

433

tribute just brought in and the sum set aside for routine expenses at once joined the reserve fund, in the charge of Athena 'for safe keeping', and later 'lent' by the goddess in the same way as the true reserve. This would be in accord with the decree of Kallias, I.G. i.[2] 92. 20–21 (Tod, 51 B)—where though κατὰ τὸν ἐνιαυτόν should certainly mean 'in the course of the year' (Tod, p. 111), the present tense, κατατιθέναι, should indicate a regulation for every year; it must be remembered, however, that this decree was passed in peacetime; and during the war the method of paying in the 'surplus' of annual revenue may have varied from time to time. Whether the products of εἰσφοραί were similarly paid into Athena's treasury and then lent is not known.[1]

If this is right, it is important that we cannot simply subtract the total sum borrowed from Athena and the Other Gods from the 5,000 tal. in the reserve in 431 (or rather, since we only have a *total* of loans, which go back to 433–432,[2] from the larger sum that was in the reserve in 433 less the 1,000 tal. special reserve), and say that only so much was left at the end of the ten years' war, because some money will have been paid in every year, and perhaps considerable sums after the reassessment of tribute in 425.

The attached tables give a summary of these logistai accounts. Table A lists the separate payments as numbered and described on the stone, but divided into Thucydidean war-years as well as into the bouleutic years used by the logistai (solar years of 366 days beginning *c.* July 2 by the Julian Calendar, and divided into ten prytanies, the first six of 37 days each, the other four of 36 days); the great majority are payments from Athena Polias, the main reserve, but there is one from Athena Nike and two from the Other Gods (who had at this time their own tamiai) in the year 423–422; I have omitted the drachmai, though I have added + and − signs where necessary—partly because in some cases the figures are doubtful.[3] Tables B and C, which record the sums borrowed in the seven years before the four-year period which is the concern of these logistai, and the grand totals, are based on Tod's tables, p. 143; in them I have included the interest, because a very large sum had

---

[1] In later years (410 to 406) a distinction is made between payments ἐκ τῶν ἐπετείον and ἐχς ὀπισθοδόμο (A.F.D. 62–64). The latter phrase occurs once on I.G. i.[2] 324 (ll. 19–20, first payment in Stratokles' year), perhaps twice (Pritchett–Neugebauer, p. 99, restoration of ll. 28–29: below, p. 592 n.); but its significance there is doubtful. It can hardly mean that all the other payments between 426 and 422 came from the annual income.

[2] They go back to this year, probably, because the decree of Kallias instituted the new method and belongs to 434–433.

[3] For some details of these doubts, as well as for the principle underlying them, see Pritchett–Neugebauer, 98–106. Some of the prytany-dates too are uncertain by a day or two, and so are the equations with the Julian calendar. But none of these doubts affect the Thucydidean problems.

accumulated, and to indicate that it was all worked out to the fractions of a drachme. The reason why the Athenians charged themselves with this payment of interest was that they hoped thereby to add one more check to their love of hasty and extravagant expenditure.

I.G. i.² 324. A. *Loans for the Period* 426–425 *to* 423–422 B.C.
From Athena Polias (lines 2–51*), from Athena Nike* (51–53)*, and from the Other Gods* (54–97)[1]

Thuc. year B.C.	Archon	Thuc. war-year	Prytany-date and destination	Amount	Annual totals Archon	Annual totals Thuc.
426–425		Year 6 (iii. 89–116)				
	Euthynos 426–425		1. ii. 4 (= Aug. 13) To Hippokrates	20 t.		
			2. ii. 31 (= Sept. 9)	50 t.		?
			3. iv. 5 (= Oct. 26)	29 t. —		
425–424		Year 7 (iv. 1–51)	4. viii. 5 (= March 18)	44½ t.		
			5. viii. 10 (= March 23)	100 t.		
			6. x. 7 (= June 1)	18½ t.	262 t. —	
	Stratokles 425–424		1. iv. 3 (= Oct. 24) To Demosthenes, περὶ Πελοπόννσον	30 t.		193 t.
424–423		Year 8 (iv. 52–116)	2. ix. 15 (= May 7) To Nikias	100 t.	130 t.	
	Isarchos 424–423		1. i. 26 (= July 30) [To Generals in Thrace?]	33 t. ±		
			2. iii. 12 (= Sept. 28)	24 t. —		163 t.
			3. vii. 2 (= Feb. 14)	6 t. +		
423–422		Year 9 (iv. 117–35)	4. viii. 30 (= April 21)	100 t.	163 t.	
	Ameinias 423–422		1. i. 11 (= July 17) To [Eurymedon?]	60 t. —		
			i. 24 (= July 29) To [Nikias?]	*31 t. —*		
			2. iii. 11 (= Sept. 28)	3 t. —		
			3. iv. 4 (= Oct. 28)	11½ t.		
			From (?) Samos iv. 4 (= Oct. 28)	*6 t.*		211½ t.
422–421		Year 10 (v. 1–24)	4. viii. 25 (= April 14)	100 t.		
			5. x. 3 (= June 3)	18 t. +		
			x. 20 (June 20)	*24 t.*	253½ t.	
						?
	426–425 to 423–422		Totals for 4 archon-years: (1) Athena Polias (2) *Nike and Other Gods*		747 t. — *61 t.*	
					808 t.	

[1] The three entries under Athena Nike (one, of 6 t.) and the Other Gods (two), all in Ameinias' year, 423–422, are printed in italics.

435

B. *Interest due for the Quadrennium, 426–425 to 423–422, on Loans made in the Previous Seven Years, 433–432 to 427–426*

Lines	Lender	Loan	Interest
98–101	Athena Polias	4,001 t., 4,522 dr.	$c.$ 195 t., 1,713$\frac{1}{3}$ dr.
102–5	Other Gods	766 t., 1,095$\frac{5}{6}$ dr.	37 t., 2,338$\frac{5}{12}$ dr.
106–8	Athena Nike	22 t., 3,098$\frac{1}{3}$ dr.	1 t., 592$\frac{5}{6}$ dr.
109–11	Hermes	1 t., 490 dr.	?

C. *Totals for Eleven Years, 433–432 to 423–422*

Lines	Lender	Loan	Interest
116–17	Athena Nike and Polias	4,777 t., 3,323$\frac{1}{3}$ dr.	$c.$ 1,248 t., 3,895$\frac{4}{12}$ dr.
119–20	Other Gods	821 t., 1,083$\frac{5}{6}$ dr.	?
122–3	Grand total	5,599 t., 4,897$\frac{1}{6}$ dr.	?

Payments in the Sixth Year of the War (426–425). It will be noticed at once how much bigger the average annual expenditure from the reserve had been in the seven years 433–432 to 427–426 than in the last four (nearly 700 tal. compared with 202 tal.). This is to be explained mainly by the greater scale of some early military expeditions, especially of the siege of Poteidaia, besides which in the first two years, 433–432 and 432–431, considerable sums for the work on the Propylaia and perhaps other buildings must have been included; but also, after 425, a much larger sum probably was handed direct to strategoi by the hellenotamiai annually, and there were to that extent smaller sums drawn from reserve. For the second half of the campaigning season of 426, however, the sums borrowed are notably small, 20, 50, and 29 tal.; and none of them can be attributed with any certainty to a known expedition. Only one strategos is named, Hippokrates, who received the first sum of 20 tal., in August; but he is not mentioned in the narrative of this year by Thucydides. (It has been conjectured that Hippokrates led the invasion into the Megarid—see Tod, p. 145—but only on the flimsy ground that he and Demosthenes commanded in the more important campaign two years later, iv. 66.) It would seem reasonable to suppose that the 50 and 29 tal. were sent to Demosthenes at Naupaktos, and perhaps the 20 tal. as well; the main financial provision for him, as for Nikias to Melos, must have been made before July, in the previous financial year.